Higher
MATHEMATICS

Mathematics in Action Group

Members of the
Mathematics in Action Group
associated with this book:

A.G. Robertson (Series Editor)
D. Brown J.L. Hodge R.D. Howat
J. Hunter E.C.K. Mullan K. Nisbet

Thomas Nelson & Sons Ltd
Nelson House
Mayfield Road
Walton-on-Thames
Surrey KT12 5PL
United Kingdom

First published by Thomas Nelson & Sons Ltd 1998
ISBN 0-17-431499-X
9 8 7 6 5 4
02 01 00 99

Editor: Margaret Cameron

Typeset by Keytec Typesetting Ltd, Bridport
Printed in China by L. Rex

Contents

Preface

This book is part of the *Maths in Action* series, and has been prepared for courses in Higher Grade Mathematics. It provides a complete and ordered coverage of Units 1(H), 2(H) and 3(H), and ensures a thorough preparation for the end-of-unit assessments and the end-of-course examination.

The book is based on a radical revision and rearrangement of the previous 5S text, and includes many more questions, new chapter reviews, summaries and revision exercises, as well as a complete set of answers. In addition, the general and course revision exercises provide the opportunity for students to integrate their knowledge across the component outcomes and units of the course.

Brief references are made throughout to the possible use of graphics calculators at appropriate points; details of a students' booklet on the use of these calculators are given in *Maths in Action* Teacher's Resource Book 4B, pages 7–10.

While the order of the chapters follows that of the outcomes in the 1997 national unit specifications, teachers may wish to vary this to some extent. For example, in Unit 1, Chapters 3.1 and 3.2 on Differentiation could be taken immediately after Chapter 1 on The Straight Line.

UNIT 1

1 The Straight Line

The length of a straight line; the distance formula

By Pythagoras' Theorem,

$$AB^2 = AC^2 + CB^2$$

$$= (x_2 - x_1)^2 + (y_2 - y_1)^2$$

$$\text{So } AB = \sqrt{(x_2 - x_1)^2 + (y_2 - y_1)^2}$$

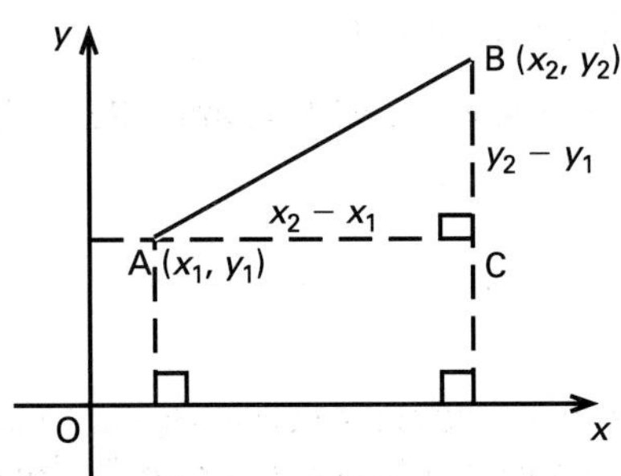

EXERCISE 1

Reminders

$2 - 3 = -1$; $2 - (-3) = 2 + 3 = 5$

$-2 - 3 = -5$; $-2 - (-3) = -2 + 3 = 1$

1 Make sure that you can do these subtractions correctly, before proceeding:

a $8 - 6$ **b** $8 - (-6)$ **c** $3 - 4$
d $3 - (-4)$ **e** $-2 - 1$ **f** $-2 - 4$
g $-4 - (-5)$ **h** $-6 - (-5)$

2 P is the point $(-1, 3)$ and Q is $(2, -4)$.
Copy and complete:
$PQ = \sqrt{(2 - (-1))^2 + (-4 - 3)^2} = \ldots = \ldots = 7.6$,
correct to 1 decimal place.

3 Calculate the length of the line joining:

a A(3, 2) and B(7, 5) **b** C(1, 0) and D(6, 12)
c E(1, 2) and F(8, 26) **d** G(−4, −2) and H(4, 4)

4 Calculate the lengths of OP, OQ and OR to find whether P, Q and R are inside, outside or on the edge of the circle. P is at (8, 6), Q(7, −7) and R(−9, 5).

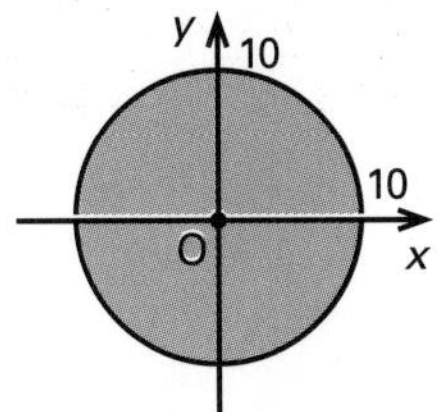

5 Sketch the triangle with vertices A(4, 6), B(5, −1) and C(10, 4). Use the distance formula to prove that the triangle is isosceles.

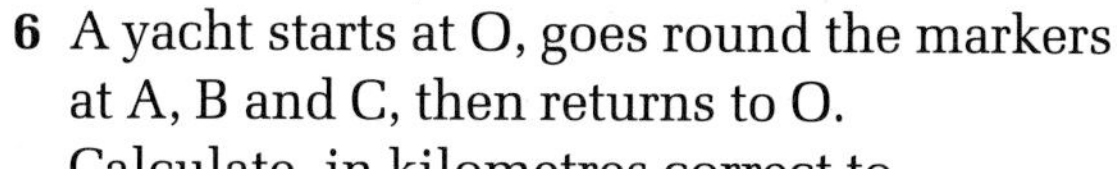

6 A yacht starts at O, goes round the markers at A, B and C, then returns to O. Calculate, in kilometres correct to 1 decimal place where necessary:
  a the length of each 'leg'
  b the total length of the course.
  Scale: 1 unit = 1 km.

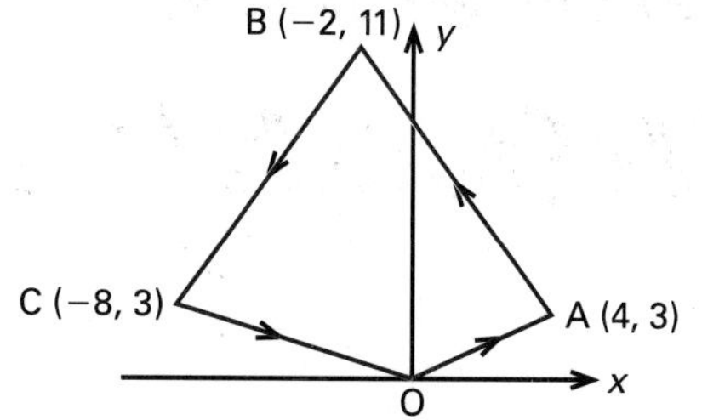

7 Find the midpoints of the lines in question **3**.

8 A is (−4, 3), B(6, 5). Find the midpoint M, and use the distance formula to show that AM = MB.

9 Repeat question **8** for A(3, 1) and B(1, −5).

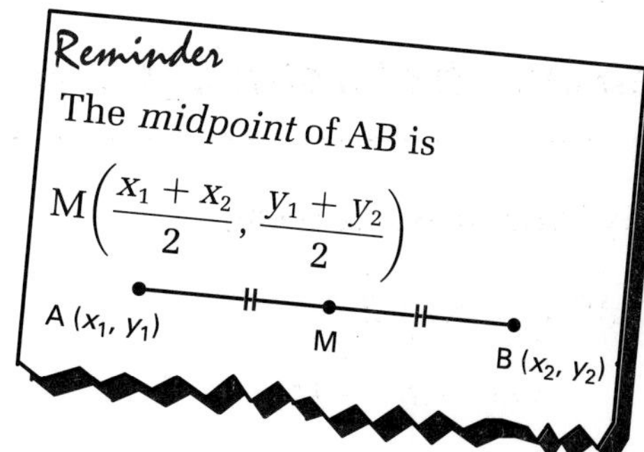

10 A triangle has vertices A(4, 6), B(−2, 2) and C(2, 0).
  a Find S, the midpoint of AB, and T, the midpoint of AC.
  b Show that ST = $\sqrt{5}$ and BC = $2\sqrt{5}$, and write down the value of ST:BC.

11 P is (−6, −4), Q(2, 2) and R(−2, 4). Use the distance formula and the converse of Pythagoras' Theorem to prove that △PQR is right-angled.

12 a Prove that A(−3, 4), K(−4, 1), V(0, 5) and T(3, −2) are vertices of a kite. (Make a sketch.)
  b Write down the coordinates of the point where its diagonals cross.

13 △ABC has vertices A(−1, −3), B(3, 0) and C(−3, 2). Prove that ∠A > ∠B > ∠C.

The gradient of a straight line; the gradient formula

The gradient of AB, m_{AB}, is

defined as $\dfrac{\text{change in } y \text{ from A to B}}{\text{change in } x \text{ from A to B}}$.

So $m_{AB} = \dfrac{y_2 - y_1}{x_2 - x_1}$, $x_2 \neq x_1$.

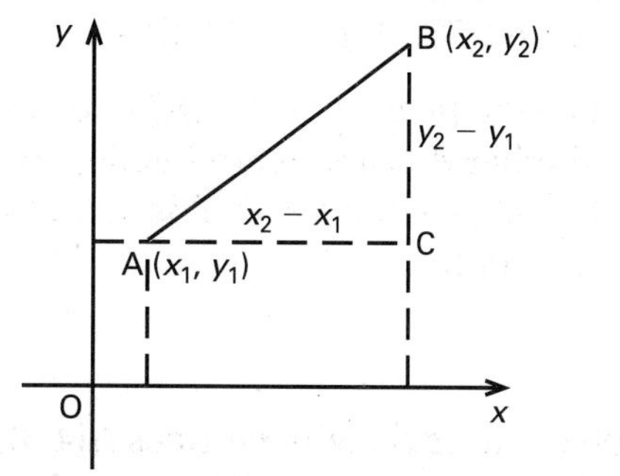

Also, $m_{AB} = \tan\theta°$, where $\theta°$ is the anti-clockwise angle from OX to AB (or AB produced).
It follows that:

(i) parallel lines have the same gradient and, conversely, lines with the same gradient are parallel
(ii) the gradient of a line parallel to the x-axis is zero
(iii) the gradient of a line parallel to the y-axis is undefined
(iv) for a line sloping *down* from left to right, $\theta°$ is an obtuse angle, $\tan\theta°$ is negative, and the gradient of the line is negative.

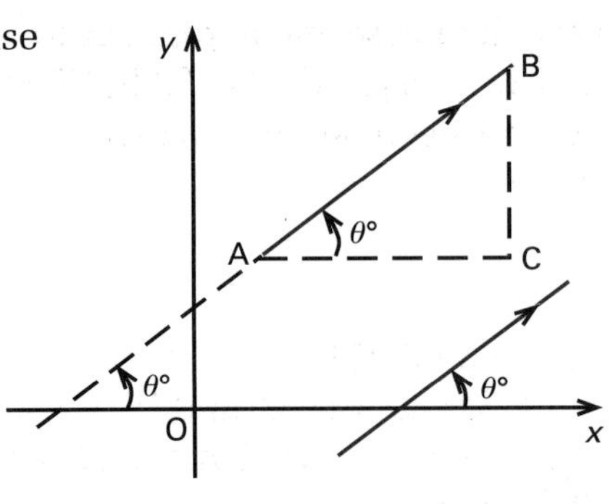

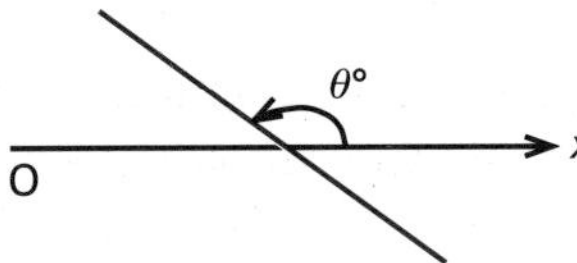

Example

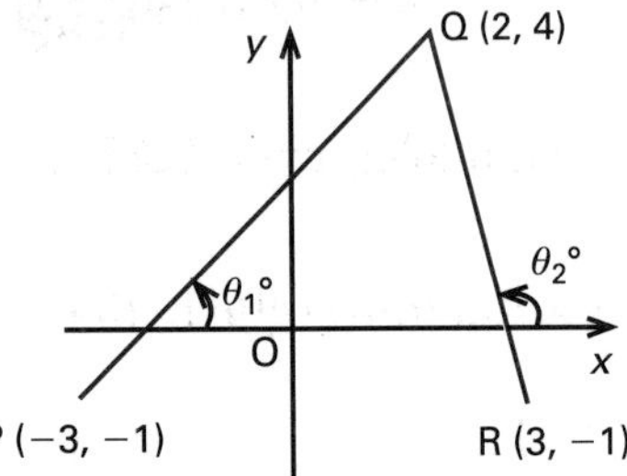

Find the gradients of PQ and QR, and the (anti-clockwise) angles $\theta_1°$ and $\theta_2°$ which the lines make with OX.

$m_{PQ} = \dfrac{4-(-1)}{2-(-3)} = \dfrac{5}{5} = 1$, so $\tan\theta_1° = 1$ and $\theta_1° = 45°$.

$m_{QR} = \dfrac{-1-4}{3-2} = \dfrac{-5}{1} = -5$, so $\tan\theta_2° = -5$;

$\theta_2°$ is obtuse, and is $180° - 79° = 101°$, to the nearest degree.

EXERCISE 2A

1 Use the gradient formula $m_{AB} = \dfrac{y_2 - y_1}{x_2 - x_1}$ to calculate the gradient of the line joining:

a A(2, 3) and B(5, 6) **b** C(0, 2) and D(2, 6) **c** E(−1, −1) and F(3, 3)
d G(1, 2) and H(−3, −6) **e** I(5, −2) and J(3, −2) **f** K(−2, 3) and L(3, −2)

2 a Write down the gradients of these lines, where possible:

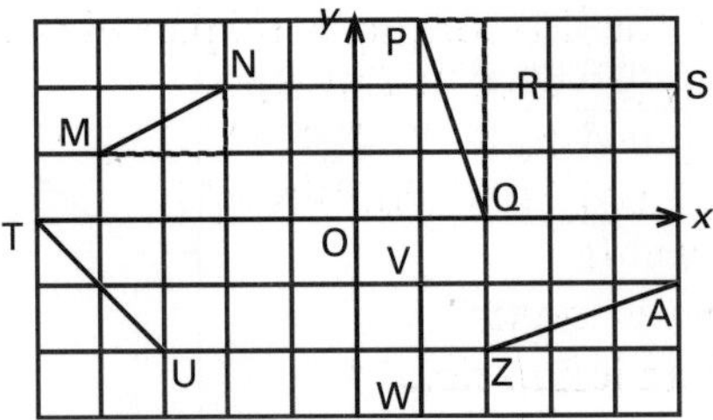

b Describe the slope of a line which has:
(i) a positive gradient **(ii)** a negative gradient.

3 Using the formula $m_{AB} = \tan \theta°$, where $\theta°$ is the anti-clockwise angle from OX to AB, write down the gradients of AB, CB and DB, correct to 1 decimal place where necessary.

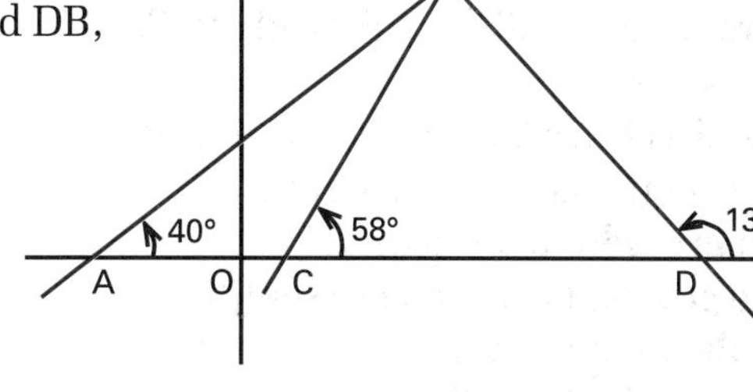

4 Quadrilateral ABCD has vertices A(−1, 0), B(3, 1), C(2, 3) and D(−2, 2). Use gradients to prove that ABCD is a parallelogram.

5 Use gradients to explain why the quadrilateral with vertices E(0, 3), F(3, 2), G(2, −3) and H(−4, −1) is a trapezium.

6 K(0, 4), L(6, 2) and M(4, 0) are three vertices, in order, of a parallelogram PKLM. Find the gradients of PK and PM.

7 Use gradients to show that the points in each of these sets are collinear (lie in the same straight line):

a A(−4, −2), B(0, 2), C(2, 4) **b** D(−6, −3), O(0, 0), E(2, 1)

8 Calculate:

(i) the gradient of the line joining each pair of points below

(ii) the anti-clockwise angle from OX to each line, to the nearest degree.

a O(0, 0), P(2, 2) **b** Q(2, 0), R(3, 2)

c S(−2, 2), T(−1, −2) **d** U(−6, 2), V(−3, 1)

9 **a** Use gradients to show that FGHK is a parallelogram.

b Now use the distance formula and the converse of Pythagoras' Theorem to show that FGHK is a rectangle.

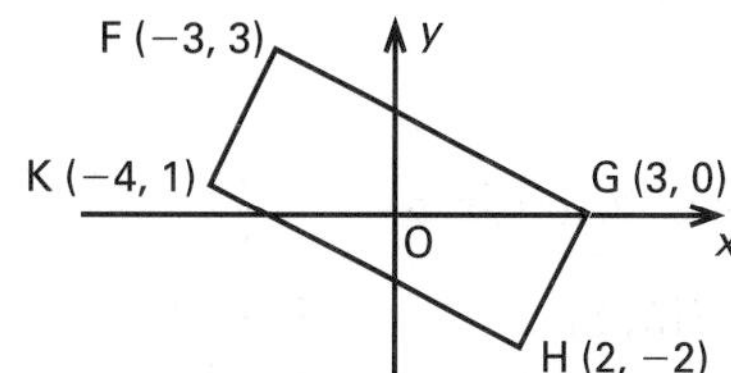

EXERCISE 2B

1 **a** Calculate the gradient of the line joining each pair of points:

(i) A(5, 3), B(8, 4) (ii) O(0, 0), C(3, 6)

(iii) D(−3, −3), E(3, 3) (iv) F(−2, 0), G(1, 1)

(v) H(−1, 5), K(2, 0) (vi) M(3, −5), N(8, −5)

b Which two lines are parallel?

c Which line is parallel to the *x*-axis?

d Which lines slope up from left to right?

2 Calculate the gradient of the line joining each pair of points, and the anti-clockwise angle that each line makes with OX, to the nearest degree:

a P(2, 1), Q(4, 7) **b** R(−3, −5), S(−7, 7)

c T(1, 4), U(−3, 8) **d** V(−4, −2), W(8, 7)

3 Prove that two pairs of the points D(2, 2), E(−3, 2), F(1, −4), G(4, −1) can be joined by parallel lines.

4 P is the point (−10, −1), Q(−4, 1), R(5, 4), S(−6, 3) and T(−1, −2). Prove that:

a P, Q, R are collinear **b** S, Q, T are collinear

c △s PQS and RQT are similar.

5 Calculate, correct to 1 decimal place where necessary, the gradient of:

a AB **b** AC **c** BC.

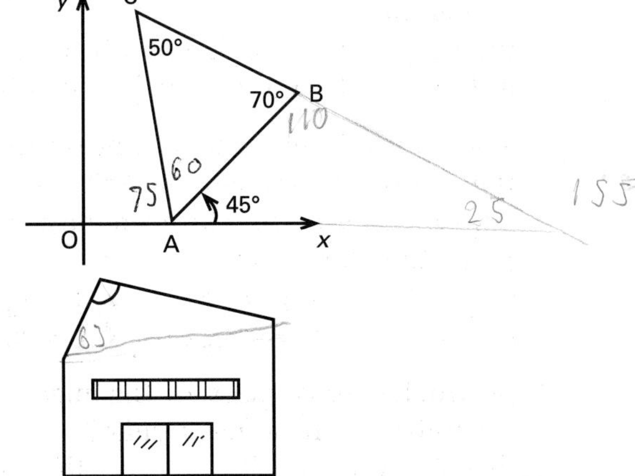

6 On an architect's plan for a factory, one side of the roof has a gradient of 2. Calculate, correct to 1 decimal place, the gradient of the other side of the roof if the angle at the apex is:

a 100° **b** 110° **c** 90°.

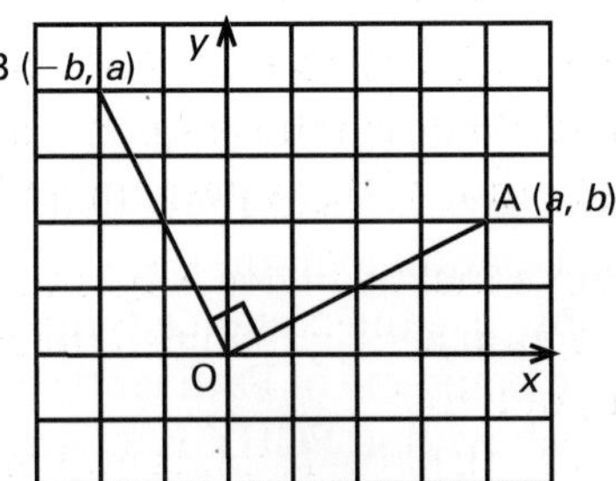

Parallel and perpendicular lines

OA is perpendicular to OB.
Under a rotation about O of 90°, A$(a, b) \rightarrow$ B$(-b, a)$.

$$m_{OA} = \frac{b-0}{a-0} = \frac{b}{a}, \text{ and}$$

$$m_{OB} = \frac{a-0}{-b-0} = -\frac{a}{b}.$$

So $m_{OA} \times m_{OB} = \frac{b}{a} \times \left(-\frac{a}{b}\right) = -1.$

The converse is also true: if $m_{OA} \times m_{OB} = -1$, then OA and OB are perpendicular.

Summary If two straight lines have gradients $\boldsymbol{m_1}$ and $\boldsymbol{m_2}$ then:
a $m_1 = m_2 \Leftrightarrow$ the lines are parallel
b $m_1 m_2 = -1 \Leftrightarrow$ the lines are perpendicular.
($\Leftrightarrow$ means that both the statement ($\Rightarrow$) and the converse ($\Leftarrow$) are true.)

Example If $m_{PQ} = \frac{2}{3}$ and PR is perpendicular to PQ, then $m_{PR} = -\frac{3}{2}$, since $\frac{2}{3} \times (-\frac{3}{2}) = -1$.

EXERCISE 3

1 Which of these pairs of numbers could be gradients of perpendicular lines?
a $3, \frac{1}{3}$ **b** $1, -1$ **c** $\frac{3}{4}, -\frac{4}{3}$ **d** $0, -1$

2 Here are some lines and their gradients:
(i) AB, $\frac{1}{2}$ **(ii)** CD, 2 **(iii)** EF, $-\frac{1}{2}$
(iv) GH, -2 **(v)** IJ, $\frac{1}{2}$ **(vi)** KL, $-\frac{1}{2}$.
Which pairs of lines are:
a parallel **b** perpendicular?

3 Write down the gradients of lines which are
(i) parallel
(ii) perpendicular to lines with gradients:
a 4 **b** -1 **c** $\frac{1}{3}$ **d** $\frac{3}{4}$ **e** $-2\frac{1}{2}$.

4 $y = mx$ is the equation of a line through the origin with gradient m. Write down the equations of lines through the origin, perpendicular to:

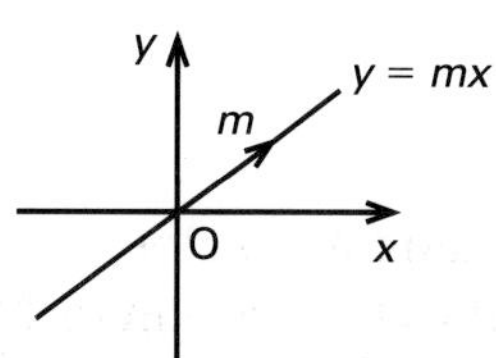

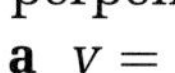
a $y = 3x$ **b** $y = -5x$ **c** $y = \frac{1}{10}x$
d $y = \frac{2}{3}x$ **e** $y = -\frac{1}{2}x$ **f** $y = x$.

5 In which of these pairs are the lines:
a parallel **b** perpendicular?
(i) $y = 2x,\ y = -\frac{1}{2}x$ **(ii)** $x + y = 0,\ x - y = 0$
(iii) $y = 4x + 3,\ y = 4x - 3$ **(iv)** $y = \frac{3}{2}x,\ 3x - 2y = 1$

6 A is the point (3, 3), B(−3, −3), C(−6, 6) and D(2, −2). Use gradients to show that AB is at right angles to CD.

7 P is (−2, −4), Q(1, 2), R(−5, 0) and S(1, k).
a Write down the gradients of PQ and RS.
b Find k, if PQ is perpendicular to RS.

8 Prove that triangles ABC and BCD in the diagram are right-angled, by means of:
a gradients
b the distance formula and the converse of Pythagoras' Theorem.

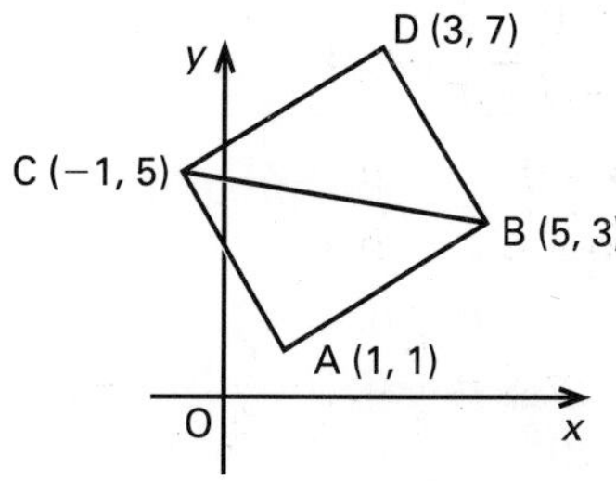

9 Use gradients to prove that the quadrilateral with vertices P(−1, 0), Q(5, −2), R(6, 1), S(0, 3), in that order, is a rectangle.

10 Prove that the triangle with vertices A(−3, 3), B(2, 4) and C(1, −1) is isosceles, and find the gradient of its axis of symmetry.

11 S(7, 1) and T(−7, −1) are ends of a diameter of a circle. Prove that K(5, −5) lies on the circle. Can you find more than one method?

The line with gradient m*, and intercept* c *on the* y*-axis,* $y = mx + c$

The line L consists of A and the set of points P(x, y) for

which $\dfrac{y - c}{x - 0} = m \quad (x \neq 0)$

i.e. $y - c = mx$

i.e. $y = mx + c$.

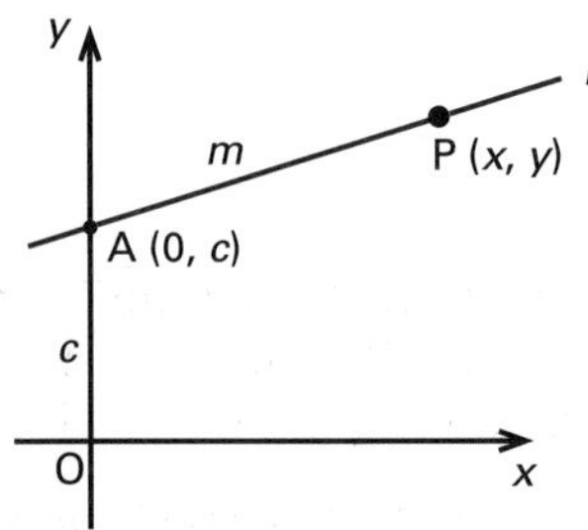

If $x = 0$, $y = c$, giving the point A. So the line L consists of the set of points P(x, y) for which $y = mx + c$.

The equation of the line is $y = mx + c$.
m is the gradient, and c is the intercept on the y-axis.

Example

a Find the equation of the line which makes an angle of 135° with OX, and passes through the point (0, 5).

b Do these points lie on the line?
(i) (3, −2) (ii) (−1, 6)

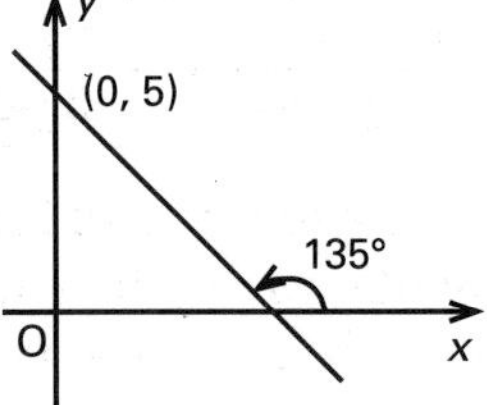

a $m = \tan\theta° = \tan 135° = -1$, and $c = 5$ in the equation $y = mx + c$.
The equation of the line is $y = -x + 5$.

b (i) If $x = 3$, $y = -3 + 5 = 2 \neq -2$, so $(3, -2)$ is not on the line.
(ii) If $x = -1$, $y = -(-1) + 5 = 6$, so $(-1, 6)$ is on the line.

Use a suitable program to draw a family of lines of the form $y = mx + c$.

a Fix c (e.g. $c = 1$) and obtain the set of lines through the point $(0, c)$ given by $m = 0, 1, -1, 2, -2$.

b Fix m (e.g. $m = 2$) and obtain the set of parallel lines using various values of c.

EXERCISE 4

In this exercise give the equations of the lines in the form $y = mx + c$.

1 Write down the equation of the line:

a with gradient 4 and y-intercept
(i) 2 (ii) −1 (iii) 0

b with gradient −1, passing through the point
(i) (0, 2) (ii) (0, −5) (iii) (0, 0)

2 Find the gradient, y-intercept and equation of:
a PQ **b** PR.

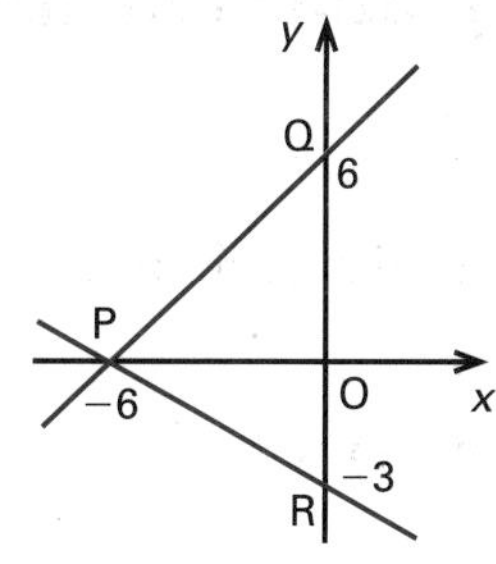

3 Find the gradient, then the equation, of the line joining:
a A (0, 4) and B (2, 6) **b** C(0, 2) and D (3, 8)
c E (0, 3) and F (6, −1) **d** G (0, −2) and H (−2, 6)

4 Find the equation of the line which passes through the point (0, −6) and makes an anti-clockwise angle with OX of:
a 45° **b** 135°.

5 Write down the equations of the lines given by m and c in the table, and find whether the given points lie on the lines.

	a	b	c	d
m	1	−2	$\frac{1}{3}$	$-\frac{2}{3}$
c	2	−1	−4	2
Point	(1, 3)	(−2, 4)	(3, −4)	(6, −2)

6 Write down the equations of the lines through the origin which are **(i)** parallel **(ii)** perpendicular to the lines with equations:
a $y = x + 4$ **b** $y = 2x - 1$ **c** $y = -3x + 4$

7 **a** A is the point (−2, 4) and B is (6, 6). Calculate the gradient of AB.
b Find the equation of the line through C (0, 5):
(i) parallel to AB **(ii)** perpendicular to AB.

8 Find the equation of the line through the first pair of points, then check whether the third point lies on the line:
a (0, 5), (4, 7); (8, 9) **b** (−1, −5), (0, −1); (3, 10).

9 Find the anti-clockwise angle $\theta°$ that each line below makes with OX, to the nearest degree.
a $y = 2x + 3$ **b** $y + 3x = 6$

10 Express each equation in the form $y = mx + c$, and hence give its gradient and y-intercept.
a $y - 2x = 4$ **b** $2y + 6x = 12$
c $3y - 2x = 6$ **d** $x + y = 5$

11 Sketch the lines in question **10**, either by using '$y = mx + c$', or by finding where the lines cut the x and y-axes.

12 Find the equation of the image of the line $y = 3x + 6$ under:
a reflection in **(i)** the x-axis **(ii)** the y-axis **(iii)** the origin
b translation of 2 units in the direction **(i)** OX **(ii)** OY.

The linear equation ax + by + c = 0

In the equation $ax + by + c = 0$:

if $a = 0$, $by + c = 0$, so $y = -\frac{c}{b}$, a straight line parallel to the x-axis;

if $b = 0$, $ax + c = 0$, so $x = -\frac{c}{a}$, a straight line parallel to the y-axis;

if $a \neq 0$ and $b \neq 0$, $y = -\frac{a}{b}x - \frac{c}{b}$, an equation of the form '$y = mx + c$', a straight line.

So, provided that a and b are not both zero, $ax + by + c = 0$ always represents a straight line, and is called a linear equation; it is of the first degree in x and y.

EXERCISE 5

1 Arrange each equation in the form $ax + by + c = 0$, where a, b and c are integers (positive or negative whole numbers, or zero).
a $2x - y = 1$ **b** $y - 2x = 1$ **c** $y = \frac{2}{3}x + 2$
d $\frac{4}{5}x + y = 1$ **e** $y = -\frac{1}{6}x - \frac{2}{3}$ **f** $\frac{1}{2}x - \frac{1}{3}y = \frac{1}{4}$

2 By finding where they cross the x and y-axes, sketch the lines with equations:
a $2x + y = 4$ **b** $4x - 3y = 12$
c $2x + y - 2 = 0$ **d** $3x - y = 0$.

3 Write down the equation of the line through the point (1, 2) which is parallel to:
a the x-axis **b** the y-axis.

4 Make a sketch in which A (4, 4) and C (2, 1) are opposite vertices of a rectangle which has its sides parallel to the x and y-axes. Write down the equations of the sides of the rectangle.

5 In the diagram, find:
a the gradients of AB and AC
b $\theta_1°$ and $\theta_2°$, correct to the nearest degree
c the size of ∠BAC, to the nearest degree.

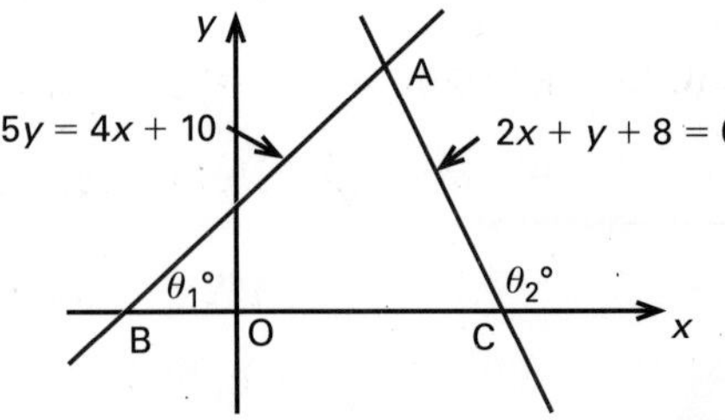

6 Which of the following equations represent straight lines?
a $x - y = 0$ **b** $x^2 + y^2 = 0$ **c** $y = \frac{1}{2}x$
d $y^2 = 4x$ **e** $3y - \frac{1}{4} = 2x$ **f** $xy = 1$

7 A straight line has equation $2x + y - 3 = 0$.
a If $(k, -1)$ lies on the line, find k.
b If (a, b) lies on the line, express b in terms of a.

8 A $(3, h)$ and B $(k, -3)$ lie on the line $3x - y - 3 = 0$.
a Find the values of h and k.
b Check, by finding the gradient of AB.

9 O is the origin and A is the point (4, 2). Show that the set of points $P(x, y)$ for which $OP = AP$ is the straight line $2x + y - 5 = 0$. (*Hint*: $OP^2 = AP^2$. Now use the distance formula.)
Note The line $2x + y - 5 = 0$ is the locus of points P for which $OP = AP$.

10 B is the point (0, 4) and C is (6, 0).
a Find the equation of the locus of $P(x, y)$ if $BP = PC$.
b Show that the locus of P is a straight line perpendicular to BC.

11 Repeat question **10** for $B(-2, 1)$ and $C(4, 3)$.

The line with gradient m, *through the point* (a, b), y − b = m(x − a)

The line L consists of A and the set of points (x, y) for which $\frac{y-b}{x-a} = m \quad (x \neq a)$

i.e. $y - b = m(x - a)$.

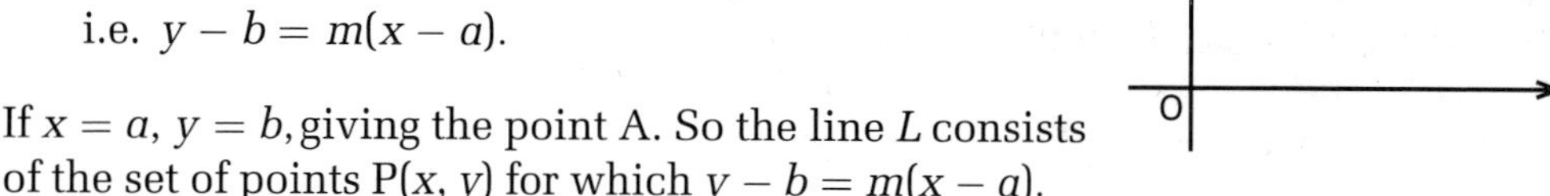

If $x = a$, $y = b$, giving the point A. So the line L consists of the set of points $P(x, y)$ for which $y - b = m(x - a)$.

The equation of the line is $y - b = m(x - a)$.

Example Find the equation of the line through $A(2, -1)$, perpendicular to the line joining $B(-2, 0)$ and $C(3, 2)$.

$$m_{BC} = \frac{2-0}{3-(-2)} = \frac{2}{5}, \text{ so } m_{AP} = -\frac{5}{2}$$

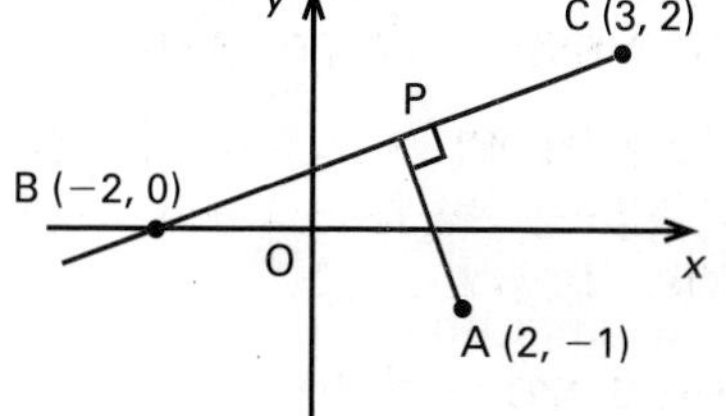

Equation of AP is $y - (-1) = -\frac{5}{2}(x - 2)$, using '$y - b = m(x - a)$'

$$2(y + 1) = -5(x - 2)$$

$$2y + 2 = -5x + 10$$

$$2y + 5x = 8$$

EXERCISE 6

In this exercise give the equations in the form $py + qx = r$, as in the worked example above.

1 Simplify these equations.

a $y + 2 = 3(x + 1)$ **b** $y - 5 = 2(x - 1)$ **c** $y = -5(x + 2)$
d $y + 1 = -(x - 3)$ **e** $y - 2 = \frac{2}{3}(x + 5)$ **f** $y - 3 = -\frac{1}{4}(x - 1)$

2 Use the equation $y - b = m(x - a)$ to find the equation of the line through the given point, with the given gradient.

a (4, 6), $m = 2$ **b** (−2, −3), $m = 3$
c (3, 4), $m = \frac{1}{3}$ **d** (3, −1), $m = -\frac{2}{5}$

3 Find the gradients, and hence the equations, of the lines through these pairs of points.

a A(−2, 1), B(4, 5) **b** C(−2, 5), D(6, 3)
c E(−1, 8), F(5, −1) **d** G(−2, −1), H(4, −3)

4 Find the equation of the line parallel to the given line, passing through the given point.

a $y = x + 4$, (5, 6) **b** $y = 3x + 2$, (4, −1)
c $x + y - 4 = 0$, (−5, 0) **d** $2y - 3x + 1 = 0$, (1, −3)

5 Find the equation of the line perpendicular to the given line, passing through the given point.

a $y = 2x - 3$, (6, −1) **b** $y - 4x = 1$, (9, 3)
c $2y - x - 5 = 0$, (3, 4) **d** $2x + 3y + 1 = 0$, (5, 0)

6 Find the equation of the line through:

a A, parallel to BC
b B, parallel to AC
c C, parallel to AB.

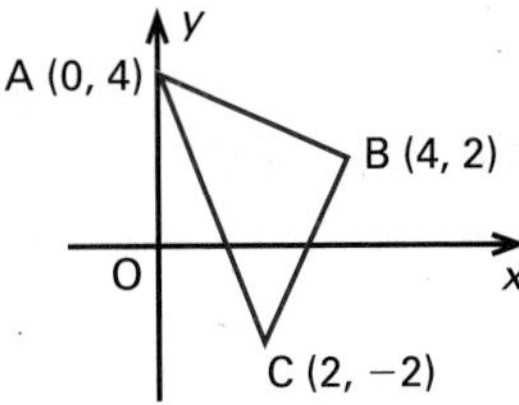

7 A median in a triangle is a line from a vertex to the midpoint of the opposite side. P is (3, 5), Q(−3, 1) and R(5, −3). Find:

a the midpoint of QR
b the gradient of the median from P
c the equation of the median from P.

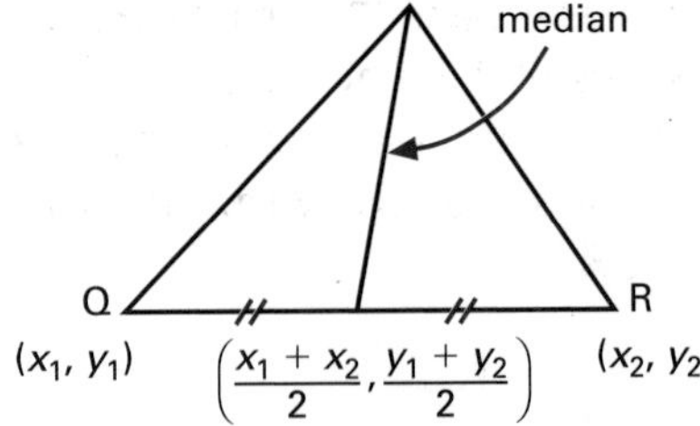

8 Find the equations of the medians of △ABC, which has vertices A(−1, 3), B(5, 5) and C(3, −3).

9 An altitude in a triangle is a line from a vertex perpendicular to the opposite side. P is (5, 2), Q(−3, 0) and R(3, −4). Find:

a the gradient of
 (i) QR **(ii)** the altitude PS
b the equation of PS.

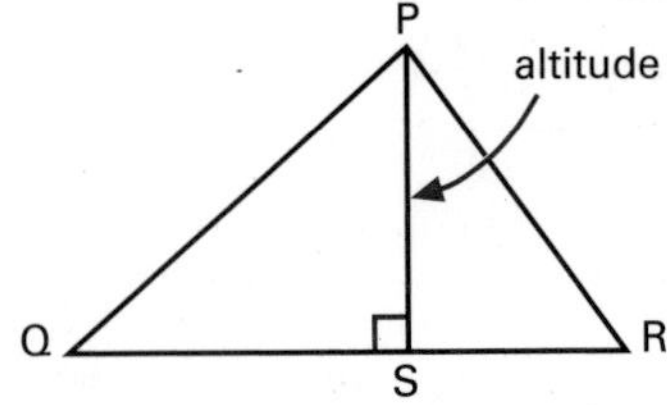

10 Find the equations of the three altitudes in △ABC in question **8**.

11 a Prove that STUV is a parallelogram, where S is (−3, 2), T(5, 6), U(2, −1) and V(−6, −5).
b Find the equations of its sides.

12 A(2, 4), B(9, 8) and C(8, 0) are vertices of a quadrilateral ABCD which has an axis of symmetry BD.

a Calculate the gradient of: **(i)** AC **(ii)** BD.

b Find the equation of BD.

c Write down the coordinates of:

(i) the midpoint of AC

(ii) D, if ABCD is a rhombus.

13 A chain drive passes round two cog wheels. In the coordinate model, the centres of the circles are A(5, 7) and B(15, 7), and the tangent SL touches one circle at S(4, 10).

Find the equations of:

a the radii AS and BL

b the tangent SL

c the axis of symmetry AB

d the tangent S′L′.

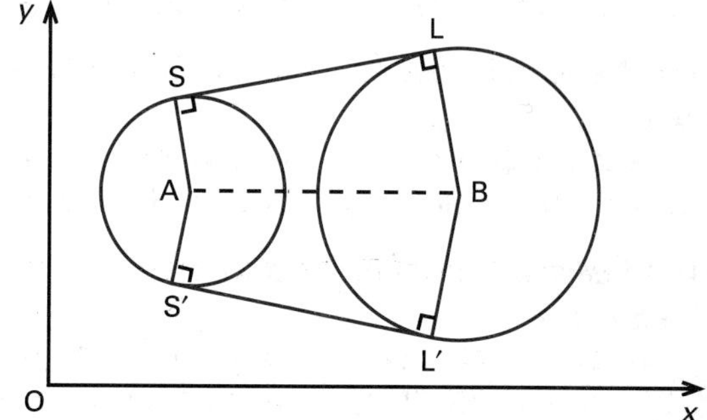

Intersecting lines

Example

a Find:

(i) the equations of the perpendicular bisectors of AB and AC in △ABC

(ii) the coordinates of S, where they meet.

b Show that S lies on the perpendicular bisector of BC.

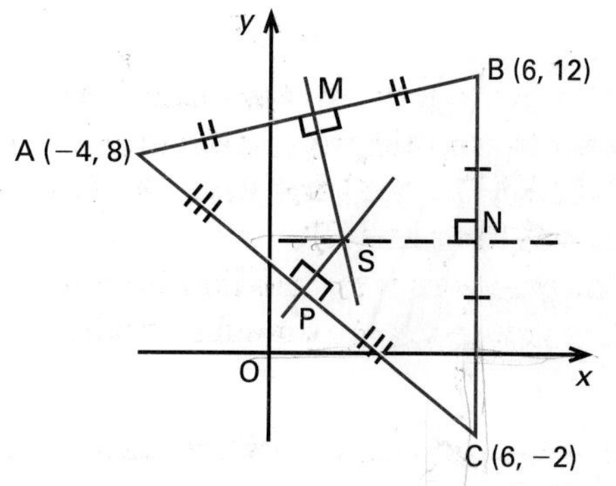

a (i) *Equation of MS*

$$m_{AB} = \frac{12-8}{6+4} = \frac{2}{5}$$

So $m_{MS} = -\frac{5}{2}$

M is $\left(\frac{-4+6}{2}, \frac{8+12}{2}\right)$, i.e. (1, 10).

Equation of MS is $y - 10 = -\frac{5}{2}(x-1)$

i.e. $\underline{2y + 5x = 25}$

Equation of PS

$$m_{AC} = \frac{-2-8}{6+4} = -1$$

So $m_{PS} = 1$

P is $\left(\frac{-4+6}{2}, \frac{8-2}{2}\right)$, i.e. (1, 3).

Equation of PS is $y - 3 = 1(x-1)$

i.e. $\underline{y - x = 2}$

(ii) See next page.

(ii) To find S, solve $\begin{cases} 2y + 5x = 25 \ldots \times 1 \\ y - x = 2 \ldots \times 2 \end{cases}$ $\quad \begin{aligned} 2y + 5x &= 25 \\ 2y - 2x &= 4 \end{aligned}$

Subtract $\quad 7x = 21$

$x = 3$, and $y = x + 2 = 5$, so S is the point (3, 5).

b *Equation of NS*
NS is parallel to the x-axis, and N is (6, 5).
The equation of NS is $y = 5$, and S(3, 5) lies on NS.
Notice that this example shows that the three perpendicular bisectors are concurrent at S.

a Draw the lines with equations $y = 3x + 1$ and $y = 6 - 2x$.
b Use the cursor to check their point of intersection, (1, 4).
c Repeat for different pairs of lines.

EXERCISE 7A

1 Find the point of intersection of the lines given by each pair of equations.

a $3y + x = 7$, $y - x = 1$ **b** $2y + 3x = 10$, $y + x = 5$ **c** $4y + 3x = 1$, $3y - 2x = 5$

2 Find the coordinates of the points of intersection of the line $2x - 3y = 12$ with the x and y-axes.

3 The sides of a triangle have equations $x = 1$, $5x + y = 5$ and $2x - y + 5 = 0$. Find the coordinates of the vertices of the triangle.

4 In diagram (i) below, the line through A is parallel to BC, which has equation $2y + x = 0$. Find:
a the equation of the line through A
b the coordinates of the points where it cuts the x and y-axes.

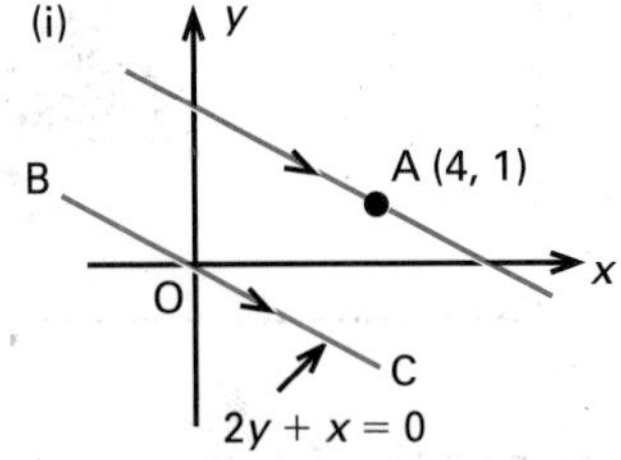

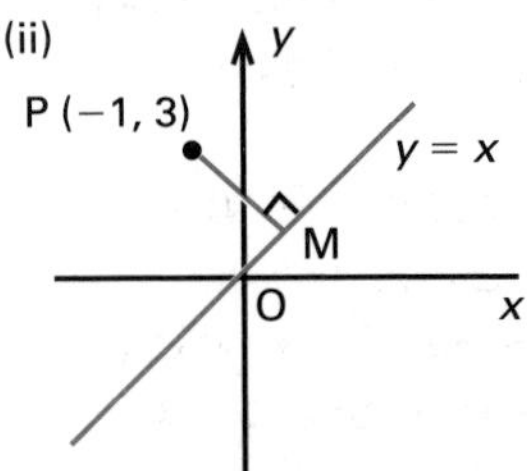

5 In diagram (ii) on page 14, the line through P is perpendicular to the line with equation $y = x$. Find:

a the equation of PM

b the coordinates of M.

6 Parallelogram STUV has vertices S(−3, 3), T(4, 7), U(5, 3) and V(−2, −1). Find:

a the equations of its diagonals

b the coordinates of their point of intersection.

7 **a** Find the equation of:

(i) the median PS

(ii) the altitude QT, in △PQR.

b Find the coordinates of their point of intersection, V.

8 Astrid and Lea are keen astronomers. They observe the movement of a star as it circles the Pole Star. With reference to their chosen axes they record the star's position at three different times as A(4, 12), B(10, 14) and C(18, 10).

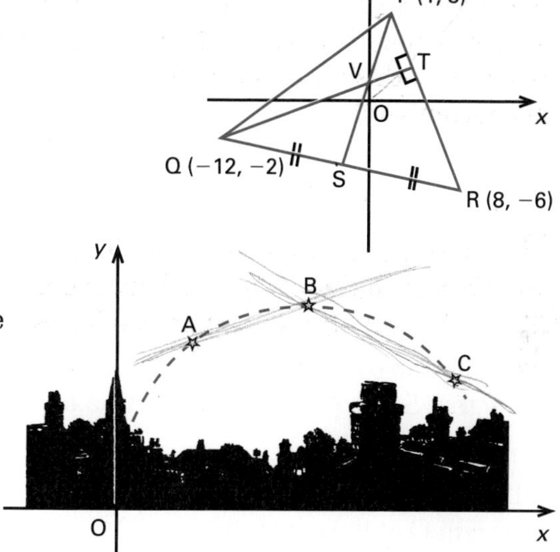

a Calculate the gradients of chords AB and BC.

b Find the equations of the perpendicular bisectors of AB and BC.

c Find the coordinates of the Pole Star, where the two perpendicular bisectors meet.

EXERCISE 7B

1 The vertices of △ABC are A(5, 5), B(−10, 0) and C(0, −10).

a Find: (i) the equations of the altitudes through A and B

(ii) the point of intersection, H, of these altitudes.

b Show that H lies on the altitude through C.

What does this tell you about the three altitudes?

2 A radar station at O detects a plane 5 km north, at A, flying in a straight line. Later the plane is noted at B, 10 km east of O. Taking OE and ON as x and y-axes:

a find the equation of (i) AB (ii) OD, which is perpendicular to AB

b find the coordinates of the point where the plane was nearest O

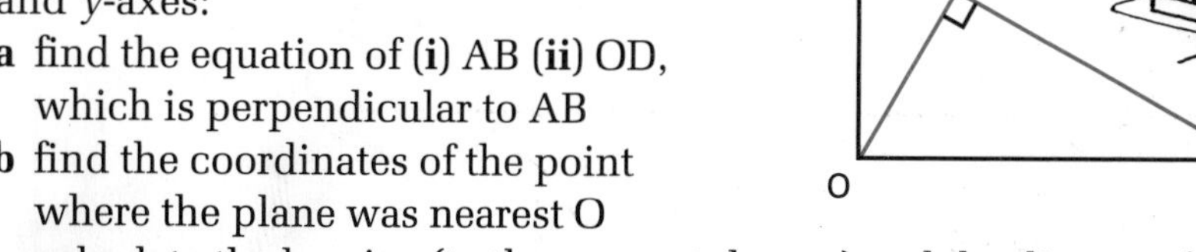

c calculate the bearing (to the nearest degree) and the distance (correct to 2 decimal places) of D from O.

3 $\triangle PQR$ has vertices P(−2, 2), Q(6, 6) and R(6, −4). Show these in a sketch.

a Find: **(i)** the equations of the perpendicular bisectors of PQ and QR

(ii) the point of intersection, S, of these lines.

b Show that S lies on the perpendicular bisector of PR (so the three perpendicular bisectors of the sides are concurrent at S).

4 In the coordinate model of this airport the origin is taken as the control tower. A is the point (−6, −2) and B is (6, 6). $\angle ABC = 90°$.

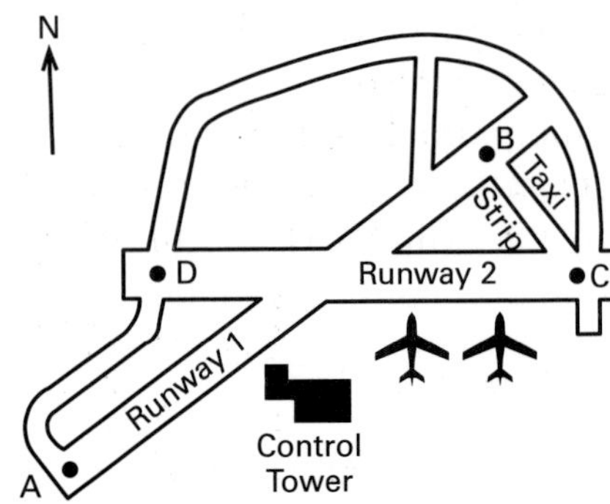

a Find the equation of:

(i) runway 1 (AB) **(ii)** the taxi strip (BC).

b Runway 2 points W-E, and D is (−2, 3). Find:

(i) the equation of DC

(ii) the coordinates of C

(iii) the length of BC, to the nearest metre (1 unit = 100 m).

5 The equations of the sides of $\triangle ABC$ are:

AB $2x - 5y + 25 = 0$, BC $3x - y - 8 = 0$ and CA $4x + 3y + 11 = 0$.

a Find: **(i)** the coordinates of A, B and C

(ii) the equations of the medians AP, BQ and CR of $\triangle ABC$.

b Show that S, the point of intersection of AP and BQ, lies on CR (so the medians are concurrent at S).

6 A ball casts a shadow on a table. With origin O at the centre of the ball, A is (−3, 4), B(4, −3) and C(0, −5).

Calculate:

a the gradients of OA and OB

b the equations of AL and LB

c the coordinates of L

d the distance LO, to the nearest cm (1 unit = 1 cm)

e the coordinates of P and Q

f the width of the shadow (PQ).

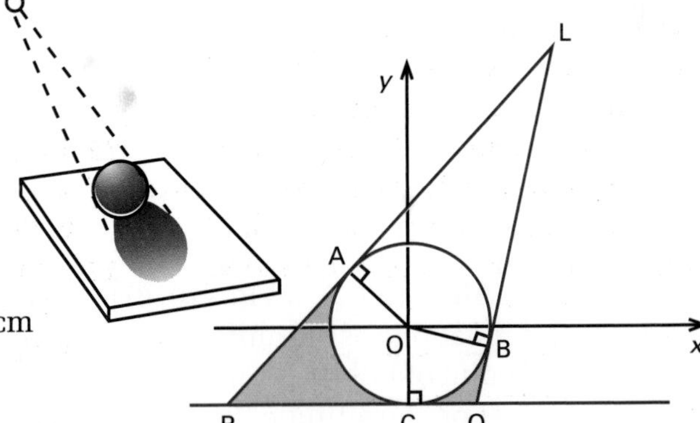

7 A computer can represent solid objects using perspective drawing and coordinate geometry. In a program, all lines going to the right converge on a vanishing point R(16, 10), and all lines to the left converge on L(0, 10). A(4, 7), E(4, 5), C(12, 7) and G(12, 5) are four vertices of a cuboid. Use intersections of lines to find the coordinates of the other vertices.

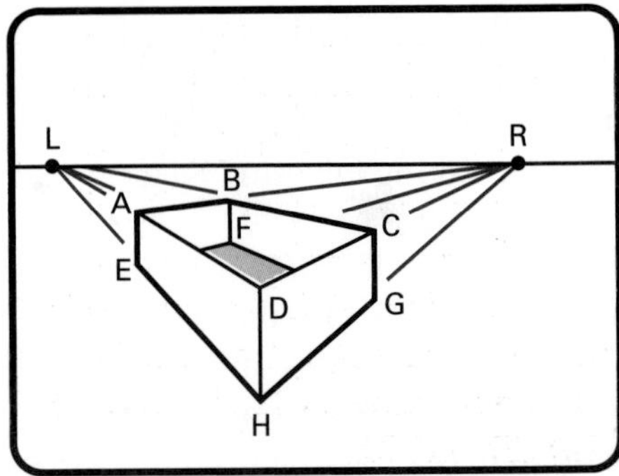

CHAPTER 1 REVIEW

1 A is the point $(-2, -3)$ and B is $(4, 5)$. Calculate:

a the length of AB

b the gradient of AB

c the angle between AB and OX, to the nearest degree.

2 G and H are the midpoints of DE and DF.

a Find the coordinates of G and H.

b Show that: **(i)** GH $\parallel$ EF **(ii)** GH $= \frac{1}{2}$EF.

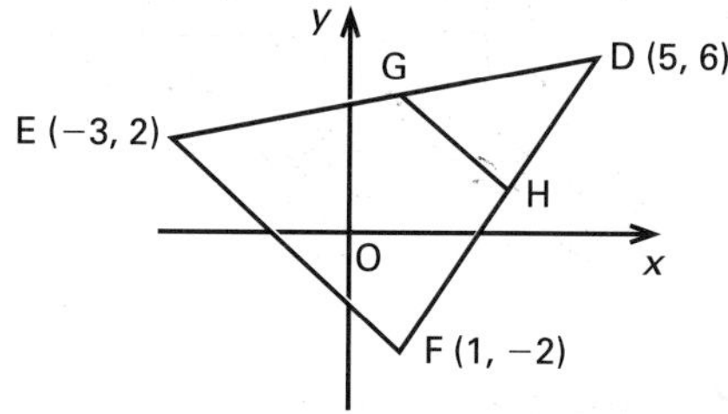

3 Say whether each line is parallel or perpendicular to the line $y = 2x + 2$:

a $y - 2x + 2 = 0$ **b** $y = -\frac{1}{2}x - 2$

c $2x - y = 4$ **d** $2y = -x - 4$

e $4x - 2y = 0$ **f** $2x + 4y = 1$

4 a Find the coordinates of the points where the line $2y - 3x = -12$ crosses the x and y-axes, and sketch the line.

b Write its equation in the form $y = mx + c$, and state its gradient.

5 Calculate the length, correct to 1 decimal place where necessary, gradient and equation of each side of kite KLMN.

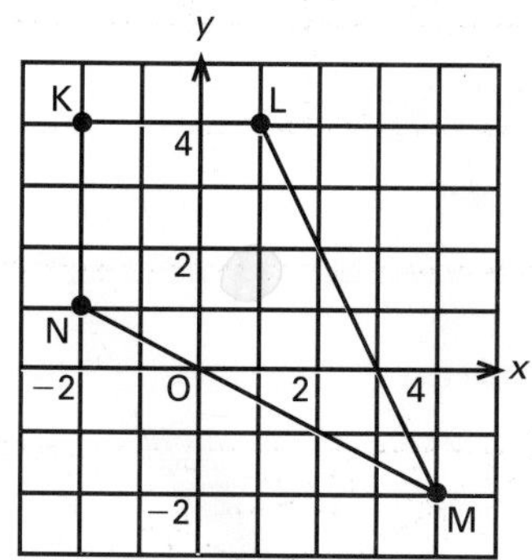

6 A is $(1, 1)$, B $(5, 3)$, C $(5, -3)$ and D $(1, 3)$. Calculate, correct to 1 decimal place:

a the angle between **(i)** AB and OX **(ii)** CD and OX

b the acute angle between AB and CD.

7 Which three of these points are collinear? $K(-2, -\frac{1}{2})$, $Z(12, 3)$, $Q(2, 1)$, $V(-4, -1)$

8 P is $(-6, 3)$ and Q is $(2, -3)$. Find the length, gradient and equation of PQ.

9 Are the lines with equations $2x - y = 3$, $3x + y = 2$ and $4x - 5y = 9$ concurrent?

10 a Find the equation of the line:

(i) with gradient $\frac{3}{4}$, passing through $(-4, 1)$

(ii) passing through $(7, 3)$ and $(10, -1)$.

b Prove that the two lines in **a** are perpendicular, and find their point of intersection.

11 In the diagram, find:

a the gradient of **(i)** AC **(ii)** altitude BP

b the equation of BP.

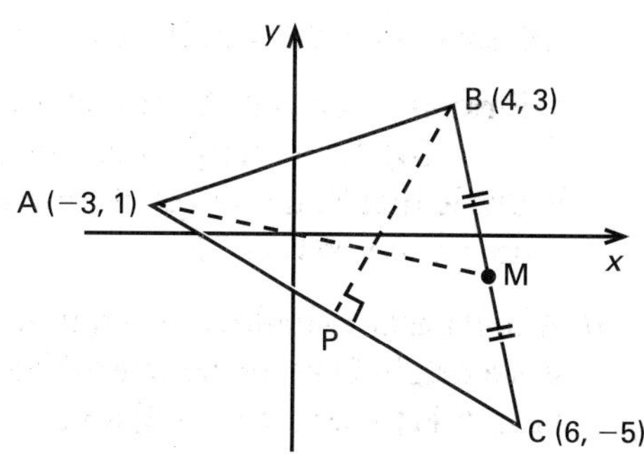

12 In the diagram for question **11**, find:

a the coordinates of M, the midpoint of BC

b the equation of median AM.

13 $A(0, 2)$, $B(3, -7)$ and $C(9, -5)$ are vertices of a rectangle ABCD.

a Find: **(i)** the equations of AD and CD

(ii) the coordinates of D.

b Check that the diagonals are equal in length.

14 The equations of the sides of $\triangle$PQR are: PQ $4y - x = 11$, QR $y - x = -1$ and PR $y + 2x = -4$. Find the coordinates of P, Q and R.

15 In $\triangle$STU, S is $(2, 6)$, T $(4, -2)$ and U $(13, 7)$. Find the coordinates of the point of intersection of altitude SF and median UE.

16 Find the equations of the lines which bisect the angles between the lines $y = x$ and $y = 2x$.

CHAPTER 1 SUMMARY

1 The distance formula

$$AB = \sqrt{(x_2 - x_1)^2 + (y_2 - y_1)^2}$$

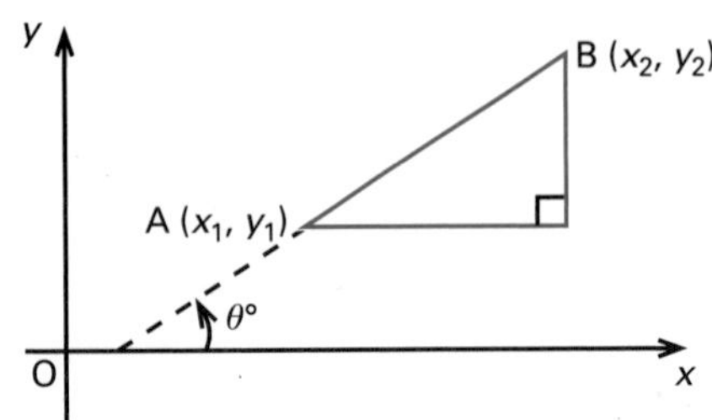

2 The midpoint of AB

The midpoint is $\left(\frac{x_1 + x_2}{2}, \frac{y_1 + y_2}{2}\right)$

3 The gradient formula

a $m_{AB} = \frac{y_2 - y_1}{x_2 - x_1}$, $x_2 \neq x_1$

b $m_{AB} = \tan\theta°$, where $\theta°$ is the anti-clockwise angle from OX to AB (or AB produced).

c A line parallel to the x-axis has zero gradient.

d A line parallel to the y-axis has no defined gradient.

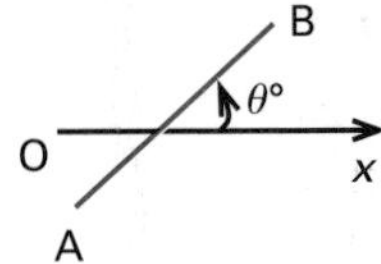

Positive gradient

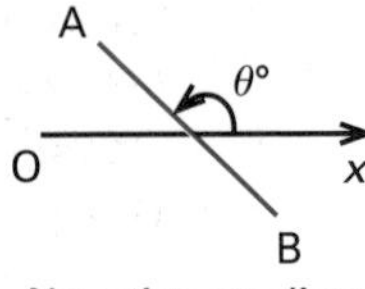

Negative gradient

4 Parallel and perpendicular lines

a

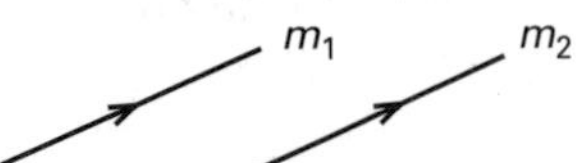

$m_1 = m_2 \Leftrightarrow$ the lines are parallel.

b

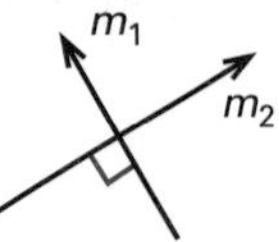

$m_1 m_2 = -1 \Leftrightarrow$ the lines are perpendicular.

If $m_1 = \frac{a}{b}$, then $m_2 = -\frac{b}{a}$.

5 Equations of a straigiht line

a Given point and gradient:

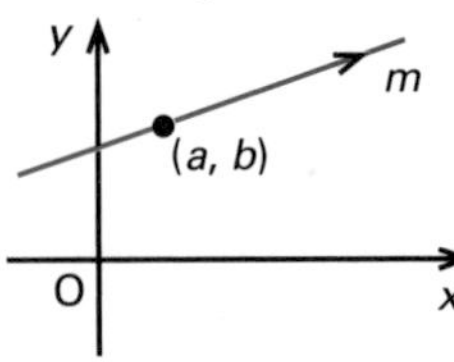

$y - b = m(x - a)$

b Given gradient and y-intercept:

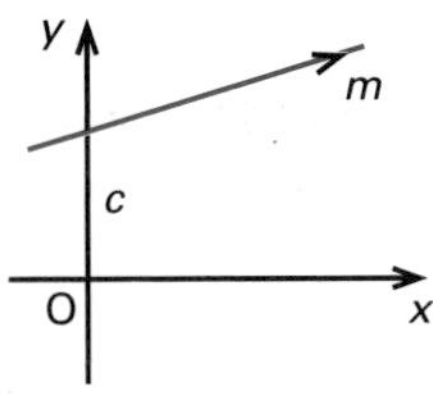

$y = mx + c$

c $ax + by + c = 0$ is a linear (straight line) equation.

6 Intersecting lines

Solve the equations of the lines simultaneously to find their point of intersection.

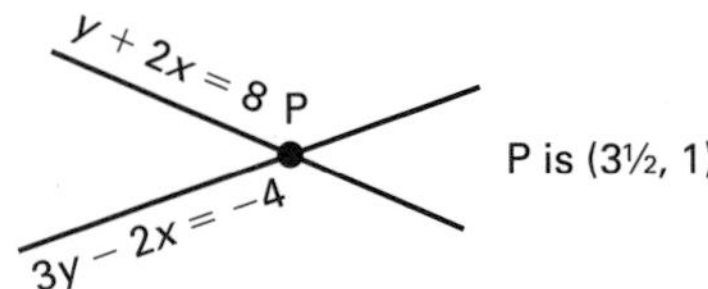

7 Sets of concurrent lines in a triangle

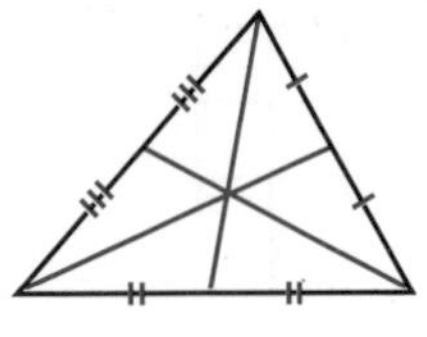
Medians

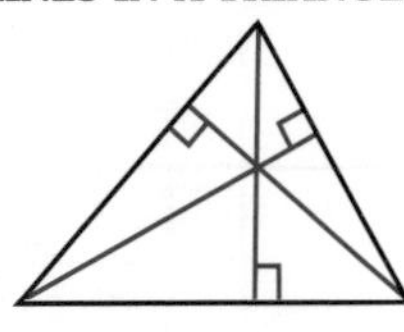
Altitudes

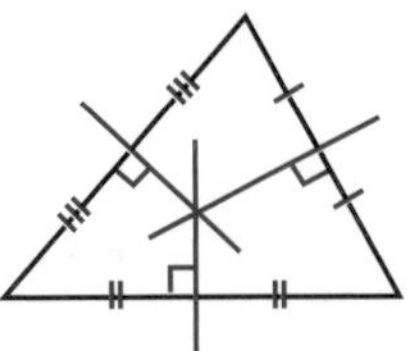
Perpendicular bisectors of sides

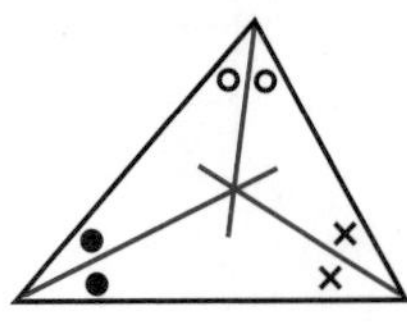
Angle bisectors

2.1 Composite and Inverse Functions

Functions

A function is defined from a set A to a set B as a rule which links each member of A to exactly one member of B.
Since a function f assigns exactly one value y to each x, we write $y = f(x)$, or f: $x \rightarrow y$ ('f maps x to y').

Examples

1

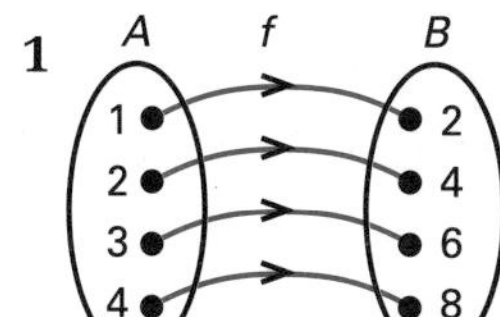

$f(x) = 2x$, or f: $x \rightarrow 2x$

2

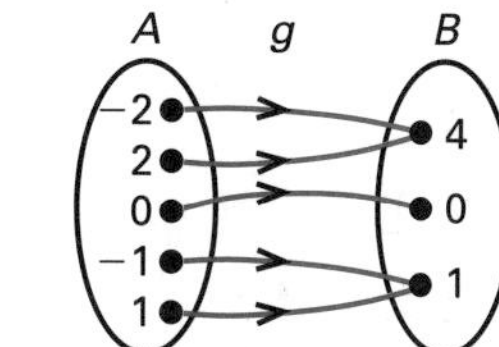

$g(x) = x^2$, or g: $x \rightarrow x^2$

3 Given $f(x) = 2x + 3$:

a $f(x + 1) = 2(x + 1) + 3 = 2x + 5$

b $f\left(\dfrac{x}{x+1}\right) = 2\left(\dfrac{x}{x+1}\right) + 3,\ x \neq -1$

$$= \frac{2x}{x+1} + \frac{3(x+1)}{x+1}$$

$$= \frac{2x}{x+1} + \frac{3x+3}{x+1}$$

$$= \frac{5x+3}{x+1}$$

Reminder

The largest domain of:

a $h(x) = \sqrt{x}$ is the set of real numbers such that $x \geqslant 0$, $\{x \in R: x \geqslant 0\}$

b $k(x) = \dfrac{1}{x-1}$ is the set of real numbers except $x = 1$, $\{x \in R: x \neq 1\}$.

EXERCISE 1

1 Copy and complete:

$f(x)$	$2x - 1$	$\frac{1}{x}$	x^2	$\frac{1}{2x^2 - 1}$
$f(1)$				
$f(0)$		undefined		
$f(-2)$				

2 Given the function and its domain, write down the range for each of these.

a $f(x) = x + 5$, domain $\{0, 1, 2\}$ **b** $f(x) = 2x - 1$, domain $\{-1, 0, 1\}$

c $f(x) = x^2$, domain $\{-2, -1, 0\}$ **d** $f(x) = \frac{1}{x}$, domain $\{1, 2, 3\}$

e $f(x) = (x + 5)^2$, domain $\{-5, 0, 5\}$

3 Decide which of these are diagrams of functions. Remember that for *every* x in the domain there is exactly *one value* of *f* in the range.

a

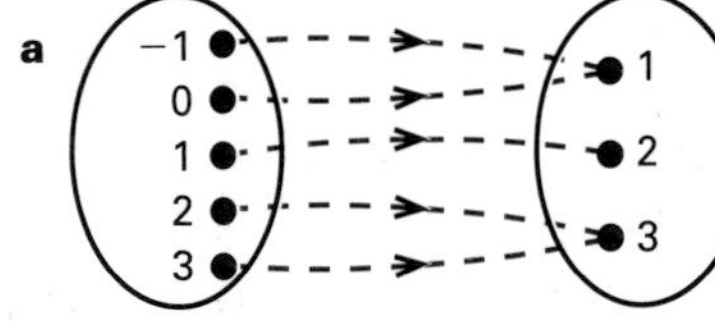

b

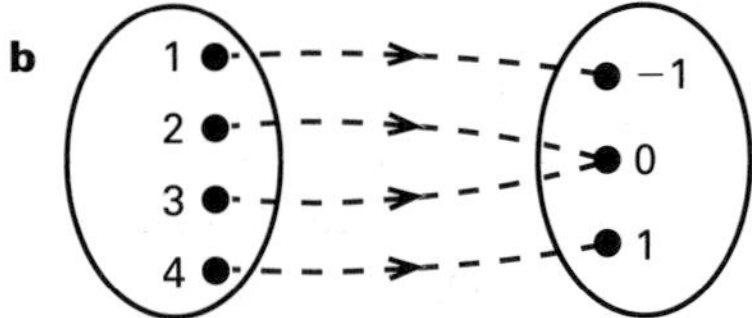

c

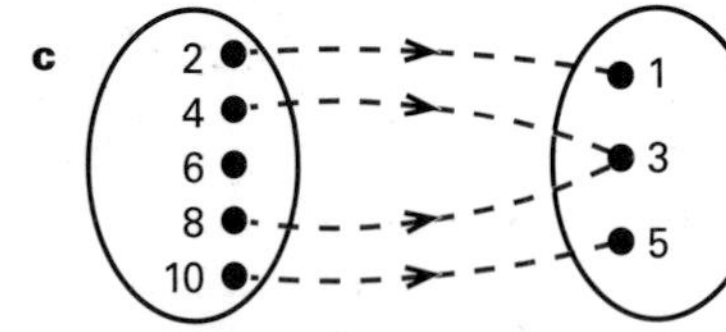

d

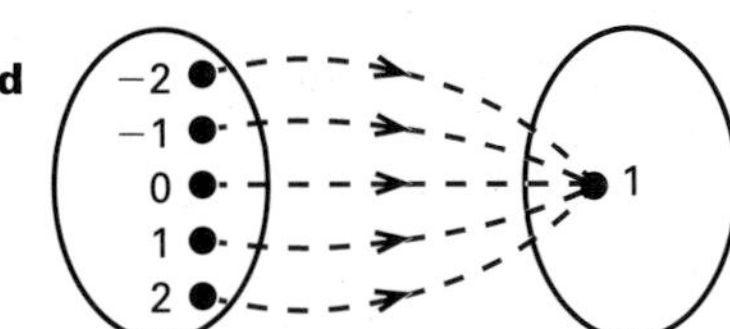

4 $f(x) = x^2$. Find formulae for:

a $f(2x)$ **b** $f(x + 1)$ **c** $f(-x)$ **d** $f\left(\frac{1}{x}\right)$.

5 $g(x) = 2x + 1$. Find formulae for:

a $g(x + 1)$ **b** $g(2x)$ **c** $g(\frac{1}{2}x)$ **d** $g(x - 1)$.

6 $h(x) = x^2 - 2x$. Show that:

a $h(2x) = 4x(x - 1)$ **b** $h(x + 1) = (x + 1)(x - 1)$.

7 $f(x) = 3x^2 + 6x + 2$.

a Show that $f(x - 1) = 3x^2 - 1$.

b Find a simplified expression for $f(x + 1)$.

c Hence simplify $\frac{f(x + 1) - f(x - 1)}{2}$.

8 For what values of x are these functions undefined?

a $f(x) = \sqrt{x}$ **b** $g(x) = \sqrt{(x - 1)}$ **c** $h(x) = \sqrt{(x + 2)}$

d $k(x) = \frac{1}{x}$ **e** $m(x) = \frac{1}{x - 5}$ **f** $n(x) = \frac{1}{x(x + 1)}$

9 $f(x) = \frac{x}{x+1}$. Simplify:

a $f(x-1)$ b $f\left(\frac{1}{x}\right)$ c $f\left(\frac{1}{x}-1\right)$ d $f\left(\frac{1}{x-1}\right)$.

10 $g(x) = \frac{x}{1-x}$. Simplify:

a $g(x+1)$ b $g\left(\frac{1}{x}\right)$ c $g\left(\frac{1}{x+1}\right)$ d $g\left(\frac{1}{1-x}\right)$.

11 $h(x) = \frac{1}{2}(x-1)$. If $h(a) = 1$, find a.

12 $k(x) = \frac{x}{2-x}$, $x \neq 2$. If $k(a) = 2$, find a.

Graphs and models

The volume, v cm^3, of a special shape of metal box is given by $v(x) = x^2 - 6x + 10$, where x cm is the length of the box. The length must be from 2 cm to 6 cm. The graph of v gives a good way to explore the design of the box. The *domain* is $2 \leqslant x \leqslant 6$, and from the graph the *range* is $1 \leqslant v \leqslant 10$.

The minimum volume is 1 cm^3 when the length is 3 cm, and the maximum volume is 10 cm^3 when the length is 6 cm.

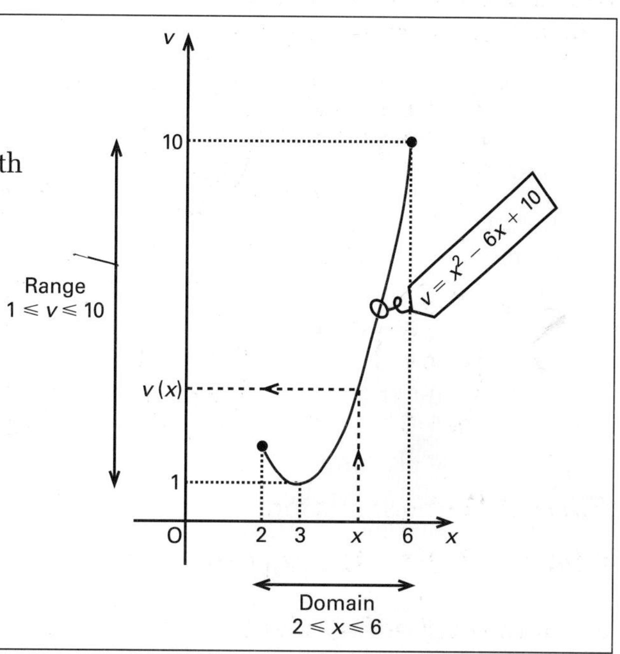

EXERCISE 2

1 For each of these graphs write down, as inequalities, the domain and range of the function illustrated.

a

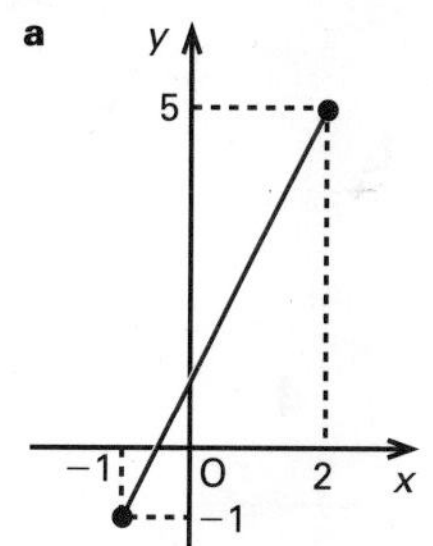

b

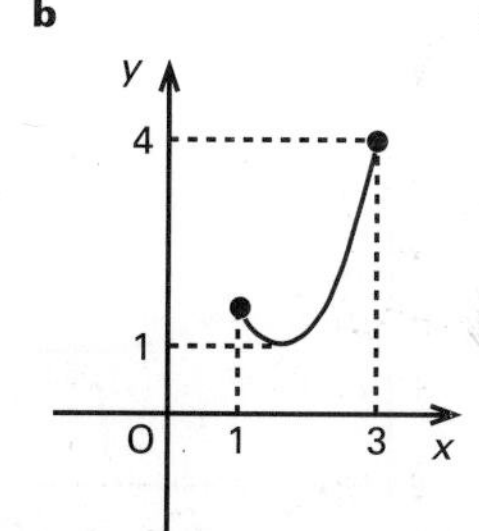

c

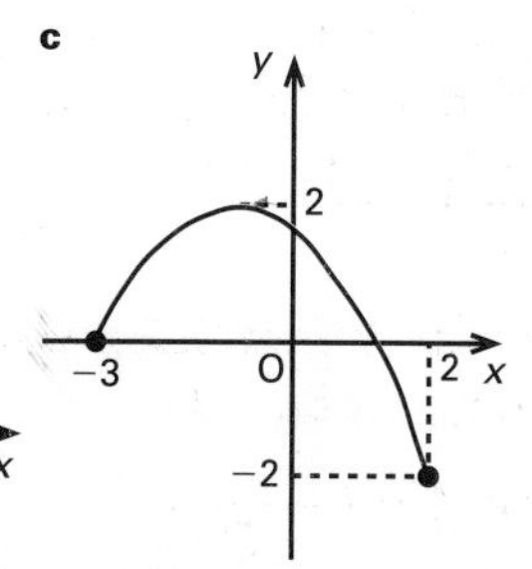

d

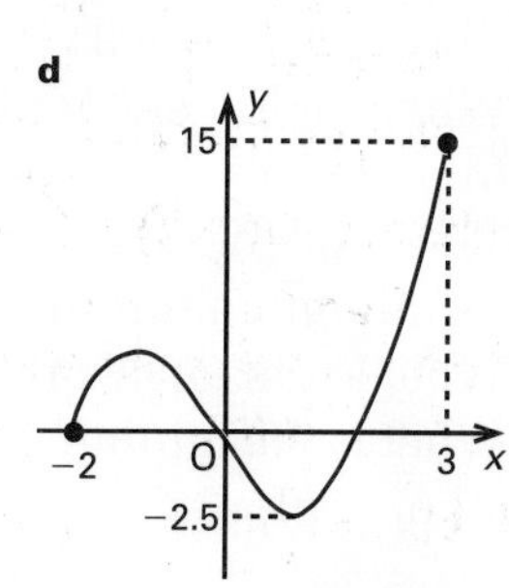

2 The domain of each function is R, the set of real numbers. Sketch the graph of each function, and state its range.
a $f(x) = 3x$ **b** $g(x) = x^2$ **c** $h(x) = 4 - x^2$

3 **a** A function g is given by the formula $g(x) = x^2 + 1$, with domain $\{x \in R: x \geqslant 0\}$. Sketch the graph of g, and state the range.
b Change the domain to R, sketch the graph now and state the range.

4 $h(x) = 3x + 1$, and the domain of h is $\{x \in R: x \geqslant 3\}$. Sketch the graph of h, and state the range.

5 Sketch the graphs of i and j, and state the range of each.
a $i(x) = x^3$, with domain $\{x \in R: -2 \leqslant x \leqslant 2\}$
b $j(x) = \frac{1}{x}$, with domain $\{x \in R: 1 \leqslant x \leqslant 4\}$

6 The volume, v cm^3, of a box is given by $v(x) = 6x - x^2$, where the length x cm has to be from 1 cm to 4 cm.
a Sketch the graph of v.
b State the domain and range of v.
c What are the maximum and minimum volumes of the box, and its corresponding lengths?

7 The support of the suspension bridge is modelled by the formula $f(x) = 8x - \frac{1}{2}x^2$, where $-3 \leqslant x \leqslant 19$, and the x-axis is the road.
a Sketch the graph of f for $-3 \leqslant x \leqslant 19$.
b State the range of f, and explain its meaning for the height of the support above: **(i)** the road **(ii)** the river (1 unit = 1 m).

8 The cost, £C million, of laying 1 km of pipe for a water main is given by the formula $C = \frac{200}{9a} + 2a$, where a is the cross-sectional area of the pipe.
a State a simple approximate formula for C when:
(i) a is very large
(ii) a is very small.
Why would neither of these be good, in practice?
b The graph of C is shown. Its minimum turning point is $(3\frac{1}{3}, 13\frac{1}{3})$. What is the range of C?
c What is the minimum cost of laying 1 km of pipe?

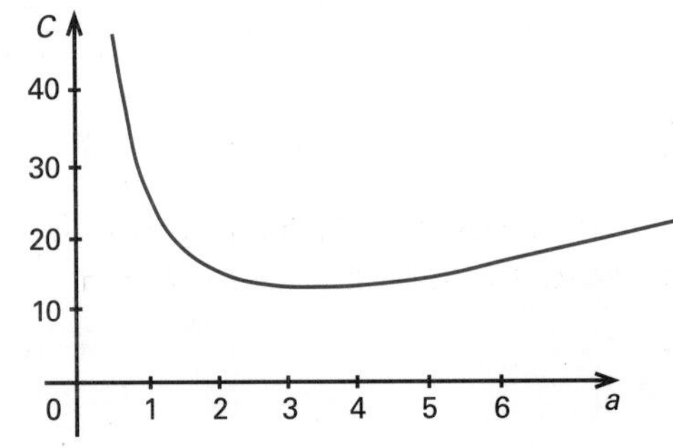

Composite functions

(i) Using the rule $\xrightarrow{f}$ Double $\xrightarrow{g}$ Add 1 applied to real numbers, check that $1 \to 3$, $2 \to 5$, $3 \to 7$, $0 \to 1$, $-1 \to -1$, and so on.
Two functions are involved: a 'doubling' function f, where $f(x) = 2x$, and an 'add 1' function g, where $g(x) = x + 1$.

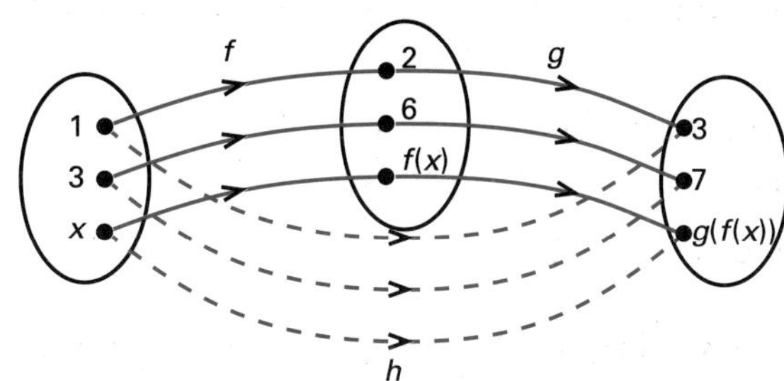

In the diagram, f and g are combined to get a new function h defined by $h(x) = g(f(x)) = g(2x) = 2x + 1$.

(ii) Now using the rule $\xrightarrow{g}$ Add 1 $\xrightarrow{f}$ Double, check that $1 \to 4$, $2 \to 6$, $0 \to 2$, $-1 \to 0$ and so on.
Combining g and f in this way gives a different function k, defined by $k(x) = f(g(x)) = f(x + 1) = 2(x + 1) = 2x + 2$.
h and k are composite functions, obtained from the compositions of f and g.

Example 1 If $f(x) = x - 2$ and $g(x) = x^2$, then:

a $f(g(x)) = f(x^2) = x^2 - 2$
b $g(f(x)) = g(x - 2) = (x - 2)^2$
c $f(f(x)) = f(x - 2) = (x - 2) - 2 = x - 4$
d $g(g(x)) = g(x^2) = (x^2)^2 = x^4$

Example 2 If $f(x) = \dfrac{x}{x-1}$, find a formula for $f(f(x))$.

$$f(f(x)) = f\left(\frac{x}{x-1}\right)$$

$$= \frac{\dfrac{x}{x-1}}{\dfrac{x}{x-1} - 1} = \frac{\dfrac{x}{x-1}}{\dfrac{x}{x-1} - \dfrac{x-1}{x-1}} = \frac{\dfrac{x}{x-1}}{\dfrac{x-(x-1)}{x-1}} = \frac{\dfrac{x}{x-1}}{\dfrac{x-x+1}{x-1}} = \frac{\dfrac{x}{x-1}}{\dfrac{1}{x-1}} = x$$

EXERCISE 3

1 List the numbers in sets B and C which correspond to the numbers in set A.

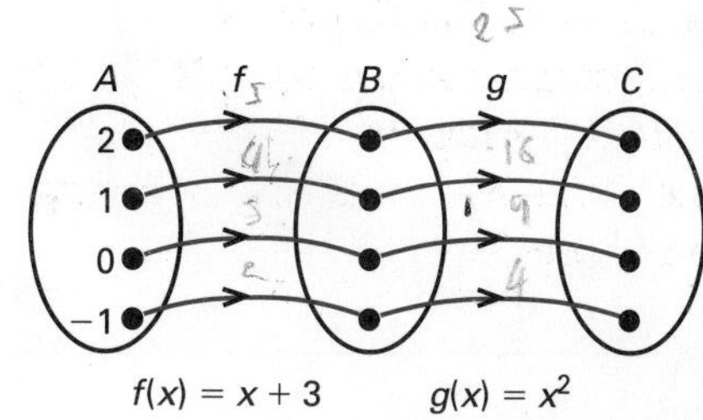

$f(x) = x + 3$ $g(x) = x^2$

2 $f(x) = x + 5$, $g(x) = 2x$ and the domain of f is $\{0, 1, 2\}$. Calculate:
- **a** $f(0)$ and $g(f(0))$
- **b** $f(1)$ and $g(f(1))$
- **c** $f(2)$ and $g(f(2))$
- **d** $g(f(x))$.

3 $f(x) = x - 2$ and $g(x) = 3x$. Calculate the values of the following composite functions. For example, $g(f(4)) = g(2) = 6$.
- **a** $g(f(3))$
- **b** $g(f(8))$
- **c** $f(g(1))$
- **d** $f(g(0))$
- **e** $f(f(5))$
- **f** $f(f(2))$
- **g** $g(g(0))$
- **h** $g(g(-2))$
- **i** $f(g(x))$
- **j** $g(f(x))$
- **k** $f(f(x))$
- **l** $g(g(x))$

4 For each pair of functions below, obtain formulae for: **(i)** $g(f(x))$ **(ii)** $f(g(x))$.
- **a** $f(x) = x + 3$, $g(x) = x + 2$
- **b** $f(x) = 2x + 3$, $g(x) = 3x + 2$
- **c** $f(x) = x^2$, $g(x) = x^3$
- **d** $f(x) = x - 2$, $g(x) = x^2$
- **e** $f(x) = x^3$, $g(x) = 3x$
- **f** $f(x) = x^2 + 3$, $g(x) = 2x + 5$
- **g** $f(x) = \sin x$, $g(x) = 2x$
- **h** $f(x) = \cos x$, $g(x) = 1 - x^2$

5 $f(x) = 3x + 1$ and $g(x) = 5x + a$, where a is a constant.
- **a** Find $f(g(x))$ and $g(f(x))$.
- **b** Find the value of a for which $f(g(x)) = g(f(x))$.

6 $g(x) = 2x$ and $h(x) = x^2 + 4$. Find in simplest form:
- **a** $h(g(x))$
- **b** $g(h(x))$
- **c** $g(g(x))$
- **d** $h(h(x))$.

7 For each pair of functions below, obtain formulae for: **(i)** $g(f(x))$ **(ii)** $f(g(x))$.
- **a** $f(x) = x + 2$, $g(x) = x^2$
- **b** $f(x) = x - 5$, $g(x) = 3x - 1$
- **c** $f(x) = x - 7$, $g(x) = x^2 - x$
- **d** $f(x) = x^2$, $g(x) = 4x^2 - 1$
- **e** $f(x) = 3x - 1$, $g(x) = x^2 + 1$
- **f** $f(x) = 3x - 1$, $g(x) = \dfrac{1}{x + 1}$
- **g** $f(x) = \dfrac{1}{x}$, $g(x) = \dfrac{2}{3x}$
- **h** $f(x) = 1 - x$, $g(x) = \dfrac{1}{x - 1}$

8 $f(x) = \dfrac{x}{1 - x}$ and $g(x) = \dfrac{1}{x}$. Find in simplest form:
- **a** $g(g(x))$
- **b** $g(f(x))$
- **c** $f(g(x))$
- **d** $f(f(x))$.

Challenges

1 Working with real numbers, you know that: $3 + 7 = 7 + 3$ and $3 \times 7 = 7 \times 3$, but $3 - 7 \neq 7 - 3$ and $3 \div 7 \neq 7 \div 3$.
So what about composition of functions?
Is $g(f(x)) = f(g(x))$? Find out from your answers in Exercise 3.

2 Check that $7 + (3 + 2) = (7 + 3) + 2$ and $7 \times (3 \times 2) = (7 \times 3) \times 2$, but $7 - (3 - 2) \neq (7 - 3) - 2$.

So what about composition of functions?
$g(f(x))$ is sometimes written $g \circ f$ ('g circle f').
Is $h \circ (g \circ f) = (h \circ g) \circ f$?
Investigate this, taking $f(x) = 2x$, $g(x) = x + 1$ and $h(x) = x^2$.
Try it again for $f(x) = 2x + 3$, $g(x) = 3x + 2$ and $h(x) = x + 4$.
Experiment with other functions of your own choice.

Functions with inverses

From the diagram, the function f that maps A to B is $f(x) = x^3$.
Is there a function g that 'undoes' f, that is, maps B back to A?
If so, $g(1^3) = 1$, $g(2^3) = 2$, $g(3^3) = 3$, and $g(4^3) = 4$. Its formula is $g(x) = x^{1/3}$, and $f(g(x)) = f(x^{1/3}) = (x^{1/3})^3 = x$.
g is the inverse of f, and its symbol is f^{-1} ('f inverse').
$f(x) = x^3$ and $f^{-1}(x) = x^{1/3}$.
For a function to have an inverse, the members of its domain and range must be in one-to-one correspondence.

EXERCISE 4

1 Decide whether each of these functions has or has not an inverse $f^{-1}: B \rightarrow A$, by checking if there is a one-to-one correspondence between members of its domain and range.

a
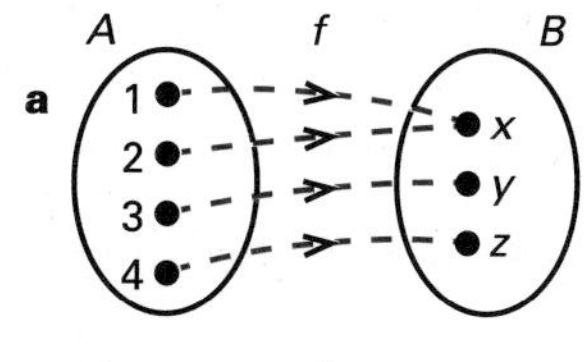

b
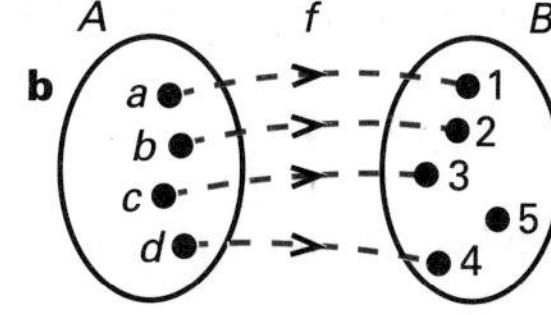

c
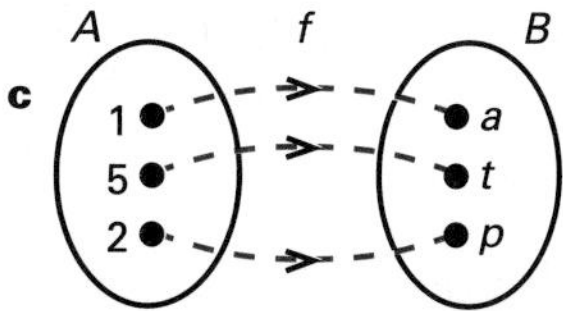

d
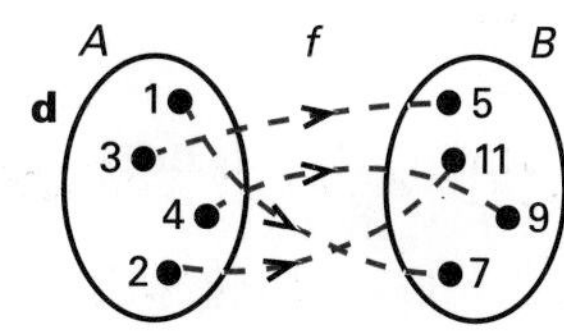

2 Here are the answers to question **1**; check yours.
a no; x has links with two members of set A.
b no; there is no link from 5 to set A.
c yes; sets A and B are in one-to-one correspondence.
d same as **c**.

3 $A = \{-2, 0, 2\}$ and $B = \{0, 4\}$. $f: A \rightarrow B$ has formula $f(x) = x^2$. Using an arrow diagram linking sets A and B, find whether or not f has an inverse f^{-1}.

4 Each table defines a function f. Which function has an inverse? Construct a table for the inverse.

a

x	-2	-1	0	1	2	3
$f(x)$	2	1	0	1	2	3

b

x	1	2	3	4	5	6
$f(x)$	10	10^2	10^3	10^4	10^5	10^6

5 Each graph below represents a function f. Neither function has an inverse. Explain why not.

a

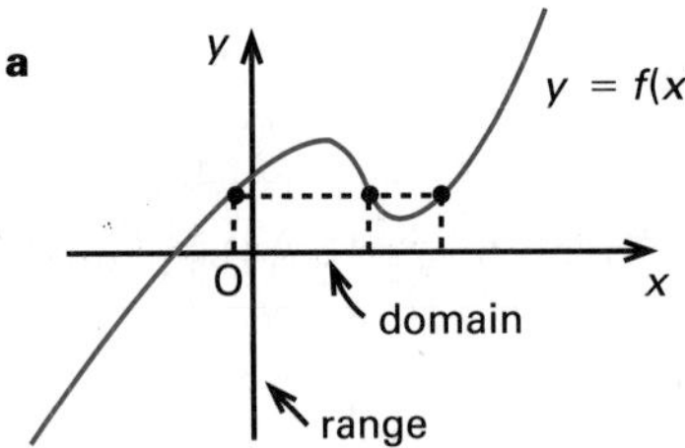

b

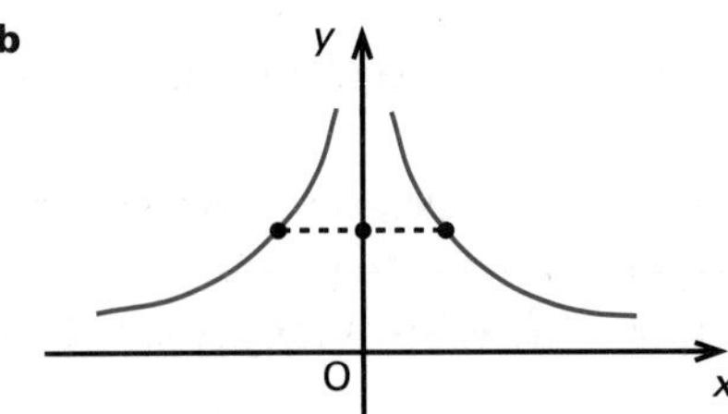

6 Use the graph of $f(x) = x^2 - 4$ to answer the following questions.

a Why does f not have an inverse?

b What is the range of f?

c How could you restrict the domain so that the new function has an inverse $f^{-1}(x)$? Can you think of other ways of doing this?

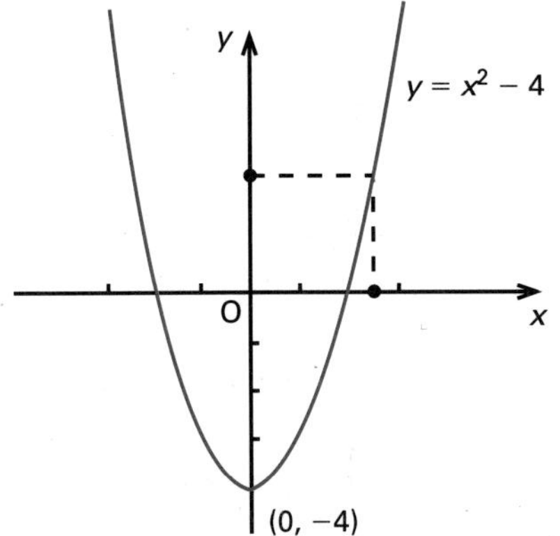

7 Sketch the graph $y = (x - 4)^2$, and answer question **6** for the function $f(x) = (x - 4)^2$.

If function f which maps A to B has an inverse function f^{-1}, then f takes x to y, and f^{-1} takes y back to x.

So $y = f(x) \Leftrightarrow x = f^{-1}(y)$.

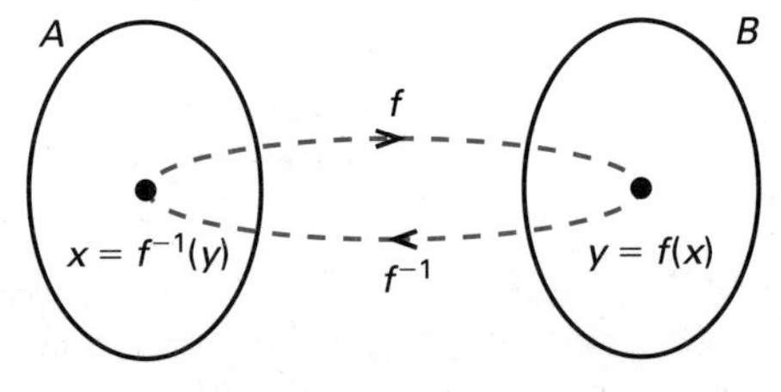

For example, the function $f: x \rightarrow 2x$ is a 'doubling' function, so its inverse is a 'halving' function, $f^{-1}: x \rightarrow \frac{1}{2}x$.
The graphs of the functions have equations $y = 2x$ and $y = \frac{1}{2}x$, and are symmetrical about the line $y = x$.

The graph $y = f^{-1}(x)$ can be found from the graph $y = f(x)$ by reflecting it in the line $y = x$.

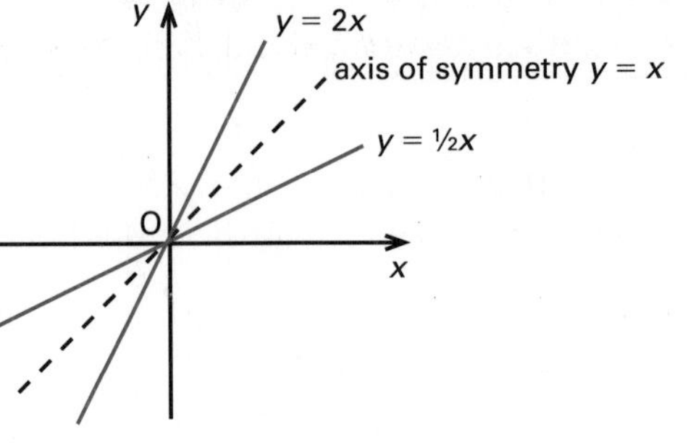

Illustrate the relationship between the graphs $y = f(x)$, $y = f^{-1}(x)$ and $y = x$ for:

a $f(x) = \sqrt{x}$, $f^{-1}(x) = x^2$ $(x \geqslant 0)$

b $f(x) = 2x + 5$, $f^{-1}(x) = \frac{1}{2}(x - 5)$.

8 Write down a formula for the inverse f^{-1} of each function, and illustrate in sketches, showing the symmetry about the line $y = x$.

a $f(x) = 4x$ **b** $f(x) = x + 2$ **c** $f(x) = x - 5$

d $f(x) = \frac{x}{5}$ **e** $f(x) = x^2 (x \geqslant 0)$ **f** $f(x) = x^3$

9 **(i)** Copy these diagrams, and sketch the graph $y = f^{-1}(x)$ by reflecting the given graphs in the line $y = x$.

(ii) Hence write down a formula for f^{-1} in each case.

a

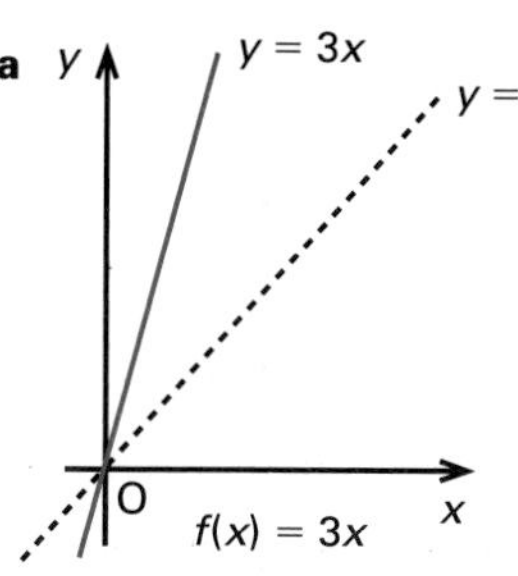

f(x) = 3x

b

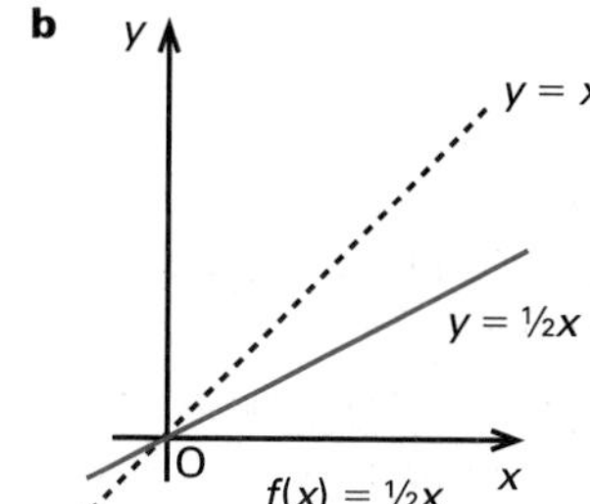

f(x) = ½x

c

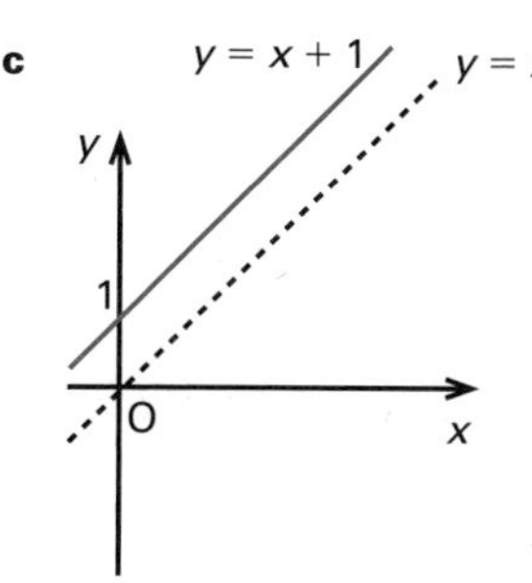

f(x) = x + 1

d

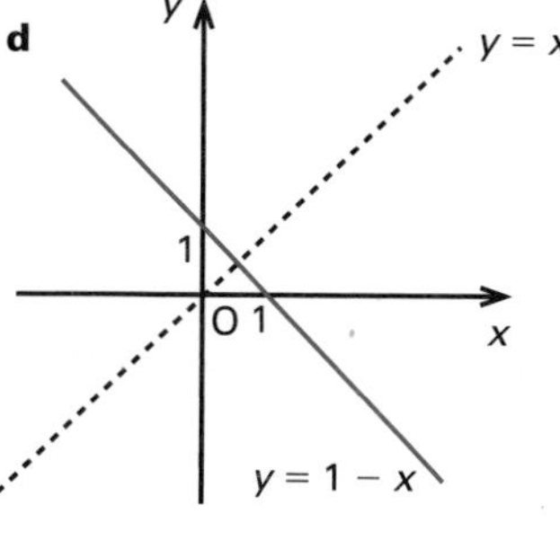

f(x) = 1 − x

10 **a** Copy and complete:

x	0	1	2	3
$f(x) = 2^x$				

b Draw the graph $y = 2^x$ for $0 \leqslant x \leqslant 3$ on squared paper.

c Make a corresponding table for the inverse function f^{-1}, and use it to draw the graph of f^{-1} on the same diagram.

d Check the symmetry about the line $y = x$.

CHAPTER 2.1 REVIEW

1 Find the range of each of these functions:

a $f(x) = 3x + 4$, domain $\{0, 1, 2, 3\}$

b $f(x) = x^{1/3}$, domain $\{0, 1, 8, 27\}$

c $f(x) = x^2 + 2$, domain $\{-3, 0, 3\}$

d $f(x) = \sin 2x°$, domain R, {all real numbers}.

2 $f(x) = \sqrt{(x + 1)}$.

a What is the largest domain of f?

b Find, and simplify:

(i) $f(x - 1)$ (ii) $f(4x - 1)$.

3 For each of these graphs, state:

(i) the domain of the function

(ii) the range.

a

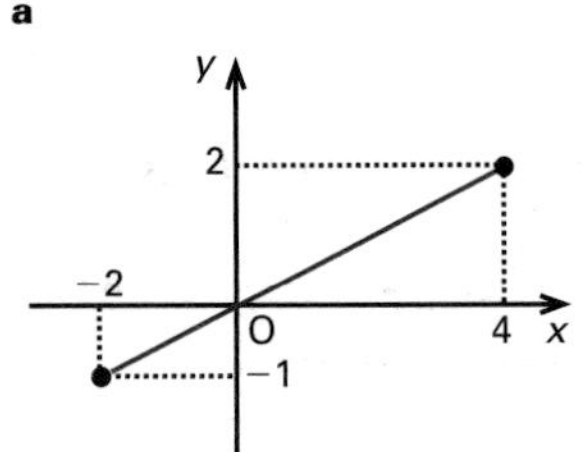

b

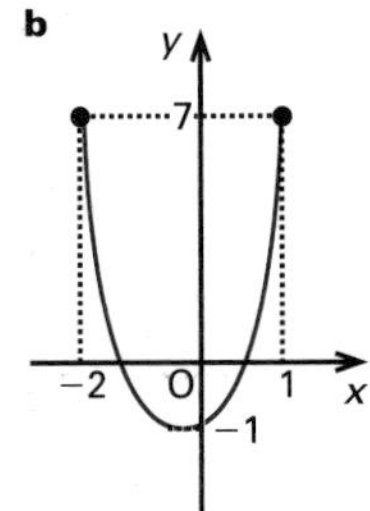

4 These formulae define functions. In each case state the largest possible domain.

a $f(x) = \sqrt{(2 - x)}$

b $g(x) = \sqrt{(x^2 - 4)}$

c $h(x) = \dfrac{3}{x + 1}$

d $k(x) = \dfrac{1}{x(x - 2)}$

5 Sketch the graphs of these functions, and state the range of each.

a $f(x) = x + 2$

b $g(x) = x^2 - 2x - 8$

6 For each pair of functions f and g find formulae for the composite functions:

(i) $g(f(x))$ **(ii)** $f(g(x))$

(iii) $f(f(x))$ **(iv)** $g(g(x))$.

a $f(x) = 3x + 5$, $g(x) = x^2$

b $f(x) = 2x - 1$, $g(x) = \dfrac{1}{x}$

c $f(x) = 1 - x$, $g(x) = 1 - 2x$

d $f(x) = \dfrac{1}{x}$, $g(x) = \dfrac{1}{x - 1}$

7 $f(x) = 2x - 1$, $g(x) = \dfrac{x^2 + 1}{x^2 - 1}$ and $h(x) = g(f(x))$.

a Find a formula for h.

b For what values of x is h undefined?

8 $f(x) = x^3 - x^2 + x$, $g(x) = x - 1$ and $h(x) = f(g(x))$.

a Show that $h(x) = (x - 1)(x^2 - 3x + 3)$.

b $k(x) = \dfrac{1}{h(x)}$. For what value of x is the function k undefined?

9 (i) Sketch the graph of each function and also the graph of its inverse on the same diagram.

(ii) Find a formula for each inverse function.

a $f(x) = 3x$ **b** $g(x) = 2x + 4$

c $h(x) = -x^3$

10 The number of cars, n per minute, passing a point in a motorway depended on their average speed, s mph, according to the formula $n(s) = \dfrac{88s}{20 + s}$.

a Suggest a suitable domain for the formula.

b Calculate the range, to the nearest whole number, for your domain.

c Rearrange the formula to express s in terms of n, and use this to find the average speed of the cars when 48 pass every minute.

CHAPTER 2.1 SUMMARY

1 FUNCTIONS

A *function* from set A to set B is a rule which links each member of A to exactly one member of B.

A function can be described by:

a a *formula*, with details of the domain. For example, $f(x) = 2x$, or $f: x \to 2x$, where $x \in R$ (x is a real number).

b an *arrow diagram*

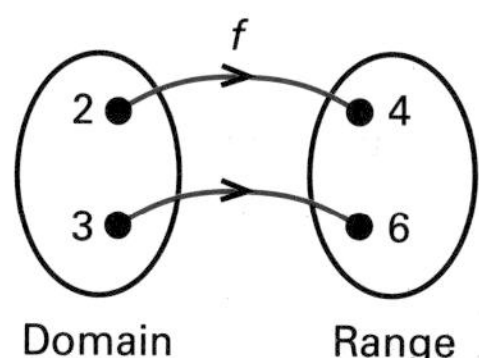

c a *graph*

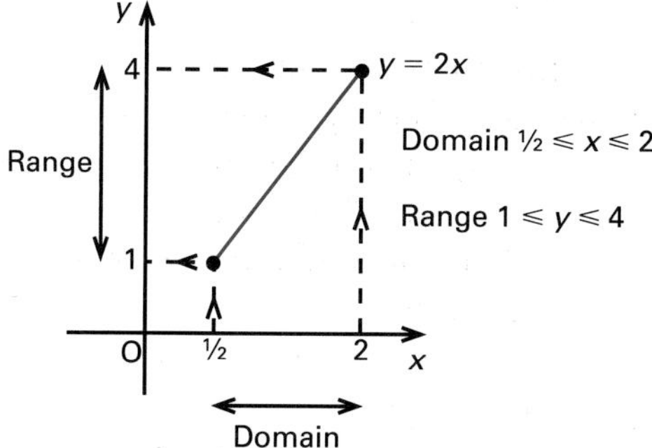

2 COMPOSITE FUNCTIONS

Functions f and g may be combined to give a new function h defined by $h(x) = g(f(x))$.

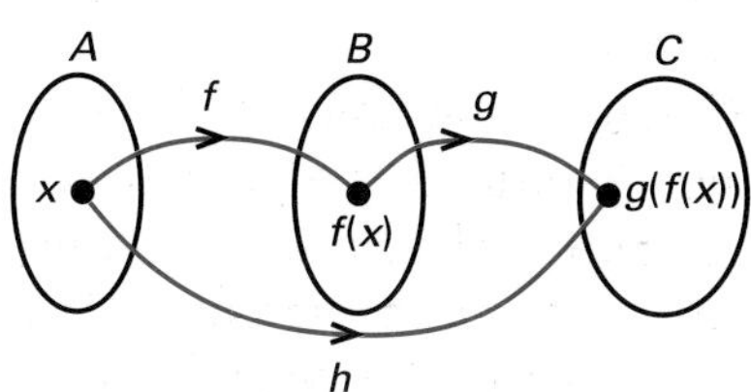

$f: A \to B$, $g: B \to C$ and $h: A \to C$.

The order of composition matters; in general $g(f(x)) \neq f(g(x))$.

3 INVERSE FUNCTIONS

a A function $f: A \to B$ has an inverse function $f^{-1}: B \to A$ if f makes a one-to-one correspondence between the sets A and B.

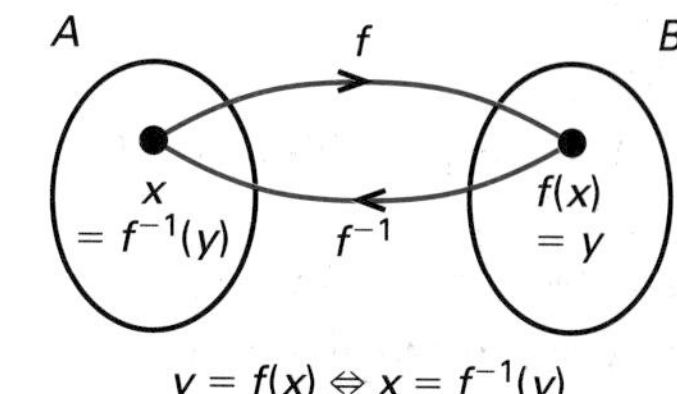

$y = f(x) \Leftrightarrow x = f^{-1}(y)$

b

The graph $y = f^{-1}(x)$ can be found from the graph $y = f(x)$ by reflecting it in the line $y = x$.

2.2 Algebraic Functions and Graphs

The quadratic function f(x) = ax² + bx + c*; completing the square*

We know that $x^2 + 2kx + k^2 = (x + k)^2$.
Rearranging, $x^2 + 2kx = (x + k)^2 - k^2$, a process called completing the square
Notice: **(i)** the coefficient of x^2 has to be 1
(ii) k is half the coefficient of x in $2kx$.

Examples Express each of these in the form $a(x + p)^2 + q$ by completing the square.

1 $x^2 + 6x = (x + 3)^2 - 3^2 = (x + 3)^2 - 9$
2 $x^2 - 4x = [x + (-2)]^2 - (-2)^2 = (x - 2)^2 - 4$
3 $x^2 + 10x + 6 = (x + 5)^2 - 5^2 + 6 = (x + 5)^2 - 19$
4 $3 - 2x - x^2 = 3 - (x^2 + 2x)$, isolating the x^2 and x terms,
$= 3 - [(x + 1)^2 - 1^2] = 3 - (x + 1)^2 + 1 = 4 - (x + 1)^2$

EXERCISE 1A

Express each of the following in the form $a(x + p)^2 + q$ by completing the square.

1 $x^2 + 8x$ **2** $x^2 + 2x$ **3** $x^2 - 6x$ **4** $x^2 - 2x$
5 $x^2 + 2x + 5$ **6** $x^2 + 6x - 1$ **7** $t^2 - 10t + 20$ **8** $p^2 - 2p - 5$
9 $u^2 + 4u - 1$ **10** $v^2 - 2v + 5$ **11** $7 - 2x - x^2$ **12** $5 + 6x - x^2$
13 $1 - 4t - t^2$ **14** $5 + 10t - t^2$ **15** $2 - 8x - x^2$ **16** $1 + 2x - x^2$

Examples Complete the square in each of the following. (Again isolate the x^2 and x terms.)
1 $4x^2 + 8x + 3 = 4(x^2 + 2x) + 3 = 4[(x + 1)^2 - 1^2] + 3 = 4(x + 1)^2 - 1$
2 $2x^2 - x + 1 = 2(x^2 - \frac{1}{2}x) + 1 = 2[(x - \frac{1}{4})^2 - \frac{1}{16}] + 1 = 2(x - \frac{1}{4})^2 + \frac{7}{8}$

EXERCISE 1B

Complete the square in each of the following. Check your answers by squaring and simplifying.

1 $2x^2 + 8x + 1$ **2** $3x^2 - 6x - 2$ **3** $2t^2 + 4t + 4$ **4** $5p^2 - 20p + 7$
5 $2c^2 + 4c + 3$ **6** $4d^2 - 16d + 3$ **7** $x^2 + x + 1$ **8** $x^2 - x + 1$
9 $2x^2 + x + 1$ **10** $2x^2 - 3x + 2$ **11** $2 + 3y - y^2$ **12** $4 - y - y^2$

Challenge

A zoo decides to fence in a rectangular-based exercise area, using 40 m of fencing.

a Taking x m for its length, show that the area of the floor, A m^2, can be written $A = 100 - (x - 10)^2$. What is the maximum floor area, and the corresponding length and breadth?

b In a similar way, find the maximum area, length and breadth of the floor if:

(i) only three sides are fenced (the fourth is bounded by a moat)

(ii) only two adjacent sides have to be fenced.

Maximum and minimum values

For all values of x, $(x + k)^2 \geqslant 0$, so the minimum value of $(x + k)^2$ is 0.

Examples

1 $x^2 + 6x + 11 = (x + 3)^2 + 2$.
So the minimum value of $x^2 + 6x + 11$ is $0 + 2 = 2$, when $x = -3$.

Also, the maximum value of the fraction $\dfrac{1}{x^2 + 6x + 11}$ occurs when $x^2 + 6x + 11$ is a minimum. The maximum value is $\frac{1}{2}$ when $x = -3$.

2 $3 - 2x - x^2 = 4 - (x + 1)^2$, from Example 4 in the box on page 30.
So the maximum value of $3 - 2x - x^2$ is $4 - 0 = 4$, when $x = -1$.

EXERCISE 2

1 By expressing each of the following in the form $a(x + p)^2 + q$, write down its minimum value and the corresponding value of x.

a $x^2 + 8x + 4$ **b** $x^2 - 4x + 6$ **c** $x^2 + 2x$ **d** $x^2 - 10x$

2 By completing the square, write down the maximum value of each of the following, and the corresponding value of x.

a $7 - 4x - x^2$ **b** $8 + 8x - x^2$

3 Express $x^2 + 2x + 7$ in the form $a(x + p)^2 + q$, and hence state the maximum value of $\dfrac{1}{x^2 + 2x + 7}$.

4 a Show that $1 - 2x - x^2 = 2 - (x + 1)^2$.

b Hence find:

(i) the maximum value of $1 - 2x - x^2$

(ii) the minimum value of $\dfrac{6}{1 - 2x - x^2}$ when $1 - 2x - x^2 > 0$.

5 The height, h metres, of a golf ball in flight is given by $h = 55 + 10t - t^2$, where t seconds is the time of flight.
a Express h in the form $a(t + p)^2 + q$.
b Find the maximum height of the ball, and the time taken to reach it.

6 The cost, c pence, of running a car for 100 miles at an average speed of x mph is given by $c = \frac{1}{2}x^2 - 50x + 1750$. Calculate:
a the most economical average speed
b the cost for 100 miles at this speed.

Sketching the graph of the quadratic function $f(x) = ax^2 + bx + c$

Example Sketch the graph $y = x^2 - 4x - 5$, using a 'completing the square' method.

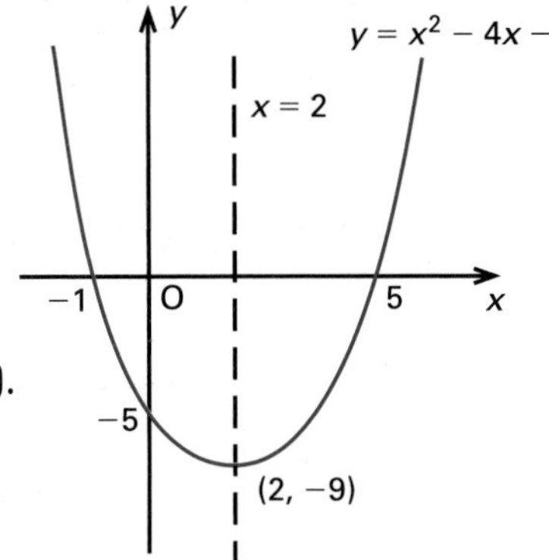

(i) Intersections with the axes
If $x = 0$, $y = -5$, giving $(0, -5)$.

If $y = 0$, $x^2 - 4x - 5 = 0$

$(x + 1)(x - 5) = 0$

$x = -1$ or 5, giving $(-1, 0)$ and $(5, 0)$.

(ii) Turning point, by completing the square
$y = x^2 - 4x - 5 = (x - 2)^2 - 2^2 - 5 = (x - 2)^2 - 9$, giving a minimum turning point $(2, -9)$.

Reminder
Turning point, from axis of symmetry:
from $(-1, 0)$ and $(5, 0)$, the axis of symmetry is $x = \frac{-1 + 5}{2} = 2$, so the turning point is $(2, -9)$.

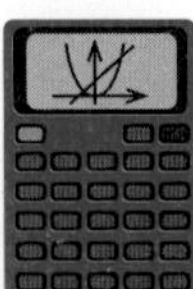

a $f(x) = 3x^2 + 6x - 1$. Express $f(x)$ in the form $3(x + p)^2 + q$.
b Draw the graph $y = f(x)$, and zoom in to find the coordinates of its minimum turning point. Compare these with the values of p and q.
c Given whole numbers a and b, use your graphics calculator to express $3x^2 - 24x + 53$ in the form $3(x + a)^2 + b$.

EXERCISE 3

1 **a** Show that $x^2 - 4x + 5 = (x - 2)^2 + 1$.
b State the minimum value of $x^2 - 4x + 5$, and the corresponding value of x.
c Sketch the graph $y = x^2 - 4x + 5$, as in the worked example on page 32.

2 **a** Show that $3 + 2x - x^2 = 4 - (x - 1)^2$.
b State the maximum value of $3 + 2x - x^2$, and the corresponding value of x.
c Sketch the graph $y = 3 + 2x - x^2$.

3 **(i)** Express each $f(x)$ below in the form $a(x + p)^2 + q$.
(ii) Write down the maximum or minimum value of f, and the corresponding value of x.
(iii) Sketch the graph $y = f(x)$ for each one.
a $f(x) = x^2 + 4x + 10$ **b** $f(x) = x^2 - 2x + 1$
c $f(x) = 8 - 2x - x^2$ **d** $f(x) = 12 + 4x - x^2$

4 Use the method of completing the square to help you to sketch these graphs.
a $y = x^2 - 6x + 8$ **b** $y = x^2 + 4x - 5$
c $y = 3x^2 + 12x + 9$ **d** $y = 15 - 2x - x^2$

Sketching the graphs of related functions

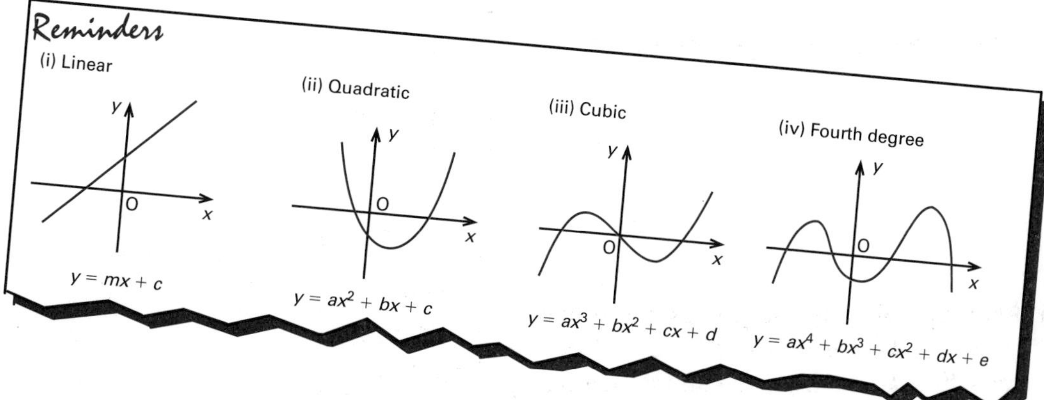

a Write a program to draw a family of parabolas of the form $y = ax^2 + b$.
b Fix b, and obtain the set of parabolas through the point $(0, b)$, using positive and negative values of a. What happens when $a < 0$, $a = 0$, $a > 0$?
c Fix a (e.g. $a = 2$), and obtain a set of 'parallel' parabolas, using various values of b.

EXERCISE 4

1 Link each equation to the most appropriate sketch below.

a $y = x^2$ **b** $y = -x^2 - 3x$ **c** $y = 4x - x^3$ **d** $y = 3 - \frac{1}{2}x$

(i)

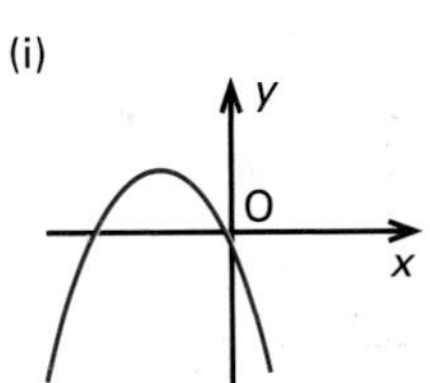

(ii)

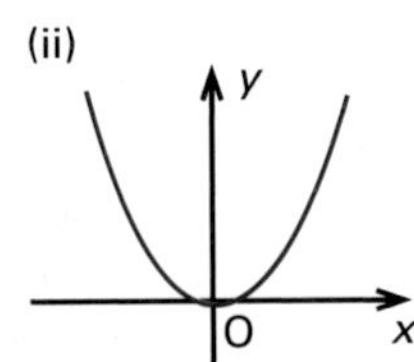

(iii)

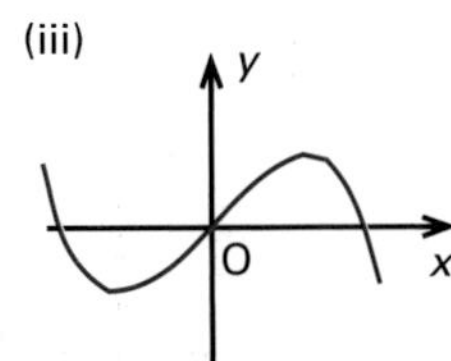

(iv)

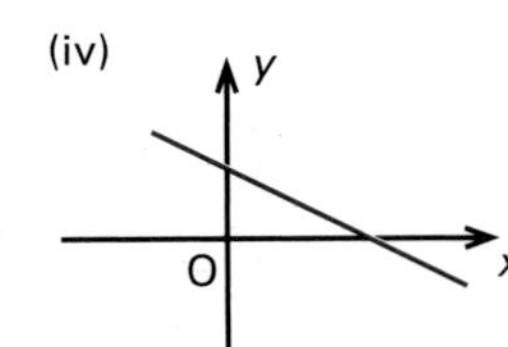

2 Study the ways in which changes to the equation $y = x^2$ produce changes to the graph $y = x^2$, as follows.

a

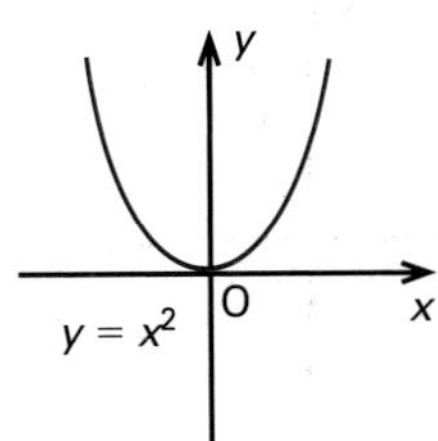

b

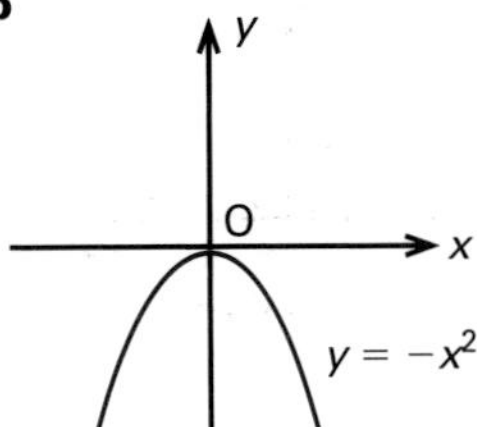

c

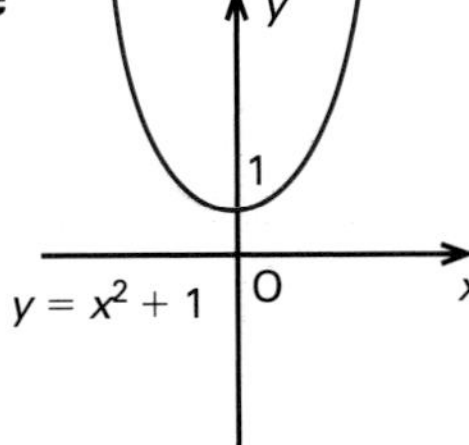

d

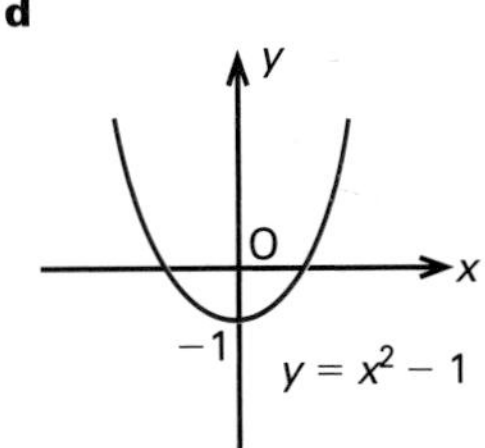

e

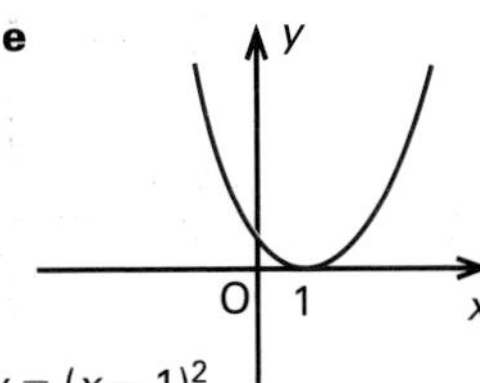

f

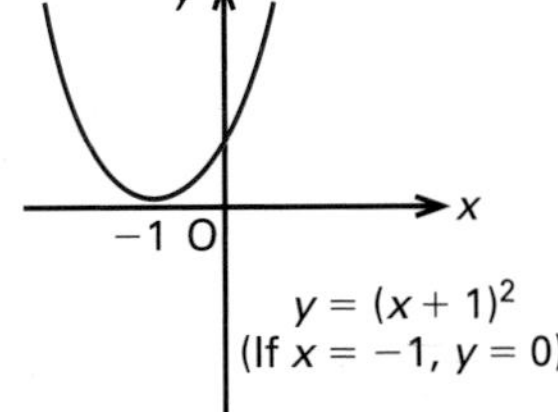

g

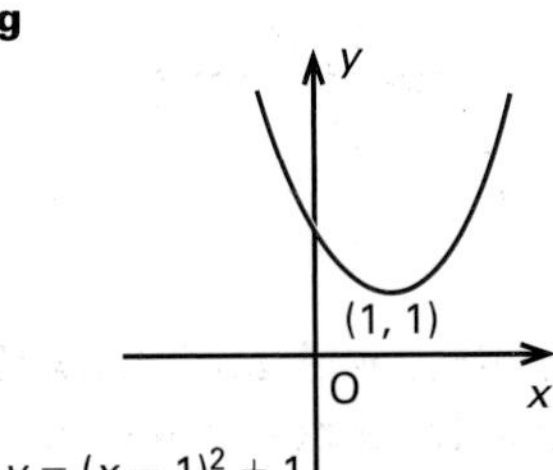

h

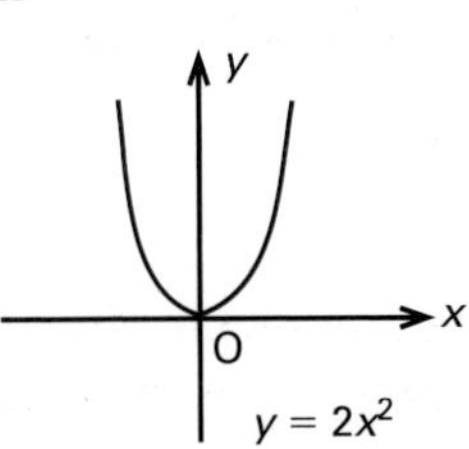

3 Match these equations with their graphs (i)–(viii).

a $y = x^2 + 1$ **b** $y = (x + 1)^2$ **c** $y = (x + 1)^2 + 1$

d $y = x^2 - 1$ **e** $y = (x - 1)^2$ **f** $y = (x - 1)^2 + 1$

g $y = (x + 1)^2 - 1$ **h** $y = (x - 1)^2 - 1$

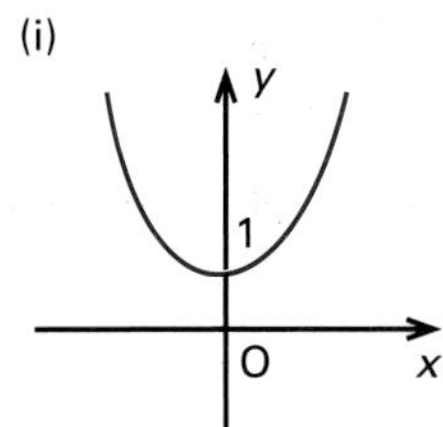

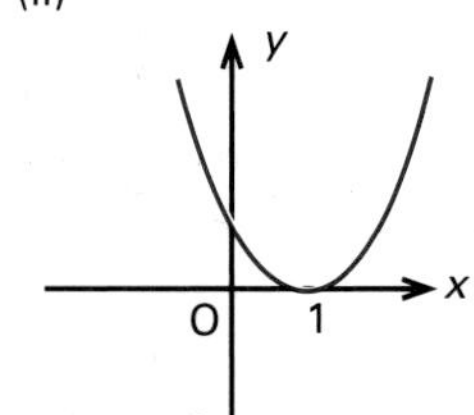

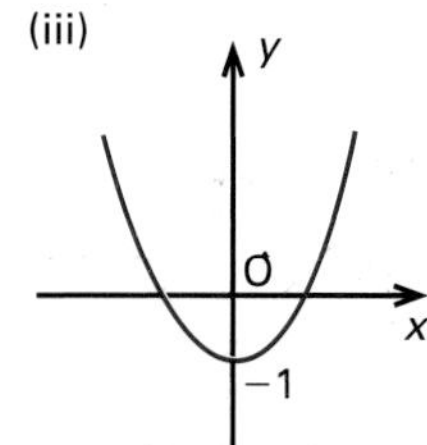

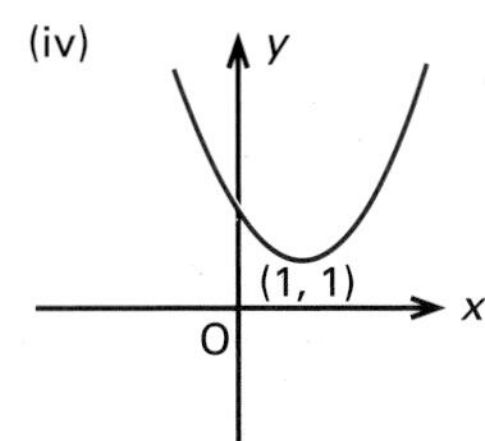

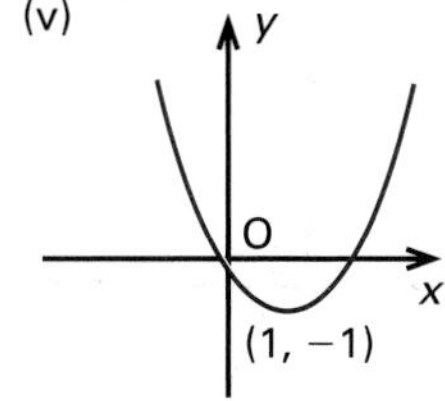

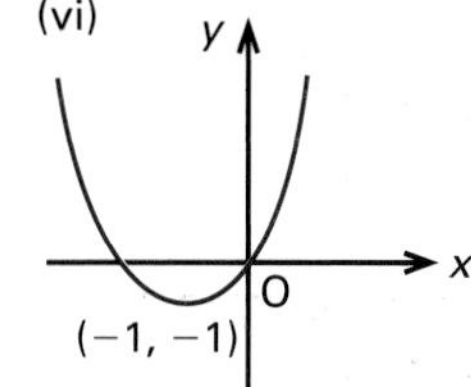

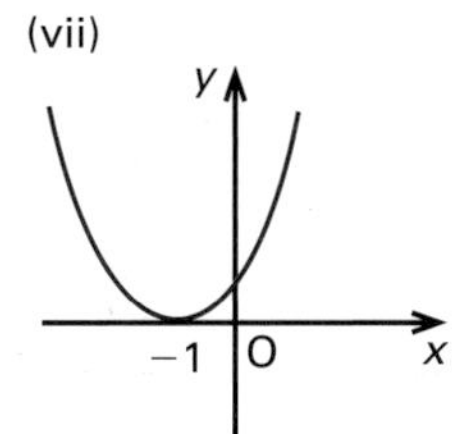

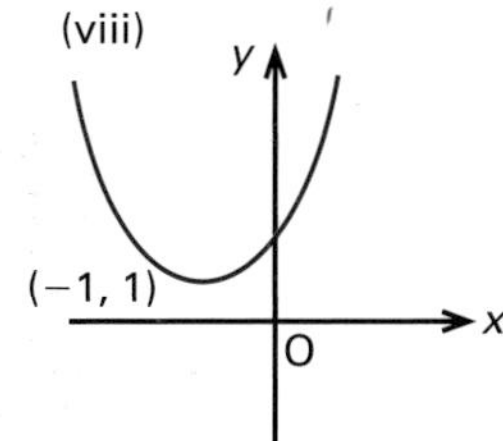

4 Given the graph $y = x^3$, sketch the graphs:

a $y = -x^3$ **b** $y = x^3 + 2$

c $y = x^3 - 2$ **d** $y = (x + 1)^3$

e $y = (x - 1)^3$ **f** $y = (x - 1)^3 + 1$.

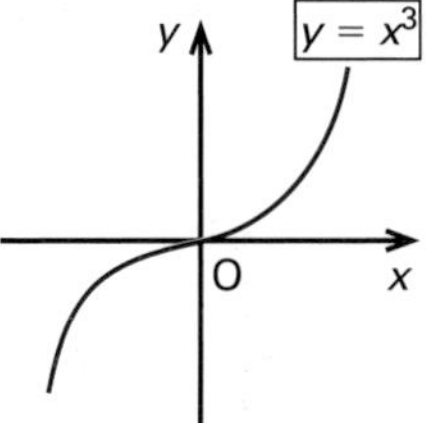

In questions **5–10**, sketch the graph of each function **a–d**, and mark the images of the points shown on the graph $y = f(x)$ etc., and also their coordinates.

5 **a** $y = f(x) + 2$

b $y = -f(x)$

c $y = -f(x) + 2$

d $y = f(x + 2)$

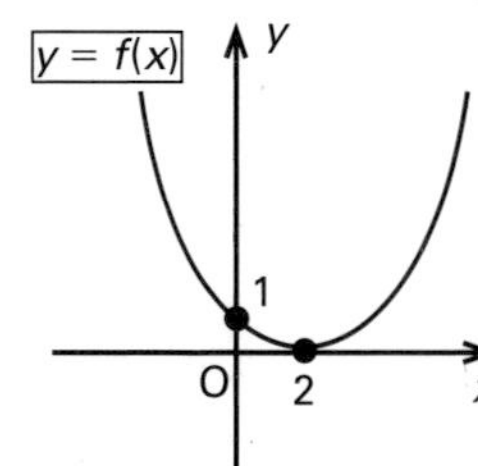

6 **a** $y = g(x) + 2$
b $y = g(x + 2)$
c $y = -g(x)$
d $y = g(-x)$

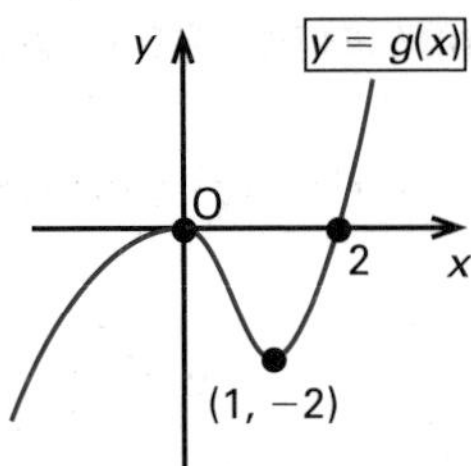

7 **a** $y = h(x - 3)$
b $y = h(x + 3)$
c $y = h(x) - 6$
d $y = -\frac{1}{2}h(x)$

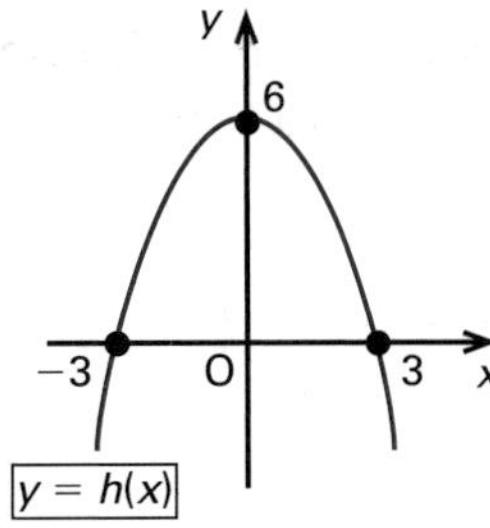

8 **a** $y = -k(x)$
b $y = k(-x)$
c $y = k(x) - 1$
d $y = 1 - k(x)$

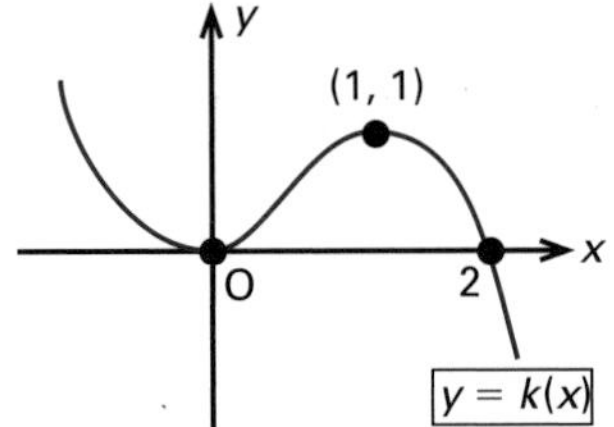

9 **a** $y = -s(x)$
b $y = 1 + s(x)$
c $y = 2s(x)$
d $y = -1 - s(x)$

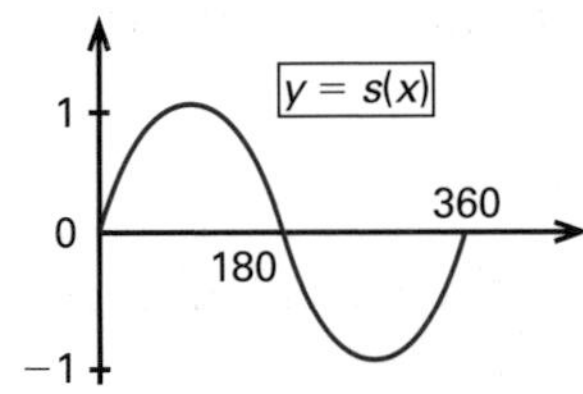

10 **a** $y = -t(x)$
b $y = t(-x)$
c $y = 5 + t(x)$
d $y = t(x - 6)$

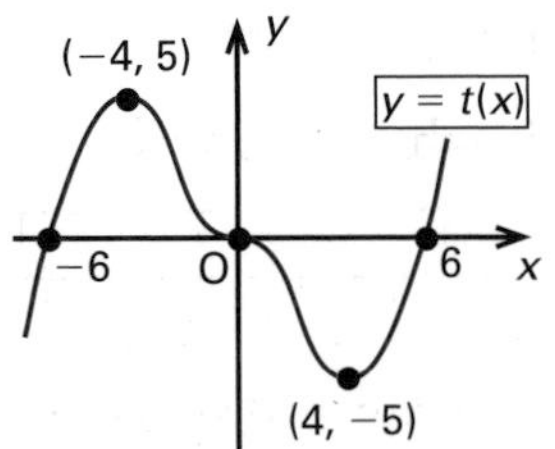

11 **a** Copy and complete the curve $y = u(x)$ so that it is symmetrical about the y-axis.
b Sketch:
(i) $y = -u(x)$
(ii) $y = u(x) + 2$
(iii) $y = u(x + 4)$
(iv) $y = \frac{1}{2}u(x)$

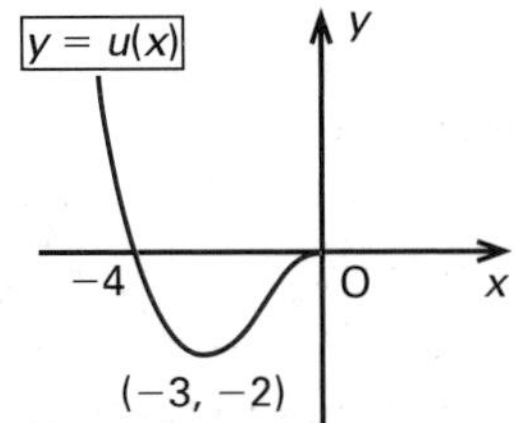

The exponential function and its graph

Using this table of values, we can draw the graph $y = 2^x$ for $-3 \leqslant x \leqslant 4$.

x	-3	-2	-1	0	1	2	3	4
2^x	0.1	0.3	0.5	1	2	4	8	16

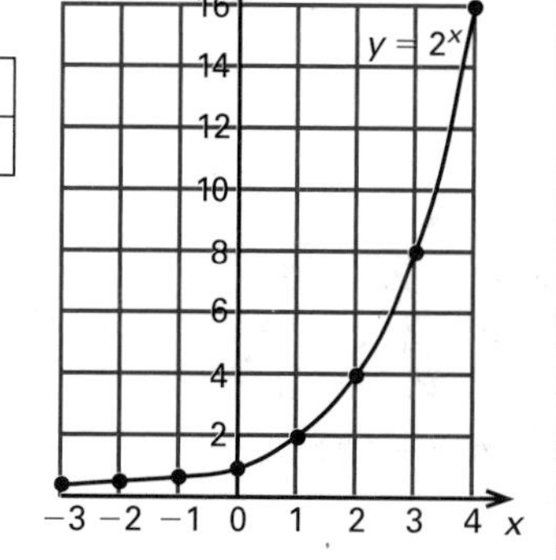

Any function of the form $f(x) = a^x$, where $a > 0$ and $a \neq 1$, is called an *exponential function* with *base a*. The graph of the function has equation $y = a^x$.

Example If $f(x) = 4^x$, then:

a $f(2) = 4^2 = 16$ **b** $f(-1) = 4^{-1} = \frac{1}{4}$

c $f(0) = 4^0 = 1$ **d** $f(\frac{1}{2}) = 4^{1/2} = 2$

a Display the graphs $y = 2^x$, $y = 3^x$, $y = 4^x$ and $y = 5^x$ on the same screen.

b Repeat **a** for $y = 1.5^x$, $y = 1.4^x$, …, and $y = 0.5^x$, $y = 0.4^x$, …

EXERCISE 5

1 $f(x) = 5^x$. Calculate:
a $f(2)$ **b** $f(1)$ **c** $f(0)$ **d** $f(-1)$

2 $f(x) = 9^x$. Calculate:
a $f(1)$ **b** $f(0)$ **c** $f(2)$ **d** $f(\frac{1}{2})$

3 $f(x) = 1.7^x$. Use the $\boxed{y^x}$ key to calculate, correct to 2 decimal places:
a $f(2)$ **b** $f(3.5)$ **c** $f(0.8)$

4 $f(x) = 25 \times 1.08^x$. Calculate, correct to 2 decimal places:
a $f(0)$ **b** $f(1)$ **c** $f(10)$.

5 a Copy and complete this table of values:

x	-2	-1	0	1	2	3
3^x	0.1	0.3	1			

b Draw the graph $y = 3^x$ on squared paper, for $-2 \leqslant x \leqslant 3$.

c What features do the graphs $y = 2^x$ (at the top of the page) and $y = 3^x$ have in common?

6 a Copy and complete this table:

x	-3	-2	-1	0	1	2	3
$(\frac{1}{2})^x$	8					0.3	0.1

b Draw the graphs $y = 2^x$ (using the table at the top of the page) and $y = (\frac{1}{2})^x$, on the same diagram, for $-3 \leqslant x \leqslant 3$.

c Which line is the axis of symmetry in the diagram?

For the exponential function $f(x) = a^x$:
(i) $a > 1$ gives an *increasing* function **(ii)** $0 < a < 1$ gives a *decreasing* function.

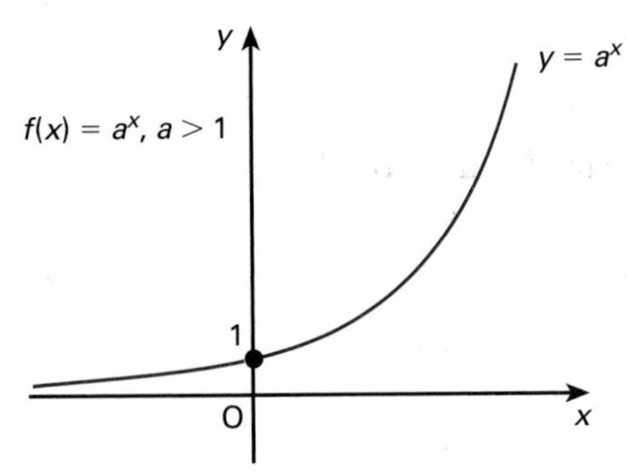

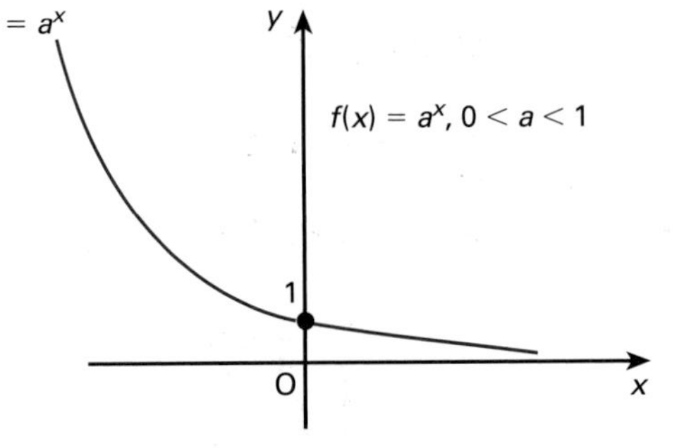

7 As a sheet of paper is folded, the number of leaves doubles each time. If L is the number of leaves, and x is the number of folds, then $L(x) = 2^x$.

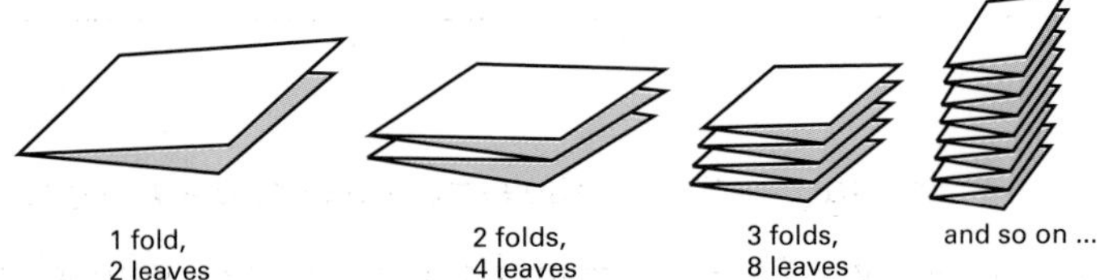

a Calculate:
(i) $L(3)$ **(ii)** $L(6)$ **(iii)** $L(10)$ **(iv)** $L(0)$.

b What does $L(0)$ mean?

c Why does $L(\frac{1}{2})$ not make sense here?

8 Starting with one bacterium, a culture trebles in number every day.

a Copy and complete this table:

Number of days (x)	0	1	2	3	4	5	6
Number of bacteria ($N(x)$)	1	3					

b Write down an exponential function which models the situation, $N(x) = \ldots$

c Calculate the number of bacteria after:
(i) 10 days **(ii)** 20 days, correct to 3 significant figures.

9 When a ball is dropped, it rebounds to half the height. It is dropped from a height of 20 m.

a Copy and complete this table:

Number of rebounds (x)	1	2	3	4	5	6
Height of rebound (H m)	10					

b Explain why this function models the situation: $H(x) = 20 \times 2^{-x}$.

c Show that the height of the ball after 11 rebounds is about 1 cm.

d In theory, should the ball ever stop bouncing? Why *does* it stop?

10 The value £V of a computer after n years is given by $V = 1500 \times 1.5^{-n}$.

a Calculate its value after: (i) 1 year (ii) 3 years.

b In which year will its value fall below £100?

Sketching graphs of exponential functions

As a guide, note the points on the graph where $x = 0$ and where $x = 1$.

Example Sketch the graphs:

a $y = 4^x$
If $x = 0$, $y = 4^0 = 1$, giving the point (0, 1)
If $x = 1$, $y = 4$, giving the point (1, 4).

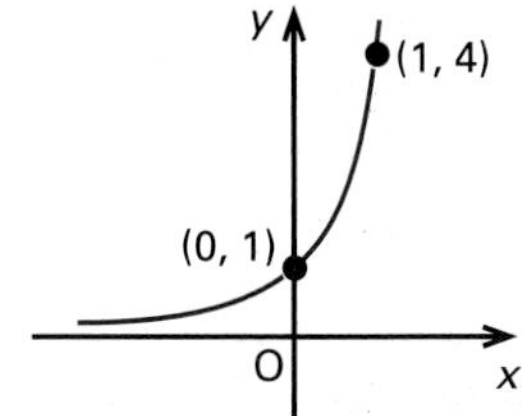

b $y = 10^{-x}$
It passes through (0, 1).
If $x = 1$, $y = 10^{-1} = \frac{1}{10}$, giving $(1, \frac{1}{10})$.

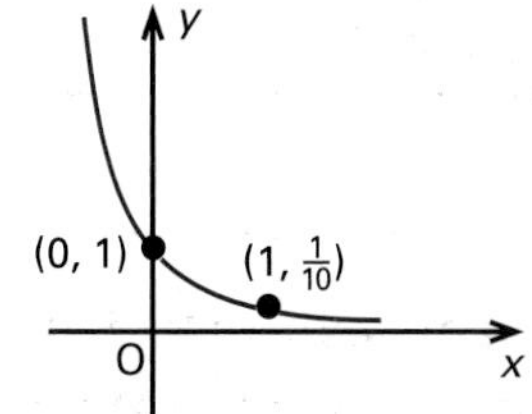

EXERCISE 6

1 Sketch the graphs $y = 3^x$ and $y = 3^{-x}$ on the same sheet of plain paper.

2 **a** Explain why the graphs $y = 2^x$, $y = 2^{2x}$ and $y = 2^{3x}$ all pass through the same point.
b Sketch the three graphs on the same diagram.

3 Sketch the graphs $y = 2^x$ and $y = 2^x - 1$ on the same diagram.

4 Find the equation of the line of symmetry in a diagram containing the graphs $y = 5^x$ and $y = 5^{-x}$.

5 Sketch the graphs $y = 3^x$ and $y = 2 \times 3^x$ on the same diagram.

6 The equation of a curve is $y = a \times 8^x$. If the curve passes through the point (0, 4), find the value of a.

7 Find the values of a and b for these curves.

a

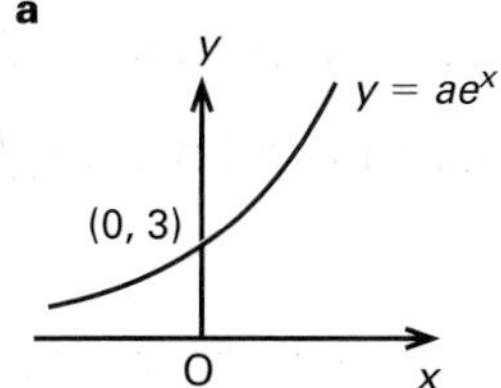

b

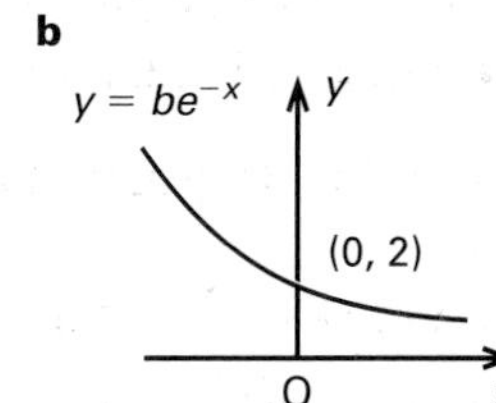

8 The line $y = 18$ cuts the graph $y = 2^x$ at P.
Use the $\boxed{y^x}$ key on your calculator and a step-by-step method to find the x-coordinate of P, correct to 1 decimal place.

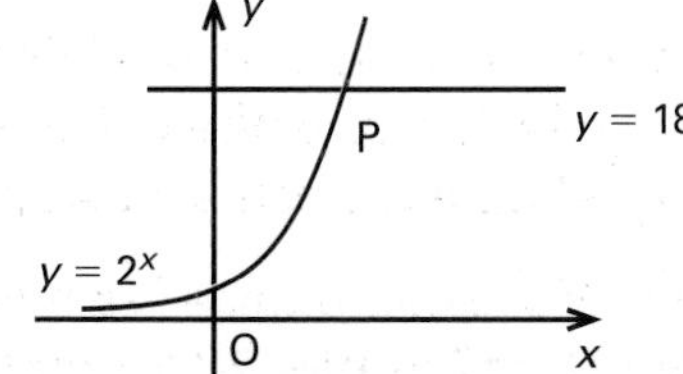

The logarithmic function and its graph

In Chapter 2.1 you saw that a function f which sets up a one-to-one correspondence between its domain A and its range B has an inverse function f^{-1} from B to A, and

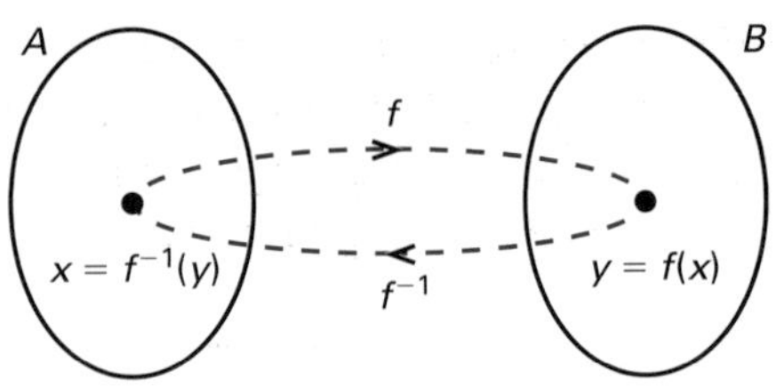

$$y = f(x) \Leftrightarrow x = f^{-1}(y)$$

Look at the graph $y = a^x$ of the exponential function $f(x) = a^x$, $a > 1$, on the right.
For each real number x, y is a positive real number. Conversely, for each positive real number y there is exactly the real number x such that $y = a^x$.
$f(x)$ sets up a one-to-one correspondence between the set of real numbers on the x-axis (the domain) and the set of positive real numbers on OY (the range).
So $f(x) = a^x$ has an inverse function, called the logarithmic function to base a, denoted by $\log_a$.

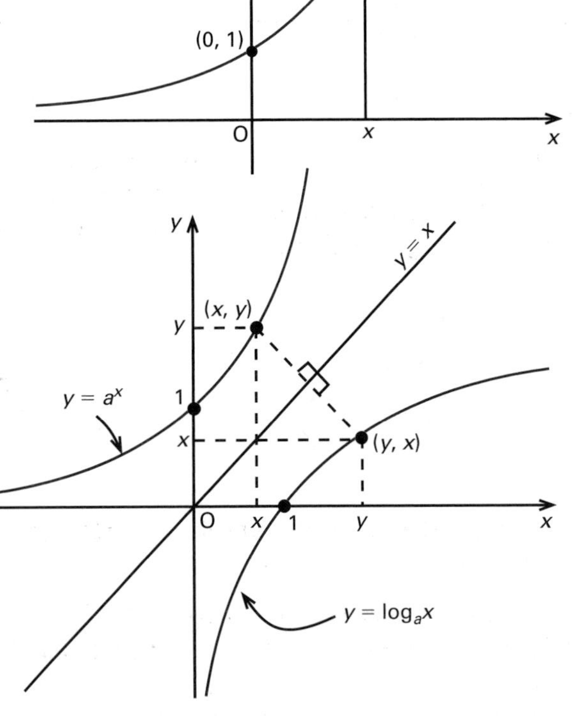

$$y = a^x \Leftrightarrow x = \log_a y$$

Notice that the graph $y = \log_a x$ is the mirror image of $y = a^x$ in the line $y = x$, as shown.

Two special logarithms
Using the form $y = a^x \Rightarrow \log_a y = x$:
(i) $1 = a^0 \Rightarrow \log_a 1 = 0$ (log 1 to any base = 0)
(ii) $a = a^1 \Rightarrow \log_a a = 1$ (log of a number to that base = 1).

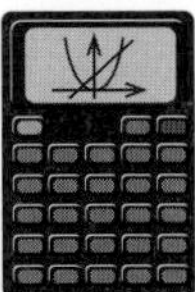

a Display the graphs $y = e^x$ and $y = \log_e x$ on the same screen ($\log_e x$ is given by ln x).
b What does the symmetry about the line $y = x$ tell you about the relationship between $y = e^x$ and $y = \log_e x$?

Sketching graphs of logarithmic functions

Using $\log_a 1 = 0$ and $\log_a a = 1$, we can obtain two points on the graph $y = \log_a x$.
If $x = 1$, $y = \log_a 1 = 0$, giving $(1, 0)$.
If $x = a$, $y = \log_a a = 1$, giving $(a, 1)$.

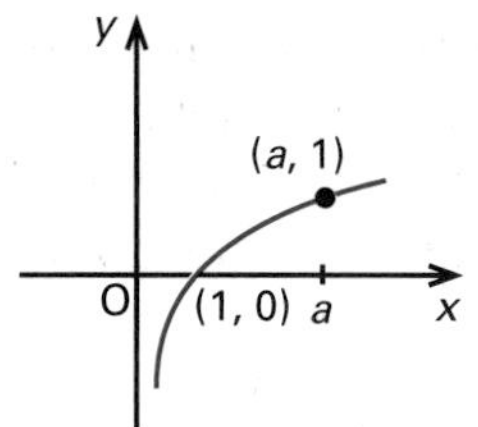

Example 1 Sketch these graphs.

a $y = \log_3 x$
If $x = 1$, $y = \log_3 1 = 0$, giving $(1, 0)$.
If $x = 3$, $y = \log_3 3 = 1$, giving $(3, 1)$.

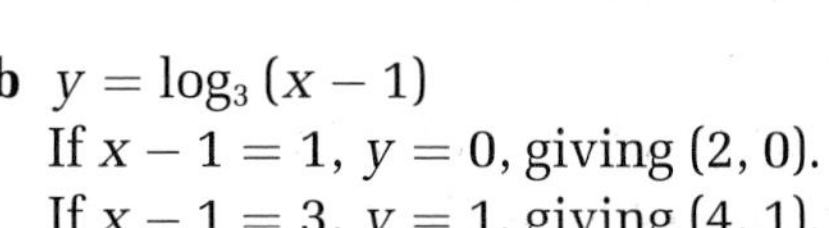

b $y = \log_3 (x - 1)$
If $x - 1 = 1$, $y = 0$, giving $(2, 0)$.
If $x - 1 = 3$, $y = 1$, giving $(4, 1)$.

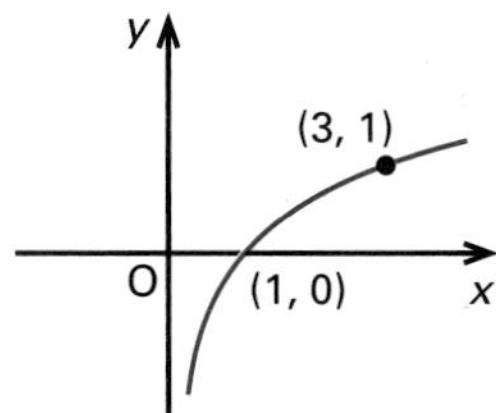

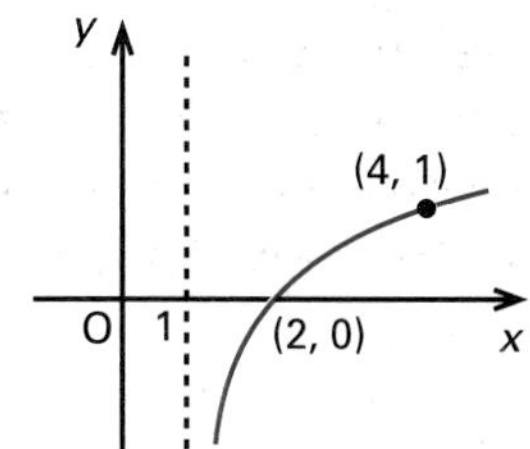

c $y = \log_3 \left(\dfrac{1}{x}\right)$.
If $x = 1$, $y = 0$, giving $(1, 0)$.
If $x = \frac{1}{3}$, $y = 1$, giving $(\frac{1}{3}, 1)$.

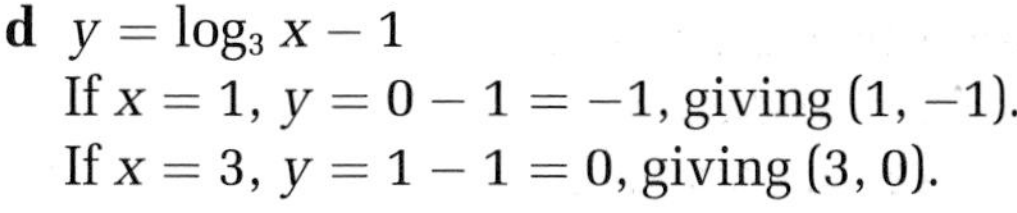

d $y = \log_3 x - 1$
If $x = 1$, $y = 0 - 1 = -1$, giving $(1, -1)$.
If $x = 3$, $y = 1 - 1 = 0$, giving $(3, 0)$.

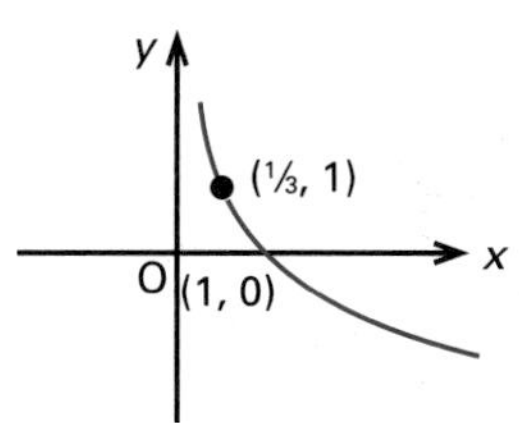

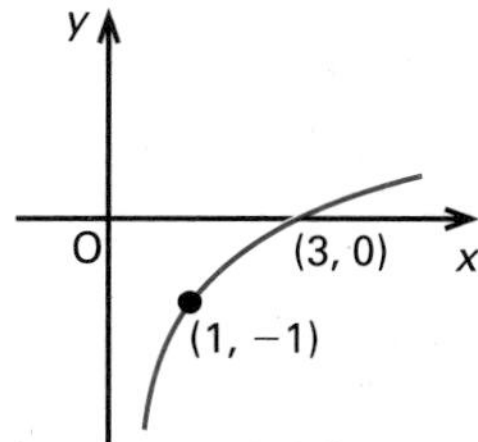

Example 2 A sketch of the graph $y = a\log_4 (x + b)$ is shown here. Find the values of a and b.

$(-2, 0)$ lies on the curve, so $0 = a\log_4 (-2 + b)$.
From $\log_4 (-2 + b) = 0$, $-2 + b = 4^0 = 1$ so $b = 3$.

$(1, 5)$ lies on the curve $y = a\log_4 (x + 3)$,
so $5 = a\log_4 4 = a$.
$a = 5$ and $b = 3$.

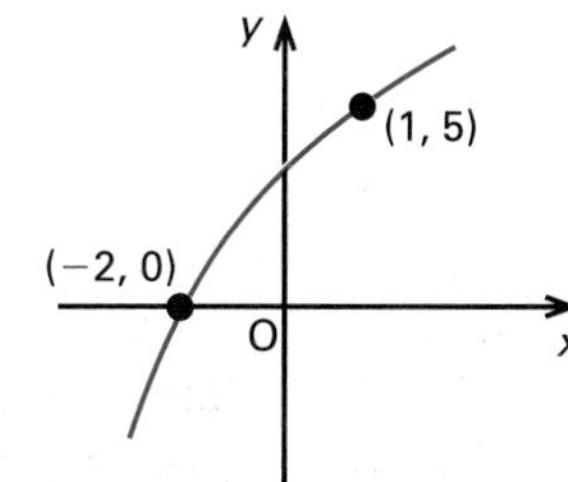

a Using X min -1, max 10, scl 1 and Y min -1, max 1, scl 0.5, draw the graphs $y = \log_{10} x$, $y = \log_{10} (x - 1)$ and $y = \log_{10} (x - 2)$. Describe the effect of changing the log function.

b Repeat part **a** for $y = \log_{10} (x + 1)$ and $y = \log_{10} (x + 2)$, and for $y = 2\log_{10} x$ and $y = 3\log_{10} x$.

EXERCISE 7

1 On the same diagram, sketch the graphs:
a $y = \log_2 x$ **b** $y = 2\log_2 x$ **c** $y = 3\log_2 x$.

2 On the same diagram, sketch the graphs:
a $y = \log_2 x$ **b** $y = \log_2 (x - 1)$ **c** $y = \log_2 (x - 2)$.

3 Sketch the graphs:
a $y = \log_4 (x + 1)$ **b** $y = \log_4 \left(\frac{2}{x}\right)$.

4 **a** Sketch the graph $y = \log_4 x + 1$.
b Where does the graph cut the x-axis?

5 Repeat question **4** for $y = \log_{10} x + 1$.

6 Study the graphs in Example 1 in the box on page 41. Which transformations take **a** to **b**, **a** to **c**, **a** to **d**?

7 Diagram (i) shows the curve $y = \log_a x$. What is the value of a?

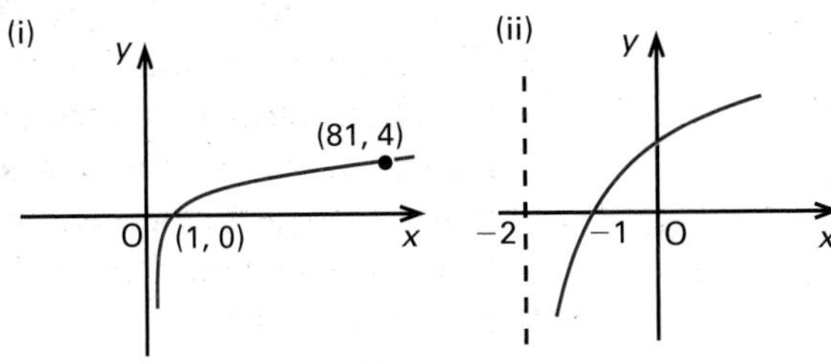

8 Diagram (ii) shows the curve $y = \log_{10} (x + p)$. What is the value of p?

9 **a** Sketch the graphs $y = 2$ and $y = \log_{10} 2x$ on the same diagram.
b Find the point of intersection of the graphs by solving the equation $\log_{10} 2x = 2$.

10 The sketch shows part of the graph $y = a\log_2 (x - b)$.
Find the values of a and b.

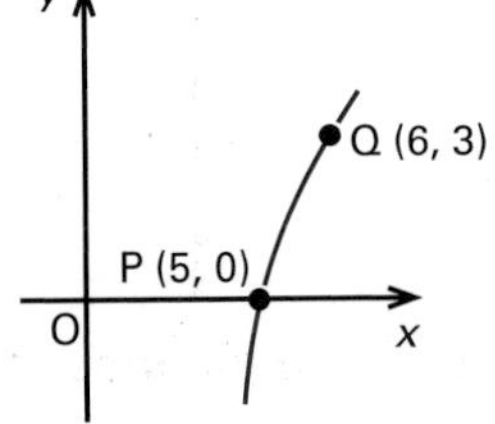

11 Repeat question **10** for the graph $y = a\log_5 (x + b)$, where P is $(-1, 0)$ and Q is $(3, 1)$.

12 **a** Sketch the graphs $y = 4 - x$ and $y = \log_{10} x$ on the same diagram.
b Write down an equation to find the x-coordinate of the point of intersection of the graphs.
c Show that x satisfies $3.4 < x < 3.5$.
d Use iteration to find x, correct to 2 decimal places.

CHAPTER 2.2 REVIEW

1 Express each of these in the form $a(x + p)^2 + q$:
a $x^2 + 10x + 15$ **b** $2x^2 - 8x - 3$.

2 **a** Complete the square in $110 - 20x + x^2$, and hence find the minimum value of $110 - 20x + x^2$, and the corresponding value of x.
b State the maximum value of $\dfrac{10}{110 - 20x + x^2}$.

3 **a** By completing the square, find the turning point of the parabola $y = x^2 - 4x - 12$.
b Sketch the parabola.

4 Write down the equation of the curve $y = f(x)$ under transformation in **a**, **b** and **c**.

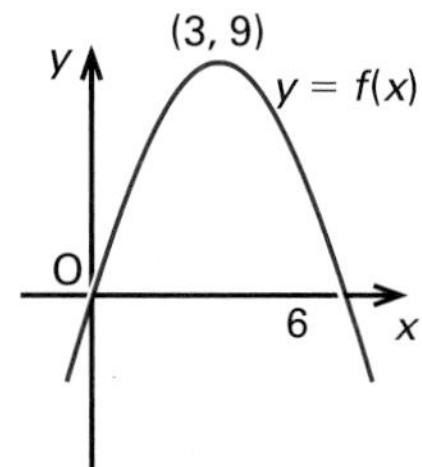

a
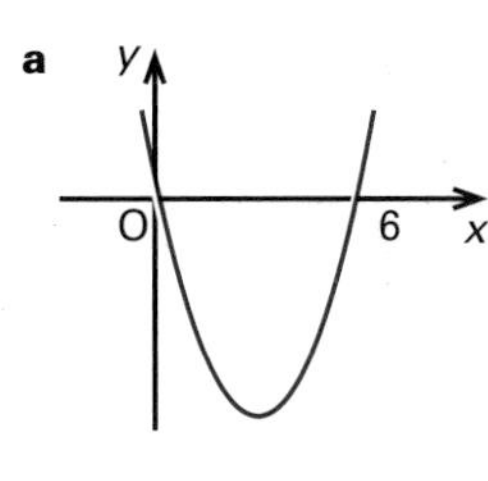

b
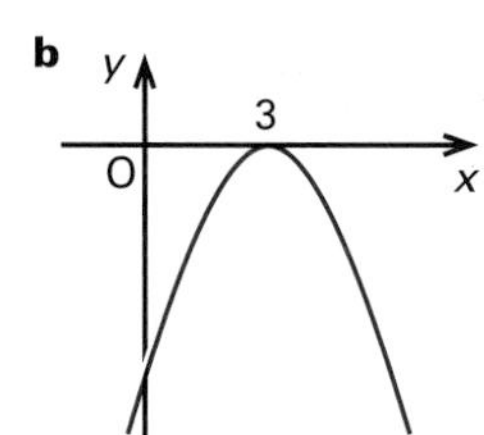

c
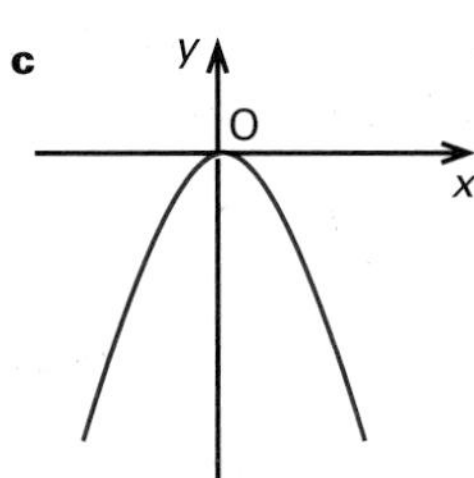

5 Pair each of the following equations with its graph.
a $y = x^2 - k^2$ **b** $y = x^3 + ax$
c $y = x^4 + ax^2$ **d** $xy = k$
e $y = k^2 - x^2$ **f** $x + y = k$

(i)
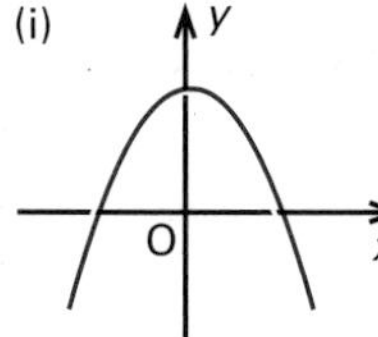

(ii)
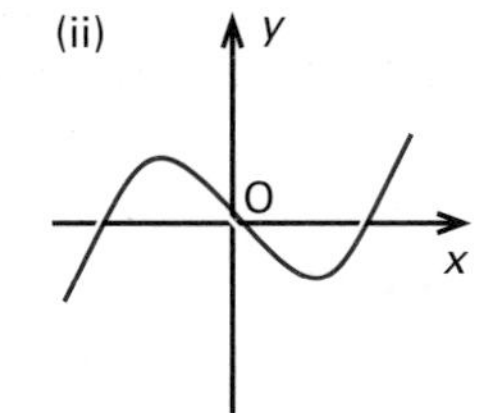

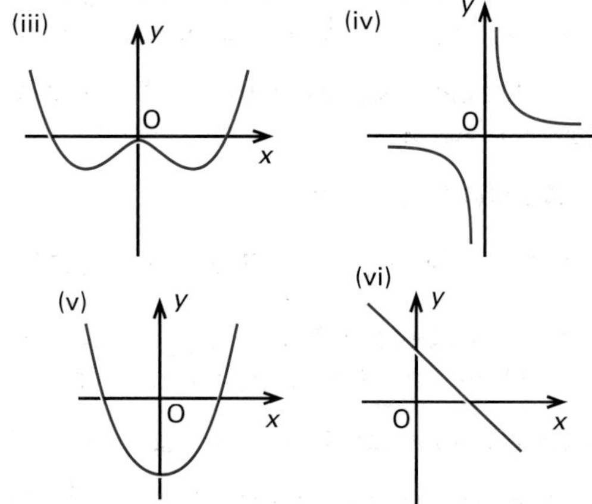

6 On the same diagram sketch graphs to illustrate the equation $y = a^x$ when:
(i) $a > 1$ **(ii)** $a = 1$ **(iii)** $0 < a < 1$.

7 The graph with equation $y = 5^x$ is sketched. Write down the equation of the graph you would sketch on the same diagram to give symmetry about the line $x = 0$. Check your answer in a diagram.

8 Sketch the graphs:
a $y = \log_2 x$ **b** $y = \log_2 x + 1$
c $y = \log_2 (x + 1)$.

9 Sketch the graphs:
a $\log_4 x$ **b** $2 \log_4 x$ **c** $3 \log_4 x$.

10 Sketch (i) shows the curve $y = \log_a x$. Find the value of a.

(i)
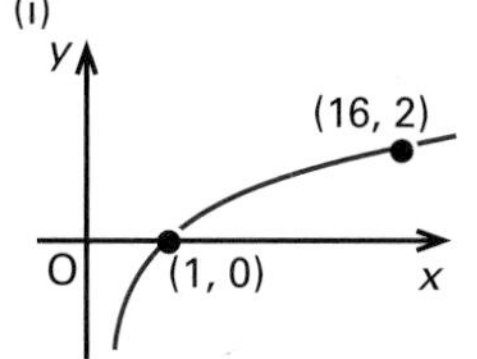

(ii)
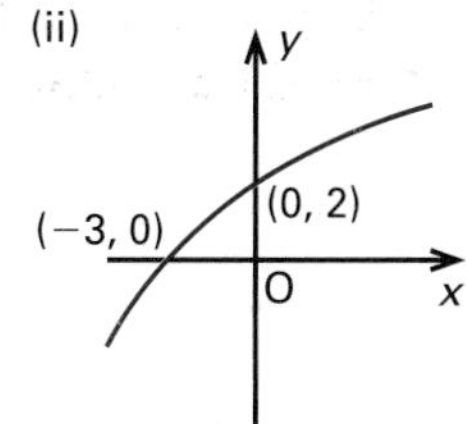

11 Sketch (ii) shows the curve $y = \log_2 (x + b)$. Find the value of b.

CHAPTER 2.2 SUMMARY

1 Completing the square of the quadratic function $f(x) = ax^2 + bx + c$
Arrange it in the form $a(x + p)^2 + q$, using $x^2 + 2kx = (x + k)^2 - k^2$.

2 Sketching the graph of the quadratic function $f(x) = ax^2 + bx + c$
Determine:
(i) intersections with the x and y-axes
(ii) its turning point, by completing the square
(iii) its axis of symmetry, if necessary.

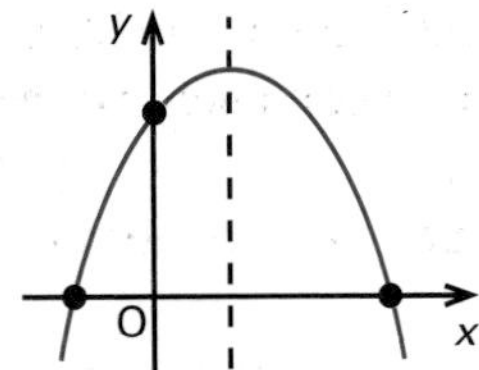

3 Sketching related graphs
Most sketches can be based on these transformations:

a

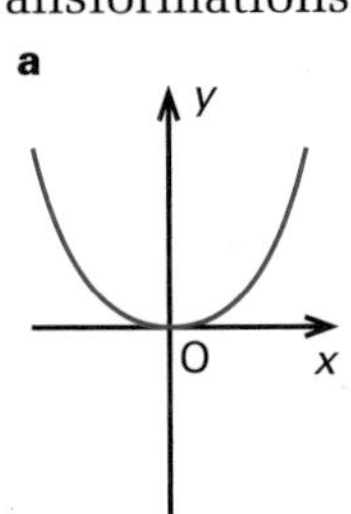

$y = f(x)$

b

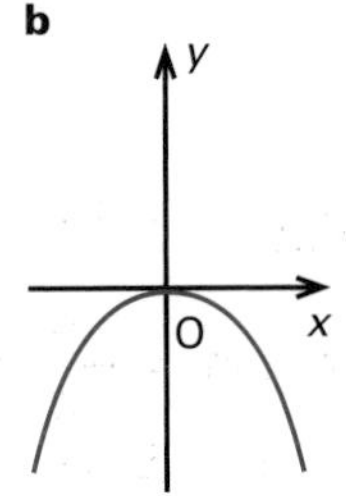

$y = -f(x)$
(reflection in x-axis)

c

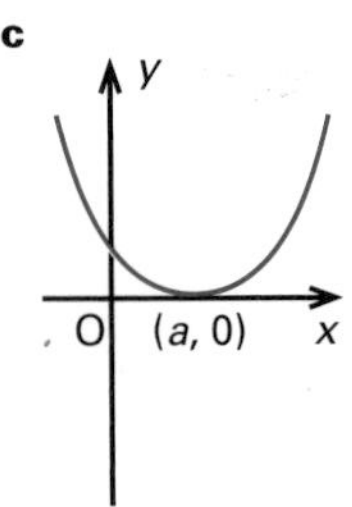

$y = f(x - a)$
(shift to right)

d

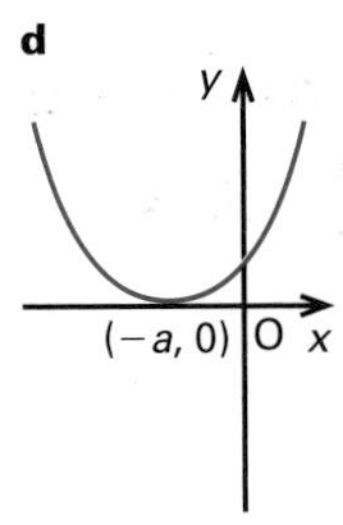

$y = f(x + a)$
(shift to left)

e

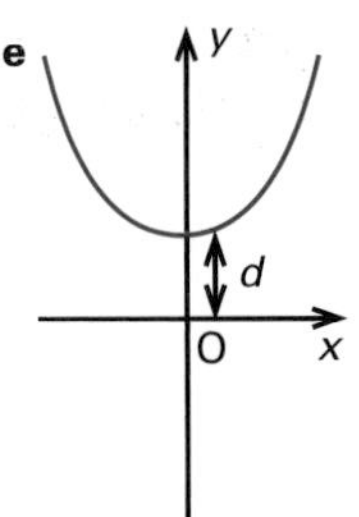

$y = f(x) + d$
(translation || y-axis)

4 a The *exponential curve* with equation $y = a^x$ $(a > 1)$ passes through the point (0, 1), like this:

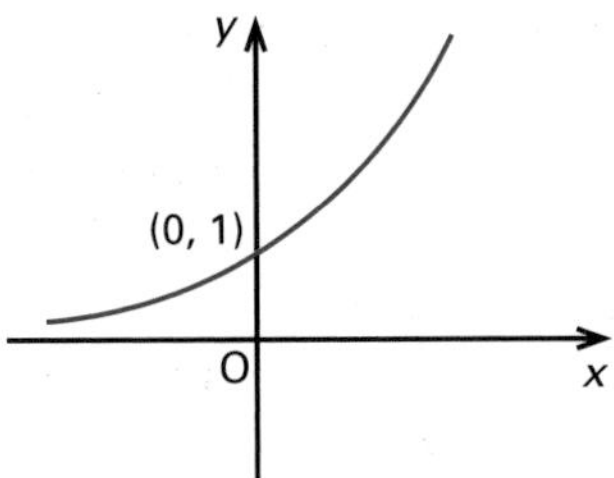

b The *logarithmic curve* with equation $y = \log_a x$ passes through the point (1, 0), like this:

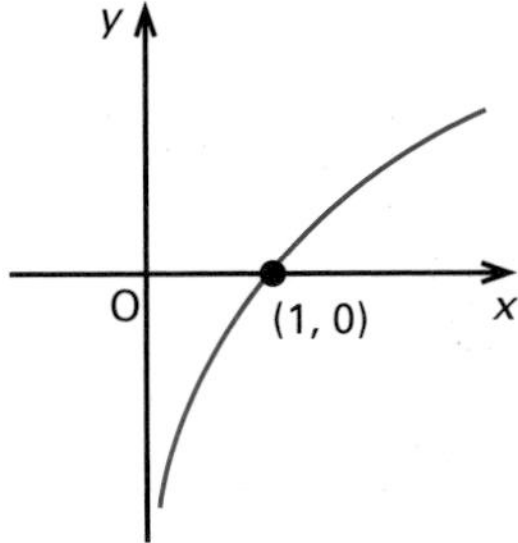

2.3 Trigonometric Functions and Graphs

Radian measure

So far you have measured angles in *degrees*. Their definition of 360 in a complete turn is possibly connected with the number of days the earth takes to circle the sun. Another useful measure for angles is the *radian*, which is closely connected with the circle, as follows.

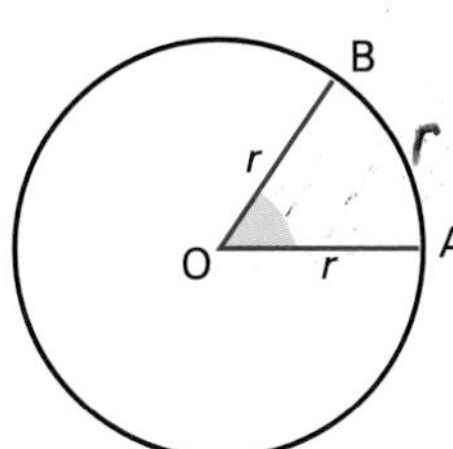

The circle has centre O, and the radii and arc AB are r units long.

$\angle AOB$ subtends an arc equal to the radius; $\angle AOB = 1$ radian.

How can you tell from the diagram that 1 radian is nearly 60°?

Radians and degrees

(i) In the diagram:

$$\frac{\angle AOB}{360°} = \frac{\text{arc AB}}{\text{circumference}}$$

i.e. $\dfrac{1 \text{ radian}}{360°} = \dfrac{r}{2\pi r}$

Cross-multiplying,

$2\ \pi$ radians $= 360°$

so π radians $= 180°$

(ii) π radians $= 180°$

So 1 radian $= \dfrac{180°}{\pi} \doteqdot 57°$

(iii) $180° = \pi$ radians

So $90° = \dfrac{\pi}{2}$ radians

(iv) $\sin\dfrac{\pi}{2}$ means $\sin\dfrac{\pi}{2}$ radians, so

$\sin\dfrac{\pi}{2} = \sin 90° = 1.$

EXERCISE 1

1 π radians $= 180°$. Change the following to degrees. For example,

$\dfrac{\pi}{4}$ radians $= \dfrac{180°}{4} = 45°.$

a $\dfrac{\pi}{2}$ radians **b** $\dfrac{\pi}{6}$ radians **c** $\dfrac{\pi}{3}$ radians **d** 2π radians **e** $\dfrac{2\pi}{3}$ radians **f** $\dfrac{3\pi}{2}$ radians

2 $180° = \pi$ radians. Change the following to radians. For example,

$20° = \frac{\pi}{180} \times 20$ radians $= \frac{\pi}{9}$ radians.

a 60° **b** 90° **c** 120° **d** 45° **e** 135°

3 Use this part of the sine graph, with angles in radians, to write down the value of:

a $\sin \frac{\pi}{2}$ **b** $\sin \pi$ **c** $\sin \frac{3\pi}{2}$ **d** $\sin 2\pi$.

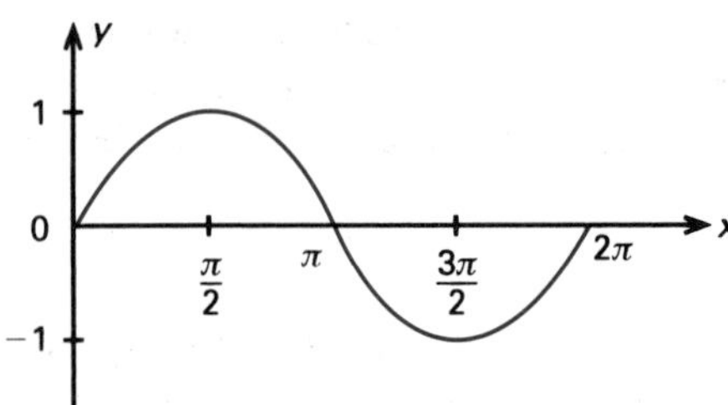

4 Sketch the cosine graph for $0 \leqslant x \leqslant 2\pi$, and write down the value of:

a $\cos \pi$ **b** $\cos 2\pi$ **c** $\cos \frac{\pi}{2}$ **d** $\cos \frac{3\pi}{2}$.

5 a Copy the triangles, and mark the lengths of the sides, in surd form where necessary.

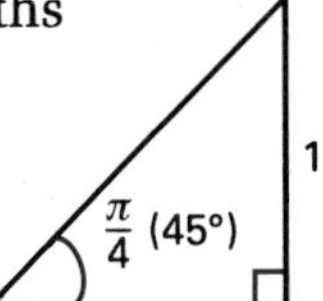

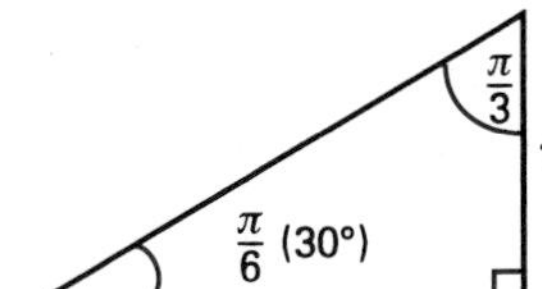

b Copy and complete this table of *exact values* of the sines, cosines and tangents of $\frac{\pi}{6}, \frac{\pi}{4}$ and $\frac{\pi}{3}$ radians.

θ	$\frac{\pi}{6}$	$\frac{\pi}{4}$	$\frac{\pi}{3}$
$\sin \theta$			$\frac{\sqrt{3}}{2}$
$\cos \theta$			
$\tan \theta$			

6 a Using your calculator, write down the values of sin 30°, cos 45° and tan 60°, correct to 2 decimal places where necessary.

b Find out how to use radians on your calculator, and write down the values of $\sin \frac{\pi}{6}$, $\cos \frac{\pi}{4}$ and $\tan \frac{\pi}{3}$, correct to 2 decimal places where necessary.

c Check that your answers to **a** and **b** are the same.

7 Remembering that $\sin \frac{\pi}{8}$ means $\sin \frac{\pi}{8}$ radians, write down, correct to 2 decimal places, the values of:

a $\sin \frac{\pi}{8}$ **b** $\cos \frac{\pi}{10}$ **c** $\tan \frac{\pi}{5}$ **d** $\sin \frac{5\pi}{6}$.

8 Use the table in question **5** to find the exact value (that is, in surd – or square root – form where necessary) of:

a $\sin x + \cos x,\ x = \frac{\pi}{6}$ **b** $\sin 2x + \cos 2x,\ x = \frac{\pi}{6}$ **c** $2 \sin x - 2 \cos x,\ x = \pi$

d $\cos x - \sin x,\ x = \frac{\pi}{4}$ **e** $4 \cos 2x,\ x = \frac{\pi}{4}$ **f** $5 \sin 3x,\ x = \frac{\pi}{6}$

g $\sin^2 \frac{\pi}{3} + \cos^2 \frac{\pi}{3}$ **h** $\tan^2 \frac{\pi}{6} + \tan^2 \frac{\pi}{3}$.

Angles of all sizes in radian measure

The definitions of the sine, cosine and tangent of an angle can be extended from acute and obtuse angles to all sizes of angle by means of these definitions:

$\sin\theta = \frac{y}{r}$, $\cos\theta = \frac{x}{r}$, $\tan\theta = \frac{y}{x}$, $x \neq 0$.

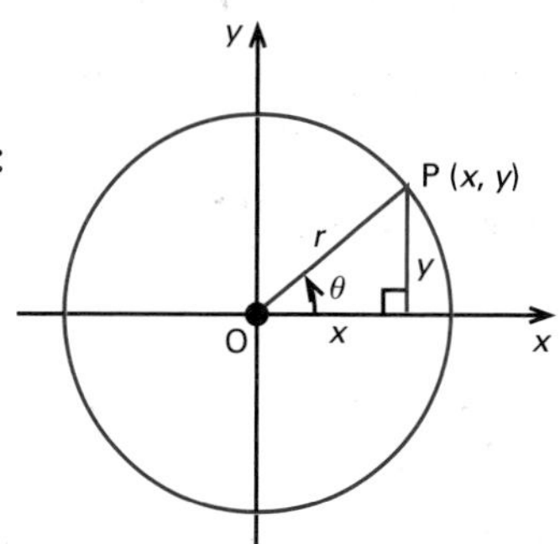

Sines, cosines and tangents of all sizes of angle can be expressed in terms of acute angles.

Example For each function in **a**, **b** and **c**, write down:

(i) its sign
(ii) its form for an acute angle
(iii) its exact value.

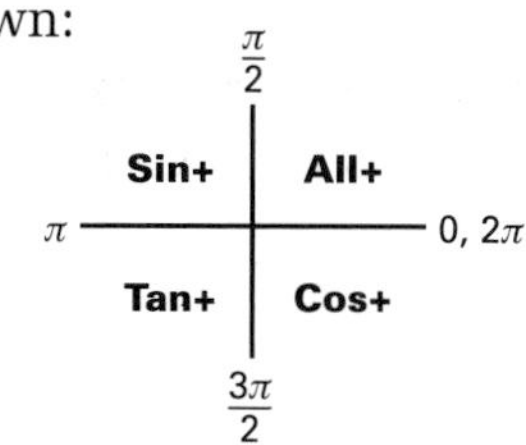

a $\sin\frac{5\pi}{6}$

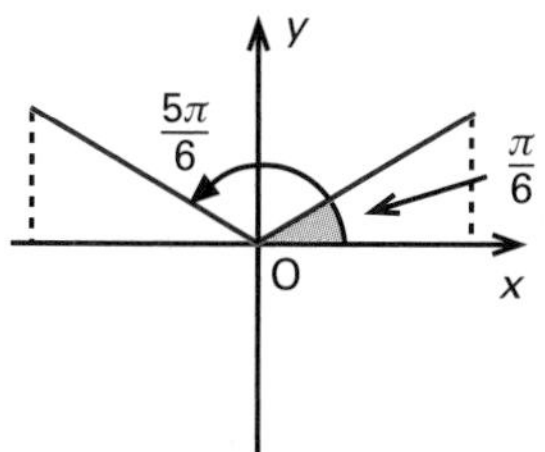

(i) $\frac{5\pi}{6}$ is in 2nd quadrant, so $\sin\frac{5\pi}{6}$ is positive.

(ii) The related acute ∠ is $\pi - \frac{5\pi}{6} = \frac{6\pi}{6} - \frac{5\pi}{6} = \frac{\pi}{6}$

(iii) $\sin\frac{5\pi}{6} = \sin\frac{\pi}{6} = \frac{1}{2}$

b $\cos\frac{5\pi}{4}$

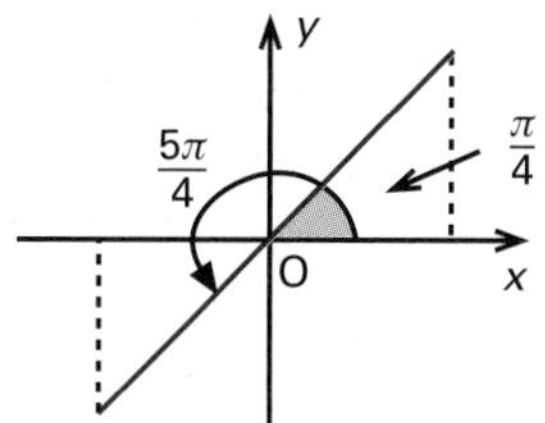

(i) $\frac{5\pi}{4}$ is in 3rd quadrant, so $\cos\frac{5\pi}{4}$ is negative.

(ii) The related acute ∠ is $\frac{5\pi}{4} - \pi = \frac{5\pi}{4} - \frac{4\pi}{4} = \frac{\pi}{4}$

(iii) $\cos\frac{5\pi}{4} = -\cos\frac{\pi}{4}$
$= -\frac{1}{\sqrt{2}}$

c $\tan\frac{5\pi}{3}$

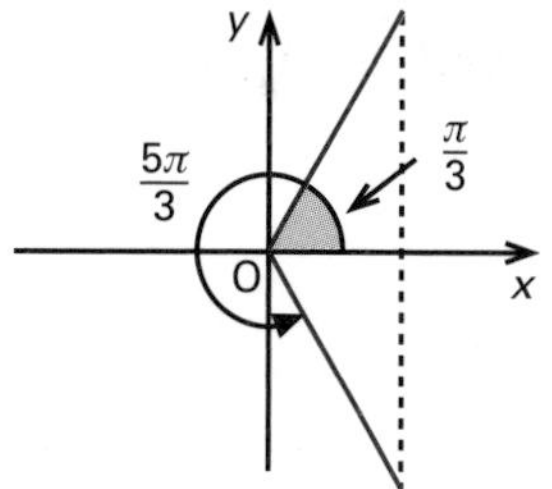

(i) $\frac{5\pi}{3}$ is in 4th quadrant, so $\tan\frac{5\pi}{3}$ is negative.

(ii) The related acute ∠ is $2\pi - \frac{5\pi}{3} = \frac{6\pi}{3} - \frac{5\pi}{3} = \frac{\pi}{3}$

(iii) $\tan\frac{5\pi}{3} = -\tan\frac{\pi}{3}$
$= -\sqrt{3}$

Hint

At stage **(ii)**, relate to π or 2π, whichever is 'nearer'.

EXERCISE 2

1 Write down, as ratios, the values of $\sin\theta$, $\cos\theta$ and $\tan\theta$ for each diagram.

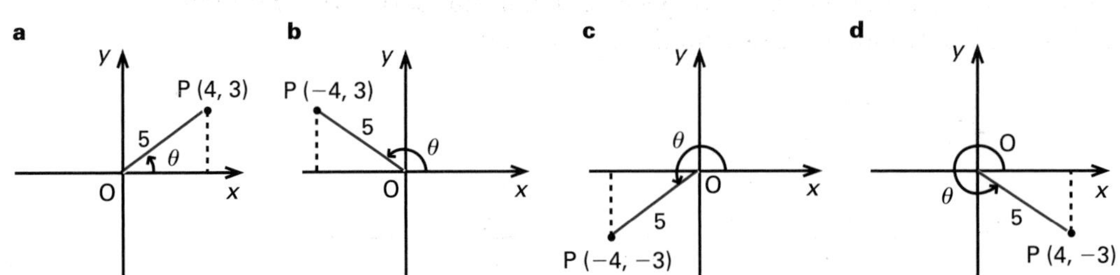

2 Check that the values you got in question **1** agree with the quadrant rule of signs in the box on page 47.

3 Say whether each of the following is positive or negative.

a $\sin\frac{\pi}{10}$ **b** $\sin\frac{11\pi}{10}$ **c** $\cos\frac{\pi}{5}$

d $\cos\frac{5\pi}{3}$ **e** $\tan\frac{4\pi}{3}$ **f** $\tan\frac{5\pi}{3}$

4 Simplify the following. For example, $\pi-\frac{\pi}{3}=\frac{3\pi}{3}-\frac{\pi}{3}=\frac{2\pi}{3}$.

a $\pi-\frac{\pi}{2}$ **b** $\pi-\frac{\pi}{6}$ **c** $\frac{3\pi}{2}-\pi$

d $\frac{5\pi}{4}-\pi$ **e** $2\pi-\frac{\pi}{3}$ **f** $2\pi-\frac{5\pi}{6}$

5 Use the method in the worked example in the box on page 47 to express each of the following in terms of an acute angle, and then to write down its exact value.

a $\sin\frac{2\pi}{3}$ **b** $\cos\frac{3\pi}{4}$ **c** $\tan\frac{4\pi}{3}$

d $\cos\frac{7\pi}{6}$ **e** $\sin\frac{5\pi}{3}$ **f** $\tan\frac{7\pi}{4}$

6 Use the general $x-y-r$ definitions for $\sin\theta$, $\cos\theta$ and $\tan\theta$, along with the diagram below, to copy and complete the table.

θ	0	$\frac{\pi}{2}$	π	$\frac{3\pi}{2}$	2π
$\sin\theta$	0	1			
$\cos\theta$	1				
$\tan\theta$	0	—		—	

$\left(\tan\theta \text{ is not defined at } \theta=\frac{\pi}{2} \text{ and } \theta=\frac{3\pi}{2}.\right)$

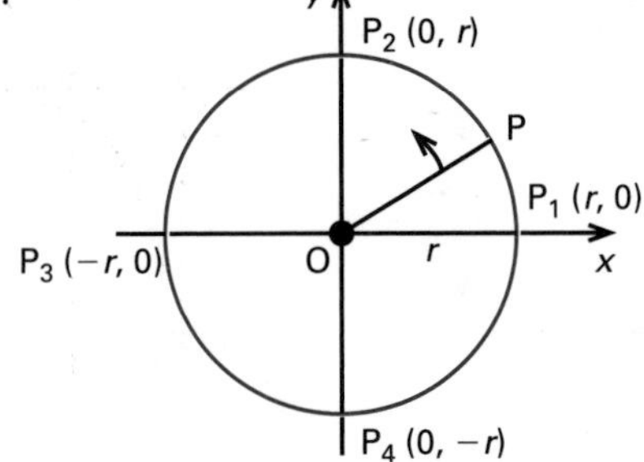

7 The rotating arm OP in the diagram in question **6** returns to its starting position after rotations about O of 2π, 4π, 6π, ... radians. So $\sin\theta$ and $\cos\theta$ have period 2π.

a Check that the data in the table in question **6** and the period of 2π for $\sin\theta$ provide sufficient data for this sketch of $y = \sin x$.

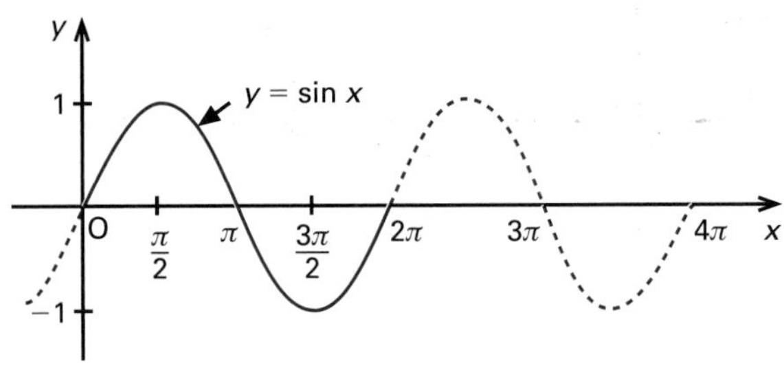

b Sketch the graph $y = \cos x$ from 0 to 4π radians in the same way.

8 Write down the maximum and minimum values of:

a $\sin x$ **b** $\cos x$ **c** $1 + \sin x$

d $2 + \cos x$ **e** $3 - \sin x$ **f** $2 - 2\cos x$

g $(1 + \sin x)^2$ **h** $1 - (1 + \sin x)^2$.

9 **a** Use the definition of $\tan\theta$, and the diagram below, to prove that $\tan(\pi + \theta) = \tan\theta$.

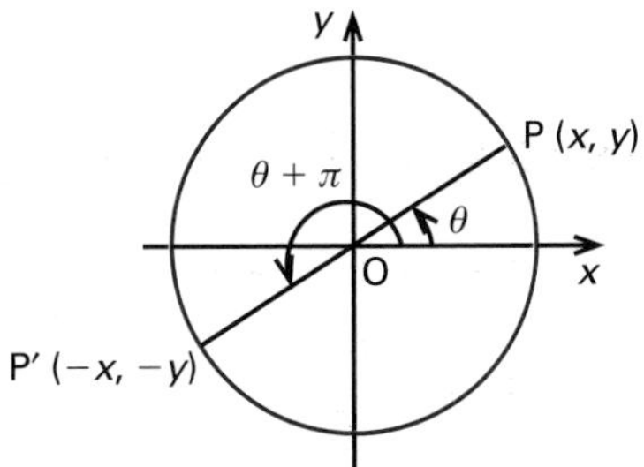

b What is the period of $\tan\theta$?

c With the help of this graph, sketch the graph $y = \tan x$ for $-\frac{3\pi}{2} < x < \frac{3\pi}{2}$, $x \neq \pm\frac{\pi}{2}$.

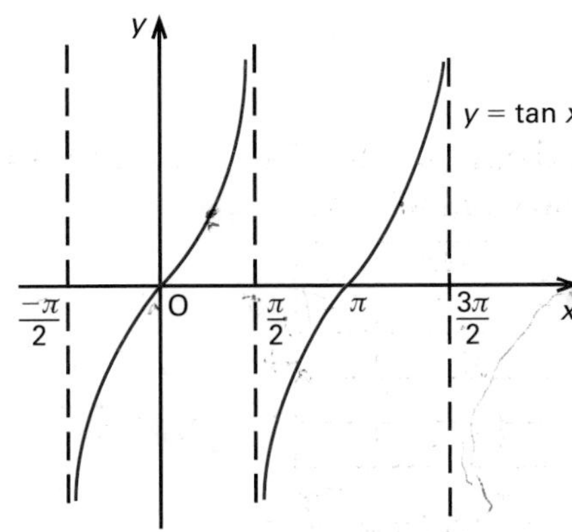

Sketching trigonometric graphs

Using degree measure, you know that for the graphs $y = a\sin nx$ and $y = a\cos nx$ $(n > 0)$:

(i) a gives the maximum and minimum values of y

(ii) n gives the number of cycles in the graph for $0 \leqslant x \leqslant 2\pi$ (x in radian measure)

(iii) the period of the graph is $\frac{2\pi}{n}$.

Check the above for these graphs, using radian measure:

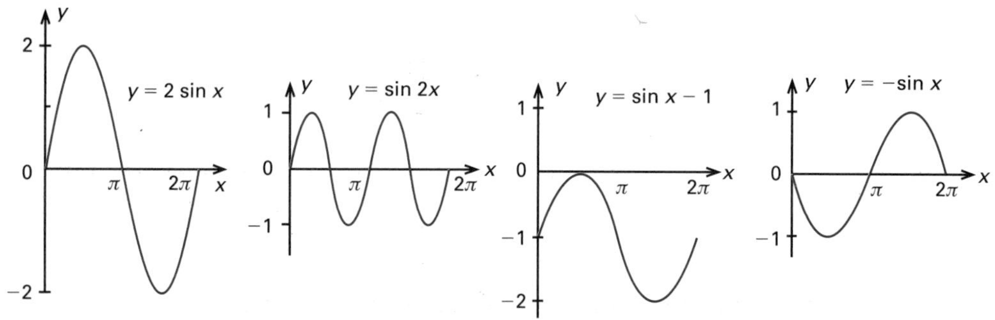

Example Find the coordinates of the maximum turning point, for $0 \leqslant x \leqslant \pi$, of the graph of $y = 3\sin\left(x - \frac{\pi}{3}\right)$.

The maximum value of y is 3, when $\sin\left(x - \frac{\pi}{3}\right) = 1$.

$\sin\left(x - \frac{\pi}{3}\right) = 1$ when $x - \frac{\pi}{3} = \frac{\pi}{2}$, i.e. $x = \frac{5\pi}{6}$.

So the maximum turning point is $\left(\frac{5\pi}{6}, 3\right)$.

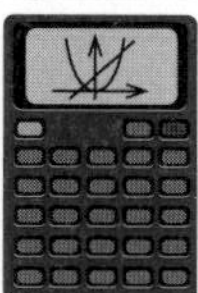

a Write a program to draw a family of graphs of the form $y = a\sin nx$.

b Keeping $n = 1$, obtain a set of sine curves by taking various values of a.

c Keeping $a = 1$, show sine curves with different periods, using $n = 1, 2, 3, 4, \frac{1}{2}, \frac{1}{3}$.

EXERCISE 3

In questions **1–3**:

(i) write down the maximum and minimum values of y, the number of cycles in the graph for $0 \leqslant x \leqslant 2\pi$ and the period of the graph

(ii) sketch the graph $y = f(x)$ for $0 \leqslant x \leqslant 2\pi$.

1 a $y = \sin x$ **b** $y = 3\sin x$ **c** $y = \sin 3x$

2 **a** $y = \cos x$ **b** $y = -\cos x$ **c** $y = \cos x - 1$

3 **a** $y = 3\sin 2x$ **b** $y = 2\cos 3x$ **c** $y = \sin \frac{1}{2}x$.

4 Each of the graphs below has an equation of the form $y = a\sin bx$ or $y = c\cos dx$. Write down the possible equation and the period of each graph.

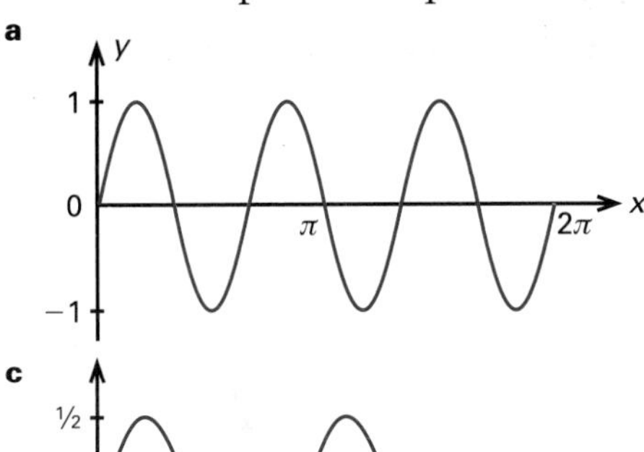

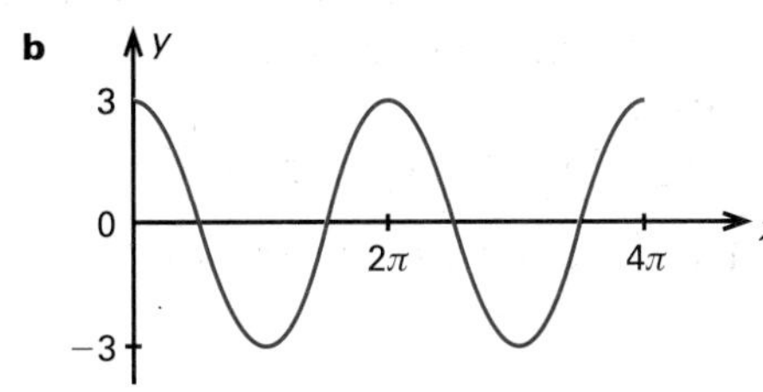

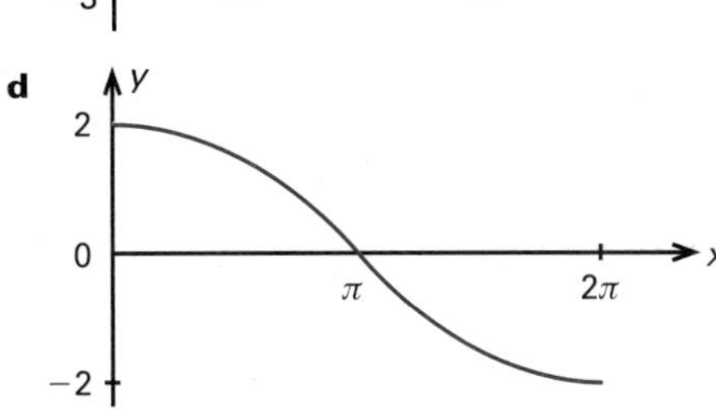

5 Write down the maximum and minimum values of each of these:
a $\sin 2x$ **b** $1 + \sin 2x$ **c** $1 - \sin 2x$
d $\cos 3x$ **e** $3 + \cos 3x$ **f** $3 - \cos 3x$.

6 Sketch the following graphs, for $0 \leqslant x \leqslant 2\pi$:
a $y = 2\sin x + 2$ **b** $y = \cos 2x - 1$
c $y = \frac{1}{2} + \frac{1}{2}\sin 4x$ **d** $y = 1 - \sin \frac{1}{2}x$.

7 Find the value of x, for $0 \leqslant x \leqslant \pi$, which gives the maximum value of:
a $\sin\left(x - \frac{\pi}{4}\right)$ **b** $\cos\left(x - \frac{\pi}{3}\right)$ **c** $2\sin\left(x + \frac{\pi}{2}\right)$.

8 Find the coordinates of the maximum turning points, for $0 \leqslant x \leqslant \pi$, of the graphs:
a $y = 2\sin\left(x + \frac{\pi}{6}\right)$ **b** $y = 5\cos\left(x - \frac{\pi}{2}\right)$.

9 An ocean tide is modelled by $y = 3\sin \frac{\pi}{6}t$, in metres above mean sea-level at time t hours.
a What is the difference in level between high tide and low tide?
b Sketch the graph $y = 3\sin \frac{\pi}{6}t$ for $0 \leqslant t \leqslant 12$.

10 A novelty toy is hanging by a spring frame from the ceiling. The toy is 1 metre above the floor. Once set bobbing, its height above the floor is given by $h(t) = 1 + \frac{1}{3}\cos 3t$ metres at time t seconds.
a Calculate the difference between its maximum and minimum heights.
b What is the period of its oscillation?
c Sketch the graph for $0 \leqslant t \leqslant \frac{2}{3}\pi$.

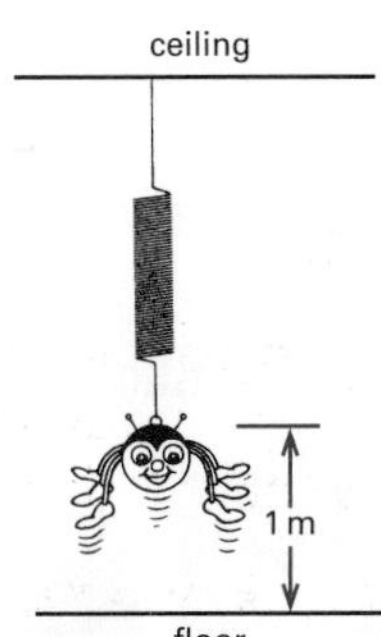

11 The Cresta Run at a theme park is based on one complete cycle of the curve $y = 20 + 20\sin\frac{x}{10}$. Units are metres.

a Sketch one cycle of the curve.

b Calculate the overall vertical and horizontal extent of the run, to the nearest metre where necessary.

Trigonometric equations

Example 1 Solve $2\sin x° = 1$, $0 \leqslant x \leqslant 360$, and illustrate the solutions in a sketch of $y = \sin x°$.

The equation is $\sin x° = \frac{1}{2}$.
Since $\sin x°$ is positive, $x°$ is in the first or second quadrants (ticked).

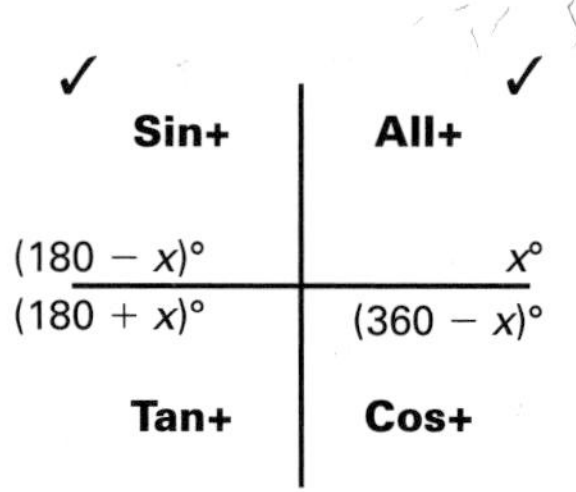

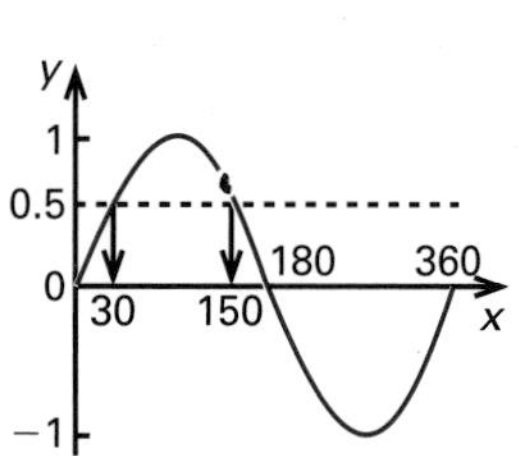

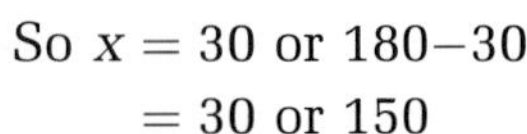

So $x = 30$ or $180 - 30$
$= 30$ or 150

Example 2 Solve $\sqrt{2}\cos\theta + 1 = 0$, $0 \leqslant \theta \leqslant 2\pi$, and illustrate the solutions in a sketch of $y = \cos\theta$.

The equation is $\cos\theta = -\dfrac{1}{\sqrt{2}}$.

From the quadrant diagram, θ is in the second or third quadrants.

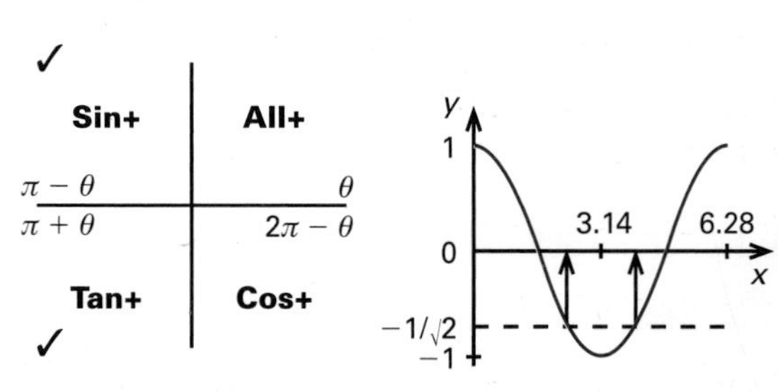

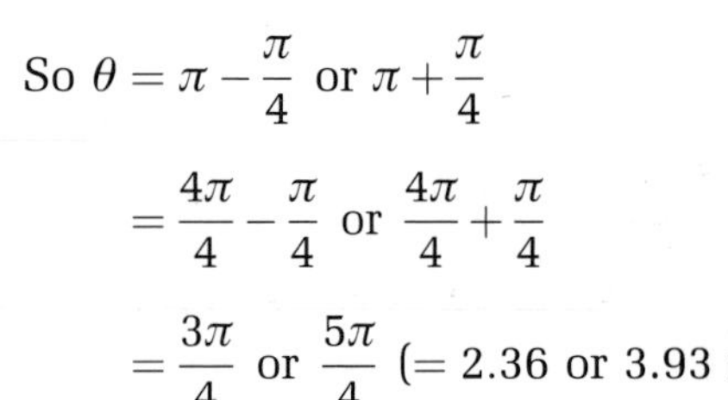

$$\text{So } \theta = \pi - \frac{\pi}{4} \text{ or } \pi + \frac{\pi}{4}$$

$$= \frac{4\pi}{4} - \frac{\pi}{4} \text{ or } \frac{4\pi}{4} + \frac{\pi}{4}$$

$$= \frac{3\pi}{4} \text{ or } \frac{5\pi}{4} \text{ (= 2.36 or 3.93 radians)}$$

Example 3 Solve $\sin 3x° = -1$, $0 \leqslant x \leqslant 360$, and illustrate the solutions in a sketch of $y = \sin 3x°$.

For $3x$, $0 \leqslant 3x \leqslant 3 \times 360$, i.e. $0 \leqslant 3x \leqslant 1080$.
If $\sin 3x = -1$,

$3x = 270, 270 + 360, 270 + 360 + 360, \ldots$
$= 270, 630, 990, \ldots$

So $x = 90, 210, 330$.

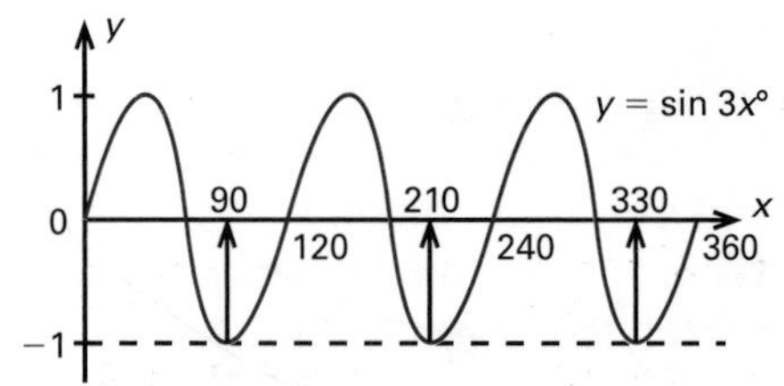

a Display the graphs $y = \cos x°$ and $y = -\frac{1}{2}$. Use the cursor to estimate the first two positive roots of the equation $2\cos x° + 1 = 0$.
b Repeat **a** for graphs $y = 2\sin x°$, $y = \cos x°$ and the equation $2\sin x° = \cos x°$.
c Repeat **b**, using radian measure (RAD).

EXERCISE 4

1 Use the sine and cosine graphs to write down the solutions of these equations.
a For $0 \leqslant x \leqslant 360$:
(i) $\sin x° = 1$ **(ii)** $\cos x° = -1$ **(iii)** $\sin x° = 0$.
b For $0 \leqslant \theta \leqslant 2\pi$:
(i) $\sin\theta = 1$ **(ii)** $\cos\theta = -1$ **(iii)** $\sin\theta = 0$.

2 Solve, for $0 \leqslant \theta \leqslant 2\pi$:
a $\sin\theta = \dfrac{1}{\sqrt{2}}$ **b** $\sin\theta = -\dfrac{1}{\sqrt{2}}$
c $\cos\theta = -\dfrac{1}{2}$ **d** $\cos\theta = \dfrac{\sqrt{3}}{2}$.

3 Solve, for $0 \leqslant \theta \leqslant 2\pi$:
a $\tan\theta = 1$ **b** $\tan\theta = -1$
c $\tan\theta = \sqrt{3}$ **d** $\sqrt{3}\tan\theta + 1 = 0$.

4 Solve, for $0 \leqslant x \leqslant 360$:
a $2\sin x° + 1 = 0$ **b** $2\cos x° - 1 = 0$
c $2\sin x° + \sqrt{3} = 0$ **d** $\sqrt{2}\cos x° - 1 = 0$.

5 Solve, for $0 \leqslant x \leqslant 360$:
a $\sin 2x° = 1$ **b** $\cos 2x° = 1$.

6 Solve, for $0 \leqslant x \leqslant 360$:
a $\sin 3x° = \dfrac{\sqrt{3}}{2}$ **b** $\cos 3x° = 0$.

7 **a** Solve, correct to the nearest degree, for $0 \leqslant x \leqslant 360$:
(i) $\sin x° = 0.7$ **(ii)** $\sin 2x° = 0.7$ **(iii)** $\sin 3x° = 0.7$.
b Illustrate the solutions in sketches of $y = \sin x°$, $y = \sin 2x°$ and $y = \sin 3x°$.

Example 4 Solve $2\sin^2 x° = 1$, $0 \leqslant x \leqslant 360$.

$\sin^2 x° = \dfrac{1}{2}$, so $\sin x° = \pm\dfrac{1}{\sqrt{2}}$.

(i) $\sin x° = \dfrac{1}{\sqrt{2}}$ **(ii)** $\sin x° = -\dfrac{1}{\sqrt{2}}$

$x = 45, 135$ $x = 225, 315$

(i) Sin+	(i) All+
$(180 - x)°$	$x°$
$(180 + x)°$	$(360 - x)°$
Tan+ (ii)	Cos+ (ii)

Example 5 Solve $4\sin^2 x + 11\sin x + 6 = 0$, correct to 2 decimal places, for $0 \leqslant x \leqslant 2\pi$.

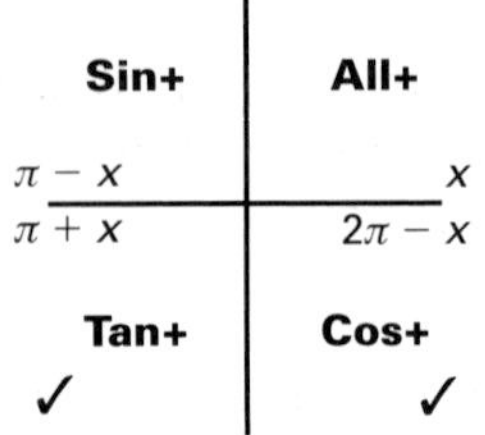

The equation is $(4\sin x + 3)(\sin x + 2) = 0$

$\sin x = -0.75$, or -2 (no solutions)

$\sin^{-1} 0.75 = 0.85$ radian, but x is in the third or fourth quadrants.

So $x = \pi + 0.85$ or $2\pi - 0.85$

$= 3.14 + 0.85$ or $6.28 - 0.85$

$= 3.99$ or 5.43

Reminder

In angle measure, π radians $= 180°$.
As a number, $\pi = 3.14$, correct to 2 decimal places.

EXERCISE 5

1 Solve these equations, for $0 \leqslant x \leqslant 360$:

a $4\sin^2 x° = 3$ $\left(\sin x° = \pm\dfrac{\sqrt{3}}{2};\ \text{four solutions}\right)$

b $3\tan^2 x° = 1$ **c** $4\cos^2 x° - 1 = 0$.

2 Solve, for $0 \leqslant x \leqslant 360$:

a $\sin^2 x° - 4\sin x° + 3 = 0$ **b** $\cos^2 x° + \cos x° - 2 = 0$

c $2\cos^2 x° + \cos x° - 1 = 0$ **d** $2\sin^2 x° - 5\sin x° - 3 = 0$.

3 Solve, correct to 2 decimal places, for $0 \leqslant \theta \leqslant 2\pi$ (calculator in RAD mode!):

a $\sin^2 \theta = 0.3$ **b** $5\cos^2 \theta = 2$

c $\tan^2 \theta = 6$ **d** $\tan^2 \theta + \tan \theta - 12 = 0$

e $6\sin^2 \theta + 5\sin \theta + 1 = 0$ **f** $15\cos^2 \theta + 7\cos \theta - 2 = 0$.

4 Solve, correct to the nearest degree where necessary, for $0 \leqslant x \leqslant 360$:

a $\sin^2 x° - \cos x° = 1$

b $\cos^2 x° + \sin x° = 1$

c $6\cos^2 x° - \sin x° - 5 = 0$

d $5\sin^2 x° - 2 = 2\cos x°$.

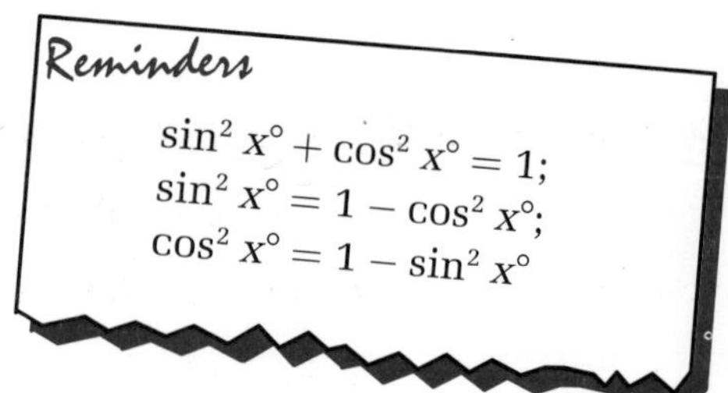

5 This is the graph $y = 2\sin\frac{1}{2}x°$, for $0 \leqslant x \leqslant 360$.

a Sketch the graph, and indicate the points of intersection with the line $y = 1$.

b Solve the equation $2\sin\frac{1}{2}x° = 1$, for $0 \leqslant x \leqslant 360$, and compare with your sketch.

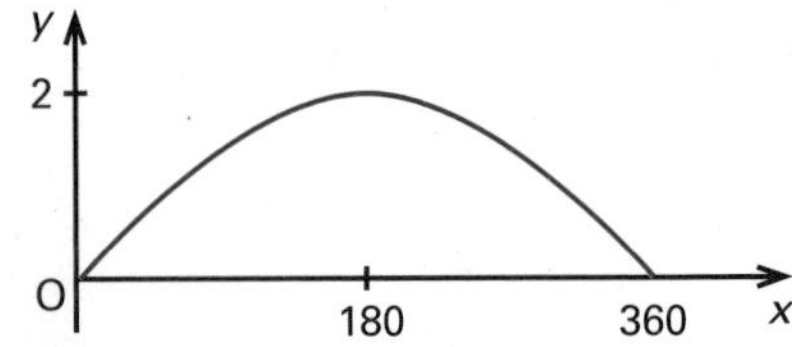

6 This is the graph $y = 2\cos 2x - 1$, for $0 \leqslant x \leqslant \pi$.

a Solve an equation to find the x-coordinates of A and B.

b Find the x-coordinates of the points of intersection of the curve and the line $y = -2$.

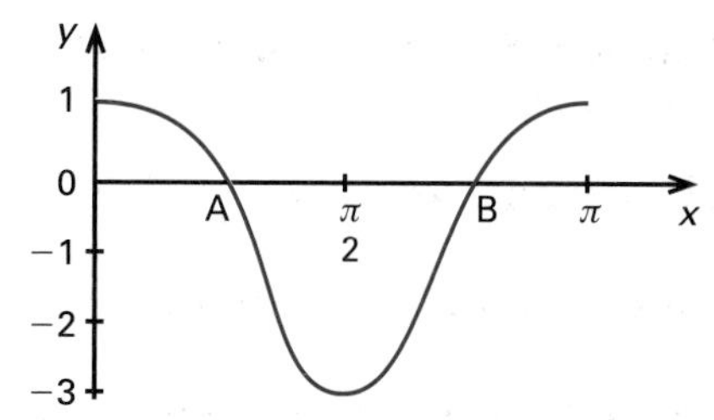

7 Find when the tide in question **9** of Exercise 3 is $1\frac{1}{2}$ metres above mean sea-level for the first time.

8 Find when the toy in question **10** of Exercise 3 is $1\frac{1}{6}$ metres from the floor for the first time.

9 Calculate the horizontal distance travelled, correct to 0.1 metre, when the height above the ground on the Cresta Run in question **11** of Exercise 3 is 30 m.

Example 6 Solve $\sin(2x - 20)° = 0.5$, $0 \leqslant x \leqslant 360$.

$2x - 20 = 30,\ 150$ or $30 + 360,\ 150 + 360$

$2x = 50,\ 170,\ 410,\ 530$

$x = 25,\ 85,\ 205,\ 265$

Example 7 Solve $3\cos\left(2x + \frac{\pi}{4}\right) = 1$, correct to 1 decimal place, for $0 \leqslant x \leqslant \pi$.

$\cos\left(2x + \frac{\pi}{4}\right) = \frac{1}{3}$

Using radian mode, to 2 decimal places,

$2x + \frac{\pi}{4} = 1.23$ or $2\pi - 1.23$

$2x = 1.23 - 0.79,\ 6.28 - 1.23 - 0.79$

$x = 0.2,\ 2.1$, correct to 1 decimal place

EXERCISE 6

Solve these equations, to the nearest degree, for $0 \leqslant x \leqslant 360$.

1 a $\sin(x - 10)° = 0.8$ b $\cos(x + 20)° = 0.4$

2 a $\sin(2x - 30)° = 1$ b $\cos(2x - 60)° = -1$

3 a $2\sin(2x - 60)° = 1$ b $4\cos(2x + 40)° = 3$

Solve these equations, correct to 1 decimal place, for $0 \leqslant x \leqslant \pi$.

4 a $\sin\left(x - \frac{\pi}{2}\right) = 0.5$ b $\cos\left(x - \frac{\pi}{3}\right) = 0.25$

5 a $3\sin\left(2x - \frac{\pi}{4}\right) = 1$ b $5\cos\left(2x + \frac{\pi}{6}\right) = -1$

*6 a $3\cos\left(2x - \frac{\pi}{2}\right) = 1$ b $2\sin\left(2x + \frac{\pi}{3}\right) = 1$

CHAPTER 2.3 REVIEW

1 Express in radian measure:
a 60° **b** 120° **c** 150° **d** 270° **e** 315°.

2 Express in degrees:
a $\frac{\pi}{2}$ radians **b** $\frac{\pi}{6}$ radians
c $\frac{3\pi}{2}$ radians **d** $\frac{\pi}{4}$ radians
e 1 radian, correct to 0.1°.

3 Find the exact value of each of the following, in surd form where necessary:
a $\sin \pi$ **b** $\tan \frac{\pi}{4}$ **c** $\cos \frac{\pi}{4}$ **d** $\sin \frac{3\pi}{4}$
e $\cos \frac{2\pi}{3}$ **f** $\tan \frac{\pi}{3}$ **g** $\sin \frac{5\pi}{6}$ **h** $\cos \frac{3\pi}{2}$.

4 With the help of the all–sin–tan–cos quadrant diagram, find the sign of:
a $\sin 100°$ **b** $\cos 200°$ **c** $\tan 300°$
d $\sin \frac{11\pi}{10}$ **e** $\cos \frac{11\pi}{10}$ **f** $\tan \frac{11\pi}{10}$.

5 Find the value, correct to 2 decimal places, of:
a $\sin 320°$ **b** $\tan 125°$ **c** $\cos 213°$
d $\sin \frac{\pi}{5}$ **e** $\cos \frac{8\pi}{5}$ **f** $\tan \frac{8\pi}{5}$.

6 For each of the following:
(i) write down the maximum and minimum values of y, the number of cycles in the graph $y = f(x)$ for $0 \leqslant x \leqslant 2\pi$, and the period of the graph
(ii) sketch the graph $y = f(x)$.
a $y = \cos 3x$ **b** $y = 3 \sin 2x$
c $y = 2 - 2 \sin x$ **d** $y = 3 + \cos \frac{1}{2}x$

7 **(i)** Write down the equation and period of each of the following graphs (each is a sine or cosine curve).

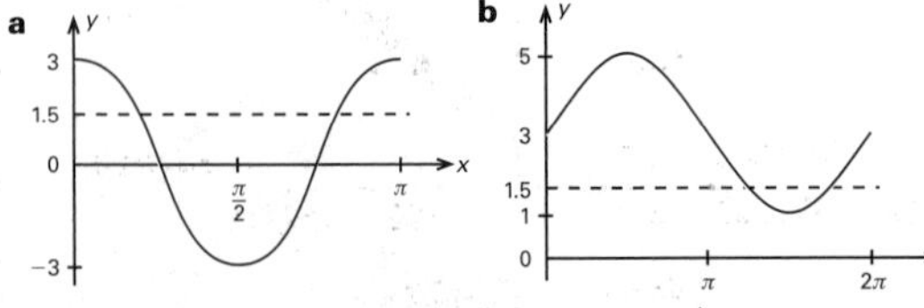

(ii) Find the values of x where the line $y = 1.5$ cuts each curve, correct to 2 decimal places for **b**.

8 The equation of this graph is of the form $y = a + b \sin cx$. Write down the values of a, b and c.

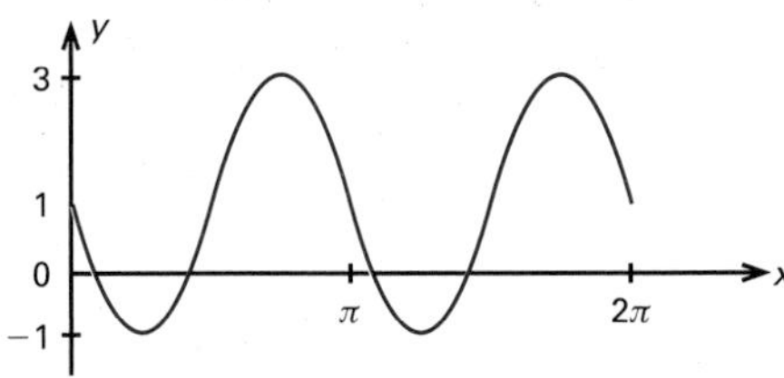

9 Solve, for $0 \leqslant x \leqslant 360$, correct to 1 decimal place where necessary:
a $\sin x° = \frac{1}{4}$ **b** $\sin^2 x° = \frac{1}{4}$
c $\tan x° = -5$.

10 Solve, for $0 \leqslant \theta \leqslant 2\pi$, correct to 2 decimal places where necessary:
a $\sin \theta = -1$
b $2 \cos \theta + \sqrt{3} = 0$
c $3 \cos^2 \theta - \cos \theta = 0$
d $12 \sin^2 \theta - 5 \sin \theta - 2 = 0$.

11 Solve, for $0 \leqslant x \leqslant 360$, to the nearest degree:
a $\sin (x + 40)° = 0.7$
b $\cos (2x + 10)° = 1$.

12 Solve, for $0 \leqslant x \leqslant \pi$, correct to 1 decimal place:
a $5 \sin \left(x - \frac{\pi}{5}\right) = 1$
b $3 \cos \left(2x + \frac{\pi}{8}\right) = -2$

13 The distance in metres moved by the piston from one end of the cylinder is given by $x(t) = \frac{1}{4} \sin 3t$, where the time t is in

seconds and $0 \leqslant t \leqslant \frac{\pi}{3}$.
a Calculate the distance moved by the cylinder in one complete cycle.
b Find the first time at which $x(t) = \frac{1}{8}$.

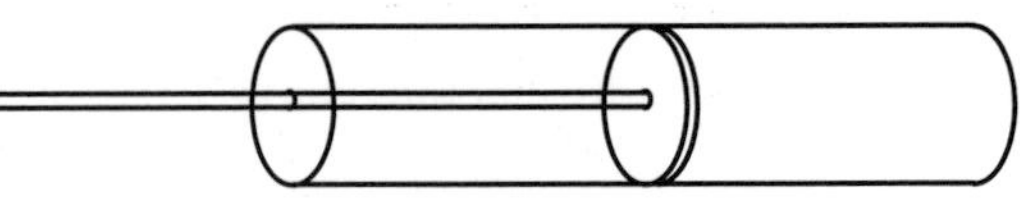

14 Write down the maximum and minimum values of:
a $1 - \sin x$ **b** $1 - \sin^2 x$
c $1 - (1 - \sin x)^2$.

CHAPTER 2.3 SUMMARY

1 Radian measure

π radians $= 180°$;
1 radian $\doteqdot 57°$

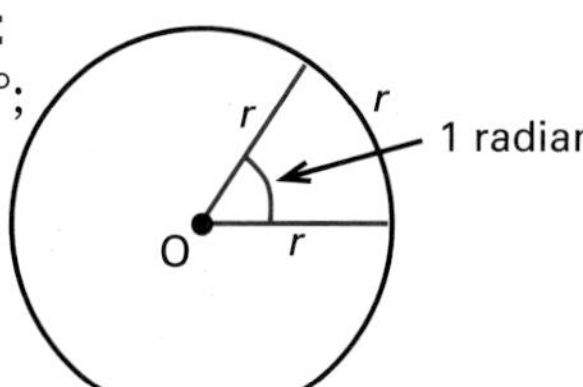

$\sin \frac{\pi}{2}$ means $\sin \frac{\pi}{2}$ radians;

$\sin \frac{\pi}{2} = \sin 90° = 1$

2 Special angles, in radian measure

a (i)

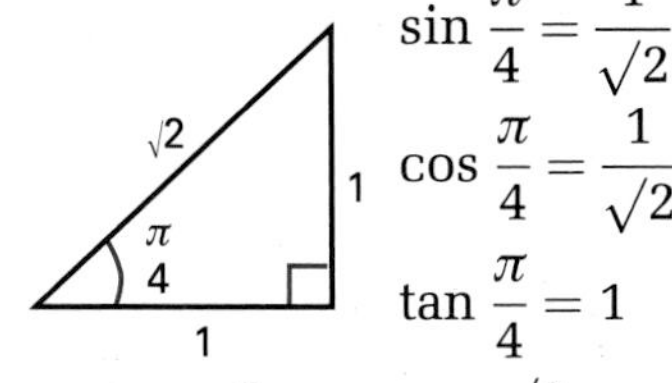

$\sin \frac{\pi}{4} = \frac{1}{\sqrt{2}}$

$\cos \frac{\pi}{4} = \frac{1}{\sqrt{2}}$

$\tan \frac{\pi}{4} = 1$

(ii) $\sin \frac{\pi}{6} = \frac{1}{2}$; $\sin \frac{\pi}{3} = \frac{\sqrt{3}}{2}$

$\cos \frac{\pi}{6} = \frac{\sqrt{3}}{2}$; $\cos \frac{\pi}{3} = \frac{1}{2}$

$\tan \frac{\pi}{6} = \frac{1}{\sqrt{3}}$; $\tan \frac{\pi}{3} = \sqrt{3}$

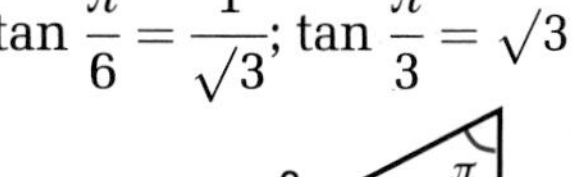
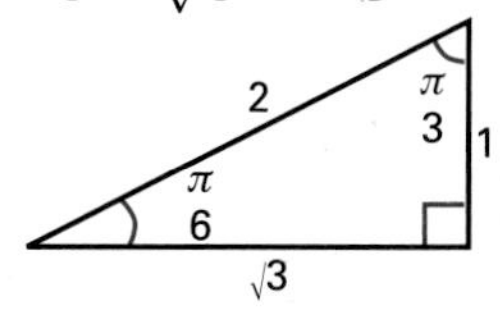

b (i)

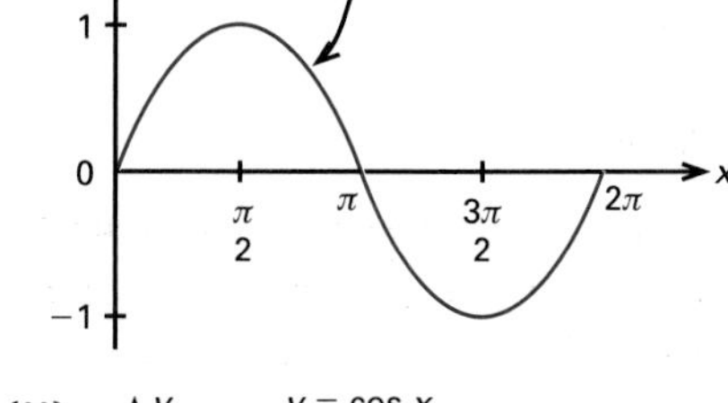

(ii)

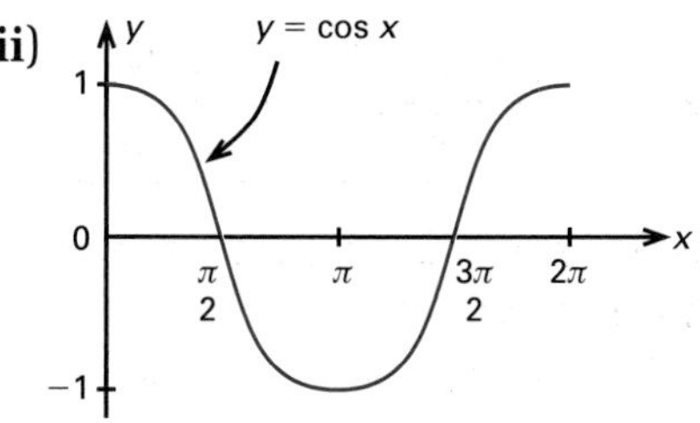

3 Trigonometric graphs

For the graphs $y = a \sin nx$ and $y = a \cos nx$ $(n > 0)$:

(i) a gives the maximum and minimum values

(ii) n gives the number of cycles for $0 \leqslant x \leqslant 2\pi$, and the period is $\frac{2\pi}{n}$.

Examples

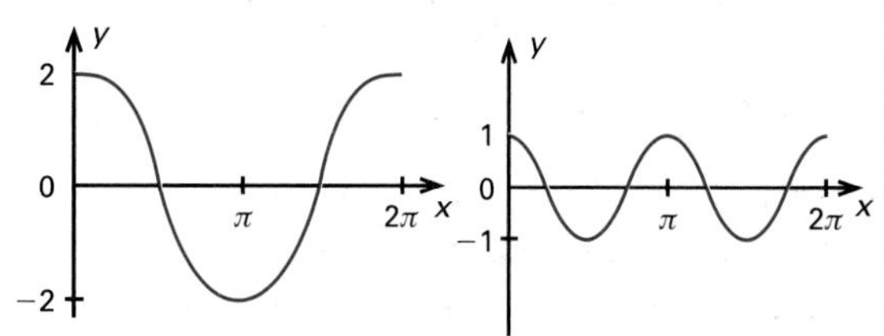

$y = 2 \cos x$
max 2, min −2
1 cycle, period 2π

$y = \cos 2x$
max 1, min −1
2 cycles, period π

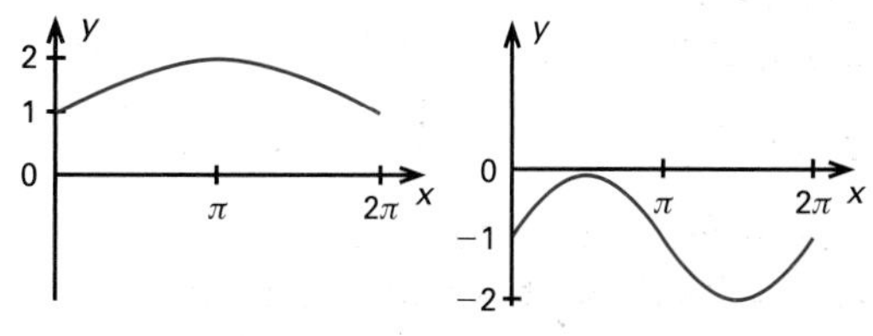

$y = 1 + \sin \frac{1}{2}x$
max 2, min 0
½ cycle, period 4π

$y = \sin x - 1$
max 0, min −2
1 cycle, period 2π

4 Trigonometric equations

Use the all–sin–tan–cos quadrant diagram to find the quadrants in which the solutions lie, and hence the actual solutions.

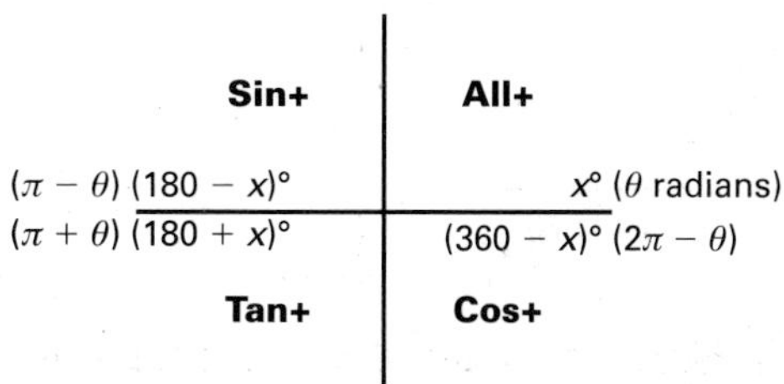

3.1 Introduction to Differentiation

Graphs and gradients

CLASS DISCUSSION/EXERCISE 1

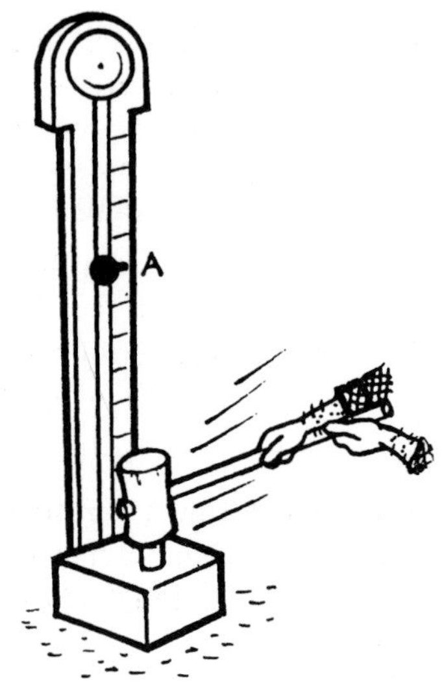

1 At the 'Test Your Strength' challenge, Bill hits the button to try to send the striker up to ring the bell. The striker's motion is modelled by the equation $h(t) = 20t - 5t^2$, where $h(t)$ is its height in metres after t seconds.

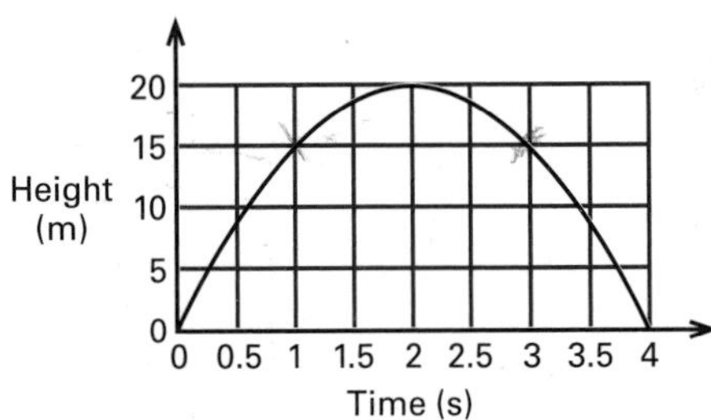

From the graph of $h(t) = 20t - 5t^2$, estimate the speed of the striker after:

a 1 second (i.e. the gradient of the graph at $t = 1$; use a ruler, but watch the scales)

b 2 seconds **c** 3 seconds.

The method above takes time and is not very accurate. In this chapter you will develop much more powerful methods for solving similar and other problems.

2 The gradient of a curve

The points P(1, 1) and Q(2, 4) lie on the parabola $y = x^2$. As Q moves along the curve towards P the gradient of the curve changes. The average gradient of the parabola from P to Q is the gradient of the chord PQ (m_{PQ}).

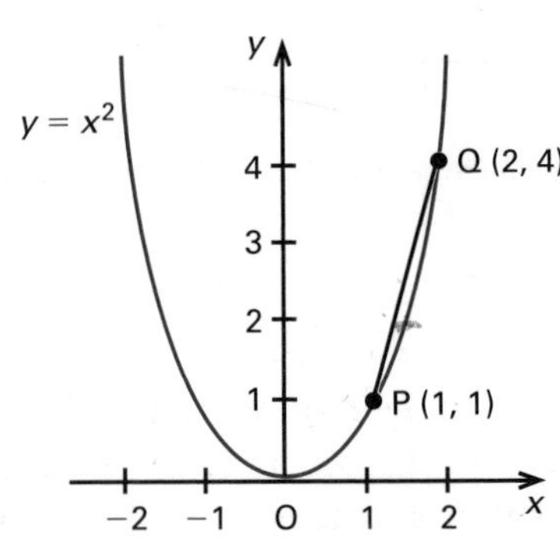

a Copy and complete:

The average gradient from $x = 1$ to $x = 2$ is

$$m_{PQ} = \frac{y_Q - y_P}{x_Q - x_P} = \frac{\dots}{\dots} = \dots$$

b (i) Keep P(1, 1) fixed, but move Q towards P. Copy and complete the table.

(ii) As Q gets closer and closer to P, what happens to the gradients of the chords?

(iii) Can you predict the gradient of the parabola at P?

x_Q	y_Q	$x_Q - x_P$	$y_Q - y_P$	Average gradient m_{PQ}
1.8	3.24	0.8	2.24	2.8
1.6	2.56	0.6	1.56	2.6
1.4	1.96	...	...	...
1.3	...	...	...	...
1.2	...	...	...	...
1.1	...	...	...	...

3 The gradient of the tangent at P(1, 1) on the parabola $y = x^2$

As lots of chords are drawn through P, with Q getting closer and closer to P, m_{PQ} gets closer and closer to the gradient of the tangent at P, the gradient of the parabola at P.

a Continue your table in **2b** for $x_Q = 1.09$, $1.08, \ldots$ as far as your calculator allows.

b Do your results suggest that the gradient of the tangent at P(1, 1) is 2?

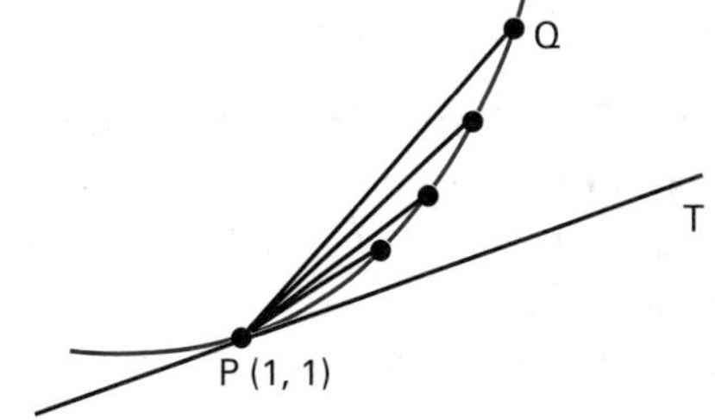

4 Proof

You can *prove* that the gradient of the tangent at P is 2, using a 'limit' method. Start at P(1, 1), and take Q on $y = x^2$ with x-coordinate $1 + h$.

$x_Q = 1 + h$, $y_Q = (1 + h)^2$. Copy and complete:

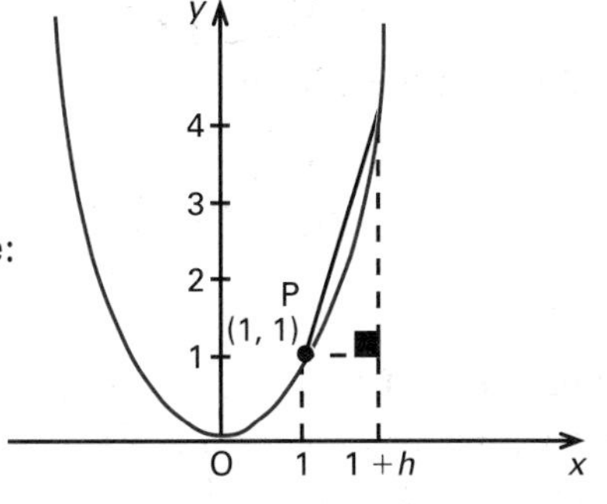

$$m_{PQ} = \frac{y_Q - y_P}{x_Q - x_p} = \frac{(1+h)^2 - \ldots}{(1+h) - \ldots} = \frac{\ldots}{\ldots}$$

$$= \frac{h(\ldots + \ldots)}{h} = 2 + h.$$

As Q $\to$ P, $h \to 0$ and $m_{PQ} \to 2$.
As Q 'disappears' at P, m_{PQ} becomes the gradient of the tangent at P.
As $h \to 0$, $m_{PQ} \to 2$. So the gradient of the tangent at P(1, 1) on the parabola $y = x^2$ is 2.

5 Using the method in **4**, calculate the gradient of the tangent to the parabola $y = x^2$ at:

a A(2, 4) **b** (5, 25) **c** (−1, 1).

You have now made a start on an important part of mathematics, called **calculus**. The subject was developed mainly by Isaac Newton (1642–1727) and Gottfried Wilhelm von Leibniz (1646–1716), working quite independently. It can be divided into two parts, **differentiation** and **integration**. This chapter deals only with differentiation.

Differentiation; the derivative of f(x)

Take points $P(x,\ f(x))$ and $Q(x+h,\ f(x+h))$ on the graph $y = f(x)$.

The gradient of the tangent at P

$$= \lim_{Q \to P} m_{PQ} = \lim_{Q \to P} \frac{y_Q - y_P}{x_Q - x_P}$$

$$= \lim_{h \to 0} \frac{f(x+h) - f(x)}{(x+h) - x} = \lim_{h \to 0} \frac{f(x+h) - f(x)}{h}.$$

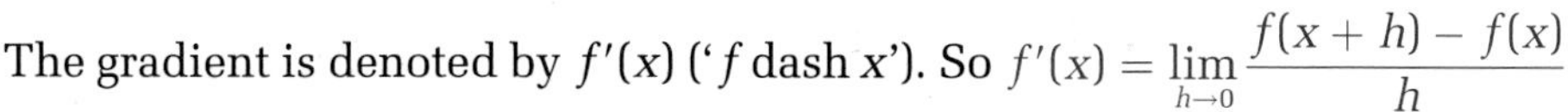

The gradient is denoted by $f'(x)$ ('f dash x'). So $f'(x) = \lim_{h \to 0} \frac{f(x+h) - f(x)}{h}$

Since the number $f'(x)$ is derived from $f(x)$, it is called the derivative of f at x.
The process of finding $f'(x)$ is called differentiation.
The formula for $f'(x)$ defines a new function f', the *derived function* of f.

Its value at $x = a$ is $f'(a) = \lim_{h \to 0} \frac{f(a+h) - f(a)}{h}$.

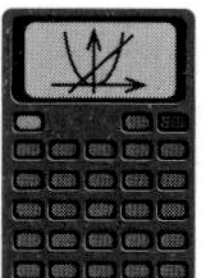

a Display the graphs:
 (i) $y = x^2$
 (ii) $y = ((x + 0.01)^2 - x^2)/0.01$.
b Use the graphs to help you to copy and complete the table.
c Comment on the entries in the table.

x	$((x + 0.01)^2 - x^2)/0.01$	$2x$
1	2.01	2
2		
3		
4		
5		

Rate of change

In the 'Test Your Strength' question on page 58 you had a function $f(t) = 20t - 5t^2$, and were asked to estimate the speed of the striker at $t = 1$, i.e. the rate of change of f at $t = 1$. This is simply the gradient of the tangent at P(1, 15) on the graph $y = 20t - 5t^2$. So the speed is $f'(1)$, i.e. the value of $f'(t)$ at $t = 1$.

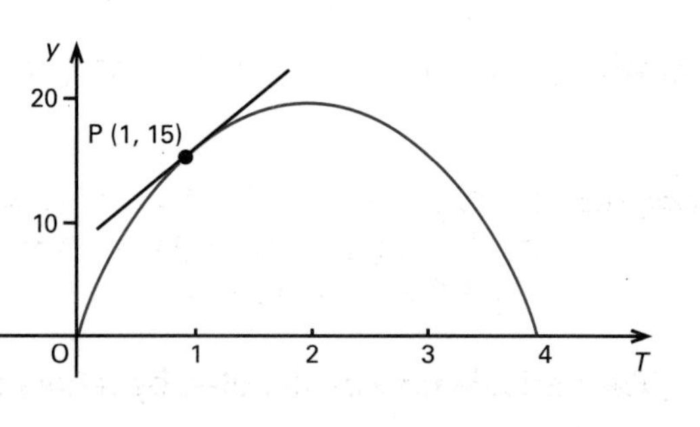

Some useful rules of differentiation

1 Derivative of $f(x) = x^n (n = 1, 2, 3, \ldots)$

The derivative of $f(x)$ is $f'(x) = \lim_{h \to 0} \frac{f(x+h) - f(x)}{h}$.

(i) $f(x) = x$. $\frac{f(x+h) - f(x)}{h} = \frac{(x+h) - x}{h} = \frac{h}{h} = 1$.

So $f'(x) = \lim_{h \to 0} 1 = 1$.

(ii) $f(x) = x^2$. $\frac{f(x+h) - f(x)}{h} = \frac{(x+h)^2 - x^2}{h} = \frac{x^2 + h^2 + 2xh - x^2}{h}$

$= \frac{h(h+2x)}{h} = h + 2x$.

So $f'(x) = \lim_{h \to 0} (h + 2x) = 2x$.

(iii) $f(x) = x^3$. $\frac{f(x+h) - f(x)}{h} = \frac{(x+h)^3 - x^3}{h} = \frac{(x+h)(x^2 + h^2 + 2xh) - x^3}{h}$

$= \frac{(x^3 + 3x^2h + 3xh^2 + h^3) - x^3}{h} = \frac{h(3x^2 + 3xh + h^2)}{h}$

$= 3x^2 + 3xh + h^2$.

So $f'(x) = \lim_{h \to 0} (3x^2 + 3xh + h^2) = 3x^2$.

Do you see the pattern for these derivatives? Copy and complete:

$f(x)$	x	x^2	x^3	x^4	x^5	x^6	x^{10}
$f'(x)$	1	$2x$	$3x^2$				

In fact, for all positive integers n, if $f(x) = x^n$, then $f'(x) = nx^{n-1}$.
Example $f(x) = x^5 \Rightarrow f'(x) = 5x^{5-1} = 5x^4$ (where $\Rightarrow$ means 'implies').

2 If $f(x) = cg(x)$, where c is a constant, $f'(x) = cg'(x)$
Example $f(x) = 6x^2 \Rightarrow f'(x) = 6 \times 2x^1 = 12x$.

3 If $f(x) = c$, where c is a constant, $f'(c) = 0$.
Example $f(x) = x^3 + 4 \Rightarrow f'(x) = 3x^2 + 0 = 3x^2$

4 If $f(x) = g(x) + h(x)$, $f'(x) = g'(x) + h'(x)$.
Examples **1** $f(x) = x^4 + 5x^2 - 1 \Rightarrow f'(x) = 4x^3 + 10x$
2 $f(x) = (2x - 3)^2 = 4x^2 - 12x + 9 \Rightarrow f'(x) = 8x - 12$, and
$f'(2) = 16 - 12 = 4$

Note The variable may be denoted by letters other than x, for example t, u, …

EXERCISE 2

Write down the derivatives in questions **1–11**.

1 **a** x^3 **b** x^2 **c** x^5 **d** x^4 **e** x

2 **a** $5x^2$ **b** $2x^3$ **c** $3x^4$ **d** $8x$ **e** 7

3 **a** $x^2 + 4x$ **b** $x^3 - 2x$ **c** $x^5 + x$

4 **a** $t^4 + 3t^2$ **b** $p^3 - 2p$ **c** $u^7 + 9$

5 **a** $x^3 + x^2 + x$ **b** $6 + 3x^2 - x^6$

6 **a** $\frac{1}{2}x^2 - x + 1$ **b** $\frac{1}{3}x^3 + 5x - 10$

7 **a** $y^3 - 2y^2 + 3y + 4$ **b** $1 + v - v^2 + v^3$

8 **a** $(x + 1)^2$ (multiply out the brackets first)
b $(x + 5)^2$ **c** $(x - 3)^2$ **d** $(2x + 1)^2$

9 **a** $(x + 3)(x + 2)$ **b** $(x - 1)(x + 1)$

10 **a** $(x - 3)(2 - x)$ **b** $(x^2 + 2)^2$

11 **a** $1 - 5u^5 + 10u^{10}$ **b** $2v^3 - 3v^2 + 5v - 7$

12 Given $f(x) = 2x^2 + 3x - 1$, find the value of:
a $f'(0)$ **b** $f'(2)$ **c** $f'(-2)$.

13 Given $f(t) = t^3 - t^2 + t - 1$, find the value of:
a $f'(0)$ **b** $f'(1)$ **c** $f'(-1)$.

14 *Reminder*: The gradient of the curve $y = f(x)$ at $x = a$ is $f'(a)$. Find the gradient at $x = a$ for:
a $f(x) = x^3$ **b** $f(x) = 2x^2 + 1$ **c** $f(x) = (x - 1)^2$.

15 Find the gradient of the curves $y = f(x)$:
a $y = x^4$ at $x = 2$ **b** $y = (x + 5)(x - 2)$ at $x = 0$.

16 *Reminder*: The rate of change of f at $x = a$ is $f'(a)$. Calculate the rate of change of:
a x^2 at $x = 4$ **b** $2x^5$ at $x = 1$
c $(3x + 1)(3x - 1)$ at $x = -2$ **d** $(3 - 2x)^2$ at $x = 3$
e $(x + 1)^3$ at $x = -1$, 0, and 2.

Making sure of indices

$$a^0 = 1;\quad a^{-m} = \frac{1}{a^m};\quad \sqrt[n]{a^m} = a^{m/n};\quad a^m \times a^n = a^{m+n};\quad a^m \div a^n = a^{m-n};\quad (a^m)^n = a^{mn}$$

EXERCISE 3

1 Write each of these with a positive index.

a x^{-5} **b** y^{-1} **c** u^{-2} **d** $\dfrac{1}{v^{-3}}$ **e** $\dfrac{2}{w^{-1}}$

2 Write each in the form ax^n. For example, $\dfrac{1}{2x^2} = \dfrac{1}{2}x^{-2}$

a $\dfrac{1}{x}$ **b** $\dfrac{1}{x^3}$ **c** $\dfrac{1}{x^4}$ **d** $\dfrac{1}{2x}$ **e** $\dfrac{1}{3x^2}$

3 Write each in the form ay^n. For example, $\dfrac{2}{\sqrt{y}} = \dfrac{2}{y^{1/2}} = 2y^{-1/2}$

a $\sqrt{y}$ **b** $\sqrt[3]{y}$ **c** $\sqrt[3]{y^4}$ **d** $\dfrac{1}{\sqrt{y}}$ **e** $\dfrac{1}{2\sqrt[3]{y}}$

4 Simplify:

a $x^4 \times x^{-2}$ **b** $y^2 \times y^{-3}$ **c** $z^{-1} \times z^{-1}$
d $t^{1/2} \times t^{-1/2}$ **e** $u^{3/2} \times u^{5/2}$ **f** $v^{1/2} \times v^{-3/2}$
g $2p^{-2} \times 3p^{-3}$ **h** $2a^{3/2} \times 5a^{1/2}$ **i** $2y \times y^{-1/2}$

5 Simplify:

a $x^4 \div x^2$ **b** $y^3 \div y^{-1}$ **c** $z^{-2} \div z^{-2}$
d $t^{3/2} \div t^{1/2}$ **e** $u \div u^{1/3}$ **f** $v \div v^{1/2}$
g $\dfrac{x^{5/2}}{x^{3/2}}$ **h** $\dfrac{y^{-1}}{2y}$ **i** $\dfrac{t}{2\sqrt{t}}$
j $\dfrac{2u}{3u^{-1}}$

6 Find the value of:

a x^{-2} when $x = 2$ **b** $y^{1/3}$ when $y = 27$
c $t^{1/3}$ when $t = -8$ **d** $u^{1/2}$ when $u = 100$
e $(p^2)^3$ when $p = 2$ **f** $4x^{-2}$ when $x = 2$.

7 Multiply out the brackets.

a $x^{1/2}(x+1)$ **b** $y^{1/3}(y^{2/3} - y^{-1/3})$ **c** $(1 + x^{1/2})^2$
d $\left(\sqrt{x} - \dfrac{1}{\sqrt{x}}\right)^2$ **e** $(t^{1/3} + 1)(t^{1/3} - 1)$

Rules of differentiation for n negative or fractional

The rules you used in Exercise 2 are true for all rational values of n.

1 $f(x) = x^n \Rightarrow f'(x) = nx^{n-1}$
2 $f(x) = cg(x) \Rightarrow f'(x) = cg'(x)$
3 $f(x) = c \Rightarrow f'(x) = 0$
4 $f(x) = g(x) + h(x) \Rightarrow f'(x) = g'(x) + h'(x)$

Examples

1 $f(x) = \dfrac{1}{x^3} = x^{-3} \Rightarrow f'(x) = -3x^{-3-1} = -3x^{-4}$

2 $f(x) = 2x + \dfrac{1}{2x} = 2x + \frac{1}{2}x^{-1} \Rightarrow f'(x) = 2 - \frac{1}{2}x^{-2}$

3 $f(y) = 2\sqrt{y} = 2y^{1/2} \Rightarrow f'(x) = 2 \times \frac{1}{2}y^{-1/2} = y^{-1/2}$

EXERCISE 4A

Write down the derivatives in questions 1–4.

1 **a** x^{-2} **b** x^{-5} **c** x^{-4} **d** x^{-1}

2 **a** x^{-3} **b** x^{-8} **c** x^{-6} **d** x^{-10}

3 **a** $x^{3/2}$ **b** $x^{5/2}$ **c** $x^{1/2}$ **d** $x^{2/3}$

4 **a** $x^{-1/2}$ **b** $x^{-1/4}$ **c** $x^{-2/3}$ **d** $x^{-1/3}$

Write each of the following (questions **5** and **6**) as a power of x, then differentiate.

5 **a** $\frac{1}{x^2}$ **b** $\frac{1}{x}$ **c** $\frac{1}{x^3}$ **d** $\frac{1}{x^5}$

6 **a** $\sqrt[3]{x^2}$ **b** $\sqrt{x}$ **c** $\frac{1}{\sqrt{x}}$ **d** $\sqrt[4]{x^5}$

7 Given $g(x) = \frac{1}{x}$, find:

a $g'(x)$ **b** $g'(1)$ **c** $g'(2)$ **d** $g'(\frac{1}{2})$.

8 $h(x) = x^{5/3}$. Find:

a $h'(x)$ **b** $h'(0)$ **c** $h'(1)$ **d** $h'(27)$.

9 $f(x) = x^{-2}$. Find the value of:
a $f'(1)$ **b** $f'(2)$ **c** the derivative of f at $x = -1$.

10 $g(x) = x^{1/2}$. Find the value of:
a $g'(1)$ **b** $g'(4)$ **c** the derivative of g at $x = 9$.

11 Express each of these in the form ax^n, then find its derivative.

a $\frac{3}{x}$ **b** $\frac{1}{2x}$ **c** $\frac{2}{\sqrt{x}}$ **d** $\frac{6}{\sqrt[3]{x}}$ **e** $\frac{2}{3x^2}$

12 Find the gradient of the curve $y = f(x)$ for:

a $f(x) = \frac{4}{x}$ at $x = -1$ **b** $f(x) = \frac{1}{x^2}$ at $x = 2$

c $f(x) = 1 + \frac{1}{x^3}$ at $x = 1$ **d** $f(x) = x + \frac{1}{x}$ at $x = 2$.

13 Calculate the rate of change of:

a $f(t) = 2t + \frac{3}{t}$ at $t = 1$ **b** $g(u) = 1 + \frac{1}{\sqrt{u}}$ at $u = 4$.

Examples

1 $f(x) = \dfrac{x^4 + 2x^2 + 3}{x}$. Find $f'(x)$.

$f(x) = \dfrac{x^4}{x} + \dfrac{2x^2}{x} + \dfrac{3}{x} = x^3 + 2x + 3x^{-1}$

So $f'(x) = 3x^2 + 2 - 3x^{-2} = 3x^2 + 2 - \dfrac{3}{x^2}$

2 $f(x) = \left(\sqrt{x} - \dfrac{1}{\sqrt{x}}\right)^2$. Find $f'(x)$.

$f(x) = x - 2 + \dfrac{1}{x} = x - 2 + x^{-1}$

So $f'(x) = 1 - x^{-2} = 1 - \dfrac{1}{x^2}$

EXERCISE 4B

Express the derivatives of the following with positive indices, as in the worked examples above.

1 **a** $2x + \dfrac{1}{x}$ **b** $4x^3 + \dfrac{1}{x^2}$ **c** $5x - \dfrac{1}{2x}$

2 **a** $\dfrac{x}{3} + \dfrac{3}{x}$ **b** $\sqrt{x} - \dfrac{1}{\sqrt{x}}$ **c** $3x - \dfrac{1}{x}$

3 **a** $2x^2 - \dfrac{1}{x^2}$ **b** $x^{1/3} + \dfrac{1}{x^{1/3}}$ **c** $\left(x + \dfrac{1}{x}\right)^2$

4 **a** $\dfrac{x-4}{x}$ **b** $\dfrac{x^2 + 3x - 1}{x}$ **c** $\dfrac{x^2 - 1}{2x}$

5 **a** $\dfrac{2x-3}{x}$ **b** $\dfrac{(x+2)^2}{x^2}$ **c** $\dfrac{(1+x)(1-x)}{x^2}$

6 **a** $x^{1/2}(1 - x^{-1/2})$ **b** $x^{3/2}(x^{1/2} - x^{-1/2})$

c $\sqrt[3]{x}\left(1 + \dfrac{1}{\sqrt[3]{x}}\right)$ **d** $(1 + \sqrt{x})^2$

7 Find the gradient at $x = \frac{1}{2}$ of the curve $y = \dfrac{(x+1)(x-1)(x^2+1)}{x}$.

8 Given $f(x) = \dfrac{(1 - x^{1/3})^2}{x^{1/3}}$, prove that $f'(x) = \dfrac{x^{2/3} - 1}{3x^{4/3}}$.

The $\frac{dy}{dx}$ notation for derivatives; the gradient of a tangent

$P(x_P, y_P)$ and $Q(x_Q, y_Q)$ are points on the graph $y = f(x)$.

(i) Replace $y_Q - y_P$, the change in y, by Δy. (Read it as 'delta y'.)

(ii) Replace $x_Q - x_P$ by Δx.

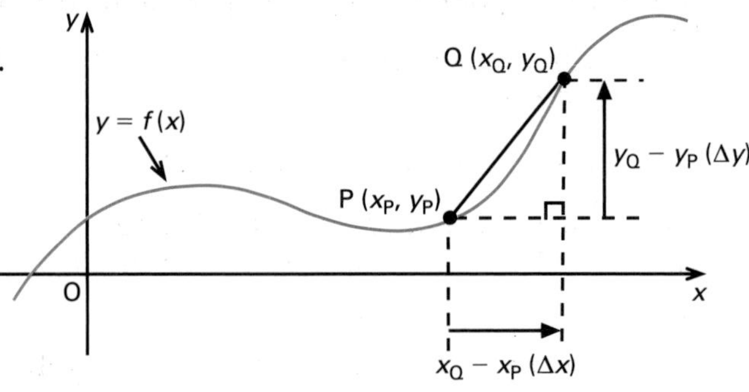

The gradient of the tangent at P

$$= f'(x) = \lim_{Q\to P} m_{PQ} = \lim_{\Delta x\to 0} \frac{\Delta y}{\Delta x}, \text{ denoted by } \frac{dy}{dx} \text{ ('}d y \text{ by } dx\text{')}.$$

So the gradient of the tangent to the curve $y = f(x)$ at the point (x, y) is $\frac{dy}{dx} = f'(x)$.

Equivalent notations: $f'(x), \frac{df}{dx}, \frac{d}{dx}(f(x)), \frac{dy}{dx}, y', y'(x)$.

Example 1 A parabola has equation $y = x^2 - 4x + 1$.
Calculate the gradient of the tangent at $x = 3$, and then find the equation of this tangent.

$\frac{dy}{dx} = 2x - 4$, so the gradient of the tangent at $x = 3$ is $2 \times 3 - 4 = 2$.

The point has coordinates $(3, 3^2 - 4 \times 3 + 1)$, i.e. $(3, -2)$.
The equation of the tangent is $y - (-2) = 2(x - 3)$, i.e. $y = 2x - 8$.

Example 2 Find the points on the curve $y = \frac{1}{2x}$ at which the tangents are parallel to the line with equation $x + 2y = 0$.

$y = \frac{1}{2x} = \frac{1}{2}x^{-1}$, so $\frac{dy}{dx} = \frac{1}{2}(-1)x^{-2} = -\frac{1}{2x^2}$.

The equation of the line is $x + 2y = 0$,
i.e. $y = -\frac{1}{2}x$, with gradient $-\frac{1}{2}$.
So the gradient of the tangents $= -\frac{1}{2}$.

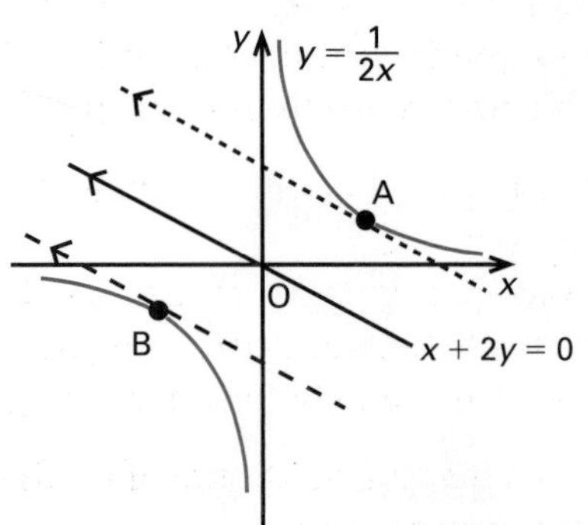

From $-\frac{1}{2x^2} = -\frac{1}{2}$, $x^2 = 1$, so $x = \pm 1$.

$y = \frac{1}{2x} = \frac{1}{2}$ or $-\frac{1}{2}$, so the points are $A(1, \frac{1}{2})$ and $B(-1, -\frac{1}{2})$.

EXERCISE 5A

1 a Use $\frac{dy}{dx}$ to find the gradient of the tangent to the parabola $y = x^2$ at:

(i) $x = -1$ (ii) $x = 0$ (iii) $x = 1$

b Illustrate in a sketch.

2 Repeat question **1** for the cubic curve $y = x^3$.

3 Find the gradient and equation of the tangent to:

a $y = 3x^2$ at $x = 2$ **b** $y = x^2 + 2x$ at $x = 1$ **c** $y = x^4$ at $x = 1$

d $y = \sqrt{x}$ at $x = 4$ **e** $y = x^{3/2}$ at $x = 1$ **f** $y = \frac{1}{x^2}$ at $x = -1$

g $y = 16 - 3x^2$ at $x = -2$ **h** $y = (x - 1)^2$ at $x = 1$.

4 a Find the point on the parabola $y = x^2 - 4x + 1$ at which the tangent has gradient 2.

b Find the equation of this tangent.

5 Find:

a the points on the curve $y = \frac{1}{3}x^3$ at which the tangents have gradient 9

b the equation of these tangents.

6 a Prove that there is only one point on the curve $y = \frac{1}{4}x^4 - 3$ at which the tangent is parallel to the line $y + 8x = 10$, and find the coordinates of this point.

b Find the equation of the tangent.

7 a Calculate, to the nearest degree, the anti-clockwise angle between the tangent to the parabola $y = x(x - 2)$ and the positive direction OX at:

(i) $x = 2$ (ii) $x = 0$ (iii) $x = 1$.

b Illustrate in a sketch.

8 Find these derivatives:

a $\frac{d}{dx}(2x^2 + 1)$ **b** $\frac{d}{dt}(4t^{3/2})$ **c** $\frac{d}{du}\left(u - \frac{1}{u}\right)$.

EXERCISE 5B

1 The curve $y = (x + 1)(x^2 + 1)$ meets the x-axis at A and the y-axis at B. Find the equations of the tangents at A and B.

2 The curve $y = (x - 2)(x^2 + 1)$ meets the x-axis at A and the y-axis at B. Find:

a the equations of the tangents at A and B

b the coordinates of their point of intersection.

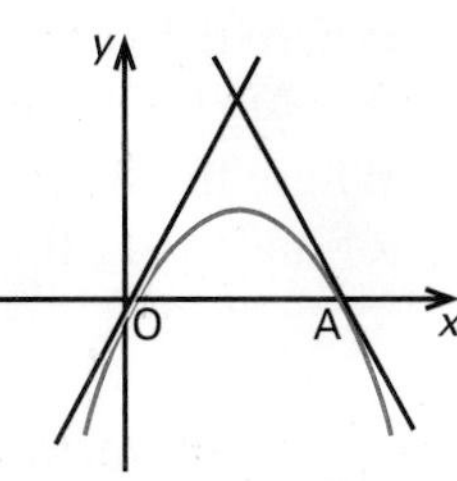

3 The parabola $y = x(3 - x)$ cuts the x-axis at O and A. Calculate:

a the gradients of the tangents at O and A

b the angle between each tangent and OX, to the nearest degree

c the acute angle between the tangents.

4 a Prove that the gradients of all the tangents to the curve $y = x^3 - 6x^2 + 12x + 1$ are never negative.

b At what point on the curve is the tangent parallel to the x-axis?

5 The tangent at A(1, 2) to the curve $y = x^3 + x^2$ meets the curve again at B.

a Show that:

(i) the equation of AB is $y = 5x - 3$

(ii) the tangent and curve meet where $x^3 + x^2 - 5x + 3 = 0$.

b Find the coordinates of B by solving the equation in **a (ii)**. (Note that A lies on the curve.)

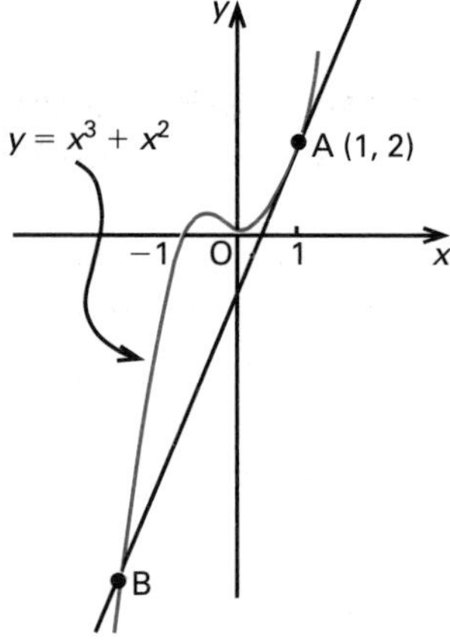

6 Find the equation of the tangent to the curve $y = 2x^4 + 1$ which makes an anti-clockwise angle of 135° with OX.

7 Simplify, giving answers with positive indices:

a $\frac{d}{dx}(1 + \sqrt[3]{x})$ **b** $\frac{d}{dx}\left(x^2 - \frac{1}{x^2}\right)$ **c** $\frac{d}{dt}\left(2t^{1/2} - \frac{2}{t^{1/2}}\right)$ **d** $\frac{d}{du}\left(1 - \frac{1}{u}\right)^2$

Challenge

a Find an expression for the gradient of the tangent at P to this curve.

b Show that the equation of the tangent is $x + a^2y = 2a$.

c Show that the area of $\triangle$OAB is constant, no matter where P lies on the curve.

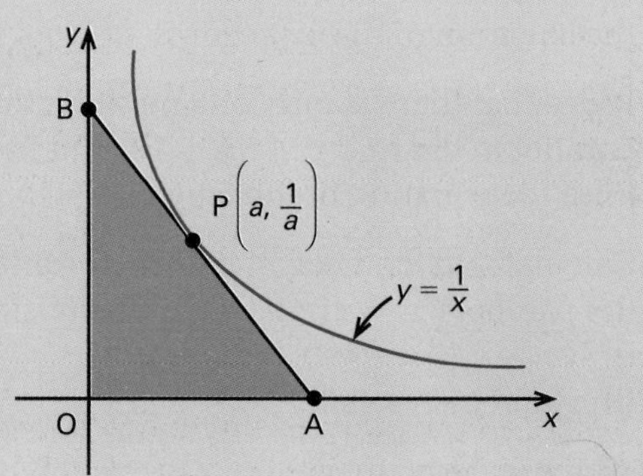

Sketching the graphs of derived functions

The graph $y = f(x)$ is shown. How can we sketch the graph of the derived function f'?

We use the fact that the gradient of the tangent at the point $(x, f(x))$ on the graph $y = f(x)$ is $f'(x)$.

(i) Where the gradient of the tangent to $y = f(x)$ is zero, $f'(x) = 0$.

(ii) Where the gradient of $y = f(x)$ is positive (or negative), the value of $f'(x)$ is positive (or negative).

Note In the illustration, f is a cubic function of the form $ax^3 + bx^2 + cx + d$, so the derived function f' is a quadratic function of the form $3ax^2 + 2bx + c$, with a parabolic graph.

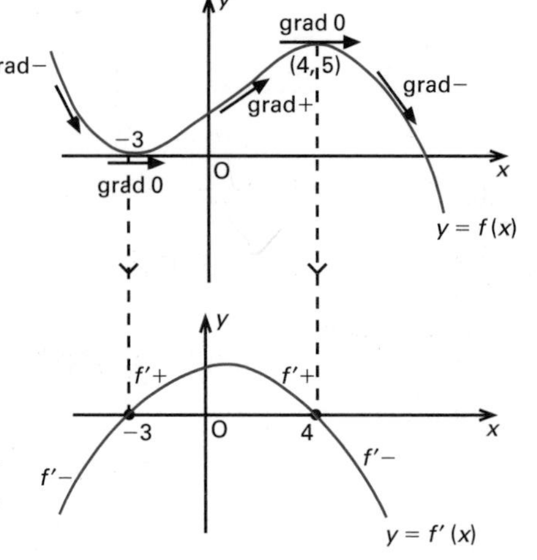

Example Sketch the graph of the derived function f' for the quadratic graph $y = f(x)$.

(i) Fix the turning point of the graph of f, and the corresponding zero of f'.
(ii) Mark +ve and −ve *gradients of f*, and corresponding positive and negative *values of f'*

Note Since $f(x)$ is of the form $ax^2 + bx + c$ here, $f'(x) = 2ax + b$, with a straight line graph.

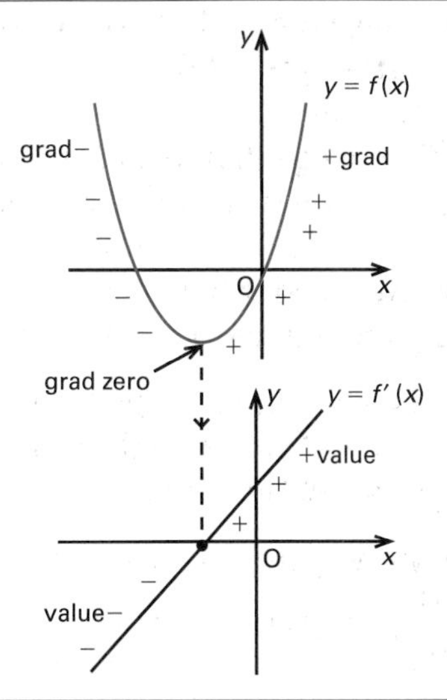

a $f(x) = x^3 + x^2$. Draw the graphs:
(i) $y = f(x)$ (ii) $y = ((x + 0.01)^3 + (x + 0.01)^2 - x^3 - x^2)/0.01$.
Graph **a(ii)** gives an approximation for the graph $y = f'(x)$.

b $g(x) = \sin x$. Set your calculator to RAD, and draw the graphs:
(i) $y = g(x)$ (ii) $y = (\sin(x + 0.01) - \sin x)/0.01$. What do you think the derivative of $\sin x$ is?

EXERCISE 6

The points where the gradient of the tangent to the curve $y = f(x)$ is zero are marked on these graphs. In questions **1–4**, sketch the graphs of the derived functions f'.

1 a Quadratic

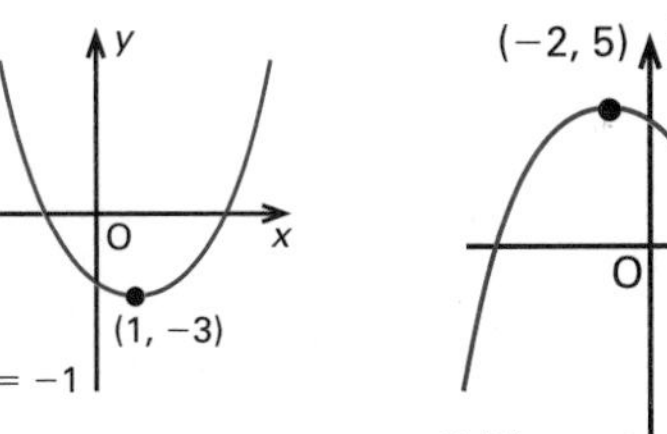

b Quadratic

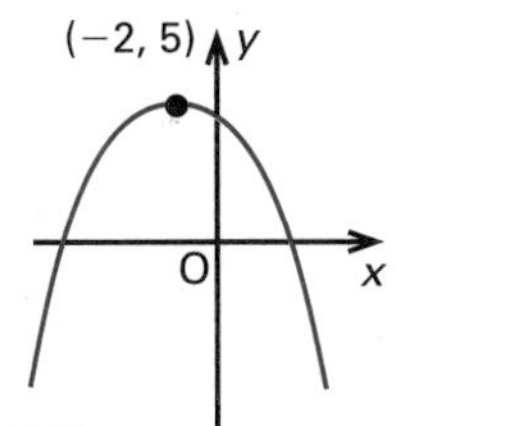

2 a Cubic

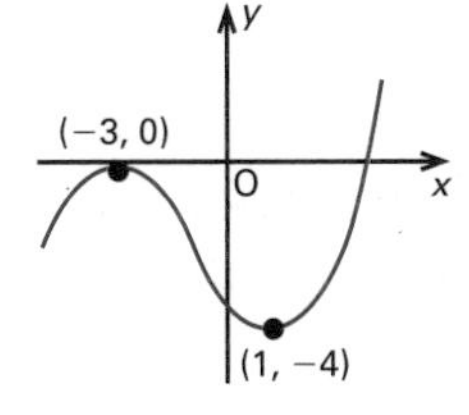

b Cubic

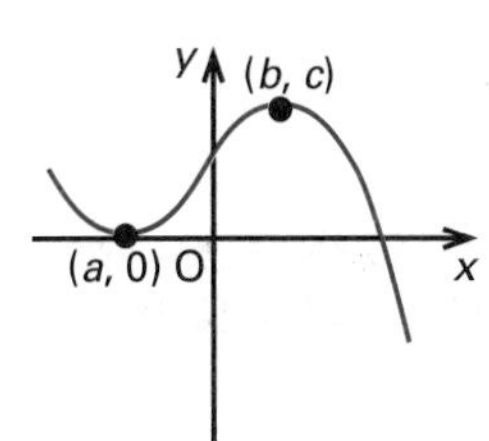

3 a Cubic

b Fourth degree

4 a Quadratic

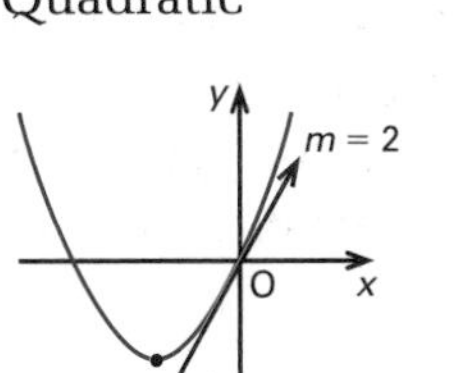

Gradient of tangent at O is 2.

b Quadratic

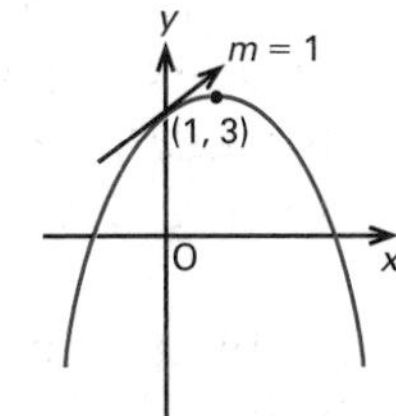

Gradient of tangent at $x = 0$ is 1.

5 **a** Given $f(x) = 2x + 2$, write down $f'(x)$.
b Sketch the graphs $y = f(x)$ and $y = f'(x)$.

6 Sketch the graph $y = f'(x)$.

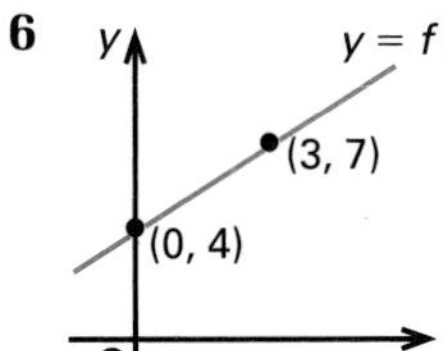

Sketch the graphs $y = f'(x)$ in questions **7** and **8**.

7 **a** Quadratic

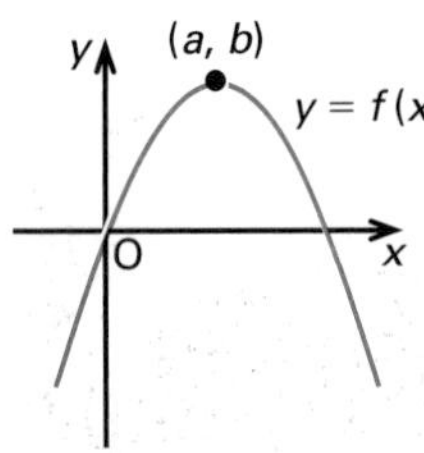

Equation of tangent at O is $y = 3x$.

b Quadratic

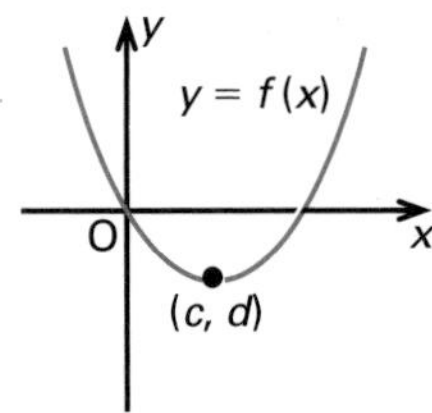

Tangent at O makes an angle of 135° with OX.

8 **a** Fourth degree

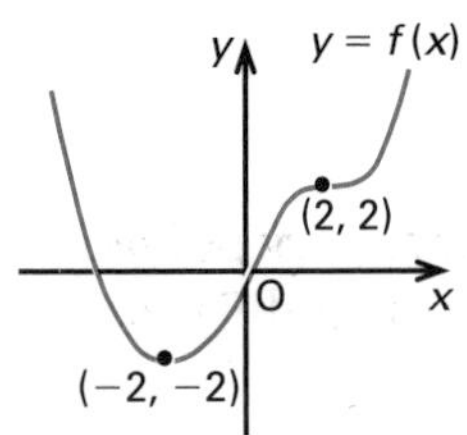

b Fifth degree

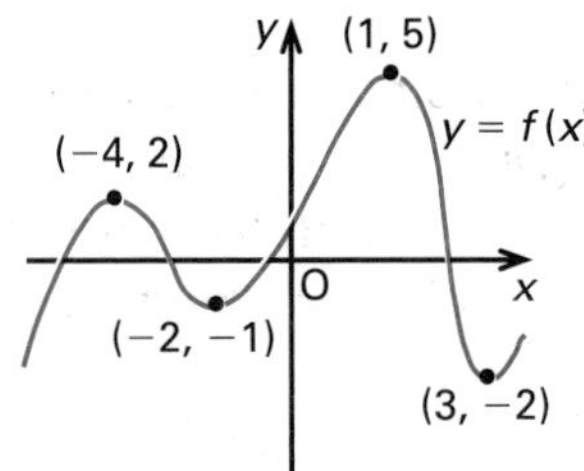

9 Given these graphs of the derived functions f', sketch possible graphs of $y = f(x)$.

a

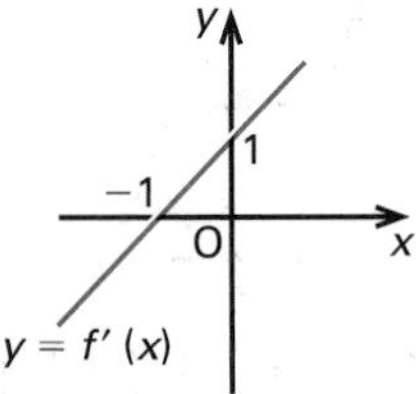

b

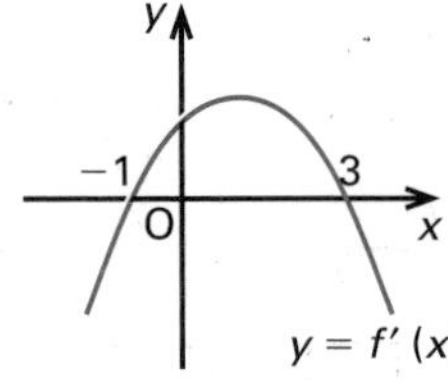

The Review and Summary for this chapter are included in those at the end of Chapter 3.2, on pages 82 and 83.

3.2 Using Differentiation

Increasing and decreasing functions; stationary points and stationary values

Examine the 'big dipper' curve below.

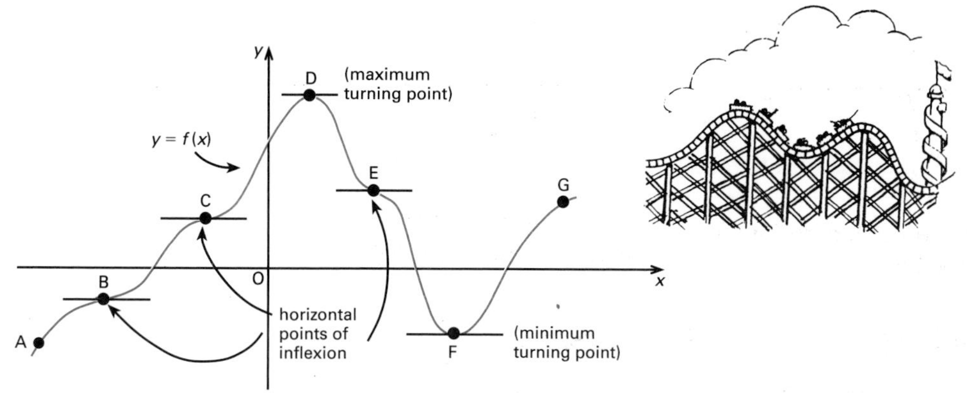

a On AB, BC, CD, FG the graph is rising and f is increasing.
b On DE, EF, the graph is falling and f is decreasing.
c At B, C, D, E and F the gradient is 0, and these are called *stationary points.*

B, C and E are *points of inflexion*, D is a *maximum turning point* and F is a *minimum turning point.*

If $(a, f(a))$ is a stationary point, $f'(a) = 0$, so a is a root of the equation $f'(x) = 0$. $f(a)$ is a stationary value of f.

The nature of a stationary point can be determined by finding the sign of $f'(x)$ to the left and to the right of $x = a$.

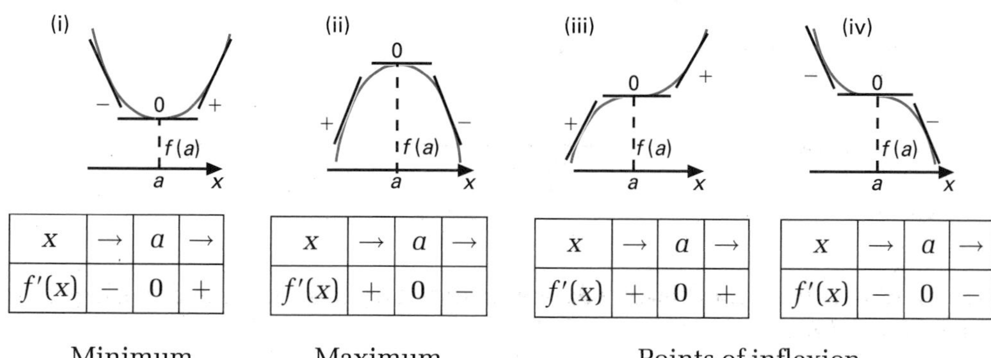

(i)

x	$\rightarrow$	a	$\rightarrow$
$f'(x)$	$-$	0	$+$

Minimum turning point

(ii)

x	$\rightarrow$	a	$\rightarrow$
$f'(x)$	$+$	0	$-$

Maximum turning point

(iii)

x	$\rightarrow$	a	$\rightarrow$
$f'(x)$	$+$	0	$+$

(iv)

x	$\rightarrow$	a	$\rightarrow$
$f'(x)$	$-$	0	$-$

Points of inflexion

Example Find the stationary point of the parabola $y = x^2 - 6x + 1$, and also its nature.

Hint
It is useful to use SP for stationary point, SV for stationary value, TP for turning point and PI for point of inflexion.

$\frac{dy}{dx} = 2x - 6$. If $\frac{dy}{dx} = 0$, $2x - 6 = 0$, and $x = 3$. When $x = 3$, $y = -8$, so $(3, -8)$ is the only stationary point.

A table of signs is a good way to investigate the nature of the SP.

x	$\rightarrow$	3	$\rightarrow$
$\frac{dy}{dx}$	–	0	+

(The arrow $\rightarrow 3$ means 'x approaching 3 from the left'; test for a suitable $x < 3$. $3 \rightarrow$ means 'x going away from 3 to the right'; test for a suitable $x > 3$.)

Shape of graph: _/

$(3, -8)$ is a minimum turning point.

a $f(x) = x^3 - 3x + 2$. Draw the graphs $y = f(x)$ and $y = f'(x) = 3x^2 - 3$.
b Use the trace facility to find where the graph $y = f'(x)$ cuts the x-axis.
c Check from the screen that:
 (i) $f(x)$ is decreasing when $-1 < x < 1$ and $f'(x) < 0$
 (ii) $f(x)$ is increasing when $x < -1$ and $f'(x) > 0$; *and* when $x > 1$ and $f'(x) > 0$.

EXERCISE 1

Find the stationary points of the curves in questions **1–8**, and determine their nature.

1 $y = x^2$ **2** $y = x^2 - 4x$ **3** $y = x^2 - 2x + 3$ **4** $y = 5 + 4x - x^2$
5 $y = 2x^3$ **6** $y = 4 - x^2$ **7** $y = (1 - 2x)(1 + 2x)$ **8** $y = (2 - x)^2$

9 a State the points where the curve $y = (x - 1)(x + 2)^2$ cuts the x-axis.
b Find the turning points of the curve, and determine their nature.
c Sketch the curve.
d Solve the inequality $x^3 + 3x^2 - 4 \geqslant 0$.

Example A function f is given by $f(x) = 5x^3 - 3x^5$. Find:
a the coordinates of its SPs
b the nature of each SP
c the intervals on which f is increasing or decreasing.

a $f'(x) = 15x^2 - 15x^4 = 15x^2(1 - x^2) = 15x^2(1 + x)(1 - x)$.
At an SP, $f'(x) = 0$, so $x = 0, -1, 1$.
So f has three SPs, $(-1, -2)$, $(0, 0)$ and $(1, 2)$ – and three SVs, $f(-1) = -2$, $f(0) = 0$ and $f(1) = 2$.

b Use a *table of sign* for $f'(x)$ to find the nature of the SPs and the intervals of increase and decrease of f.

x	$\rightarrow$	-1	$\rightarrow$	0	$\rightarrow$	1	$\rightarrow$
$15x^2$	$+$	$+$	$+$	0	$+$	$+$	$+$
$1+x$	$-$	0	$+$	$+$	$+$	$+$	$+$
$1-x$	$+$	$+$	$+$	$+$	$+$	0	$-$
$f'(x)$	$-$	0	$+$	0	$+$	0	$-$

Shape of graph:

$(-1, -2)$ is a minimum TP, $(0, 0)$ is a PI, and $(1, 2)$ is a maximum TP.

c f is increasing for $-1 < x < 0$ and $0 < x < 1$, and f is decreasing for $x < -1$ and $x > 1$.

EXERCISE 2

For each function in questions **1–8**, find:

a the coordinates of its SPs, and the nature of each SP

b the intervals in which f is increasing or decreasing.

1 $f(x) = x^2 + 1$ **2** $f(x) = 3 - 2x^2$ **3** $f(x) = x^3$

4 $f(x) = 3x - x^3$ **5** $f(x) = 3x^4 - 4x^3$ **6** $f(x) = x^4 - 2x^2 + 5$

7 $f(x) = x^3 + 3x$ **8** $f(x) = 3x^5 - 5x^3 + 2$

9 A hyperbola has equation $y = \frac{4}{x}$.

a Show that the gradient of every tangent to the hyperbola is negative.

b Find the equation of the tangent at A(2, 2).

c If the tangent meets the x and y-axes at M and N, show that A is the midpoint of MN.

d Sketch the hyperbola and the tangent at A.

Challenge

The cost £C of extracting a million barrels of oil from a North Sea Field depends on the cost £C_1 of pipe-laying and the cost £C_2 of pumping. These are related to the diameter, d metres, of the pipe by the formulae

$C_1 = d + a$ and $C_2 = \frac{4}{d}$,

where a is a positive constant.

a If d is increased, do C_1 and C_2 increase or decrease?

b The total cost $C = C_1 + C_2$. Find the stationary value of C, and deduce the minimum total cost, and the corresponding diameter of the pipe.

Curve sketching

A useful guide

Determine:

(i) points of intersection with the x and y-axes
(ii) stationary points and their nature
(iii) the behaviour of y for large positive and negative x
(iv) any other useful points on the graph.

Example Sketch the graph $y = 8x^3 - 3x^4$.

(i) *Intersections with axes*
If $x = 0$, $y = 0$, giving $(0, 0)$.
If $y = 0$, $8x^3 - 3x^4 = 0$,
i.e. $x^3(8 - 3x) = 0$, so $x = 0$ or $2\frac{2}{3}$, giving $(0, 0)$ and $(2\frac{2}{3}, 0)$.

x	$\rightarrow$	0	$\rightarrow$	2	$\rightarrow$
$12x^2$	+	0	+	+	+
$2 - x$	+	+	+	0	−
$\frac{dy}{dx}$	+	0	+	0	−

(ii) *Stationary points*

For SPs, $\frac{dy}{dx} = 0$.

Here $\frac{dy}{dx} = 24x^2 - 12x^3 = 12x^2(2 - x)$.

If $\frac{dy}{dx} = 0$, $x = 0$ or 2, giving SPs $(0, 0)$ and $(2, 16)$.
From the table of signs, $(0, 0)$ is a point of inflexion and $(2, 16)$ is a maximum TP.

(iii) *Large positive and negative x*
$y = 8x^3 - 3x^4$ behaves like $y = -3x^4$ for large positive and negative values of x.
If x is large positive, y is large negative; if x is large negative, y is large negative.

(iv) *Useful points*
For example: $(1, 5)$, $(-1, -11)$.

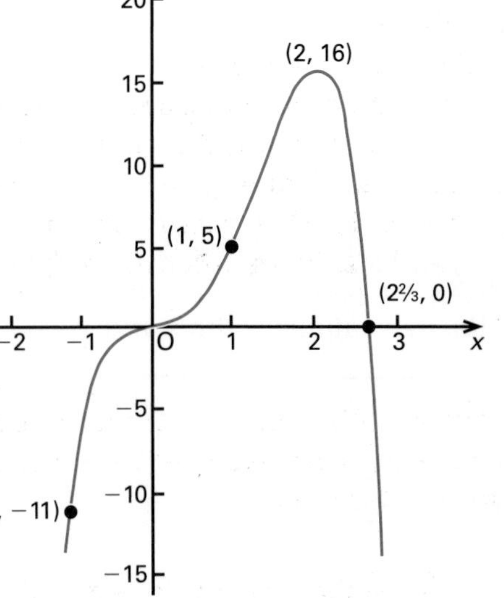

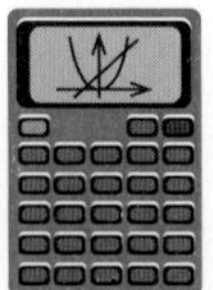

a $f(x) = x^3 - 6x$. Draw the graphs: **(i)** $y = f(x)$ **(ii)** $y = f'(x)$.
b Check that the stationary points on $y = f(x)$ occur where the graph $y = f'(x)$ crosses the x-axis.
d Use the zoom facility to estimate the x-coordinates of the SPs, correct to 2 decimal places.

EXERCISE 3

Follow the guide on page 74 to sketch the graphs in questions **1–15**.

1 $y = x^2 - 4x + 5$ **2** $y = 8 + 2x - x^2$ **3** $y = x^2 + 2$

4 $y = 4 - x^2$ **5** $y = x^3$ **6** $y = 3x - x^3$

7 $y = x(x + 2)$ **8** $y = x^2(3 - 2x)$ **9** $y = x(x - 3)^2$

10 $y = x^3 - 3x$ **11** $y = x^3(4 - x)$ **12** $y = 4x^3 + 6x^2$

13 $y = 3x^5 - 5x^3$ **14** $y = x^6 - 6x^4$ **15** $y = 6x^4 - x^6$

Maximum and minimum values on a closed interval

The graph $y = f(x)$ of a function f is shown below for $-4 \leqslant x \leqslant 3$, that is on the closed interval $[-4, 3]$.

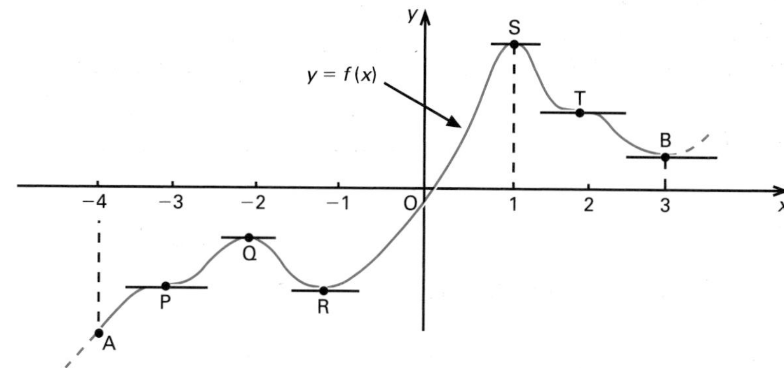

Check these facts:

(i) The end points are A, B.

(ii) The stationary points are P, Q, R, S, T, B.

(iii) The maximum turning points are Q, S, the minimum turning points R, B and the horizontal points of inflexion P, T.

(iv) On $[-4, 3]$, f has *maximum value* $f(1)$ (given by the maximum turning point S) and *minimum value* $f(-4)$ (given by the end point A).

Notice that the maximum and minimum values of f on a closed interval can occur at end points or at stationary points in the interval.

Example Find the maximum value and the minimum value of $f(x) = 2x^3 - 3x^2 - 12x + 5$ on $[-2, 1]$, i.e. for $-2 \leqslant x \leqslant 1$.

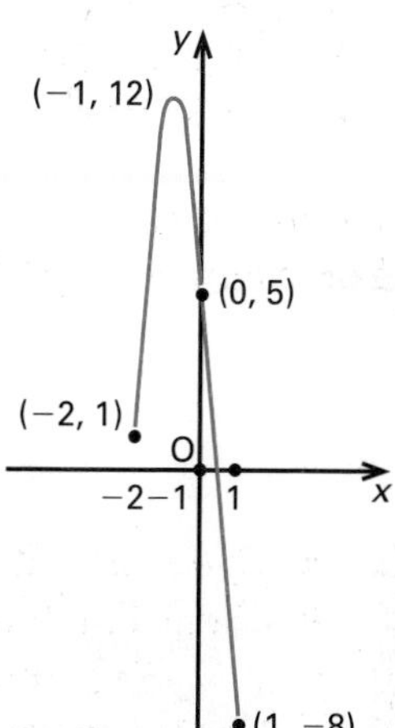

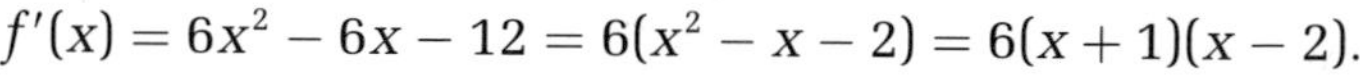

$f'(x) = 6x^2 - 6x - 12 = 6(x^2 - x - 2) = 6(x + 1)(x - 2)$.

For stationary values, $f'(x) = 0$, so $x = -1$ or $x = 2$.

$x = 2$ does not lie in the interval, so is discarded.

$f(-1) = 2(-1)^3 - 3(-1)^2 - 12(-1) + 5 = 12$.

The values at the end points are:

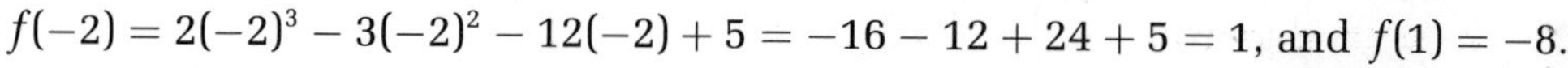

$f(-2) = 2(-2)^3 - 3(-2)^2 - 12(-2) + 5 = -16 - 12 + 24 + 5 = 1$, and $f(1) = -8$.

The maximum value of f on $[-2, 1]$ is 12, and the minimum value is -8.

EXERCISE 4

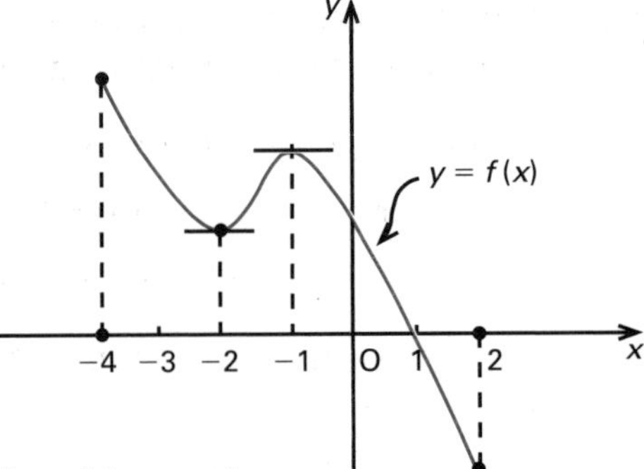

1 The graph $y = f(x)$ of function f is shown for $-4 \leqslant x \leqslant 2$.

a In $[-4, -1]$, the maximum value is $f(-4)$. Write down the minimum value.

b Write down the maximum and minimum values of f on the interval $[0, 2]$.

c Write down the maximum and minimum values on $[-2, 1]$.

2 Calculate for each function:

(i) the values of $f(x)$ at the end points of the closed interval

(ii) the stationary value(s) lying within the interval.

Then **(iii)**, write down the maximum and minimum values of f in the interval.

a $f(x) = 5 - 2x^2$ on $[-1, 2]$ **b** $f(x) = x^3 - 3x$ on $[-2, 3]$

c $f(x) = 3x^5 - 20x^3$ on $[-1, 3]$ **d** $f(x) = x^3 - 3x^2 - 9x + 27$ on $[-4, 3]$

e $f(x) = 8x^3 - 3x^4$ on $[-1, 3]$ **f** $f(x) = 5x^3 - 3x^5$ on $[-2, 2]$

Problem solving

Example 100 metres of fence are available for making the three sides of a rectangular enclosure against an existing wall.
Find the greatest area that can be enclosed.

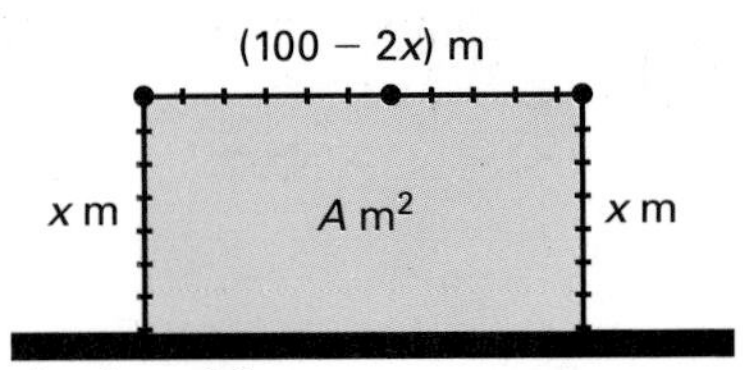

A mathematical model will help us to solve this kind of problem.

If the breadth of the rectangle is x m, the length must be $(100 - 2x)$ m. The area, A m², is given by $A = x(100 - 2x)$.

$$A = x(100 - 2x) = 100x - 2x^2, \text{ and } \frac{dA}{dx} = 100 - 4x.$$

For maximum and minimum values of A, $\dfrac{dA}{dx} = 0$, so $100 - 4x = 0$, and $x = 25$.

x	$\rightarrow$	25	$\rightarrow$
$\frac{dA}{dx}$	+	0	−
	/	—	\

From the table, $x = 25$ gives a maximum value of $A = 25(100 - 50) = 1250$.
The maximum possible area is 1250 m².

EXERCISE 5A

1 The sum of two numbers x and y is 12.

a Explain why their product can be given by $P = x\,(12 - x)$.

b Find the values of x and y which maximise P.

2 The difference $y - x$ between two numbers x and y is 50.
a Show that their product is given by $P = x(x + 50)$.
b Find the values of x and y which minimise P.

3 The product of two positive numbers x and y is 36.
a Prove that their sum is given by $S = x + \frac{36}{x}$.
b Find the values of x and y which minimise S.

4 A rectangle has length x cm and breadth y cm. Its perimeter is 60 cm and its area is A cm^2.
a Prove that $A = x(30 - x)$.
b Calculate the maximum area of the rectangle, and its corresponding length and breadth.

5 A rectangle has length x cm, breadth y cm and perimeter P cm. Its area is 100 m^2.
a Prove that $P = 2x + \frac{200}{x}$.
b Find the length and breadth of the rectangle with the smallest perimeter.

6 A rectangular sheet of metal 44 cm wide is bent to form a rectangular rain gutter. AB = DC = x cm.
a Show that the area, A cm^2, of the gutter's cross-section is given by $A = 44x - 2x^2$.
b Find the dimensions of the cross-section for a maximum flow of water.

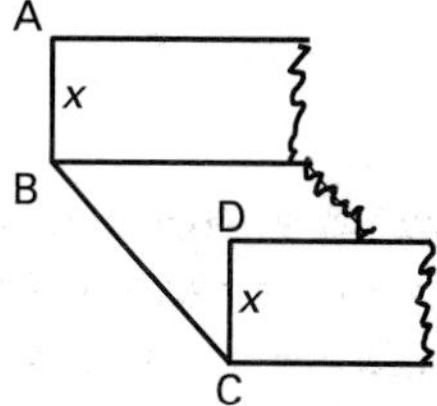

7 A metal plate consists of a rectangle and an isosceles triangle.
a Write down a formula for the area, A cm^2, of the plate.
b If $2x + y = 12$, show that $A = 24x - 3x^2$.
c Find x and y for the plate to have maximum area.

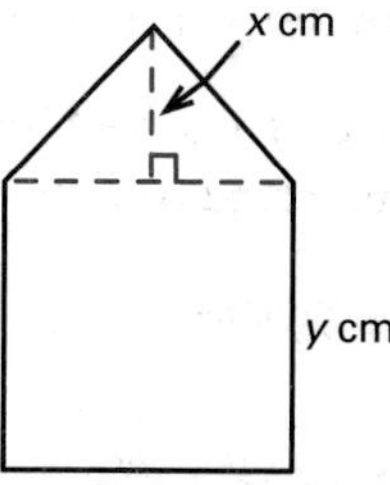

EXERCISE 5B

1 Four congruent squares of side x cm are cut from the corners of a cardboard square of side 12 cm. The cardboard is then folded to make a small open tray of volume V cm^3.

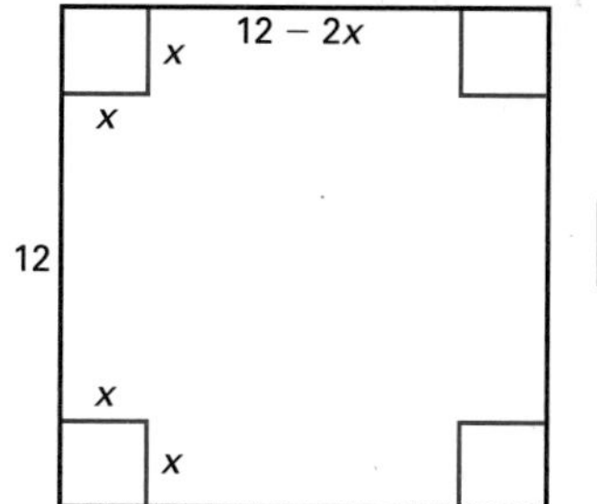

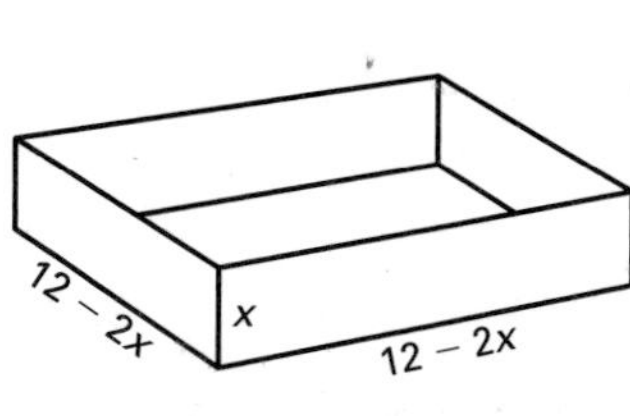

a Prove that $V = 144x - 48x^2 + 4x^3$.
b What value of x maximises V?

2 A cuboid is open at the top. It has a square base of side x cm, a height y cm and volume of 13.5 cm³.

a Prove that:

(i) $y = \dfrac{13.5}{x^2}$

(ii) the outer surface area, S cm², of the cuboid is given by $S = x^2 + \dfrac{54}{x}$.

b Find the dimensions which give a minimum surface area.

3 The dimensions marked on square ABCD are in centimetres.

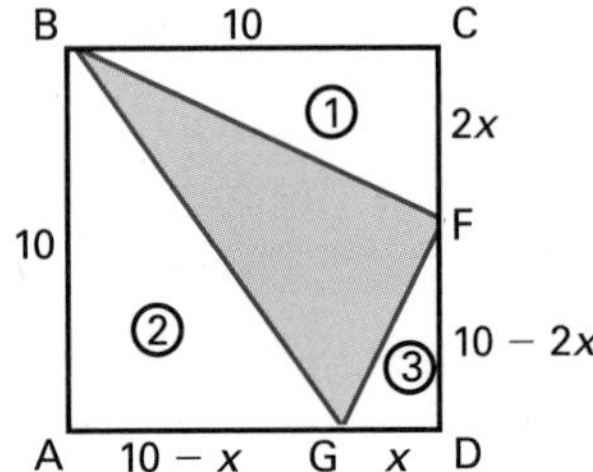

a Prove that the area A cm² of △BFG is given by $A = 50 - 10x + x^2$. (*Hint*: A = area of square – areas 1, 2 and 3.)

b Find the value of x which gives a minimum value of A.

4 In this rectangle, PQ = 12 cm and QR = 8 cm.

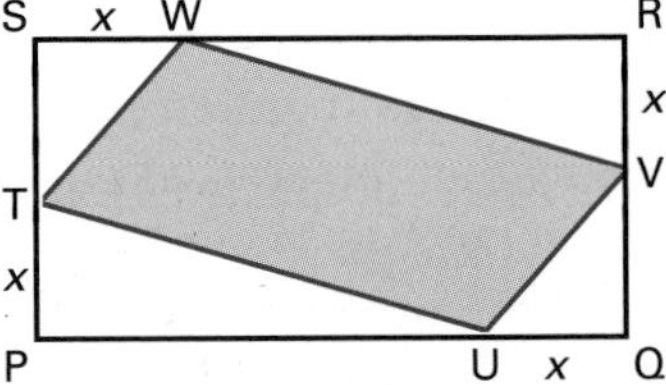

a Prove that the area of quadrilateral TUVW is given by $A = 96 - 20x + 2x^2$.

b Find the minimum area of TUVW.

5 Each end of this solar greenhouse is parabolic in shape.
The equation of the parabola is $y = 6 - \frac{1}{2}x^2$.

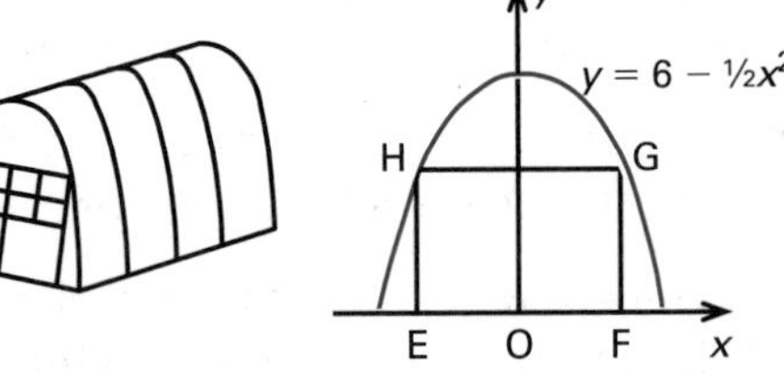

a If EF = $2x$ metres, show that the area of the door EFGH, A m², is given by $A = 12x - x^3$.

b Find the area of the largest possible door.

6 Sunshine Fruits want to redesign their tins to reduce costs. The tins have to be cylindrical and hold 128 π cm³ of juice.

a Show that the total surface area of a tin is given by

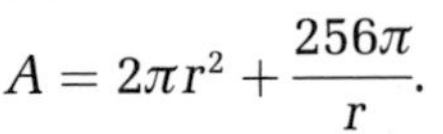

$$A = 2\pi r^2 + \frac{256\pi}{r}.$$

(Volume of cylinder = $\pi r^2 h$, curved surface area = $2\pi rh$.)

b Find the best dimensions for reducing the cost of metal to a minimum.

Rate of change

To solve a problem we often have to make a mathematical model in the form of an equation, or a graph, or a formula, etc. Many useful models involve rates of change which can be written as derivatives. Here is an example.

Statement The rate of decrease in temperature T of a body at time t is proportional to the difference between the temperature of the body and the temperature of the surroundings (T_0).

Model $\frac{\mathrm{d}T}{\mathrm{d}t} = -k(T - T_0)$, where k is a positive constant. The rate of change is negative since T is decreasing.

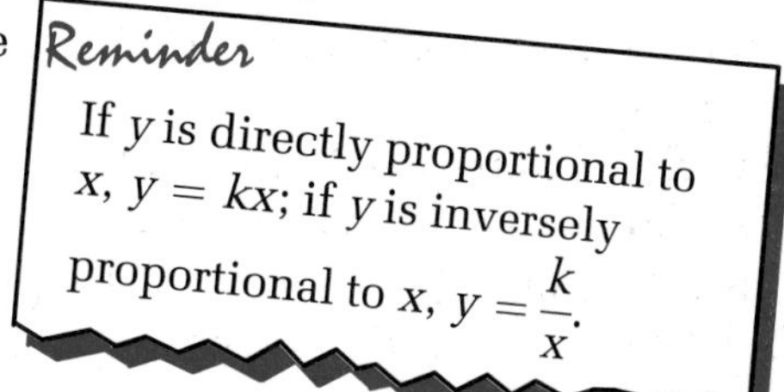

EXERCISE 6

In questions **1–7**, express the rates of change in terms of suitable derivatives.

1 The rate of change of y with respect to x is:
a directly proportional to x^2
b inversely proportional to $\sqrt{x}$.

2 The rate of *increase* of the number N of bacteria in a culture at time t is directly proportional to the number, N, present at the time.

3 The rate of *decrease* of the quantity Q of radium in a substance at time t is directly proportional to the amount, Q, present at the time.

4 A square sheet of metal has area A cm^2 and length of edge x cm.
a Write down a formula for A in terms of x.
b Find the rate of increase of A with respect to x as the metal is heated.

5 A metal cube has volume V cm^3 and length of edge x cm.
a Write down a formula for V in terms of x.
b Find the rate of decrease of V with respect to x as the metal is cooled.

6 A spherical balloon has volume V cm^3 and radius r. Using $V = \frac{4}{3}\pi r^3$, find:
a the rate of increase of V as the balloon is inflated
b the rate of decrease of V as the balloon is deflated.

7 The force F between two objects in space is inversely proportional to the square of the distance x between them.
a Write down a formula for F in terms of x.
b Find the rate of change of F with respect to x.

8 An insect population has a mass m grams at time t seconds. If $m = 6t^2$, calculate its rate of growth in g/s when $t = 2$.

9 Memory tests show that the number N of words that a person can memorise in t minutes is $N = 10\sqrt{t}$. Calculate the rate at which N is increasing when $t = 16$.

10 The number N of bacteria in an experiment varies directly with time t seconds according to the formula $N = 2000 + 300t + 18t^2$. How fast is the population growing when $t = 10$?

11 Water seeps into soil to a depth of y metres in t hours according to the formula $y = \sqrt{t}$.
a Calculate the rate of seepage in metres per hour when $t = 4$.
b What happens to the rate as t increases? Is the answer surprising?

12 The area A mm² of a circular metal disc of radius r mm increases as the disc is put under pressure. Calculate the rate of increase of its area with respect to r when $r = 12$.

Velocity and acceleration

The point P moving along the x-axis has displacement x (OP) at time t. Then:

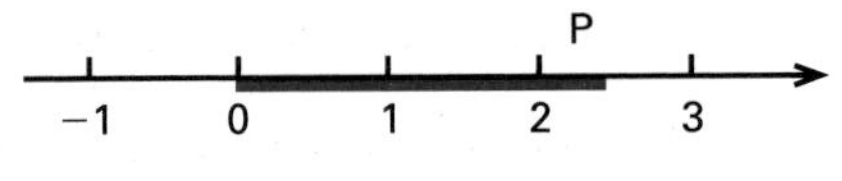

(i) the *velocity* of P is the rate of change of its displacement x at time t, given by

$$v = \frac{dx}{dt}$$

(ii) the *acceleration* of P is the rate of change of its velocity v at time t, given by

$$a = \frac{dv}{dt}.$$

Example The model engine runs on a straight track. Its displacement x metres from the signal at O after t seconds is given by $x = 1 - 4t + t^3$, $t \geqslant 0$. Calculate:
a its velocity and acceleration at time t
b its displacement, velocity and acceleration at $t = 1$
c the time at which the velocity is 8 m/s.

a $v = \frac{dx}{dt} = -4 + 3t^2$; $a = \frac{dv}{dt} = 6t$
b $x = 1 - 4 + 1 = -2$ (2 m to the left of O); $v = -1$ (moving to the left on x-axis); $a = 6$
c $-4 + 3t^2 = 8$, so $3t^2 = 12$, $t^2 = 4$, $t = \pm 2$. But $t \geqslant 0$, so $t = 2$.

EXERCISE 7

1 The displacement x cm at time t seconds of a point moving on the x-axis is given by $x = 5 - 14t + 2t^2$, $t \geqslant 0$.

a Find formulae for its velocity v cm/s and its acceleration a cm/s^2 at time t seconds.

b Calculate v and a when $t = 3$.

c In which direction is P moving when $t = 3$?

2 Repeat question **1** for $x = 3 + 7t - t^2$, $t \geqslant 0$.

3 The displacement x cm of a point moving along the x-axis at time t seconds is $x = 1 + 6t - 2t^3$, $t \geqslant 0$.

a Calculate the velocity v cm/s and the acceleration a cm/s^2 when $t = 0$.

b Find: **(i)** t when $v = 0$ **(ii)** x when $a = 0$.

4 Repeat question **3** for $x = t(t^2 - 12)$, $t \geqslant 0$.

5 $v = 12t - 3t^2$. Calculate:

a the acceleration at each of the times when $v = 9$

b the velocity when $a = 0$.

6 A displacement x cm from O at time t seconds is $x = 20 - 24t + 2t^3$, $t \geqslant 0$. Calculate the time and acceleration when the velocity is zero.

7 A projectile is fired vertically upwards. Its height h m after t seconds is given by $h = 80t - 4t^2$. Calculate:

a its velocity, v m/s, at t seconds

b the greatest height that it reaches.

8 Repeat question **7** for $h = 120t - 3t^2$.

9 In an experiment, a mass of 1 kg is rotated in a circle of radius 1 m. It rotates through an angle of θ radians in t seconds, where $\theta = 4t + \frac{3}{2}t^2 - \frac{1}{3}t^3$. The force on the mass is given by $F = \left(\frac{d\theta}{dt}\right)^2$.

a Find a formula for $\frac{d\theta}{dt}$.

b Calculate F at $t = 3$.

10 What can you say about the position, velocity and acceleration of a point P moving along the x-axis, if:

a $x > 0, v > 0, a > 0$ **b** $x < 0, v < 0, a < 0$?

CHAPTER 3 REVIEW

Differentiate in questions **1–5**.

1 a ax^6 **b** $10x^2$ **c** $x^3 - 3x^2 + 4x - 1$

2 a x^{-1} **b** $5x^{-4}$ **c** $\frac{1}{x^2}$ **d** $\frac{1}{2x}$

3 a $y^{1/2}$ **b** $\frac{1}{y^{1/3}}$ **c** $\sqrt[3]{y^2}$ **d** $\frac{4}{\sqrt[4]{y}}$

4 a $t + \frac{1}{t}$ **b** $\frac{t^2 + t + 2}{t}$ **c** $t^{-2} + t^{-1/2}$

5 a $u(1 - u)$ **b** $(u + 3)(u - 2)$
c $(2u + 5)^2$

6 Given $f(x) = 2x^2 - 8x + 3$, find:
a (i) $f'(0)$ **(ii)** $f'(1)$ **(iii)** $f'(-1)$
b x for which $f'(x) = 0$, and the corresponding value of f.

7 Find $\frac{dy}{dx}$, given:
a $y = x^4$ **b** $y = \frac{1}{x^3}$ **c** $y = 2\sqrt{x}$.

8 Find the equation of the tangent at $x = -1$ to the curve:
a $y = x^2 - 3$ **b** $y = x + \frac{1}{x}$.

9 a Find the equations of the tangents to the curve $y = x^2 - 2x + 2$ at $x = 0$ and at $x = 2$.
b Find the point of intersection of the tangents.

10 The tangent to the curve $y = 4\sqrt{x}$ at the point A (4, 8) cuts the x-axis at B.
a Find the equation of the tangent.
b Prove that AB is bisected by the y-axis.

11 Find the rate of change of g, where $g(x) = \frac{1}{4x^2}$, at:
a $x = -2$ **b** $x = \frac{1}{2}$

12 A curve has equation $y = ax^2 + b$. It passes through P(−2, −1), where the tangent has gradient 8. Find a and b.

13 The height h metres of a projectile at time t seconds is given by $h(t) = 50 + 40t - 5t^2$. Find:
a the time it takes to reach its maximum height
b the maximum height
c the times when the projectile is above its initial height and
(i) rising **(ii)** falling.

14 Determine the stationary points of these functions, and decide their nature:
a $f(x) = 9 - x^2$
b $f(x) = 2x^3 - 6x$
c $f(x) = 4x^3$.

15 Find the intervals in which the functions in question **14** are:
(i) increasing **(ii)** decreasing.

16 Sketch the graphs:
a $y = x(x - 4)$
b $y = x(3 - x)^2$
c $y = 3x^4 - 4x^3$.

17 $f(x) = x^4 - 2x^2 + 1$. Find the maximum value of f for $-1 \leqslant x \leqslant 1$, and for $-2 \leqslant x \leqslant 2$.

18 The displacement x mm of a point at time t seconds is $x = t^3 + t^2 - 6$. Calculate:
a its displacement at $t = 4$
b its velocity and acceleration at $t = 2$
c its velocity when its acceleration is 11 mm/s^2.

19 The tangent at A to the cubic graph $y = f(x)$ is parallel to the line $y = 2x$. Sketch the graph of f'.

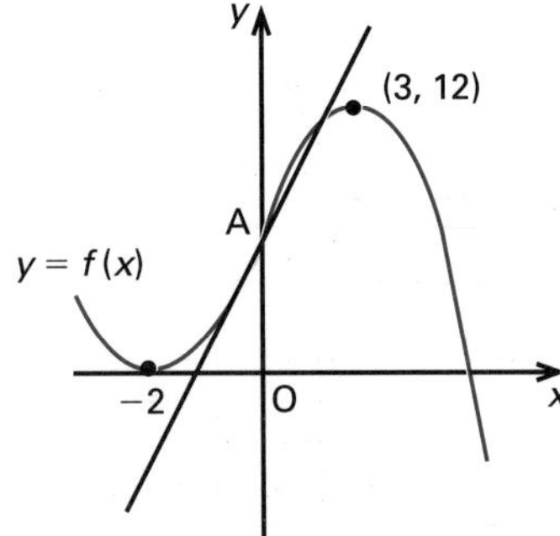

20 a State the points where the curve $y = (x + 1)^2(x - 2)$ cuts the x-axis.
b Find the turning points of the curve, and determine their nature.
c Sketch the curve.
d Solve the inequality $x^3 - 3x - 2 \leqslant 0$.

CHAPTER 3 SUMMARY

1 Derived function, or derivative

The derived function, or derivative, of f is given by

$$f'(x) = \lim_{h \to 0} \frac{f(x+h) - f(x)}{h}$$

2 Particular derivatives

If $f(x) = x^n$, then $f'(x) = nx^{n-1}$, n a rational number.

3 Rate of change

The rate of change of a function f at $x = a$ is $f'(a)$.

4 Gradient of tangent

The gradient of the tangent to the curve $y = f(x)$ at the point (x, y) is denoted by $\frac{dy}{dx}$, where $\frac{dy}{dx} = f'(x)$.

5 Stationary value of a function

If $f'(a) = 0$, then $f(a)$ is a stationary value of f, and $(a, f(a))$ is a stationary point.

6 Nature of a stationary point (maximum, minimum, point of inflexion)

The nature is found from the sign of $f'(x)$ near $x = a$.

(i)

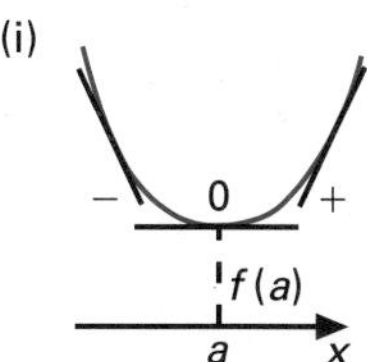

x	→	a	→
$f'(x)$	−	0	+

Minimum TP

(ii)

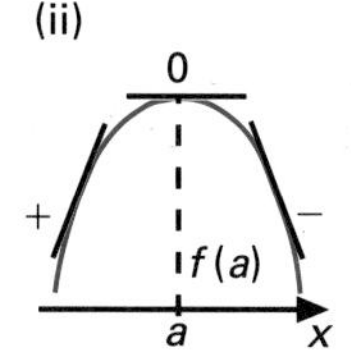

x	→	a	→
$f'(x)$	+	0	−

Maximum TP

(iii)

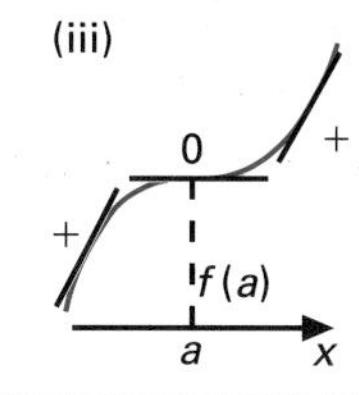

x	→	a	→
$f'(x)$	+	0	+

(iv)

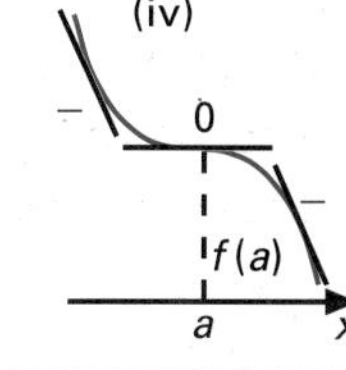

x	→	a	→
$f'(x)$	−	0	−

Points of inflexion

7 Increasing and decreasing functions

In **(i)** above, f is decreasing for $x < a$ (where $f'(x) < 0$), and increasing for $x > a$ (where $f'(x) > 0$).
In **(iii)** f is increasing for all values of x except $x = a$.

8 Curve sketching

To sketch a curve, find:

(i) points of intersection with the x and y-axes
(ii) stationary points and their nature
(iii) the behaviour of y for large positive and negative x
(iv) any other useful points on the graph.

9 Velocity and acceleration

Velocity v = rate of change of displacement s, so $v = \frac{ds}{dt}$.
Acceleration a = rate of change of velocity v, so $a = \frac{dv}{dt}$.

4 Sequences

Class discussion

Some sequences have definite patterns, based on rules for their formation; others have not. Which of the following have obvious rules? What are the rules?

a 1, 3, 5, 7, ...

b 10, 9, 8, 7, ...

c 11, 4, −1, 13, ...

d $\sqrt{2}$, 2, 4, 16, ...

e 1, −3, 9, −27, ...

f 2, 3, 8, 1, ...

g 121, 131, 141, ...

h −7, −3, 1, 5, ...

This chapter deals with sequences which have definite patterns, and which have two ways of defining them, by giving:

(i) a formula for their *n*th term, or
(ii) one term and a method for finding each of the following terms.

Formula for the nth term of a sequence $u_1, u_2, u_3, \ldots, u_n, \ldots$

a Given a formula for the *n*th term, we can calculate all of the terms.

For example, if $u_n = 4n + 5$, then $u_1 = 4 \times 1 + 5 = 9$

$u_2 = 4 \times 2 + 5 = 13$

$u_3 = 4 \times 3 + 5 = 17$, and so on.

b Conversely, given a sequence (for example 2, 5, 8, 11, ...) based on a rule for forming the sequence ('add 3 to the previous term'), we can find a formula for its *n*th term (here $u_n = 3n - 1$; the terms are multiples of 3, minus 1).

EXERCISE 1

1 Given these formulae for the nth terms, calculate the first five terms of each sequence.

a $u_n = 2n$ **b** $u_n = 3n + 1$ **c** $u_n = 2^n + 1$

d $u_n = n^2 + 1$ **e** $u_n = \frac{1}{3^n}$ **f** $u_n = 1 - n$

2 A knockout tournament starts with 32 teams, and half the teams are eliminated in each round. u_n is the number of teams after round n.

a Calculate u_1, u_2 and u_3.

b For what value of n is $u_n = 1$?

3 Find a formula for the nth term of each sequence. For example, for 1, 3, 5, ..., $u_n = 2n - 1$.

a 5, 10, 15, 20, ... **b** 4, 9, 14, 19, ...

c 3, 5, 7, 9, ... **d** −1, 1, 3, 5, ...

e 2, 4, 8, 16, ... **f** 3, 9, 27, 81, ...

g 0, 7, 14, 21, ... **h** −10, 0, 10, 20, ...

i 10, 8, 6, 4, ... ($u_n = -2n + \ldots$)

j 20, 17, 14, 11, ... **k** 10, 9, 8, 7, ...

Recurrence relations

a Given the first term of a sequence and a formula for calculating u_{n+1} from u_n, we can calculate all of the terms.
For example, if $u_1 = 7$ and $u_{n+1} = u_n + 3$, then:
$u_1 = 7$, $u_2 = u_1 + 3 = 7 + 3 = 10$, $u_3 = u_2 + 3 = 10 + 3 = 13$, and so on, giving the sequence 7, 10, 13, ...
$u_{n+1} = u_n + 3$ is called a recurrence relation since successive terms of the sequence can be found by recurring use of it.

b Conversely, given the sequence, we may be able to define it by giving the first term u_1 and the relation between u_{n+1} and u_n. For example:
(i) for 13, 10, 7, 4, ... $u_1 = 13$ and $u_{n+1} = u_n - 3$
(ii) for 5, 10, 20, 40, ... $u_1 = 5$ and $u_{n+1} = 2u_n$.

4 Use these recurrence relations to list the first four terms of each sequence.

a $u_{n+1} = 2u_n$ and $u_1 = 3$ **b** $u_{n+1} = u_n + 2$ and $u_1 = 5$

c $u_{n+1} = u_n - 2$ and $u_1 = 10$ **d** $u_{n+1} = \frac{1}{2}u_n$ and $u_1 = 256$

e $u_{n+1} = 3u_n + 1$ and $u_1 = 1$

5 Write down a recurrence relation, including the first term u_1, for each sequence in question **3**.

6 A mushroom bed has 60 mushrooms. Each morning their number has doubled, and the gardener picks 50 mushrooms. If u_n = number of mushrooms after n days, then u_0 = number at the beginning, after 0 days. So $u_0 = 60$ and $u_{n+1} = 2u_n - 50$. Use this recurrence relation to calculate u_1, u_2, u_3 and u_4.

7 There are three trees in Jim's garden. He plants two more trees each day for the next six days.

a Taking u_n as the number of trees after n days, so that $u_0 = 3$, write down a recurrence relation for the number of trees.

b Calculate the number of trees after 1, 2, 3, 4 and 5 days.

c Write down a *formula* for the number of trees after n days, $u_n = \ldots$

8 Calculate:

a the first ten terms of the Fibonacci sequence given by $u_{n+2} = u_{n+1} + u_n$ and $u_2 = u_1 = 1$.

b $\frac{u_2}{u_1}, \frac{u_3}{u_2}, \frac{u_4}{u_3}, \ldots, \frac{u_{10}}{u_9}, \ldots$. Comment on this sequence.

Linear recurrence relations

These are of the form $u_{n+1} = mu_n + c$, where m and c are constants (compare $y = mx + c$). Special sequences are obtained if $m = 1$ or $c = 0$.

(i) Arithmetic sequences

If $m = 1$ in the recurrence relation $u_{n+1} = mu_n + c$, then $u_{n+1} = u_n + c$, which gives *arithmetic sequences* like 2, 4, 6, 8, 10, ... in which the *difference* between successive terms is constant.

Example By June 30 a castle had 1500 visitors. After that, a bus load of 20 visitors arrived each day. u_n is the total number of visitors n days after June 30.

a Find a recurrence relation for the sequence of visitors.

b Calculate u_1, u_2 and u_3.

c Write down a formula for u_n.

d When will the total number of visitors reach 2000?

a $u_{n+1} = u_n + 20$ and $u_0 = 1500$

b $u_1 = u_0 + 20 = 1520$, $u_2 = 1540$, $u_3 = 1560$

c $u_n = 20n + 1500$

d $20n + 1500 = 2000$, so $n = 25$.
The total reaches 2000 after 25 days.

Write a program to generate the sequence $u_{n+1} = au_n + b$. Use it to generate several sequences. ([1] [=] sets up 1 as u_0; [3] [Ans] [+] [4] [=] [=] generates terms of the recurrence relation $u_{n+1} = 3u_n + 4$.)

EXERCISE 2

1 Find a formula for u_n, the nth term of each of these arithmetic sequences.

a 4, 6, 8, 10, ...

b 1, 7, 13, 19, ...

c 90, 80, 70, 60, ...

d 9, 2, −5, −12, ...

2 Using each recurrence relation, write down:
(i) u_1, u_2, u_3, u_4 (ii) a formula for u_n.
a $u_{n+1} = u_n + 3$, and $u_0 = 4$
b $u_{n+1} = u_n + 1$, and $u_0 = 0$
c $u_{n+1} = u_n - 2$, and $u_0 = 10$
d $u_{n+1} = u_n - 1$, and $u_0 = 100$
e $u_{n+1} = u_n + 9$, and $u_0 = 17$
f $u_{n+1} = u_n + 7$, and $u_0 = -10$

3 Susan bought a computer on hire purchase. She paid a deposit of £200 and makes a payment of £25 at the end of each month.
a If p_n is the amount she has paid by the end of the nth month, copy and complete this recurrence relation: $p_{n+1} = p_n + \ldots$ and $p_0 = \ldots$ (the deposit)
b Calculate p_1, p_2, p_3, p_4.
c Write down a formula for p_n.
d Payments are complete after 24 months. How much did the computer cost?

4 Sam is a courier, travelling 200 km each week. His mileometer reads 12 340 when he begins.
a If r_n is the reading after n weeks, copy and complete: $r_{n+1} = r_n + \ldots$ and $r_0 = \ldots$
b Calculate r_1, r_2, r_3, r_4.
c Write down a formula for r_n.
d When will the reading be 14 140?

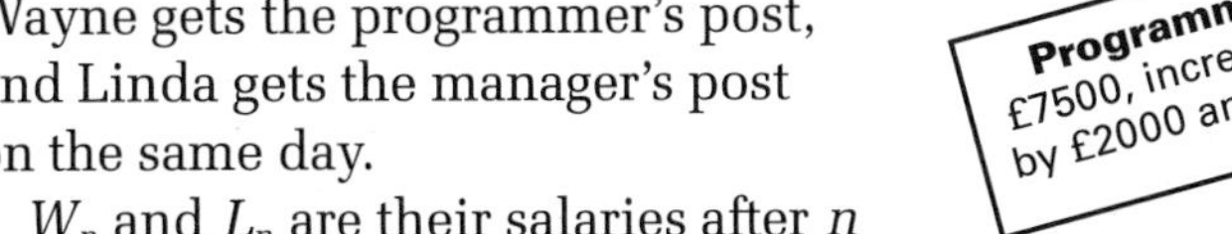

5 Wayne gets the programmer's post, and Linda gets the manager's post on the same day.
a W_n and L_n are their salaries after n years. $W_{n+1} = W_n + 2000$ and $W_0 = 7500$. Write down a similar result for Linda.
b Calculate W_1, W_2, W_3, W_4, and write down a formula for W_n.
c Calculate L_1, L_2, L_3, L_4, and write down a formula for L_n.
d After how many years will their salaries be equal?

(ii) Geometric sequences

If $c = 0$ in the recurrence relation $u_{n+1} = mu_n + c$, then $u_{n+1} = mu_n$, which gives *geometric sequences* like 1, 3, 9, 27, 81, ... in which the *ratio* of successive terms is constant.

Example Every year a typical bag of groceries rises in price by 5%. Its initial value, V_0, is £20.
a Describe the prices by a recurrence relation.
b Calculate V_1, V_2 and V_3.
c Write down a formula for V_n.
d Find the year in which the price first exceeds £30.

a $V_{n+1} = 1.05 \times V_n$ and $V_0 = 20$
b $V_1 = 1.05 \times V_0 = 1.05 \times 20 = 21$, $V_2 = 1.05 \times 21 = 22.05$, $V_3 = 23.15$, to the nearest penny
c $V_n = (1.05)^n \times 20$
d Using **c** and trial-and-improvement, $V_8 = 29.55$ and $V_9 = 31.03$, so the answer is the ninth year.

EXERCISE 3

1 The value of a car falls by 10% each year from an initial value of £10 000. V_n is its value after n years.
a Copy and complete $V_{n+1} = 0.9 \times V_n$ and $V_0 = \dots$
b Calculate V_1, V_2, V_3, V_4.
c Write down a formula for V_n.
d Calculate the value of the car after ten years, to the nearest £100.

2 u_n is the number of bacteria in a culture after n hours. At present there are 100, but their number doubles every hour.
a Complete this recurrence relation: $u_{n+1} = \dots \times u_n$, and $u_0 = 100$.
b Calculate u_1, u_2, u_3, u_4.
c Write down a formula for u_n.

3 Kirsty has £800 in a bank which pays 10% compound interest each year. If A_n is the amount in her account after n years:
a state the value of A_0
b write down a recurrence relation
c calculate A_1, A_2, A_3, A_4
d write down a formula for A_n
e calculate the amount after 25 years.

4 An office plant is 100 cm tall, and its height increases each month by 5% of its height at the beginning of the month. If H_n is the height after n months:
a make a recurrence relation
b calculate H_1, H_2, H_3, to the nearest cm
c write down a formula for H_n
d check that the height will double in the fifteenth month.

5 The Ultra Bank pays 7% compound interest, and Sarah invests £1000. If A_n is the amount after n years:
a write down a recurrence relation
b calculate A_1, A_2, A_3
c write down a formula for A_n
d find when she will have £2000.

6 Ahmed receives 40 units of a drug in hospital. His body destroys 6% of the drug every hour. u_n is the number of units of drug left in his body after n hours.
a Write down a recurrence relation, and use it to find the amount of drug left after 4 hours, correct to 1 decimal place.
b Write down a formula for u_n, and calculate the amount of drug left after 24 hours.

7 Separate populations of 200 caterpillars are treated weekly with these pesticides.
a Write down formulae for T_n, P_n and N_n, the number of caterpillars left after n weeks' treatment.
b After how many weeks in each case is the population reduced to ten or fewer?

Laboratory Report
TRITOX: 60% destroyed
PILLARY: 90% destroyed
NOPEST: 40% destoyed

8 James wants to buy the CD player, but has only £190. He invests this in Monex to increase his cash. But the price of the CD rises with inflation at 4.5% per annum.
a Write down formulae for P_n and M_n, the price of the CD and the value of his money after n years.
b After how many years can he purchase the CD?

9 Each microscope filter cuts out 10% of the light reaching the slide. A_0 is the amount of light reaching the slide with no filter.
a Obtain a recurrence relation connecting A_n, A_{n+1}, where A_n is the amount of light getting through n filters.
b Find a formula for A_n in terms of A_0.
c How many filters would be needed to cut out at least 50% of the light?

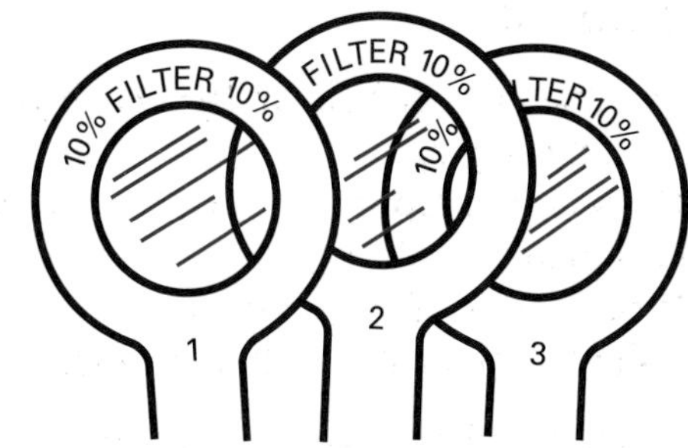

Finite and infinite sequences

EXERCISE 4

1 The first three terms of a sequence are 1, 2, 4. What is the next term? You need some clue to the pattern. Write down the fourth term of the above sequence, using the following rules. The sequence is:
a 1, followed by even numbers, in order
b powers of 2, i.e. $2^0, 2^1, \ldots$
c factors of 20, in increasing order
d factors of 44, in increasing order.

2 Two of the sequences in question **1** are finite (with a definite number of terms) and two are infinite.
a Identify these.
b Write out the finite sequences completely.

3 A sequence is given by $u_n = \dfrac{n-1}{n}$, $n \geqslant 1$.
a Write down u_1, u_2, u_3, u_4 and u_5.
b Write down u_{10}, u_{100}, u_{1000}, $u_{10\,000}$, $u_{100\,000}$ and $u_{1000\,000}$.
c Write down the value which u_n approaches as n gets larger and larger, i.e. as $n \to \infty$.
d $u_n = 1 - \dfrac{1}{n}$. Why does this make it clearer that $u_n \to 1$ as $n \to \infty$ ('u_n tends to 1 as n tends to infinity')?

4 Old Ben went panning for gold. After panning n times he found he had extracted $0.65\,(1 - (0.25)^n)$ grams of gold.

a How much gold did he extract on his first panning, correct to 2 decimal places?
b How much did he extract on his second panning (to 2 decimal places)?
c What is the maximum amount he could hope to extract?

5 Each of the sequences defined by the formulae below is convergent, i.e. has a limit value as $n \to \infty$. State the limit for each.

a $u_n = \left(\dfrac{1}{2}\right)^n$ **b** $u_n = 2 - \dfrac{1}{n^2}$ **c** $u_n = 3 + \dfrac{1}{n^3}$

d $u_n = 1 - 0.5^n$ **e** $u_n = \dfrac{2n+1}{n}$ **f** $u_n = \dfrac{n}{n+1}$

6 **a** Copy the following to find the sum, S_n, of the first n terms of the geometric sequence $a, ar, ar^2, ar^3, \ldots$ where r is the common ratio between successive terms.

$$S_n = a + ar + ar^2 + \ldots + ar^{n-1}$$
$$rS_n = \quad ar + ar^2 + \ldots + ar^{n-1} + ar^n$$
$$S_n - rS_n = \ldots - \ldots$$
$$S_n(1 - r) = a(\ldots - \ldots)$$
$$S_n = \frac{a(1 - r^n)}{1 - r}, \; r \neq 1.$$

b If $-1 < r < 1$, $r^n \to 0$ as $n \to \infty$. Write down the formula for the limit of S_n as $n \to \infty$.

c Use your formula to calculate the limit of S_n for:

(i) 100, 50, 25, . . . **(ii)** 9, 3, 1, . . .

(iii) 8, −4, 2, −1, . . . **(iv)** 10, 9, 8.1, . . .

The linear recurrence relation $u_{n+1} = mu_n + c$, *with* $m \neq 1, c \neq 0$

Example A loch contains 10 tonnes of toxic waste. Tidal action removes 50% of the waste each week, but a local factory discharges 8 tonnes of waste into the loch at the end of each week.

a Write down a linear recurrence relation, and calculate u_1, u_2, u_3, u_4, where u_n is the weight of waste in the loch after n weeks.

b What is the weight levelling out at?

a $u_{n+1} = 0.5u_n + 8$ and $u_0 = 10$; $u_1 = 0.5 \times 10 + 8 = 13$, $u_2 = 0.5 \times 13 + 8 = 14.5$, $u_3 = 15.25$, $u_4 = 15.625$.

b About 16 tonnes.

Limits If $-1 < m < 1$, u_{n+1} and u_n will each tend to a limit L.
In the above example, $u_{n+1} = 0.5u_n + 8$ becomes $L = 0.5L + 8$, so $0.5L = 8$, and $L = 16$.

In general, if $-1 < m < 1$, $u_{n+1} \to L$ and $u_n \to L$, so $u_{n+1} = mu_n + c$ becomes

$$L = mL + c$$
$$L(1 - m) = c$$
$$\text{so } L = \frac{c}{1 - m}.$$

Using the program you wrote for the graphics calculator in the work which preceded Exercise 2, generate several sequences using $-1 < a < 1$ in order to see how each converges to a limit.

EXERCISE 5

1 For each of these linear recurrence relations:

(i) list the values of u_1, u_2, u_3

(ii) say whether or not a limit exists, giving a reason

(iii) calculate the limit of the corresponding sequence, if it exists.

a $u_{n+1} = 0.5u_n + 5$, and $u_1 = 6$

b $u_{n+1} = 1.5u_n + 1$, and $u_1 = 16$

c $u_{n+1} = -0.4u_n + 30$, and $u_1 = 38$

d $u_{n+1} = 1.1u_n + 4$, and $u_1 = 5.1$

e $u_{n+1} = 0.9u_n + 3$, and $u_1 = 48$

f $u_{n+1} = -0.8u_n + 10$, and $u_1 = 30$

g $u_{n+1} = 0.6u_n - 4$, and $u_1 = -1$

h $u_{n+1} = -4u_n - 2$, and $u_1 = 38$

2 A mushroom bed has 1000 mushrooms ready for picking. Each morning 70% of the crop are picked, and each night another 300 are ready for picking. Let M_n be the number ready for picking after n days.

a Write down a recurrence relation to model the situation.

b How many are ready for picking after three days?

c How do you know that the number of mushrooms will become constant?

d Calculate the limit of the sequence.

3 Dr Sharma is studying a large flock of 200 birds. Every minute 10% of the birds leave the flock and 30 birds return.

a Using B_n for the number of birds at the end of minute n, write down a recurrence relation to model the situation.

b How many birds are in the flock at the end of 5 minutes?

c What can you say about the size of the flock in the long run?

4 At present, just after high tide, a harbour has 1 metre of silt. A dredger removes 70% of the silt between high tides, but each tide deposits an extra 1.2 metres of silt. A depth of silt greater than 1.8 metres will make the harbour unusable.

a Taking d_n for the depth of silt in metres after n tides, write down a recurrence relation.

b Find the depth of silt, to the nearest centimetre, after four tides.

c Will the harbour become unusable? Give reasons.

5 For safety reasons, tyres must have a pressure over 25 and under 28 units. A slow puncture makes a tyre lose 11% of its pressure every day, but every morning, before use, 3 units of pressure are put in the tyre. Will the pressure remain within safe limits if it starts at 26 units? Give reasons.

6 A farmer has a new irrigation system in his greenhouses. The water tank can hold 2000 gallons, and must have at least 1340 gallons when the system starts up. 75% of the stored water is used each day, but during the night water is pumped back in according to one of these options:

a 1600 gallons **b** 1300 gallons **c** 1000 gallons.

The farmer starts up the system with 1750 gallons in the tank. Which night-time option should he choose? Explain fully.

New sequences from old

Andrew has challenged his friends to find the next term of the sequence 1, 2, 7, 32, ... They decide to see whether these four terms fit a linear recurrence relation $u_{n+1} = mu_n + c$, where m and c are constants.
For u_1 and u_2, $u_2 = mu_1 + c$, so $2 = m \times 1 + c$, giving $m + c = 2$.
For u_2 and u_3, $u_3 = mu_2 + c$, so $7 = m \times 2 + c$, giving $2m + c = 7$.
Solving these simultaneous equations, $m = 5$ and $c = -3$, so the recurrence relation $u_{n+1} = 5u_n - 3$ fits in with $u_1 = 1$, $u_2 = 2$ and $u_3 = 7$.
Then $u_4 = 5u_3 - 3 = 5 \times 7 - 3 = 32$. So 1, 2, 7, 32 are the first four terms of the sequence defined by $u_{n+1} = 5u_n - 3$, with $u_1 = 1$, and the next term is $5 \times 32 - 3 = 157$.

EXERCISE 6

1 For each sequence, find a recurrence relation $u_{n+1} = mu_n + c$, and determine the next term.

a 5, 10, 30, 110, ... **b** 1, 5, 17, 53, ...
c 8, 36, 50, 57, ... **d** 93, 39, 21, 15, ...
e 11, 20, 110, 1010, ... **f** 30, 21, 15, 11, ...

2 **a** Which of the sequences in question **1** have a limit? Give a reason in each case.
b Calculate the limits.

3 A sequence is given by the formula $u_n = an + b$, where a and b are constants.
a If $u_1 = 5$ and $u_2 = 8$, find a and b.
b Calculate u_3, u_4, u_5.

4 For an arithmetic sequence, $u_n = an + b$. Its third term is 13 and its seventh term is 33.
a Find a and b.
b Calculate the first six terms.

5 For a geometric sequence, $u_n = ar^n$. Its second term is 6 and its fourth term is 54.
a Find r (two values) and a.
b Write down the first four terms of the two possible sequences.

6 For a sequence, $u_{n+1} = mu_n + c$, $u_0 = 1$, $u_1 = 3$ and $u_2 = 7$.
a Form two equations, and solve them simultaneously to find m and c.
b Calculate u_5.

7 For another sequence, $u_{n+1} = 3u_n + b$, $u_1 = 1$ and $u_3 = 21$. Find the value of b, and calculate u_5.

8 **a** Andrew's friends found the recurrence relation $u_{n+1} = 5u_n - 3$, with $u_1 = 1$, for the sequence starting 1, 2, 7, 32, ... Check that $u_5 = 157$ and $u_6 = 782$.
b But there are many sequences which begin 1, 2, 7, 32, ..., each with a different rule for its formation. Find the first six terms of the sequences given by:
(i) $u_{n+1} = u_n + 5^{n-1}$, with $u_1 = 1$
(ii) $u_n = \frac{1}{3}(8n^3 - 42n^2 + 73n - 36)$, $n \geqslant 1$.

CHAPTER 4 REVIEW

1 For each recurrence relation, find:
(i) u_1, u_2, u_3, u_4 (ii) a formula for u_n.
a $u_{n+1} = u_n + 5$, and $u_0 = 3$
b $u_{n+1} = u_n - 4$, and $u_1 = 5$
c $u_{n+1} = 2u_n$, and $u_0 = 1$
d $u_{n+1} = \frac{1}{2}u_n$, and $u_1 = 6$

2 Duncan was training for the half marathon. Initially he ran ten laps of the circuit. Thereafter he added two laps daily to his run. If u_n is the number of laps after n days:
a copy and complete: $u_{n+1} = u_n + \ldots$ and $u_0 = \ldots$
b calculate u_1, u_2, u_3, u_4
c write down a formula for u_n.

3 The Golden Bank pays 12% compound interest. Theo deposits £2000.
a If A_n is the amount in his account after n years, write down a recurrence relation.
b Calculate A_1, A_2, A_3, A_4.
c Write down a formula for A_n.
d Calculate the amount after ten years.

4 Iain Jansen borrowed £600 from a company that charged him interest of 2% at the end of each month.
a If B_n is the balance he is due to pay after n months, write down a recurrence relation.
b Write down a formula for B_n.
c How much was he due to pay after one year?

5 I have saved £120. Each month I receive £100 in wages, and spend 35% of all my money. I hope to buy a TV set costing £290. Will I be able to do so?

6 Kim is studying for her French exam. At present she knows 600 words. In each hour of study she learns 40 new words and forgets 5% of the words she knew. Her aim is to know 750 words.
a If u_n is the number of words she knows after n hours, write down a recurrence relation.
b How many words will she know after 4 hours of study?
c In the long run, with enough work, will she achieve her aim?

7 For each of the following relations:
(i) calculate the first three terms of the sequence
(ii) explain how you know that a limit exists
(iii) calculate the limit as $n \to \infty$.
a $u_{n+1} = 0.7u_n + 3$ and $u_1 = 5$.
b $u_{n+1} = -0.82u_n + 9$ and $u_1 = 100$.

8 In the sequences in question **7** calculate the smallest value of n for which:
a $u_n > 9$ in sequence **a**
b $u_n < 40$ in sequence **b**, and is positive.

9 For a sequence, $u_{n+1} = au_n + b$, $u_0 = -1$, $u_1 = 5$ and $u_2 = -7$.
a Form two equations and solve them simultaneously to find a and b.
b Calculate u_4.

10 $t_{n+1} = \frac{1}{2}t_n + \frac{1}{2}$ and $t_1 = \frac{1}{4}$. What happens to t_n as $n \to \infty$?

CHAPTER 4 SUMMARY

1 A *sequence* may be defined by:
 a a formula for the nth term; for example, $u_n = n + 5$, giving $u_1 = 6$, $u_2 = 7$, $u_3 = 8, \ldots$
 b a recurrence relation and an initial term; for example, $u_{n+1} = u_n + 1$ and $u_0 = 5$, giving $u_1 = 6$, $u_2 = 7$, $u_3 = 8, \ldots$.

2 A *linear recurrence relation* is of the form $u_{n+1} = mu_n + c$, where m and c are constants.
 a If $m = 1$, $u_{n+1} = u_n + c$, giving an *arithmetic sequence.*
 b If $c = 0$, $u_{n+1} = mu_n$, giving a *geometric sequence.*

3 The *sequence generated by the recurrence relation* $u_{n+1} = mu_n + c$ will 'level out' at a *limit* L if $-1 < m < 1$. In this case, $u_{n+1} = mu_n + c$ leads to $L = mL + c$, and $L = \dfrac{c}{1-m}$, $-1 < m < 1$.
For example, for $u_{n+1} = \frac{1}{3}u_n + 8$, the limit is $\dfrac{8}{1-\frac{1}{3}} = 12$.

4 If some terms of a sequence are known, it may be possible to find a recurrence relation for the sequence.
For example, for 5, 6, 6.8, …, $u_{n+1} = au_n + b$ gives $6 = 5a + b$ and $6.8 = 6a + b$, from which $a = 0.8$, $b = 2$ and the relation could be $u_{n+1} = 0.8u_n + 2$, since $u_3 = 0.8 \times 6 + 2 = 6.8$.

5 Revision Exercises

CHAPTER REVISION EXERCISES

CHAPTER 1 REVISION

1 A is the point $(-5, -2)$ and B is $(7, 3)$. Find:

a the midpoint of AB

b the length of AB

c the gradient of AB

d the gradients of CD, parallel to AB, and EF, perpendicular to AB.

2 a Write down the gradients of lines with equations $y = 3x - 6$ and $x - 4y = -7$.

b Calculate, correct to 1 decimal place:

(i) the angle which each line makes with OX

(ii) the acute angle between the lines.

3 a Prove that:

(i) D$(-9, 3)$, E$(-4, 2)$, F$(1, 1)$ are collinear

(ii) E is the midpoint of DF.

b Find the equation of the line through E, perpendicular to DF.

4 a Show that the quadrilateral with vertices A$(3, 3)$, B$(7, 2)$, C$(6, -2)$ and D$(-3, -4)$ is a kite.

b *Write down* the coordinates of the point where its diagonals cross.

5 A is the point $(0, 2)$, B is $(8, 2)$ and C is $(8, 6)$, as in the diagram.

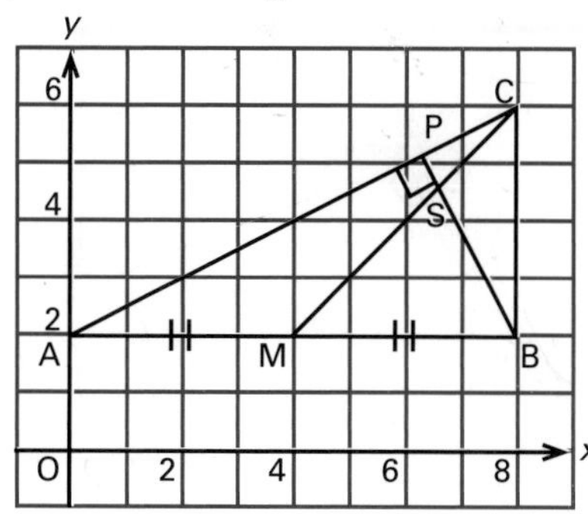

a Find the equation of:

(i) median CM

(ii) altitude BP, in $\triangle$ABC.

b Find the coordinates of S, the point of intersection of CM and BP.

6 STUV is a rhombus. S is $(-2, -4)$ and U is $(6, 2)$. Find:

a the equation of diagonal

(i) SU **(ii)** TV

b the value of k if T is the point $(8, k)$

c the coordinates of V.

7 The equation of the straight line AB which represents a coastline is $4y - 3x = 24$. The ship at P has to take the shortest route to the coastline.

a Find the equation of the course the ship should follow.

b Calculate the shortest distance. (The units are km.)

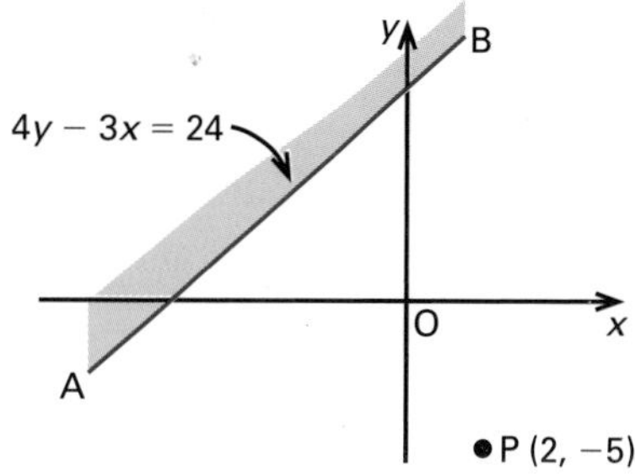

8 See next page.

8 A cylinder, whose circular end has its centre at (12, 24), rests on a slope with gradient $\frac{1}{3}$.

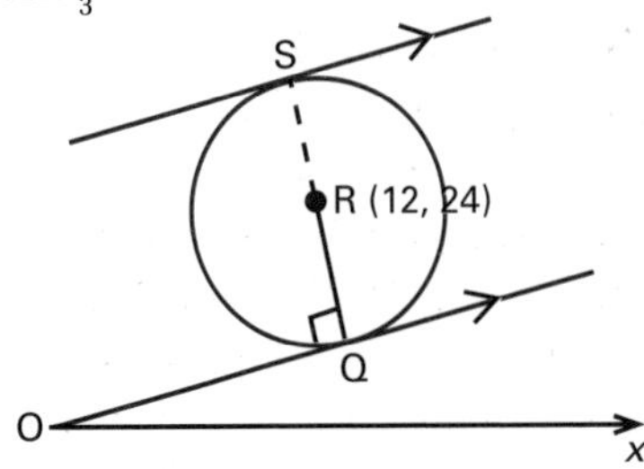

Find:

a the equation of radius RQ

b the coordinates of Q

c the equation of the parallel tangent at S.

9 The vertices of △ABC are A (−6, 2), B (10, 10) and C (12, −4).

a Find the equation of the perpendicular bisectors of AB and BC.

b Find the point of intersection P of the two lines in **a**.

c Show that P lies on the perpendicular bisector of AC.

10 In a computer-simulated golf game, the tee is at (0, 30) and the hole is at (350, 80).

a Calculate the distance from the tee to the hole, to the nearest metre.

b The parallel edges of the stream have equations $y = 4x - 800$ and $y = 4x - 950$. If a shot lands at (250, 80) has it crossed the stream or not?

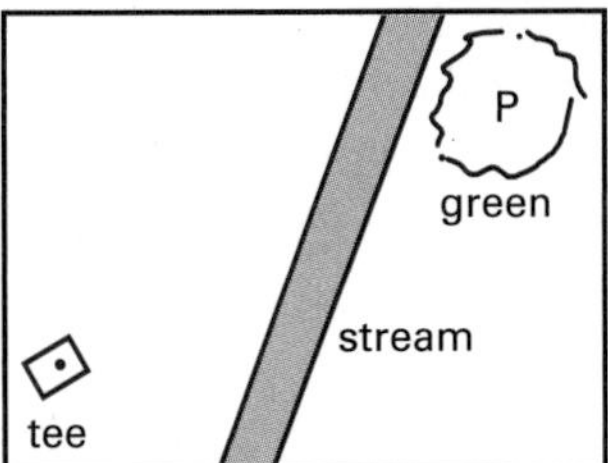

CHAPTER 2.1 REVISION

1 Copy and complete this table:

$g(x)$	$2 - 3x$	$\frac{1}{x+1}$	$\sqrt{(x-1)}$	$(2x-1)^2$
$g(1)$				
$g(-2)$			–	
$g(0)$			–	

2 Formulae and domains are given for these functions. Express the ranges as inequalities.

a $f(x) = 2x, -1 \leqslant x \leqslant 3$

b $g(x) = x^2, x \in R$ (all real numbers)

c $h(x) = \sqrt{x}, 1 \leqslant x \leqslant 16$

d $k(x) = 5 + 2x, x > 3$

3 $f(x) = 1 - 2x$. Simplify:

a $f(x + 1)$ **b** $f(\frac{1}{2}x)$

c $f(1 - x)$ **d** $f(-x)$.

4 $g(x) = \dfrac{1}{1 - x}$. Simplify:

a $g(x + 1)$ **b** $g(1 - x)$

c $g\left(\dfrac{1}{x}\right)$ **d** $g\left(\dfrac{1}{1 + x}\right)$.

5 $f(x) = 2x^2 - 5x + 7$, and the domain of f is $-1 \leqslant x \leqslant 11$.

a Calculate, where possible:

(i) $f(2)$ **(ii)** $f(-2)$

(iii) $f(-1)$ **(iv)** $f(0)$.

b Find k if $f(k) = 10$.

6 For each of these graphs, state:

(i) the domain

(ii) the range

(iii) whether or not the function has an inverse function.

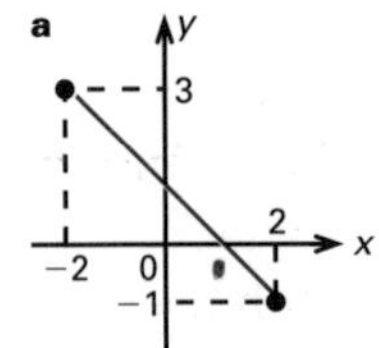

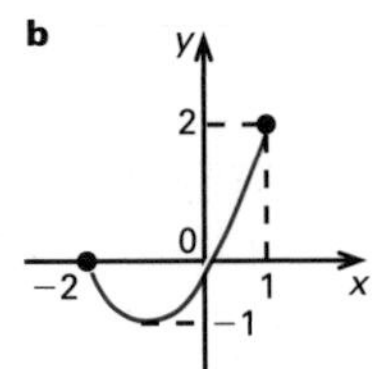

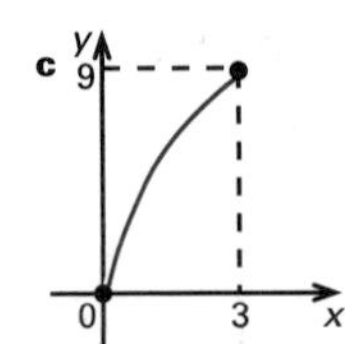

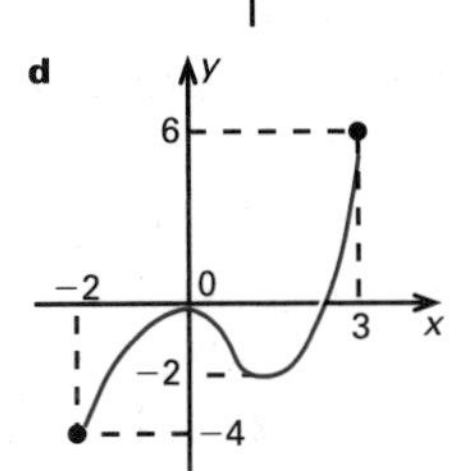

7 For each pair of functions obtain a formula for:
(i) $g(f(x))$ (ii) $f(g(x))$
(iii) $f(f(x))$ (iv) $g(g(x))$.
a $f(x) = x + 2$, $g(x) = 2x$
b $f(x) = x^2$, $g(x) = x - 1$
c $f(x) = \frac{1}{x}$, $g(x) = 1 - x$
d $f(x) = x - 1$, $g(x) = \frac{1}{x - 1}$

8 $f(x) = ax + b$, $f(-3) = -9$ and $f(2) = 1$. Find a and b, and hence calculate $f(-1)$.

9 Copy these sketches, and draw the graph $y = f^{-1}(x)$ in each. Write down the formula for $f^{-1}(x)$ for each.

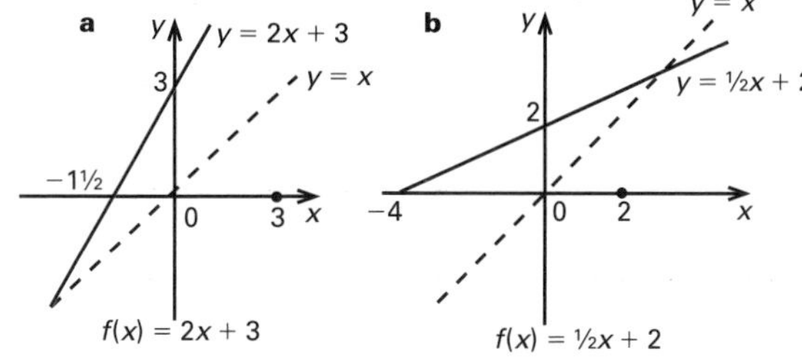

10 $f(x) = 1 - 2x$ and $g(x) = x^2$. Find:
a formulae for $f(g(x))$ and $g(f(x))$
b x for which
(i) $f(g(x)) = -7$
(ii) $f(g(x)) = g(f(x))$.

11 $f(x) = x^2 - 2x + 4$.
a Find x, given $f(x + 1) - f(x - 1) = 0$.
b Find $f(f(x))$ in its simplest form.

12 The gradient of the tightrope must not be more than $\frac{1}{10}$, or less than zero.
a Find a formula for $L(x)$, the length of the rope.
b Find an expression for the gradient of the rope, and use it to determine the domain of $L(x)$.
c Calculate the range of $L(x)$, correct to 2 decimal places where necessary.

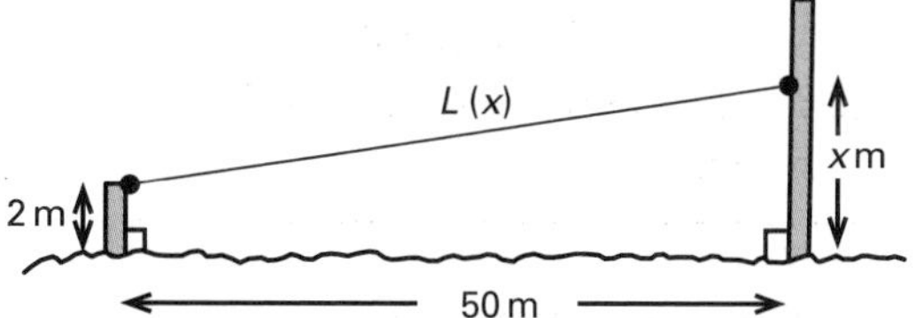

CHAPTER 2.2 REVISION

1 Express each of the following in the form $a(x + p)^2 + q$:
a $x^2 + 2x + 5$
b $x^2 - 6x$
c $3 - 4x - x^2$.

2 By completing the square, find the maximum or minimum value of each of the following, and the corresponding value of x:
a $x^2 - 8x + 6$ b $5 + 10x - x^2$.

3 Use completing the square to find the turning point of the parabola $y = x^2 - 2x - 3$, and sketch the parabola.

4 Given the graph $y = x^4$, sketch the graphs:
a $y = x^4 - 1$
b $y = (x + 2)^4$
c $y = -x^4$
d $y = (x - 1)^4 - 2$.

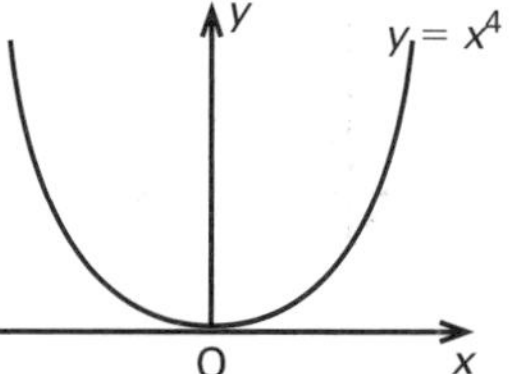

5 Sketch the graphs:
a $y = -f(x)$
b $y = f(x + 2)$
c $y = f(x) - 2$
d $y = f(-x)$.

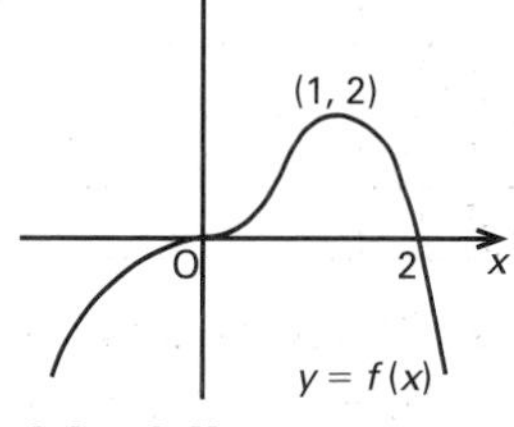

6 Find the equations of the following curves.

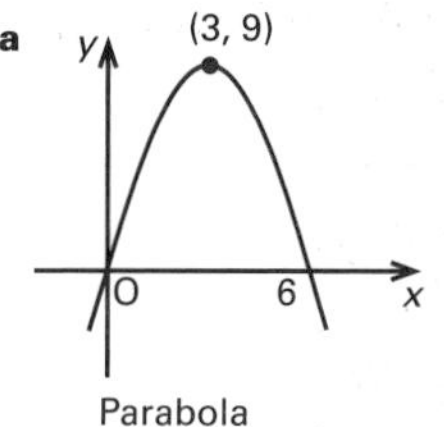

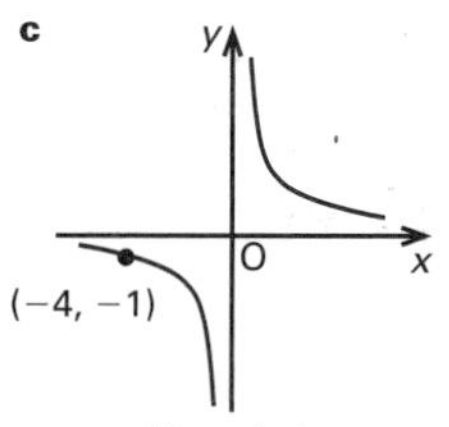

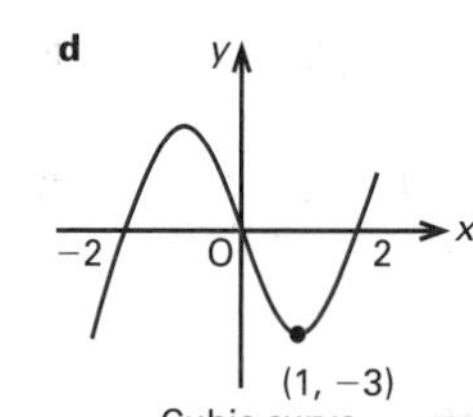

7 On the same diagram, sketch the curves:

a $y = 10^x$

b $y = 10^x + 1$

c $y = 10^{2x}$.

8 The equation of graph (**i**) below is $y = k \times 2^x$. Find the value of k.

(i)

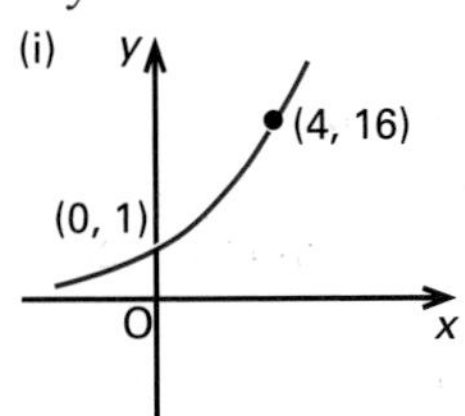

(ii)

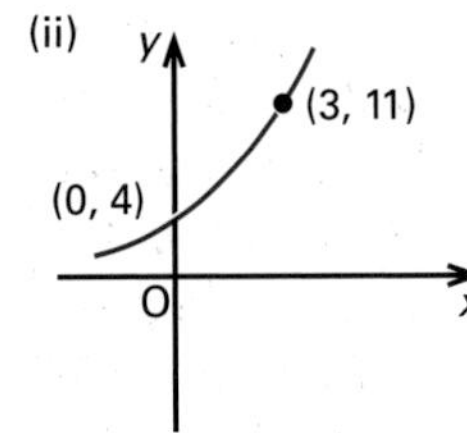

9 The equation of graph (**ii**) above is $y = 2^x + n$. Find the value of n.

10 Pair these equations with their graphs.

a $y = \log_2 x$ **b** $y = \log_2 (x - 1)$

c $y = \log_2 \left(\frac{1}{x}\right)$ **d** $y = \log_2 x - 1$

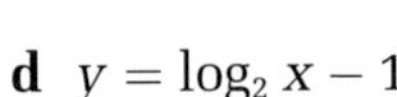

(i)

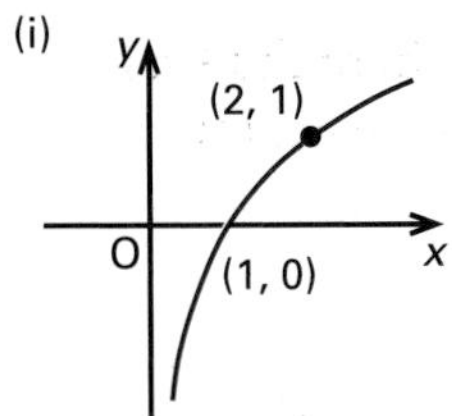

(ii)

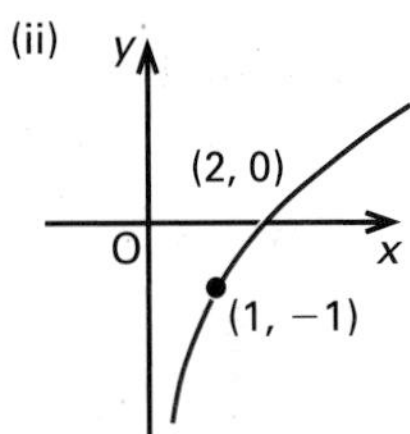

(iii)

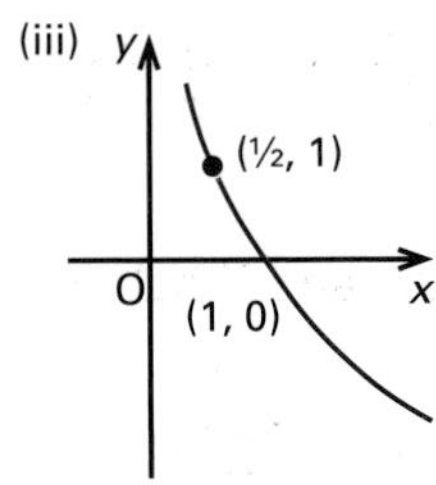

(iv)

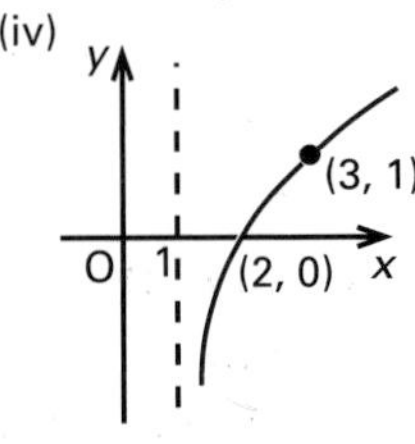

11 The sketch below shows the graph $y = \log_{10} (x + c)$. Find the value of c.

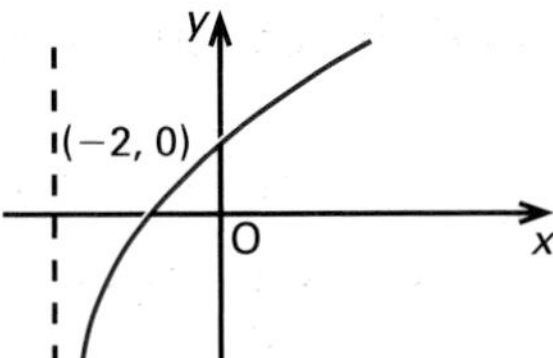

12 The sketch below shows the graph $y = a \log_2 (x + b)$. Find the values of a and b.

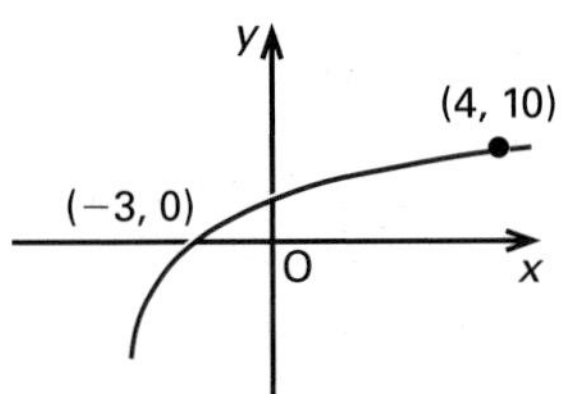

CHAPTER 2.3 REVISION

1 Copy and complete:

$x(°)$	180	60	300			
x (radians)				$\frac{\pi}{2}$	$\frac{3\pi}{4}$	$\frac{11\pi}{6}$

2 Find the exact value of:

a $\cos \frac{3\pi}{4}$ **b** $\tan \frac{5\pi}{4}$ **c** $\sin \frac{2\pi}{3}$ **d** $\sin \frac{5\pi}{3}$

e $\tan \frac{\pi}{3}$ **f** $\tan \frac{4\pi}{3}$ **g** $\cos \frac{\pi}{6}$ **h** $\cos \frac{7\pi}{6}$.

3 a Sketch a right-angled triangle ABC in which $\tan A = \frac{\sqrt{5}}{2}$.

b Find the exact value of cos A.

4 If $90° < x° < 180°$, and $\sin x° = \frac{3}{\sqrt{10}}$, find the exact value of $\tan x°$.

5 Find the values of the following, correct to 3 significant figures:

a $\sin 190°$ b $\cos 290°$ c $\tan 125°$

d $\sin \frac{\pi}{5}$ e $\cos \frac{5\pi}{8}$ f $\tan \frac{9\pi}{5}$.

6 Simplify, without using a calculator:

a $\sin^2 \frac{\pi}{4} + \sin^2 \frac{\pi}{6}$

b $\cos^2 \frac{\pi}{3} + \cos^2 \frac{\pi}{6}$

c $\tan^2 \frac{\pi}{4} + \tan^2 \frac{\pi}{3}$

d $\sin^2 \frac{\pi}{2} + \cos^2 \frac{\pi}{2}$.

7 Sketch the graphs:

a $y = \sin\theta$ for $0 \leqslant \theta \leqslant 4\pi$

b $y = \cos\theta$ for $-2\pi \leqslant \theta \leqslant 2\pi$

c $y = \tan\theta$ for $-\frac{\pi}{2} < \theta < \frac{\pi}{2}$.

8 Write down the equations of these sine and cosine graphs:

a

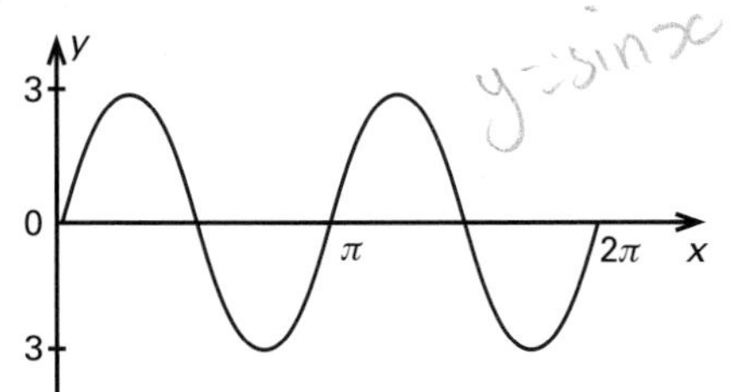

b

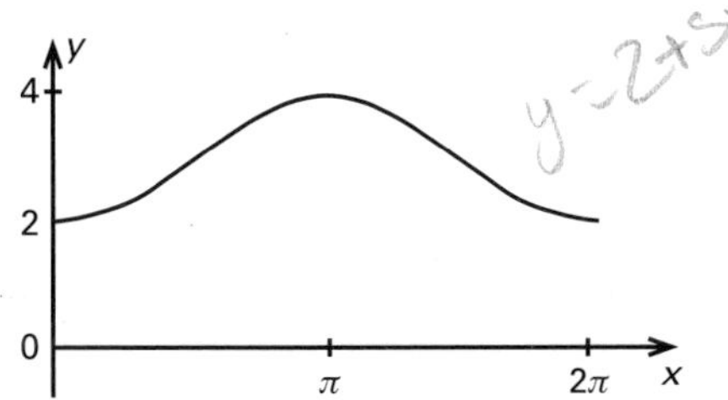

9 For each of the following:

(i) write down the maximum and minimum values of y, the number of cycles in the graph for $0 \leqslant x \leqslant 2\pi$ and the period of the graph

(ii) sketch the graph.

a $y = \sin 2x$ b $y = 2\cos\frac{1}{2}x$

c $y = 3 + \cos 4x$ d $y = -1 - \sin x$

10 Solve, for $0 \leqslant \theta \leqslant 2\pi$:

a $\cos\theta = -1$ b $4\sin^2\theta - 1 = 0$.

11 Solve, for $0 \leqslant x \leqslant 360$:

a $2\cos^2 x° + \cos x° - 1 = 0$

b $2\cos^2 x° + \sin x° = 1$.

12 Solve, for $0 \leqslant \theta \leqslant 2\pi$, correct to 2 decimal places:

a $3\sin^2\theta - 2\sin\theta - 1 = 0$

b $9\sin^2\theta + 3\cos\theta = 7$.

13 Solve, for $0 \leqslant x \leqslant 360$, correct to the nearest degree:

a $3\cos(x - 80)° = -1$

b $\sin(2x - 80)° = -1$.

14 Solve, for $0 \leqslant x \leqslant \pi$, correct to 1 decimal place:

a $4\cos\left(x + \frac{\pi}{6}\right) = 1$

b $2\sin\left(2x - \frac{\pi}{4}\right) = 1$.

15 Find the values of x where the line $y = 4$ cuts this cosine curve, for $0 \leqslant x \leqslant \frac{\pi}{2}$.

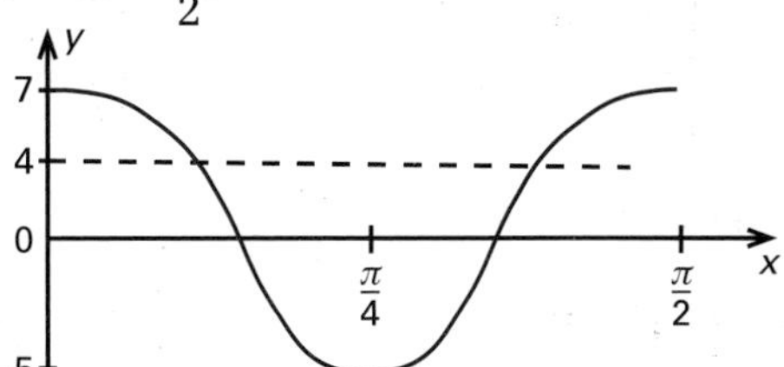

16 Find the coordinates of A and B below.

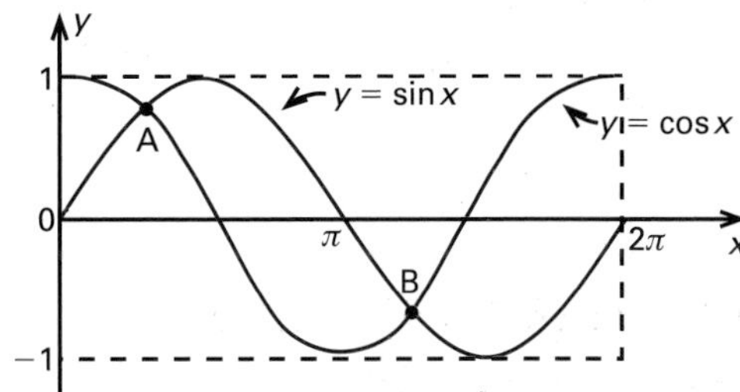

17 Find the maximum and minimum turning points, for $0 \leqslant x \leqslant 2\pi$, of the graphs:

a $y = 3\sin\left(x - \frac{\pi}{6}\right)$

b $y = 2\cos\left(x + \frac{\pi}{3}\right)$

CHAPTER 3 REVISION

Differentiate in questions **1–3**.

1 a $4x^2 - 5x + 6$ **b** $\frac{1}{2}x^2 + \frac{3}{4}x^4$ **c** $4x^{1/4}$

2 a $(x - 2)(2 - x)$ **b** $(3x + 1)^2$ **c** $x(x - 1)^2$

3 a $\dfrac{2}{x^3}$ **b** $\dfrac{1}{4x}$ **c** $\dfrac{4}{\sqrt{x}}$ **d** $(1 + \sqrt{x})^2$

4 Calculate $\dfrac{dy}{dx}$, given:

a $y = x^3 + \dfrac{1}{x^3}$

b $y = \dfrac{2x^2 + 3x + 4}{x}$

c $y = x^{1/3}(x^{2/3} - x^{-1/3})$

d $y = 2\sqrt{x} + \dfrac{1}{2\sqrt{x}}$.

5 Given $f(x) = 2x^2 + 8x - 7$, calculate:
a $f'(0)$ **b** $f'(-4)$ **c** $f'(\frac{1}{2})$.

6 A curve has equation $y = \sqrt{x} + 1$. Find:
a the gradient of the tangent at $x = 4$
b the equation of the tangent.

7 The equation of a curve is $y = \frac{1}{4}x^4 + 6x$. The gradient of the curve at A(a, b) is -2. Find:
a the coordinates of A
b the equation of the tangent at A.

8 Find the equations of the tangents to the curve $y = x + \dfrac{1}{x}$ which are perpendicular to the line $9x + 8y = 0$.

9 The distance s metres travelled by a train in t seconds is given by the formula $s = t^3 - 5t^2 + 6t$. Calculate the speed (rate of change of distance) of the train at $t = 5$.

10 Given $y = x^3 - 9x^2 + 27x$:
a show that $\dfrac{dy}{dx} = 3(x - 3)^2$
b describe the gradients of all the tangents to the curve.

11 The tangent to the curve $y = x^3$ at A (1, 1) meets the y-axis at B. Find:
a the equation of the tangent
b the coordinates of B.

12 Find the equations of the tangents to the curve $y = x(x^2 - 3)$ which have a gradient of 9.

13 The tangents to the parabola $y = x(2 - x)$ at O and A intersect at B.

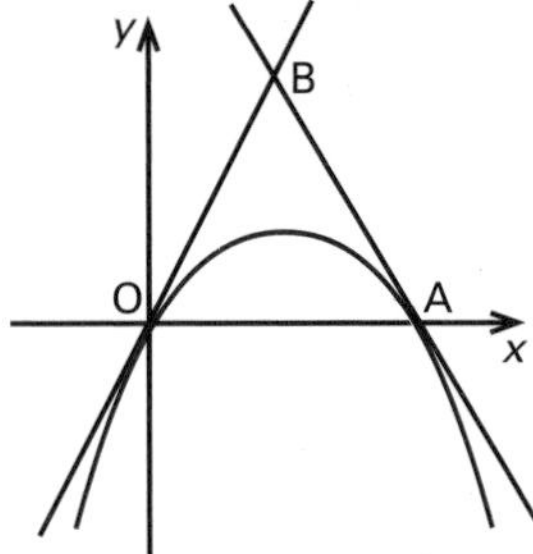

Find:
a the equations of the tangents
b the coordinates of B
c the size of ∠OBA, to the nearest degree.

14 Find the stationary points and their nature for the following curves:
a $y = x^2 - 8x + 12$
b $y = (x^2 - 4)^2$.

15 State the range of values of x for which the tangents to the curves in question **14** have positive gradients.

16 Sketch these curves. (Use your answers to question **14** for **a** and **b**).
a $y = x^2 - 8x + 12$ **b** $y = (x^2 - 4)^2$
c $y = 3x^2 - x^3$ **d** $y = (x - 1)^3$

17 The area of a rectangular plot of ground is 9 m^2.
a If one edge is x m long, show that the perimeter P m is given by $P = 2x + \dfrac{18}{x}$.
b Find the minimum length of fence needed to enclose the plot.

18 a Sketch the curve $y = \frac{1}{4}x^2 - 3x + 8$.
b If the curve cuts the x-axis at A and B, and the tangents at A and B meet at C, find the size of ∠ACB.

19 The displacement s metres at time t seconds of an object moving in a straight line is $s = 3 - 6t + 2t^3$.

a Calculate its displacement at $t = 1$ and $t = 2$.

b Show that its velocity is 0 at $t = 1$.

c Calculate its velocity when its acceleration is zero.

CHAPTER 4 REVISION

1 Calculate u_1, u_2 and u_3 for each formula or recurrence relation.

a $u_n = 3n - 3$

b $u_n = 2^n + 3$

c $u_n = 14 - 2n$

d $u_n = 0.4^n \times 100$

e $u_{n+1} = 2u_n + 3$, and $u_0 = 4$

f $u_{n+1} = 0.1u_n + 30$, and $u_0 = 100$

g $u_{n+1} = 0.6u_n$, and $u_0 = 50$

2 For each recurrence relation below, find: **(i)** u_1, u_2, u_3, u_4 **(ii)** a formula for u_n.

a $u_{n+1} = u_n + 2$, and $u_0 = 5$

b $u_{n+1} = u_n - 3$, and $u_0 = 30$

c $u_{n+1} = u_n + 10$, and $u_0 = 1$

d $u_{n+1} = u_n - 5$, and $u_0 = 20$

3 At midday the floodwater was 4 m deep, and each hour thereafter the level fell by 30% of the depth at the beginning of the hour. D_n was the depth n hours after midday.

a Write down the value of D_0.

b Calculate D_1, D_2 and D_3.

c Write down a recurrence relation to model the situation.

d Write down a formula for D_n.

e When was the floodwater less than 50 cm deep?

4 It is estimated that Sunnyside Farm has an average 280 slugs per acre. The farmer has to reduce this within a week to less than 100 per acre to protect his crops, and has a choice of three types of slug control.

Comparison Report
(Percentage removed per daily application)
SLUGONE: 14%
SLUGOFF: 15%
SLUGRID: 13%

Analyse the population, P_n, of slugs after n days for each control method. Which treatment(s) could the farmer choose?

5 For each of these recurrence relations:
(i) calculate u_1, u_2, u_3
(ii) state, with a reason, whether a limit exists, and if it does calculate it.

a $u_{n+1} = 0.9u_n + 1$, and $u_0 = 4$

b $u_{n+1} = 1.1u_n - 1$, and $u_0 = 50$

c $u_{n+1} = -\frac{1}{2}u_n + 6$, and $u_0 = 2$

d $u_{n+1} = \frac{3}{4}u_n - 2$, and $u_0 = 8$

6 Each month 35% of the poultry on Sunnyside Farm die from disease, and each month 500 new birds are introduced. The farm had 4500 birds at the beginning. B_n is the number of live birds n months later.

a Write down B_0.

b Calculate B_1, B_2, B_3 to the nearest whole number.

c Describe the situation by a recurrence relation.

d The farmer calculates that if the number eventually falls below 1500, his business will collapse. Will this happen? Explain.

7 Which of these annual plans will maintain at least 10 000 trees in a forest?

A. Cut down 8% of the trees, and replant 810.

B. Cut down 6%, and replant 590.

C. Cut down 4%, and replant 400.

8 A sequence satisfies the recurrence relation $u_{n+1} = au_n + b$. If $u_1 = 33$, $u_2 = 9$ and $u_3 = 3$, find the values of a and b, and hence calculate u_4.

GENERAL REVISION EXERCISES

REVIEW A

1 ΔABC has vertices A(2, 4), B(−2, 2) and C(4, −2). Find the equation of:
  a the median AM
  b the altitude AD.

2 Complete the square of $E = x^2 - 2x + 3$, and hence write down the minimum value of E.

3 a $f(x) = x + \frac{1}{x}$. Find $f'(2)$ and $f'(\frac{1}{2})$.
  b Find x for which $f'(x) = 0$.

4 This is the curve $y = f(x)$ for $-3 \leqslant x \leqslant 3$.

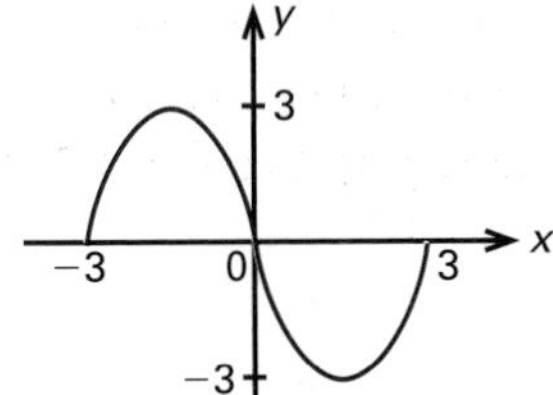

Sketch:
  a $y = f(x) + 3$
  b $y = f(x + 3)$.

5 $u_{n+1} = mu_n + c$ is a recurrence relation, where m and c are constants. If $u_0 = 64$, $u_1 = 48$ and $u_2 = 36$:
  a find the values of m and c
  b calculate the limit of the corresponding sequence.

6 A country's population was 85 million in 1995. Assuming an annual growth rate of 1%, what would the population be, to the nearest million, in 2005?

7 $f(x) = x^2$ and $g(x) = x + \frac{1}{x}$. Show that $f(g(x)) - g(f(x)) = 2$.

8 a Prove that A(4, −1), B(7, 4), C(−2, 2) and D(−5, −3) are vertices of a parallelogram.
  b Find the coordinates of the point of intersection of its diagonals.

9 a Express $x^2 + 6x - 3$ in the form $(x + p)^2 + q$.
  b Hence write down the coordinates of the turning point of the curve $y = x^2 + 6x - 3$.
  c Sketch the curve.

10 Find the equation of the tangent to the curve:
  a $y = x^4 - x^2$ at $(-1, 0)$
  b $y = x^{1/2}(x + 4)$ at (4, 16).

11 This is a sketch of a cosine curve for $0 \leqslant x \leqslant 90$.

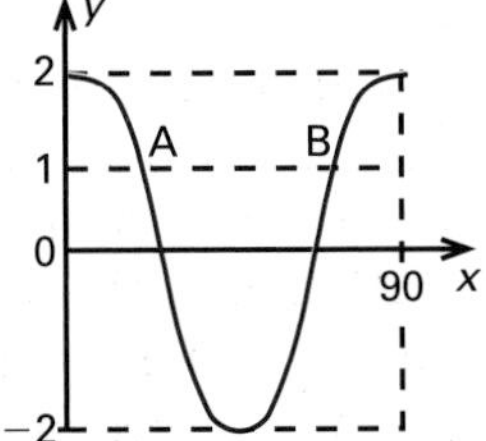

  a State the equation of the curve.
  b The line $y = 1$ cuts the curve at A and B. Find the x-coordinates of A and B.

12 Calculate, to the nearest degree, the acute angle between OX and the tangent to the curve $y = x^4 - 2x^3 + 3x^2 - 4x + 1$ at the point where $x = 2$.

13 a Sketch the graphs $y = 2\sin 2x$ and $y = 1 - \cos x$ for $0 \leqslant x \leqslant 2\pi$.
  b Write down the maximum and minimum values, and the corresponding values of x $(0 \leqslant x \leqslant 2\pi)$ of:
  (i) $2\sin 2x$ (ii) $1 - \cos x$.

14 The equations of the sides of ΔABC are: AB $y + x = 2$, AC $y - x = 2$ and BC $3y - x = 14$.
  a Find the coordinates of A, B and C.
  b Prove, by two different methods, that ΔABC is right-angled.

15 The equation of a curve is $y = (x + 1)(x^2 - 4x - 5)$.

a Find: **(i)** where it meets the x-axis
(ii) its stationary points and their nature.

b Sketch the curve.

16 Solve the equations:

a $2\sin^2\theta - \sin\theta = 0, 0 \leqslant \theta \leqslant 2\pi$

b $6\sin^2 x° + \cos x° - 5 = 0, 0 \leqslant x \leqslant 360$, correct to 0.1°.

17 The height, h metres, of a ball after t seconds is given by $h = 25t - 5t^2$.

a Find its height and velocity at:
(i) $t = 0$ **(ii)** $t = 2$.

b What is its maximum height?

REVIEW B

1 a $P(x, y)$ lies on the line $x + y = 1$. Express OP^2 as a quadratic expression in x.

b Show that the quadratic can be written $\frac{1}{2} + 2(x - \frac{1}{2})^2$.

c Deduce the minimum distance from O to the line $x + y = 1$, in exact form.

2 The height of a rocket, h metres, is given by $h = 200 + 20t - t^2$, where t seconds is the time of flight. Express h in the form $a(t + p)^2 + q$, and hence find the maximum height of the rocket and when this occurs.

3 A ladder leans against a sloping wall.

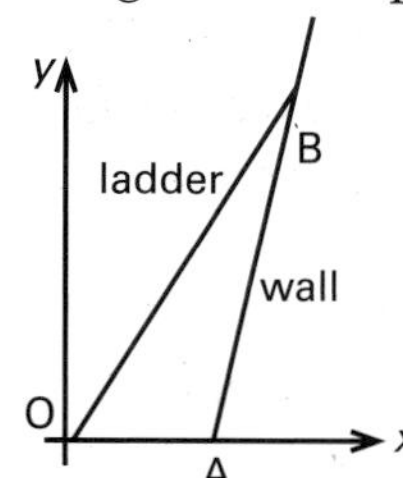

The equations of OB and AB are $3y - 4x = 0$ and $2y - 3x + 6 = 0$. Calculate:

a the angle between the ladder and the ground, to the nearest degree

b the length of the ladder (units are feet).

4 a Find the equations of the tangents to the curve $y = 3x^2 - 12x + 6$ at $P(1, -3)$ and $Q(3, -3)$.

b Show that the point of intersection of the tangents lies on the line $9x + 2y = 0$.

5 The equations of the sides of ΔABC are: AB $3x - 2y + 1 = 0$, BC $x + 8y + 9 = 0$ and CA $2x + 3y - 8 = 0$.

a Find the coordinates of A, B and C.

b Show that:
(i) ΔABC is right-angled
(ii) $AC = 2AB$.

6 Sketch (i) shows the curve $y = f(x)$. Write down the equations of the related congruent graphs (ii) and (iii).

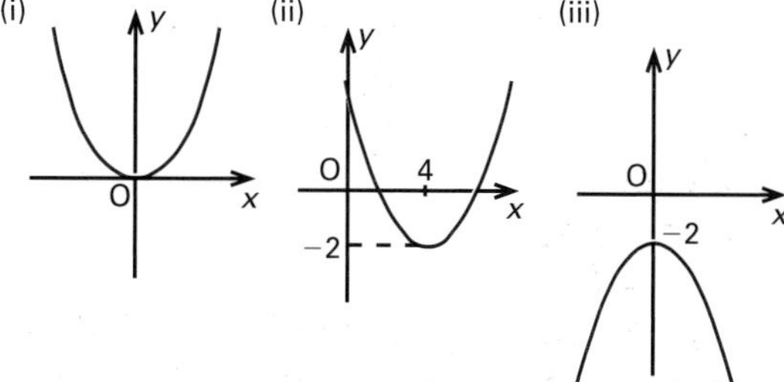

7 Differentiate:

a $2x^2 + \dfrac{1}{2x^2}$ **b** $\dfrac{(x^{1/2} + 1)^2}{x}$.

8 The outline of the cross-section of a new plant container is part of the curve $y = x^4 - 4x^2$. Sketch the curve, marking the turning points and intersections with the axes.

9 Western Wines have 50 litres of wine in stock. Each day they make 10 litres and sell 10% of the wine already in stock.

a If u_n is the number of litres in stock after n days, state the value of u_0 and write down a recurrence relation for u_{n+1}.

b How many litres have they after three days?

c Their store holds 120 litres. Will they ever run out of storage space? Justify your answer.

10 Prove that the quadrilateral with vertices A(2, −5), B(4, −1), C(0, 1) and D(−2, −3) is a square.

11 a Express $1 - 8x - 2x^2$ in the form $a(x + p)^2 + q$.

b Hence write down the maximum or minimum value (say which) of:

(i) $1 - 8x - 2x^2$

(ii) $\dfrac{4}{1 - 8x - 2x^2}$ when $1 - 8x - 2x^2 > 0$.

12 a Sketch the graph $y = \sin\dfrac{2x}{3}$ for $0 \leqslant x \leqslant 3\pi$.

b On the same diagram as in **a**, sketch:

(i) $y = 2\sin\dfrac{2x}{3}$

(ii) $y = \sin\dfrac{2x}{3} - 1$.

13 Calculate, correct to 0.1°, the acute angle between the tangents to the curve $y = \dfrac{x^2 + 1}{x}$ at the points where $x = 1$ and $x = \frac{1}{2}$.

14 A displacement s cm at time t seconds is given by $s = t^3 + t^2 - 1$. Calculate:

a the velocity and acceleration at $t = 2$

b the velocity when the acceleration is 20 cm/s².

15 A parabola has equation $y = ax^2 + bx + c$. It passes through the origin, and the tangent at (1, 0) on it makes an angle of 45° with OX. Find the actual equation of the parabola.

16 Solve the equations:

a $\sin(2x - 40)^\circ = 0$ for $0 \leqslant x \leqslant 360$

b $5\cos\left(2\theta - \dfrac{\pi}{4}\right) = 2$, for $0 \leqslant \theta \leqslant \pi$, correct to 1 decimal place.

REVIEW C

1 Functions f and g are defined by $f(x) = 2x + 1$ and $g(x) = x^2$.

a Show that $g(f(x)) - f(g(x)) = 2x^2 + 4x$.

b Solve $g(f(x)) - f(g(x)) = 0$, and show the solutions on a sketch of $y = g(f(x)) - f(g(x))$.

c Hence solve the inequality $g(f(x)) - f(g(x)) \leqslant 0$.

2 A sequence is defined by the relation $u_{n+1} = -0.3u_n + 1.5$, with $u_1 = 2$. Calculate:

a u_2, u_3, u_4

b the limit of u_n as $n \to \infty$.

3 A is the point (2, 5). P lies on the line $y = -1$, and the gradient of AP is $-\frac{1}{2}$. Find the x-coordinate of P.

4 a Find the equation of the tangent to the parabola $y = 1 - \frac{1}{9}x^2$ at C.

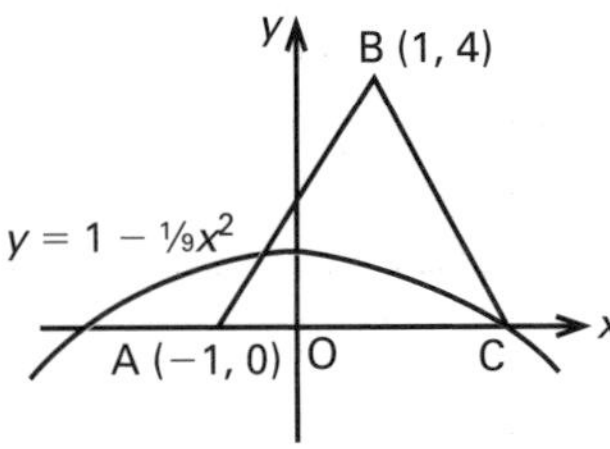

b Show that the tangent is a median of ΔABC.

c Find the point of intersection of the medians of ΔABC.

5 $f(x) = 2x^2 + 4ax + 1$, where a is a constant.

a Complete the square of the quadratic.

b The minimum value of the quadratic is −7. Find the possible values of a.

6 Solve these equations:

a $4\cos^2 x^\circ = 3$, for $0 \leqslant x \leqslant 360$

b $\tan\left(\theta + \dfrac{\pi}{6}\right) = -2$, correct to 2 decimal places, for $0 \leqslant \theta \leqslant 2\pi$.

7 **a** Determine the stationary points, and their nature, of the curve $y = x^3 - 12x$.
b Sketch the curve.
c Show that the tangent to the curve at $x = -1$ passes through the minimum turning point of the curve.

8 The parabola $y = f(x)$ has a maximum TP at $x = 1$, and the gradient of the tangent at $x = 6$ is -4.

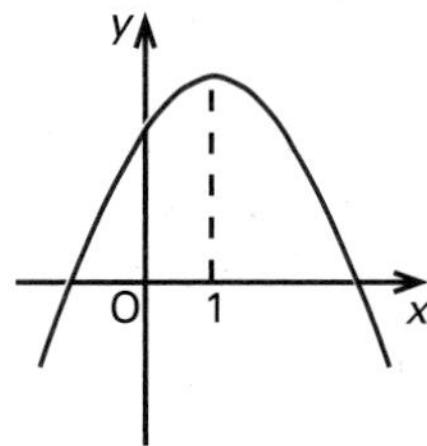

a Sketch the graph $y = f'(x)$, and find its equation.
b Find the gradient of the parabola where it cuts the y-axis.

9 The equation of the curve is $y = a\sin(x - b)$ for $0 \leqslant x \leqslant 2\pi$.

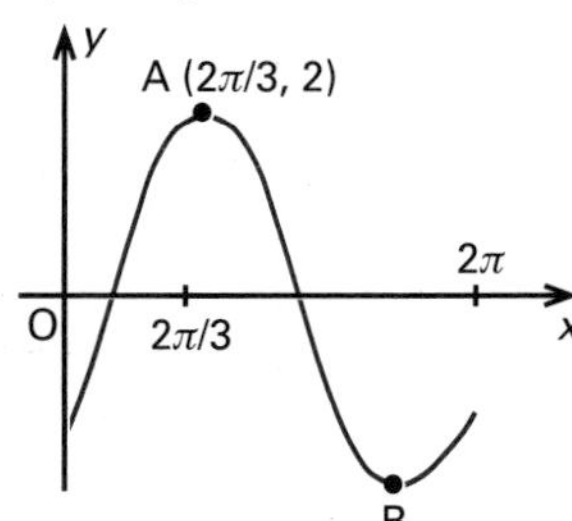

a Write down the value of a, and calculate the value of b.
b Write down the coordinates of B.
c Solve the equation $a\sin(x - b) = 1$, with your values of a and b, and show the solutions on a sketch.

10 Each stroke of a pump increases a tyre's pressure by 3 units. But the valve is leaking, and at the start of each stroke the pressure falls by 8%.
a If P_n is the pressure in the tyre after n strokes, write down a recurrence relation.
b The tyre pressure's safety range is 30 to 37 units inclusive. If the pressure is 28 units, how many strokes are needed for the pressure to reach the safety range?
c Is it safe to continue to operate the pump indefinitely?

11 **a** Find the equations of the straight lines through P$(-2, 3)$ which are parallel and perpendicular to the line $3y = 2x + 4$.
b The lines you have found cut the line $11x + 3y = 26$ at Q and R. Find:
(i) the coordinates of Q and R
(ii) the exact length of QR.

12 $f(x) = x^{3/2} + x^{1/2}$. Find x for which $f'(x) = 2$.

13 A window consists of a rectangle and a semicircle of glass.

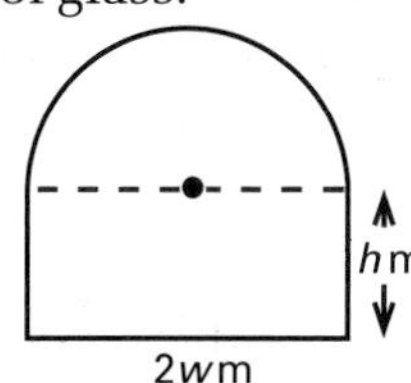

a If its perimeter is 6 m, show that $2h = 6 - 2w - \pi w$.
b Show that the area, A m^2, of the window is given by $A = 6w - 2w^2 - \frac{1}{2}\pi w^2$.
c Find w and h, correct to 2 decimal places, for maximum area of glass.

14 For a geometric sequence, $u_n = ar^{n-1}$, $n \geqslant 1$.
a Give formulae for u_1, u_2, u_3, u_4 in terms of a and r.
b If $u_2 = 6$ and $u_4 = 54$, find a and r.
c Write down the first four terms of the two possible sequences.

U·N·I·T·2

1.1 Polynomials

Introduction

An expression of the form $a_n x^n + a_{n-1}x^{n-1} + \ldots + a_3x^3 + a_2x^2 + a_1x + a_0$, with $a_0, \ldots, a_n$ constants and $a_n \neq 0$, is called a *polynomial* of degree n.

Examples of polynomials: $x^2 + 2x - 5$, $x^3 - x^2 + x + 3$, $4x - 1$.

If $f(x) = 4x^3 - 3x^2 + 2x - 7$, its value for $x = 5$ is

$f(5) = 4 \times 5^3 - 3 \times 5^2 + 2 \times 5 - 7 = 428$.

A very useful way to calculate $f(5)$ is by means of the *nested form* of the polynomial, where

$4x^3 - 3x^2 + 2x - 7 = (4x^2 - 3x + 2)x - 7 = [(4x - 3)x + 2]x - 7$.

The calculation can be arranged like this, using the coefficients of the terms and adding the numbers in each column:

5	4		−3		2		−7	
	↓	×5 ↗	20	×5 ↗	85	×5 ↗	435	
	4		17		87		428	$= f(5)$

Example Calculate the value of $2x^3 + 4x^2 - 10$ when $x = -3$.

There is no x-term, so the coefficients are 2, 4, 0, −10.

−3	2	4	0	−10	
	↓	−6	6	−18	
	2	−2	6	−28	$= f(-3)$.

The value of the polynomial is −28.

EXERCISE 1

1 Use the nested calculation scheme to calculate the value of each polynomial.

a $x^2 + 3x + 1$, $x = 4$
b $3x^2 - 2x + 5$, $x = 2$
c $5x^2 - 3x - 11$, $x = -1$
d $x^3 + x^2 + 3x - 6$, $x = 3$
e $x^3 - 2x^2 - 2x - 3$, $x = 4$
f $u^3 - 3u^2 - 9u - 3$, $u = -2$
g $5t^3 - 2t + 3$, $t = 5$ (coefficient of $t^2 = 0$!)
h $t^3 + 3t^2 - 5$, $t = -2$
i $x^4 - 3x^3 + 2x^2 + x + 1$, $x = -3$

2 Use nested calculation to check that each equation has the given number as a root.

a $x^3 - 2x - 4 = 0$, $x = 2$ (show that $f(2) = 0$)
b $2x^4 - 3x^3 - 17x^2 + 27x - 9 = 0$, $x = 1$
c $2t^3 + t^2 - 25t + 12 = 0$, $t = 3$
d $6u^3 + 13u^2 - 14u + 3 = 0$, $u = -3$

3 $f(x) = x^4 + 3ax^3 - 3a^2x^2 - 11a^3x - 6a^4$. Show that $x = -a$, $x = 2a$ and $x = -3a$ are all roots of the equation $f(x) = 0$.

4 Use a calculator and the nested calculation scheme to evaluate:

a $3x^3 - 2x^2 + 5x - 4$, when $x = 1.2$

b $2x^4 - x^2 + 2x - 1$, when $x = 2.5$

c $2x^3 - 3x^2 + 2x - 1$, when $x = 0.43$.

Division of polynomials

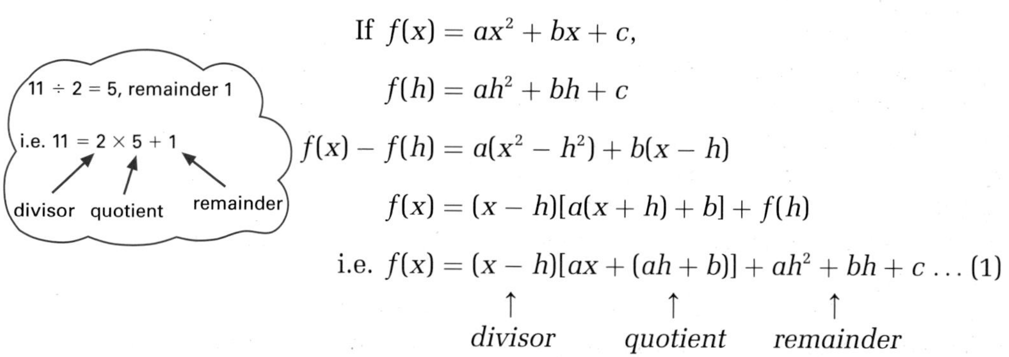

$$\text{If } f(x) = ax^2 + bx + c,$$

$$f(h) = ah^2 + bh + c$$

$$f(x) - f(h) = a(x^2 - h^2) + b(x - h)$$

$$f(x) = (x - h)[a(x + h) + b] + f(h)$$

$$\text{i.e. } f(x) = \underset{\text{divisor}}{(x - h)}\,[\underset{\text{quotient}}{ax + (ah + b)}] + \underset{\text{remainder}}{ah^2 + bh + c} \ldots (1)$$

Using the nested calculation scheme for $f(h)$:

$$\begin{array}{c|ccc} h & a & b & c \\ & \downarrow & ah & (ah+b)h \\ \hline & a & ah+b & ah^2+bh+c \end{array}$$

coefficients of quotient in (1) (a, $ah + b$); *remainder in* (1) ($ah^2 + bh + c$)

So the nested calculation scheme provides the quotient and the remainder when $f(x)$ is divided by $x - h$. This process is called *synthetic division*.

Example Find the quotient and remainder when $x^3 + 6x^2 + 3x - 15$ is divided by $x + 3$.

The divisor is $x - (-3)$.

$$\begin{array}{c|cccc} -3 & 1 & 6 & 3 & -15 \\ & \downarrow & -3 & -9 & 18 \\ \hline & 1 & 3 & -6 & 3 \end{array}$$

The quotient is $x^2 + 3x - 6$, and the remainder is 3.
So $x^3 + 6x^2 + 3x - 15 = (x + 3)(x^2 + 3x - 6) + 3$.

EXERCISE 2

Use synthetic division to find the quotient and remainder when each polynomial is divided by the given divisor.

	Polynomial	Divisor		Polynomial	Divisor
1	$x^2 + 2x - 2$	$x - 1$	**7**	$2x^2 + x - 2$	$x - \frac{1}{2}$
2	$2x^2 - x - 3$	$x + 2$ (i.e. $x - (-2)$)	**8**	$4x^2 + 2x + 3$	$x + \frac{1}{2}$
3	$x^3 + x^2 + x - 1$	$x + 1$	**9**	$x^3 - 1$	$x - 1$
4	$x^3 - x^2 + 3x - 4$	$x - 2$	**10**	$x^3 + 8$	$x + 2$
5	$2t^3 + 6t^2 + 33$	$t + 4$	**11**	$t^6 + 1$	$t - 1$
6	$3u^3 - 13u^2 - 50$	$u - 5$			

Division by ax + b

Example Find the quotient and remainder when $4x^3 - 2x + 5$ is divided by $2x + 1$.

$2x + 1 = 2(x + \frac{1}{2}) = 2(x - (-\frac{1}{2}))$

$$\begin{array}{r|rrrr} -\frac{1}{2} & 4 & 0 & -2 & 5 \\ & \downarrow & -2 & 1 & \frac{1}{2} \\ \hline & 4 & -2 & -1 & \boxed{5\frac{1}{2}} \end{array}$$

So $4x^3 - 2x + 5 = (x + \frac{1}{2})(4x^2 - 2x - 1) + 5\frac{1}{2}$

$= (2x + 1)(2x^2 - x - \frac{1}{2}) + 5\frac{1}{2} \ldots$

to return to the original divisor, $2x + 1$ ($\times 2$, $\div 2$).

The quotient is $2x^2 - x - \frac{1}{2}$ and the remainder is $5\frac{1}{2}$.

12 Find the quotients and remainders for:

	Polynomial	Divisor		Polynomial	Divisor
a	$2x^2 - x - 3$	$2x - 1$	**c**	$4t^3 + 6t^2 - 2t - 1$	$2t + 1$
b	$3x^2 - 5x + 7$	$3x + 1$	**d**	$3x^3 - 2x + 5$	$2x + 1$

The remainder theorem and the factor theorem

(i) In the last section you saw that when a quadratic polynomial $f(x) = ax^2 + bx + c$ is divided by $x - h$, the remainder is $f(h)$. It is easy to prove that this is true for all polynomials.

Proof If R is the remainder and $q(x)$ the quotient when polynomial $f(x)$ is divided by $x - h$, R is a constant (of degree 0).

Then $f(x) = (x - h)q(x) + R$, an *identity*, i.e. true for all values of x,

and $f(h) = (h - h)q(h) + R$

$= 0 \times q(h) + R$

$f(h) = R$. So $f(x) = (x - h)q(x) + f(h)$

The remainder theorem: When a polynomial $f(x)$ is divided by $x - h$ the remainder is $f(h)$.

(ii) If $f(h) = 0$, then $f(x) = (x - h)q(x)$; so $x - h$ is a factor of $f(x)$. Conversely, if $f(x) = (x - h)q(x)$, then $f(h) = 0$.
The factor theorem: $x - h$ is a factor of polynomial $f(x) \Leftrightarrow f(h) = 0$.

Example Find the factors of $f(x) = 2x^3 - 11x^2 + 17x - 6$.

Try factors of 6, i.e. $\pm1, \pm2, \pm3, \pm6$.

1	2	−11	17	−6
	↓	2	−9	8
	2	−9	8	2 ≠ 0

$x - 1$ *is not a factor.*

−1	2	−11	17	−6
	↓	−2	13	−30
	2	−13	30	−36 ≠ 0

$x + 1$ *is not a factor.*

2	2	−11	17	−6
	↓	4	−14	6
	2	−7	3	0

$x - 2$ *is a factor.*

So $f(x) = (x - 2)(2x^2 - 7x + 3)$

$= (x - 2)(2x - 1)(x - 3)$, by factorising the quadratic.

Only rational factors, like $x - 3$ and $2x + 1$, in which the coefficients are rational numbers, are included here.

EXERCISE 3

1 Show by means of the factor theorem that:
- **a** $x - 3$ and $x + 2$ are factors of $x^2 - x - 6$
- **b** $x - 2$ is a factor of $2x^3 + x^2 - 13x + 6$
- **c** $x + 1$ is a factor of $x^5 + 1$.

2 Which of the following are factors of $x^3 - 3x^2 - 10x + 24$?

a $x - 1$ **b** $x + 1$ **c** $x - 2$ **d** $x + 2$
e $x - 3$ **f** $x + 3$ **g** $x - 4$ **h** $x + 4$

Factorise the polynomials in questions **3–12**.

3 $x^3 - x^2 - x + 1$

4 $x^3 - 3x - 2$

5 $x^3 - 7x + 6$

6 $x^3 - 2x^2 + 4x - 8$

7 $3x^3 - 2x^2 - 19x - 6$

8 $x^3 + 3x^2 - 9x - 27$

9 $x^3 + 3x^2 + 3x + 1$

10 $6x^3 + 13x^2 + x - 2$

11 $x^4 - 5x^2 + 4$

12 $x^4 - 1$

13 Show that $x - h$ is a factor of $x^n - h^n$.

14 $x + 1$ is a factor of $f(x) = x^3 + x^2 - 4x + a$. Find a, and factorise $f(x)$ fully.

15 $x - 3$ is a factor of $g(x) = 2x^3 - 9x^2 + kx - 3$. Find k, and factorise $g(x)$ fully.

16 Find a so that $x - 4$ is a factor of $h(x) = x^3 - 5x^2 - ax + 80$, then factorise $h(x)$ fully.

17 Find b so that $x + 3$ is a factor of $k(x) = x^3 + bx^2 + 7x - 15$, then factorise $k(x)$ fully.

18 When $x^4 - x^3 + x^2 + ax + b$ is divided by $x - 1$ the remainder is 0, and when divided by $x - 2$ the remainder is 11. Find a and b.

19 Show that $2x + 1$ is a factor of $2x^3 - 5x^2 + x + 2$, and find the other factors.

20 Show that $3x - 2$ is a factor of $12x^3 - 20x^2 - x + 6$ and find the other factors.

21 $2x - 1$ is a factor of $f(x) = 2x^3 - 17x^2 + 40x + p$. Find p, and factorise $f(x)$ fully.

Solving polynomial equations

We use the fact that:
$x - h$ is a factor of $f(x) \Leftrightarrow h$ is a root of the equation $f(x) = 0$.

Example Solve the equation $x^3 - 2x^2 - x + 2 = 0$.

Let $f(x) = x^3 - 2x^2 - x + 2$. To find a factor of $f(x)$, try factors of 2, i.e. $\pm1, \pm2$.

$$\begin{array}{c|cccc} 1 & 1 & -2 & -1 & 2 \\ & \downarrow & 1 & -1 & -2 \\ \hline & 1 & -1 & -2 & \boxed{0} \end{array}$$

So $x - 1$ is a factor, and $f(x) = (x - 1)(x^2 - x - 2) = (x - 1)(x + 1)(x - 2)$.
The equation is $(x - 1)(x + 1)(x - 2) = 0$, so $x = 1, -1$ or 2.

EXERCISE 4

Solve the equations in questions **1–6**.

1 $x^3 + x^2 - x - 1 = 0$

2 $x^3 - 2x^2 - 2x + 4 = 0$

3 $x^3 + 2x^2 - 4x - 8 = 0$

4 $x^3 - 3x^2 - 16x + 48 = 0$

5 $x^3 + 3x^2 + 6x + 18 = 0$

6 $2x^3 - 3x^2 - 18x + 27 = 0$

7 $x = 1$ is a root of the equation $x^3 - 4x^2 + 5x + k = 0$. Find k, and the other two roots of the equation.

8 Show that $x^3 + x^2 + 2x + 2 = 0$ has only one real root.

9 $x = 2$ is a root of $x^3 - 10x^2 + 31x - k = 0$. Find k, and the other two roots of the equation.

10 $x - 1$ is a factor of the polynomial $f(x) = x^3 + kx^2 + 5x - 14$.
a Find k, then factorise $f(x)$ fully. **b** Solve the equation $f(x) = 0$.

11 **a** Solve the equation $x^3 - 9x^2 + 26x - 24 = 0$.
b State the coordinates of the points where the curve $y = x^3 - 9x^2 + 26x - 24$ cuts the x-axis.

12 Find the points where the curve $y = x^3 + 3x^2 - 4$ cuts the x-axis.

13 This rectangular crate has a volume of 36 m³.
a Form a polynomial equation in x.
b Solve the equation, and find the length of a side of the base.

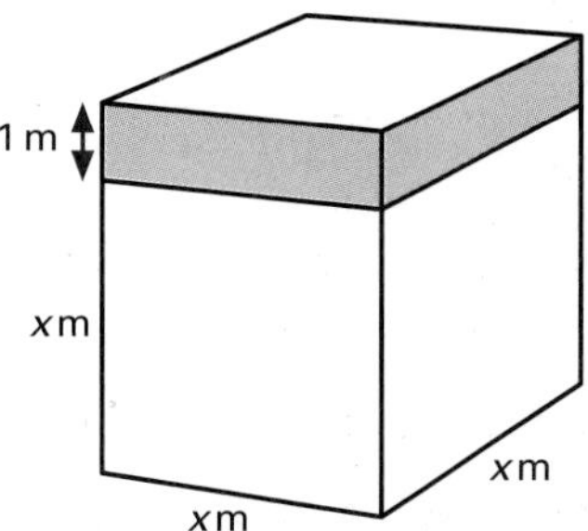

14 The value £V million of the daily print run of the *Daily Cheer* in year y is given by the formula $V = y^3 - 6y^2 + 11y + 4$. Make a polynomial equation, and solve it to find the years in which the value was £10 million.

15 t seconds after the van hits the motorway crash barrier the sideways displacement d cm is given by $d = 15t(t^3 - 6t - 9)$. How long after impact does the barrier take to return to its original position?

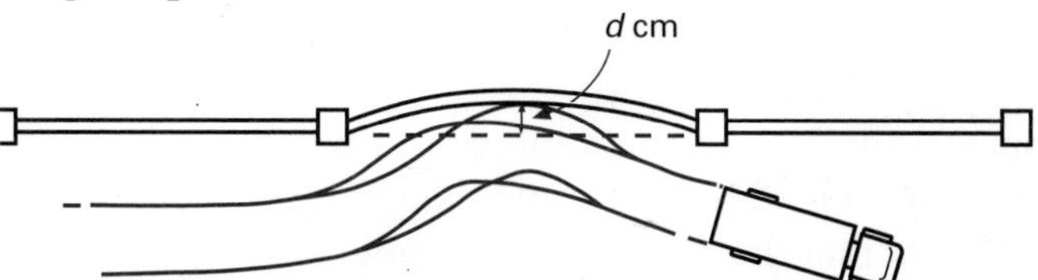

16 A planet's sun is becoming warmer. Its surface temperature t °C after y million years is given by $t = 10y^3 - 100y^2 + 270y - 180$.
a How long will it be until the present ice age on the planet ends (i.e. the ice melts)?
b **(i)** When will the next ice age begin?
(ii) How long will it last?

17 An iceberg under tow from Antarctica to Africa has volume V after n days, given by $V = \frac{500\pi}{3}(2000 - 100n + 20n^2 - n^3)$.
How long will it be until the ice melts completely?

Approximate roots of f(x) = 0

The last section gave a technique for solving the equation $f(x) = 0$, provided that the roots are rational. If they are not, then a step-by-step method can be used in order to find approximate values of the roots.

Example Show that $x^3 - 3x + 1 = 0$ has a real root between 1 and 2. Find an approximation for the root, correct to 1 decimal place.
Let $f(x) = x^3 - 3x + 1$.

Step 1 $\left.\begin{array}{l} f(1) = -1 \\ f(2) = 3 \end{array}\right\}$ so graph $y = f(x)$ crosses the x-axis between $x = 1$ and $x = 2$, indicating a root α there.

Step 2 $\left.\begin{array}{l} f(1.5) \doteqdot -0.13 \\ f(1.6) \doteqdot 0.30 \end{array}\right\} 1.5 < \alpha < 1.6.$

$f(1.55) \doteqdot 0.07$

$\left.\begin{array}{l} f(1.54) \doteqdot 0.03 \\ f(1.53) \doteqdot -0.01 \end{array}\right\} 1.53 < \alpha < 1.54.$

So $\alpha = 1.5$, correct to 1 decimal place.

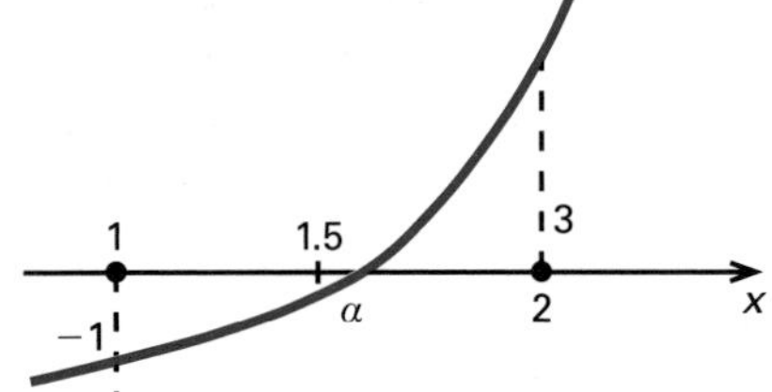

EXERCISE 5

1 Show that $x^3 - x - 1 = 0$ has a real root between 1 and 2. Find an approximation for the root, correct to 1 decimal place.

2 Show that $x^3 + x - 3 = 0$ has a real root between 1 and 1.5, and find an approximation, correct to 1 decimal place.

3 Show that $x^3 - 4x + 2 = 0$ has a real root between 0.5 and 1, and find an approximation, correct to 1 decimal place.

4 The Allshapes Manufacturing Company makes containers for fruit juice. Its design department is struggling with three orders.

a The first customer wants cuboid containers holding 200 ml of juice, with each edge differing in length by 1 cm as shown. Show that the design department has to solve the equation $x^3 + 3x^2 + 2x - 200 = 0$, and help them to find x, to the nearest millimetre.

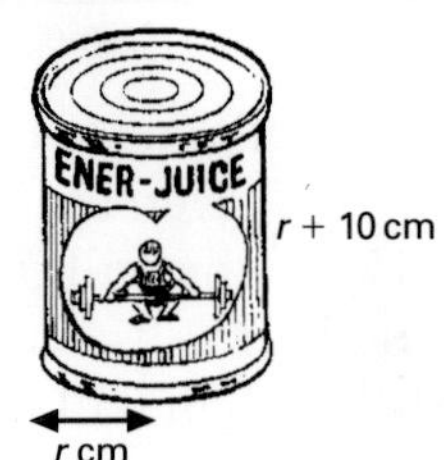

b The second customer wants his product to be sold in cylindrical cans holding 1 litre, with height 10 cm more than the radius. Show that the equation this time is $r^3 + 10r^2 - 318 = 0$, and find r, to the nearest millimetre. $\left(\text{Take 318 as an approximation for } \dfrac{1000}{\pi}.\right)$

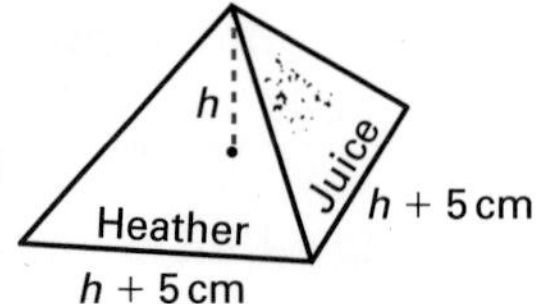

c The third customer has asked for containers in the shape of square pyramids, holding 250 ml, with side of base 5 cm more than the height. Find an equation, and hence an approximation for h, correct to the nearest millimetre.

CHAPTER 1.1 REVIEW

1 $f(x) = x^2 - 5x + 6$. Calculate:
 a $f(0)$ b $f(2)$ c $f(-2)$.

2 $g(x) = x^3 - 2x^2 + 3x - 4$. Calculate:
 a $g(1)$ b $g(-1)$ c $g(10)$.

3 Use the nested calculation scheme to calculate the value of:
 a $2x^3 - x + 7$ when $x = 5$ (no x^2 term!)
 b $t^4 - 3t^3 + 5t^2 + 4$ when $t = -2$.

4 Use synthetic division to find the quotient and remainder in each case.
 a $3x^3 - x^2 + 2x - 5$, divided by $x - 2$
 b $2x^4 + 5x^3 + x + 7$, divided by $x + 3$
 c $2x^4 + x^3 - 3x^2 + 3x - 4$, divided by $2x - 1$

5 Factorise:
 a $x^3 - x^2 - 5x - 3$
 b $x^3 - 4x^2 - 11x + 30$
 c $2x^4 - 5x^2 - 12$
 d $x^3 - 2x^2 - 2x - 3$.

6 Find a if $2x^3 + x^2 + ax - 8$ is divisible by $x + 2$.

7 $2x^3 - 3x^2 + px + q$ has a factor $x + 1$. Show that $q = p + 5$.

8 Find m and n if $x - 1$ and $x + 1$ are factors of $2x^3 + 3x^2 + mx + n$.

9 When $x^3 + x^2 + ax + b$ is divided by $x - 2$ the remainder is 0, and when it is divided by $x + 2$ the remainder is 12. Find the values of a and b.

10 Solve the equations:
 a $x^3 - 19x + 30 = 0$
 b $x^4 - 3x^2 - 2x = 0$

11 Find the roots of these equations:
 a $x^3 + 3x^2 + 2x + 6 = 0$
 b $x^3 + 4x^2 + x - 6 = 0$.

12 Find the points where the curve $y = x^3 + 7x^2 + 4x - 12$ cuts the x-axis.

13 Find the coordinates of the points where the line $y = 4x - 2$ meets the curve $y = x^3 + x$.

14 Show that:
 a $x = 1$ is a solution of the equation $x^3 - 3x^2 + 2 = 0$
 b there is another solution of the equation between $x = 2$ and $x = 3$, and find it, correct to 1 decimal place.

15 a Show that the equation $x^3 - x^2 + x + 1 = 0$ has a root between -1 and 0.
 b Use iteration (step-by-step process) to find the root, correct to 2 decimal places.

16 The height, h metres, of a toy rocket t seconds after firing, is given by $h(t) = 3t - t^3$. Show that the rocket reaches a height of 1 metre between $t = 0.3$ and $t = 0.4$, and use iteration to find this time, correct to 2 decimal places.

17 Find, correct to 1 decimal place, the solution of the equation $x^3 - 2x + 3 = 0$ which lies between -1 and -2.

CHAPTER 1.1 SUMMARY

1 $a_nx^n + a_{n-1}x^{n-1} + \ldots + a_2x^2 + a_1x + a_0$, where $a_0, a_1, \ldots, a_n$ are constants and $a_n \neq 0$, is a *polynomial* in x of degree n.

2 If a polynomial $f(x)$ is divided by $x - h$ to give a quotient $q(x)$ and a remainder R, then $f(x) = (x - h)q(x) + R$.

3 If $ax^3 + bx^2 + cx + d$ is divided by $x - h$ the quotient and remainder can be found using the following scheme, called *synthetic division*:

4 THE REMAINDER THEOREM
When a polynomial $f(x)$ is divided by $x - h$, the remainder is $f(h)$.

5 THE FACTOR THEOREM
If $f(x)$ is a polynomial, $f(h) = 0 \Leftrightarrow x - h$ is a factor of $f(x)$.

6 POLYNOMIAL EQUATIONS $f(x) = 0$
If $x - h$ is a factor of $f(x)$, h is a root of the equation $f(x) = 0$. Approximate solutions can be found by an iterative (step-by-step) process.

h	a	b	c	d
	$\downarrow$	ah	$ah^2 + bh$	$ah^3 + bh^2 + ch$
	a	$ah + b$	$ah^2 + bh + c$	$ah^3 + bh^2 + ch + d$
	coefficients of quotient			*remainder* $= f(h)$

(Arrows marked $\times h$ lead diagonally from each bottom-row entry to the next column.)

1.2 Quadratic Theory

Introduction

1 A sky rocket rises s metres vertically in t seconds, where $s = 80t - 5t^2$.
What is the maximum height that it reaches?

2 Is the line $y = 2x - 1$ a tangent to the parabola $y = x^2$?

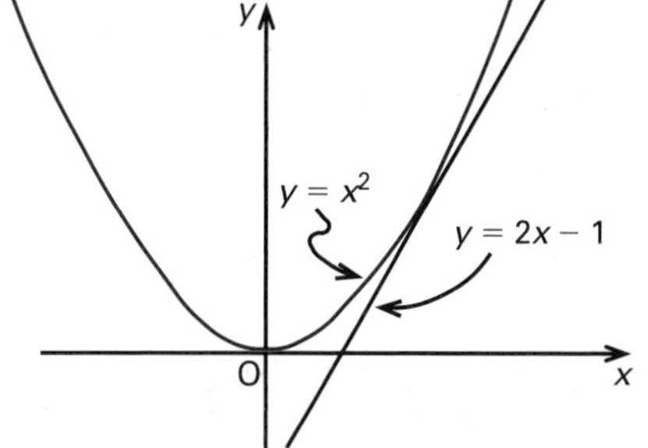

3 The cost (in £) to a small firm of making x guitars is $C = 10x + 500$.
The income (in £) arising from the sale of these guitars is $I = 15x + x^2$.
How many guitars does the firm need to sell to break even?

The solution to these and many other questions can be found by using 'quadratic theory'.

Reminders

(i) $f(x) = ax^2 + bx + c$, $a \neq 0$, is a *quadratic function.*

(ii) $3x^2 + 2x - 1$ is a *quadratic expression*, with $a = 3$, $b = 2$ and $c = -1$.

(iii) $3x^2 + 2x - 1 = 0$ is a quadratic equation, and this one can be solved by factors:

$(3x - 1)(x + 1) = 0$

$3x - 1 = 0$ or $x + 1 = 0$

$x = \frac{1}{3}$ or -1

(iv) A quadratic equation with roots 2 and -3 is $(x - 2)(x + 3) = 0$, i.e. $x^2 + x - 6 = 0$.

EXERCISE 1 (REVISION)

1 Comparing each quadratic expression with $ax^2 + bx + c$, write down the values of a, b, c in:

a $6x^2 - 7x + 1$ **b** $x^2 + 2x - 3$ **c** $2x^2$
d $4 + 3x - x^2$ **e** $7 - 3x^2$ **f** $4x - 10x^2$.

2 Factorise:

a $t^2 + t - 2$ **b** $p^2 - 6p + 8$ **c** $n^2 - 2n + 1$
d $2x^2 + x - 3$ **e** $x^2 - 14x + 49$ **f** $2y^2 - 7y + 6$
g $m^2 - 1$ **h** $4n^2 - 9$ **i** $16 - 25r^2$.

3 Solve these quadratic equations by factors:

a $t^2 + 2t - 3 = 0$ **b** $x^2 + 5x + 6 = 0$ **c** $p^2 + 16p + 15 = 0$
d $y^2 - 2y - 8 = 0$ **e** $9x^2 - 6x + 1 = 0$ **f** $y^2 - 9 = 0$
g $2r^2 - r = 0$ **h** $2q^2 + 4q = 0$ **i** $2x^2 - 5x - 3 = 0$
j $4d^2 - 12d + 9 = 0$ **k** $x(x-1) = 12$ **l** $y(y+2) = 15$
m $t^2 = t + 2$ **n** $3x^2 + 5x = -2$.

4 Write down, then simplify, quadratic equations with roots:

a 1, 2 **b** −3, −4 **c** −1, 3 **d** 0, −5.

Solving quadratic equations in general

When the quadratic expression cannot be factorised easily we have to use other methods of solving the quadratic equation.

Method 1	*Method 2*	*Example*
Completing the square	*The quadratic formula*	*Using the formula*
$x^2 - 2x - 4 = 0$	$ax^2 + bx + c = 0$	Solve $3x^2 + 4x - 5 = 0$. Here $a = 3$, $b = 4$, $c = -5$.
$(x-1)^2 - 1^2 - 4 = 0$	$x^2 + \frac{b}{a}x + \frac{c}{a} = 0$	$x = \frac{-b \pm \sqrt{b^2 - 4ac}}{2a}$
$(x-1)^2 = 5$	$\left(x + \frac{b}{2a}\right)^2 - \left(\frac{b}{2a}\right)^2 + \frac{c}{a} = 0$	$= \frac{-4 \pm \sqrt{4^2 - 4 \times 3 \times (-5)}}{2 \times 3}$
$(x-1) = \sqrt{5}$ or $-\sqrt{5}$	$\left(x + \frac{b}{2a}\right)^2 = \frac{b^2 - 4ac}{4a^2}$	$= \frac{-4 \pm \sqrt{76}}{6}$
$x = 1 + \sqrt{5}$ or $1 - \sqrt{5}$	$x + \frac{b}{2a} = \frac{\pm\sqrt{b^2 - 4ac}}{2a}$	$= 0.79$ or -2.12,
$= 3.24$ or -1.24, correct to 2 decimal places.	$x = \frac{-b \pm \sqrt{b^2 - 4ac}}{2a}$	correct to 2 decimal places.

EXERCISE 2

1 Solve these equations by factors *and* by the quadratic formula, for practice.
a $x^2 + 3x + 2 = 0$ **b** $x^2 - x - 6 = 0$

2 Solve these, correct to 2 decimal places.
a $x^2 + 2x - 4 = 0$ **b** $x^2 + 5x + 2 = 0$
c $2x^2 + 3x - 4 = 0$ **d** $3x^2 - 6x + 2 = 0$

3 Arrange these equations in standard form, $ax^2 + bx + c = 0$, and solve them by factors, or by formula if necessary, correct to 2 decimal places.
a $y(3y + 5) + 2 = 0$ **b** $x(x + 3) = 1$
c $(2t - 1)^2 - 1 = 0$ **d** $(c - 1)(4 - c) = 2$
e $\frac{x^2 + 1}{x} = 2$ **f** $\frac{x}{2} + \frac{2}{x} = 3$

4 In question **3** of the Introduction, $C = 10x + 500$ and $I = 15x + x^2$. To break even, $C = I$. Make a quadratic equation and solve it to find the break-even number of guitars the firm must sell.

5 Prove that one root of the equation $x^2 + x - 3 = 0$ lies between 1 and 2, and then find it, correct to 2 decimal places, using the quadratic formula.

6 In the painting, the horizon is at B where
$\frac{AB}{BC} = \frac{AC}{AB}$, i.e. at the 'golden section' ratio.
a Taking $AC = 1$ and $AB = x$, show that $x^2 + x - 1 = 0$.
b Calculate the value of x exactly (in surd form).

Challenges

1 Solve the equation $x^4 - 2x^2 - 1$, giving the roots correct to 2 decimal places.

2 Investigate the relationships between the sum and the product of the roots of the equation $ax^2 + bx + c = 0$ and the coefficients a, b and c.

The discriminant

The solutions, or roots, of the quadratic equation $ax^2 + bx + c = 0$ are

$$x = \frac{-b + \sqrt{b^2 - 4ac}}{2a} \text{ and } x = \frac{-b - \sqrt{b^2 - 4ac}}{2a}.$$

When: (i) $b^2 - 4ac < 0$, there are no real roots

(ii) $b^2 - 4ac = 0$, the roots are equal; each root is $-\dfrac{b}{2a}$

(iii) $b^2 - 4ac > 0$, there are two real and distinct roots.

Since $b^2 - 4ac$ discriminates between the different types of roots, it is called the *discriminant* of the equation. These illustrations show the relations between the parabola $y = ax^2 + bx + c$ with $a > 0$, the roots of the equation $ax^2 + bx + c = 0$ and the discriminant $b^2 - 4ac$.

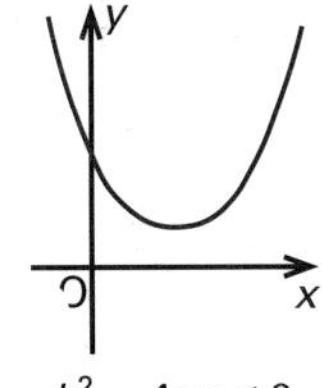

$b^2 - 4ac < 0$

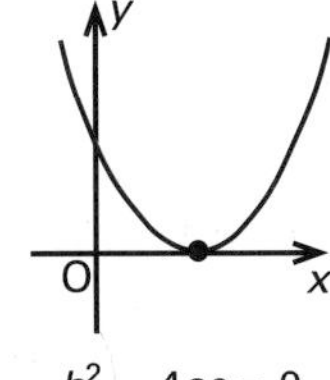

$b^2 - 4ac = 0$

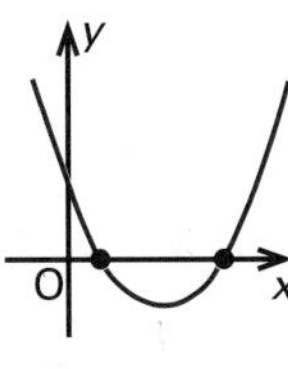

$b^2 - 4ac > 0$

Example Find m if the roots of $9x^2 - 12x + m = 0$ are: **a** equal **b** real and distinct.

$b^2 - 4ac = (-12)^2 - 4 \times 9 \times m = 144 - 36m$

a For equal roots, $144 - 36m = 0$, so $36m = 144$ and $m = 4$.

b For real and distinct roots, $144 - 36m > 0$, $36m < 144$ and $m < 4$.

EXERCISE 3

1 Decide the nature of the roots of each equation ('no real roots', 'equal roots' or 'real and distinct roots') by calculating its discriminant.

a $x^2 + 4x + 1 = 0$ **b** $t^2 - 3t + 4 = 0$

c $y^2 + y + 1 = 0$ **d** $9x^2 + 6x + 1 = 0$

e $3u^2 + u - 5 = 0$ **f** $3t^2 - 6t + 3 = 0$

g $2p(p + 1) = 3$ **h** $(t + 1)^2 + 2t^2 = 8t$

2 One of these equations has real and distinct roots, one has equal roots, one has no real roots. Which is which?

a $t^2 + 4t + 1 = 0$ **b** $x^2 - 8x + 16 = 0$ **c** $p^2 - 2p + 3 = 0$

3 Repeat question **2** for these three equations.

a $3y^2 - 5y + 4 = 0$ **b** $3 - 8t + 2t^2 = 0$ **c** $4u(u - 3) = -9$

4 For what values of p does the equation $x^2 - 2x + p = 0$ have:

a equal roots **b** real and distinct roots **c** no real roots?

5 Find m, given that $x^2 + (m + 1)x + 9 = 0$ has equal roots.

6 **(i)** Find the values of a, b and c if these equations have equal roots.
(ii) Calculate the value of the root in each case.
a $ax^2 + 4x + 2 = 0$ **b** $3x^2 + bx + 3 = 0$ **c** $x^2 + 6x + c = 0$

7 Show that the roots of the equation $(x - 2)(x - 3) = k^2$ are always real.

8 **a** For what values of t does $tx^2 + 6x + t = 0$ have equal roots?
b Find the nature of the roots if t lies between these values ($t \neq 0$).

9 **a** Find q for which $x^2 + (q - 3)x + 1 = 0$ has equal roots.
b Hence match each equation with its graph:
(i) $x^2 - x + 1 = 0$
(ii) $x^2 - 2x + 1 = 0$
(iii) $x^2 - 3x + 1 = 0$

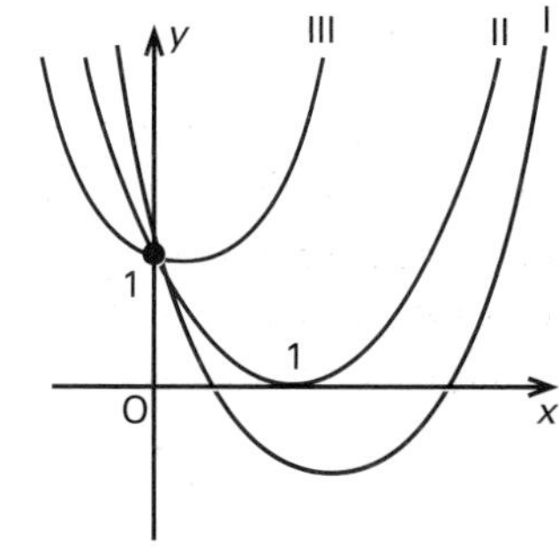

10 Find the values of a for which the equation $ax^2 + (a - 1)x + (7a - 2) = 0$ has equal roots.

11 Find the range of values of m for which $5x^2 - 3mx + 5 = 0$ has two real and distinct roots.

12 For what value of k does the graph $y = kx^2 - 3kx + 9$ touch the x-axis?

13 Find the values of n which ensure that these equations have equal roots.
a $\dfrac{x^2 + 1}{x} = n$ **b** $\dfrac{(x - 2)^2}{x^2 + 2} = n$

Tangents to curves

Example Find the value of c if the line $y = 5x + c$ is a tangent to the parabola $y = x^2 + 3x + 4$.

At their points of intersection, $x^2 + 3x + 4 = 5x + c$.
This is the quadratic equation
$x^2 - 2x + (4 - c) = 0 \ldots (1)$
Its discriminant is $(-2)^2 - 4 \times 1 \times (4 - c)$
$= 4 - 16 + 4c$
$= -12 + 4c$
For tangency, the line meets the curve in one point, so the quadratic equation has equal roots.
In this case, '$b^2 - 4ac = 0$', so $-12 + 4c = 0$, or $c = 3$, and the tangent is $y = 5x + 3$.

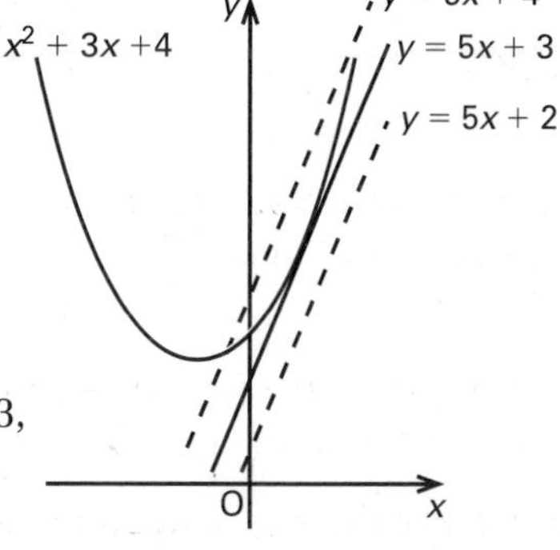

Note Equation (1) is now $x^2 - 2x + 1 = 0$, i.e. $(x - 1)^2 = 0$, from which $x = 1$. So the line $y = 5x + 3$ touches the parabola at the point $(1, 8)$.

a Draw the graphs $y = 2x^2 + 1$ and $y = 4 - x$. Use the cursor to find estimates for the x-coordinates of the points of intersection of the parabola and the straight line. Compare these with their exact values.
b Alter the term '$a =$' (4 in **a**) systematically to find when the line $y = a - x$ is a tangent to the curve.

EXERCISE 4

1 Show that the line $y = 4x - 4$ is a tangent to $y = x^2$, and find the point of contact.

2 Find out which of the lines $y = x + 2$ and $y = 6x - 9$ is a tangent to $y = x^2$, and find its point of contact.

3 Prove that $4x + y + 4 = 0$ is a tangent to $y = x^2$, and find the point of contact.

4 Show that each of these lines is a tangent to the parabola, and find its point of contact.
a $y = 1$, $y = x^2 + 1$ **b** $y = 4x$, $y = x^2 + 4$
c $y = 2x + 1$, $y = 4x - x^2$ **d** $y = 6 + 2x$, $y = 5 - x^2$

5 Prove that $y = 4(1 - x)$ is a tangent to the hyperbola $xy = 1$, and find the point of contact.

6 a Which of the lines $y = 4 - 2x$ and $y = 3 + 2x$ is a tangent to the hyperbola $xy = 2$?
b Find the point of contact of the tangent and the points of intersection with the hyperbola for the other line.

7 Find the point, or points, of intersection of the line $x + y + 3 = 0$ and the parabola $y = x^2 + x - 2$.

8 Answer question **2** in the Introduction on page 115.

9 a Show that the line $y = mx$ meets the parabola $y = x^2 + 1$ at points given by $x^2 - mx + 1 = 0$.
b For the line to be a tangent, this quadratic equation has equal roots, so '$b^2 - 4ac = 0$'. Find possible values of m, and write down the equations of the tangents.

10 a Show that the line $y = x + c$ meets the parabola $y = x^2 - 3x$ where $x^2 - 4x - c = 0$.
b Find c for the line to be a tangent to the parabola.
c Find the coordinates of the point of contact.

11 a Show that the line $y = 5x + c$ meets the parabola $y = 2x^2 + x - 5$ where $2x^2 - 4x + (-5 - c) = 0$.
b Find c for the line to be a tangent.
c Find the point of contact.

12 For what value of t is the line $x - y + t = 0$ a tangent to the curve $y^2 = 4x$?

13 a Find k if $y = x - k$ is a tangent to $x^2 + y^2 = 8$.
b Find the point of contact for each value of k.

14 **a** Find c if $y = c - x$ is a tangent to $x^2 + y^2 = 2$.
b What is the point of contact for each value of c?

Challenge

Can you sketch a line which crosses a curve but which is still a tangent to the curve? Try the line $x + y = 0$ and the curve $y = x^3 - 2x^2$.

Quadratic inequalities

Example 1 In making x machines, a firm's profit £P is given by $P = 100x - x^2$. How many machines will make:
a a profit **b** the maximum profit?

For a profit, $P(x) > 0$, so $100x - x^2 > 0$.
The graph $y = 100x - x^2$ will help us to solve the inequality.
When $x = 0$, $y = 0$.
When $y = 0$, $100x - x^2 = 0$

$$x(100 - x) = 0$$
$$x = 0 \text{ or } 100.$$

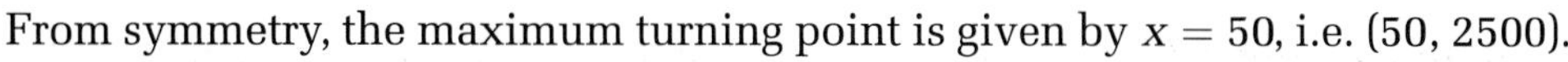

From symmetry, the maximum turning point is given by $x = 50$, i.e. (50, 2500).
a For a profit, $100x - x^2 > 0$, when $0 < x < 100$. So 1 to 99 machines will make a profit.
b For maximum profit, $x = 50$. So 50 machines will make the maximum profit.

Example 2 Solve the inequalities:
a $x^2 - 6x + 5 > 0$ **b** $x^2 - 6x + 5 \leqslant 0$
First sketch the parabola $y = x^2 - 6x + 5$.
When $x = 0$, $y = 5$; when $y = 0$, $(x - 1)(x - 5) = 0$ so $x = 1$ or 5, etc.

a Emphasise the curve where $y > 0$, and the corresponding values of x. Read off $x < 1$ or $x > 5$.

b Emphasise the curve where $y \leqslant 0$, and the corresponding values of x. Read off $1 \leqslant x \leqslant 5$.

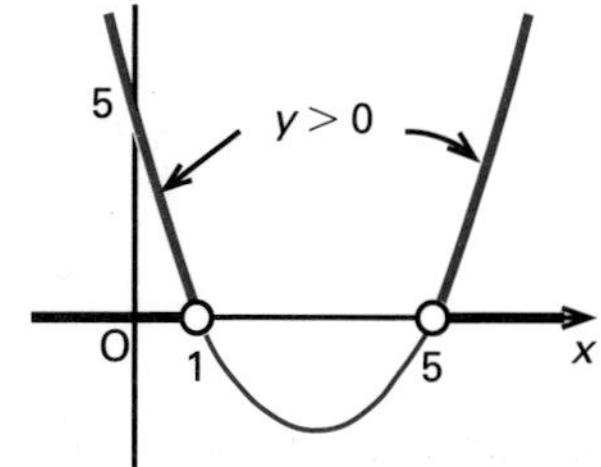

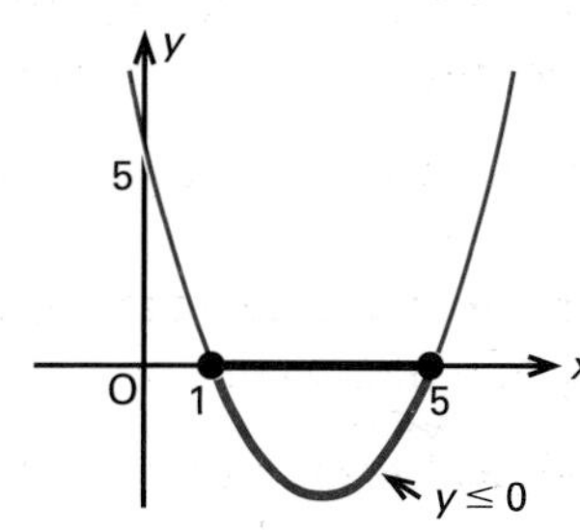

EXERCISE 5

1 Write down the values of x for which:
a $x^2 - 2x - 3 = 0$
b $x^2 - 2x - 3 > 0$.

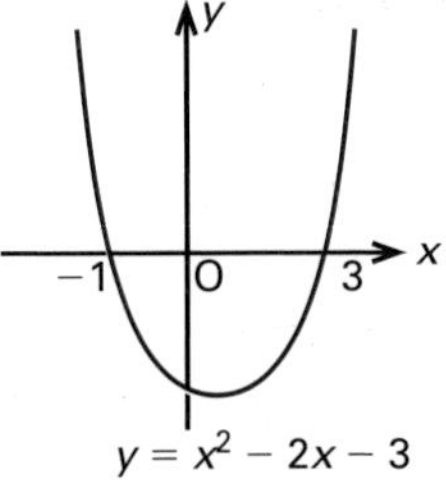

2 Write down the values of x for which:
a $-4 - 5x - x^2 = 0$
b $-4 - 5x - x^2 \leqslant 0$.

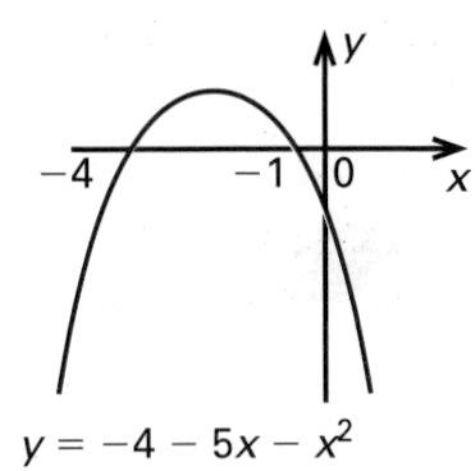

3 Write down the values of x for which:
a $x^2 - 9 = 0$
b $x^2 - 9 > 0$
c $x^2 - 9 \leqslant 0$.

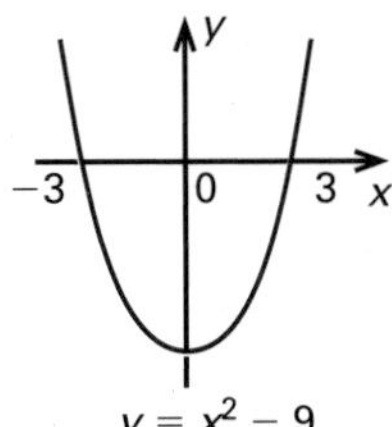

In questions **4–13**: **a** make a sketch **b** solve the inequality.

4 $y = (x + 1)(x - 1)$; $(x + 1)(x - 1) < 0$

5 $y = (x - 1)(x - 4)$; $(x - 1)(x - 4) > 0$

6 $y = (2 + x)(3 - x)$; $(2 + x)(3 - x) \geqslant 0$

7 $y = x(4 - x)$; $x(4 - x) \leqslant 0$

8 $(x + 5)(5 - x) > 0$

9 $(2x - 1)(x + 2) \geqslant 0$

10 $x^2 - x - 2 < 0$

11 $x - x^2 \leqslant 0$

12 $x^2 > 2x - 1$

13 $x(x + 4) \geqslant 5$

14 Two numbers differ by 1, and their product is less than 6. Construct an inequality, and solve it to find the possible range of values of the smaller number.

15 For each pair of functions f and g, solve these inequalities:
(i) $f(x) \geqslant g(x)$ **(ii)** $f(x) < g(x)$.
Deal with $f(x) - g(x)$ in each case.
a $f(x) = 5 - x^2$, $g(x) = x^2 - 3$ **b** $f(x) = 2x^2 + x - 3$, $g(x) = 4x + 2$

16 In the construction of an oil rig, the designers laid down these conditions for a rectangular helicopter landing pad:
(i) length to be 10 m more than breadth
(ii) area of pad to lie between 375 m^2 and 600 m^2.
Calculate the limits for the breadth of the pad.

CHAPTER 1.2 REVIEW

1 Factorise:
a $x^2 + 2x - 3$ **b** $p^2 - p - 12$
c $3t^2 - 2t - 5$.

2 Solve these quadratic equations:
a $x^2 + x - 6 = 0$ **b** $y^2 - 7y + 12 = 0$
c $6n^2 + n - 2 = 0$.

3 Write down, and simplify, quadratic equations with roots:
a 4, 2 **b** −3, −2 **c** −1, 5 **d** $\frac{1}{2}, \frac{1}{3}$

4 The area of a rectangular floor is 144 m^2. Its length is 10 m more than its breadth. Taking x m for the breadth, make an equation, and solve it to find the breadth and length.

5 Solve these equations, giving the roots correct to 2 decimal places. (First rearrange **c** and **d** in 'standard form'.)
a $x^2 - 2x - 4 = 0$ **b** $t^2 - 8t + 5 = 0$
c $3 + 2u - 2u^2 = 0$ **d** $(x - 1)(3x - 2) = 1$

6 For each of the following equations:
(**i**) calculate the discriminant
(**ii**) determine the nature of the roots.
a $2x^2 + 3x + 1 = 0$
b $3x^2 + 2x + 1 = 0$
c $4t^2 - 12t + 9 = 0$
d $y^2 - 5y + 1 = 0$
e $x(2x - 3) + 1 = 0$
f $(u - 1)^2 + 3(u - 1) - 3 = 0$

7 Find k if $(2k - 2)x^2 + 24x + k = 0$ has:
a equal roots
b real and distinct roots.

8 The flight of a comet as viewed from earth can be modelled by the equation $y = 5 - 4x - 2x^2$. The horizon can be represented by the line $y = k$, where k is a constant which depends on the observer's position.
A shows a location where the comet rises above the horizon and sets again.

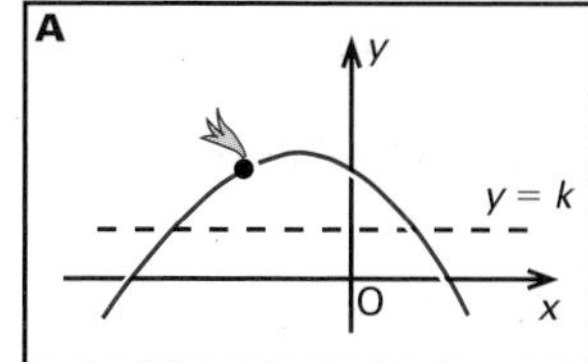

B shows a location where the observer is not going to see the comet.

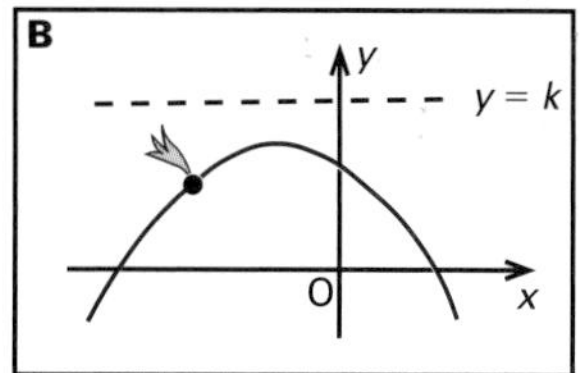

Solving the equation $(5 - k) - 4x - 2x^2 = 0$ will give the x-coordinates of the rising and setting points on the horizon. What values of k ensure a sighting of the comet?

9 Find a if the roots of the quadratic equation $x^2 + (2a + 1)x + a^2 = 0$ are not real.

10 Find the coordinates of the points in which each line meets the curve.
a $y = 2x - 5$, circle $x^2 + y^2 = 10$
b $y = -5x - 13$, parabola $y = 2x^2 + 3x - 5$
c $y = 4(x - 1)$, hyperbola $xy = 8$
What is the relationship between the line and the curve in **b**?

11 **a** Prove that the line $y = 3x + t$ meets the parabola $y = x^2 + 4$ where $x^2 - 3x + (4 - t) = 0$.
b Find the value of t for which the line is a tangent, and also find the point of contact.

12 Solve these quadratic inequalities.
a $4x^2 + 5x + 1 \leqslant 0$
b $x^2 + x + 2 > 0$
c $6 + x - x^2 \geqslant 0$
d $x^2 - 10x + 25 > 0$

13 The equation of this parabola is $y = x^2 + ax + b$.

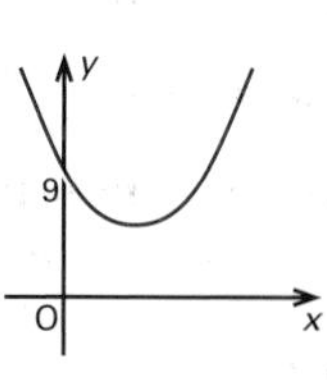

a What is the value of b?
b For what values of a does the parabola:
(**i**) touch the x-axis
(**ii**) cut the x-axis in two distinct points?

14 A toy firm has profits £P given by $P = -100 + 20x - 0.1x^2$. Find its maximum profit and the corresponding value of x.

CHAPTER 1.2 SUMMARY

1 Solving the quadratic equation
$ax^2 + bx + c = 0$
Methods: **(i)** factorisation
(ii) completing the square
(iii) using the quadratic formula

$$x = \frac{-b \pm \sqrt{b^2 - 4ac}}{2a}$$

(iv) drawing a graph, possibly on a graphics calculator.

2 The nature of the roots of the quadratic equation $ax^2 + bx + c = 0$
Use the discriminant $b^2 - 4ac$:
(i) $b^2 - 4ac < 0 \Rightarrow$ no real roots
(ii) $b^2 - 4ac = 0 \Rightarrow$ equal roots
(iii) $b^2 - 4ac > 0 \Rightarrow$ two real and distinct roots.

3 Tangents to curves
A tangent touches a curve at one point, so for this diagram the equation
$\frac{1}{x} = 2 - x$, i.e. $x^2 - 2x + 1 = 0$, or
$(x - 1)^2 = 0$, has equal roots. Notice that '$b^2 - 4ac$' $= (-2)^2 - 4 \times 1 \times 1 = 0$.

The tangent touches the curve at the point (1, 1).

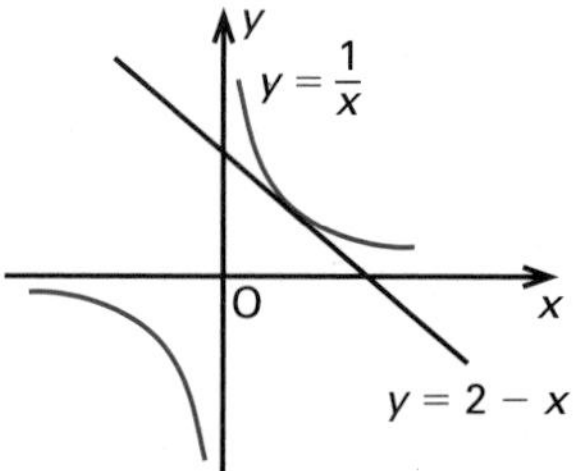

4 Solving the quadratic inequality
$ax^2 + bx + c > 0$ (or ≥ 0, < 0, ≤ 0)
(i) Sketch the curve $y = ax^2 + bx + c$.
(ii) Check the relevant parts of the curve and the corresponding values of x.

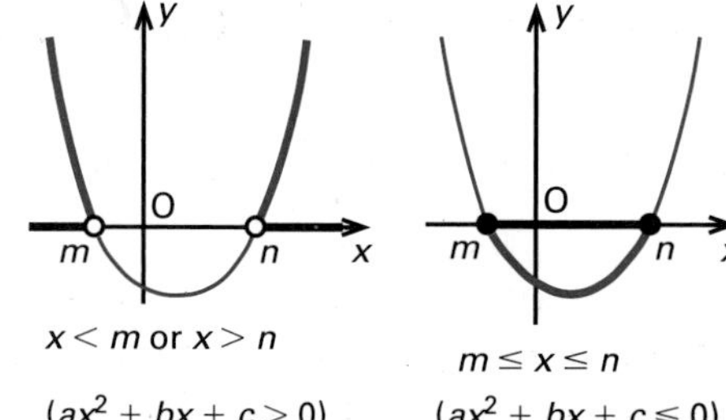

2 Integration

Differential equations

The gradient of the tangent to a parabola at the point (x, y) is given by $\frac{dy}{dx} = 8x$.

The equation of the parabola could be:

$y = 4x^2$, since $\frac{dy}{dx} = 8x$; or

$y = 4x^2 + 1$, since $\frac{dy}{dx} = 8x$; or

$y = 4x^2 - 3$, since $\frac{dy}{dx} = 8x$; and so on.

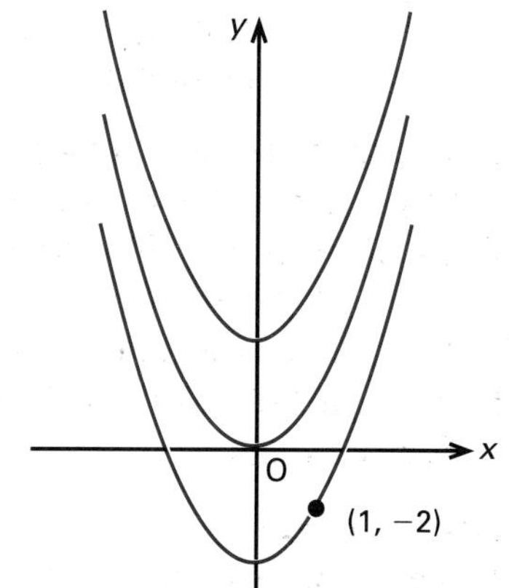

In fact there is a family of parabolas with equation $y = 4x^2 + c$, where c is a constant.
To choose a particular member of the family, more information is needed. For example, if it passes through the point $(1, -2)$, then $-2 = 4 \times 1^2 + c$, from which $c = -6$, and this parabola is $y = 4x^2 - 6$.

Notation

$\frac{dy}{dx} = 8x$ is a *differential equation.*

$y = 4x^2 + c$ is the *general solution* of the differential equation.

$y = 4x^2 - 6$ is a *particular solution* of the differential equation.

Example Find the particular solution of the differential equation $\frac{dy}{dx} = 8x - 1$ given by $y = 5$ when $x = 1$.

The general solution is $y = 4x^2 - x + c$.
When $y = 5$, $x = 1$. So $5 = 4 \times 1^2 - 1 + c$, from which $c = 2$.
The particular solution is $y = 4x^2 - x + 2$.

EXERCISE 1

1 Find the general solutions of these differential equations.

a $\frac{dy}{dx} = 2x$ **b** $\frac{dy}{dx} = 4x$ **c** $\frac{dy}{dx} = 6x + 1$

Check each answer by differentiation.

2 Find the particular solutions of these differential equations for the given values of x and y.

a $\frac{dy}{dx} = 3 + 6x$, given that $y = 2$ when $x = -1$

b $\frac{dy}{dx} = 12x + 1$, given that $y = 16$ when $x = 2$

c $\frac{dy}{dx} = 5 - 8x$, given that $y = -2$ when $x = 1$.

3 The table gives the gradients of the tangents at (x, y) to six curves, and a point on each curve. Find the equations of the curves.

	$\frac{dy}{dx}$	Curve passes through the point
a	$6x$	$(1, 5)$
b	$8x$	$(-2, 4)$
c	$2x - 1$	$(2, 1)$
d	$4x - 3$	$(1, 0)$
e	$1 - 3x^2$	$(2, 2)$
f	$4x^3$	$(-1, -1)$

4 Kate and Mike make a simultaneous parachute jump. Their velocity after x seconds is $v = 5 + 10x$ m/s. If they have fallen y metres, then $v = \frac{dy}{dx}$, so $\frac{dy}{dx} = 5 + 10x$.

a Find the distance y metres they fall in x seconds, given $y = 0$ when $x = 0$.

b Calculate the distance they fall in 10 seconds.

Integration

$3x^2 - 4x + c$ is called an *anti-derivative* of $6x - 4$, since
$\frac{d}{dx}(3x^2 - 4x + c) = 6x - 4$. It comes from $6x - 4$ by 'undoing' differentiation.
Leibnitz invented a useful notation for anti-derivatives, namely
$\int(6x - 4)\,dx = 3x^2 - 4x + c$.
In general, $\int f(x)\,dx = F(x) + c$ means $F'(x) = f(x)$.

Notation

The process of calculating an anti-derivative is called *integration*.
The anti-derivative $F(x)$ is called the *integral* and c is the *constant of integration*.
$F(x)$ is obtained from $f(x)$ by *integrating with respect to x*.

Some useful rules

1 In the chapter Introduction to Differentiation, you used the rule
$\frac{d}{dx}(x^n) = nx^{n-1}$.

So $\frac{d}{dx}(x^{n+1}) = (n+1)x^n$, from which $\frac{d}{dx}\left(\frac{x^{n+1}}{n+1}\right) = x^n,\ n \neq -1$.

It follows that $\int x^n\,dx = \frac{x^{n+1}}{n+1} + c,\ n \neq -1$.

2 $\int(f(x) + g(x))\,dx = \int f(x)\,dx + \int g(x)\,dx$

3 $\int kf(x)\,dx = k\int f(x)\,dx$, k a constant.

Examples

1 a $\int x\,dx = \frac{x^2}{2} + c$ **b** $\int x^2\,dx = \frac{x^3}{3} + c$ **c** $\int x^3\,dx = \frac{x^4}{4} + c$

2 If $n = 0$, $\int x^0\,dx = \frac{x^1}{1} + c = x + c$, that is $\int 1\,dx = x + c$

3 $\int(\sqrt[3]{x} - 5)\,dx = \int(x^{1/3} - 5)\,dx = \frac{x^{4/3}}{\frac{4}{3}} - 5x + c = \frac{3}{4}x^{4/3} - 5x + c$

EXERCISE 2A

Integrate the expressions in questions **1–3**. Remember to include c in each answer.

1 a x^2 **b** x^3 **c** x^4 **d** x^5

2 a x **b** $4x$ **c** $6x^2$ **d** $12x^3$

3 a 5 (i.e. $5x^0$) **b** 8 **c** $2x$ **d** $3x^2$

In questions **4–8**, find:

4 a $\int(x^2 + x)\,dx$ **b** $\int(2x + 1)\,dx$

5 a $\int(3 - 4x)\,dx$ **b** $\int(3x^2 - 4)\,dx$

6 a $\int(4x^3 + 4x)\,dx$ **b** $\int(1 - 5x^4)\,dx$

7 a $\int(6x^2 - 4x + 2)\,dx$ **b** $\int(3x^2 + 8x - 5)\,dx$

8 a $\int(x + 3)^2\,dx$ **b** $\int(x + 4)(x - 4)\,dx$

9 Find the general solutions of these differential equations:

a $\frac{dy}{dx} = 3x^2 - 4$ **b** $\frac{dy}{dx} = 8x^3 + 2x$

c $\frac{dy}{dx} = 6x^5 - 6x^2$ **d** $\frac{dy}{dx} = 1 - x + x^2 - x^3$

10 Given the gradient $\frac{dy}{dx}$ of the curve at the point (x, y) and a point on the curve, find the equation of each curve.

a $\frac{dy}{dx} = 3x^2 - 6x + 1$, $(3, 4)$

b $\frac{dy}{dx} = 4x^3 - 6x^2 + 5$, $(1, 9)$

c $\frac{dy}{dx} = (x + 2)(x - 3)$, $(0, -1)$

11 As point P moves along OX, its displacement from O is x, and its velocity at time t is given by $v = \frac{dx}{dt}$.

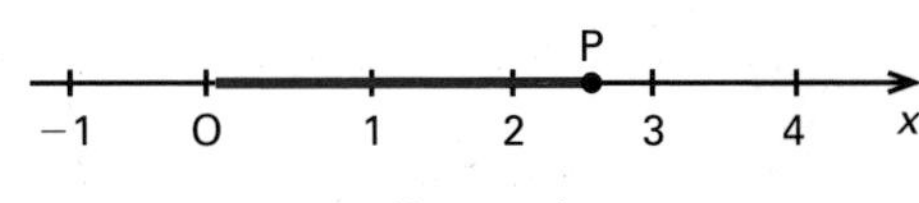

Find the displacement x, given:

a $\frac{dx}{dt} = 4t + 2$, and $x = 0$ when $t = 0$

b $\frac{dx}{dt} = 3t^2 - 2t$, and $x = 8$ when $t = 2$

c $v = 1 - 8t + 6t^2$, and $x = 0$ when $t = 1$

d $v = (t - 1)^2$, and $x = 12$ when $t = 3$.

EXERCISE 2B

In this exercise, give the answers with positive indices.

Integrate the expressions in questions **1–3**.

1 a x^{-3} **b** x^{-2} **c** $\frac{1}{x^4}$ **d** $\frac{1}{x^5}$

2 a $x^{1/3}$ **b** $x^{3/4}$ **c** $x^{-1/2}$ **d** $x^{-3/2}$

3 a $\frac{6}{x^2}$ **b** $6x^{1/2}$ **c** $\frac{1}{2x^3}$ **d** $\frac{1}{2x^{1/2}}$

In questions **4–7**, find:

4 a $\int t^{1/4}\,dt$ **b** $\int 3t^{-4}\,dt$ **c** $\int \frac{2}{t^2}\,dt$

5 a $\int(\sqrt{u} - 3)\,du$ **b** $\int u^{1/2}(u^{1/2} + u^{-1/2})\,du$

6 a $\int\left(x^2 + \frac{1}{x^2}\right)dx$ **b** $\int\left(\sqrt{x} - \frac{1}{\sqrt{x}}\right)dx$

7 a $\int\left(1+\frac{2}{t^3}\right)\mathrm{d}t$ **b** $\int 2t\left(3t-\frac{1}{t}\right)\mathrm{d}t$

8 Find $f(x)$, given:

a $f'(x) = 2x - 1$ and $f(3) = 20$ **b** $f'(x) = 9x^2$ and $f(0) = 5$

c $f'(x) = 2 - \frac{1}{x^2}$ and $f(1) = 8$ **d** $f'(x) = x + \frac{1}{\sqrt{x}}$ and $f(4) = 10$

e $f'(x) = \frac{1}{2}x^{1/2} - 5x^{3/2}$ and $f(0) = 3$.

9 Find the particular solutions which satisfy these differential equations.

a $\frac{\mathrm{d}y}{\mathrm{d}x} = 4x^3 + \frac{2}{x^3}$ and $y = 0$ when $x = 1$

b $\frac{\mathrm{d}y}{\mathrm{d}u} = \frac{u^2+1}{u^2}$ and $y = 4$ when $u = 2$

10 Integrate with respect to the relevant variables.

a $p^2\left(p^2 - \frac{1}{p^2}\right)$ **b** $(2t+1)^2$ **c** $\left(u - \frac{1}{u}\right)^2$

d $\frac{v^3+v}{v}$ **e** $\frac{t^2+2}{\sqrt{t}}$ **f** $\frac{(u^2+1)^2}{u^2}$

EXERCISE 3

1 The rate of growth per month (t) of the population $P(t)$ of Carlos Town is given by the differential equation $\frac{\mathrm{d}P}{\mathrm{d}t} = 5 + 8t^{1/3}$.

a Find the general solution of this equation.
b Find the particular solution, given that at present ($t = 0$), $P = 5000$.
c What will the population be 8 months from now?

2 Mr Isaacs produces x jewel boxes each week. His weekly profit function $P(x)$, in £, is such that $\frac{\mathrm{d}P}{\mathrm{d}x} = 70 - 0.4x$.

a Given $P(0) = -1200$ (i.e. fixed costs are £1200 per week), find $P(x)$.
b Calculate his profit in a week when he makes 20 boxes.

3 A dam begins to release water into a stream at time $t = 0$. The total volume of water released by time t satisfies the differential equation $\frac{\mathrm{d}V}{\mathrm{d}t} = 1400 + 60t$.

a Solve this equation to find V.
b Calculate V at $t = 10$.

4 A flu epidemic hits the small town of Wilmore. On a certain day there are 42 cases. The medical officer estimates that x days later there will be $7 + 6x$ new cases per day. The total number of cases after x days is N, so that $\frac{\mathrm{d}N}{\mathrm{d}x} = 7 + 6x$.

a Solve the equation to find a formula for N.
b Calculate N after 5 days.

5 A weight on the beam x m from A causes the beam to sag y cm. The model for this, when A is fixed, is $\frac{dy}{dx} = 2x(4 - \frac{1}{2}x)$. Solve this equation, and find the sag at B, 4 m from A.

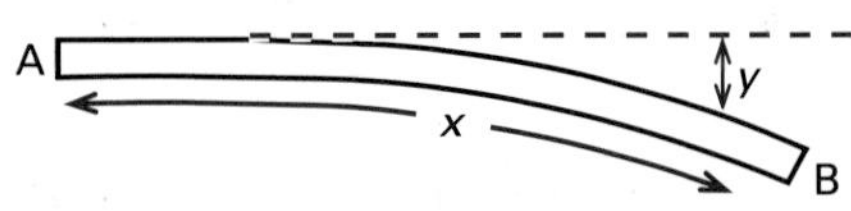

6 A white mouse weighed 10 g at birth, and its weight $w(t)$, in grams, at week t increased at a rate of $\frac{3}{4}(2 + t)$g per week.

a Make a differential equation, and hence find a formula for the weight after t weeks.

b Calculate the weight after 12 weeks.

7 The velocity of a car after t seconds has the formula $v(t) = 30 + 6t$ m/s. The distance travelled in t seconds is $s(t)$ metres.

a Construct a differential equation for $s(t)$, and solve it. $\left(\text{Remember, } v = \frac{ds}{dt}.\right)$

b Calculate the distance travelled in the first 3 seconds.

8 A single-stage rocket is launched vertically from rest at ground-level. Its engines burn for 100 seconds, producing an acceleration $a(t) = 400 - 2t$ m/s² during the time interval $0 \leqslant t \leqslant 100$.

a Find the velocity $v(t)$ at time t. $\left(v(0) = 0;\ \text{remember } a(t) = \frac{dv}{dt}.\right)$

b If $y(t)$ is the height at time t, write down a differential equation for $y(t)$.

c Solve the equation in **b**, and find the height $y(100)$ at burnout, to the nearest 100 m.

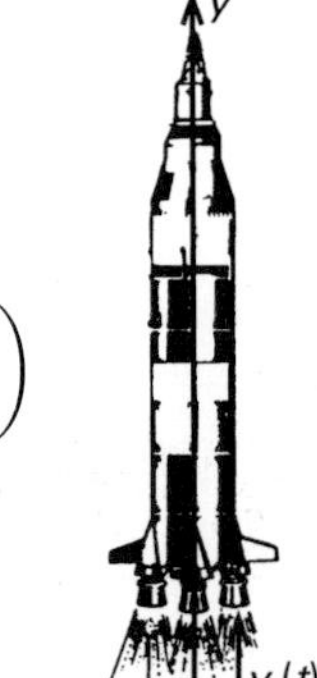

The area under a curve – notation

You have calculated many areas bounded by straight lines, including rectangles, triangles and parallelograms. For example, the shaded area is $\frac{1}{2}b^2 - \frac{1}{2}a^2$.

It is not so easy to calculate an area bounded by a curve. We'll work out a method for calculating the area bounded by the x-axis, the lines $x = a$ and $x = b$, and the curve $y = f(x)$.

We take $A(x)$ = the area under the curve up to x, starting at $x = a$, and use this to find the area of a strip under the curve, h wide.

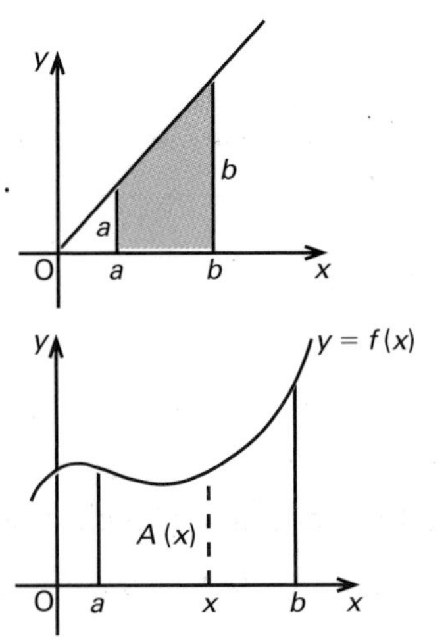

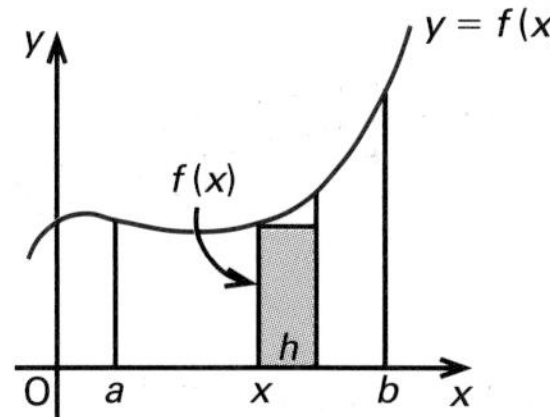

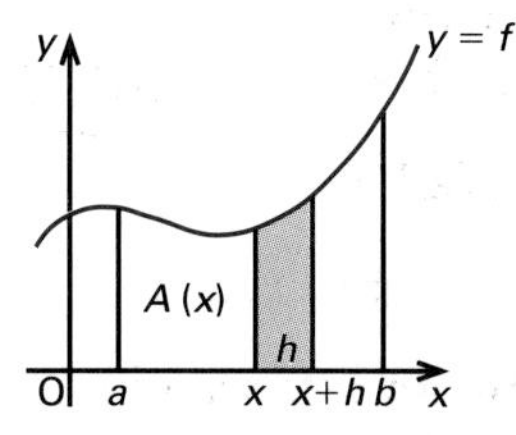

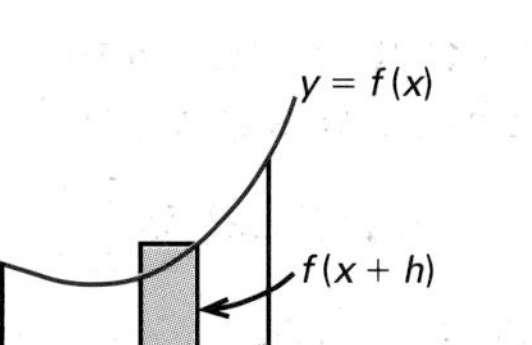

Comparing areas, $h \times f(x) \leqslant A(x+h) - A(x) \leqslant h \times f(x+h)$

Dividing by h $(\neq 0)$, $f(x) \leqslant \dfrac{A(x+h) - A(x)}{h} \leqslant f(x+h)$

As $h \to 0$, $f(x) \leqslant \lim\limits_{h \to 0} \dfrac{A(x+h) - A(x)}{h} \leqslant f(x)$

So $f(x) = A'(x)$, by the definition of a derived function

and $A(x) = \displaystyle\int f(x)\,dx$, by the definition of integration.

The area we wish to calculate, bounded by the x-axis, the lines $x = a$ and $x = b$, and the curve $y = f(x)$, is denoted by $\int_a^b f(x)\,dx$.
In one sense, this integral represents the summing of all the strips of area under the curve from $x = a$ to $x = b$, and, in fact, $\int$ is an elongated form of the letter S.

Example Show, by shading in sketches, the areas associated with:

a $\displaystyle\int_1^4 2x\,dx$ **b** $\displaystyle\int_{-2}^2 x^3\,dx$ **c** $\displaystyle\int_0^{\pi/2} \sin x\,dx$

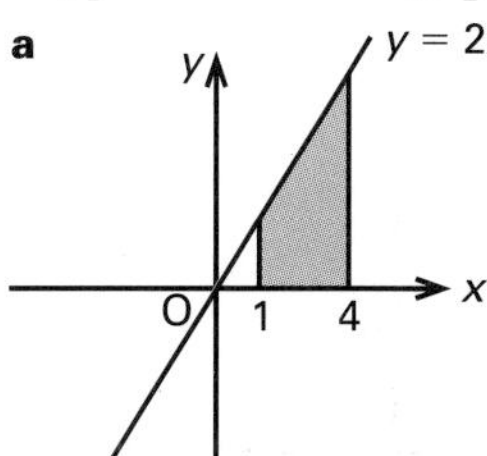

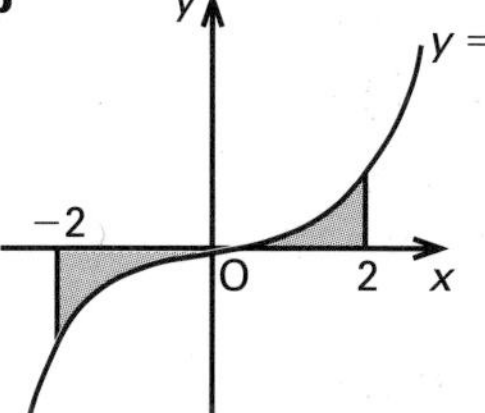

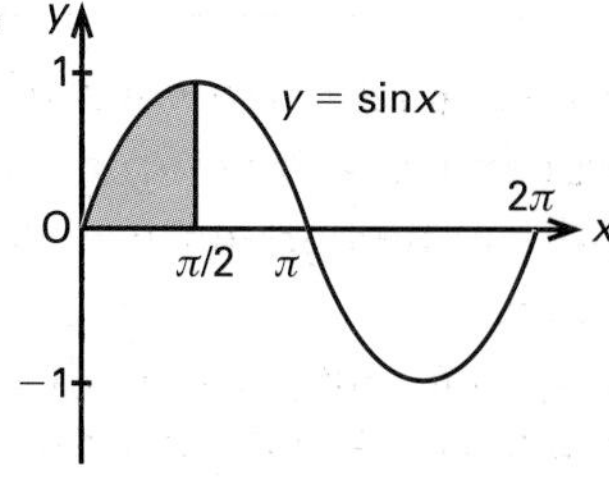

EXERCISE 4

Show, by shading in sketches, the areas associated with the integrals in questions **1–3**.

1 a $\displaystyle\int_0^3 x\,dx$ **b** $\displaystyle\int_0^2 \tfrac{1}{2}x\,dx$ **c** $\displaystyle\int_1^4 (x+3)\,dx$

2 a $\displaystyle\int_0^2 x^2\,dx$ **b** $\displaystyle\int_{-4}^4 x^2\,dx$ **c** $\displaystyle\int_0^5 x^3\,dx$

3 **a** $\int_0^{\pi/2} \cos x \, dx$ **b** $\int_0^{\pi} \sin x \, dx$ **c** $\int_{3\pi/4}^{5\pi/4} \cos 2x \, dx$ **d** $\int_0^{2\pi} \sin \frac{1}{2}x \, dx$

Write down integrals associated with the shaded regions in questions **4–8**.

4 **a**

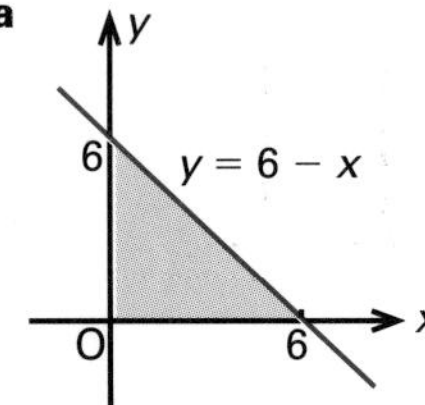

b

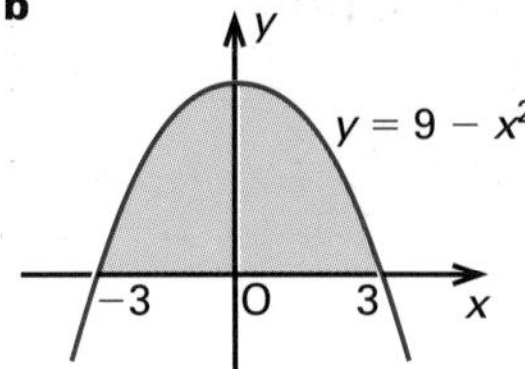

5 **a**

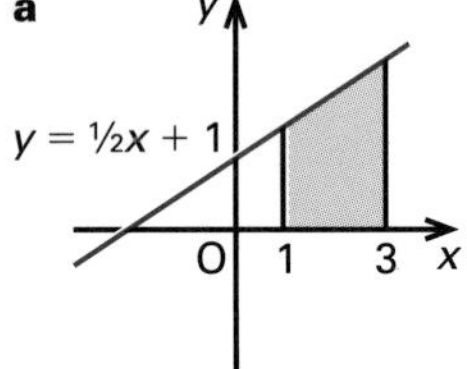

b

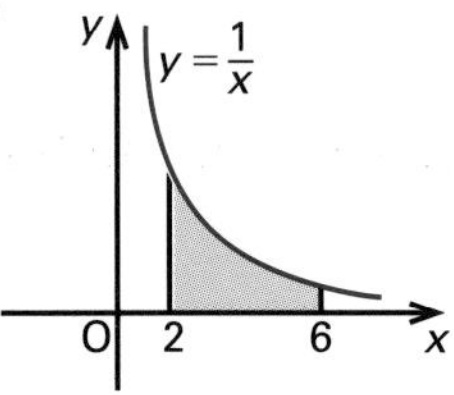

6 **a**

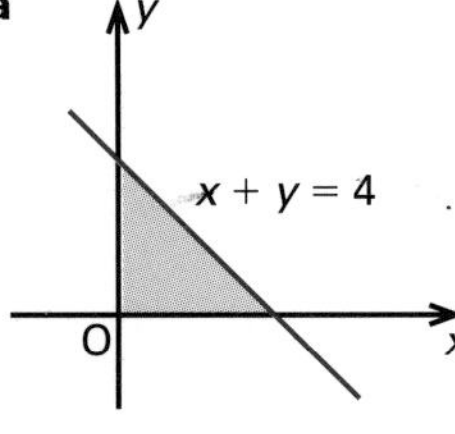

b

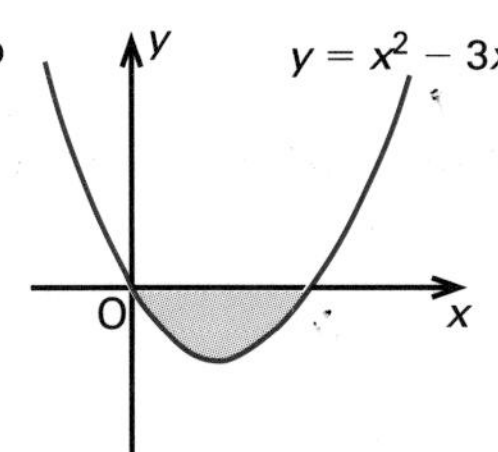

7 **a**

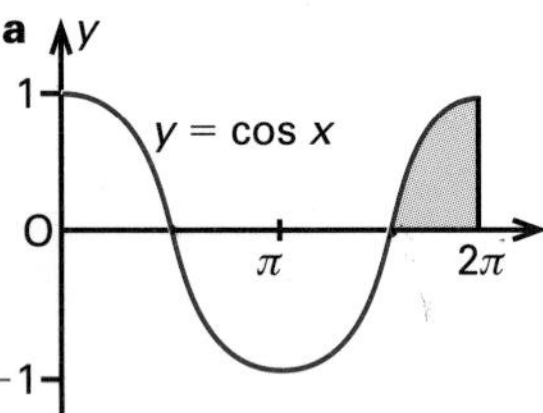

b

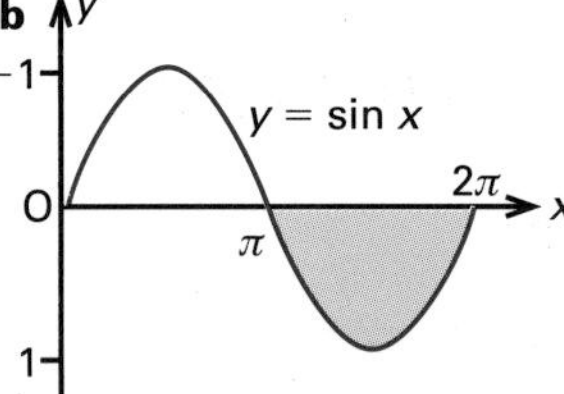

8 **a**

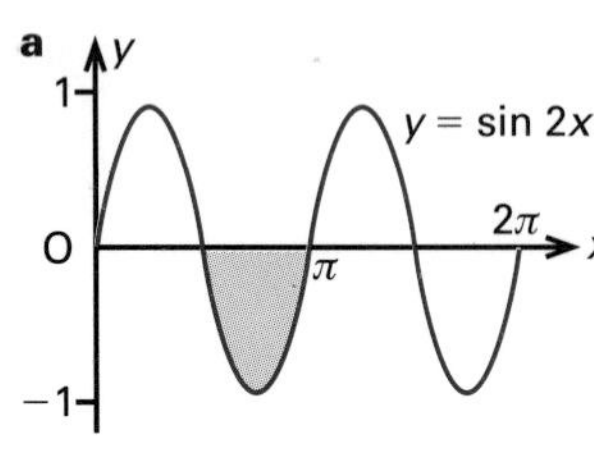

b

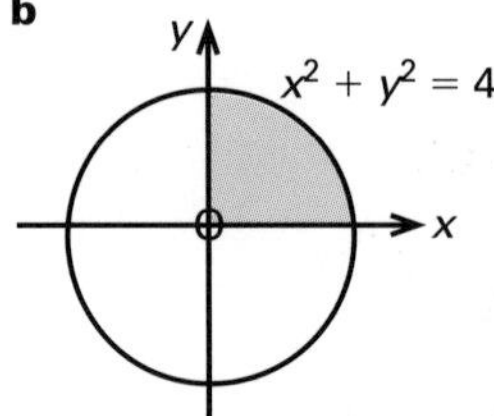

The area under a curve – a formula; definite integrals

$A(x)$ = the area under the curve up to x, starting at $x = a$, and $A(b)$ = the area under the curve from $x = a$ to $x = b$, which is the area we wish to find.
From the last section, $A(x) = \int f(x)\,dx$.

Let $\int f(x)\,dx = F(x) + c$, where $F'(x) = f(x)$.

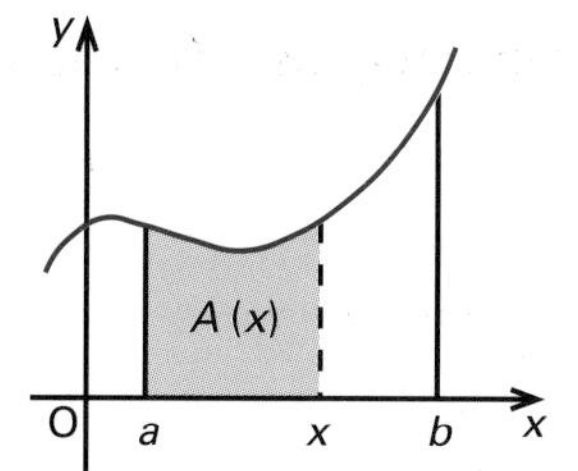

Then $A(x) = F(x) + c$, and

$A(a) = 0$ (from the diagram) $= F(a) + c$, so $c = -F(a)$.

Now $A(x) = F(x) - F(a)$

and $A(b) = F(b) - F(a)$, the area we are trying to find.

$F(b) - F(a)$ is denoted by $[F(x)]_a^b$.

The area under the curve $y = f(x)$ from $x = a$ to $x = b$ is
$$\int_a^b f(x)\,dx = [F(x)]_a^b = F(b) - F(a).$$

$\int_a^b f(x)\,dx$ is a *definite integral*, with *lower limit a* and *upper limit b*.

Examples Evaluate these integrals:

1 $\int_1^3 x^3\,dx = \left[\frac{x^4}{4}\right]_1^3 = \frac{1}{4}(3^4 - 1^4) = \frac{1}{4} \times 80 = 20$

2 $\int_{-1}^2 2x(3x + 1)\,dx = \int_{-1}^2 (6x^2 + 2x)\,dx = [2x^3 + x^2]_{-1}^2$

$= (16 + 4) - (-2 + 1) = 20 + 1 = 21$

EXERCISE 5

Evaluate the integrals in questions **1–12**.

1 a $\int_0^2 4x\,dx$ **b** $\int_1^3 3x^2\,dx$ **c** $\int_1^2 4x^3\,dx$

2 a $\int_1^2 x\,dx$ **b** $\int_0^1 2x\,dx$ **c** $\int_{-1}^2 2x\,dx$

3 a $\int_0^2 3\,dx$ **b** $\int_{-1}^1 4\,dx$ **c** $\int_0^1 x^2\,dx$

4 a $\int_0^1 (4x + 3)\,dx$ **b** $\int_{-2}^2 (2x + 1)\,dx$

5 a $\int_0^2 (8 - 2x)\,dx$ **b** $\int_{-1}^1 (5 - 3x^2)\,dx$

6 a $\int_0^1 (u^2 + 2u + 1)\,du$ **b** $\int_{-1}^1 (u^2 + 2u + 1)\,du$

7 a $\int_0^2 (x + 1)(x - 1)\,dx$ **b** $\int_{-2}^0 (x - 1)^2\,dx$

8 a $\int_{-1}^1 (3t^2 - 5t^4)\,dt$ **b** $\int_{-1}^0 (4t^3 + 3t^2)\,dt$

9 a $\int_0^4 x^{1/2}\,dx$ **b** $\int_1^2 \frac{dx}{x^2}$ **c** $\int_1^4 \frac{dx}{\sqrt{x}}$

10 a $\int_1^3 \left(x^2 - \frac{1}{x^2}\right) dx$ **b** $\int_1^2 \left(2t + \frac{2}{t^3}\right) dt$

11 a $\int_0^1 u^{1/2}(u^{1/2} + u^{-1/2})\,du$ **b** $\int_1^4 \frac{1 + \sqrt{t}}{\sqrt{t}}\,dt$

12 a $\int_0^1 x(1 - x)\,dx$ **b** $\int_{-1}^1 (x + 1)(3x - 1)\,dx$

13 Check that: $\int_{-1}^0 (2x - 1)\,dx + \int_0^1 (2x - 1)\,dx = \int_{-1}^1 (2x - 1)\,dx.$

14 Find a, greater than zero, given:

a $\int_0^a (2x + 2)\,dx = 8$ **b** $\int_0^a 3x^{1/2}\,dx = 16.$

The area under a curve – calculations

We now know that:

(i) the area A bounded by the x-axis, the lines $x = a$ and $x = b$, and the curve $y = f(x)$ is denoted by

$$\int_a^b f(x)\,dx$$

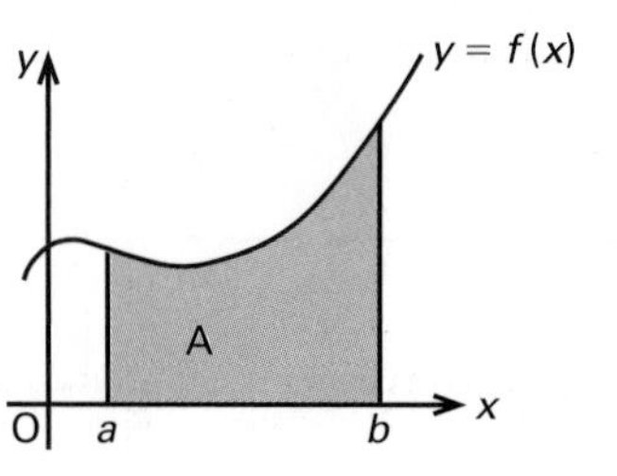

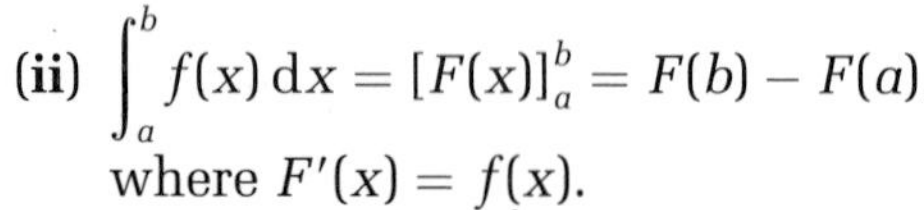

(ii) $\int_a^b f(x)\,dx = [F(x)]_a^b = F(b) - F(a)$, where $F'(x) = f(x)$.

It follows that $A = \int_a^b f(x)\,dx = [F(x)]_a^b = F(b) - F(a)$,

where $f(x) \geqslant 0$ and $a \leqslant x \leqslant b$.

Example Calculate the area of the region:

a bounded by the x-axis, the line $x = 2$ and the parabola $y = x^2 - 1$ (A)

b enclosed by the parabola and the x-axis (B).

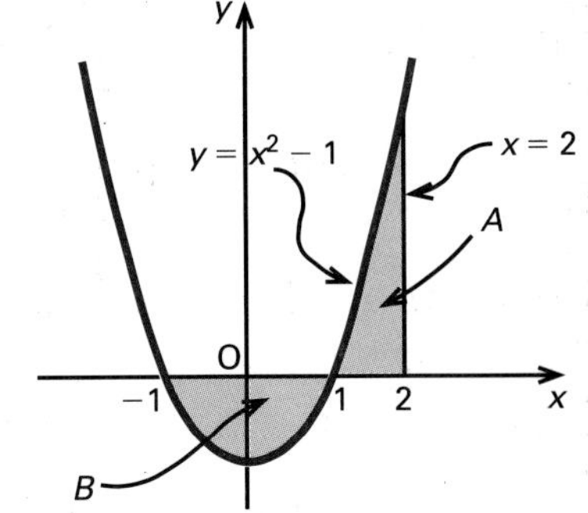

a Area $A = \int_1^2 (x^2 - 1)\,dx = [\tfrac{1}{3}x^3 - x]_1^2 = (\tfrac{8}{3} - 2) - (\tfrac{1}{3} - 1) = 1\tfrac{1}{3}$

b Area $B = \int_{-1}^{1} (x^2 - 1)\,dx = [\tfrac{1}{3}x^3 - x]_{-1}^{1} = (\tfrac{1}{3} - 1) - (-\tfrac{1}{3} + 1) = -1\tfrac{1}{3}$.

This definite integral is negative, but the area has measure $1\tfrac{1}{3}$.

Note

(i) Integration will give negative values for areas under the x-axis since, for the shaded strip, $f(x) < 0$ and $h > 0$, so $h \times f(x)$ is negative.

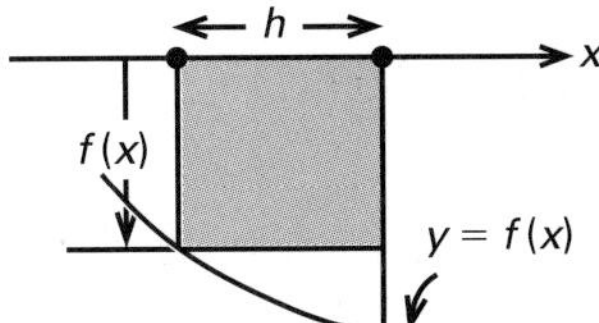

(ii) In the above example, the total area cannot be found by evaluating $\int_{-1}^{2} (x^2 - 1)\,dx$; its value would be $1\tfrac{1}{3} + (-1\tfrac{1}{3}) = 0$. Areas for $f(x) \geqslant 0$ and $f(x) < 0$ must be calculated separately, and the numerical values added together. In the example, the total area $= 1\tfrac{1}{3} + 1\tfrac{1}{3} = 2\tfrac{2}{3}$.

EXERCISE 6

Calculate the areas of the shaded regions in questions **1–5**.

1 **a**

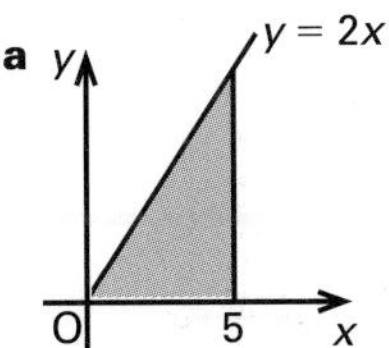

b

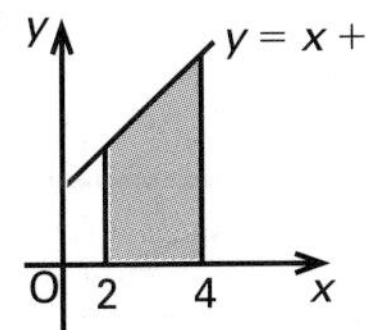

2 **a**

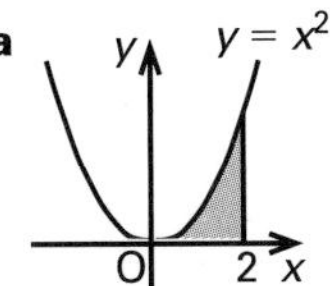

b

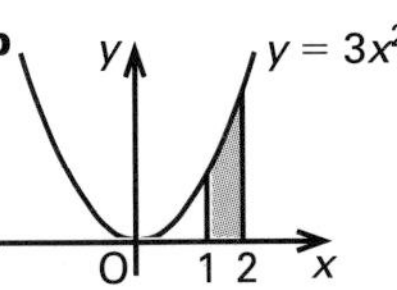

3 **a**

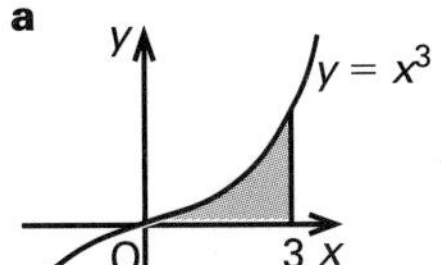

b

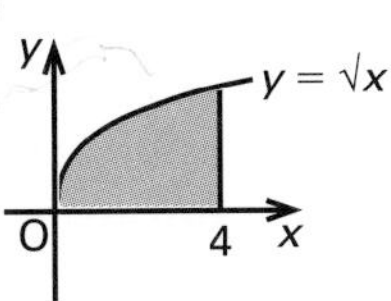

4 a

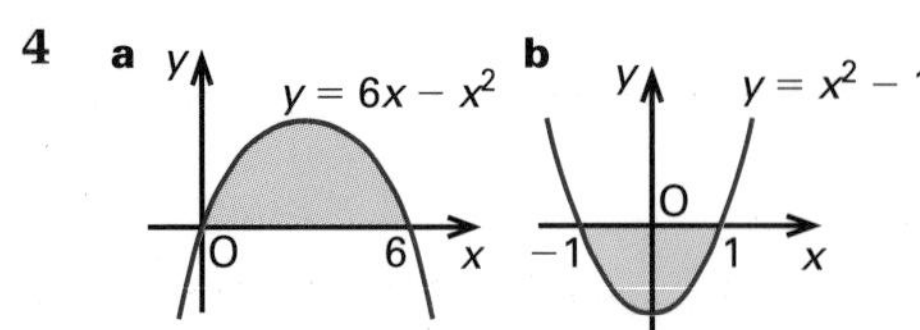

5 a

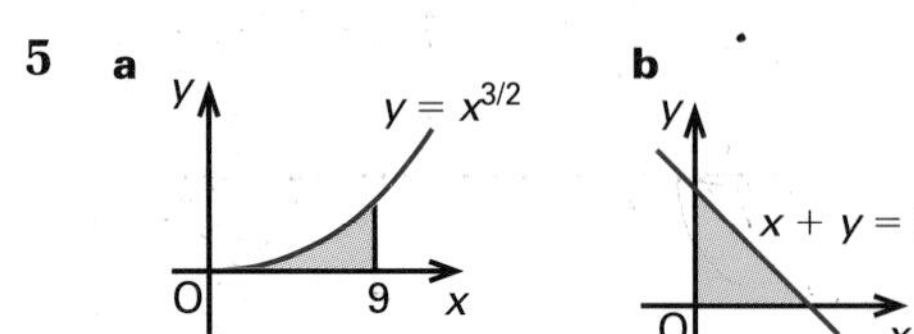

6 Calculate the area enclosed by the curve $y = (1 - x)^2$, the x-axis and the y-axis.

7 Calculate the area enclosed by the curve $y = 1 - x^2$ and the x-axis.

8 Calculate the areas of the shaded regions M and N, and deduce the total area $M + N$.

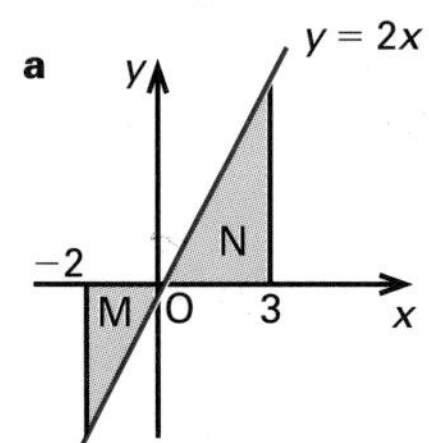

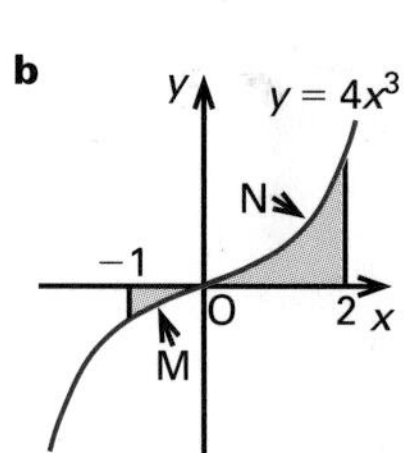

9 Find the x-coordinates of A, B and C, and then the total shaded area in each diagram.

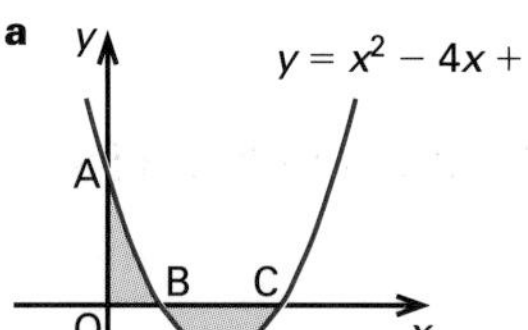

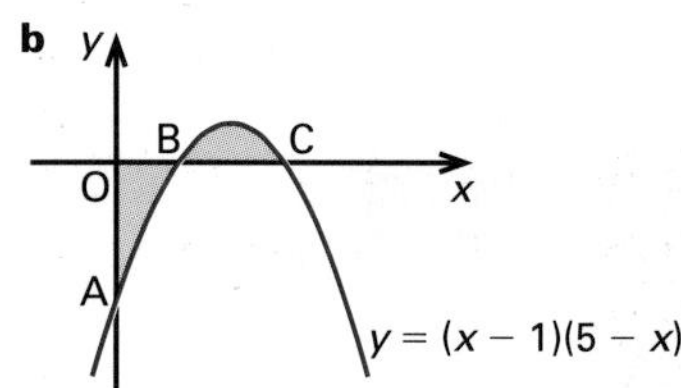

10 Sketch the line $y = 4x - 4$, and find the total area bounded by the line, the x-axis and the lines $x = -1$ and $x = 2$.

11 Sketch the curve $y = x^3$, and find the area enclosed by the curve, the x-axis and the lines $x = -1$ and $x = 2$.

12 **a** Calculate $\int_{-2}^{2} (x^3 - 4x)\,dx$. Explain your answer with the help of a sketch.
b Calculate the area enclosed by the curve and the x-axis.

13 **a** Find the area bounded by the curve $y = 6\sqrt{x}$, the x-axis and the line $x = 4$.
b The line $x = a$ divides this area in half. Find a, correct to 1 decimal place.

14 **a** For the curve $y = 3x - x^3$, find:
  (i) its points of intersection with the x and y-axes
  (ii) its maximum and minimum turning points.
b Sketch the curve.
c Calculate the area enclosed by:
  (i) the curve and the x-axis
  (ii) the x-axis, the lines through the turning points perpendicular to the x-axis and the part of the curve between the turning points.

The area between two curves

The area between the curves $y = f(x)$ and $y = g(x)$ from $x = a$ to $x = b$

$=$ the area from the x-axis to the part of the upper curve

$-$ the area from the x-axis to the part of the lower curve

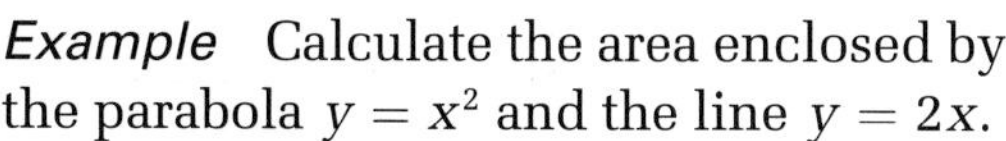

$$= \int_a^b (f(x) - g(x))\,dx.$$

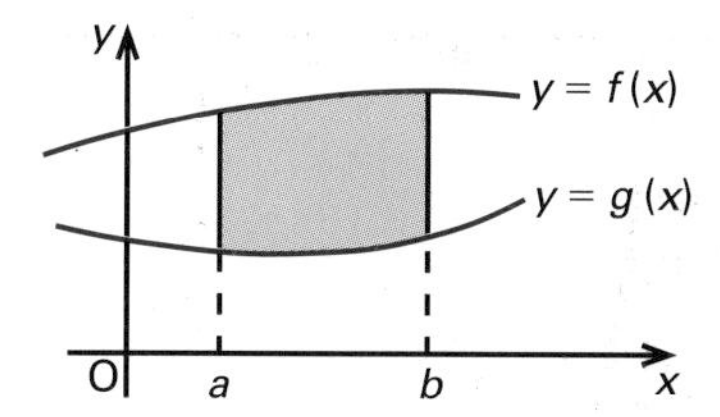

Example Calculate the area enclosed by the parabola $y = x^2$ and the line $y = 2x$.

$y = x^2$ meets $y = 2x$ where $x^2 = 2x$, i.e. $x(x - 2) = 0$, so $x = 0$ or $x = 2$.
The area of the shaded region

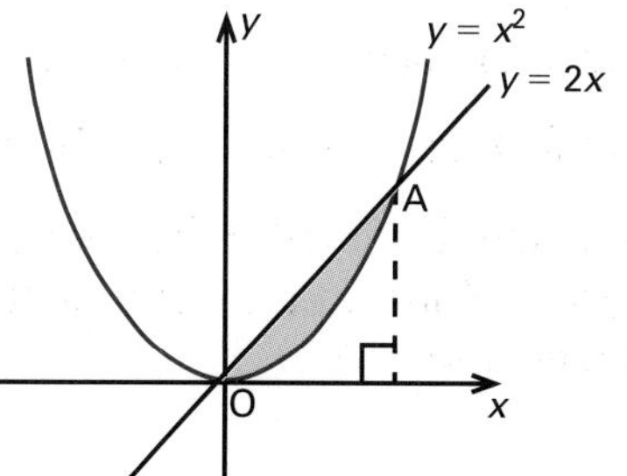

$$= \int_0^2 2x\,dx - \int_0^2 x^2\,dx = \int_0^2 (2x - x^2)\,dx$$

$$= [x^2 - \tfrac{1}{3}x^3]_0^2 = (4 - \tfrac{8}{3}) - (0 - 0) = 1\tfrac{1}{3}.$$

Display as many pairs of graphs in Exercise 7 as you can to show the relevant areas.

EXERCISE 7

Make a sketch for each question, and shade the region showing the required area.
In questions **1–11**, calculate the areas enclosed by the lines and curves with the given equations.

1 $y = x^2$, $y = x$

2 $y = 3x^2$, $y = 6x$

3 $y = x^2$, $y = 9$

4 $y = x^2$, $y = 2 - x^2$

5 $y = x^3$, $y = x$

6 $y = x^2$, $y = \sqrt{x}$

7 $y = x^2 - 3x$, $y = 3x$

8 $y = 4 - x^2$, $y = 4 - 2x$

9 $y = 2 + x - x^2$, $y = 3x - 1$

10 $y = 4x - x^2$, $y = x^2 - 6$

11 $y = 9x - x^3$, $y = 5x$

12 **a** Calculate the area A bounded by the curve $y = -8x - x^2$ and the x-axis.
b Find the points of intersection of the curve and $y = x^2$, and show that the curve $y = x^2$ divides A in the ratio 3:1.

13 **a** Find the equation of the tangent to the parabola $y = x(3 - x)$ at the point P (2, 2).

b Calculate the area enclosed by the tangent, the x-axis and the arc of the curve to the right of P.

14 **a** Find the point of intersection of the tangents to the parabola $y = x^2 + 4$ at A(−4, 20) and B(1, 5).

b Calculate the area bounded by the tangents and the arc AB (the sum of two areas).

Areas in action

EXERCISE 8

1 When a bridge is designed, the area presented to the wind must be calculated in order to forecast the forces on the bridge.

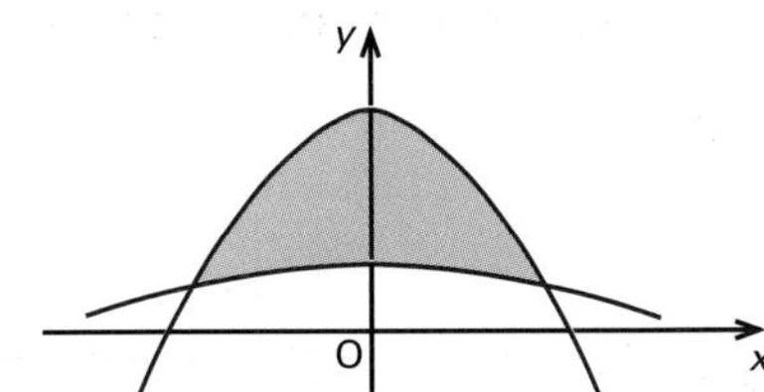

For this bridge the area is modelled by the region between the parabolas $y = 10 - x^2$ and $y = 19 - 2x^2$. Calculate its area (1 unit = 10 m).

2 A logo is made from the region between the parabolas $y = x^2 - 4$ and $y = 2x - x^2$. Calculate the area of the logo (1 unit = 1 cm).

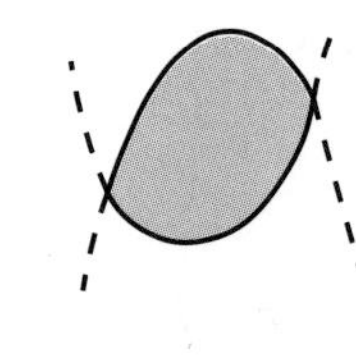

3 The playground slide is shaped like part of a parabola.

a Calculate the shaded area of the side (1 unit = 1 m).

b A half-height slide for smaller children has equation $y = \frac{1}{100}x^2 - \frac{1}{5}x + 1$. Is its area half that of the larger one?

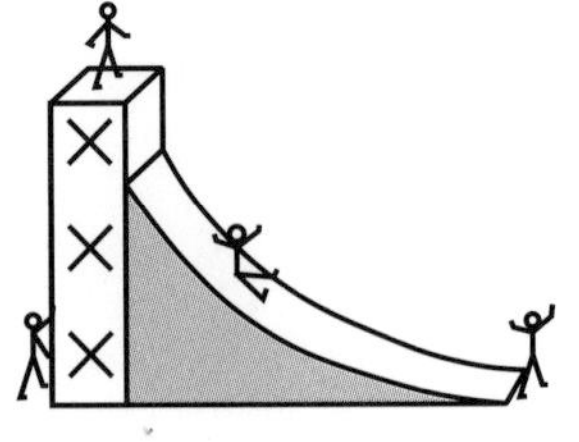

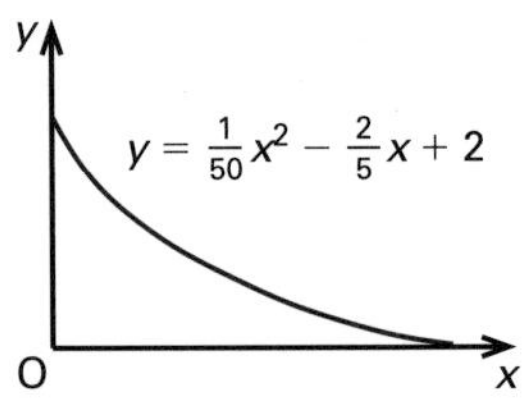

4 The fire-surround is rectangular, with a parabolic opening for the fire.

a Find the coordinates of A and B.

b Calculate the tiled area (1 unit = 10 cm).

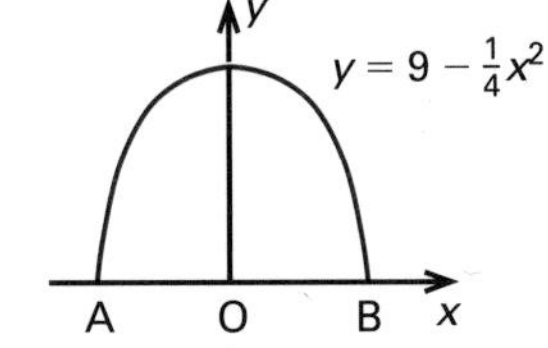

5 The curved edge of the rain-gutter is parabolic.

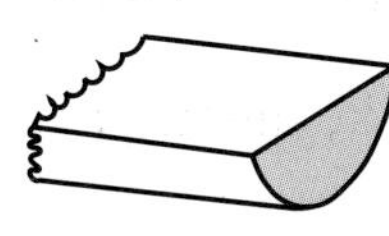

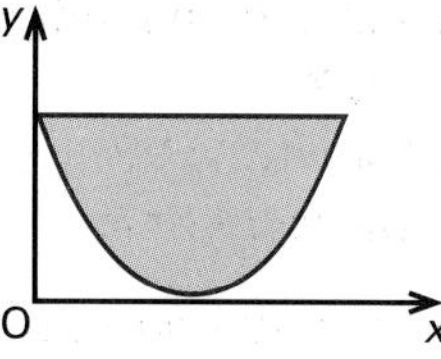

The equation of the parabola is $y = 0.24x^2 - 2.4x + 6$. Calculate the area of the cross-section of the gutter (1 unit = 1 cm).

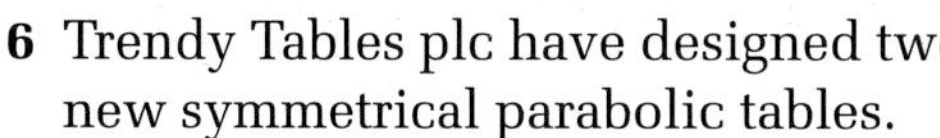

6 Trendy Tables plc have designed two new symmetrical parabolic tables.

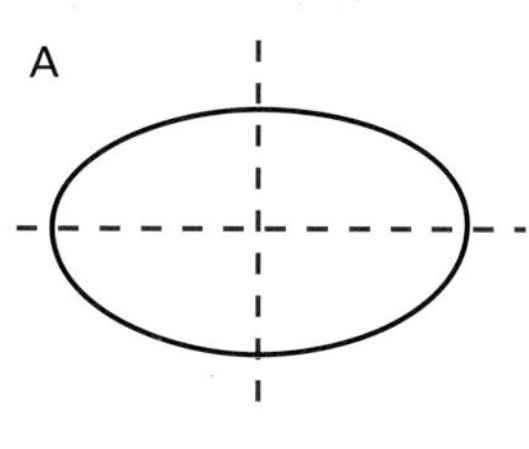

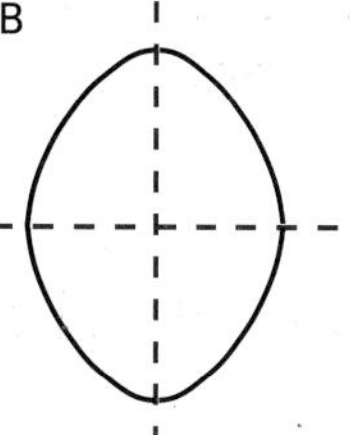

The outlines of one half of each table are shown on the coordinate diagram. If 1 unit = 20 cm, calculate, to the nearest 100 cm² the area of each table.

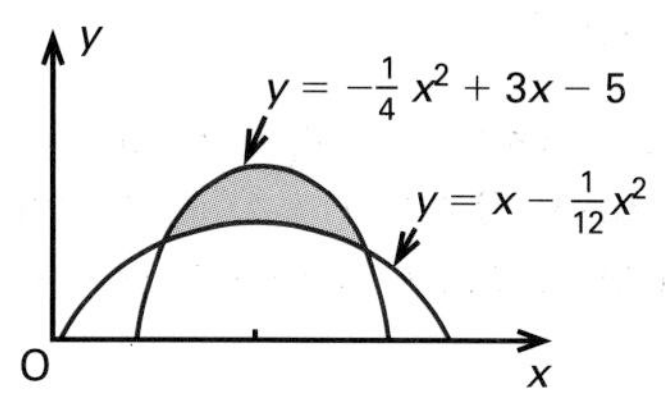

7 Millennium Park is based on two parabola shapes.

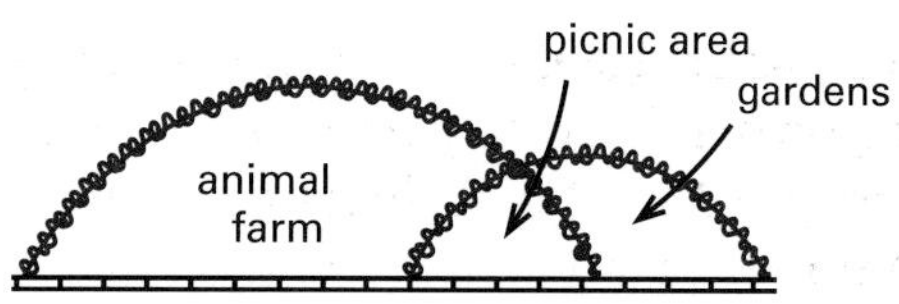

A plan is laid out in the coordinate diagram. Calculate the areas of the three parts of the park on the diagram.

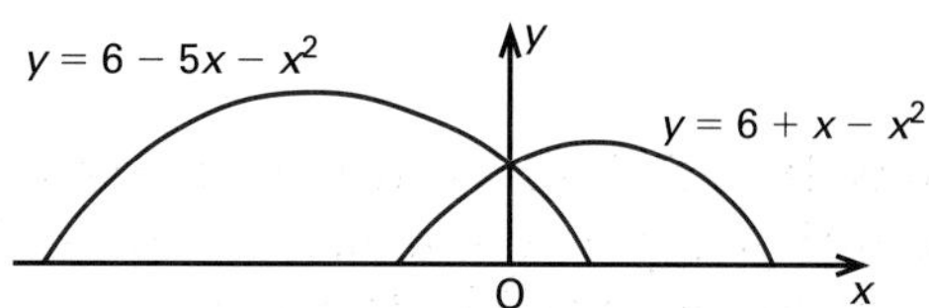

CHAPTER 2 REVIEW

1 Integrate:

a $x^2 + x + 1$ **b** $8x^3 - 4x - 2$

c $x^{1/2} + x^{-1/2}$ **d** $\frac{1}{x^2} + \frac{1}{x^3}$.

2 Find:

a $\int(3 - 3x^2)\,dx$

b $\int x^4\left(3x + \frac{2}{x^3}\right)dx$.

3 Find $f(x)$, given:

a $f'(x) = 6x^2 - 8x$

b $f'(x) = \frac{2 - x^4}{x^2}$.

4 Find the general solution of:

a $\frac{dy}{dx} = 1 - x$

b $\frac{dy}{dx} = (x + 1)(x - 1)$.

5 Solve the differential equations:

a $\frac{dy}{dx} = 3 - 2x + 6x^2$, where $y = 5$ when $x = 1$

b $\frac{dy}{dx} = \sqrt[3]{x}$, where $y = 3$ when $x = 1$.

6 Evaluate:

a $\int_1^2 10x\,dx$ **b** $\int_{-2}^2 5\,dx$ **c** $\int_{-1}^0 3x^2\,dx$.

7 Evaluate:

a $\int_0^1 (4 + 2x)\,dx$ **b** $\int_{-1}^1 (6x^2 - 1)\,dx$

c $\int_{-1}^0 (t + 1)^2\,dt$ **d** $\int_1^3 \frac{2v^2 + 3}{v^2}\,dv$.

8 Find:

a $\int\left(3x^2 + \frac{2}{x^3}\right)dx$

b $\int\left(3x^{1/2} + \frac{1}{3x^{1/3}}\right)dx$

c $\int\left(x + \frac{1}{x}\right)^2 dx$

d $\int(x + 1)(x + 2)(x + 3)\,dx$.

9 Write down integrals to represent the shaded regions of these diagrams.

a

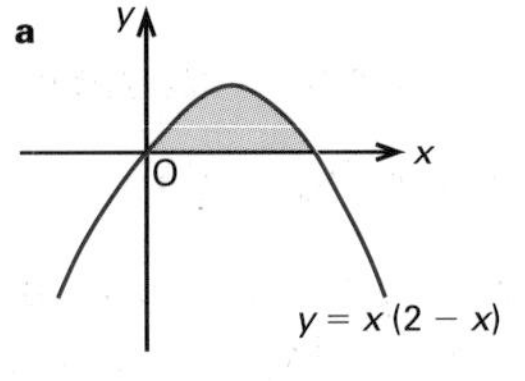

b

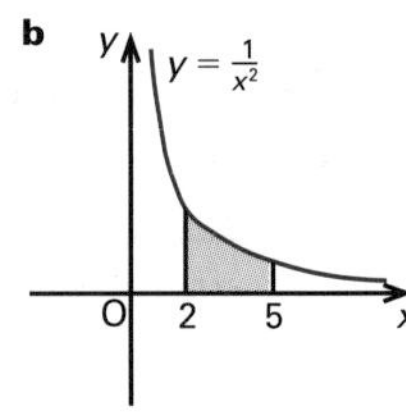

c

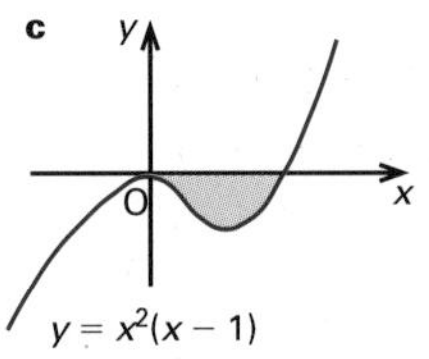

d

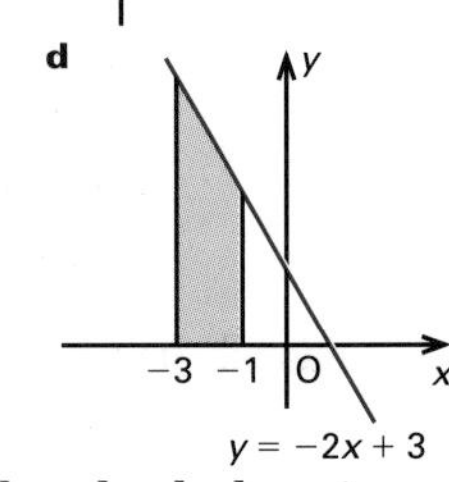

10 Calculate the areas of the shaded regions in question **9**.

Make sketches in questions **11–16** before calculating the areas.

11 Calculate the area enclosed by the x-axis and the parabola $y = 8 - 2x^2$.

12 Calculate the area enclosed by the x-axis, the curve $y = \sqrt{x}$ and the line $x = 9$.

13 Calculate the area enclosed by the x-axis and the curve $y = x(x^2 - 1)$.

14 a Use integration to calculate the area enclosed by the lines $y = x + 1$, $y = -2x + 4$ and $x = 3$.

b Check your answer by calculating the area of the triangle in another way.

15 Calculate the area enclosed by the line $y = 3(x - 1)$ and the parabola $y = 3 + 2x - x^2$.

16 The tangents at A(0, 2) and B(2, 6) on the parabola $y = x^2 + 2$ meet at C. Calculate the area enclosed by the tangents and the arc AB of the parabola.

17 A doorway is symmetrical about a central vertical line, and is 6 m wide. The curve of its top is part of the parabola $y = 5 - \frac{1}{5}x^2$. Calculate the area of the door.

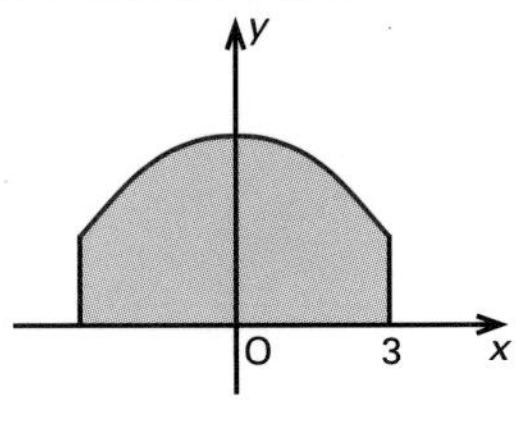

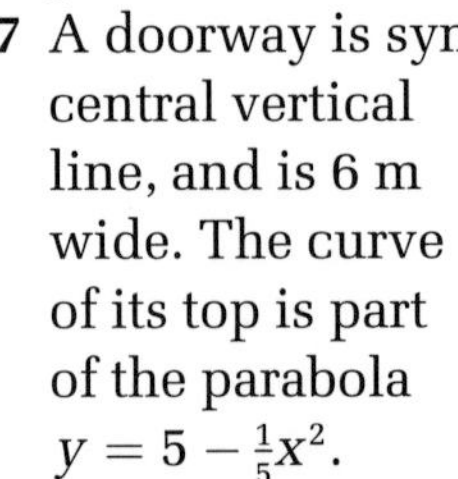

CHAPTER 2 SUMMARY

1 DIFFERENTIAL EQUATIONS; INTEGRALS

(i) $\frac{dy}{dx} = f(x)$ is a differential equation, with general solution $y = \int f(x)\,dx = F(x) + c$, where $F'(x) = f(x)$.

(ii) $\int f(x)\,dx = F(x) + c$ is an indefinite integral of $f(x)$, and c is the constant of integration.

(iii) If $f(x) = x^n$, $\int x^n\,dx = \frac{x^{n+1}}{n+1} + c$, $n \neq -1$.

2 AN AREA FORMULA

$A = \int_a^b f(x)\,dx = [F(x)]_a^b = F(b) - F(a)$, where $F'(x) = f(x)$.

$\int_a^b f(x)\,dx$ is a definite integral.

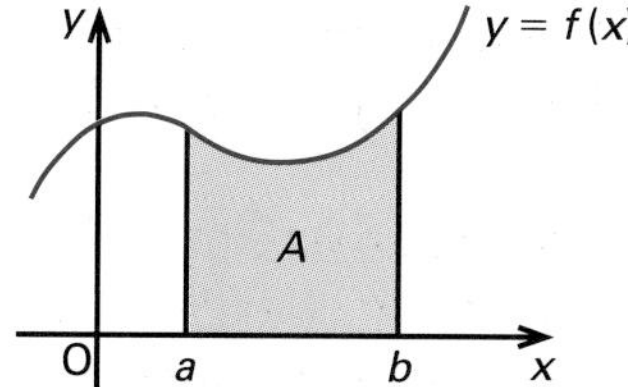

For example, $\int_{-1}^{2} 6x^2\,dx$

$= \left[\frac{6x^3}{3}\right]_{-1}^{2} = [2x^3]_{-1}^{2}$

$= 2 \times 2^3 - 2 \times (-1)^3$

$= 2 \times 8 - 2 \times (-1)$

$= 18.$

3 THE AREA UNDER A CURVE

The magnitude of the area in each shaded region is $\int_a^b f(x)\,dx$.

In **a**, the sign of the integral is positive; in **b**, the sign is negative.

a

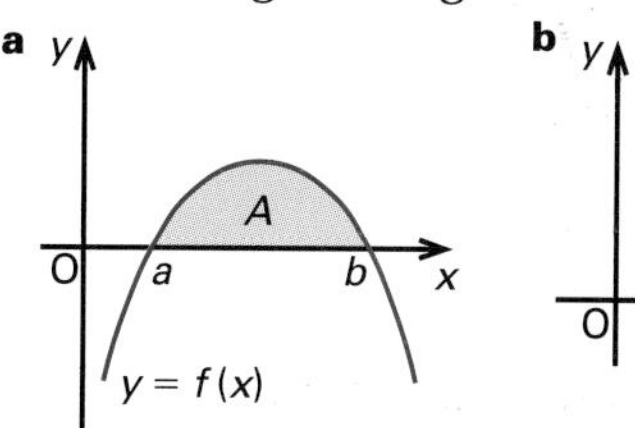

b

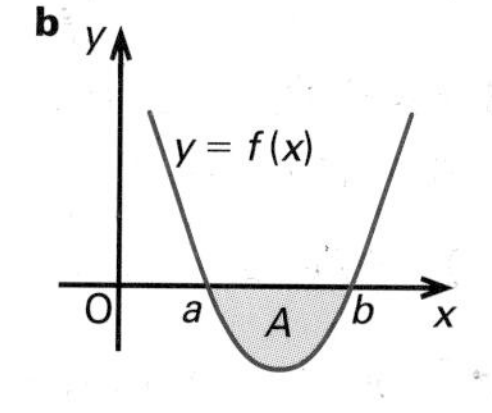

4 THE AREA BETWEEN TWO CURVES

The area of the shaded region between the two curves is $\int_a^b (f(x) - g(x))\,dx$.

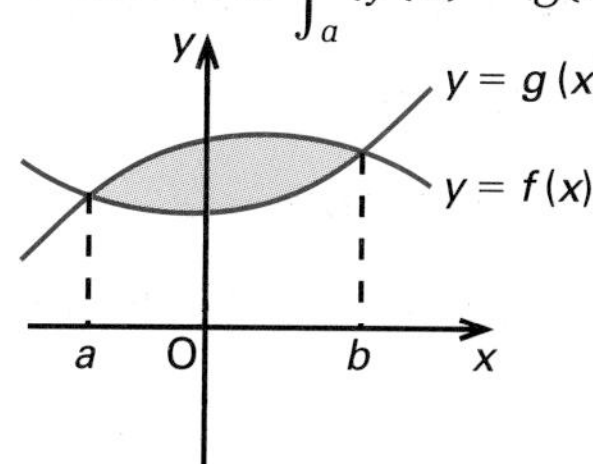

3.1 Calculations in 2 and 3 Dimensions

Two dimensions

Reminders

1 Definitions

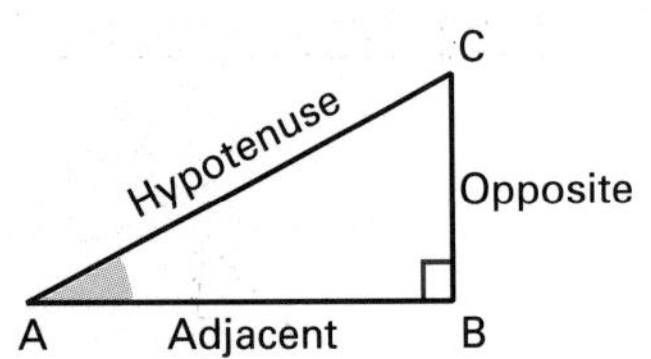

$$\text{Sin A} = \frac{\textbf{Opposite}}{\textbf{Hypotenuse}}$$

$$\text{Cos A} = \frac{\textbf{Adjacent}}{\textbf{Hypotenuse}}$$

$$\text{Tan A} = \frac{\textbf{Opposite}}{\textbf{Adjacent}}$$

2 Triangle formulae

Sine rule $\dfrac{a}{\sin \text{A}} = \dfrac{b}{\sin \text{B}} = \dfrac{c}{\sin \text{C}}$

Cosine rule $a^2 = b^2 + c^2 - 2bc \cos \text{A}$

$$\cos \text{A} = \frac{b^2 + c^2 - a^2}{2bc}$$

Area of $\triangle$ ABC $\triangle = \frac{1}{2}ab \sin \text{C}$

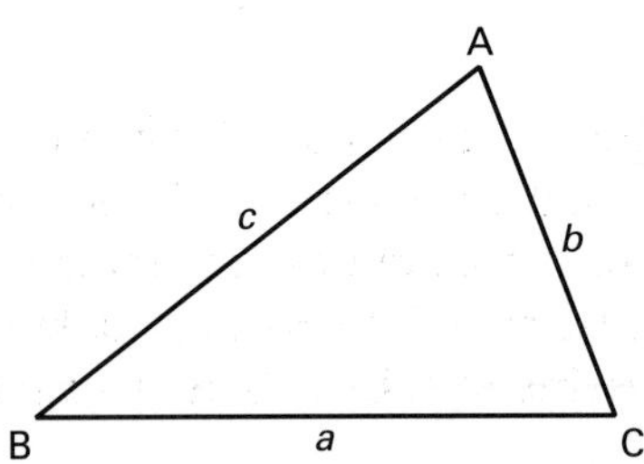

EXERCISE 1

1 Calculate x, correct to 1 decimal place.

a

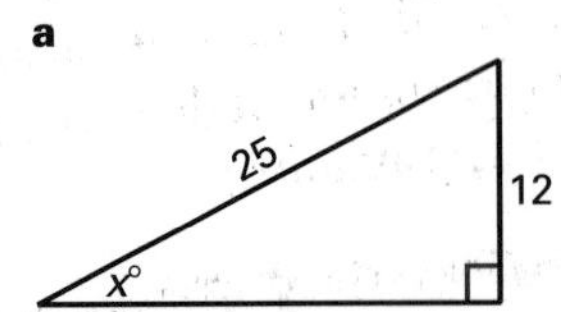

b

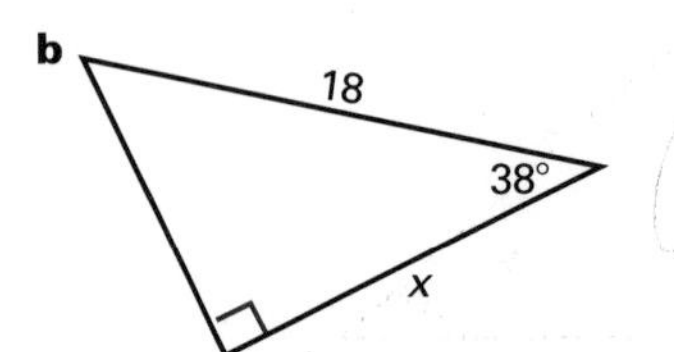

2 This trigometer reads distances and angles when pointed at objects.

Calculate, to the nearest metre:

a the distance d m

b the height h m.

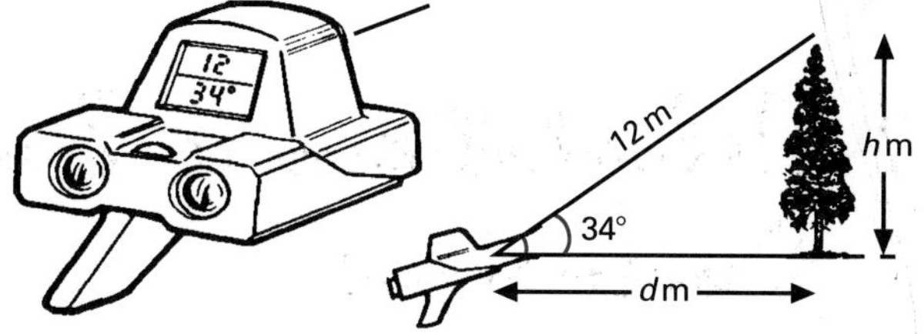

3 In $\triangle$ABC, $\angle B = 35°$, $\angle C = 66°$ and $a = 8.5$ cm. Calculate b, correct to 1 decimal place.

4 Calculate, correct to 0.1°, the size of the largest angle in the triangle with sides 7.5 cm, 9.5 cm and 15.5 cm long.

5 This is part of the Newtown road system. Calculate:

a the acute angle between Rose Street and Graham Avenue, correct to 0.1°

b the area of the triangular traffic island surrounded by the three roads, to the nearest m^2.

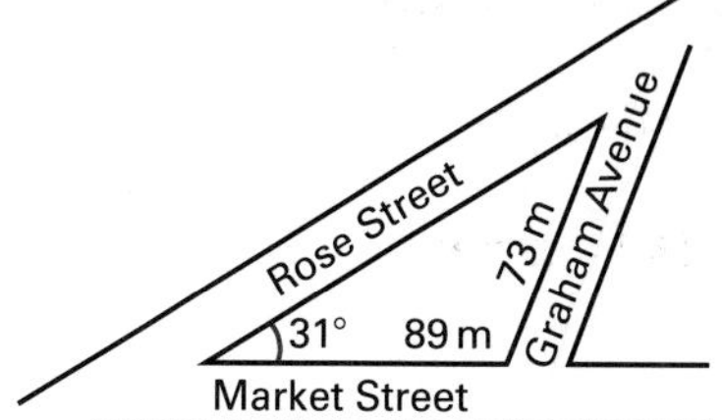

6 Given the measurements in the diagram, calculate, to the nearest metre:

a QC **b** AC.

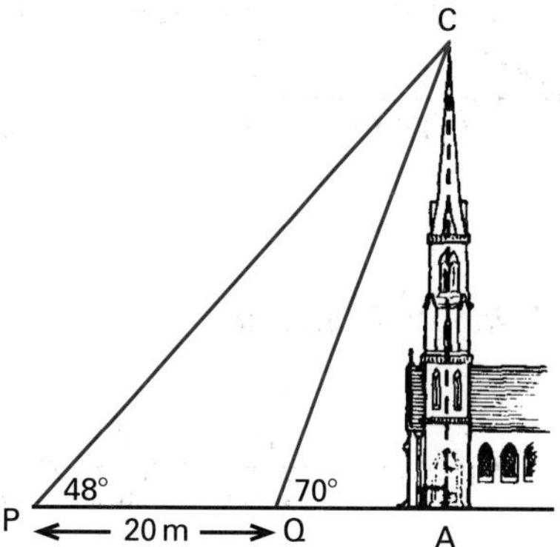

7 Two ships sail from port O. The first follows a course 050° for 80 km to A. The second steers 315° for 40 km to B. Calculate:

a the distance AB, to the nearest km

b the bearing of A from B, to the nearest degree.

8 Prove that:

a the area of $\triangle PQR = \frac{1}{2}qr\sin(\alpha + \beta)$

b $p = \dfrac{q\sin(\alpha + \beta)}{\sin\alpha}$

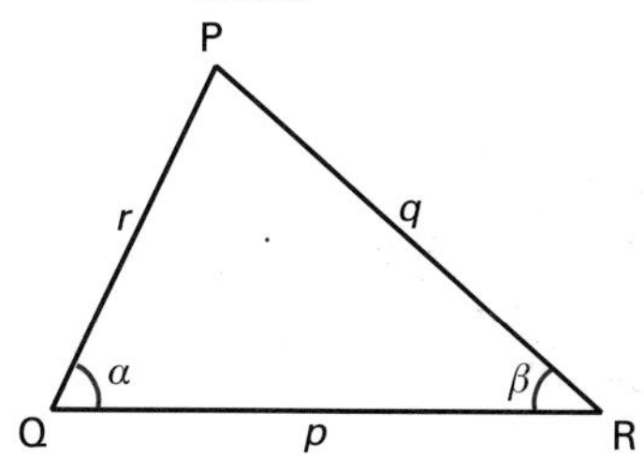

Reminders

(i) In $\triangle$ABC, $A = 180° - (B + C)$

(ii) $\sin(180° - A) = \sin A$. (The sine of an angle = the sine of its supplement.)

9 Point R bears $a°$ from P and $b°$ from Q.
Prove that:

a $d_1 = \dfrac{d_2 \sin a°}{\sin b°}$

b $d_2 = \dfrac{d_3 \sin b°}{\sin (b - a)°}$

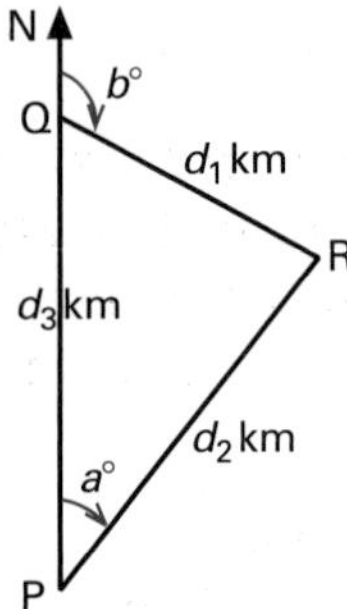

10 Prove that:

a $QC = \dfrac{d \sin x}{\sin (y - x)}$

b $AC = \dfrac{d \sin x \sin y}{\sin (y - x)}$.

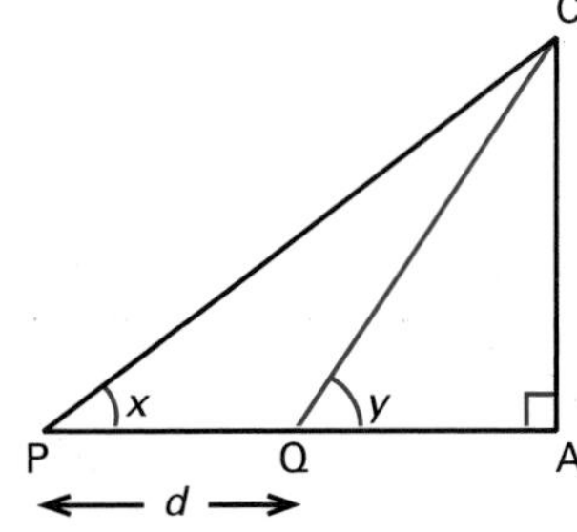

11 In △ABC, AB = AC and ∠B = $x°$.

a Prove that $a \sin x° = b \sin 2x°$.

b Find the exact value of $a{:}b$ when:

(i) $x = 30$ (ii) $x = 45$ (iii) $x = 60$.

12 In △ABC, AB = AC = 4 cm and BC = 2 cm.

Show that the exact value of sin A is $\dfrac{\sqrt{15}}{8}$.

Can you find more than one method?

Three dimensions

We live in a 3-dimensional world – a world of length, breadth and height. Even this sheet of paper has 3 dimensions, although its thickness is very small in comparison with its length and breadth. We start our study by returning to the basic 3-dimensional shape of the cuboid, and calculating angles and lengths associated with it.

(i) *Angle between line and plane*
To find the angle between HB and ABCD, find the perpendicular HD from H to ABCD. *∠HBD is the required angle.*

(ii) *Angle between two planes*
To find the angle between planes ABGH and ABCD, find their line of intersection AB, then a line in each plane (BC and BG) perpendicular to AB. *∠CBG is the required angle*; ∠DAH would also do.

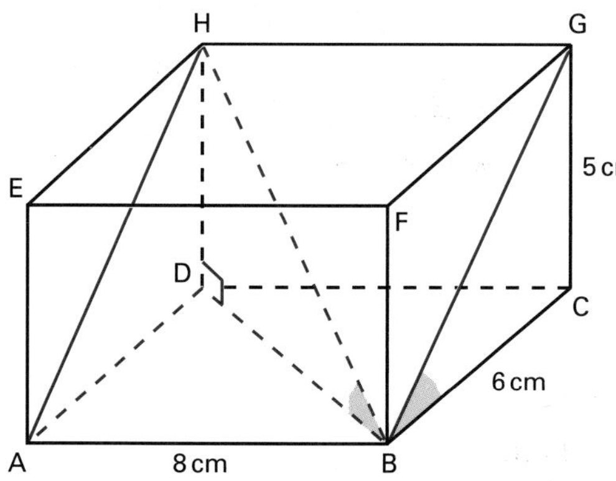

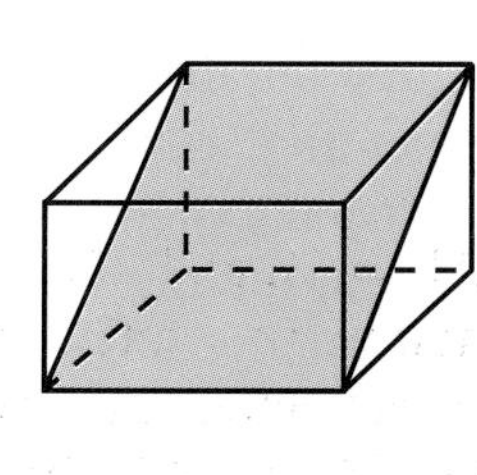

EXERCISE 2

1 In the cuboid in the box above, calculate (angles correct to 0.1°):
a BD **b** ∠HBD **c** ∠CBG.

2 In this cube, name the angle between:

a *line* and *plane*

TQ	PQRS
QV	PQRS
QT	PSWT

b *plane* and *plane*

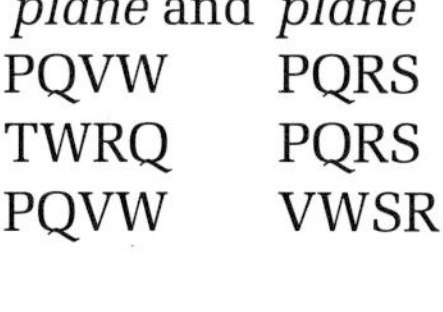

PQVW	PQRS
TWRQ	PQRS
PQVW	VWSR

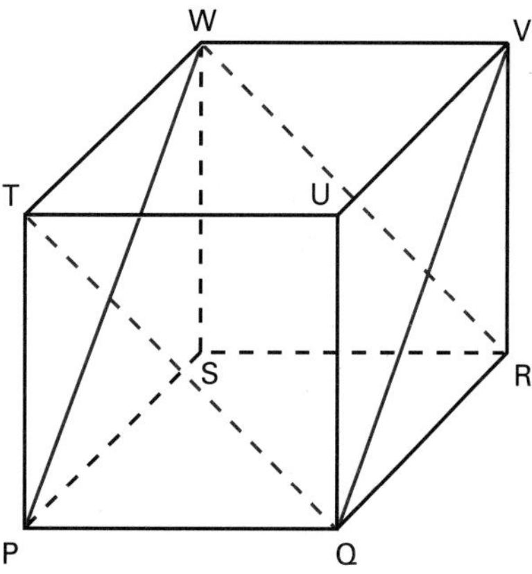

3 This cube has side 1 unit long. Calculate, correct to 0.1°, the size of the angle between:

a planes AFGD and ABCD

b face diagonal AF and space diagonal AG.

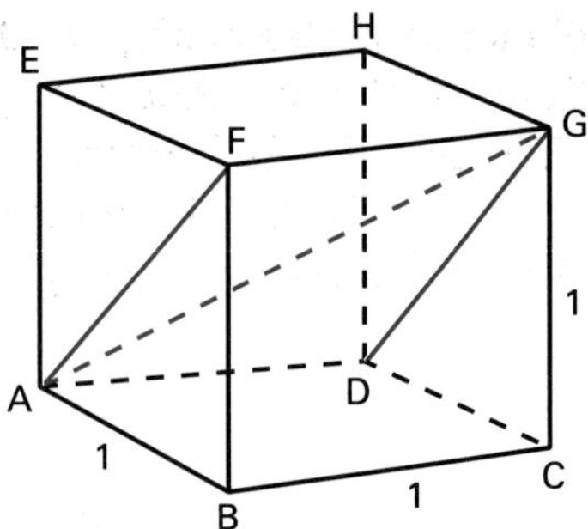

4 The measurements on the bungalow shown in the diagram are in metres. Calculate:

a (i) RQ (ii) OR

(iii) the angle between the side OEF of the roof and the horizontal plane DEFG, to the nearest degree

b (i) DF, to 1 decimal place

(ii) the angle between OD and the plane DEFG, to the nearest degree.

5 ABCD is a regular tetrahedron of side 2 m. AO is the perpendicular from A to base BCD, and DO is produced to meet BC at M.

a Why is M the midpoint of BC?

b Calculate the lengths of DM and MO, to 1 decimal place (assume that $MO = \frac{1}{3}MD$).

c Calculate the size of the angle between the faces ABC and BCD (i.e. angle AMD), to 0.1°.

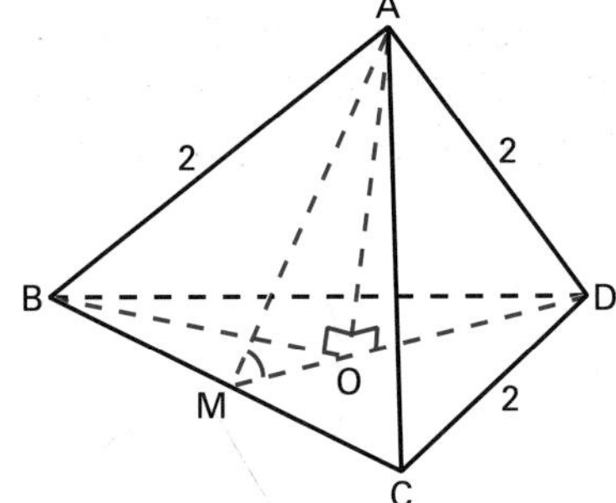

6 This viewer is sitting directly in front of the bottom left-hand corner of the screen. Satisfactory viewing in a cinema requires the eyes to rise through no more than 30° from the bottom to the top of the screen. Calculate, correct to 1 decimal place:

a OA **b** OD

c the angle between planes OAB and ABCD

d the angle the viewer's eyes rise through from D to C. Is this satisfactory?

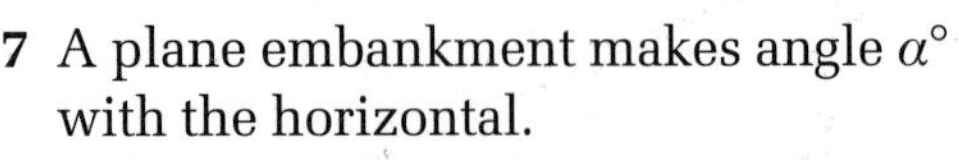

7 A plane embankment makes angle $\alpha°$ with the horizontal.
A drainage channel makes angle $\beta°$ with the fence, and angle $\gamma°$ with a horizontal plane.

a Copy the triangular pyramid part ABCD, and mark angles $\alpha°$, $\beta°$ and $\gamma°$.

b Show that $\sin\gamma° = \sin\alpha° \cos\beta°$.

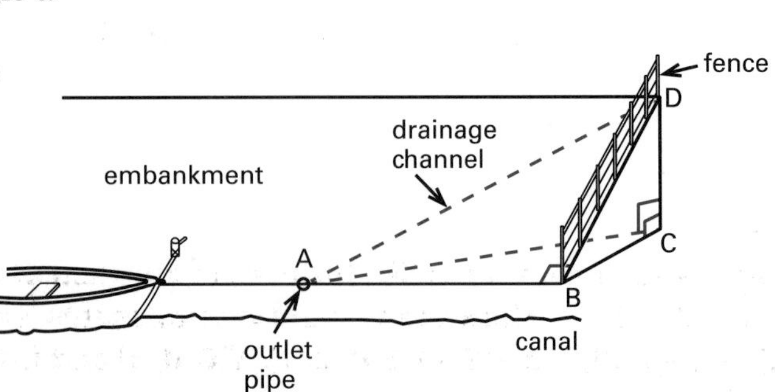

8 OP makes angles of $\alpha°$, $\beta°$ and $\gamma°$ with OX, OY and OZ respectively. OABCRSPQ is a cuboid.

a Express: **(i)** OB^2 in terms of x and y

(ii) OP^2 in terms of x, y and z (use $\triangle OBP$).

b Prove that $\cos^2 \alpha° + \cos^2 \beta° + \cos^2 \gamma° = 1$.

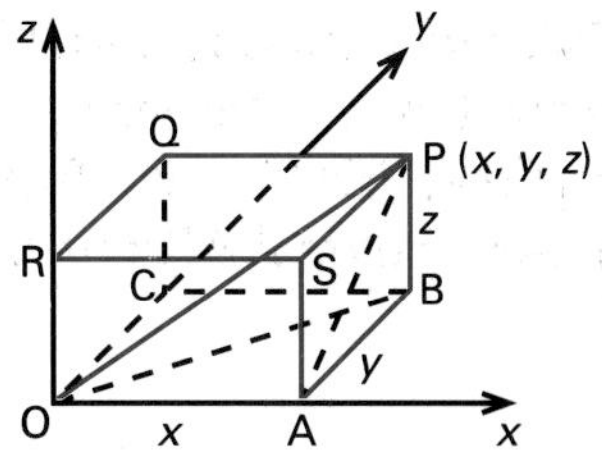

Coordinates in 3 dimensions

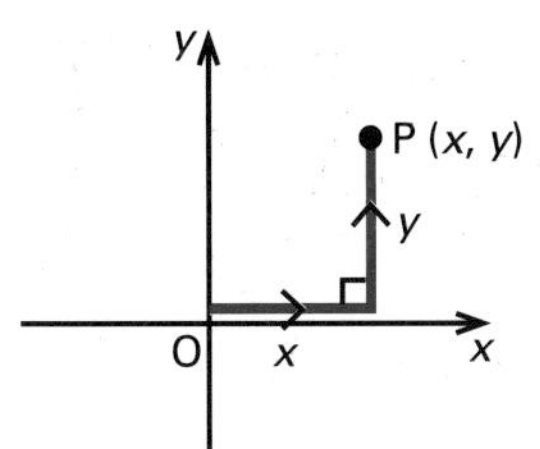

To fix the position of a point on the plane you need two axes OX and OY, and two coordinates x and y. P is the point (x, y).

When you move out of that plane all you need is one other axis OZ (perpendicular to OX and OY), and one other coordinate z, to fix the position of $Q(x, y, z)$.

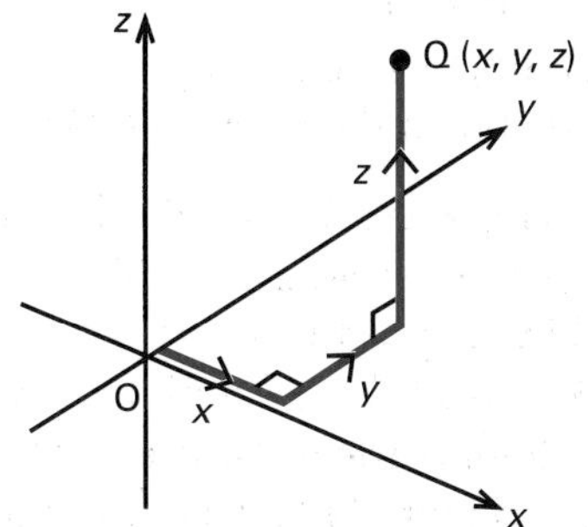

EXERCISE 3

1 Check the positions of the points A(3, 2, 1), B(−1, −2, 3), C(0, 2, 0) and D(0, 0, −3) by following the trail from O in the x-direction, then in the y-direction, then in the z-direction.

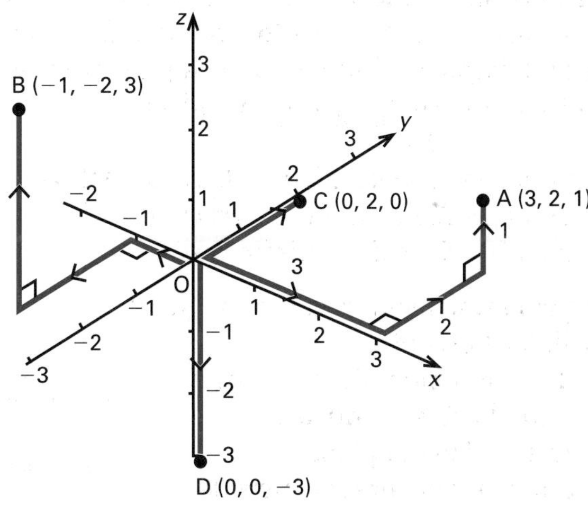

2 Draw a set of three axes like the ones in question **1**, and mark the scales 1, 2, 3, …, −1, −2, −3, …. Show the x, y and z-components leading to the points P(3, 1, 1), Q(−1, −1, 2), R(2, −1, 0), S(0, 2, 1), T(0, 0, 3) and U(0, −2, −3).

3 a P is the point (3, 2, 2). What are the coordinates of the point on the XOY plane directly below P?

b Write down the coordinates of A, B and C.

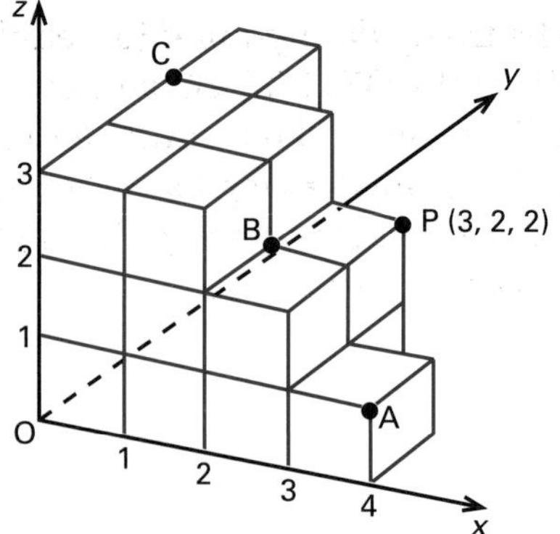

4 The cuboid sits in the OX, OY, OZ corner. P is the point (2, 1, 3).

a Write down the coordinates of the other seven vertices of the cuboid (x-direction, then y-direction, then z-direction).

b Calculate, correct to 1 decimal place:
(i) OQ **(ii)** OS **(iii)** OU.

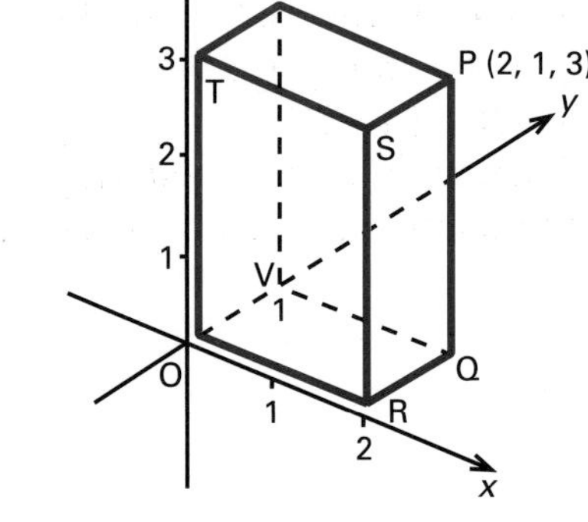

5 The edges of this cuboid are parallel to the axes. AB = 4 units, BC = 2 units and CG = 3 units. A is the point (−1, 2, 0).

a Write down the coordinates of the other vertices.

b Calculate, in simplest surd form, the lengths of:

(i) the face diagonals of the cuboid BG, AC and AF

(ii) the space diagonal AG.

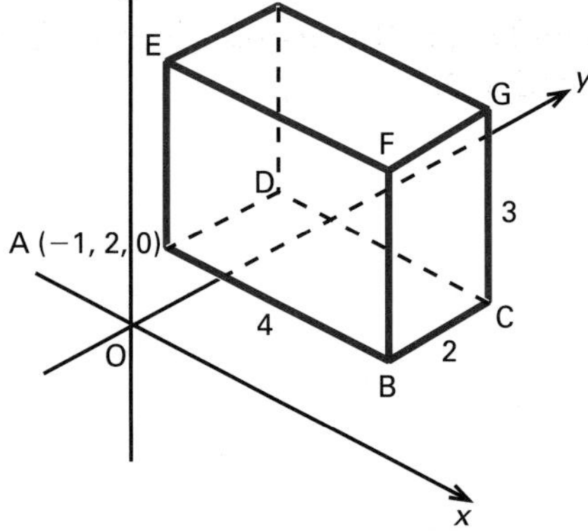

6 P is the point (12, 10, 8) and PR is perpendicular to plane XOY. OQRS is a rectangle.

a Write down the coordinates of Q, R, S and T.

b Calculate, correct to 1 decimal place:

(i) the length of OR

(ii) the angle between OP and plane OQRS.

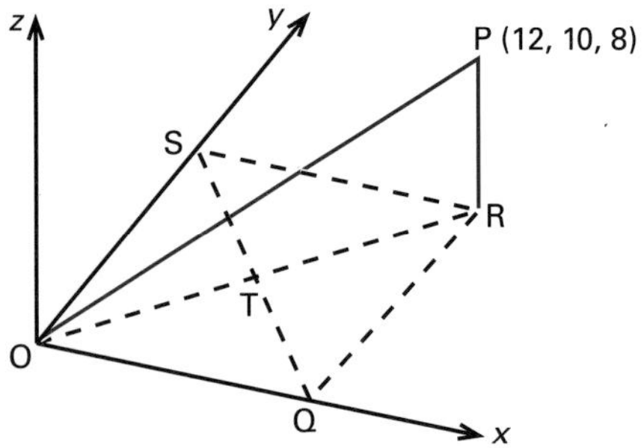

7 The triangular pyramid (or tetrahedron) OABC sits in the OX, OY′, OZ corner.

a Write down the coordinates of its vertices.

b Calculate the lengths of the sides of △ABC as surds, and the sizes of the angles of △ABC to the nearest degree.

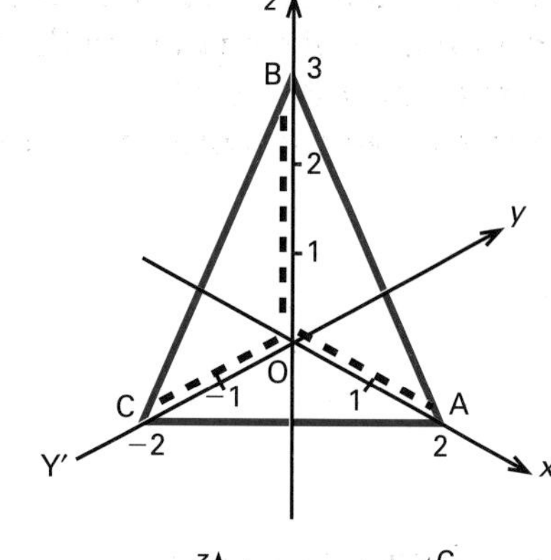

8 A is (4, 0, 0), B(4, 3, 0) and C(4, 3, 12).

a Calculate the length of:

(i) OB **(ii)** OC.

b Calculate the size of the angle between OC and plane XOY, to the nearest degree.

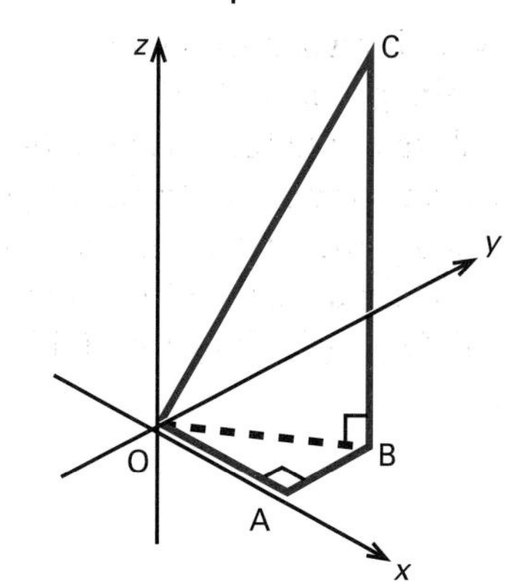

9 Calculate, to the nearest degree, the angle between the planes ABC and XOY′ in question **7**.

CHAPTER 3.1 REVIEW

1 Calculate the distance, correct to 0.1 km, between the ship S and the lighthouse L. H is the harbour.

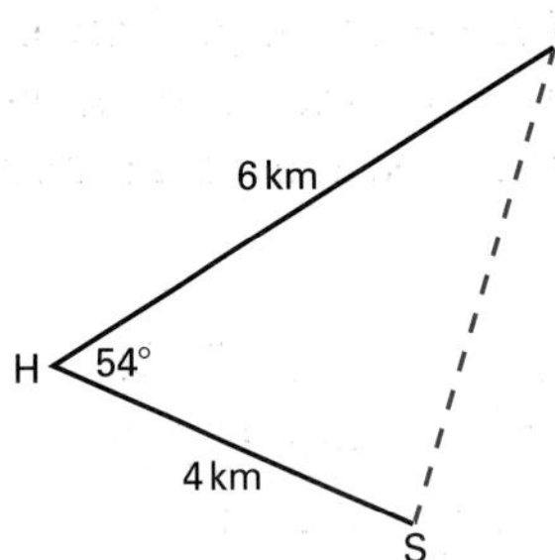

2 Calculate the size of angle A, correct to 0.1°.

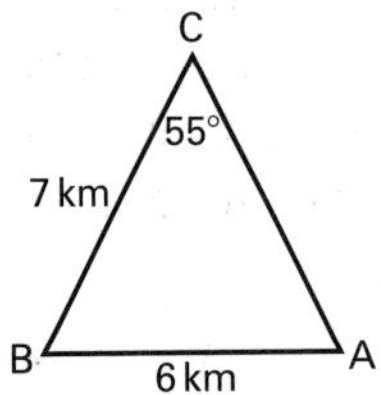

3 Calculate the area of △ABC in question 2, correct to 1 decimal place.

4 Show that, in the diagram:

a PQ = 8 cm

b PS = $8\sqrt{3}$ cm

c $\sin y° = \dfrac{15 - 8\sqrt{3}}{34}$

5 A tower OP stands on horizontal ground.

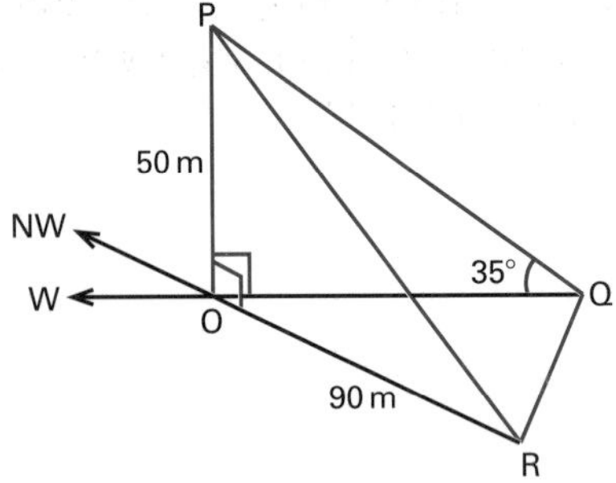

Calculate, to the nearest degree or metre:

a the angle of elevation of the sun (∠ORP) when it shines from the north-west

b the length of the tower's shadow OQ when the sun is due west

c the distance QR.

6 ABCDPQRS is a cuboid. Calculate, correct to 1 decimal place where necessary:

a the lengths QC and PC

b the angle between

(i) PC and CD

(ii) PC and the plane CBQR.

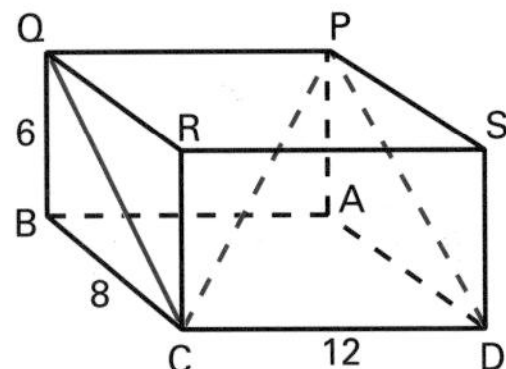

7 OABCEFGH is a cuboid, and P(4, 3, 8) is vertically above M. AF = 6.

a Give the coordinates of A, B, C, E, F, G and H.

b Calculate the length of AP, correct to 1 decimal place.

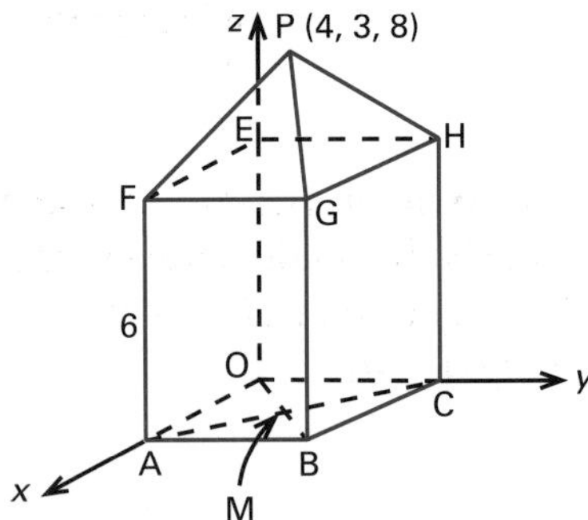

8 An aircraft is 9 km east and 12 km north of its base, and at a height of 8 km.

a Sketch a set of three perpendicular axes, and write down the coordinates of the aircraft's position.

b Calculate the distance and bearing from the base of the point on the ground below the aircraft.

CHAPTER 3.1 SUMMARY

1 Triangle formulae

Sine rule $\dfrac{a}{\sin A} = \dfrac{b}{\sin B} = \dfrac{c}{\sin C}$

Cosine rule $a^2 = b^2 + c^2 - 2bc\cos A$

$$\cos A = \frac{b^2 + c^2 - a^2}{2bc}$$

Area of $\triangle$ ABC $\triangle = \frac{1}{2}ab\sin C$

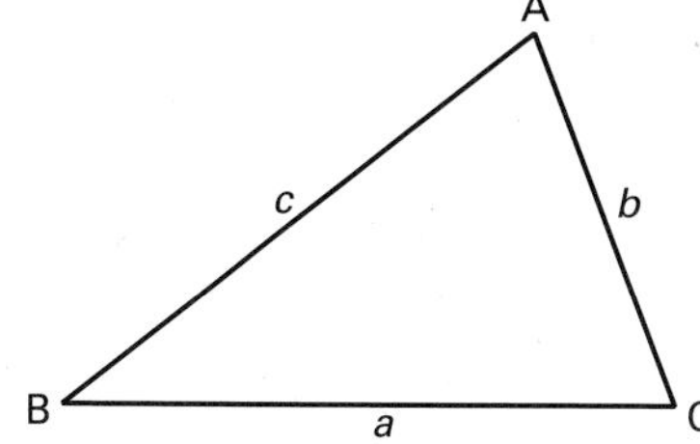

2 Related angles

$\sin(180° - A) = \sin A$

$\sin(-A) = -\sin A$

$\cos(180° - A) = -\cos A$

$\cos(-A) = \cos A$

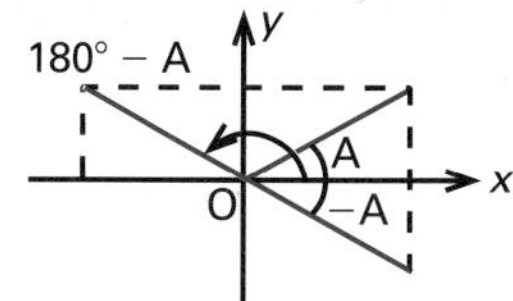

3 The angle between a line and a plane

This is the angle between the line and its projection in the plane, i.e. ∠PRQ in diagram (**ii**).

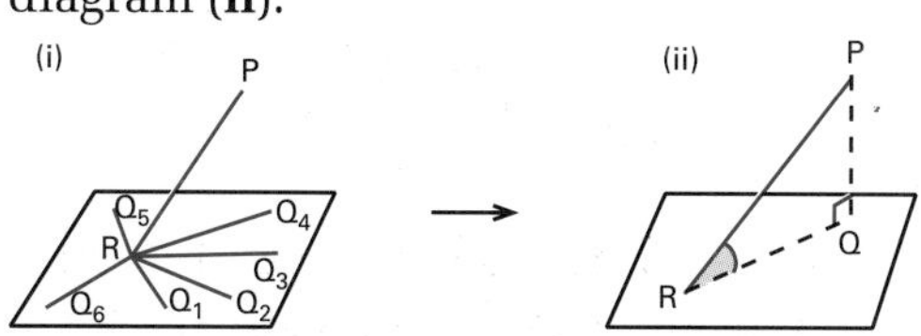

4 The angle between two planes

The angle between two planes which meet at AB is the angle between two lines, one in each plane, perpendicular to AB and meeting on AB, as shown below.

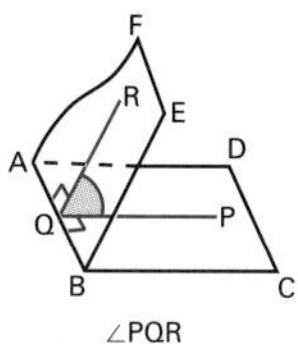

∠PQR (planes ABCD, ABEF)

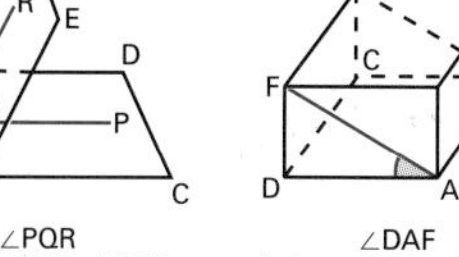

∠DAF (planes ABCD, ABEF)

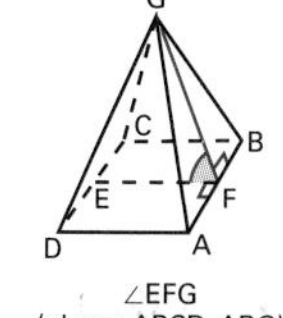

∠EFG (planes ABCD, ABG)

5 Coordinates in 2 and 3 dimensions

To fix the position of a point on the plane you need two axes, OX and OY, and two coordinates x and y. P is the point (x, y).

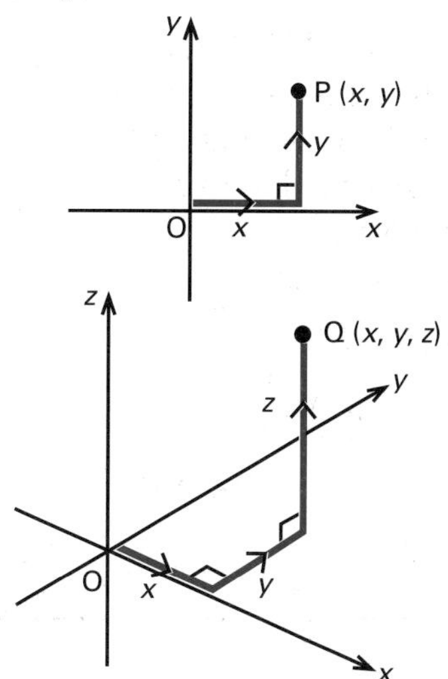

To fix the position of a point in space you need three axes, OX, OY and OZ, and three coordinates x, y and z. Q is the point (x, y, z).

3.2 Compound Angle Formulae

Reminders

1 Related angles

(i) $-A$  (ii) $90° - A$ (iii) $180° - A$

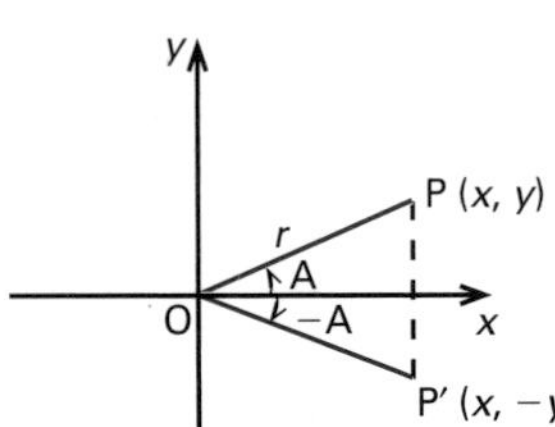

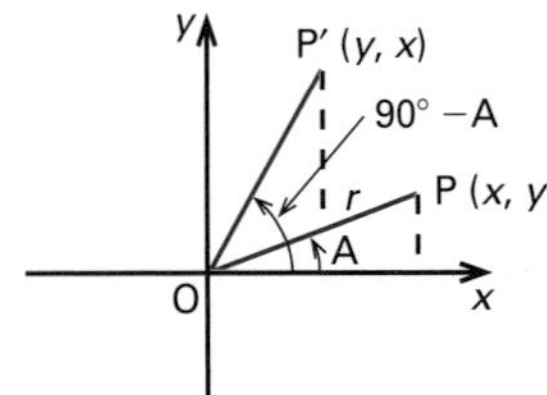

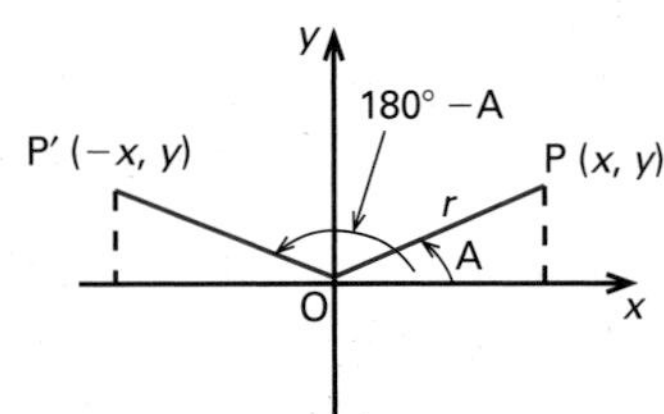

$\sin(-A) = \dfrac{-y}{r} = -\sin A$ $\quad \sin(90° - A) = \dfrac{x}{r} = \cos A$ $\quad \sin(180° - A) = \dfrac{y}{r} = \sin A$

$\cos(-A) = \dfrac{x}{r} = \cos A$ $\quad \cos(90° - A) = \dfrac{y}{r} = \sin A$ $\quad \cos(180° - A) = \dfrac{-x}{r} = -\cos A$

2 Sin–cos–tan formulae

(i) $$\frac{\sin A}{\cos A} = \frac{\frac{y}{r}}{\frac{x}{r}} = \frac{y}{x} = \tan A$$

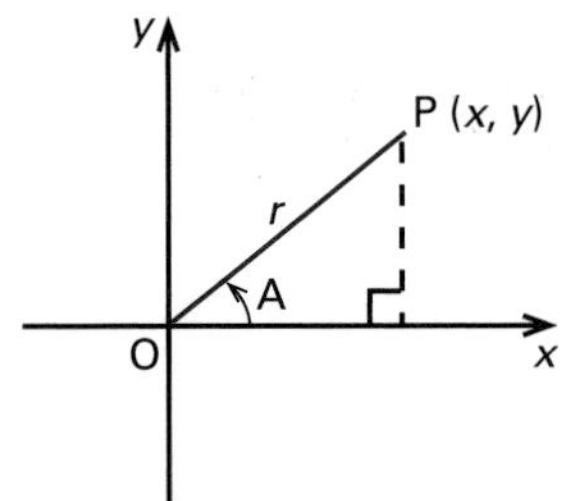

(ii) $$\sin^2 A + \cos^2 A = \frac{y^2}{r^2} + \frac{x^2}{r^2} = \frac{y^2 + x^2}{r^2} = 1$$

(Pythagoras' Theorem)

Summary

a **(i)** $\left.\begin{array}{l}\sin(-A) = -\sin A \\ \cos(-A) = \cos A\end{array}\right\}$ **(ii)** $\left.\begin{array}{l}\sin(90° - A) = \cos A \\ \cos(90° - A) = \sin A\end{array}\right\}$

(iii) $\left.\begin{array}{l}\sin(180° - A) = \sin A \\ \cos(180° - A) = -\cos A\end{array}\right\}$ **(iv)** π radians $= 180°$

b **(i)** $\dfrac{\sin A}{\cos A} = \tan A$

(ii) $\sin^2 A + \cos^2 A = 1$ (and $\sin^2 A = 1 - \cos^2 A$, $\cos^2 A = 1 - \sin^2 A$)

EXERCISE 1

1 Simplify:

a $\sin(-x)^\circ$ **b** $\cos(-y)^\circ$ **c** $\sin(90 - a)^\circ$

d $\sin(180 - a)^\circ$ **e** $\cos(90 - b)^\circ$ **f** $\cos(180 - b)^\circ$.

2 Simplify (using radian measure):

a $\sin(\pi - \theta)$ **b** $\cos(\pi - \theta)$ **c** $\sin(-\theta)$

d $\cos\left(\frac{\pi}{2} - \theta\right)$ **e** $\sin\left(\frac{\pi}{2} - \theta\right)$ **f** $\cos(-\theta)$.

3 Use your calculator to check that:

a $\cos(-10)^\circ = \cos 10^\circ$ **b** $\sin^2 50^\circ + \cos^2 50^\circ = 1$

c $\sin 160^\circ = \sin 20^\circ$ **d** $\cos 160^\circ = -\cos 20^\circ$

e $\sin 75^\circ = \cos 15^\circ$ **f** $\frac{\sin 40^\circ}{\cos 40^\circ} = \tan 40^\circ$.

4 Simplify:

a $\sin x^\circ + \sin(-x)^\circ + \sin(180 - x)^\circ$

b $\cos x^\circ + \cos(-x)^\circ + \cos(180 - x)^\circ$.

5 Write each of these in its simplest form:

a $\frac{\sin A}{\cos A}$ **b** $\frac{\sin B}{\cos B}$ **c** $\frac{\sin 2C}{\cos 2C}$

d $\sin^2 u^\circ + \cos^2 u^\circ$ **e** $\sin^2 3t^\circ + \cos^2 3t^\circ$

f $1 - \sin^2 A$ **g** $1 - \cos^2 B$ **h** $1 - \cos^2 2C$.

6 Without using a calculator, check by using exact values of $\sin\frac{\pi}{4}\left(= \frac{1}{\sqrt{2}}\right)$ etc., that:

a $\sin^2\frac{\pi}{4} + \cos^2\frac{\pi}{4} = 1$ **b** $\cos^2 30^\circ = 1 - \sin^2 30^\circ$

c $\frac{\sin 45^\circ}{\cos 45^\circ} = \tan 45^\circ$ **d** $\frac{\sin\frac{\pi}{3}}{\cos\frac{\pi}{3}} = \tan\frac{\pi}{3}$.

Cos (A + B) and cos (A − B)

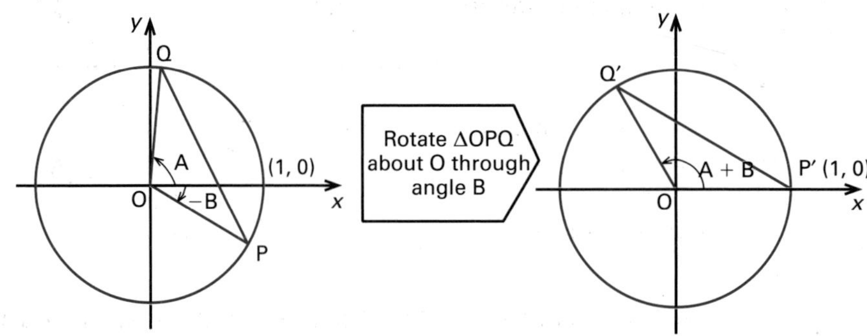

P is $(\cos(-B), \sin(-B))$, i.e. P is $(\cos B, -\sin B)$
Q is $(\cos A, \sin A)$
$PQ^2 = (\cos A - \cos B)^2 + (\sin A + \sin B)^2$

$$= \cos^2 A + \sin^2 A + \cos^2 B + \sin^2 B - 2\cos A\cos B + 2\sin A\sin B$$

$$= 2 - 2(\cos A\cos B - \sin A\sin B)$$

P′ is (1, 0)
Q′ is $(\cos(A+B), \sin(A+B))$
$(P'Q')^2 = (1 - \cos(A+B))^2 + (\sin(A+B))^2$

$$= 1 + \cos^2(A+B) + \sin^2(A+B) - 2\cos(A+B)$$

$$= 2 - 2\cos(A+B).$$

But $PQ^2 = (P'Q')^2$.
It follows that $\cos(A+B) = \cos A\cos B - \sin A\sin B$.
The formula is true for all sizes of angles A and B, whether in degrees or in radians.
Replacing B by −B, the formula becomes
$\cos(A-B) = \cos A\cos(-B) - \sin A\sin(-B)$, that is:

$$\cos(A-B) = \cos A\cos B + \sin A\sin B$$

EXERCISE 2

1 Write down formulae for:
a $\cos(X+Y)$ **b** $\cos(C-D)$
c $\cos(M+N)$ **d** $\cos(P-Q)$.

2 Prove that:
a $\cos(U+V) + \cos(U-V) = 2\cos U\cos V$
b $\cos(U-V) - \cos(U+V) = 2\sin U\sin V$.

3 **a** Write down a formula for cos (C + D).
b Use the triangles to show that $\cos(C + D) = \frac{16}{65}$.
c Find the value of cos (C – D) as a fraction.

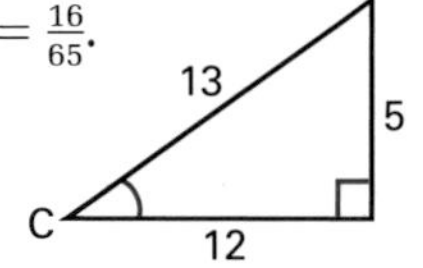

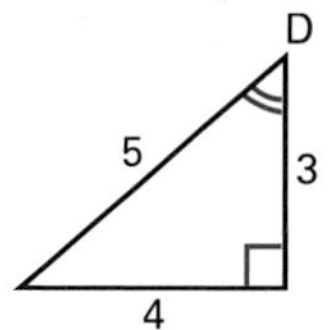

4 **a** Sketch right-angled triangles for which:
(i) $\sin A = \frac{3}{5}$ (ii) $\sin B = \frac{7}{25}$.
b Show that $\cos(A + B) = \frac{3}{5}$.
c Find the value of cos (A – B) as a fraction.

5 Sketch:
a 30°, 60°, 90° and 45°, 45°, 90° triangles, marking the side lengths 1, 2, $\sqrt{3}$ and 1, 1, $\sqrt{2}$
b the sine and cosine graphs $y = \sin x°$, $y = \cos x°$ for $0 \leqslant x \leqslant 360$.

Use the above in the following questions. Don't use a calculator.

6 Check the formula for cos (A + B) using:
a A = B = 90° **b** A = 30°, B = 60°.

7 Check the formula for cos (A – B) using:
a $A = B = \frac{\pi}{4}$ radians **b** $A = \frac{\pi}{3}$, B = 0 radians.

8 Use the formulae for cos (A ± B) to simplify:
a $\cos(180 + x)°$ **b** $\cos(360 - y)°$
c $\cos(2\pi + \theta)$ **d** $\cos\left(\frac{\pi}{2} - \theta\right)$.

9 Using 75° = 45° + 30°, show that $\cos 75° = \frac{\sqrt{3} - 1}{2\sqrt{2}}$.

10 Using 15° = 60° – 45°, show that $\cos 15° = \frac{\sqrt{6} + \sqrt{2}}{4}$.

11 Are these true or false?
a $\cos(x - 30)° - \cos(x + 30)° = \sqrt{3} \sin x°$
b $\cos(x + 45)° + \cos(x - 45)° = \sqrt{2} \cos x°$

12 Simplify:
a $\cos P \cos Q - \sin P \sin Q$
b $\cos A \cos 2A + \sin A \sin 2A$
c $\cos 55° \cos 35° - \sin 55° \sin 35°$
d $\cos 75° \cos 15° + \sin 75° \sin 15°$.

13 Prove that:
$(\cos A + \cos B)^2 + (\sin A - \sin B)^2 = 2(1 + \cos(A + B))$.

14 In engineering, the problem of making bends in pipes often arises. One view of this pipe is seen by projecting vertically down onto the drawing board.

a Find the lengths of AB and BC.

b State the relation between $x°$, $y°$ and $\angle$ABC.

c Find the exact value of cos ABC.

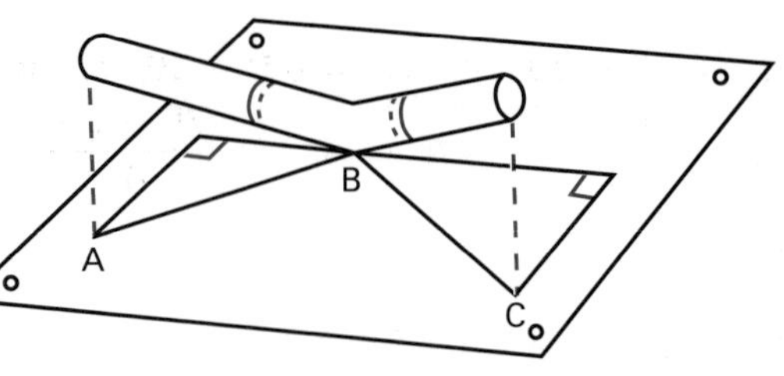

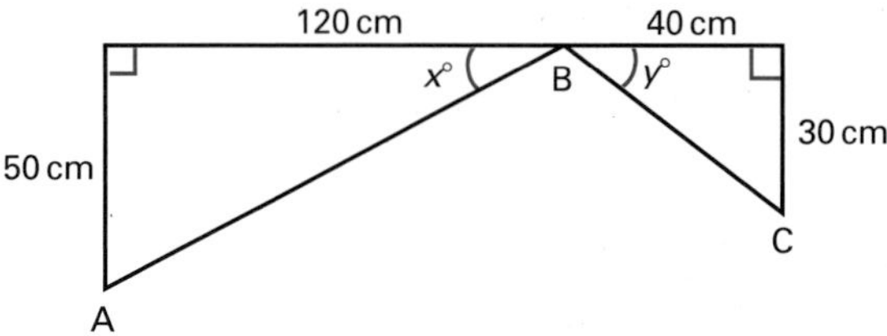

Sin (A + B) *and* sin (A – B)

Reminder

1(ii) on page 152 tells you how to change a sine to a cosine.

So, $\sin(A + B) = \cos(90° - (A + B)) = \cos((90° - A) - B)$

$$= \cos(90° - A)\cos B + \sin(90° - A)\sin B$$

$$= \sin A \cos B + \cos A \sin B$$

$$\sin(A + B) = \sin A \cos B + \cos A \sin B$$

Similarly, $\sin(A - B) = \sin A \cos B - \cos A \sin B$

EXERCISE 3

1 Write down formulae for:
a $\sin(P + Q)$ **b** $\sin(X - Y)$.

2 Prove that:
a $\sin(M + N) + \sin(M - N) = 2 \sin M \cos N$
b $\sin(M + N) - \sin(M - N) = 2 \cos M \sin N$.

3 a Sketch a right-angled triangle in which $\cos A = \frac{5}{13}$, and another in which $\sin B = \frac{4}{5}$.
b Write down ratios for sin A and cos B.
c Show that $\sin(A + B) = \frac{56}{65}$.
d Find the value of $\sin(A - B)$ as a fraction.

4 a Check the formula for $\sin(A + B)$ using $A = B = 45°$.
b Check the formula for $\sin(A - B)$ using $A = \frac{\pi}{6}$ and $B = \frac{\pi}{3}$ radians.

5 Use the formulae for $\sin(A \pm B)$ to simplify:
a $\sin(360 + x)°$ **b** $\sin(90 - y)°$
c $\sin(\pi + \theta)$ **d** $\sin(2\pi - \theta)$.

6 Using $75° = 45° + 30°$ and $15° = 45° - 30°$, show that:

a $\sin 75° = \dfrac{\sqrt{6}+\sqrt{2}}{4}$ **b** $\sin 15° = \dfrac{\sqrt{6}-\sqrt{2}}{4}$.

7 Prove that:

a $\sin\left(\theta + \dfrac{\pi}{6}\right) = \frac{1}{2}(\cos\theta + \sqrt{3}\sin\theta)$

b $\sin(x + 60)° - \cos(x + 30)° = \sin x°$

c $\cos\left(\dfrac{\pi}{4} + \theta\right) - \sin\left(\dfrac{\pi}{4} - \theta\right) = 0.$

8 Prove that:

a $\tan A - \tan B = \dfrac{\sin(A - B)}{\cos A \cos B}$

b $\tan 3A + \tan A = \dfrac{\sin 4A}{\cos 3A \cos A}$.

9 Prove that $\sin(x + 30)° + \cos(x - 120)° = \sqrt{3}\sin x°$.

a Use $\tan(B - A) = \dfrac{\sin(B - A)}{\cos(B - A)}$ to find a formula for $\tan(B - A)$ in terms of $\tan B$ and $\tan A$.

b The gradients of the lines in the diagram are m_1 and m_2. Prove that $\tan\theta° = \dfrac{m_2 - m_1}{1 + m_1 m_2}$.

c Find the acute angle between the lines $y = 2x + 1$ and $y = -3x + 2$, using the formula in **b**.

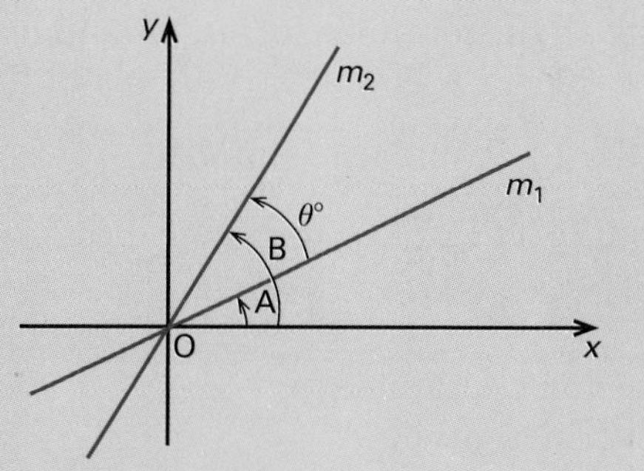

Sin 2A and cos 2A

(i) $\sin 2A = \sin(A + A) = \sin A\cos A + \cos A\sin A = 2\sin A\cos A$

(ii) $\cos 2A = \cos(A + A) = \cos A\cos A - \sin A\sin A = \cos^2 A - \sin^2 A$

Also, $\cos^2 A - \sin^2 A = \cos^2 A - (1 - \cos^2 A) = 2\cos^2 A - 1$

and $\cos^2 A - \sin^2 A = (1 - \sin^2 A) - \sin^2 A = 1 - 2\sin^2 A$

(iii) From $\cos 2A = 2\cos^2 A - 1$, $\cos^2 A = \frac{1}{2}(1 + \cos 2A)$

$\cos 2A = 1 - 2\sin^2 A$, $\sin^2 A = \frac{1}{2}(1 - \cos 2A)$

So:

$$\sin 2A = 2\sin A\cos A$$
$$\cos 2A = \cos^2 A - \sin^2 A$$
$$= 2\cos^2 A - 1$$
$$= 1 - 2\sin^2 A$$
$$\cos^2 A = \tfrac{1}{2}(1 + \cos 2A)$$
$$\sin^2 A = \tfrac{1}{2}(1 - \cos 2A)$$

EXERCISE 4A

Do not use a calculator in this exercise.

1 Write down a formula for each of these:
a $\sin 2X$ **b** $\sin 2\theta$ **c** $\sin 4\theta$.

2 Write down three formulae for each of these:
a $\cos 2Y$ **b** $\cos 2\theta$ **c** $\cos 4\theta$.

3 **a** Sketch a right-angled triangle in which $\sin A = \frac{3}{5}$, and show that $\cos 2A = \frac{7}{25}$.
b Find a fraction for $\sin 2A$.

4 $\sin A = \dfrac{1}{\sqrt{5}}$ and $0 < A < \dfrac{\pi}{2}$. Find the exact values of:
a $\cos A$ **b** $\sin 2A$ **c** $\cos 2A$.
Check that $\sin^2 2A + \cos^2 2A = 1$.

5 $\cos x° = \dfrac{3}{\sqrt{10}}$ and $0 < x < 90$. Find the exact values of:
a $\sin x°$ **b** $\sin 2x°$ **c** $\cos 2x°$ **d** $\sin 4x°$.

6 $\tan\theta = \dfrac{1}{\sqrt{15}}$ and $0 < \theta < \dfrac{\pi}{2}$. Find the exact values of:
a $\sin 2\theta$ **b** $\cos 2\theta$.

7 Check all the formulae for $\sin 2A$ and $\cos 2A$ for:
a $A = 30°$ **b** $A = 45°$ **c** $A = \pi$ radians.

8 Use the 2A formulae to simplify:
a $2\sin 15° \cos 15°$ **b** $2\cos^2 \dfrac{\pi}{6} - 1$
c $2\sin 45° \cos 45°$ **d** $1 - 2\sin^2 \dfrac{\pi}{12}$.

9 Write down formulae for:
a $\sin A$ in terms of $\frac{1}{2}A$
b $\cos A$ in terms of $\frac{1}{2}A$ (3 formulae).

10 **a** Show that:
(i) $\sin^2 A = \frac{1}{2}(1 - \cos 2A)$ **(ii)** $\cos^2 A = \frac{1}{2}(1 + \cos 2A)$.
b Given $\cos 2A = \frac{1}{4}$, and $0 < A < \dfrac{\pi}{2}$, use the results of **a** to show that:
(i) $\sin A = \dfrac{\sqrt{3}}{2\sqrt{2}}$ **(ii)** $\cos A = \dfrac{\sqrt{5}}{2\sqrt{2}}$.
Check that, for these values, $\sin^2 A + \cos^2 A = 1$.

11 Prove that:
a $(\sin A + \cos A)^2 = 1 + \sin 2A$ **b** $\sin^3 x \cos x + \sin x \cos^3 x = \frac{1}{2}\sin 2x$.

12 Using $3A = 2A + A$, prove that:
a $\sin 3A = 3\sin A - 4\sin^3 A$ **b** $\cos 3A = 4\cos^3 A - 3\cos A$.

13 Using $\tan\theta = \dfrac{\sin\theta}{\cos\theta}$, prove that:
a $\dfrac{2\tan\theta}{1 + \tan^2\theta} = \sin 2\theta$ **b** $\dfrac{1 - \tan^2\theta}{1 + \tan^2\theta} = \cos 2\theta$.

Challenge

a Express $\cos^4 x$ in the form $a + b\cos 2x + c\cos 4x$. (Start with $\cos^2 x = \frac{1}{2}(1 + \cos 2x)$.)

b Find a corresponding expression for $\sin^4 x$.

Example In $\triangle$ABC, prove that $a = 4b\cos x\cos 2x$.

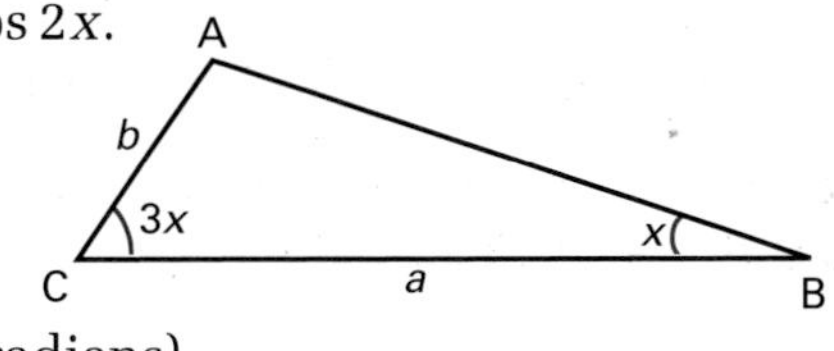

Using the sine rule,

$$\frac{b}{\sin x} = \frac{a}{\sin(\pi - 4x)} \quad \text{(sum of angles of } \triangle = \pi \text{ radians)}$$

$$\text{so } a = \frac{b\sin 4x}{\sin x} = \frac{2b\sin 2x\cos 2x}{\sin x} = \frac{2b(2\sin x\cos x)\cos 2x}{\sin x}$$

i.e. $a = 4b\cos x\cos 2x$.

EXERCISE 4B

1 Using a formula for $\sin(a + b)°$ to prove that in the diagram, $a + b = 45$.

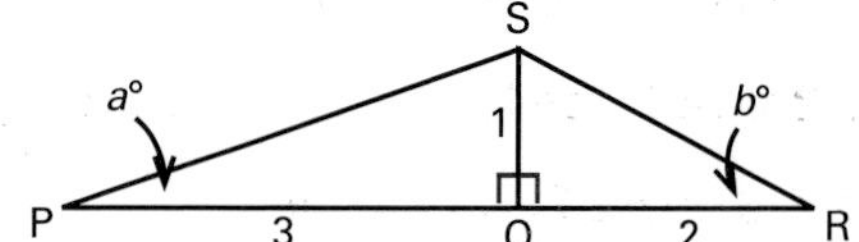

2 Use a formula for $\cos(a + b)°$ to calculate $\angle$ADC, correct to 1 decimal place.

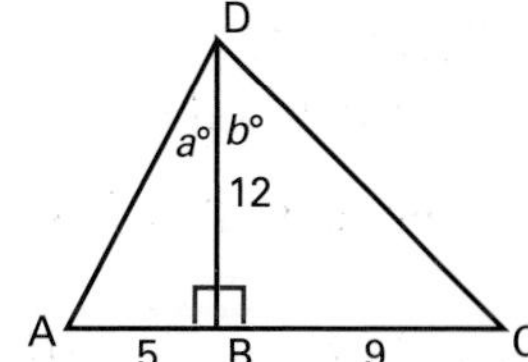

3 For this snooker shot,

a prove that:

(i) $\sin y° = \sin 2x°$

(ii) $\cos y° = -\cos 2x°$.

b Show that:

(i) $\sin y° = \dfrac{336}{625}$

(ii) $\cos y° = -\dfrac{527}{625}$.

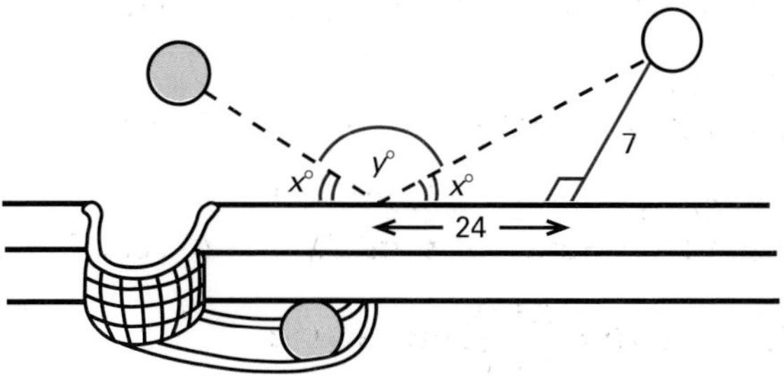

4 $\triangle$ABC is isosceles. Show that:

a $\sin A° = \sin 2\theta°$

b $a = 2b\cos\theta°$, by

(i) using the Sine Rule

(ii) drawing AD perpendicular to BC.

5 Show that in $\triangle$ABC in question **4**:

a the area of the triangle is $b^2 \sin\theta° \cos\theta°$

b $\cos 2\theta° = \dfrac{a^2}{2b^2} - 1$.

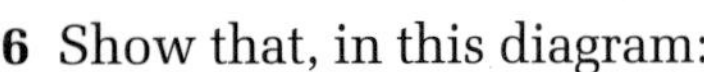

6 Show that, in this diagram:

a $\angle XBC = (45 - \theta)°$

b $XC = a(\cos\theta° - \sin\theta°)$.

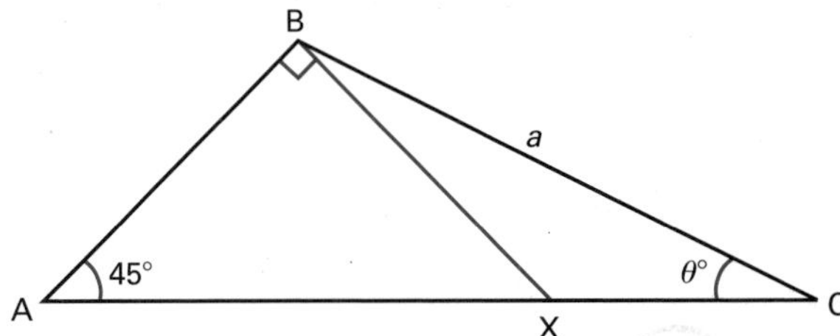

7 a Assuming a formula for $\cos 2\theta°$, prove that $\cos^2\theta° = \frac{1}{2}(1 + \cos 2\theta°)$.

b O is the centre of this circle, with radius 2 units. Prove that:

(i) $OD = 2\cos\theta°$

(ii) $AD^2 = 2(5 + 3\cos 2\theta°)$.

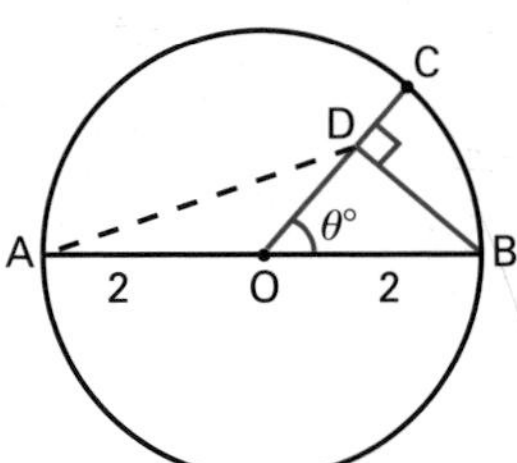

8 Light meets a plate glass surface at $i°$ to the perpendicular, and leaves at $r°$ to the perpendicular. The refractive index $\dfrac{\sin i°}{\sin r°}$ is a constant.

The glass surface is rotated through angle $\theta°$, so that the light meets the glass at $(i - \theta)°$ to the perpendicular, and leaves at $R°$ to the perpendicular.

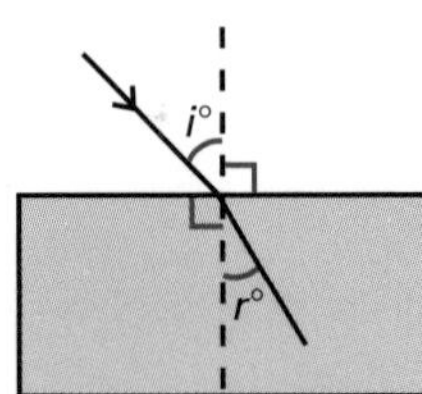

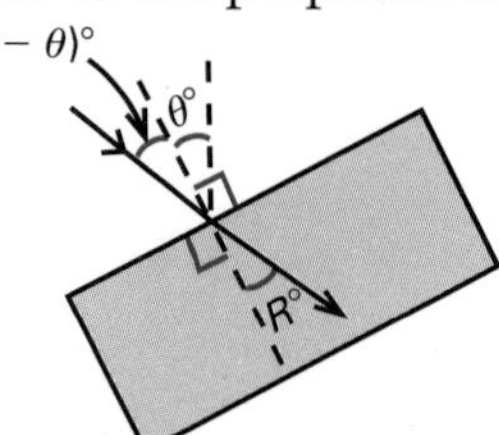

a Write down an equation, equating two expressions for the refractive index.

b Prove that $\sin R° = \left(\cos\theta° - \dfrac{\sin\theta°}{\tan i°}\right)\sin r°$.

9 Two mirrors are at $x°$ to each other. A ray of light strikes one mirror at $x°$ and is reflected at B onto the second mirror at C. Prove that $\sin BCD = -\sin 4x°$.

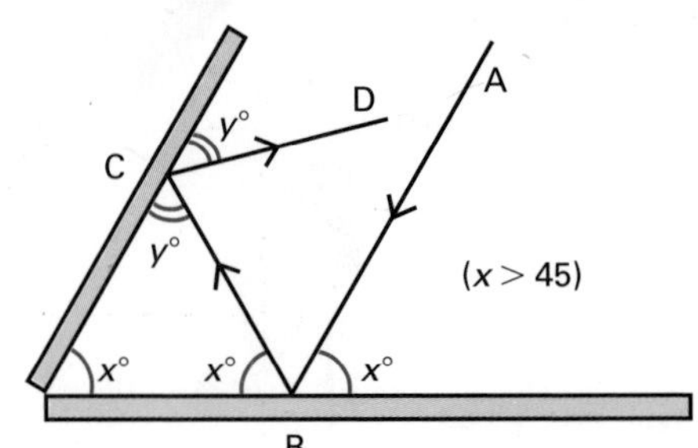

Solving equations containing sin 2A and cos 2A terms

Example Solve the equation $\cos 2x° - \cos x° + 1 = 0$, for $0 \leqslant x \leqslant 360$.

$$\cos 2x° - \cos x° + 1 = 0$$
$$(2\cos^2 x° - 1) - \cos x° + 1 = 0$$
$$2\cos^2 x° - \cos x° = 0$$
$$\cos x°(2\cos x° - 1) = 0$$

Sin+	All+ ✓ $x°$
Tan+	$(360 - x)°$ Cos+ ✓

So $\cos x° = 0$ or $2\cos x° - 1 = 0$

$\cos x° = 0$ $\qquad \cos x° = \frac{1}{2}$

$x = 90, 270$ $\qquad x = 60$, or $360 - 60 = 300$

$x = 60, 90, 270$ and 300

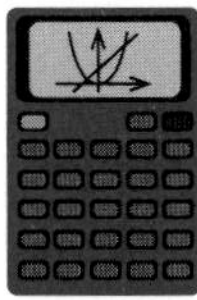

Display the graph $y = \cos 3x + 2\cos x$. Use the cursor to estimate the smallest positive root of the equation $\cos 3x + 2\cos x = 0$. Compare your estimate with the exact value, $\frac{1}{3}\pi$.

EXERCISE 5

Solve the equations in questions **1–8** for $0 \leqslant x \leqslant 360$.

1 $\sin 2x° - \cos x° = 0$

2 $\sin 2x° - 3\sin x° = 0$

3 $\cos 2x° + \cos x° = 0$

4 $\cos 2x° + \sin x° = 0$

5 $\cos 2x° + \cos x° + 1 = 0$

6 $\cos 2x° - 5\sin x° + 2 = 0$

7 $\cos 2x° + 5\cos x° - 2 = 0$

8 $\cos 2x° - 7\sin x° - 4 = 0$

9 Find algebraically the coordinates of the points of intersection of the two graphs ($0 \leqslant x \leqslant 360$).

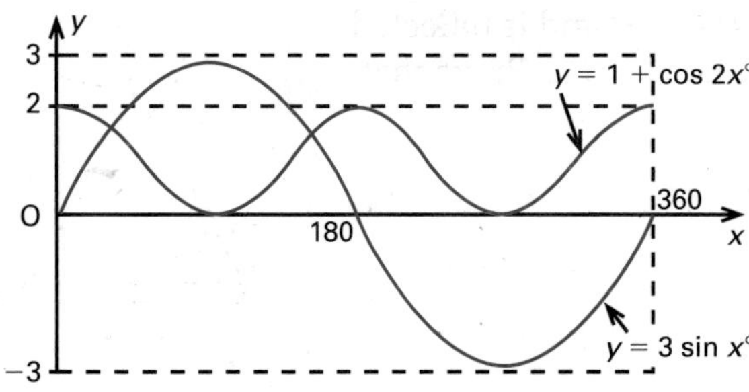

Solve the equations in questions **10–15** for $0 \leqslant \theta \leqslant 2\pi$.

10 $\cos 2\theta + \sin\theta = 0$

11 $\cos 2\theta - \sin\theta = 0$

12 $\sin 2\theta - \sin\theta = 0$

13 $\sin 2\theta + \cos\theta = 0$

14 $\cos 2\theta + \cos\theta = 0$

15 $\cos 2\theta - 4\cos\theta = 5$

16 The diagram contains parts of two cosine curves.

a Write down the equations of the curves.

b Find algebraically the coordinates of the points of intersection of the curves $(0 \leqslant x \leqslant 2\pi)$.

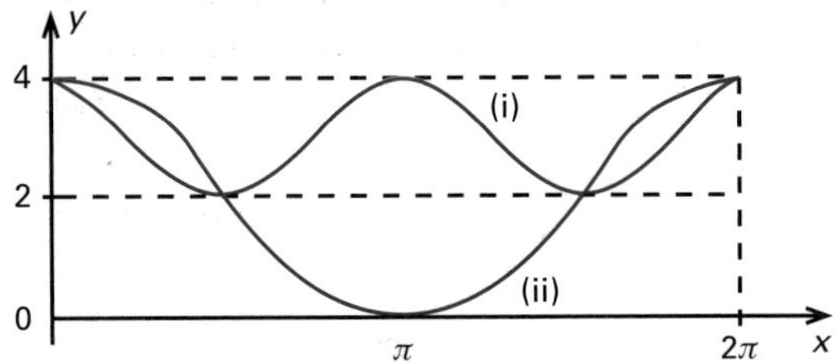

Solve these equations, correct to 1 decimal place where necessary, for $0 \leqslant x \leqslant 360$, or $0 \leqslant \theta \leqslant 2\pi$.

17 $2\cos 2x° - 3\cos x° + 1 = 0$

18 $3\cos 2x° + \sin x° - 2 = 0$

19 $5\cos 2\theta - \cos\theta + 2 = 0$

20 $6\cos 2\theta - 5\cos\theta + 4 = 0$

a Solve the equation $3\sin 2x = 2\cos x$ in these two different ways:

(i) Draw the graphs $y = 3\sin 2x$ and $y = 2\cos x$, and explore their points of intersection.

(ii) Draw the graphs $y = 3\sin 2x - 2\cos x$, and explore its intersections with the x-axis.

b Solve $3\sin 2x - 2\cos x = 2$ by drawing the graph $y = 3\sin 2x - 2\cos x$, and moving the cursor until $y = 2$.

Waves and graphs

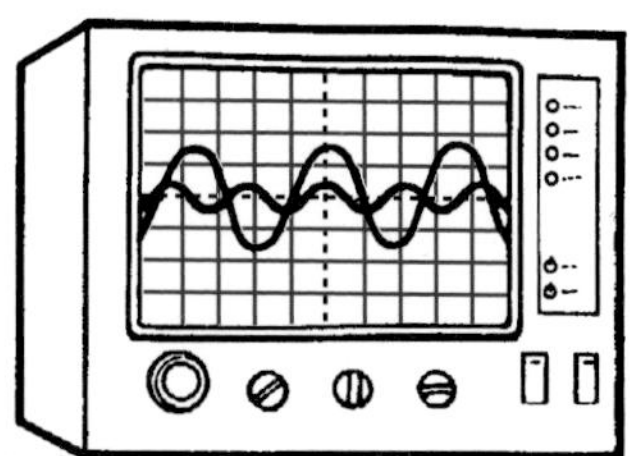

A ship at sea, a current passing through an oscilloscope, a singer in full voice – these all involve patterns of waves, mostly very complex. The study of waves is based on their graphs. Do you recognise these graphs, for $0 \leqslant x \leqslant 2\pi$ (radians)?

(i) $y = \cos x$ **(ii)** $y = 2\cos x$ **(iii)** $y = \cos 2x$

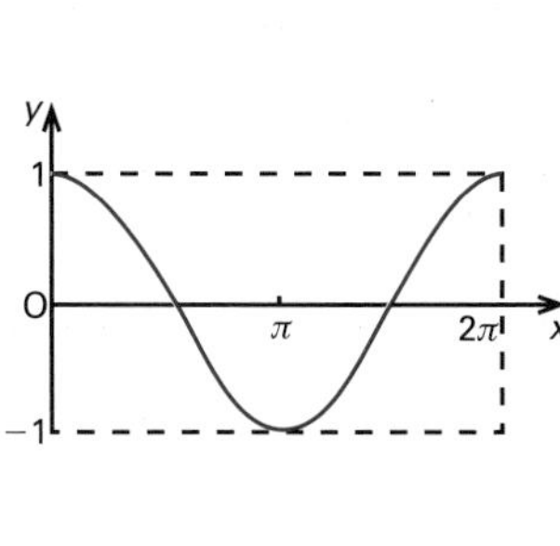

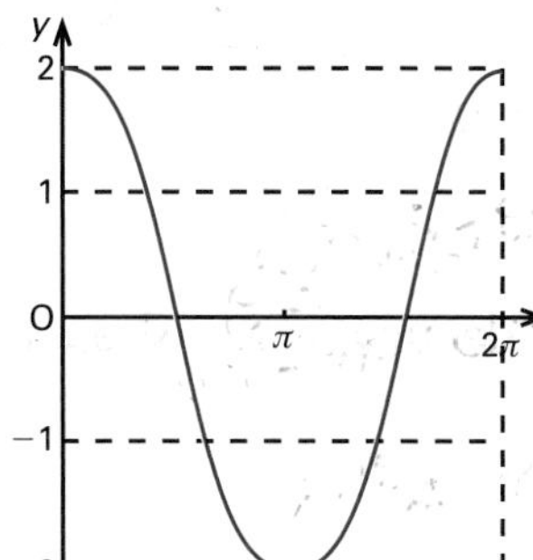

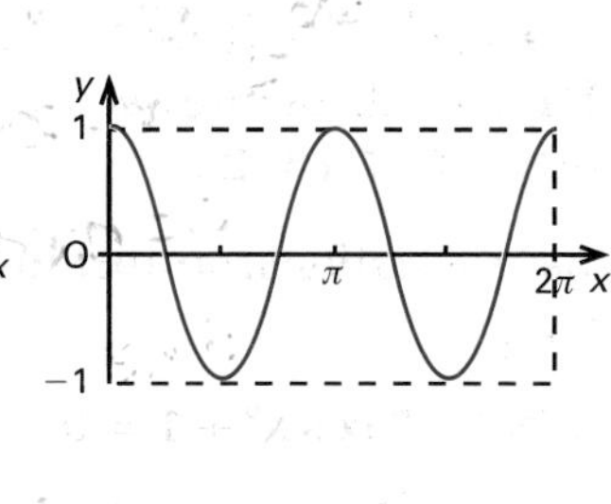

The *amplitude* of a wave is its maximum height above its mean height: 1, 2 and 1 for the graphs above.
The *period* of a wave is the interval on the x-axis for one complete wave; 2π, 2π, π radians above.

Reminders
For the graphs $y = a\sin nx$ and $y = a\cos nx$ $(n > 0)$:
(i) a gives the maximum and minimum values
(ii) n gives the number of cycles for $0 \leqslant x \leqslant 2\pi$, and the period is $\frac{2\pi}{n}$.

EXERCISE 6

1 Sketch these graphs, for $0 \leqslant x \leqslant 2\pi$ radians, and state their amplitudes and periods:
a $y = \sin x$ **b** $y = 2\sin x$ **c** $y = \sin 2x$.

2 Repeat question **1** for the graphs:
a $y = \cos x$ **b** $y = 4\cos x$ **c** $y = \cos 3x$.

3 For each of the following sine and cosine graphs, write down its:
(i) amplitude **(ii)** period **(iii)** equation.

a

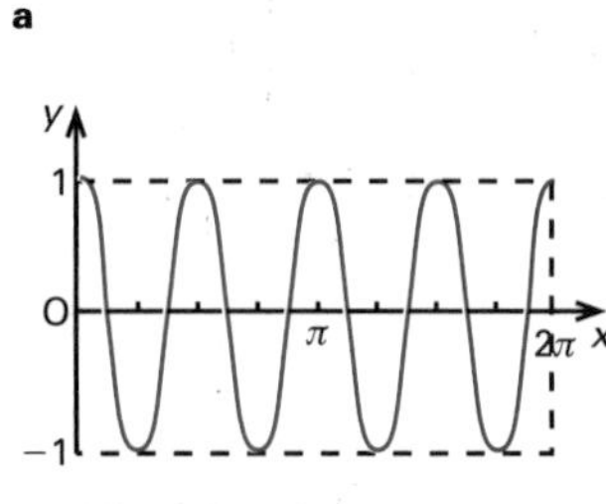

b

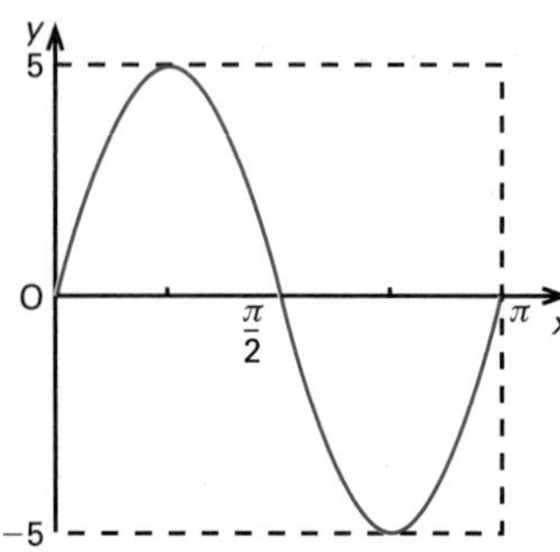

4 **(i)** Sketch the graphs **a** $y = \cos\frac{1}{2}x$ and **b** $y = 2\cos 2x$, for $0 \leqslant x \leqslant 2\pi$.
(ii) Write down their maximum and minimum values, and the corresponding values of x.

5 Repeat question **4** for the graphs $y = 3\sin x$ and $y = \sin 3x$.

Example Sketch the graph $y = \cos\left(x - \frac{\pi}{4}\right)$ for $0 \leqslant x \leqslant 2\pi$.

(i) One cycle of a cosine curve, period 2π radians.
(ii) Intersection with the axes

If $x = 0$, $y = \cos\left(-\frac{\pi}{4}\right) = \cos\left(\frac{\pi}{4}\right) \doteqdot 0.7$.

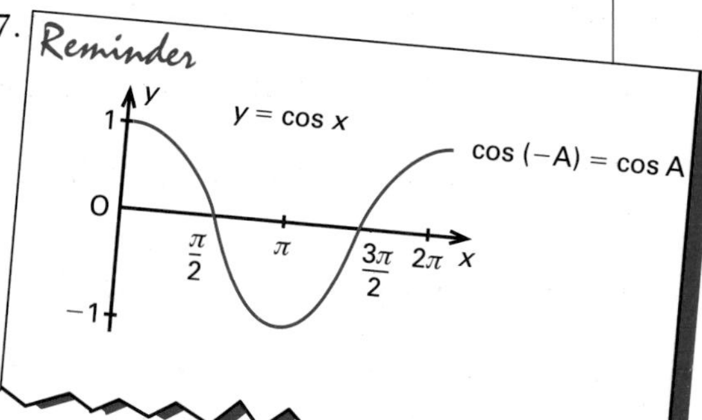

If $y = 0$, $\cos\left(x - \frac{\pi}{4}\right) = 0$

$$x - \frac{\pi}{4} = \frac{\pi}{2}, \frac{3\pi}{2}, \ldots$$

$$x = \frac{3\pi}{4}, \frac{7\pi}{4}, \ldots$$

(iii) Maximum and minimum values

Maximum value of $\cos\left(x - \frac{\pi}{4}\right) = 1$,

when $x - \frac{\pi}{4} = 0, 2\pi, \ldots$, i.e. $x = \frac{\pi}{4}, \frac{9\pi}{4}, \ldots$

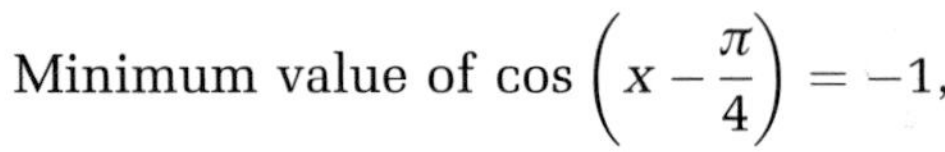
Minimum value of $\cos\left(x - \frac{\pi}{4}\right) = -1$,

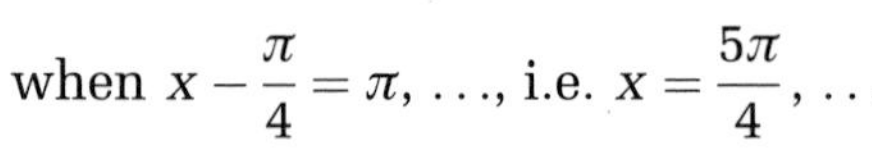
when $x - \frac{\pi}{4} = \pi, \ldots$, i.e. $x = \frac{5\pi}{4}, \ldots$

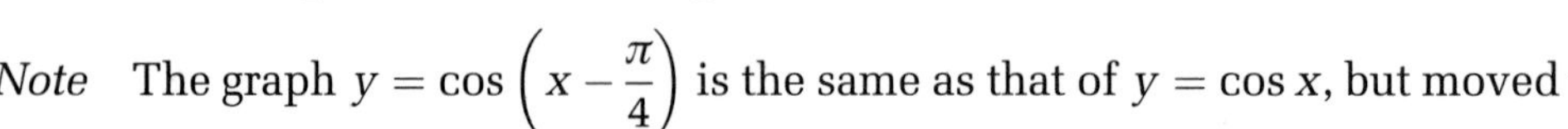
Note The graph $y = \cos\left(x - \frac{\pi}{4}\right)$ is the same as that of $y = \cos x$, but moved to the right by the *phase angle* $\frac{\pi}{4}$ radians.

Explore the effect on amplitude and period of these graphs, in relation to $y = \sin x$ and $y = \cos x$:

a $y = 2\sin x,\ y = -\sin x,\ y = \sin 2x,\ y = \sin\left(x - \frac{\pi}{4}\right)$

b $y = 3\cos x,\ y = -2\cos x,\ y = \cos 3x,\ y = \cos\left(x + \frac{\pi}{4}\right)$

EXERCISE 7

1 Sketch the graphs $y = \sin x$ and $y = \cos x$, $0 \leqslant x \leqslant 2\pi$ radians (or 360°), for reference in this exercise.

In questions **2–5**, follow the steps in the worked example above to analyse and sketch the graphs.

2 $y = \cos\left(x - \frac{\pi}{2}\right),\ 0 \leqslant x \leqslant 2\pi$

3 $y = \sin\left(x - \frac{\pi}{2}\right),\ 0 \leqslant x \leqslant 2\pi$

4 $y = \cos(x + 90)^\circ,\ 0 \leqslant x \leqslant 360$

5 $y = \sin(x + 90)^\circ,\ 0 \leqslant x \leqslant 360$

6 Notice the shift of $y = \cos x$ and $y = \sin x$ to the right by $\frac{\pi}{2}$ radians in questions **2** and **3**, and to the left in questions **4** and **5**. (Compare $y = f(x) \rightarrow y = f(x - a)$ or $f(x + a)$.)
Describe the shift in each of the following, and draw sketches (without any working).

a $y = \cos\left(x - \frac{\pi}{6}\right)$ **b** $y = \sin\left(x + \frac{\pi}{6}\right)$

c $y = \cos(x + 45)^\circ$ **d** $y = \sin(x - 45)^\circ$

7 **a** Show that, for $0 \leqslant x \leqslant 360$, the graph $y = \sin(2x + 90)^\circ$:
  (i) cuts the y-axis at (0, 1) and the x-axis at (45, 0), (135, 0), (225, 0) and (315, 0)
  (ii) has maximum turning points at $x = 0$, 180 and 360, and minimum turning points at $x = 90$ and 270.

b Sketch the graph, and write its equation in terms of a cosine function.

8 Repeat the method in question **7a** for the graph $y = \sin(2x - 90)^\circ$.

9 Use the method in question **7a** to sketch the graphs for $0 \leqslant x \leqslant 2\pi$:

a $y = \cos\left(2x - \frac{\pi}{2}\right)$ **b** $y = \cos\left(2x + \frac{\pi}{2}\right)$.

CHAPTER 3.2 REVIEW

Do not use a calculator in questions **1–12**.

1 Simplify:
  a $\sin(-A)$
  b $\sin(180 - x)°$
  c $\cos(-B)$
  d $\cos(180 - y)°$
  e $\sin(90 - a)°$
  f $\cos(90 - a)°$.

2 Verify the formulae for $\cos(A + B)$ and $\sin(A + B)$ for $A = 45°$ and $B = 90°$.

3 Verify the formulae for $\cos(A - B)$ and $\sin(A - B)$ for $A = \frac{\pi}{6}$ and $B = \pi$ radians.

4 P and Q are acute angles, $\sin P = \frac{4}{5}$ and $\sin Q = \frac{5}{13}$. Show that $\sin(P + Q) = \frac{63}{65}$, and find the exact value of $\cos(P + Q)$.

5 α and β are acute angles, $\cos\alpha = \frac{4}{5}$ and $\tan\beta = \frac{5}{12}$. Find the exact values of $\sin(\alpha + \beta)$, $\cos(\alpha + \beta)$ and $\tan(\alpha + \beta)$.

6 a Simplify:
  (i) $\sin(X + Y) - \sin(X - Y)$
  (ii) $\cos(X - Y) - \cos(X + Y)$.
  b Show that: $\sin(X - Y) + \cos(X + Y) = (\sin X + \cos X)(\cos Y - \sin Y)$.

7 Check the formula for $\sin 2A$, and three formulae for $\cos 2A$, using

$A = \frac{\pi}{6}$ radians.

8 Angle A is acute, and $\sin A = \frac{1}{\sqrt{5}}$. Show that $\sin 2A = \frac{4}{5}$, and find the exact values of $\cos 2A$, $\sin 4A$ and $\cos 4A$.

9 $\tan B = \frac{1}{3}$, and $0 < B < 90$. Find exact values (as fractions) of:
  a $\sin 2B$ **b** $\cos 2B$ **c** $\tan 2B$.

10 Prove that:
  $(\cos\theta + \sin\theta)(\cos\theta - \sin\theta) = \cos 2\theta$.

11 Change the subject of:
  a $\cos 2x = 1 - 2\sin^2 x$ to $\sin^2 x$
  b $\cos 2x = 2\cos^2 x - 1$ to $\cos^2 x$.

12 Express as functions of acute angles:
  a $\sin\frac{2\pi}{3}$ **b** $\cos\frac{3\pi}{4}$
  c $\sin\frac{5\pi}{4}$ **d** $\cos\frac{5\pi}{3}$.

13 Solve, for $0 \leqslant x \leqslant 360$:
  a $\sin 2x° - 3\cos x° = 0$
  b $\cos 2x° - \sin x° - 1 = 0$
  c $\cos 2x° - 5\cos x° = 2$.

14 Solve, for $0 \leqslant \theta \leqslant 2\pi$, correct to 1 decimal place:
  a $\cos 2\theta + \sin\theta + 2 = 0$
  b $2\cos 2\theta + \cos\theta - 1 = 0$.

15 Find algebraically the coordinates of the points of intersection of these graphs.

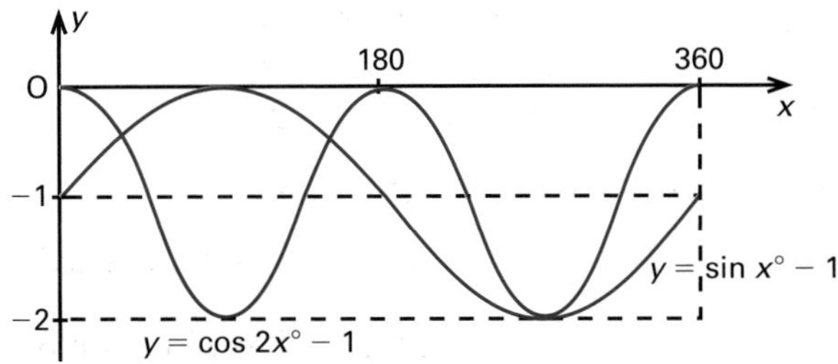

16 Sketch these graphs, for $0 \leqslant x \leqslant 2\pi$, and give their amplitudes and periods:
  a $y = 4\sin x$
  b $y = \sin 4x$
  c $y = 2\sin\frac{1}{2}x$.

17 a Find the intersections of the graph $y = 2\cos\left(x - \frac{\pi}{6}\right)$ with the x and y-axes, for $0 \leqslant x \leqslant 2\pi$. Also find its maximum and minimum turning points.
  b Sketch the graph.

18 Use the method of question **17** to sketch the graph $y = 2\sin\left(x - \frac{\pi}{6}\right)$, for $0 \leqslant x \leqslant 2\pi$.

19 Show that:

$$\sin\theta + \sin\left(\frac{2\pi}{3} + \theta\right) + \sin\left(\frac{4\pi}{3} + \theta\right) = 0.$$

CHAPTER 3.2 SUMMARY

1 Some useful reminders

a (i) $\sin(-A) = -\sin A$

$\cos(-A) = \cos A$

(ii) $\sin(90° - A) = \cos A$

$\cos(90° - A) = \sin A$

(iii) $\sin(180° - A) = \sin A$

$\cos(180° - A) = -\cos A$

b (i) $\dfrac{\sin A}{\cos A} = \tan A$

(ii) $\sin^2 A + \cos^2 A = 1$

(and $\sin^2 A = 1 - \cos^2 A$,

$\cos^2 A = 1 - \sin^2 A$)

2 cos (A ± B) and sin (A ± B)

$\cos(A + B) = \cos A \cos B - \sin A \sin B$

$\cos(A - B) = \cos A \cos B + \sin A \sin B$

$\sin(A + B) = \sin A \cos B + \cos A \sin B$

$\sin(A - B) = \sin A \cos B - \cos A \sin B$

3 sin 2A and cos 2A

$\sin 2A = 2 \sin A \cos A$

$\cos 2A = \cos^2 A - \sin^2 A$

$= 2\cos^2 A - 1$

$= 1 - 2\sin^2 A$

$\cos^2 A = \frac{1}{2}(1 + \cos 2A)$

$\sin^2 A = \frac{1}{2}(1 - \cos 2A)$

4 Trigonometric equations with sin 2A and cos 2A

Use the all–sin–tan–cos quadrant diagram to find the quadrants in which the solutions lie, and hence the actual solutions.

Sin +	All +
$(\pi - \theta)$ $(180 - x)°$	$x°$ (θ radians)
$(\pi + \theta)$ $(180 + x)°$	$(360 - x)°$ $(2\pi - \theta)$
Tan +	Cos +

5 Graphs with equations $y = \sin(x \pm \alpha)$ and $y = \cos(x \pm \alpha)$

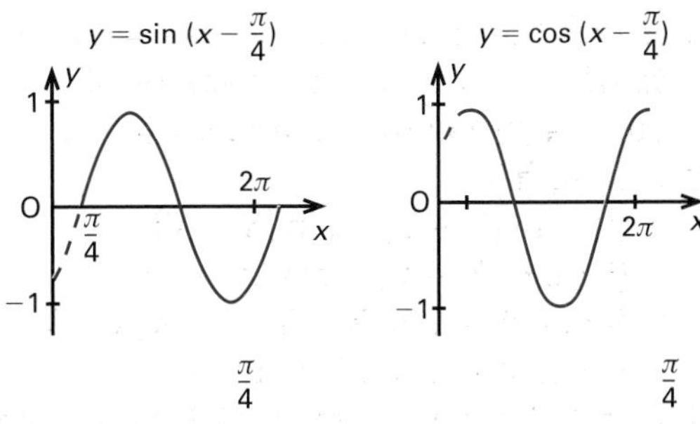

Graphs $y = \sin x$ and $y = \cos x$ moved $\frac{\pi}{4}$ to right.

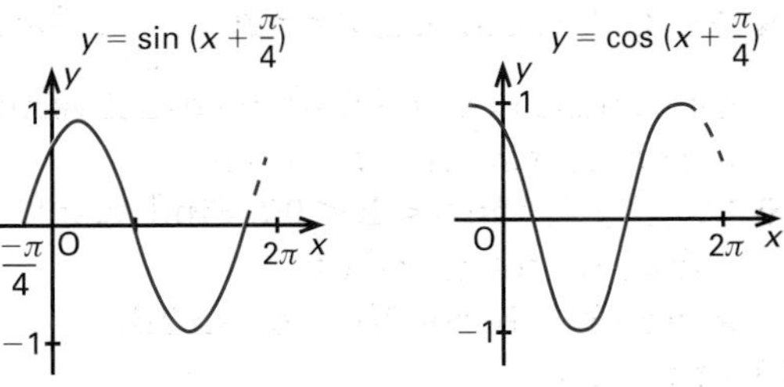

Graphs $y = \sin x$ and $y = \cos x$ moved $\frac{\pi}{4}$ to left.

4 The Circle

The circle, centre O(0, 0) *and radius* r, $x^2 + y^2 = r^2$

The circle consists of the set of points $P(x, y)$ for which $OP = r$, or $OP^2 = r^2$, so $x^2 + y^2 = r^2$.
The equation of the circle is $x^2 + y^2 = r^2$.

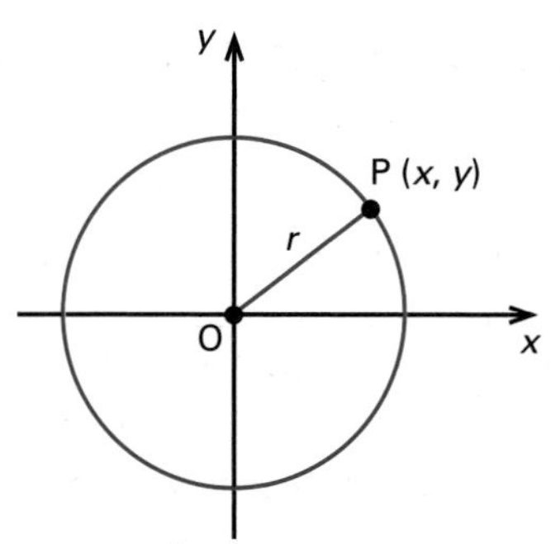

Note The *locus* of P is the circle with equation $x^2 + y^2 = r^2$.

Example Find the equation of the circle, centre O, passing through the point A(6, −8).

Here $r^2 = OA^2 = (6 - 0)^2 + (-8 - 0)^2 = 36 + 64 = 100$.
The equation of the circle is $x^2 + y^2 = 100$.

To draw a circle, the x-scale has to be multiplied by factor 1.5. For example, use X min −7.5, max 7.5, scl 1; Y min −5, max 5, scl 1. Draw the graphs $y = \sqrt{(16 - x^2)}$ and $y = -\sqrt{(16 - x^2)}$ to obtain an 'acceptable' picture of the circle $x^2 + y^2 = 16$.

EXERCISE 1

1 Write down the centre and radius of each circle. (Arrange **e** and **f** in the form $x^2 + y^2 = r^2$ first.)
a $x^2 + y^2 = 9$ **b** $x^2 + y^2 = 16$ **c** $x^2 + y^2 = 64$
d $x^2 + y^2 = 1$ **e** $y^2 = 36 - x^2$ **f** $3x^2 + 3y^2 = 12$

2 Write down the equation of the circle with centre O and radius:
a 5 **b** 7 **c** 12 **d** 20 **e** $\sqrt{3}$.

3 Find the equation of the circle, centre O, passing through the point:
a (3, 4) **b** (−5, 4) **c** (−3, −3) **d** (0, 7).

4 Find the equation of the circle with the same centre as $x^2 + y^2 = 100$, but with radius twice as long.

5 **a** Sketch the square whose sides have equations $x = 5$, $y = 5$, $x = -5$ and $y = -5$.
b Find the equation of the circle, centre O:
(i) touching all the sides of the square
(ii) passing through all the vertices of the square.

6 **a** Check that the point $(12, -9)$ lies on the circle $x^2 + y^2 = 225$.
b Find p if the given point lies on the circle:
(i) $(p, 3)$, $x^2 + y^2 = 13$ **(ii)** (p, p), $x^2 + y^2 = 72$.

7 **a** Check that A(3, 4), B(−4, 3) and C(5, 0) are all at the same distance from the origin.
b Write down the equation of the circle, centre O, passing through A, B and C.
c Find the equation of the circle, centre O, with radius half that of the circle in **b**.

8 A stone is dropped into water. A circular ripple travels out at a rate of 2 cm per second. Using the point where the stone entered the water as the origin, write down an equation for the ripple after:
a 1 second **b** 5 seconds **c** 7 seconds.

9 By calculating OA^2, OB^2, …, find whether each of the points A, B, … lies inside, outside or on the circle $x^2 + y^2 = 100$:
A(8, 6), B(7, 7), C(−9, 5), D(−6, 8), E(0, −10), F(4, 9).

10 Dr Shepherd, an astronomer, focuses her telescope on the crescent moon, setting the crosswires of the telescope at the moon's centre. The photograph is faulty, with white flecks on it. The radius of the moon's photograph is 3.6 cm.
a Write down the equation of the moon's outer rim using the crosswires as axes. (The 'unseen' part is shown dotted.)
b White flecks are found at these points on the plate. Which of them cannot be stars?
(i) (3, 1) **(ii)** (2, −3) **(iii)** (1.5, 2)
(iv) (3.5, −1.5) **(v)** (2.5, −2.5)

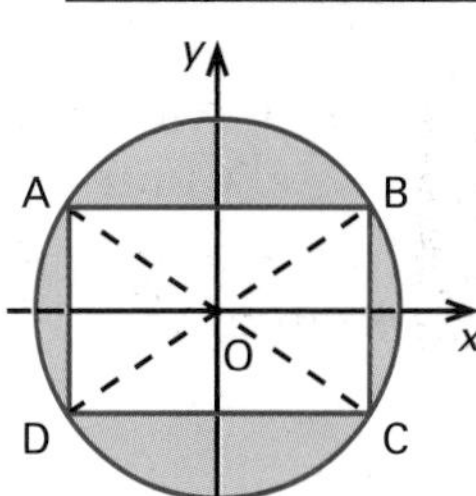

11 A rectangular indoor pitch 30 m by 16 m is marked out in a circular arena. Find the equation of the edge of the arena, shown in the diagram.

12 Calculate, to the nearest m², the area of the shaded part of the arena in question **11**.

Challenge

In a computer simulation, arrows land randomly on the archery target. The bull has a radius of 1 unit, and scores 5. Each ring is 3 units broad, and the inner scores 3, the middle 2 and the outer 1, as shown.

A shot (a, b) would score 1 point if $(a, b) \in \{(x, y): 49 < x^2 + y^2 \leqslant 100\}$, i.e. '$(a, b)$ belongs to the set of points (x, y) such that $x^2 + y^2$ is greater than 49 and less than or equal to 100'.

1 Find the scores of shots $(a, b) \in$:
a $\{(x, y): x^2 + y^2 \leqslant 1\}$
b $\{(x, y): x^2 + y^2 > 100\}$
c $\{(x, y): 16 < x^2 + y^2 \leqslant 49\}$.

2 Use the above 'set notation' to describe the regions where the scores are:
a 1 **b** 3 **c** greater than 2
d less than 3 **e** 1 or more.

The circle, centre C(a, b) *and radius* r, $(x - a)^2 + (y - b)^2 = r^2$

The circle consists of the set of points $P(x, y)$ for which $CP = r$, or $CP^2 = r^2$, so
$(x - a)^2 + (y - b)^2 - r^2$.
The equation of the circle is $(x - a)^2 + (y - b)^2 = r^2$.

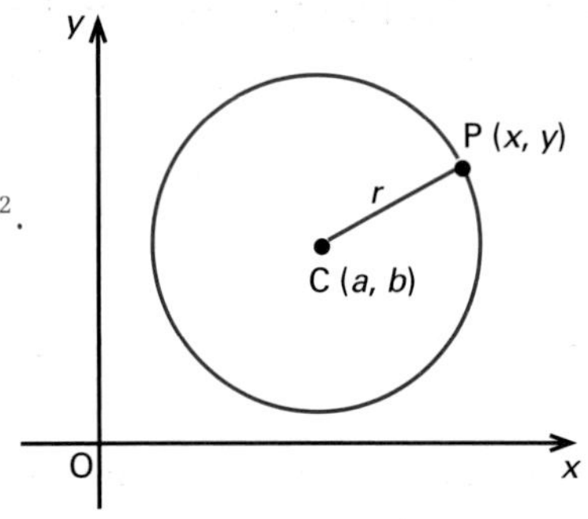

Example Find the equation of the circle, centre C(1, −2), passing through the point A(4, 7).

$r^2 = CA^2 = (4 - 1)^2 + (7 - (-2))^2 = 9 + 81 = 90.$

The equation of the circle is $(x - 1)^2 + (y + 2)^2 = 90$.

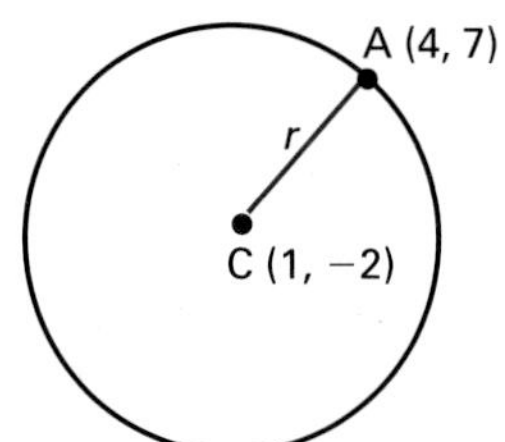

EXERCISE 2A

1 Write down the equations of the circles with these centres and radii:
a $(2, 7)$, $r = 4$ **b** $(3, -1)$, $r = 7$
c $(-1, 0)$, $r = 10$ **d** $(-5, -6)$, $r = 1$.

2 State the centre and radius of each of these circles:
a $(x - 3)^2 + (y - 1)^2 = 25$ **b** $(x - 4)^2 + (y - 4)^2 = 1$
c $(x + 5)^2 + (y - 2)^2 = 4$ **d** $(x + 2)^2 + (y + 1)^2 = 9$
e $(x - 1)^2 + y^2 = 16$ **f** $x^2 + (y + 3)^2 = 36$.

3 Find the equation of each circle, centre C, passing through the point P:
a C(2, 2), P(5, 4) **b** C(1, −5), P(3, 1)
c C(−2, −3), P(6, 1) **d** C(−3, 0), P(3, −2).

4 Write down the centres and equations of the four circles which touch both the x and y-axes, and have radius 5.

5 Find the equation of the circle concentric with the circle $(x - 1)^2 + (y + 1)^2 = 16$, but with radius twice as long.

6 Find the centres and $(\text{radii})^2$, and hence the equations, of the circles on the lines joining the following pairs of points as diameters:
a O(0, 0) and A(2, 4)
b P(−1, −2) and Q(−1, 4).

7 David took a photograph of the big wheel at the fairground. Using the axes shown, he estimated A to be (1, 6) and B(11, 10). Find the equation of the circular edge through A and B.

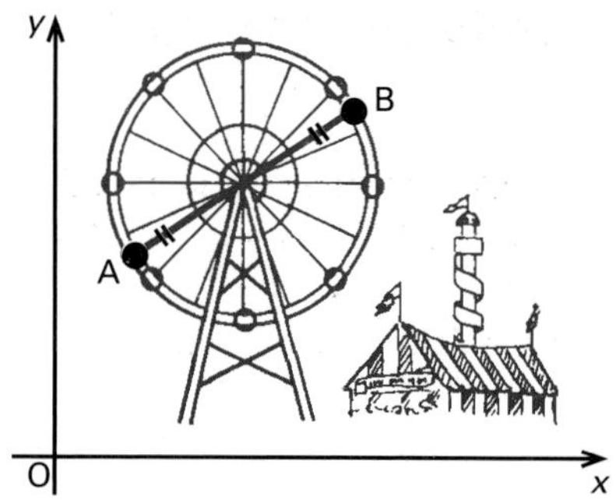

8 Find the centre and radius, and hence the equation, of the circle passing through the vertices O(0, 0), A(0, 4), B(6, 4) and C(6, 0) of the rectangle OABC.

EXERCISE 2B

1 D is the point (1, 2), E(5, 6) and F(1, 6).
a Prove that $\angle DFE = 90°$.
b Find the equation of the circle passing through D, E and F.

2 Find the shortest distance from the point A(−4, 3) to the circle $(x - 4)^2 + (y + 3)^2 = 9$.

3 Find the equation of the image of the circle $(x + 2)^2 + (y - 2)^2 = 4$ under:
a reflection in **(i)** the x-axis **(ii)** the y-axis **(iii)** the origin
b translation of 2 units in the direction **(i)** OX **(ii)** OY.

4 a Show that the distance between the centres of the circles $x^2 + y^2 = 4$ and $(x - 3)^2 + (y - 4)^2 = 9$ is equal to the sum of the radii.
b What does this tell you about the circles?

5 The small circle, centre C, has equation $(x + 2)^2 + (y + 1)^2 = 25$. The large circles, centres A and B, touch the small circle, and AB is parallel to the x-axis. Find:
a the centre and radius of each circle
b the equations of the large circles.

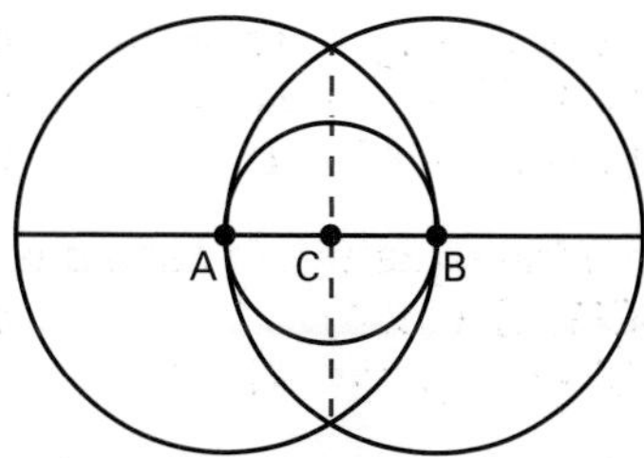

6 In a computer game, the rim of the front wheel of the tractor has equation $(x - 5)^2 + (y - 3)^2 = 4$.
a The ground line is parallel to the x-axis. Write down its equation.
b The rear wheel's radius is 3 times the front one's. If the wheels touch the ground 10 units apart, find the equation of the rear wheel's rim.
c The tractor moves forward 2 units. Find the new equation of: **(i)** the front wheel **(ii)** the rear wheel.

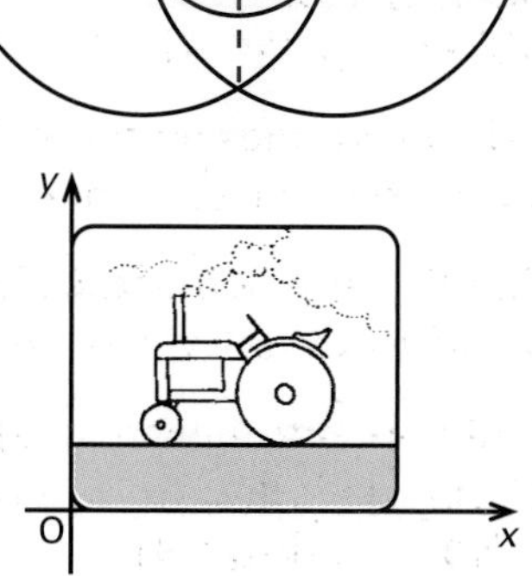

The general equation of a circle, $x^2 + y^2 + 2gx + 2fy + c = 0$

The equation $(x-4)^2 + (y+3)^2 = 4$ represents a circle with centre $(4, -3)$ and radius 2.
Multiplying out, $x^2 - 8x + 16 + y^2 + 6y + 9 = 4$,
so $x^2 + y^2 - 8x + 6y + 21 = 0$ represents the same circle.
What about the other way round?
Can we show that $x^2 + y^2 + 2gx + 2fy + c = 0$ represents a circle?
Rearranging, $(x^2 + 2gx) + (y^2 + 2fy) = -c$

$$(x+g)^2 - g^2 + (y+f)^2 - f^2 = -c \text{ ... completing the squares}$$

$$(x+g)^2 + (y+f)^2 = g^2 + f^2 - c$$

$$(x-(-g))^2 + (y-(-f))^2 = g^2 + f^2 - c$$

So $x^2 + y^2 + 2gx + 2fy + c = 0$ represents a circle with centre $(-g, -f)$ and radius $\sqrt{g^2 + f^2 - c}$, provided that $g^2 + f^2 - c > 0$.

Note The coefficients of x^2 and y^2 must be 1.

Example Show that the equation $3x^2 + 3y^2 - 12x + 24y - 36 = 0$ represents a circle, and find its centre and radius.

The equation is $x^2 + y^2 - 4x + 8y - 12 = 0$. This represents a circle, since:
(i) the coefficients of x^2 and y^2 are equal
(ii) $g = -2$, $f = 4$ and $c = -12$, so that $g^2 + f^2 - c = 4 + 16 + 12 = 32 > 0$.
The centre is $(-g, -f)$, i.e. $(2, -4)$, and the radius is $\sqrt{32}$, or $4\sqrt{2}$ in simplest form.

EXERCISE 3A

1 Check which of these equations represent circles. Where they do, find the centres and radii of the circles.

a $x^2 + y^2 - 4x - 8y + 16 = 0$
b $x^2 + y^2 - 6x - 10y + 35 = 0$
c $x^2 + y^2 - 8x - 2y + 13 = 0$
d $x^2 + y^2 - 2x + 2y - 5 = 0$
e $x^2 + y^2 + 6x - 2y + 11 = 0$
f $x^2 + y^2 + 4x + 6y + 4 = 0$
g $x^2 + y^2 + 2x + 4y + 13 = 0$
h $2x^2 + 2y^2 + 4x + 4y - 14 = 0$

2 Match each circle with its equation below, (Do you *need* to find each radius as well as the centre?)

a $x^2 + y^2 + 6x - 8y + 24 = 0$
b $x^2 + y^2 + 2x - 2y - 2 = 0$
c $x^2 + y^2 + 2x + 2y - 14 = 0$
d $x^2 + y^2 - 6x - 2y + 1 = 0$
e $x^2 + y^2 - 10x + 8y + 32 = 0$

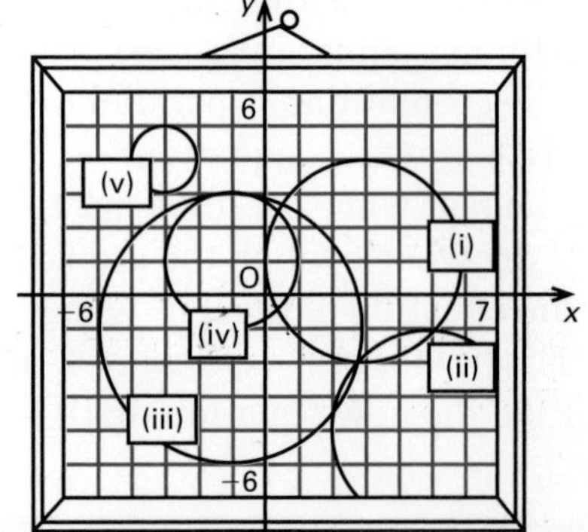

3 **a** Find the centre and radius of the circle $x^2 + y^2 - 2x - 8y - 8 = 0$.
b Say whether each of the points A(1, 1), B(4, 8), C(−1, −1), D(3, 2) lies inside, outside or on the circle.

4 Find p, given that:
a A(8, p) lies on the circle $x^2 + y^2 - 8x - 6y + 9 = 0$
b B(p, 1) lies on the circle $x^2 + y^2 + 2x + 2y - 11 = 0$.

5 A circle, centre B, has equation $x^2 + y^2 - 6x - 4y - 12 = 0$.
a What are the coordinates of B?
b Check that A(−1, 5) lies on the circle.
c Find the point on the circle diametrically opposite A.

6 A(2, 1) and B(−2, 9) lie on the circle $x^2 + y^2 + 4x - 8y - 5 = 0$.
a Find the equation of the perpendicular bisector of AB.
b Show that the perpendicular bisector passes through the centre of the circle.

7 **a** Find the equations of the perpendicular bisectors of AB and BC in the diagram.
b Find their point of intersection, S.
c Hence find the equation of the circle through A, B and C.

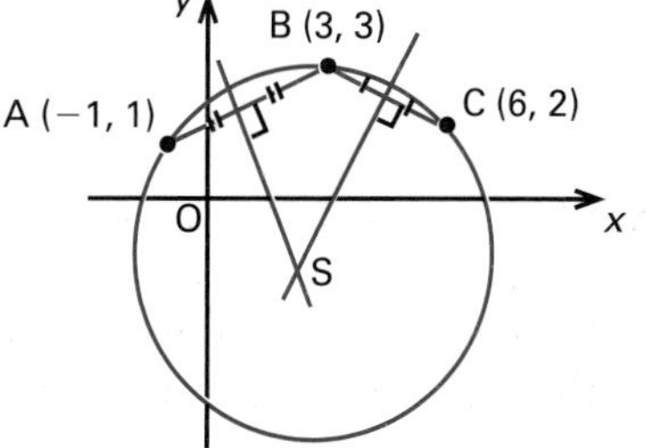

8 Find the equation of the circle through the points:
a (−5, −2), (−2, 7), (7, 4) **b** (−1, −1), (1, 3), (0, 6).

9 The equations of the sides of a triangle are AB $y = x - 2$, BC $x = 7$, AC $x - 7y - 14 = 0$. Find the equation of the circle through A, B and C.

Challenge

On the watchmaker's plan the rim of the medium cog, B, has equation $4x^2 + 4y^2 - 28x - 28y + 97 = 0$.
a Show that the radius of this cog is 0.5 unit.
b The radii of the rims of the three cogs are in the ratio 4:2:1. Find the equations of the rims of cogs A and C.

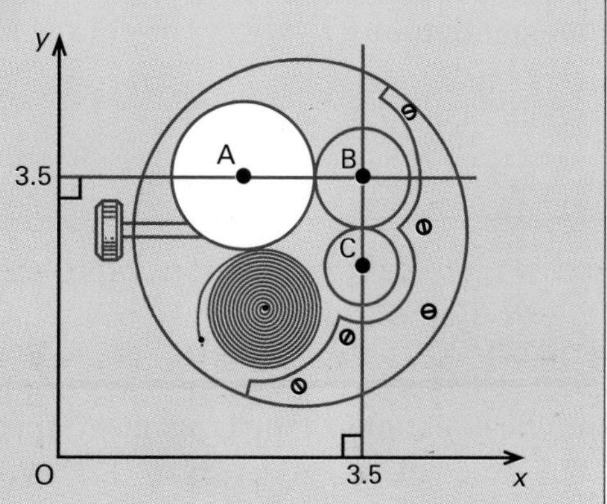

EXERCISE 3B

1 **a** Find the centres and radii of the circles $x^2 + y^2 = 4$ and $x^2 + y^2 - 8x + 6y + 24 = 0$.
b Sketch the circles, and calculate the shortest distance between their circumferences.

2 a Find the centres and radii of the circles $x^2 + y^2 = 9$ and $x^2 + y^2 - 14x + 33 = 0$.
b Explain why the circles touch each other externally.

3 Prove that the circles $x^2 + y^2 = 4$ and $x^2 + y^2 + 6x - 16 = 0$ touch internally.

4 A is the point $(-2, 0)$ and B is $(4, 3)$.
a Show that the set of points $P(x, y)$ for which $2AP = PB$, that is the locus of P, is the circle $x^2 + y^2 + 8x + 2y - 3 = 0$. (Use $4AP^2 = PB^2$.)
b Write down its centre and radius, and illustrate in a sketch.

5 A is the point $(0, 3)$ and B is $(6, 0)$.
a Find the equation of the locus of $P(x, y)$ for which $AP = 2PB$.
b Show that this is the equation of a circle, and write down its centre and radius.

Tangents to a circle

Example Find the equation of the tangent to the circle $x^2 + y^2 - 4x + 6y - 12 = 0$ at the point $P(5, 1)$.

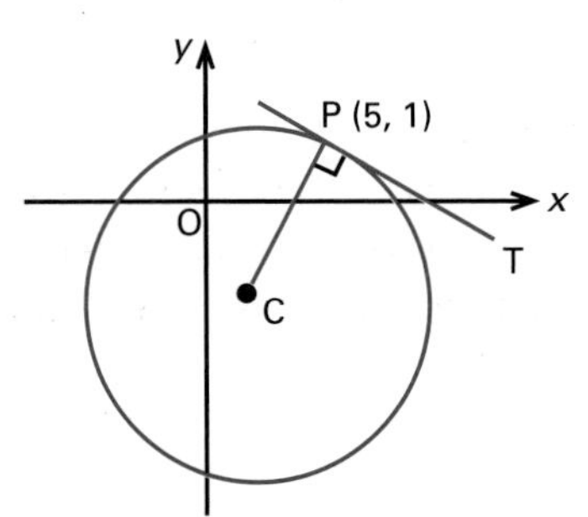

The centre C is the point $(2, -3)$.

$$m_{PC} = \frac{1 - (-3)}{5 - 2} = \frac{4}{3}.$$

Since the tangent is perpendicular to the radius at P, $m_{PT} = -\frac{3}{4}$.

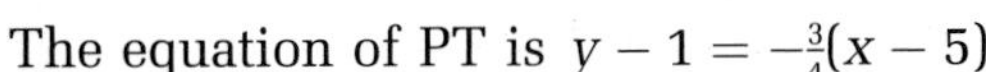

The equation of PT is $y - 1 = -\frac{3}{4}(x - 5)$

$$4y - 4 = -3x + 15$$

$$4y + 3x = 19$$

EXERCISE 4

1 Find the equations of the tangents to these circles at the given points:
a $x^2 + y^2 = 10$, $(3, -1)$ **b** $x^2 + y^2 = 13$, $(-2, 3)$.

2 The tangent at $P(-2, 2)$ to the circle $x^2 + y^2 = 8$ meets the x-axis at A and the y-axis at B. Find:
a the equation of the tangent
b the coordinates of A and B
c the length of AB.

3 a Find the equations of the tangents at $C(-2, 1)$ and $D(1, 2)$ on the circle $x^2 + y^2 = 5$.
b Find the point of intersection of the tangents.

4 A tangent is drawn from A(9, −4) to the circle $x^2 + y^2 + 8x + 2y - 8 = 0$.

a Find the centre and radius of the circle.

b Calculate the exact length of:

(i) AC **(ii)** the tangent AB.

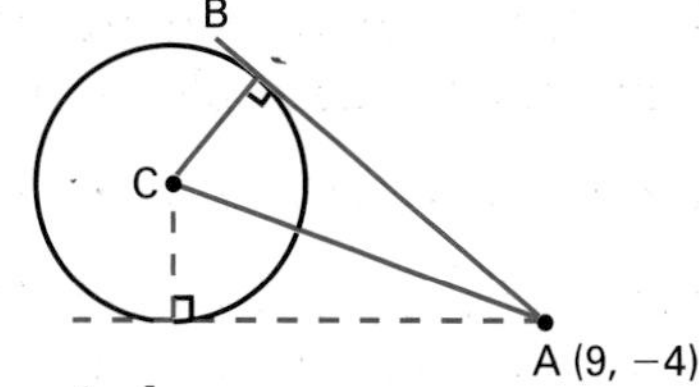

5 Calculate the length of the tangent from P(−4, −1) to the circle $x^2 + y^2 - 10x - 7 = 0$.

6 Find the equations of the tangents to these circles at the given points.

a $(x - 2)^2 + (y + 1)^2 = 2$, $(3, -2)$

b $(x - 2)^2 + (y - 6)^2 = 9$, $(2, 3)$

c $x^2 + y^2 + 8x - 6y - 40 = 0$, $(3, -1)$

d $x^2 + y^2 - 2x - 3y - 1 = 0$, $(-1, 2)$

7 **a** Find the point of intersection, P, of the tangents to the circle $x^2 + y^2 - 8x - 4y + 10 = 0$ at the points A(1, 1) and B(5, 5).

b Verify that PA = PB.

8 **a** Find the equations of the tangents to the circle, centre (−4, 3) and radius 5, at the points where the circle cuts the x and y-axes.

b Show that two of the tangents are parallel, and find the equation of the fourth tangent which completes a tangent parallelogram.

Intersections of lines and circles

Example Find the coordinates of the points of intersection of the line $5y - x + 7 = 0$ and the circle $x^2 + y^2 + 2x - 2y - 11 = 0$.

The line $5y - x + 7 = 0$ and the circle $x^2 + y^2 + 2x - 2y - 11 = 0$ meet where

$5y - x + 7 = 0$, i.e. $x = 5y + 7 \ldots (1)$

and $x^2 + y^2 + 2x - 2y - 11 = 0 \ldots (2)$

At the points of intersection, substituting (1) into (2),

$$(5y + 7)^2 + y^2 + 2(5y + 7) - 2y - 11 = 0$$

$$25y^2 + 70y + 49 + y^2 + 10y + 14 - 2y - 11 = 0$$

$$26y^2 + 78y + 52 = 0$$

$$y^2 + 3y + 2 = 0 \ldots \text{(A)}$$

So $(y + 2)(y + 1) = 0$ and $y = -2$ or $y = -1$.
From (1), $x = -3$ when $y = -2$, and $x = 2$ when $y = -1$.
The line meets the circle at the points $(-3, -2)$ and $(2, -1)$.

Note We can interpret the intersection of a line and a circle both algebraically and geometrically as follows.

Line meets circle:	*Quadratic equation at* (**A**) *has:*	*Discriminant:*
(i) in two distinct points	two distinct real roots	$b^2 - 4ac > 0$
(ii) in one point*	equal roots*	$b^2 - 4ac = 0$*
(iii) in no points	no real roots	$b^2 - 4ac < 0$

* *tangency*

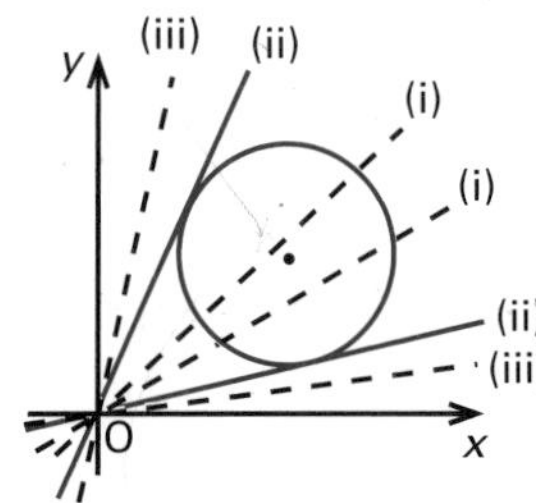

Example Find the values of k for $y = x + k$ to be a tangent to the circle $x^2 + y^2 = 8$.

The line and circle intersect where $x^2 + (x + k)^2 = 8$. In standard form, this quadratic equation is $2x^2 + 2kx + (k^2 - 8) = 0$.
For tangency, '$b^2 - 4ac = 0$', so $(2k)^2 - 8(k^2 - 8) = 0$.
So $4k^2 = 64$, $k^2 = 16$ and $k = \pm 4$ (giving tangents $y = x \pm 4$).

EXERCISE 5A

1 Do these lines and circles intersect? If they do, find the coordinates of the points of intersection.

a $y = 1,\ x^2 + y^2 = 10$ **b** $y = 2,\ x^2 + y^2 = 4$
c $y = 4,\ x^2 + y^2 = 9$ **d** $y = x,\ x^2 + y^2 = 8$
e $y = x + 1,\ x^2 + y^2 = 5$ **f** $2x + y = 5,\ x^2 + y^2 = 5$

2 For each circle, calculate the length of the chord cut off by:
(i) the x-axis **(ii)** the y-axis.

a $x^2 + y^2 - 6x - 8y = 0$ **b** $x^2 + y^2 - 24x + 10y = 0$
c $x^2 + y^2 - 7x + 8y + 12 = 0$ **d** $x^2 + y^2 - 6x - 10y + 9 = 0$

What is special about **d**?

3 Stars revolve in circles round the Pole Star once each night. One star S traces out the circle $x^2 + y^2 + 2x - 8y + 4 = 0$, in a chosen set of coordinate axes.

a Write down the coordinates of the Pole Star.
b The equation of the horizon is $y = 1$. Find the coordinates of the rising and setting points A and B of the star S.

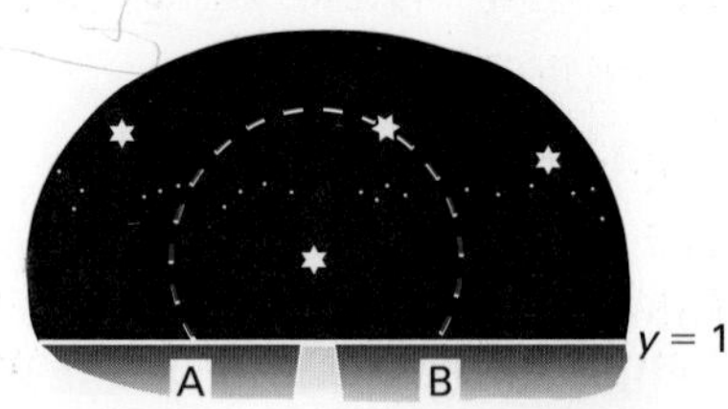

4 The line $y = x$ cuts the circle $x^2 + y^2 - 8x - 4y + 10 = 0$ at P and Q. Find:
a the coordinates of P and Q
b the equation of the circle on PQ as diameter.

5 The line $y = x + 1$ cuts the circle $x^2 + y^2 + 2x + 2y + 1 = 0$ at V and W. Find the exact length of VW.

6 The line $x = 4$ cuts the circle $x^2 + y^2 = 25$ at A and B. Find:
a the coordinates of A and B
b the equations of the tangents at A and B
c the point P of intersection of the tangents
d the length of each tangent from P.

7 The line $x - 2y + 5 = 0$ meets the circle $x^2 + y^2 = 10$ at C and D. Find:
a the coordinates of C and D
b the equation of the circle, centre $(-2, 4)$, passing through C and D.

EXERCISE 5B

1 Prove that the line is a tangent to the circle in each case, and find the point of contact.
a $x = 3$, $x^2 + y^2 = 9$
b $y = 3x - 10$, $x^2 + y^2 = 10$
c $y = 3x + 10$, $x^2 + y^2 - 8x - 4y - 20 = 0$
d $4x - y + 7 = 0$, $x^2 + y^2 - 6x - 4y - 4 = 0$

2 **a** Show that at the points of intersection of the line $y = c - x$ and the circle $x^2 + y^2 = 8$, $2x^2 - 2cx + (c^2 - 8) = 0$.
b Find the values of c for the line to be a tangent to the circle.
c Find the coordinates of the points of contact of the tangents and the circle.

3 Find the value of k if $y = 2x - 5$ is a tangent to the circle $x^2 + y^2 = k$.

4 **a** Show that the line $y = mx$ meets the circle $x^2 + y^2 - 4x - 2y + 4 = 0$ at points with x-coordinates given by $(m^2 + 1)x^2 - 2(m + 2)x + 4 = 0$.
b Find values of m if the line:
(i) is a tangent to the circle
(ii) does not cut the circle
(iii) cuts the circle in real and distinct points.

5 **a** Show that the equation of the tangent at A$(8, -6)$ to the circle $x^2 + y^2 + 20y + 20 = 0$ is $y = 10 - 2x$.
b Prove that it is also a tangent to the circle $x^2 + y^2 = 20$, and find the coordinates of the point of contact.

6 **a** Show that the equation of the tangent at B$(-3, -1)$ to the circle $x^2 + y^2 = 10$ is $y = -3x - 10$.
b Prove that it is also a tangent to the circle $x^2 + y^2 - 20y + 60 = 0$, and find the coordinates of the point of contact.

7 For the diagram below, find:

a the equation of the tangent to the inner circle $x^2 + y^2 = 8$ at P(−2, 2)

b the points of intersection, Q and R, of the tangent and the outer circle $x^2 + y^2 = 26$

c the length of QR, in simplest form.

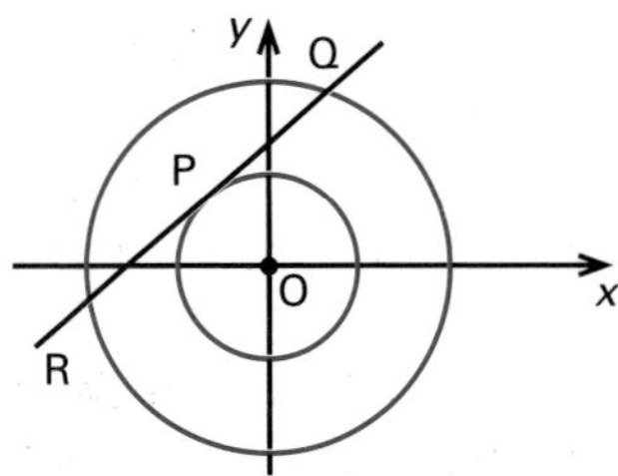

8 **a** Prove that the line $x - 3y + 20 = 0$ is a common tangent to the circles $x^2 + y^2 = 40$ and $x^2 + y^2 - 22x - 14y + 160 = 0$.

b Find the coordinates of the two points of contact, A and B.

c Calculate the exact length of the common tangent AB.

9 The position of a quayside derrick is monitored by a computer, which calculates angle α. The locus of the end of the arm is a circle with equation $x^2 + y^2 - 10x - 8y + 31 = 0$ for the axes chosen. The line representing the quayside passes through the points (0, 4) and (4, 6). Find:

a the equation of the quayside

b the coordinates of A and B

c the range of values of α, to the nearest degree, for which the end of the derrick's arm projects beyond the edge of the quay.

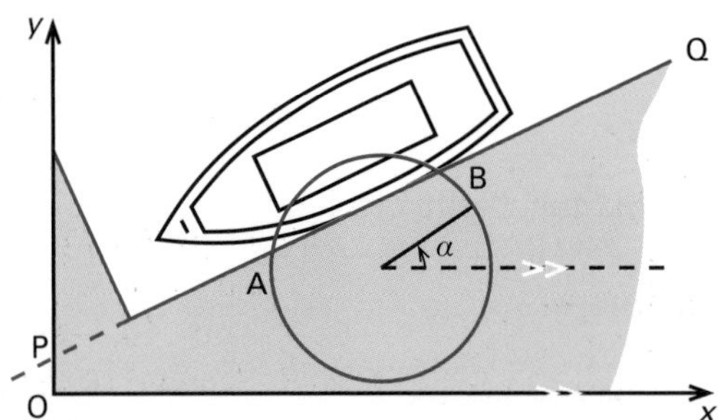

Challenge

Prove that each of the following lines is a tangent to the circle, and find the point of contact.

a $3y - 4x = 25$, $x^2 + y^2 = 25$

b $4y + 3x = 25$, $x^2 + y^2 = 25$

c $3x + 2y = 6$, $x^2 + y^2 + 2x + 4y - 8 = 0$

d $3x - 4y + 9 = 0$, $x^2 + y^2 - 8x + 2y - 8 = 0$

CHAPTER 4 REVIEW

1 Write down:

a the equation of the circle, centre O, radius 7

b the centre and radius of the circle $4x^2 + 4y^2 = 36$.

2 Find the points of intersection of these circles with the x and y-axes:

a $x^2 + y^2 = 100$ **b** $2x^2 + 2y^2 = 50$.

3 a Write down the centre and radius of the circle $x^2 + y^2 - 6x - 2y - 15 = 0$.

b Say whether each of these points lies inside, outside or on the circle: A(3, 6), B(−1, 3), C(8, 0).

4 Write down:

a the centre and radius of the circle $(x - 4)^2 + (y + 3)^2 = 16$

b the equation of the circle with centre (−5, 7) and radius 2.

5 On a street plan, two roads are represented by straight lines with equations $y = -x + 4$ and $y = x$.
The intersection of these lines marks the centre of a roundabout whose diameter is 2 units on the plan. Find the equation of the circle representing the roundabout.

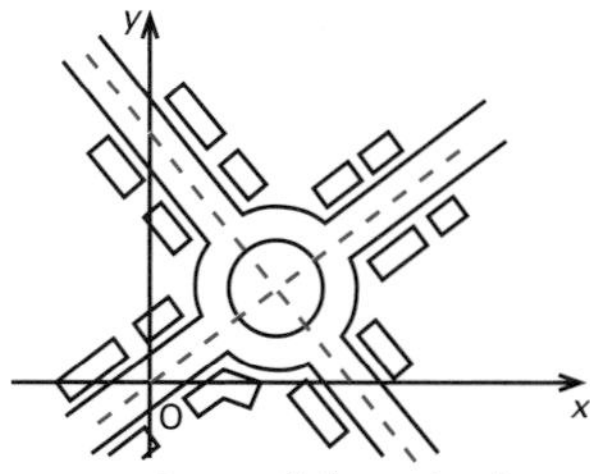

6 Find the equation of the circle, centre (−3, −5), passing through the origin.

7 Write down the equation of:

a the circle, centre (1, 3), touching the x-axis

b the image of the circle under reflection in

(i) the x-axis
(ii) the y-axis
(iii) the origin
(iv) the line $y = x$.

8 Check that the point P(−2, 4) lies on the circle $x^2 + y^2 = 20$, and find the equation of the tangent at P.

9 The line $x = 3$ cuts the circle $x^2 + y^2 = 25$ at A and B. Find the co-ordinates of the point of intersection of the tangents at A and B.

10 a Find the centre and radius of the circle $x^2 + y^2 + 8x - 2y - 8 = 0$.

b Calculate the length of a tangent to the circle from the point P(2, 4), in its simplest form.

11 a Sketch the circles $x^2 + y^2 = 4$ and $x^2 + y^2 - 8x - 6y + 16 = 0$.

b Prove that the circles touch each other.

12 Find the points in which the line $y = x + 1$ cuts the circle $x^2 + y^2 - 4x - 8y + 7 = 0$.

13 a Find the equation of the circle, centre C(4, 2), passing through the origin.

b The midpoint of the chord DF is E(1, 5). Find the coordinates of D and F.

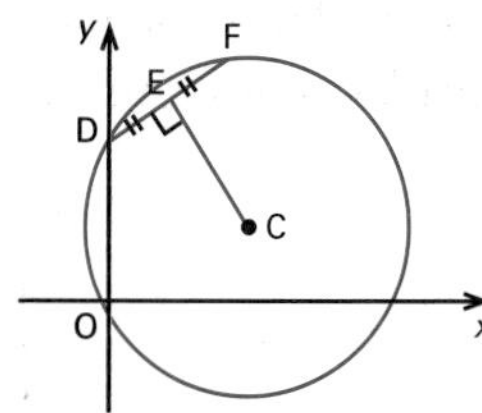

14 Find the equation of the tangent to the circle $x^2 + y^2 - 6x - 8y - 9 = 0$ at the point (0, −1).

15 Prove that the line $x - 7y - 50 = 0$ is a tangent to the circle $x^2 + y^2 = 50$, and find the point of contact.

16 Find the equation of the circle which passes through the points T(2, 0), U(6, 0) and V(6, −4).

17 A is the point (−4, 8), B is (6, 12) and C is (6, −2). Find:

a the equations of the perpendicular bisectors of AB and BC

b their point of intersection

c the equation of the circumcircle of △ABC.

CHAPTER 4 SUMMARY

1 The circle, centre O and radius r, has equation $x^2 + y^2 = r^2$.

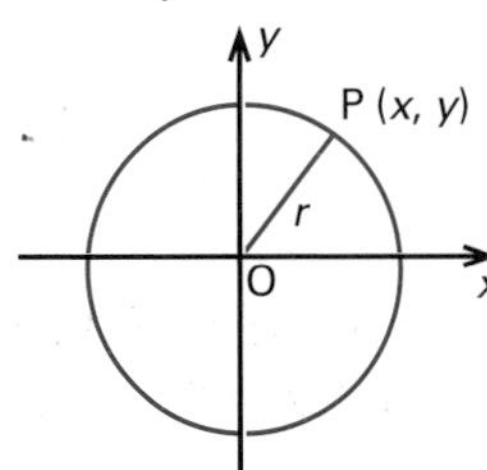

2 The circle, centre C(*a*, *b*), radius r, has equation $(x - a)^2 + (y - b)^2 = r^2$.

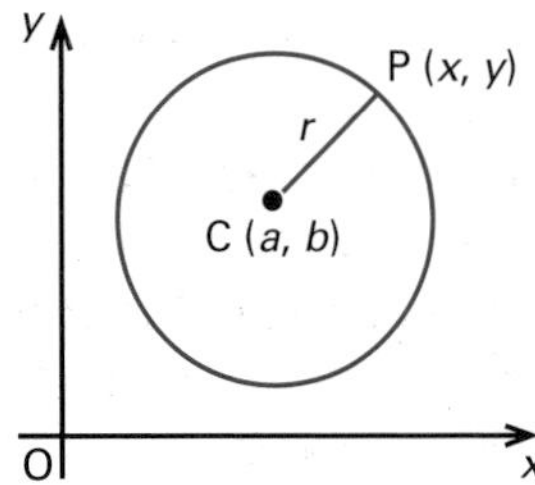

3 The general equation of a circle is is $x^2 + y^2 + 2gx + 2fy + c = 0$, $g^2 + f^2 - c > 0$. The centre is $(-g, -f)$ and the length of the radius is $\sqrt{g^2 + f^2 - c}$, $g^2 + f^2 - c > 0$.

4 Tangents to a circle at a given point
The tangent is perpendicular to the radius, so $m_{PQ} \times m_{OP} = -1$.
Hence the gradient and equation of the tangent at P can be found.

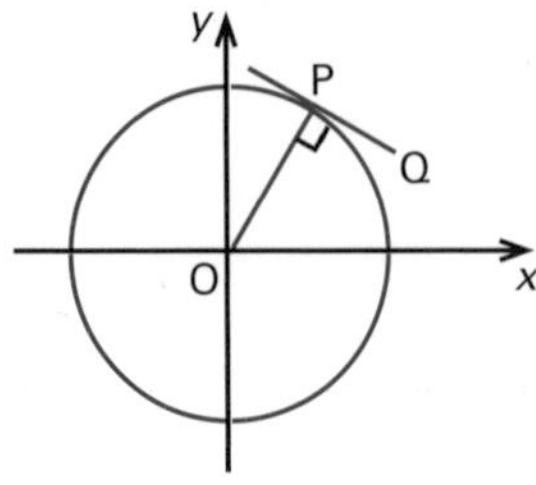

5 Intersections of lines and circles
Line meets circle:
(i) in two distinct points
(ii) at a point*
(iii) in no points
Quadratic equation has:
two distinct real roots
equal roots*
no real roots
Discriminant:
$b^2 - 4ac > 0$
$b^2 - 4ac = 0$*
$b^2 - 4ac < 0$
*The line is a tangent to the circle.

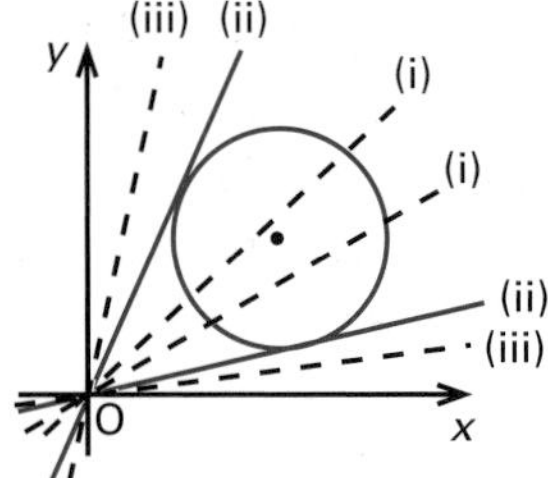

For example, for the line $y = x + k$ to be a tangent to the circle $x^2 + y^2 = 8$, the quadratic equation $x^2 + (x + k)^2 = 8$, i.e. $2x^2 + 2kx + (k^2 - 8) = 0$, has equal roots.
So $(2k)^2 - 4 \times 2 \times (k^2 - 8) = 0$, i.e. $4k^2 = 64$, or $k = \pm 4$.
The lines $y = x \pm 4$ are tangents to the circle.

5 Revision Exercises

CHAPTER REVISION EXERCISES

CHAPTER 1.1 REVISION

1 $g(x) = 8x^3 - 4x^2 + 2x - 1$. Calculate:
a $g(0)$ **b** $g(1)$ **c** $g(-1)$ **d** $g(\frac{1}{2})$.

2 Evaluate by nested calculations:
a $f(4)$, where $f(x) = 3x^3 + 2x^2 + 4x - 1$
b $g(-2)$, where $g(x) = x^4 - 3x^3 + 2x - 1$
c $h(0.4)$, where $h(x) = x^3 - 2x + 1$.

3 Find the remainder when $3x^3 + 2x^2 + x - 1$ is divided by $x - 2$.

4 Express $f(x) = x^3 + 6x^2 - 3x + 4$ in the form $(x - 3)q(x) + R$, where q is a quadratic function and R is a constant.

5 Which of the following are factors of $x^3 - x^2 + 2x - 2$?
a $x - 1$ **b** $x + 1$
c $x - 2$ **d** $x + 2$

6 Factorise:
a $x^3 - 7x + 6$
b $2x^3 + 7x^2 + 2x - 3$.

7 $x + 2$ is a factor of $x^3 + ax^2 - x - 2$. Find a, and factorise the polynomial fully.

8 $x - 1$ and $x + 3$ are factors of $x^4 + 2x^3 - 7x^2 + px + q$. Find p and q, and factorise the polynomial fully.

9 Prove that $2x - 1$ is a factor of $2x^3 + 3x^2 - 8x + 3$, and factorise the polynomial fully.

10 **a** Show that $2x - 3$ is a factor of $8x^3 - 27$.
b Explain why $8x^3 - 27$ has no other factors of the form $ax + b$.

11 Show that 1 is a root of the equation $x^3 - 2x^2 - x + 2 = 0$, and find the other roots.

12 Solve these equations:
a $x^3 - 3x + 2 = 0$
b $x^3 + 4x^2 + x - 6 = 0$.

13 **a** Show that $3x - 1$ is a factor of $3x^3 - x^2 - 3x + 1$.
b Solve the equation $3x^3 - x^2 - 3x + 1 = 0$.

14 **a** Find the points of intersection of the curves $y = x^3 - 8x^2 + 19x - 10$ and $y = x^2 - 5x + 6$.
b What can you deduce?

15 Show that the equation $3x^4 - 8x^3 = 0$ has a root between 2.6 and 2.7, using:
a factors **b** nested calculations.

16 Show that $x^3 + x^2 - 2x + 1 = 0$ has a root between -3 and -2.

17 Show that $2x^3 - x^2 - 3x + 1 = 0$ has a root between -2 and -1, a second root between 0 and 1, and a third root between 1 and 2.

18 Find the root of $x^3 + 2x^2 - 5 = 0$ between 1 and 2, correct to 1 decimal place.

CHAPTER 1.2 REVISION

1 Factorise:
a $x^2 + 3x - 10$
b $2x^2 - 5x + 2$
c $4x^2 - 12x + 9$.

2 Solve these quadratic equations:
a $x^2 - 7x + 6 = 0$
b $3x^2 + 4x + 1 = 0$
c $(y - 10)^2 = 0$
d $2t^2 - 3t - 5 = 0$.

3 The sides about the right angle in a set-square differ by 4 cm. The area of the set-square is 48 cm^2. Taking x cm for the shorter length, make a quadratic equation and solve it to find the lengths of the two sides.

4 Solve these equations, correct to 2 decimal places where necessary:
a $9x^2 - 6x + 1 = 0$
b $2x^2 - x - 6 = 0$
c $4x^2 - 6x + 1 = 0$
d $4 - 2x + x^2 = 0$.

5 The profile of an artificial ski slope is based on the equation
$y = 0.004x^2 - 0.8x$.
a For what values of x is $y = 0$?
b The lowest point on the slope is midway between the points given by the roots of the slope's equation. Find the coordinates of this point.

6 Determine the nature of the roots of these quadratic equations:
a $2x^2 - 3x + 2 = 0$
b $3x^2 + 2x - 2 = 0$
c $2x^2 + 4x + 1 = 0$
d $9x^2 - 12x + 4 = 0$.

7 Find k if the equation $2x^2 + 3x + k = 0$ has equal roots.

8 Find the values of p which ensure that $3x^2 + (p + 3)x + p = 0$ has:
a equal roots **b** no real roots.

9 **a** Show that the line $y = mx$ meets the circle $x^2 + y^2 - 4x + 2 = 0$ at points given by $(1 + m^2)x^2 - 4x + 2 = 0$.
b Find m if the line is a tangent to the circle.

10 Find m if $y = mx$ is a tangent to the circle $x^2 + y^2 - 6x - 8y = 0$.

11 **a** Write down the equation of a line through the point $(0, -4)$ with gradient m.
b If the line is a tangent to the parabola $y = x^2$, find m, and write down the equations of the two possible tangents.

12 Sketch the graphs of f below, and solve the inequalities
(i) $f(x) > 0$ **(ii)** $f(x) \leqslant 0$ for:
a $f(x) = x^2 + 3x - 10$
b $f(x) = 10x - x^2 - 21$.

13 The length of this rectangle is given by
$$y = \frac{x^2 + 3x + 5}{x - 1} \cdots (1).$$

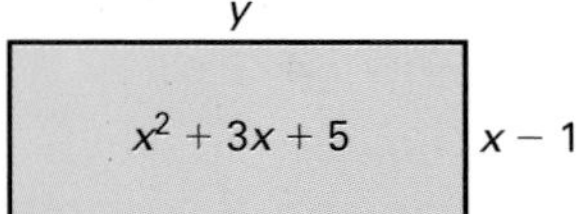

a Rearrange (1) as a quadratic equation in x.
b Show that for real roots $y \geqslant 11$ (or $y \leqslant -1$).
c Find the length, breadth and area of the rectangle for which (1) has equal roots.

14 The flight path of the rugby ball is given by $y = \frac{1}{150}(600 + 10x - x^2)$.
The units are metres.

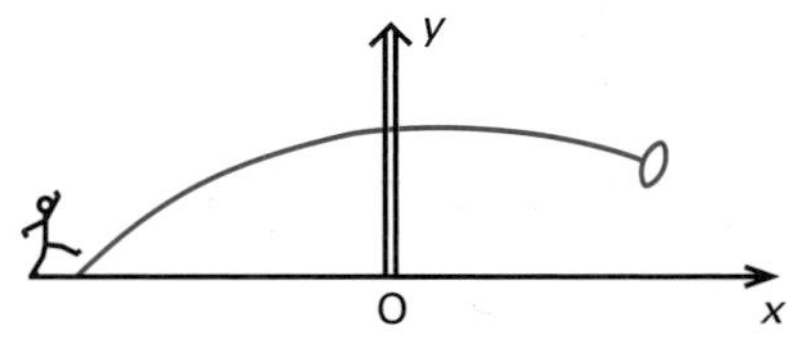

a How far from the goal posts (OY):
(i) is the player
(ii) will the ball land?
b The cross-bar is 3 m high. Will the ball go over?
c Calculate:
(i) the maximum height of the ball
(ii) the distance of the ball from the goal-line then.

CHAPTER 2 REVISION

1 Integrate:

a $4x^3 + 2x^2 + 1$ **b** $x^4 - x + 3$

c $2 - 4x + 6x^2$ **d** $(x + 1)(x - 2)$.

2 Integrate:

a $x^{-1/2} + x^{1/2} + x^{3/2}$

b $t^{1/4}(t^{3/4} - t^{-1/4})$

c $\dfrac{1}{x^2} + \dfrac{2}{x^3}$

d $\dfrac{x^2 + 4}{x^2}$

e $\dfrac{t^{3/2} + t^{1/2}}{t}$.

3 Given $f'(x)$, find $f(x)$:

a $f'(x) = 6x + 5$ and $f(1) = 10$

b $f'(x) = \dfrac{x^3}{4} + \dfrac{4}{x^3}$ and $f(-2) = 4$.

4 Find:

a $\displaystyle\int \left(6t^2 - \frac{4}{t^3}\right) dt$

b $\displaystyle\int u^{1/2}(u + u^2)\, du$

c $\displaystyle\int \left(3x^2 + \frac{1}{3x^2}\right) dx$

d $\displaystyle\int (\sqrt{x} + 1)^2\, dx$.

5 The gradient of the tangent to a curve at (x, y) is given by $\dfrac{dy}{dx} = 2x + \dfrac{1}{x^2}$.
If the curve passes through $(-1, 0)$, find its equation.

6 Evaluate:

a $\displaystyle\int_0^4 (x + 5)\, dx$ **b** $\displaystyle\int_{-1}^2 6x\, dx$

c $\displaystyle\int_{-1}^2 6x^2\, dx$.

7 Check that:

a $\displaystyle\int_0^2 (4x + 1)\, dx = -\int_2^0 (4x + 1)\, dx$

b $\displaystyle\int_1^2 (3x^2 - 2x)\, dx + \int_2^3 (3x^2 - 2x)\, dx = \int_1^3 (3x^2 - 2x)\, dx$.

8 Evaluate:

a $\displaystyle\int_0^2 (8x^3 + 2x)\, dx$

b $\displaystyle\int_1^3 (3x^2 - 2x + 5)\, dx$

c $\displaystyle\int_{-2}^0 (6x^2 - 1)\, dx$

d $\displaystyle\int_{-1}^1 t^2(t - 1)\, dt$.

9 Find a, given:

a $\displaystyle\int_1^a (2x + 1)\, dx = 4$ **b** $\displaystyle\int_a^1 \frac{dx}{x^2} = 2$

c $\displaystyle\int_a^4 \sqrt{x}\, dx = 0$.

10 Sketch and shade the areas associated with the following integrals, and then calculate each area:

a $\displaystyle\int_1^3 (2x - 1)\, dx$ **b** $\displaystyle\int_{-1}^1 (x^2 + 3)\, dx$

c $\displaystyle\int_{-2}^2 4x^3\, dx$ **d** $\displaystyle\int_{-3}^3 (x^3 - 9x)\, dx$.

11 Find the areas enclosed by these curves and the x-axis:

a $y = (x + 2)(x - 4)$

b $y = 6 + x - x^2$.

12 **a** Find the area enclosed by the x-axis, the y-axis and the curve $y = (x - 6)^2$.

b Find the ratio (> 1) in which the line $x = 3$ divides the area.

Make sketches in questions **13–16**, and calculate the area enclosed by each pair of curves.

13 $y = x^2$ and $y = 4$

14 $y = x^2 - 4x$ and $y = 8x - 2x^2$

15 $y = x^2 + 1$ and $y = 3 - x$

16 $y = (x - 2)^2$ and $y = 10 - x^2$

17 Calculate the area bounded by the parabola $y = x^2 + 4$, the lines $y = 10 - x$ and $x = 4$, and the x and y-axes.

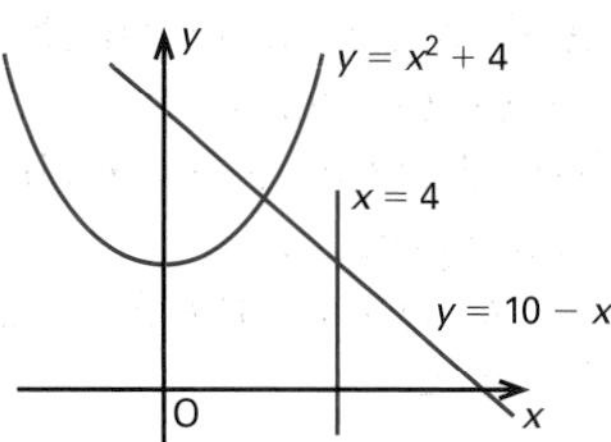

18 Calculate the area enclosed by the tangent at A(1, 1) to the parabola $y = x(4 - 3x)$, the y-axis, and the arc OA, where O is the origin.

CHAPTER 3.1 REVISION

1 O is the centre of the sphere, radius R cm. The shaded circular cross-section has radius r cm, and is d cm from O. Express:

a r in terms of R and d

b $\sin\theta°$, $\cos\theta°$ and $\tan\theta°$ in terms of R and d

c the angle between the radius R and the shaded cross-section in terms of $\theta°$.

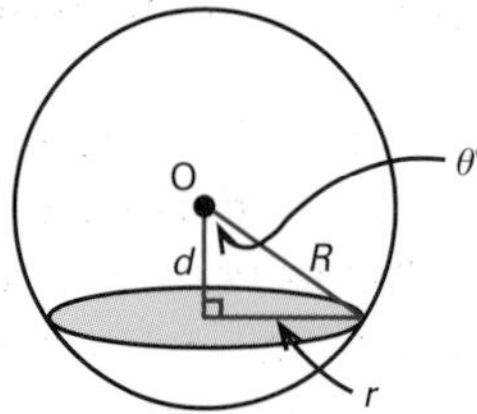

2 The equal sides of an isosceles triangle are each a cm long, and the angles opposite them are $\alpha°$. Prove that the area of the triangle is $\frac{1}{2}a^2 \sin 2\alpha°$.

3 Rectangle ABCD is tilted in a vertical plane above the horizontal line PAQ. Calculate:

a ∠CAQ, to the nearest degree

b the height of C above PQ, correct to 0.1 cm.

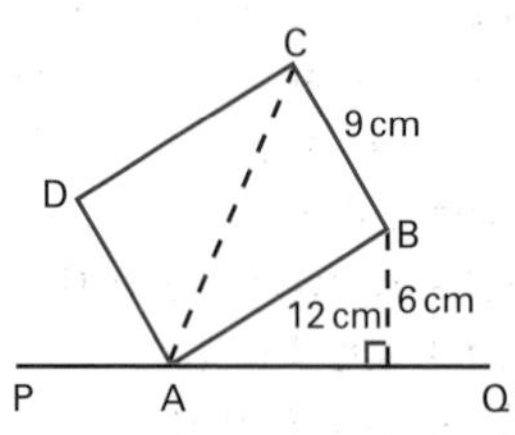

4 In △ABC, $a = 4$, $b = 5$ and $c = 6$. Prove that angle C is double angle A.

5 OPQRSTUV is a cuboid. U is the point (5, 4, 3).

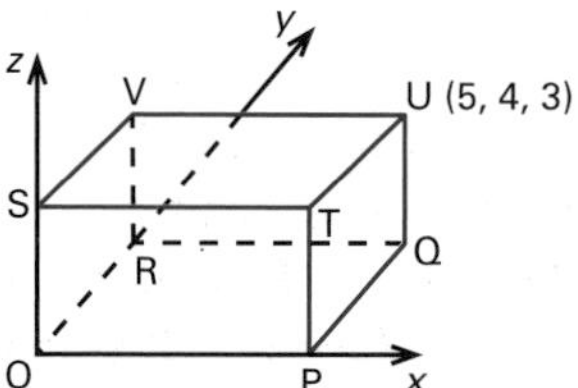

a Write down the coordinates of P, Q, R, S, T and V, and the point of intersection, W, of the space diagonals.

b Calculate, correct to 0.1°, the angle between:

(i) OU and plane OPQR

(ii) planes OPUV and OPQR.

6 The diagram below represents a symmetrical house roof.

a Write down the coordinates of B, C, D, M and E.

b Calculate the angle between the side BCF and the base ABCD, correct to 0.1°.

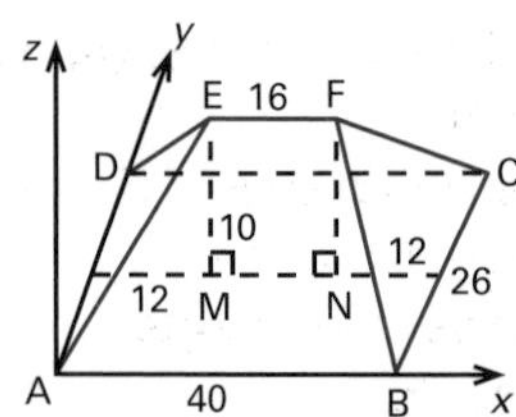

7 In the diagram below, OBCD is a square, with OB on OX and OD on OY.
A(4, 4, 10) is vertically above E, the centre of the square. F is the midpoint of BC.

a Write down the coordinates of B, C, D, E and F.

b Calculate:

(i) EF

(ii) the angle between the planes ABC and OBCD, correct to 0.1°.

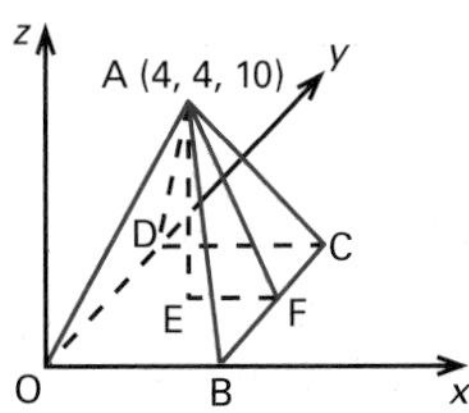

8 Calculate, correct to 0.1 m or the nearest degree:

a the length of the chalk line

b the angle between the chalk line and the top of the board

c the height of the top of the blackboard above the ground

d the angle between the front and back blackboards

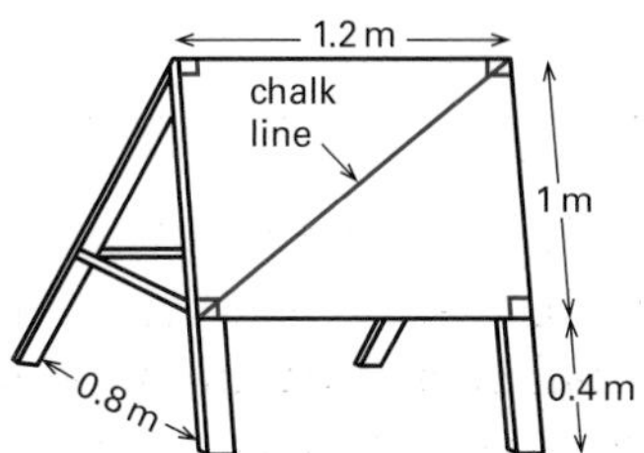

CHAPTER 3.2 REVISION

1 Write down formulae for:

a cos (U − V) **b** sin (H − K)

c sin $2t°$ **d** cos $2t°$ (three formulae)

e sin $4t°$.

2 Express these as functions of acute angles:

a sin 160° **b** cos 320° **c** tan 200°

d cos 100° **e** sin 280° **f** tan 350°.

3 Express each of the following in the form cos (A ± B) or sin (A ± B), and hence give their exact values:

a sin 54° cos 36° + cos 54° sin 36°

b cos 67° cos 22° + sin 67° sin 22°

c $\sin\frac{5\pi}{8}\cos\frac{\pi}{8} - \cos\frac{5\pi}{8}\sin\frac{\pi}{8}$

d $\cos\frac{5\pi}{8}\cos\frac{\pi}{8} - \sin\frac{5\pi}{8}\sin\frac{\pi}{8}$.

4 A and B are acute angles, with $\cos A = \frac{4}{5}$ and $\cos B = \frac{7}{25}$.

a Show that $\cos(A - B) = \frac{4}{5}$ and $\sin(A - B) = -\frac{3}{5}$

b Find the exact value of:

(i) sin 2A

(ii) cos 2A

(iii) sin 4A.

5 $\tan\alpha = \frac{2}{3}$ and $\tan\beta = \frac{1}{2}$, where $0 < \alpha < 90$ and $0 < \beta < 90$. Calculate the exact value of:

a $\cos(\alpha - \beta)$ **b** $\sin(\alpha - \beta)$

c $\sin 2\alpha$ **d** $\cos 2\alpha$.

6 Write $\cos 3x°$ as $\cos(2x + x)°$, and hence show that $\cos 3x° = 4\cos^3 x° - 3\cos x°$.

7 Change the subject of:

a $\cos 2A = 2\cos^2 A - 1$ to $\cos^2 A$

b $\cos 2A = 1 - 2\sin^2 A$ to $\sin^2 A$.

8 In △ABC, $b = 2$, $c = 3$, ∠B = $x°$ and ∠C = $(x + 30)°$.

a Use the Sine Rule to show that

$$\tan x° = \frac{1}{3 - \sqrt{3}}.$$

b Hence calculate x, correct to 0.1°.

9 Solve, for $0 \leqslant x \leqslant 360$, correct to 1 decimal place where necessary:

a $2\sin 2x° + 3\cos x° = 0$

b $\cos 2x° + 3\sin x° - 2 = 0$

c $\cos 2x° + \cos^2 x° - 2 = 0$.

10 Solve, for $0 \leqslant \theta \leqslant 2\pi$:

a $\cos 2\theta - 9\sin\theta + 4 = 0$

b $\cos 2\theta + \sin\theta = 1$

c $\cos 2\theta + \sin^2\theta = 0$.

11 Find the coordinates of the four points of intersection of these graphs ($0 \leqslant x \leqslant 360$):

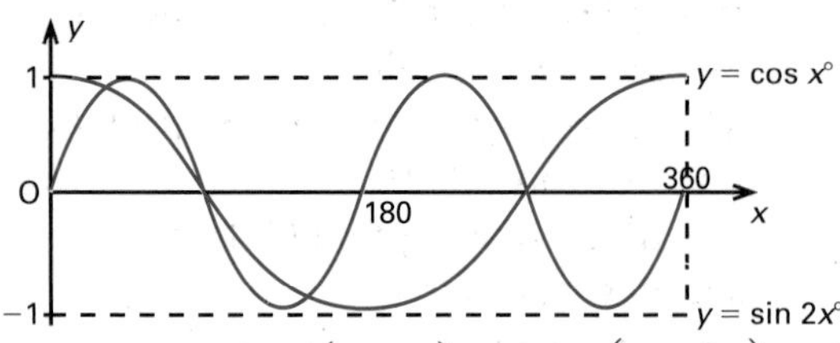

12 Simplify $\cos\left(\theta + \frac{\pi}{3}\right) + \cos\left(\theta + \frac{2\pi}{3}\right)$.

13 Use the formula $\triangle = \frac{1}{2}ab\sin C$ three times in this diagram to prove that $\sin(x + y) = \sin x \cos y + \cos x \sin y$.

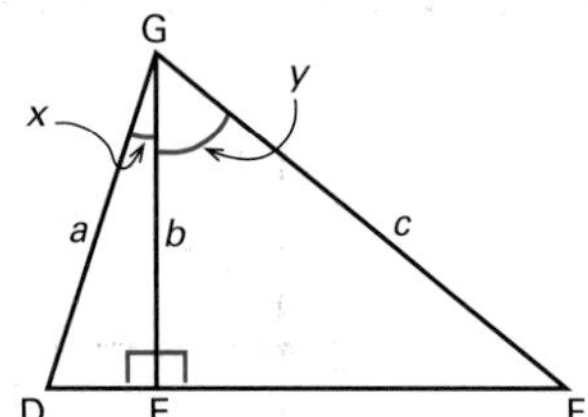

14 In the diagram below, (i) is part of the graph of a sine function and (ii) is part of the graph of a cosine function.

a Determine the equations of the graphs.

b Find the coordinates of A, B, C and D (C and D correct to 1 decimal place).

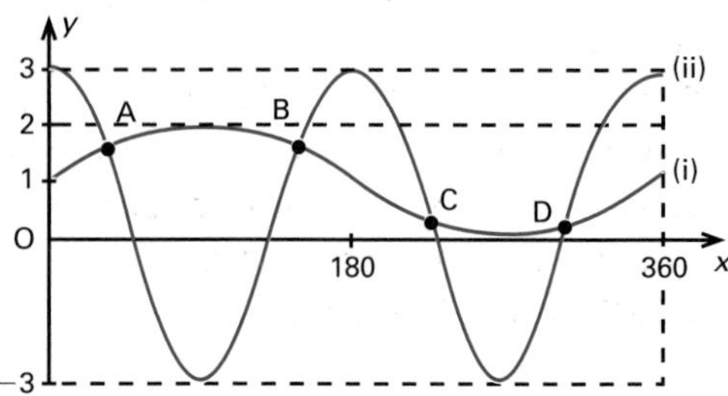

15 Sketch the graph $y = 4\sin\left(2x - \frac{\pi}{6}\right)$ for $0 \leqslant x \leqslant 2\pi$.

CHAPTER 4 REVISION

1 Find the equation of the circle, centre O, and:

a radius 6

b radius half that of $x^2 + y^2 = 64$

c passing through the point $(-2, 5)$.

2 Find the equation of the circle, centre $(-1, 2)$, and:

a radius 7

b passing through the origin

c touching the x-axis

d touching the y-axis.

3 Find the centre and radius, and hence the equation, of the circle through the vertices of the square $A(-1, 5)$ $B(1, 7)$ $C(3, 5)$ $D(1, 3)$.

4 These three circles touch the y-axis at O, and pass through the points $A(2, 0)$, $B(4, 0)$ and $C(6, 0)$ as shown.

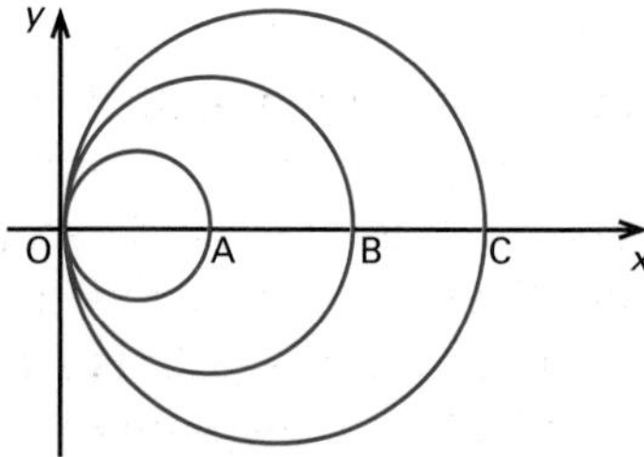

a Find the ratio of:

(i) the radii of the circles

(ii) the areas of the circles.

b Find the equations of the circles.

c What is the equation of:

(i) their common tangent

(ii) their axis of symmetry?

5 Find the coordinates of the centre and the length of the radius of the circle:

a $x^2 + y^2 - 10x - 2y - 10 = 0$

b $3x^2 + 3y^2 + 12x - 18y + 12 = 0$.

6 Prove that the circles $x^2 + y^2 = 20$ and $x^2 + y^2 + 4x + 6y - 7 = 0$ are equal in area.

7 Find p if the point $(p, -3)$ lies on the circle $x^2 + y^2 + 13x + 15y + 6 = 0$.

8 Show that the circles $x^2 + y^2 = 32$ and $x^2 + y^2 - 8x - 8y - 96 = 0$ touch internally.

9 The circles $(x + 5)^2 + y^2 = 25$, centre C, and $(x - 8)^2 + y^2 = 144$, centre D, intersect at M and N. Use the converse of Pythagoras' Theorem to prove that $\angle$CMD is a right angle.

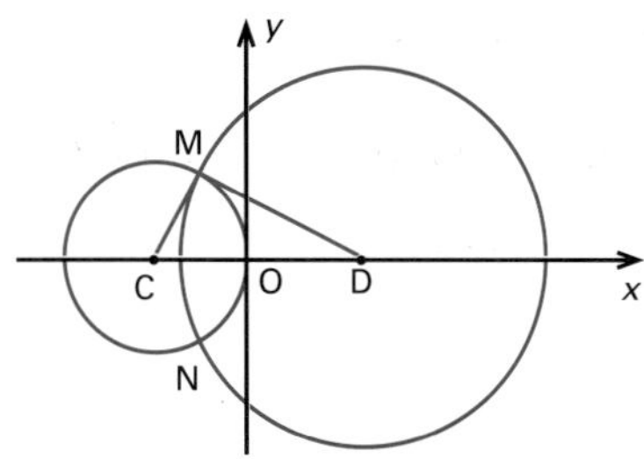

10 Find the length of the chord cut off on:

a the line $3x - y + 5 = 0$ by the circle $x^2 + y^2 = 5$

b the x-axis by the circle $x^2 + y^2 + 10x - 8y - 11 = 0$.

11 **a** Show that the point P(1, –4) lies on the circle $x^2 + y^2 + 4x + 10y + 19 = 0$.

b Find the equation of the tangent at P.

12 **a** Find the points of intersection of the line $y = 4$ and the circle $x^2 + y^2 = 25$.

b Find the equations of the tangents to the circle at these points, and also the coordinates of the point of intersection of the tangents.

13 Find k, given that $x = 2y - k$ is a tangent to the circle $x^2 + y^2 = 5$.

14 **a** Show that the tangent to the circle $x^2 + y^2 = 10$ at M(–3, –1) is also a tangent to the circle $x^2 + y^2 - 20y + 60 = 0$, and find the point of contact, N.

b Calculate the length of MN, in simplest surd form.

15 **a** Find the equation of the circle on A(–1, 0) C(7, 4) as diameter.

b Find the coordinates of B and D where the perpendicular diameter meets the circle.

c Check that ABCD is a square.

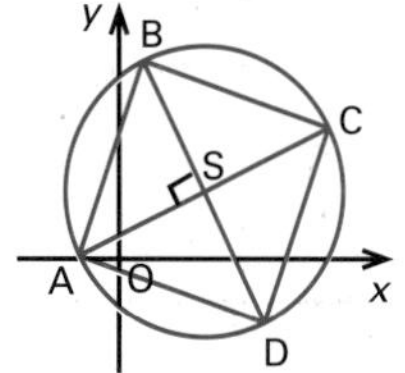

16 Find the equation of the circle:

a through O(0, 0), P(2, 6) and Q(10, –10)

b through O(0, 0) and A(0, 4), and having the line $x = -2$ as a tangent.

GENERAL REVISION EXERCISES

REVIEW A

1 Simplify:

a $\int(3x^2 - 2x + 1)\,dx$

b $\int(x^{1/2} - x^{-1/2})\,dx$.

2 Find, correct to 2 decimal places, the coordinates of the points of intersection of the parabola $y = x^2$ and the line $y = 2x + 1$.

3 a Write down the equation of the circle with centre O and radius $2\sqrt{5}$.

b Find:

(i) the equation of the tangent to the circle at the point $(2, -4)$

(ii) the coordinates of the points where the tangent cuts the x and y-axes.

4 $\sin\alpha = \frac{3}{5}$ and $\tan\beta = \frac{5}{12}$, with α and β acute angles. Find exact values of:

a $\sin(\alpha + \beta)$ **b** $\sin 2\alpha$.

5 Evaluate:

a $\int_0^1 (x^2 + x - 1)\,dx$

b $\int_1^3 \left(x^2 + \frac{1}{x^2}\right)dx$.

6 $f(x) = 1 - x^2$ and $g(x) = 2x + 1$.

a Find formulae for $f(g(x))$ and $g(f(x))$.

b Given $f(g(a)) = -24$, find the values of a.

7 a Prove that the equation $x^2 - 2x + 3 = 0$ has no real roots.

b Find the turning point of the parabola $y = x^2 - 2x + 3$, and sketch the parabola.

8 a Find the equation of the circle with centre $(2, 3)$, passing through the point $(5, 6)$.

b Prove that the line $y = x + 7$ is a tangent to the circle, and find the point where they touch.

9 a Write down a formula for:

(i) $\sin 2x°$

(ii) $\cos 2x°$ in terms of $\cos x°$.

b Solve these equations, for $0 \leqslant x \leqslant 360$:

(i) $\sin 2x° + \sin x° = 0$

(ii) $\cos 2x° - \cos x° - 2 = 0$.

10 a Show by shading in sketches the areas represented by:

(i) $\int_{-2}^{0} x\,dx$

(ii) $\int_{-1}^{1} x^2\,dx$

(iii) $\int_{0}^{4} x^3\,dx$.

b Calculate the three areas.

11 In the cuboid, OA = 12, AB = 5 and BF = 4.

a Write down the coordinates of A, B and F.

b Calculate the angle, correct to 0.1°, between:

(i) OF and plane OABC

(ii) planes ABCO and ABGD.

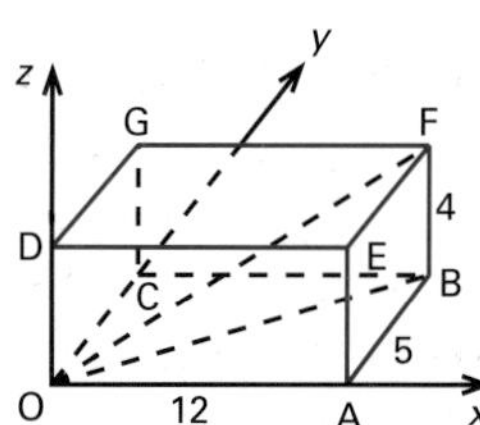

12 a Sketch the parabola $y = 3 + 2x - x^2$, and hence solve the inequality $3 + 2x - x^2 \geqslant 0$.

b Repeat the method in **a** to solve $x^2 - 9 > 0$.

13 a Find the points of intersection of the line $y = x + 1$ and the circle $x^2 + y^2 = 13$.

b Find c for the line $y = x + c$ to be a tangent to the circle.

14 a Sketch the curve $y = x^3 + 3x^2$.

b Find the area enclosed between the curve and the x-axis.

15 A straight railway line, represented by the x-axis, crosses a river at A, B and C.

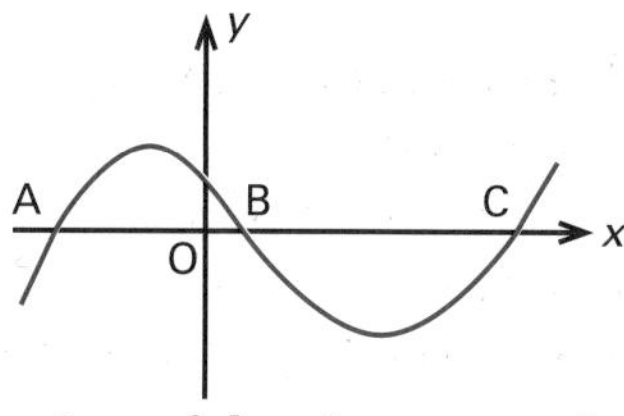

The equation of the river curve is $y = 2x^3 - 5x^2 - 14x + 8$.

a Find the coordinates of A, B and C.

b If each unit represents 5 km, calculate the distances AB and BC between the bridges.

16 Find the equation of the circle through the origin and the points (0, 6) and (4, 2).

17 Find p if the roots of $(p+1)x^2 + 2px + (p-2) = 0$ are:

a equal **b** real and distinct.

REVIEW B

1 Find the values of m if the line $y = mx + 1$ is a tangent to the curve $y = x^2 - 2x + 5$.

2 Evaluate:

a $\displaystyle\int_1^3 \left(x^2 - 1 + \frac{1}{x^2}\right) dx$

b $\displaystyle\int_0^8 x^{1/3}(x^{2/3} - x^{-2/3})\, dx$.

3 a Show that the circle with centre O and radius $2\sqrt{5}$ intersects the parabola $y = x^2$ at points with x-coordinates given by $x^4 + x^2 - 20 = 0$.

b Solve this equation to find the points of intersection.

4 A function f is given by $f(x) = x^3 - 3x + 2$.

a Solve the equation $f(x) = 0$.

b Find the stationary points of the curve $y = f(x)$.

c Sketch the curve $y = f(x)$.

d Write down the intervals in which f is:

(i) increasing **(ii)** decreasing.

5 a Show that $\cos(A - 45)^\circ - \cos(A + 45)^\circ = \sqrt{2}\sin A^\circ$.

b If $\cos\alpha = \frac{4}{5}$, and $270 < \alpha < 360$, find the value of $\tan\alpha$.

6 a Find the equation of the tangent at A(−2, 1) to a circle, centre O.

b Under a translation parallel to the y-axis the tangent is a line through the origin. Write down:

(i) the y component of the translation

(ii) the equations of the images of the tangent and the circle.

7 a Factorise $x^3 - 6x^2 + 9x - 4$.

b Find the TPs of the curve $y = x^3 - 6x^2 + 9x - 4$, and sketch the curve.

c Find the area enclosed between the curve and the x-axis.

8 Solve these equations:

a $\tan(4x - 5)^\circ + 1 = 0,\ 0 \leqslant x \leqslant 180$

b $2\cos 2x + \cos x - 1 = 0,\ 0 \leqslant x \leqslant 2\pi$, correct to 2 decimal places.

9 An architect bases his Millennium Arch on the curve $y = 75 + 44x - 4x^2$, where the x-axis represents level ground at the base of the arch. Taking 1 unit to represent 1 metre, calculate the greatest width and height of the arch.

10 A machine part (shaded) is bounded by the circle, centre C(5, 4), which touches the y-axis, and the parabola $y = 4 - \frac{4}{9}(x - 5)^2$.

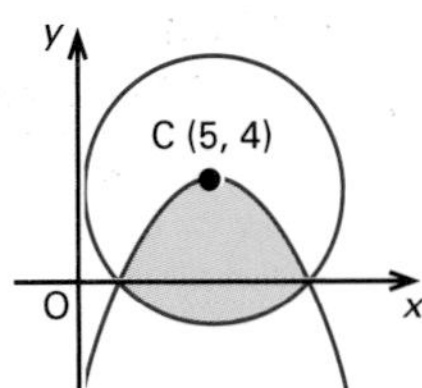

a Show that the maximum turning point of the parabola is at C.

b Prove that the circle and the parabola cut the x-axis at the same points.

11 **a** Show the line $y = 2x + 1$ crossing the parabola $y = 4 - x^2$ in a sketch.

b Calculate the area enclosed by them.

12 **a** Prove that $r = \dfrac{s \sin \beta}{\cos(\alpha - \beta)}$. Remember that $\sin(90° - A) = \cos A$.

b Find, in simplest factorised form, an expression for the area of the quadrilateral.

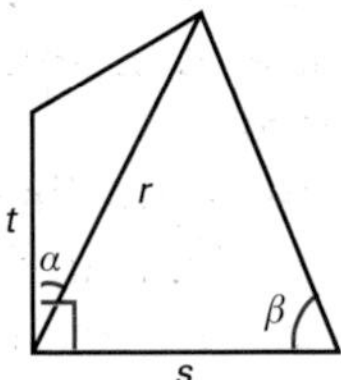

13 Write down a formula for the inverse f^{-1} of each function, and sketch the graphs $y = f(x)$ and $y = f^{-1}(x)$ for each pair on the same diagram:

a $f(x) = \frac{1}{2}x$ **b** $f(x) = x - 1$

c $f(x) = x^4 (x \geqslant 0)$.

14 The circle $x^2 + y^2 - 8x - 6y = 0$ cuts the x-axis at A and B. The tangents to the circle at A and B meet at C. Find the coordinates of C.

15 $f(x) = 1 - x$ and $g(x) = \dfrac{1}{x - 1}$.

a Find, in simplest form, $f(g(x))$ and $g(f(x))$.

b Find x, correct to 1 decimal place, if $f(g(x)) = g(f(x))$.

16 A is the point $(-2, -1)$ and B is $(3, 1)$.

a Find the equation of the locus of $P(x, y)$ which moves so that $AP = 3PB$.

b Show that this is the equation of a circle.

REVIEW C

1 Find $f(x)$, given $f'(x) = x + \dfrac{2}{\sqrt{x}}$ and $f(4) = 17$.

2 **a** Show that the line $y = x + 1$ is a tangent to the circle $x^2 + y^2 - 6x + 1 = 0$, and find the point of contact.

b Determine the equation of the parallel tangent to the circle.

3 **a** Find the equation of the tangent to the parabola $y = 5 - x^2$ at P(2, 1).

b Calculate the area of the shaded region bounded by the tangent, the parabola and the y-axis.

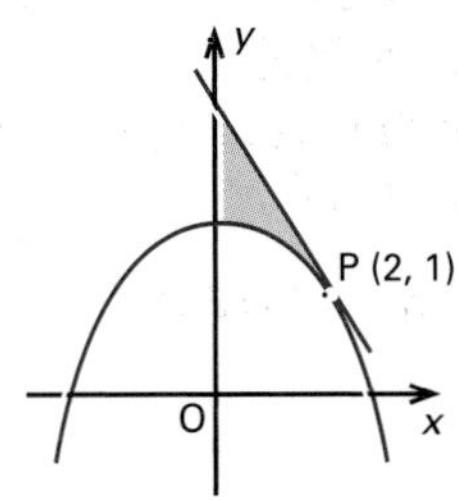

4 **a** Find k if $kx^2 + 2(k - 1)x + (k + 2) = 0$ has:
(i) equal roots
(ii) no real roots.
b Find the equal roots in case **a(i)**.

5 $f(x) = x^2 + x$ and $g(x) = x^2 + 2x$.
a Find formulae for $f(g(x))$ and $g(f(x))$.
b Solve the equation $f(g(x)) = g(f(x))$.

6 **a** Find the equation of the tangent to the circle $x^2 + y^2 + 4x - 2y - 8 = 0$ at P(1, 3).
b The tangent is also a tangent at P to a circle with centre (4, 5). Find the equation of this circle.

7 $f(x) = (\cos x° + 2\sin x°)^2 + (2\cos x° + \sin x°)^2$.
a Show that $f(x) = 5 + 4\sin 2x°$.
b State the maximum and minimum values of f, and sketch the graph $y = f(x)$ for $0 \leqslant x \leqslant 180$.
c Find x for which $f(x) = 3$.

8 A design for a stained glass window shows two sets of parabolic curves. One set is based on the parabola $y = x^2 - 2x$, and the other is based on $y = 4x - x^2$. Calculate the shaded region where a pair of the parabolas overlap.

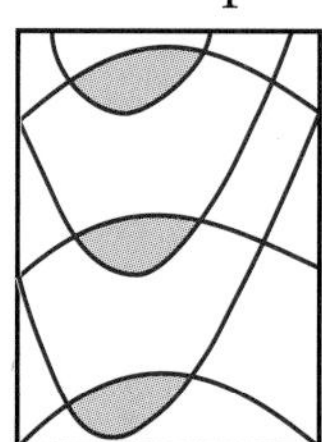

9 Solve, correct to 1 decimal place where necessary:
a $2\sin 2x° = \cos x°$, for $0 \leqslant x \leqslant 360$
b $\cos 2\theta + 2\cos\theta = 1$, for $0 \leqslant \theta \leqslant 2\pi$.

10 $f(x) = x^2$, $g(x) = \sin x$ and $h(x) = \cos x$.
a Express $g(a + b)$ in terms of $g(a)$, $g(b)$, $h(a)$ and $h(b)$.
b Show that $f(h(x)) - f(g(x)) = h(2x)$.
c Show also that

$$g(x)h(x) = \tfrac{1}{2}g(2x).$$

11 AC and AD are edges of roller-blade runs from level A to the ground.
a Calculate: (i) AD (ii) AC.
b Show that:
(i) $BC = 15\sqrt{3}$ m
(ii) $\sin CAD = \dfrac{12 - 5\sqrt{3}}{26}$.

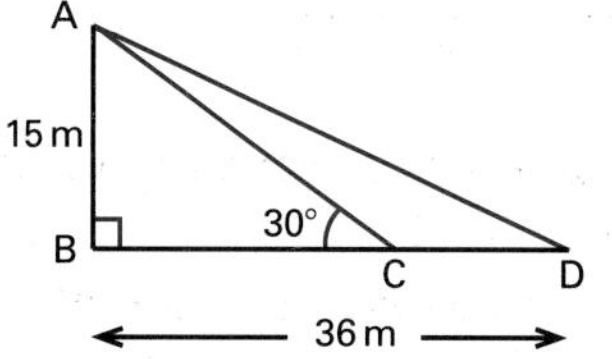

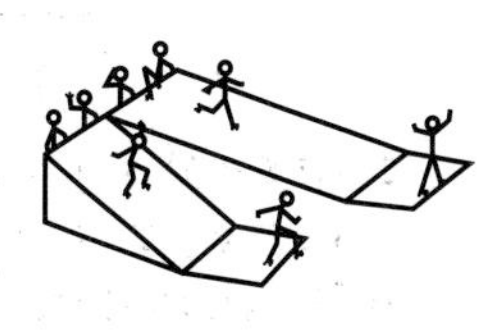

12 Find the equation of the circle which touches the line $x - 4y + 4 = 0$ at (4, 2), and the line $4x + y - 1 = 0$ at (1, −3).

13 **a** Write down formulae in terms of $2x$ for:
(i) $2\sin x\cos x$
(ii) $\sin^2 x$.
b Express $8\sin^3 x\cos x$ in the form $a\sin 2x - b\sin 4x$.

14 The curve $y = x^3 + 2x^2 - x - 2$ meets the x-axis at A, B and C, where $x_A < x_B < x_C$.
a Find the x-coordinates of A, B and C.
b If the gradients of the tangents at A, B and C are m_A, m_B and m_C, show that $m_A m_B + m_C = 0$.

15 The arc length AB is given by

$$s = \int_a^b \sqrt{\left(1 + \left(\frac{dy}{dx}\right)^2\right)}\,dx.$$

a Show that for the curve

$$y = \tfrac{1}{3}x^3 + \frac{1}{4x},\quad 1 + \left(\frac{dy}{dx}\right)^2 = \left(x^2 + \frac{1}{4x^2}\right)^2.$$

b Calculate the length of arc from $x = 1$ to $x = 2$.

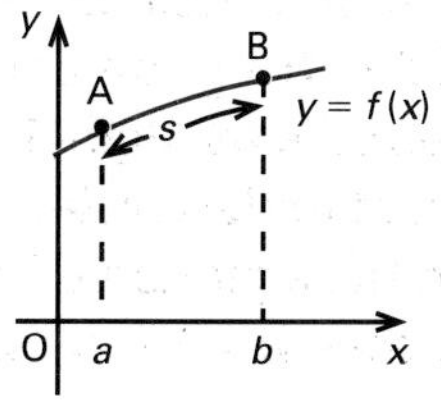

UNIT 3

1 Vectors

CLASS DISCUSSION

1 The definition of a vector

a Consider:

- the number of students in the class
- the amount of money you have with you
- the time of day
- the temperature in the classroom
- the width of this page.

All of these quantities have one thing in common – size, or *magnitude*. The magnitude of each can be shown on the number scale so they are called *scalars*.

b Concorde takes off from Heathrow, and flies in a straight line for 60 km. Why are you unable to say exactly where its final position is?
Its course is 090°, due east. Can you fix its position now?
'60 km due east' involves distance, or *magnitude*, and *direction*.

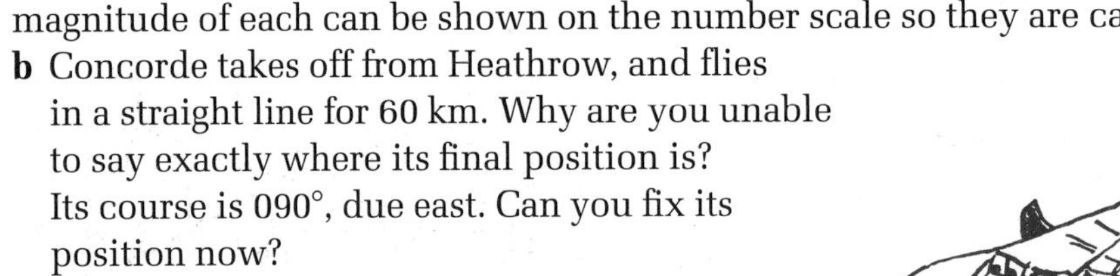

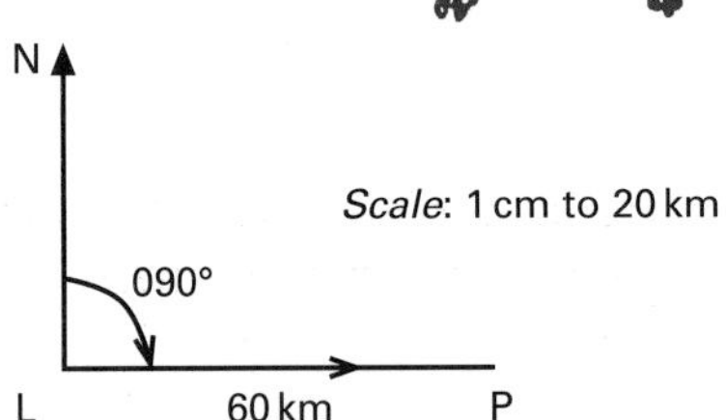

A quantity which has magnitude and direction is a *vector*.

One example of a vector is a *displacement*, that is the distance moved by a point in a certain direction. Concorde's displacement of 60 km due east is represented in *distance* and *direction* by the arrowed line drawn *from* L *to* P above, 3 cm long.

2 Directed line segments

A vector $\boldsymbol{u}$ can be represented in magnitude and direction by a directed line segment $\overrightarrow{AB}$.
The length of $\overrightarrow{AB}$ is proportional to the magnitude of $\boldsymbol{u}$, and the arrow shows the direction of $\boldsymbol{u}$.
In the diagram, $\overrightarrow{AB}$ and $\overrightarrow{CD}$ have the same magnitude and direction, so $\overrightarrow{AB} = \overrightarrow{CD}$. Both represent the vector $\boldsymbol{u}$, and we write $\boldsymbol{u} = \overrightarrow{AB}$ or $\boldsymbol{u} = \overrightarrow{CD}$.

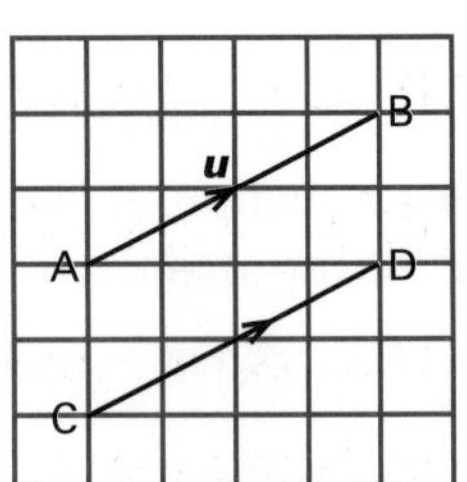

3 Components of a vector in 2 dimensions

The displacement from A to B can be made by moving 2 units in the x-direction, then 4 units in the y-direction.

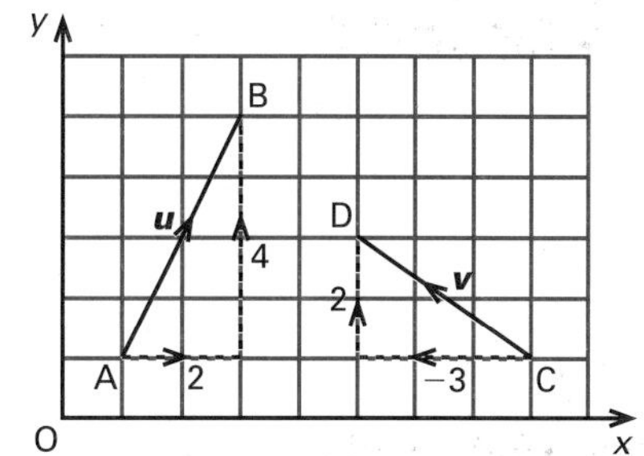

The vector $\overrightarrow{AB} = \begin{pmatrix} 2 \\ 4 \end{pmatrix}$, **or** $\boldsymbol{u} = \begin{pmatrix} 2 \\ 4 \end{pmatrix}$.

2 is the x-component of $\overrightarrow{AB}$, and 4 is the y-component. In the same way,

$\overrightarrow{CD} = \begin{pmatrix} -3 \\ 2 \end{pmatrix}$, or $v = \begin{pmatrix} -3 \\ 2 \end{pmatrix}$.

EXERCISE 1

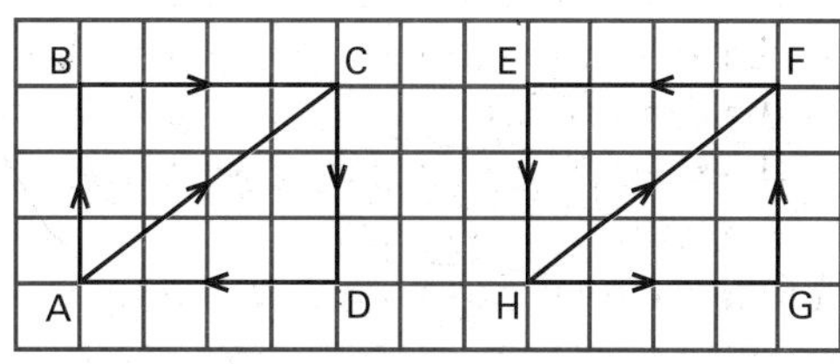

1 Name the directed line segments in both rectangles which are equal to each of the following vectors. (Remember to check directions as well as lengths.)

a $\overrightarrow{AB}$ **b** $\overrightarrow{BC}$ **c** $\overrightarrow{CD}$ **d** $\overrightarrow{AC}$

2 Name all the directed line segments in the squares which represent vector:

a $\boldsymbol{u}$ **b** v **c** $\boldsymbol{w}$.

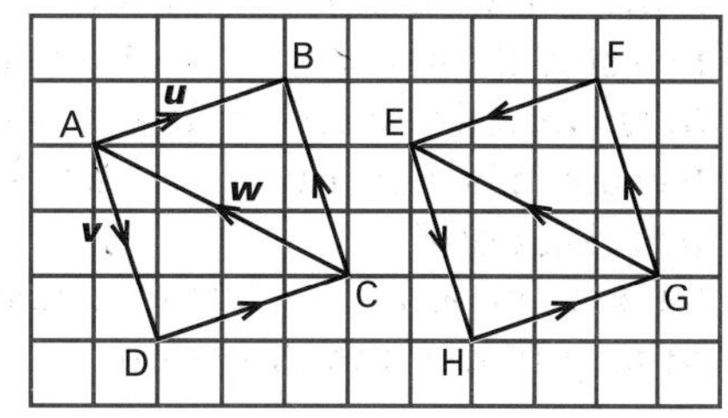

3 Write each vector below in component form like this: $\boldsymbol{a} = \begin{pmatrix} 2 \\ 3 \end{pmatrix}$. As you cannot write a bold type of a, underline it like this: $\underset{\sim}{a}$.

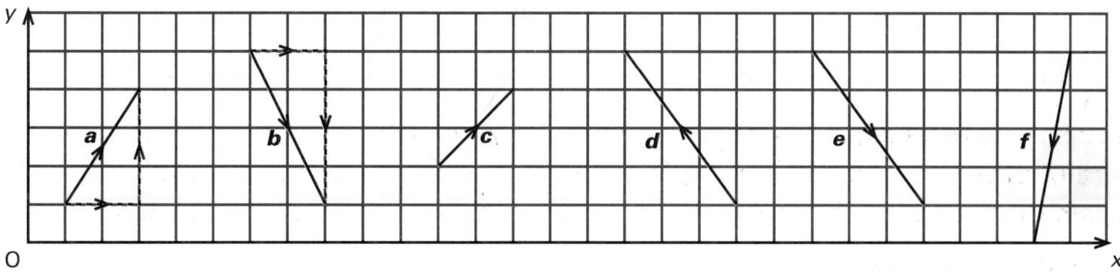

4 **a** Draw a directed line segment on squared paper to represent each of these vectors.

(i) $\boldsymbol{p} = \begin{pmatrix} 3 \\ 2 \end{pmatrix}$ (ii) $\boldsymbol{q} = \begin{pmatrix} 3 \\ -2 \end{pmatrix}$ (iii) $\boldsymbol{r} = \begin{pmatrix} -4 \\ -1 \end{pmatrix}$

b Draw two directed line segments for $\begin{pmatrix} 2 \\ 1 \end{pmatrix}$. What can you say about their lengths and directions?

5 $\overrightarrow{AB} = \begin{pmatrix} 2 \\ 1 \end{pmatrix}$, $\overrightarrow{CD} = \begin{pmatrix} -3 \\ 4 \end{pmatrix}$ and $\overrightarrow{EF} = \begin{pmatrix} -1 \\ -6 \end{pmatrix}$. Write down the components of $\overrightarrow{BA}$, $\overrightarrow{DC}$ and $\overrightarrow{FE}$.

6 $\overrightarrow{PQ} = \begin{pmatrix} 3 \\ 2 \end{pmatrix}$. Find the coordinates of Q, given that P is the point:

a (0, 0) **b** (1, 4) **c** (−4, 3) **d** (5, −2)

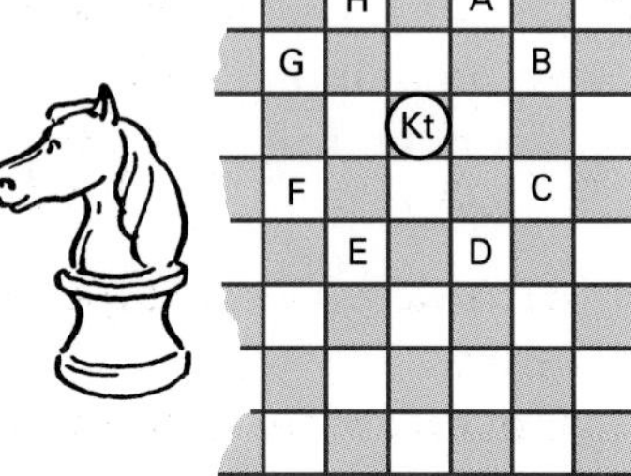

7 In chess, the knight can move 2 squares left or right then 1 square up or down, or 1 square left or right then 2 squares up or down. Write down the components for his moves from square Kt to squares A, B, … H.

For example, $\overrightarrow{KG} = \begin{pmatrix} -2 \\ 1 \end{pmatrix}$.

8 Irma drives a bus. She selects gears by sliding the gear-lever along the grooves. The distance between gear positions (shown by dots) is 3 cm.

a Use components, with N as origin, to describe the displacement of the gear lever from:

(i) N to 3 (ii) N to 4 (iii) N to 1 (iv) 1 to 2 (v) 4 to 3.

b Express:

(i) $\overrightarrow{NR}$ (ii) $\overrightarrow{RN}$

in component form.

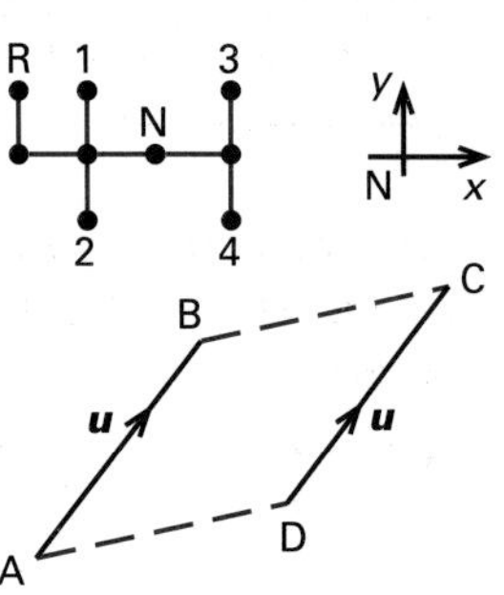

9 $\boldsymbol{u} = \overrightarrow{AB} = \overrightarrow{DC}$.

a Prove that ABCD is a parallelogram in this diagram.

b If $\overrightarrow{AB} = \overrightarrow{BE}$, what can you say about A, B and E?

The magnitude of a vector in 2 dimensions

The situation

Pat is pulling a trolley across the floor. He pulls with a *force* $\boldsymbol{F}$ which has size and direction. So force is another example of a vector.

The horizontal component of the force is 8 newtons, and the vertical component is 4 newtons.

The vector diagram

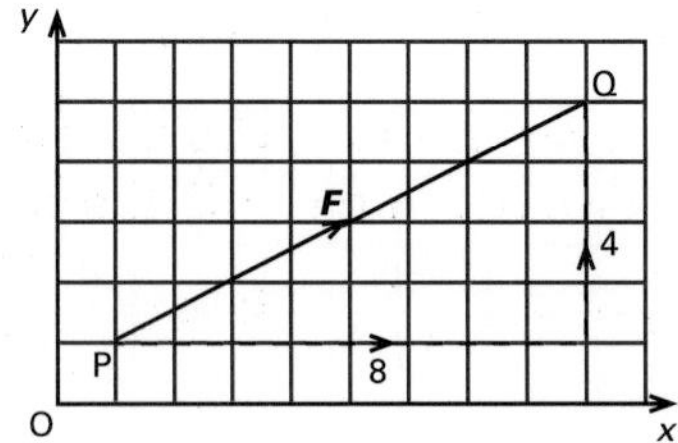

$\overrightarrow{PQ} = \begin{pmatrix} 8 \\ 4 \end{pmatrix}$, and the length of PQ is written $|\overrightarrow{PQ}|$. By Pythagoras' Theorem, $|\overrightarrow{PQ}|^2 = 8^2 + 4^2$, and $|\overrightarrow{PQ}| = 8.9$, correct to 1 decimal place.

So Pat pulls the trolley with a force $\boldsymbol{F}$ of magnitude 8.9 newtons.

The magnitude of vector u is written $|u|$.

If $\boldsymbol{u} = \begin{pmatrix} -9 \\ 12 \end{pmatrix}$, $|\boldsymbol{u}|^2 = (-9)^2 + (12)^2 = 225$. So $|\boldsymbol{u}| = 15$.

Throughout this chapter, give lengths and angles correct to 1 decimal place where necessary.

EXERCISE 2

1 Draw each vector on squared paper, then calculate its magnitude. Write your answer like this: $|\underset{\sim}{y}| = 6$.

a $\boldsymbol{u} = \begin{pmatrix} 4 \\ 3 \end{pmatrix}$ **b** $v = \begin{pmatrix} 6 \\ 8 \end{pmatrix}$ **c** $\boldsymbol{w} = \begin{pmatrix} 12 \\ -5 \end{pmatrix}$

2 **(i)** Write down the components of the forces represented by $\overrightarrow{AB}$ in the diagrams below.

(ii) Calculate the magnitude of each force.

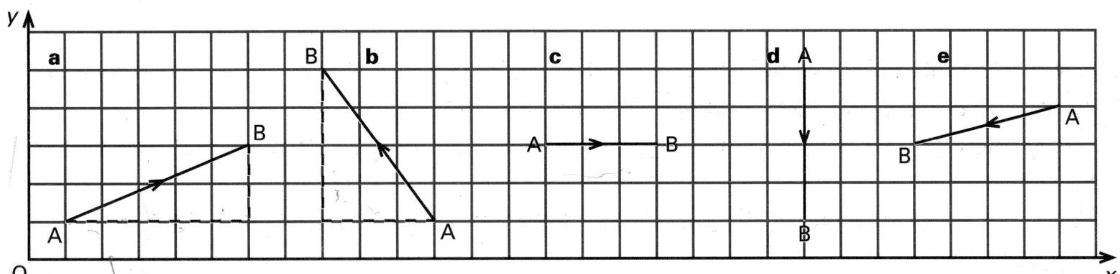

3 An orienteering course requires a distance and a direction, so is yet another example of a vector. Calculate the lengths of the courses, to the nearest km, given by these vectors.

a $\overrightarrow{PQ} = \begin{pmatrix} 5 \\ 5 \end{pmatrix}$ **b** $\overrightarrow{RS} = \begin{pmatrix} 3 \\ 7 \end{pmatrix}$ **c** $\overrightarrow{TU} = \begin{pmatrix} 6 \\ 2 \end{pmatrix}$

4 A velocity has a magnitude (speed) and a direction, so it is also a vector. Calculate the magnitude, to the nearest m/s where necessary, of the velocities given by these vectors.

a $v = \begin{pmatrix} 7 \\ 24 \end{pmatrix}$ **b** $v = \begin{pmatrix} 12 \\ -9 \end{pmatrix}$ **c** $v = \begin{pmatrix} 10 \\ 10 \end{pmatrix}$

5 In each of these pairs of vectors, which vector has:
(i) the greater magnitude **(ii)** the steeper slope?

a $\boldsymbol{u} = \begin{pmatrix} 5 \\ 8 \end{pmatrix}, v = \begin{pmatrix} 3 \\ 9 \end{pmatrix}$ **b** $\boldsymbol{u} = \begin{pmatrix} 5 \\ -4 \end{pmatrix}, v = \begin{pmatrix} 3 \\ -6 \end{pmatrix}$

6 $\boldsymbol{p} = \begin{pmatrix} 2 \\ x \end{pmatrix}$ has the same magnitude as $\boldsymbol{q} = \begin{pmatrix} 4 \\ -3 \end{pmatrix}$. Calculate x.

Vectors in 3 dimensions

Components

The edges of the cuboid are parallel to the axes. The displacement from A to B can be made by moving 4 units in the x-direction, 3 units in the y-direction, then 2 units in the z-direction.
The x-component of $\overrightarrow{AB}$ is the step AP, parallel to OX $= x_B - x_A = 5 - 1 = 4$.
The y-component of $\overrightarrow{AB} = y_B - y_A = 6 - 3 = 3$.
The z-component of $\overrightarrow{AB} = z_B - z_A = 4 - 2 = 2$.

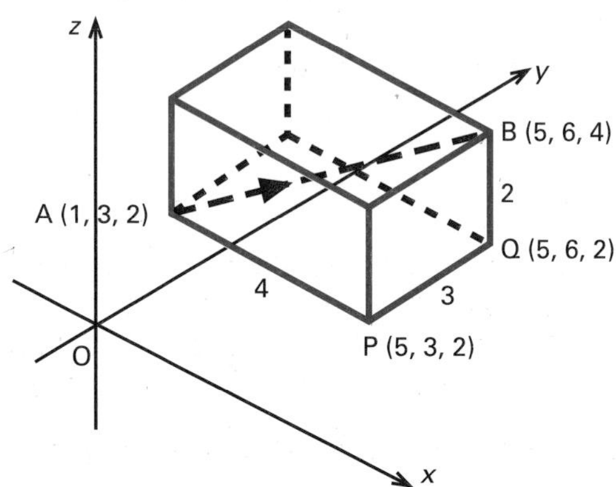

In component form, $\overrightarrow{AB} = \begin{pmatrix} 4 \\ 3 \\ 2 \end{pmatrix} = \begin{pmatrix} x\text{-component} \\ y\text{-component} \\ z\text{-component} \end{pmatrix}$

In general, $\overrightarrow{AB} = \begin{pmatrix} x_B - x_A \\ y_B - y_A \\ z_B - z_A \end{pmatrix}$, a column vector

Example If P is (6, 2, 0) and Q is (8, −3, 1), then $\overrightarrow{PQ} = \begin{pmatrix} 8-6 \\ -3-2 \\ 1-0 \end{pmatrix} = \begin{pmatrix} 2 \\ -5 \\ 1 \end{pmatrix}$.

Magnitude

$$\begin{aligned} AB^2 &= AQ^2 + BQ^2 \text{ (Pythagoras' Theorem)} \\ &= (AP^2 + PQ^2) + BQ^2 \\ &= (x_B - x_A)^2 + (y_B - y_A)^2 + (z_B - z_A)^2 \\ &= 4^2 + 3^2 + 2^2 \\ &= 29 \end{aligned}$$

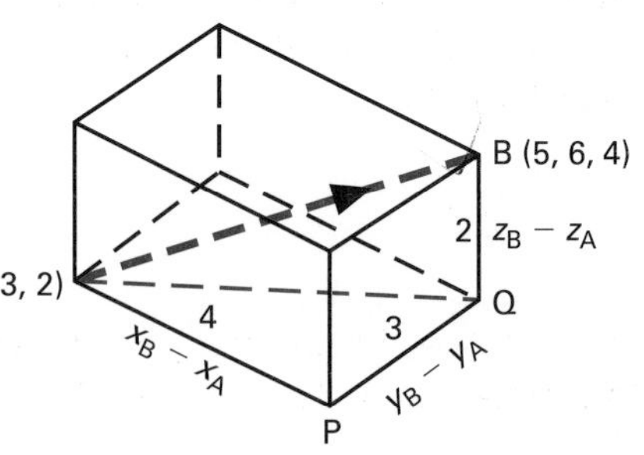

If $\boldsymbol{u} = \overrightarrow{AB}$, the magnitude of $\boldsymbol{u}$, $|\boldsymbol{u}| = AB = \sqrt{29} = 5.4$, correct to 1 decimal place.

If $\boldsymbol{u} = \overrightarrow{AB}$, then $|\boldsymbol{u}| = AB = \sqrt{[(x_B - x_A)^2 + (y_B - y_A)^2 + (z_B - z_A)^2]}$.

This is the distance formula for 3 dimensions.

EXERCISE 3

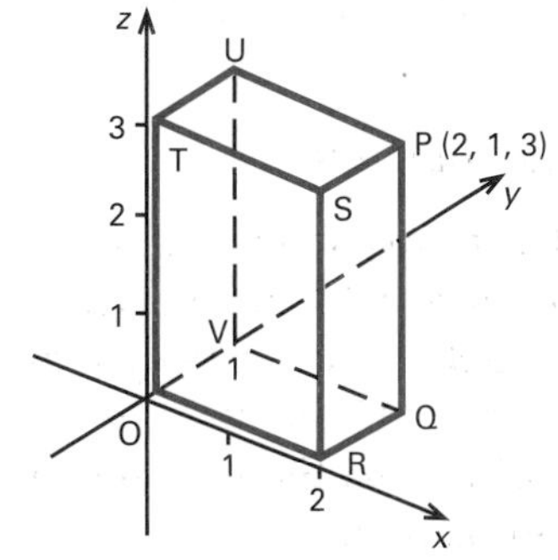

1 For the cuboid shown:

a write down the components of the space diagonal vector $\overrightarrow{OP}$

b calculate the length of OP.

2 Write down the components of $\overrightarrow{AB}$ as a column vector:

a A(0, 1, −2) B(2, 1, 3) **b** A(1, 1, 1) B(2, 4, −5)

c A(1, 2, 4) B(1, 2, 6) **d** A(0, 2, 0) B(−3, 1, −2)

e A(7, 5, −1) B(2, 7, −3) **f** A(−2, 1, 6) B(5, −2, 3).

3 Calculate the length of AB in **a–d** of question **2**.

4 A is (x_A, y_A, z_A) and B is (x_B, y_B, z_B). Write down in column form the components of:

a $\overrightarrow{AB}$ **b** $\overrightarrow{BA}$.

5 P is the point (6, 4, 2), Q(8, 6, 4) and R(2, 2, 2).

a Show that $\overrightarrow{OP} = \overrightarrow{RQ}$, where O is the origin.

b What type of quadrilateral is OPQR?

6 A is the point (2, 4, 6), B(7, 5, 0), C(6, 10, −6) and D(1, 9, 0).

a Show that:

(i) $\overrightarrow{AB} = \overrightarrow{DC}$ (ii) $|\overrightarrow{AB}| = |\overrightarrow{BC}|$.

b What type of quadrilateral is ABCD?

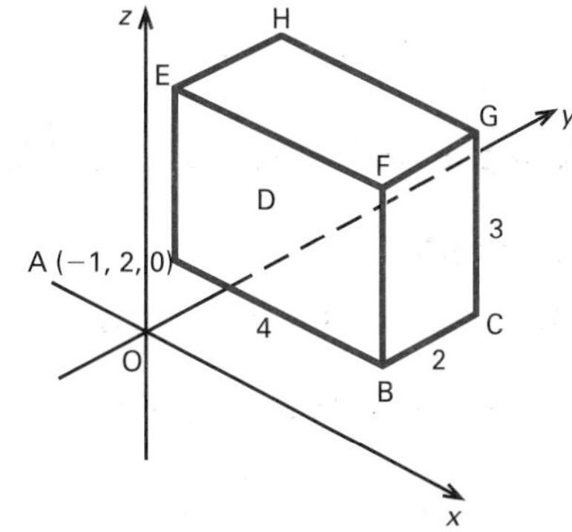

7 The edges of the cuboid are parallel to the axes, and A is the point (−1, 2, 0).

a Write down the coordinates of G.

b Express $\overrightarrow{AG}$ as a column vector.

c Calculate $|\overrightarrow{AG}|$.

8 Show that A(4, 11, 2), B(2, −3, 10) and C(0, 5, −4) lie on the surface of a sphere with centre S(2, 3, 4).

9 Show that △P(3, 4, −1) Q(9, 8, 11) R(−9, −2, 3) is isosceles.

10 △LMN has vertices L(4, 7, −3), M(5, 7, −5) and N(2, 7, −4). Prove that the triangle is: **a** isosceles **b** right-angled.

11 If $\overrightarrow{AB} = \begin{pmatrix} 7 \\ 5 \\ 3 \end{pmatrix}$, and A is (3, 2, −1), find the coordinates of B.

12 A is (1, 3, −1), B(3, 5, 0), D(−1, 4, 1). If ABCD is a parallelogram, find the coordinates of C.

13 A vector has only one set of components.

If $\begin{pmatrix} a \\ b \\ c \end{pmatrix} = \begin{pmatrix} d \\ e \\ f \end{pmatrix}$, then $a = d$, $b = e$ and $c = f$. Find the values of x, y and z, given:

a $\begin{pmatrix} 2x \\ y+3 \\ z-1 \end{pmatrix} = \begin{pmatrix} 6 \\ 8 \\ 2 \end{pmatrix}$ **b** $\begin{pmatrix} x+2 \\ 5 \\ -2z \end{pmatrix} = \begin{pmatrix} 2y+1 \\ x+y \\ -2 \end{pmatrix}$

14 ABCD is a tetrahedron.

a Express $\overrightarrow{AD}$ in component form.

b Calculate the length of AD.

c If $\overrightarrow{AC} = \begin{pmatrix} 3 \\ 1 \\ -1 \end{pmatrix}$ find C.

d $\overrightarrow{DB} = \begin{pmatrix} -1 \\ -1 \\ 3 \end{pmatrix}$. Find B.

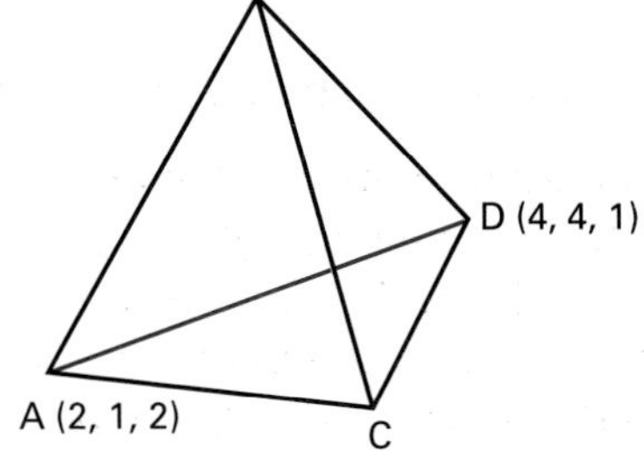

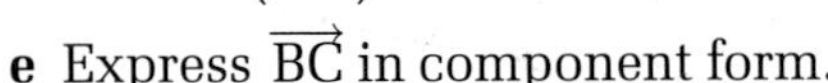

e Express $\overrightarrow{BC}$ in component form.

f Calculate the length of BC.

15 When lightning strikes the old tower at A, it is directed safely to ground by the lightning conductor. A is (1, 1, 6), B(0, 0, 3), E(2, 2, 0).

a Write down the coordinates of C and D.

b Express $\overrightarrow{AB}$ in component form, and calculate $|\overrightarrow{AB}|$.

c Find the total length of the conductor.

d Find the components and magnitude of $\overrightarrow{AE}$.

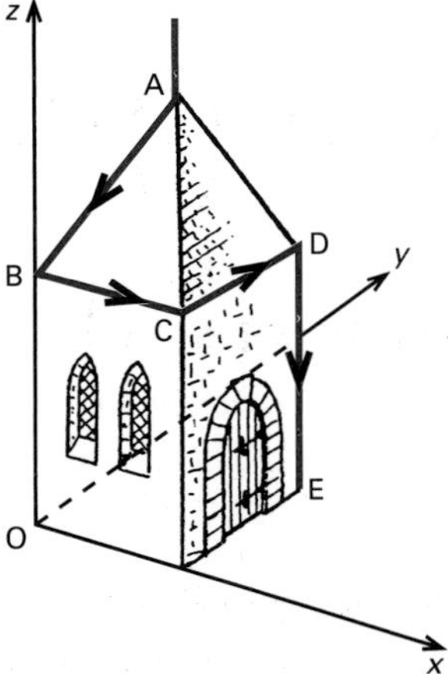

Addition and subtraction of vectors, and multiplication by a number

Personal stereo £25

Batteries £2.50

Total £27.50

Temperature at 10 pm = −1°C

Temperature at 2 am = −5°C

Fall in temperature = 4°C

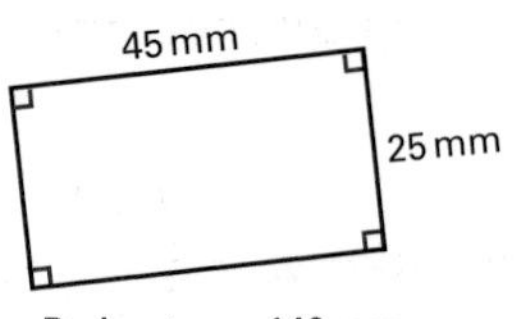

Perimeter = 140 mm

It's easy to add and subtract scalars. But what about vectors, which have *direction* as well as *size*, or *magnitude*?

For example, an aircraft is flying at 400 km/h in an easterly direction, in a wind blowing at 50 km/h from the north. How can you find the actual track of the aircraft over the ground?

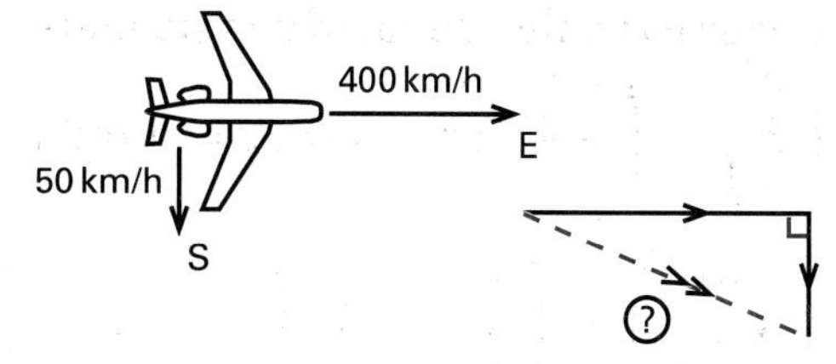

Or, two tugs are towing a liner with equal force, acting at an angle of 30°. How can these be combined?

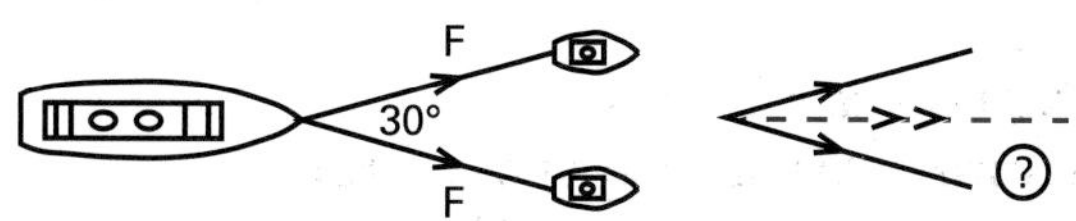

A commonsense solution

Concorde is pinpointed at A(1, 1, 1), then at B(3, 3, 3), then at C(4, 6, 7).
Instead of flying from A to B, then from B to C, it could have flown directly from A to C.
In this sense, $\overrightarrow{AB} + \overrightarrow{BC} = \overrightarrow{AC}$.

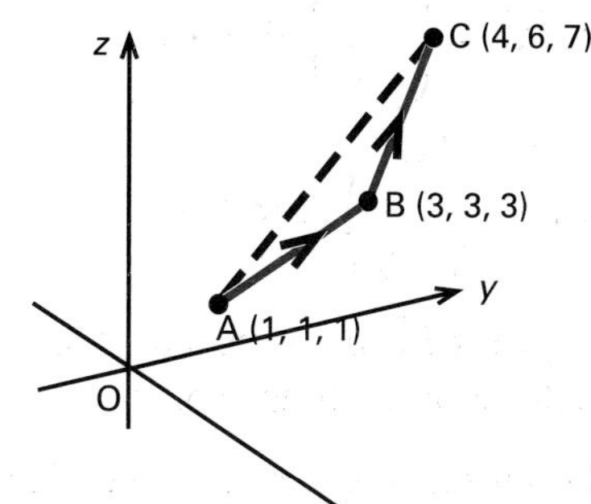

Vectors are, in fact, added like this, 'nose-to-tail'.

$$\overrightarrow{AB} + \overrightarrow{BC} = \begin{pmatrix} 2 \\ 2 \\ 2 \end{pmatrix} + \begin{pmatrix} 1 \\ 3 \\ 4 \end{pmatrix} = \begin{pmatrix} 3 \\ 5 \\ 6 \end{pmatrix},$$

and $\overrightarrow{AC} = \begin{pmatrix} 4-1 \\ 6-1 \\ 7-1 \end{pmatrix} = \begin{pmatrix} 3 \\ 5 \\ 6 \end{pmatrix}$.

So $\overrightarrow{AB} + \overrightarrow{BC} = \overrightarrow{AC}$.

Adding two vectors

1 Triangle rule for adding vectors:

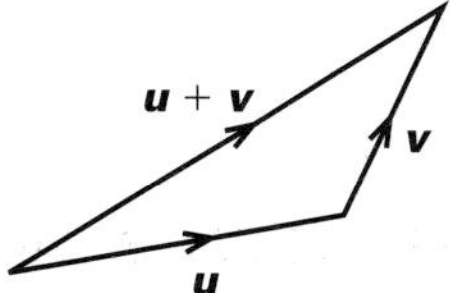

2 Using components: $\begin{pmatrix} a \\ b \\ c \end{pmatrix} + \begin{pmatrix} p \\ q \\ r \end{pmatrix} = \begin{pmatrix} a+p \\ b+q \\ c+r \end{pmatrix}$

Example $\boldsymbol{u} = \begin{pmatrix} 1 \\ 1 \\ 1 \end{pmatrix}$ and $\boldsymbol{v} = \begin{pmatrix} 2 \\ -3 \\ 0 \end{pmatrix}$. Calculate: **(i)** $\boldsymbol{u}+\boldsymbol{v}$ **(ii)** $|\boldsymbol{u}+\boldsymbol{v}|$

(i) $\boldsymbol{u}+\boldsymbol{v} = \begin{pmatrix} 1 \\ 1 \\ 1 \end{pmatrix} + \begin{pmatrix} 2 \\ -3 \\ 0 \end{pmatrix} = \begin{pmatrix} 1+2 \\ 1-3 \\ 1+0 \end{pmatrix} = \begin{pmatrix} 3 \\ -2 \\ 1 \end{pmatrix}$

(ii) $|\boldsymbol{u}+\boldsymbol{v}|^2 = 3^2 + (-2)^2 + 1^2 = 14$, so $|\boldsymbol{u}+\boldsymbol{v}| = 3.7$, correct to 1 decimal place

EXERCISE 4

1 Calculate:
(i) $\boldsymbol{u}+\boldsymbol{v}$ (ii) $|\boldsymbol{u}+\boldsymbol{v}|$ for:

a $\boldsymbol{u}=\begin{pmatrix}2\\1\\-1\end{pmatrix}$, $\boldsymbol{v}=\begin{pmatrix}-2\\1\\3\end{pmatrix}$ **b** $\boldsymbol{u}=\begin{pmatrix}3\\4\\5\end{pmatrix}$, $\boldsymbol{v}=\begin{pmatrix}0\\-4\\5\end{pmatrix}$.

2 On squared paper, construct vector triangles to add the vectors shown in the diagram.
a $\boldsymbol{p}+\boldsymbol{q}$ **b** $\boldsymbol{p}+\boldsymbol{r}$ **c** $\boldsymbol{p}+\boldsymbol{s}$
d $\boldsymbol{q}+\boldsymbol{r}$ **e** $\boldsymbol{q}+\boldsymbol{s}$ **f** $\boldsymbol{r}+\boldsymbol{s}$

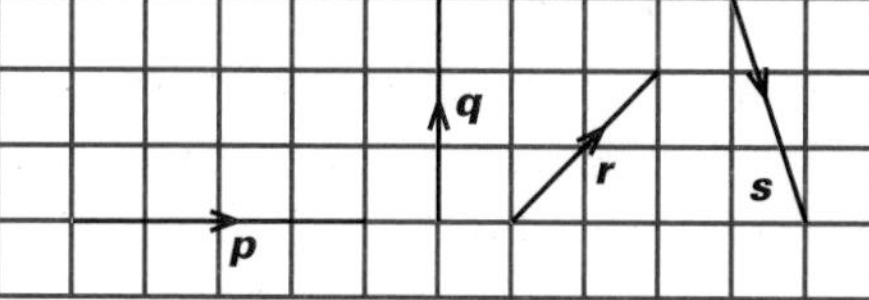

The negative of a vector

If $\boldsymbol{u}=\begin{pmatrix}5\\0\\-1\end{pmatrix}$ and $\boldsymbol{v}=\begin{pmatrix}-5\\0\\1\end{pmatrix}$, then $\boldsymbol{u}+\boldsymbol{v}=\begin{pmatrix}0\\0\\0\end{pmatrix}$, the zero vector $\boldsymbol{0}$.

$\boldsymbol{v}$ is called the negative of $\boldsymbol{u}$, and is written $\boldsymbol{v}=-\boldsymbol{u}$. So $\boldsymbol{u}+(-\boldsymbol{u})=\boldsymbol{0}$.

3 Write down the negative of each of these vectors:

a $\begin{pmatrix}3\\2\\1\end{pmatrix}$ **b** $\begin{pmatrix}-1\\0\\4\end{pmatrix}$ **c** $\begin{pmatrix}-2\\-3\\-4\end{pmatrix}$ **d** $\begin{pmatrix}a\\b\\c\end{pmatrix}$.

4 $\overrightarrow{AB}+\overrightarrow{BA}=\overrightarrow{AA}=\boldsymbol{0}$. $\overrightarrow{BA}$ is the negative of $\overrightarrow{AB}$, i.e. $\overrightarrow{BA}=-\overrightarrow{AB}$. What can you say about the length and direction of $\overrightarrow{BA}$ compared to $\overrightarrow{AB}$?

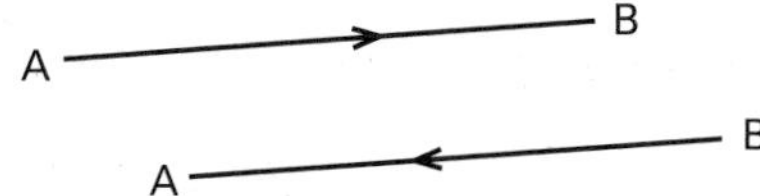

Subtracting two vectors

You'll remember that $5-3=5+(-3)$, that is subtracting 3 is the same as adding negative 3. The same idea is used for vectors:

$\boldsymbol{u}-\boldsymbol{v}=\boldsymbol{u}+(-\boldsymbol{v})$.

For example, if $\boldsymbol{u}=\begin{pmatrix}1\\2\\-5\end{pmatrix}$ and $\boldsymbol{v}=\begin{pmatrix}1\\-2\\3\end{pmatrix}$,

then $\boldsymbol{u}-\boldsymbol{v}=\begin{pmatrix}1\\2\\-5\end{pmatrix}+\begin{pmatrix}-1\\2\\-3\end{pmatrix}=\begin{pmatrix}0\\4\\-8\end{pmatrix}$.

5 $\boldsymbol{u}=\begin{pmatrix}5\\3\\1\end{pmatrix}$, $\boldsymbol{v}=\begin{pmatrix}-1\\-2\\0\end{pmatrix}$ and $\boldsymbol{w}=\begin{pmatrix}2\\0\\-1\end{pmatrix}$. Calculate:

a $\boldsymbol{u}-\boldsymbol{v}$ **b** $\boldsymbol{v}-\boldsymbol{w}$ **c** $\boldsymbol{u}-\boldsymbol{w}$.

6 The diagram shows the construction of $\boldsymbol{u} + \boldsymbol{v}$, and also $\boldsymbol{u} - \boldsymbol{v}$ based on $\boldsymbol{u} + (-\boldsymbol{v})$. Use the vectors in question **2** to construct vector triangles on squared paper for:

a $\boldsymbol{p} - \boldsymbol{q}$ **b** $\boldsymbol{p} - \boldsymbol{r}$ **c** $\boldsymbol{p} - \boldsymbol{s}$
d $\boldsymbol{q} - \boldsymbol{r}$ **e** $\boldsymbol{q} - \boldsymbol{s}$ **f** $\boldsymbol{r} - \boldsymbol{s}$

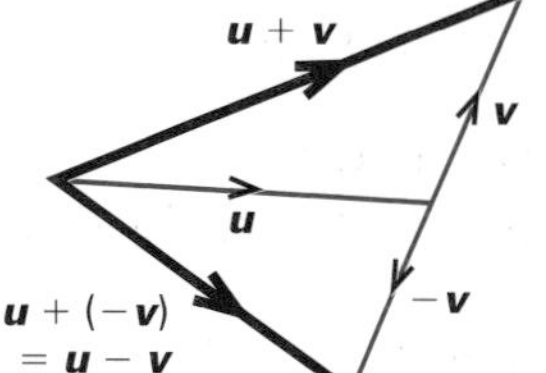

Multiplying by a number

Given vector $\boldsymbol{v}$, and number k, then $k\boldsymbol{v}$ has the same direction as $\boldsymbol{v}$ if $k > 0$, and the opposite direction if $k < 0$.

In component form, $k\begin{pmatrix} a \\ b \\ c \end{pmatrix} = \begin{pmatrix} ka \\ kb \\ kc \end{pmatrix}$.

$\boldsymbol{u} = k\boldsymbol{v} \Leftrightarrow \boldsymbol{u}$ and $\boldsymbol{v}$ are parallel, $k \neq 0$.

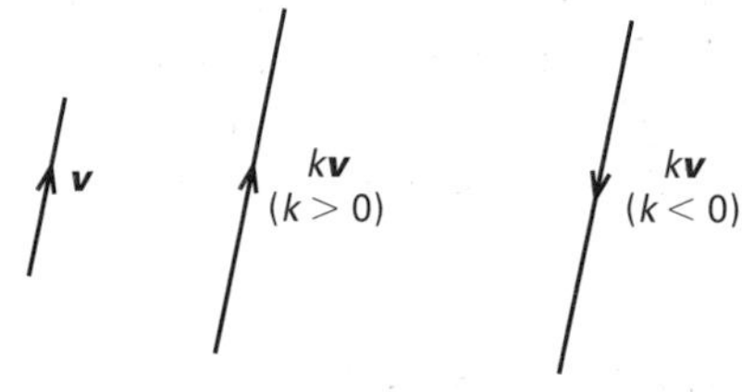

7 Calculate: **(i)** $2\boldsymbol{u}$ **(ii)** $3\boldsymbol{v}$ **(iii)** $2\boldsymbol{u} + 3\boldsymbol{v}$, for:

a $\boldsymbol{u} = \begin{pmatrix} 1 \\ -1 \\ 3 \end{pmatrix}, \boldsymbol{v} = \begin{pmatrix} 2 \\ 4 \\ -2 \end{pmatrix}$ **b** $\boldsymbol{u} = \begin{pmatrix} 0 \\ 1 \\ 2 \end{pmatrix}, \boldsymbol{v} = \begin{pmatrix} 6 \\ -2 \\ 0 \end{pmatrix}$.

8 Given $\boldsymbol{p} = \begin{pmatrix} 0 \\ 1 \\ 0 \end{pmatrix}$ and $\boldsymbol{q} = \begin{pmatrix} -2 \\ -1 \\ 4 \end{pmatrix}$:

a express $\boldsymbol{p} + 2\boldsymbol{q}$ in component form **b** find the value of $|\boldsymbol{p} + 2\boldsymbol{q}|$.

9 Given this vector, $\xrightarrow{\boldsymbol{u}}$, draw vectors $-\boldsymbol{u}$, $2\boldsymbol{u}$ and $-3\boldsymbol{u}$. Remember to mark arrows on them.

10 $\boldsymbol{a} = \begin{pmatrix} 2 \\ 3 \\ -1 \end{pmatrix}, \boldsymbol{b} = \begin{pmatrix} 8 \\ 12 \\ -4 \end{pmatrix}$ and $\boldsymbol{c} = \begin{pmatrix} -2 \\ -3 \\ 1 \end{pmatrix}$.

a If $\boldsymbol{b} = m\boldsymbol{a}$, $\boldsymbol{c} = n\boldsymbol{a}$ and $\boldsymbol{c} = p\boldsymbol{b}$, find the numbers m, n and p.
b What can you say about the directions and magnitudes of the vectors in the pairs: **(i)** $\boldsymbol{a}$ and $\boldsymbol{b}$ **(ii)** $\boldsymbol{a}$ and $\boldsymbol{c}$ **(iii)** $\boldsymbol{b}$ and $\boldsymbol{c}$?

11 **a** Express each of these pairs of vectors in the form $\boldsymbol{u} = k\boldsymbol{v}$, where k is a number.

(i) $\boldsymbol{u} = \begin{pmatrix} 3 \\ 9 \\ 6 \end{pmatrix}, \boldsymbol{v} = \begin{pmatrix} 1 \\ 3 \\ 2 \end{pmatrix}$ **(ii)** $\boldsymbol{u} = \begin{pmatrix} -8 \\ -2 \\ 4 \end{pmatrix}, \boldsymbol{v} = \begin{pmatrix} 4 \\ 1 \\ -2 \end{pmatrix}$

b Describe the relations between the directions and magnitudes of $\boldsymbol{u}$ and $\boldsymbol{v}$ in each part.

12 $\overrightarrow{AB} = \begin{pmatrix} 4 \\ 6 \\ 8 \end{pmatrix}$ and $\overrightarrow{DC} = \begin{pmatrix} 6 \\ 9 \\ 12 \end{pmatrix}$. Which type of quadrilateral is ABCD, assuming that the points A, B, C, D are not collinear?

13 A circus tent support pole is held in position by three guy ropes, exerting forces

$\boldsymbol{F}_1 = \begin{pmatrix} -3 \\ -2 \\ -5 \end{pmatrix}$, $\boldsymbol{F}_2 = \begin{pmatrix} 4 \\ -1 \\ -5 \end{pmatrix}$ and $\boldsymbol{F}_3 = \begin{pmatrix} 7 \\ 3 \\ -5 \end{pmatrix}$.

Calculate:

a the components of the total force at O

b the magnitude of this total force.

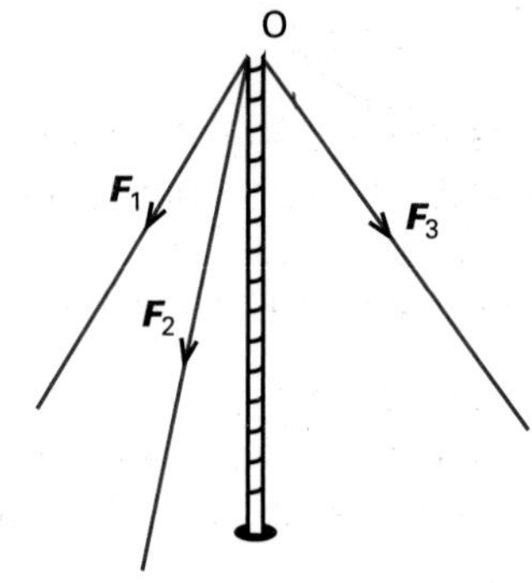

Position vectors

$\overrightarrow{OP}$ is the *position vector* of the point P(x, y, z).

In component form, $\overrightarrow{OP} = \begin{pmatrix} x \\ y \\ z \end{pmatrix}$. So $\boldsymbol{p} = \overrightarrow{OP} = \begin{pmatrix} x \\ y \\ z \end{pmatrix}$.

The coordinates (x, y, z) give the position of the point P,

while the components $\begin{pmatrix} x \\ y \\ z \end{pmatrix}$ give instructions for a 'journey' from O to P, with displacements x, y and z parallel to the x, y and z-axes.

The coordinates of P are the components of its position vector.

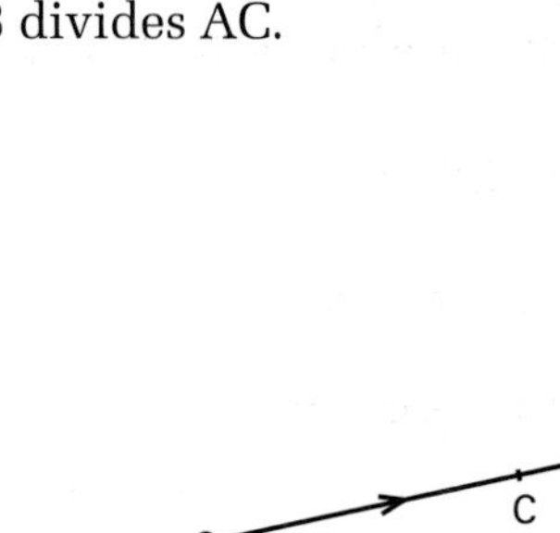

A useful result

In the diagram, $\overrightarrow{OB} = \overrightarrow{OA} + \overrightarrow{AB}$

so $\overrightarrow{AB} = \overrightarrow{OB} - \overrightarrow{OA}$,

that is $\overrightarrow{AB} = \boldsymbol{b} - \boldsymbol{a}$.

where $\boldsymbol{a}$, $\boldsymbol{b}$ are the position vectors of A, B.

Similarly, $\overrightarrow{PQ} = \boldsymbol{q} - \boldsymbol{p}$, $\overrightarrow{ST} = \boldsymbol{t} - \boldsymbol{s}$, etc.

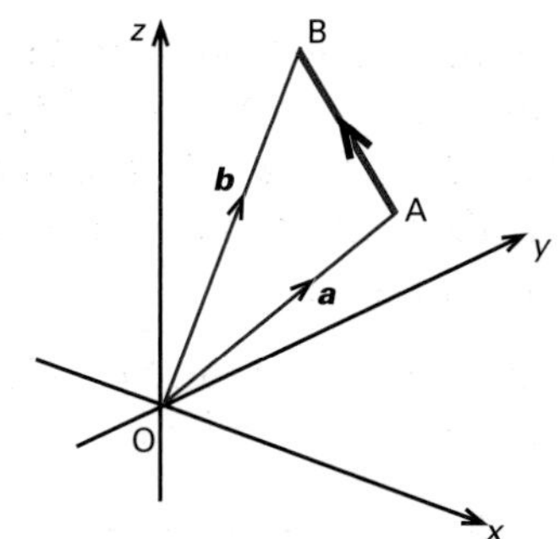

Example Prove that the points A(2, −3, 4), B(8, 3, 1) and C(12, 7, −1) are collinear, and find the ratio $\frac{AB}{BC}$, i.e. the ratio in which B divides AC.

$$\overrightarrow{AB} = \boldsymbol{b} - \boldsymbol{a} = \begin{pmatrix} 8 \\ 3 \\ 1 \end{pmatrix} - \begin{pmatrix} 2 \\ -3 \\ 4 \end{pmatrix} = \begin{pmatrix} 6 \\ 6 \\ -3 \end{pmatrix} = 3\begin{pmatrix} 2 \\ 2 \\ -1 \end{pmatrix}$$

$$\overrightarrow{BC} = \boldsymbol{c} - \boldsymbol{b} = \begin{pmatrix} 12 \\ 7 \\ -1 \end{pmatrix} - \begin{pmatrix} 8 \\ 3 \\ 1 \end{pmatrix} = \begin{pmatrix} 4 \\ 4 \\ -2 \end{pmatrix} = 2\begin{pmatrix} 2 \\ 2 \\ -1 \end{pmatrix}$$

$2\overrightarrow{AB} = 3\overrightarrow{BC}$, or $\overrightarrow{AB} = \frac{3}{2}\overrightarrow{BC}$, so $\overrightarrow{AB}$ is parallel to $\overrightarrow{BC}$.

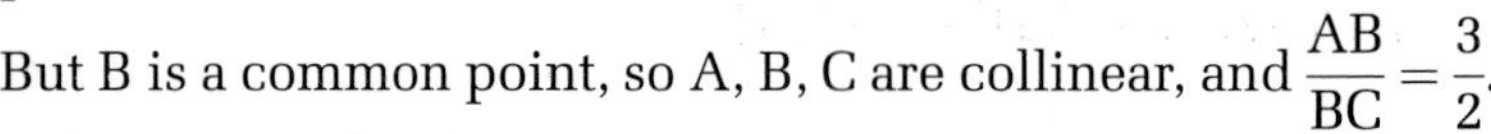

But B is a common point, so A, B, C are collinear, and $\frac{AB}{BC} = \frac{3}{2}$.

EXERCISE 5

1 A is the point (1, 4, 5), B(2, 7, 8), C(0, 12, 15) and D(3, 21, 24).
a Calculate the components of:
(i) $\overrightarrow{AB}$ **(ii)** $\overrightarrow{CD}$.
b Prove that $\overrightarrow{CD} = 3\overrightarrow{AB}$. What does this tell you about $\overrightarrow{CD}$ and $\overrightarrow{AB}$?

2 P is (0, 1, 1), Q(1, 1, 0), R(−5, −4, −5) and S(−3, −4, −7).
a Show that $\overrightarrow{RS} = k\overrightarrow{PQ}$ for some value of k.
b How are $\overrightarrow{RS}$ and $\overrightarrow{PQ}$ related?

3 A is (0, 1, 2), B(1, 3, −1) and C(3, 7, −7).
a Find $\overrightarrow{AB}$ and $\overrightarrow{BC}$ as column vectors.
b Show that: (i) A, B, C are collinear **(ii)** $\dfrac{AB}{BC} = \dfrac{1}{2}$.

4 **a** Show that O (0, 0, 0), A(1, 2, 3) and B(2, 4, 6) are collinear.
b Calculate: (i) $\dfrac{OA}{AB}$ **(ii)** $\dfrac{OA}{OB}$.

5 O is the origin, D is (−2, −1, 1) and E(6, 3, −3).
a Show that $\overrightarrow{OE} = -3\overrightarrow{OD}$.
b What does this tell you about:
(i) the directions of $\overrightarrow{OD}$ and $\overrightarrow{OE}$ **(ii)** $\dfrac{OD}{OE}$?

6 The transmitter T broadcasts to the receiver R. At three different times a ship S has locations S_1 (2, −2, 4), S_2 (2, −3, 4) and S_3 (2, −4, 4). Prove that one of these locations is in the line of transmissions.

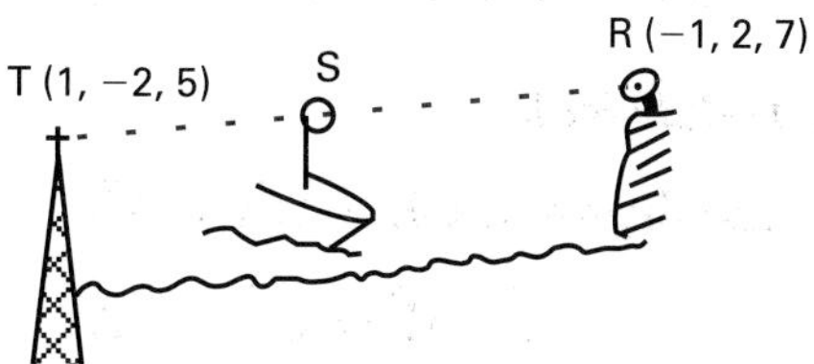

7 L is the point (2, 4, 6), M is (6, 6, 2) and N is (14, 10, −6). Show that L, M and N are collinear, and calculate the ratio in which M divides LN.

> *Position vector of the midpoint of AB*
>
> M is the midpoint of AB, and $\boldsymbol{a}$, $\boldsymbol{m}$ and $\boldsymbol{b}$ are the position vectors of A, M and B.
>
> $\overrightarrow{AM} = \overrightarrow{MB}$, so
>
> $\boldsymbol{m} - \boldsymbol{a} = \boldsymbol{b} - \boldsymbol{m}$
>
> $\boldsymbol{m} = \frac{1}{2}(\boldsymbol{a} + \boldsymbol{b})$

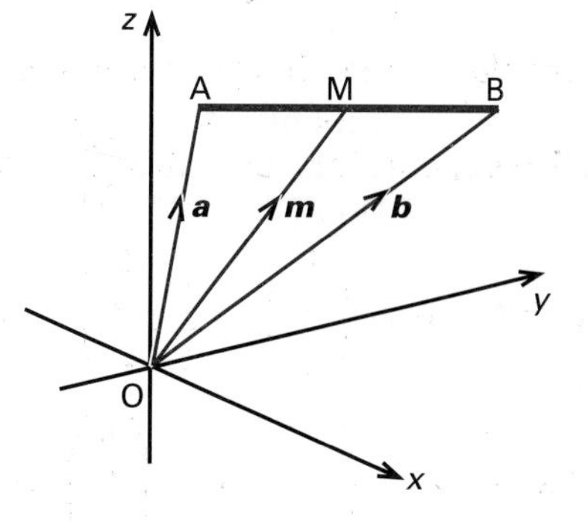

8 Use the above result to write down the coordinates of the midpoints of the lines joining:
a A(4, 2, 3), B(6, 8, 1) **b** C(−2, 3, −1), D(−8, −7, 1)

9 a In this diagram, find the coordinates of:
 (i) P, the midpoint of AB
 (ii) Q, the midpoint of BC.
b Show that $\overrightarrow{PQ} = \frac{1}{2}\overrightarrow{AC}$.
c Deduce the geometrical relationship between PQ and AC.

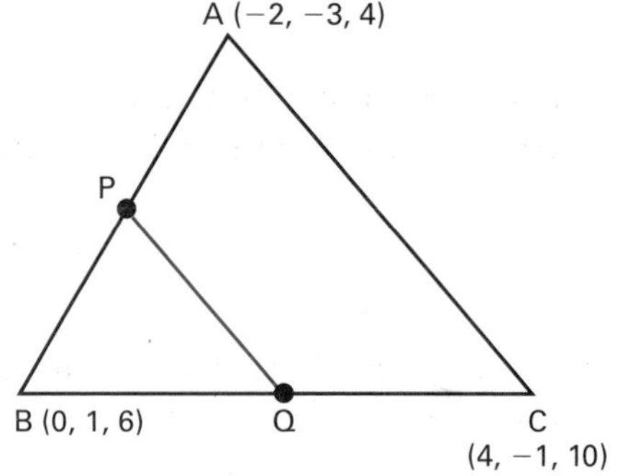

10 O is (0, 0, 0), P(2, 2, 2), Q(8, 6, 4) and R(6, 4, 2).
a Show that OPQR is a parallelogram.
b A, B, C, D are the midpoints of OP, PQ, QR and OR respectively. Show that ABCD is also a parallelogram.

11 a Show that D, E, F are collinear, and calculate k if $\overrightarrow{DE} = k\overrightarrow{EF}$, given:
 (i) D(1, 3, −4), E(3, 2, −3), F(9, −1, 0) **(ii)** D(1, −2, 5), E(2, −4, 4), F(−1, 2, 7).
b Illustrate in sketches.

12 There are three stations for the chairlift to the ski slopes:
A (base) has grid reference 575637 and is 0.09 unit above sea-level (A is point (57.5, 63.7, 0.09)).
B (nursery slope) has reference 581645 and is 0.14 above sea-level.
C (main slope) has reference 593661 and is 0.24 above sea-level.
a Obtain the components of:
 (i) $\overrightarrow{AB}$ **(ii)** $\overrightarrow{BC}$.
b Prove that A, B, C are collinear.
c Calculate the magnitude of:
 (i) $\overrightarrow{AB}$ **(ii)** $\overrightarrow{BC}$.

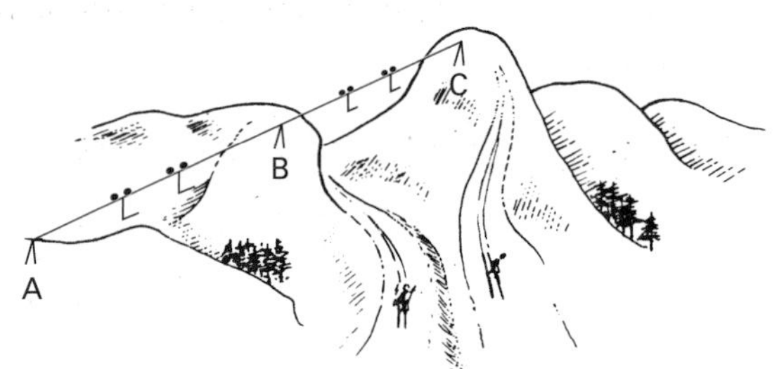

Points dividing lines in given ratios

Example P divides AB in the ratio 3:2.
Find the coordinates of P.

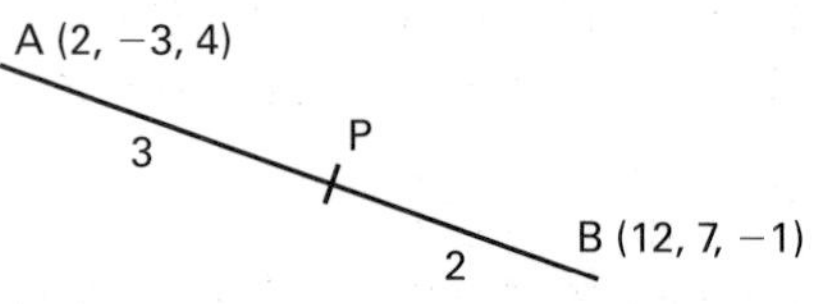

The vector form of $\dfrac{AP}{PB} = \dfrac{3}{2}$ is $\overrightarrow{AP} = \frac{3}{2}\overrightarrow{PB}$,

i.e. $2\overrightarrow{AP} = 3\overrightarrow{PB}$.

So $2(\boldsymbol{p} - \boldsymbol{a}) = 3(\boldsymbol{b} - \boldsymbol{p})$

$$2\boldsymbol{p} - 2\boldsymbol{a} = 3\boldsymbol{b} - 3\boldsymbol{p}$$

$$5\boldsymbol{p} = 2\boldsymbol{a} + 3\boldsymbol{b}$$

$$\boldsymbol{p} = \frac{1}{5}(2\boldsymbol{a} + 3\boldsymbol{b}) = \frac{1}{5}\left[\begin{pmatrix}4\\-6\\8\end{pmatrix} + \begin{pmatrix}36\\21\\-3\end{pmatrix}\right] = \begin{pmatrix}8\\3\\1\end{pmatrix}.$$

P is the point (8, 3, 1).

Hint
A useful scheme

AP:PB
3:2

$$\boldsymbol{p} = \frac{3\boldsymbol{b} + 2\boldsymbol{a}}{3 + 2} = \tfrac{1}{5}(3\boldsymbol{b} + 2\boldsymbol{a}) \text{ etc.}$$

EXERCISE 6

1 P divides AB in the ratio 1:2.
Use the equation AP:PB = 1:2 to find the coordinates of P.

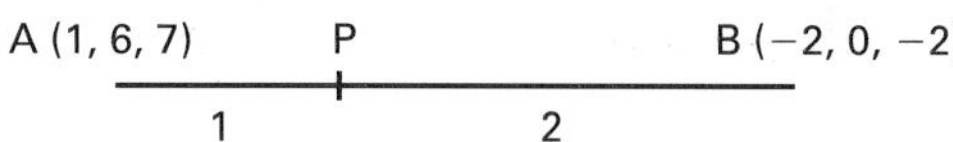

2 Draw the line AB in question **1** and mark point Q which divides AB in the ratio 2:1. Find the coordinates of Q.

3 Find the coordinates of P which divides:
a A(1, 0, 2) B(5, 4, 10) in the ratio 3:1
b C(2, 2, 3) D(2, −2, −1) in the ratio 1:3
c E(2, −3, 4) F(12, 7, −1) in the ratio 2:3.

4 △PQR has vertices P(3, −2, 6), Q(−2, 3, −4) and R(3, 3, 1). S divides PQ in the ratio 4:1, and T divides PR in the ratio 4:1.
a Find the coordinates of S and T.
b Show that ST∥QR, and calculate $\frac{\text{ST}}{\text{QR}}$.

5 A is (−2, −2, −2), B(1, −2, 1) and C(1, 0, −1).
a Show that the point D dividing AB in the ratio 2:1 is (0, −2, 0).
b Use the distance formula and the converse of Pythagoras' Theorem to prove that ∠BDC = 90°.

6 P divides AB externally, in the ratio 3:1 so that $\frac{\text{AP}}{\text{PB}} = \frac{3}{-1}$.
Use $\overrightarrow{\text{AP}} = -3\,\overrightarrow{\text{PB}}$, or $\overrightarrow{\text{AP}} = 3\,\overrightarrow{\text{BP}}$, to show that P is the point (4, 2, −3).

A (−2, −1, 3)   B (2, 1, −1)   P

7 Q divides MN externally in the ratio 4:3, so that $\frac{\text{MQ}}{\text{QN}} = \frac{4}{-3}$. If M is (−3, −2, −1) and N is (0, −5, 2), find the coordinates of Q.

8 △ABC has vertices A(3, 0, 6), B(0, 3, −3) and C(1, 0, −4). P divides AB in the ratio 1:2, Q is the midpoint of AC, and R divides BC externally in the ratio 2:1 $\left(\text{so that } \frac{\text{BR}}{\text{RC}} = \frac{2}{-1}.\right)$
a Find the coordinates of P, Q and R.
b Show that P, Q, R are collinear, and find the value of PQ:QR.

9 A is (1, 4, 6) and B(1, 0, 2). S divides AB internally in the ratio 3:1, and T divides AB externally in the ratio 3:1.
a Find the coordinates of S and T.
b Show that AB:ST = 4:3.

10 Prove the formula $\boldsymbol{p} = \frac{m\boldsymbol{b} + n\boldsymbol{a}}{m + n}$ for the position vector of the point P which divides AB in the ratio m:n.

Unit vectors i, j, k

A unit vector has magnitude 1. If $\boldsymbol{u} = \overrightarrow{AB} = \begin{pmatrix} a \\ b \\ c \end{pmatrix}$ is a unit vector, then $a^2 + b^2 + c^2 = 1$.

The unit vectors in the directions OX, OY, OZ are denoted by:

$\boldsymbol{i} = \begin{pmatrix} 1 \\ 0 \\ 0 \end{pmatrix}$, $\boldsymbol{j} = \begin{pmatrix} 0 \\ 1 \\ 0 \end{pmatrix}$, $\boldsymbol{k} = \begin{pmatrix} 0 \\ 0 \\ 1 \end{pmatrix}$.

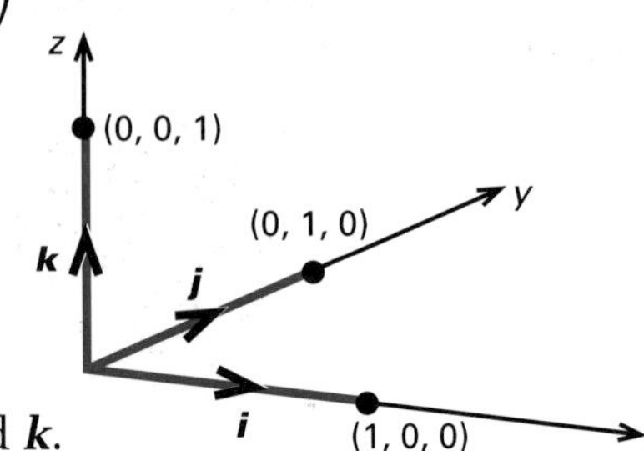

Every vector can be expressed in terms of $\boldsymbol{i}$, $\boldsymbol{j}$ and $\boldsymbol{k}$. For example, the position vector

of the point P(a, b, c) is $\begin{pmatrix} a \\ b \\ c \end{pmatrix} = a\begin{pmatrix} 1 \\ 0 \\ 0 \end{pmatrix} + b\begin{pmatrix} 0 \\ 1 \\ 0 \end{pmatrix} + c\begin{pmatrix} 0 \\ 0 \\ 1 \end{pmatrix} = a\boldsymbol{i} + b\boldsymbol{j} + c\boldsymbol{k}$.

The unit vectors $\boldsymbol{i}$, $\boldsymbol{j}$, $\boldsymbol{k}$ form a basis for 3-dimensional space.

EXERCISE 7

1 Write down the position vectors of the points A, B and C below in the form:

(i) $\begin{pmatrix} a \\ b \\ c \end{pmatrix}$ **(ii)** $a\boldsymbol{i} + b\boldsymbol{j} + c\boldsymbol{k}$.

a A(1, 2, 8) **b** B(−1, −5, 2) **c** C(6, 0, −7)

2 Write these in component form:

a $\boldsymbol{i}$ **b** $2\boldsymbol{j}$ **c** $-\boldsymbol{k}$ **d** $\boldsymbol{i} + \boldsymbol{j}$

e $\boldsymbol{i} + \boldsymbol{j} + \boldsymbol{k}$ **f** $\boldsymbol{i} - \boldsymbol{j}$ **g** $2\boldsymbol{i} - 2\boldsymbol{k}$.

3 $\boldsymbol{a} = \begin{pmatrix} 1 \\ 1 \\ 2 \end{pmatrix}$, $\boldsymbol{b} = \begin{pmatrix} 1 \\ 4 \\ 3 \end{pmatrix}$, $\boldsymbol{c} = \begin{pmatrix} 0 \\ -1 \\ -2 \end{pmatrix}$.

a Write $\boldsymbol{a}$, $\boldsymbol{b}$ and $\boldsymbol{c}$ in terms of $\boldsymbol{i}$, $\boldsymbol{j}$ and $\boldsymbol{k}$.

b Express $\boldsymbol{a} + \boldsymbol{b} + \boldsymbol{c}$ in components, and in terms of $\boldsymbol{i}$, $\boldsymbol{j}$ and $\boldsymbol{k}$.

4 $\boldsymbol{u} = 2\boldsymbol{i} - \boldsymbol{j} + \boldsymbol{k}$ and $\boldsymbol{v} = 4\boldsymbol{i} + 2\boldsymbol{j} - \boldsymbol{k}$.

a Express $\boldsymbol{u} + \boldsymbol{v}$ and $\boldsymbol{u} - \boldsymbol{v}$ in component form.

b Calculate the exact values of $|\boldsymbol{u} + \boldsymbol{v}|$ and $|\boldsymbol{u} - \boldsymbol{v}|$.

5 $\boldsymbol{p} = 3\boldsymbol{i} + 4\boldsymbol{j} + 12\boldsymbol{k}$, and $\boldsymbol{q} = 2\boldsymbol{i} + 2\boldsymbol{j} + \boldsymbol{k}$. Calculate:

a $|\boldsymbol{p}|$ **b** $|\boldsymbol{q}|$ **c** $|\boldsymbol{p} + \boldsymbol{q}|$ **d** $|\boldsymbol{p} - \boldsymbol{q}|$.

6 Calculate the lengths of these vectors:

a $\boldsymbol{u} = 3\boldsymbol{i} - 2\boldsymbol{j} + 6\boldsymbol{k}$

b $\boldsymbol{v} = 5\boldsymbol{i} - 2\sqrt{2}\boldsymbol{j} - 4\sqrt{3}\boldsymbol{k}$.

7 $a\boldsymbol{i} + \frac{1}{2}\boldsymbol{j} - \frac{1}{2}\boldsymbol{k}$ is a unit vector. Calculate the two possible values of a.

8 $a\boldsymbol{i} + b\boldsymbol{j} + \frac{1}{2}\boldsymbol{k}$ is a unit vector. Find the relation between a and b.

9 $\boldsymbol{u} = \boldsymbol{i} - \boldsymbol{j} + 3\boldsymbol{k}$ and $\boldsymbol{v} = -2\boldsymbol{i} + 2\boldsymbol{j} - 6\boldsymbol{k}$. Prove that vectors $\boldsymbol{u}$ and $\boldsymbol{v}$ are parallel.

10 Three forces are acting on Bud Jones on his space walk: $\boldsymbol{e} = 2\boldsymbol{i} + \boldsymbol{j} + \boldsymbol{k}$, $\boldsymbol{m} = 3\boldsymbol{i} + \boldsymbol{j} + 2\boldsymbol{k}$ and $\boldsymbol{s} = \boldsymbol{i} + \boldsymbol{j} - \boldsymbol{k}$.

a Find the resultant force (the sum of $\boldsymbol{e}$, $\boldsymbol{m}$ and $\boldsymbol{s}$).

b Calculate its magnitude.

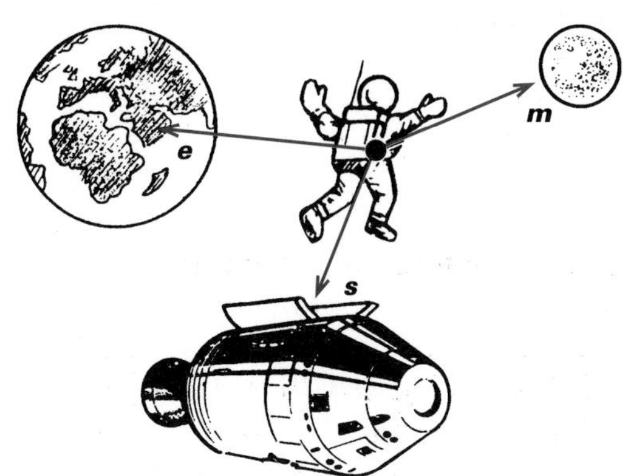

11 P and Q have position vectors $\boldsymbol{p} = -\boldsymbol{i} + 2\boldsymbol{k}$ and $\boldsymbol{q} = 2\boldsymbol{i} + 6\boldsymbol{j} - 4\boldsymbol{k}$. Find, in terms of $\boldsymbol{i}$, $\boldsymbol{j}$, $\boldsymbol{k}$, the position vector of the point R which divides PQ in the ratio 2:1.

The scalar product of two vectors

CLASS DISCUSSION

You have added and subtracted vectors, and multiplied vectors by real numbers. But so far there has been no need to multiply two vectors together.
Here is an example of how this can arise.
Tom is pulling the crate across the factory floor with force $\boldsymbol{F}$ (in magnitude and direction). He moves it through the displacement $\mathbf{x}$ (also in magnitude and direction).
Physicists will tell you that the work done is $|\boldsymbol{F}||\mathbf{x}|\cos\theta$. In a sense they are 'multiplying' two vectors together, even though the product is a real number. Hence the name *scalar product*.
$|\boldsymbol{F}||\mathbf{x}|\cos\theta$ is called the *scalar product* $\boldsymbol{F}.\mathbf{x}$ of the vectors $\boldsymbol{F}$ and $\mathbf{x}$.

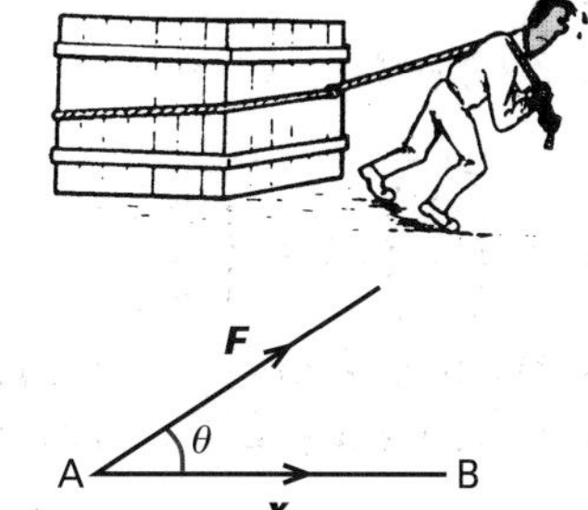

Definition The scalar product of two vectors $\boldsymbol{a}$ and $\boldsymbol{b}$, denoted by $\boldsymbol{a}.\boldsymbol{b}$ ('$\boldsymbol{a}$ dot $\boldsymbol{b}$'), is $\boldsymbol{a}.\boldsymbol{b} = |\boldsymbol{a}||\boldsymbol{b}|\cos\theta$, neither $\boldsymbol{a}$ nor $\boldsymbol{b}$ being zero.

Component form of a.b

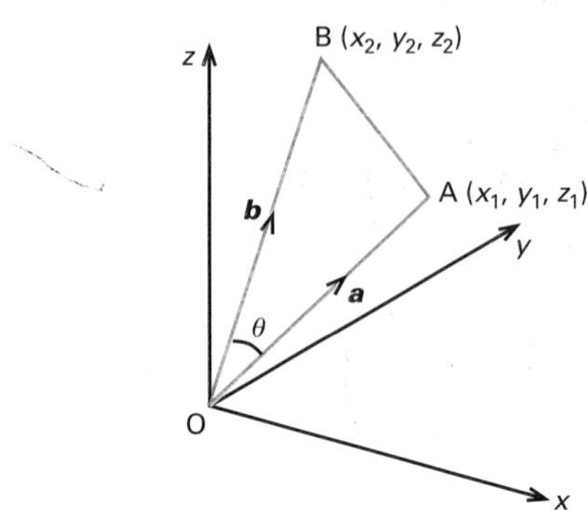

In $\triangle$OAB, $AB^2 = OA^2 + OB^2 - 2\,OA\,OB\cos\theta$ (Cosine Rule)

$$= (x_1^2 + y_1^2 + z_1^2) + (x_2^2 + y_2^2 + z_2^2) - 2|\boldsymbol{a}||\boldsymbol{b}|\cos\theta \ldots \quad (1)$$

But $AB^2 = (x_1 - x_2)^2 + (y_1 - y_2)^2 + (z_1 - z_2)^2$ (Distance Formula)

$$= (x_1^2 + y_1^2 + z_1^2) + (x_2^2 + y_2^2 + z_2^2) - 2(x_1x_2 + y_1y_2 + z_1z_2) \ldots \quad (2)$$

From (1) and (2), $|\boldsymbol{a}||\boldsymbol{b}|\cos\theta = x_1x_2 + y_1y_2 + z_1z_2$.
So $\boldsymbol{a}.\boldsymbol{b} = x_1x_2 + y_1y_2 + z_1z_2$.

Either of the definitions

$\boldsymbol{a}.\boldsymbol{b} = |\boldsymbol{a}||\boldsymbol{b}|\cos\theta$, or
$\boldsymbol{a}.\boldsymbol{b} = x_1x_2 + y_1y_2 + z_1z_2$

can be taken to define the scalar product of ***a*** and ***b***.

The sign of the number ***a.b*** ***(a ± 0, b ± 0)***

From its definition, ***a.b*** is a real number whose sign is determined by the size of θ as follows.

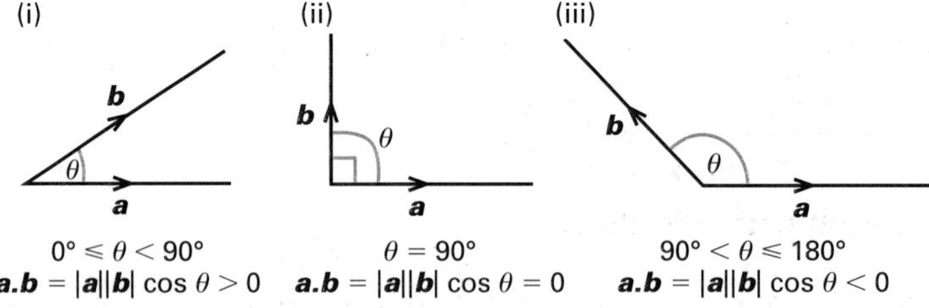

θ is the angle between vectors pointing *out* from the vertex:

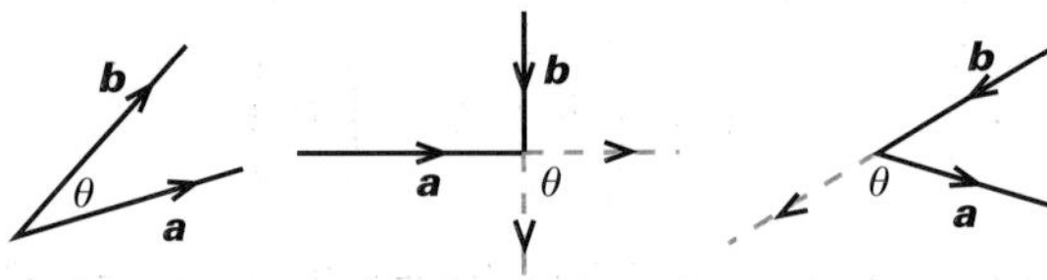

Example P is the point (1, 2, 3), Q(5, −3, 0) and R(−1, 0, 4). If $\boldsymbol{a} = \overrightarrow{PQ}$ and $\boldsymbol{b} = \overrightarrow{QR}$, calculate $\boldsymbol{a}.\boldsymbol{b}$.

$$\boldsymbol{a} = \overrightarrow{PQ} = \boldsymbol{q} - \boldsymbol{p} = \begin{pmatrix} 5 \\ -3 \\ 0 \end{pmatrix} - \begin{pmatrix} 1 \\ 2 \\ 3 \end{pmatrix} = \begin{pmatrix} 4 \\ -5 \\ -3 \end{pmatrix} \text{ and}$$

$$\boldsymbol{b} = \overrightarrow{QR} = \boldsymbol{r} - \boldsymbol{q} = \begin{pmatrix} -1 \\ 0 \\ 4 \end{pmatrix} - \begin{pmatrix} 5 \\ -3 \\ 0 \end{pmatrix} = \begin{pmatrix} -6 \\ 3 \\ 4 \end{pmatrix}.$$

$$\boldsymbol{a}.\boldsymbol{b} = \begin{pmatrix} 4 \\ -5 \\ -3 \end{pmatrix} \cdot \begin{pmatrix} -6 \\ 3 \\ 4 \end{pmatrix} = -24 - 15 - 12 = -51.$$

EXERCISE 8

1 Use $\boldsymbol{a}.\boldsymbol{b} = |\boldsymbol{a}||\boldsymbol{b}|\cos\theta$ to calculate $\boldsymbol{a}.\boldsymbol{b}$ for each of these diagrams.

a

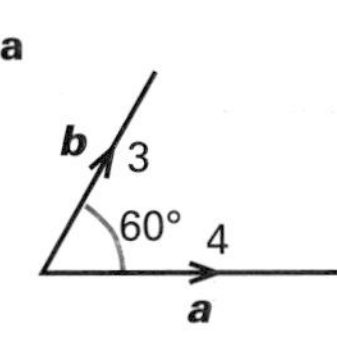

b

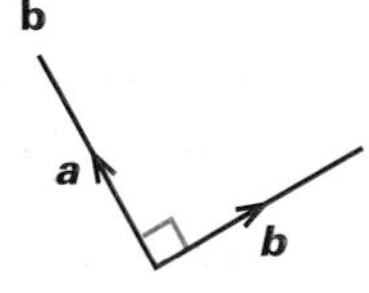

c

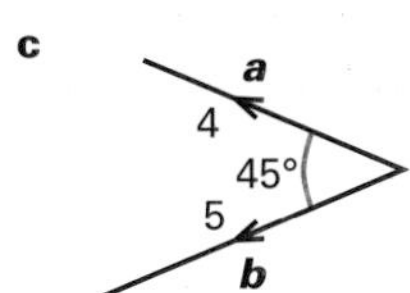

d

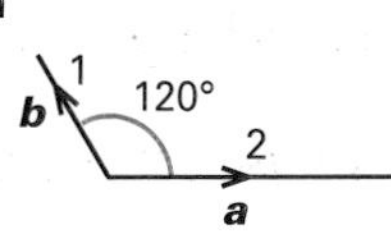

2 Calculate $\boldsymbol{a}.\boldsymbol{b}$ for:

a $|\boldsymbol{a}| = 2$, $|\boldsymbol{b}| = 1$, $\theta = \frac{\pi}{6}$

b $|\boldsymbol{a}| = 2$, $|\boldsymbol{b}| = 5$, $\theta = \frac{\pi}{4}$

c $|\boldsymbol{a}| = 2$, $|\boldsymbol{b}| = 5$, $\theta = \frac{3\pi}{4}$

d $\theta = \frac{\pi}{2}$.

3 Calculate $\boldsymbol{a}.\boldsymbol{b}$ for each pair of vectors.

a $\boldsymbol{a} = \begin{pmatrix} 2 \\ -1 \\ -3 \end{pmatrix}$, $\boldsymbol{b} = \begin{pmatrix} 1 \\ 0 \\ -2 \end{pmatrix}$

b $\boldsymbol{a} = \begin{pmatrix} 1 \\ 2 \\ 4 \end{pmatrix}$, $\boldsymbol{b} = \begin{pmatrix} -3 \\ -2 \\ 2 \end{pmatrix}$

c $\boldsymbol{a} = \begin{pmatrix} 3 \\ -2 \\ 1 \end{pmatrix}$, $\boldsymbol{b} = \begin{pmatrix} -2 \\ -4 \\ 3 \end{pmatrix}$

d $\boldsymbol{a} = \begin{pmatrix} a \\ b \\ c \end{pmatrix}$, $\boldsymbol{b} = \begin{pmatrix} 1 \\ 0 \\ 0 \end{pmatrix}$

4 $\boldsymbol{a}$ is the position vector of A(1, 2, 3) and $\boldsymbol{b}$ is the position vector of B(−2, 4, −1). Calculate $\boldsymbol{a}.\boldsymbol{b}$.

5 Repeat question **4** for A(3, −1, 0) and B(2, 4, 6).

6 In the formula $\boldsymbol{a}.\boldsymbol{b} = |\boldsymbol{a}||\boldsymbol{b}|\cos\theta$, θ is the angle between the vectors pointing out from the vertex.

a Copy these diagrams, and draw the lines necessary to show θ in each case.

b If $|\boldsymbol{a}| = |\boldsymbol{b}| = 5$, calculate $\boldsymbol{a}.\boldsymbol{b}$ in each, correct to 1 decimal place.

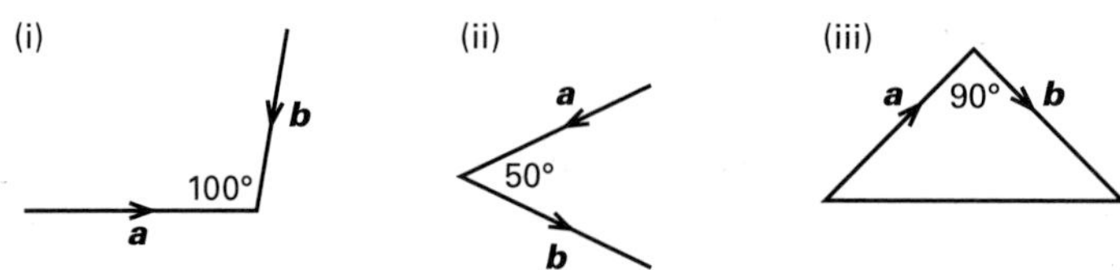

7 Calculate $\boldsymbol{a}.\boldsymbol{b}$ for:

a $\boldsymbol{a} = \boldsymbol{i} - 2\boldsymbol{j} + 3\boldsymbol{k}$, $\boldsymbol{b} = 2\boldsymbol{i} - 3\boldsymbol{j} + 2\boldsymbol{k}$

b $\boldsymbol{a} = 3\boldsymbol{i} - \boldsymbol{j}$, $\boldsymbol{b} = 2\boldsymbol{j} + \boldsymbol{k}$

c $\boldsymbol{a} = \boldsymbol{i} + \boldsymbol{j} + \boldsymbol{k}$, $\boldsymbol{b} = \boldsymbol{j} + \boldsymbol{k}$

d $\boldsymbol{a} = 3\boldsymbol{i} + \boldsymbol{j} - 2\boldsymbol{k}$, $\boldsymbol{b} = \boldsymbol{i} - \boldsymbol{k}$.

8 P is the point (1, 1, 1), Q is (−1, 1, 0) and R is (3, −2, −1). If $\boldsymbol{a} = \overrightarrow{PQ}$ and $\boldsymbol{b} = \overrightarrow{QR}$, calculate $\boldsymbol{a}.\boldsymbol{b}$.

9 Repeat question **8** for P(0, 1, 0), Q(−1, 0, 1) and R(2, −1, −2).

10 S is the point (1, 2, −3) and T is (11, −3, 7). U divides ST in the ratio 3:2. $\boldsymbol{a} = \overrightarrow{SU}$ and $\boldsymbol{b} = \overrightarrow{UT}$. Find:

a the coordinates of U

b the value of $\boldsymbol{a}.\boldsymbol{b}$.

11 $\triangle$ABC has vertices A(3, 0, 2), B(2, 1, 0) and C(0, −1, 4). M is the midpoint of AB and N is the midpoint of AC. Find:

a the coordinates of M and N

b $\boldsymbol{a}.\boldsymbol{b}$ and $\boldsymbol{c}.\boldsymbol{d}$, where $\boldsymbol{a} = \overrightarrow{MA}$, $\boldsymbol{b} = \overrightarrow{MN}$, $\boldsymbol{c} = \overrightarrow{BA}$ and $\boldsymbol{d} = \overrightarrow{BC}$.

Calculating the angle between two vectors

From the definitions

$$\left.\begin{aligned}\boldsymbol{a}.\boldsymbol{b} &= |\boldsymbol{a}||\boldsymbol{b}|\cos\theta, \text{ and}\\ \boldsymbol{a}.\boldsymbol{b} &= x_1x_2 + y_1y_2 + z_1z_2\end{aligned}\right\} \quad \boxed{\cos\theta = \frac{\boldsymbol{a}.\boldsymbol{b}}{|\boldsymbol{a}||\boldsymbol{b}|} = \frac{x_1x_2 + y_1y_2 + z_1z_2}{|\boldsymbol{a}||\boldsymbol{b}|}}, \quad \begin{aligned}\boldsymbol{a} &\neq 0,\\ \boldsymbol{b} &\neq 0\end{aligned}$$

Note $\boldsymbol{a}.\boldsymbol{b} = 0 \Leftrightarrow \theta = 90°$ or $\frac{\pi}{2}$, i.e. $\boldsymbol{a}$ is perpendicular to $\boldsymbol{b}$, assuming $\boldsymbol{a} \neq 0$, $\boldsymbol{b} \neq 0$.

Example 1 Calculate, correct to 1 decimal place, the size of the angle between

the vectors $\boldsymbol{a} = \begin{pmatrix} 1 \\ 2 \\ -1 \end{pmatrix}$ and $\boldsymbol{b} = \begin{pmatrix} -2 \\ 3 \\ 1 \end{pmatrix}$.

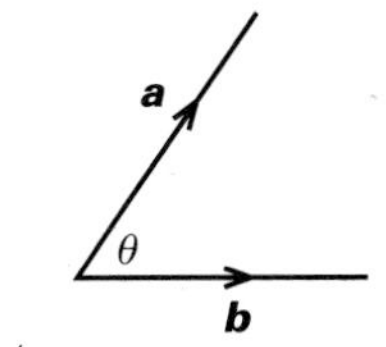

$$\boldsymbol{a.b} = \begin{pmatrix} 1 \\ 2 \\ -1 \end{pmatrix} \cdot \begin{pmatrix} -2 \\ 3 \\ 1 \end{pmatrix} = -2 + 6 - 1 = 3.$$

$|\boldsymbol{a}| = \sqrt{(1^2 + 2^2 + (-1)^2)} = \sqrt{6}$, and $|\boldsymbol{b}| = \sqrt{((-2)^2 + 3^2 + 1^2)} = \sqrt{14}$.

$\cos\theta = \dfrac{\boldsymbol{a.b}}{|\boldsymbol{a}||\boldsymbol{b}|} = \dfrac{3}{\sqrt{6}\sqrt{14}}$, so $\theta = 70.9°$, correct to 1 decimal place.

Example 2 P is (3, 5, −3), Q(5, 8, −9) and R(0, 7, −3).
Show that $\angle QPR = \dfrac{\pi}{2}$.

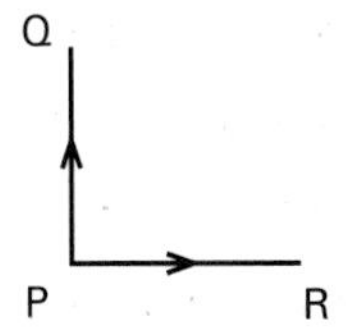

Notice that in $\angle$QPR the directions of the vectors away from the vertices (as in the scalar product definition) are $\overrightarrow{PQ}$ and $\overrightarrow{PR}$.

$$\overrightarrow{PQ} = \boldsymbol{q} - \boldsymbol{p} = \begin{pmatrix} 5 \\ 8 \\ -9 \end{pmatrix} - \begin{pmatrix} 3 \\ 5 \\ -3 \end{pmatrix} = \begin{pmatrix} 2 \\ 3 \\ -6 \end{pmatrix}, \text{ and}$$

$$\overrightarrow{PR} = \boldsymbol{r} - \boldsymbol{p} = \begin{pmatrix} 0 \\ 7 \\ -3 \end{pmatrix} - \begin{pmatrix} 3 \\ 5 \\ -3 \end{pmatrix} = \begin{pmatrix} -3 \\ 2 \\ 0 \end{pmatrix}.$$

$$\boldsymbol{a.b} = \overrightarrow{PQ}.\overrightarrow{PR} = \begin{pmatrix} 2 \\ 3 \\ -6 \end{pmatrix} \cdot \begin{pmatrix} -3 \\ 2 \\ 0 \end{pmatrix} = -6 + 6 + 0 = 0.$$

So $\cos QPR = \dfrac{\overrightarrow{PQ}.\overrightarrow{PR}}{|\overrightarrow{PQ}||\overrightarrow{PR}|} = 0$, and $\theta = \dfrac{\pi}{2}$.

EXERCISE 9

For angles, use degrees unless radians are indicated.

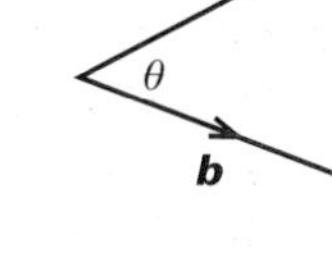

1 Use the formula $\cos\theta = \dfrac{\boldsymbol{a}.\boldsymbol{b}}{|\boldsymbol{a}||\boldsymbol{b}|}$ to calculate θ for:

a $\boldsymbol{a} = \begin{pmatrix} 2 \\ -1 \\ 0 \end{pmatrix}, \boldsymbol{b} = \begin{pmatrix} 3 \\ 1 \\ 0 \end{pmatrix}$ **b** $\boldsymbol{a} = \begin{pmatrix} 1 \\ -1 \\ 2 \end{pmatrix}, \boldsymbol{b} = \begin{pmatrix} 2 \\ 0 \\ 2 \end{pmatrix}$

c $\boldsymbol{a} = 2\boldsymbol{i} - 2\boldsymbol{j} - \boldsymbol{k}, \boldsymbol{b} = 2\boldsymbol{i} - 2\boldsymbol{k}$

d $\boldsymbol{a} = 2\boldsymbol{i} + 3\boldsymbol{j} + \boldsymbol{k}, \boldsymbol{b} = 3\boldsymbol{i} - 5\boldsymbol{j} + 9\boldsymbol{k}$.

2 Calculate $\angle$AOB, where O is the origin and:

a A is (4, −1, 2), B(1, 2, −1)

b A is (1, 1, 0), B(0, −1, 1)

c A is (3, 0, 3), B(−3, 0, −3).

3 Calculate the angle between the vectors $\boldsymbol{u} = 2\boldsymbol{i} + \boldsymbol{j} - \boldsymbol{k}$ and $\boldsymbol{v} = 3\boldsymbol{i} - 2\boldsymbol{j} + 2\boldsymbol{k}$.

4 Show that the vectors $\boldsymbol{p} = 2\boldsymbol{i} + 3\boldsymbol{j} - \boldsymbol{k}$ and $\boldsymbol{q} = 4\boldsymbol{i} - 2\boldsymbol{j} + 2\boldsymbol{k}$ are perpendicular.

5 The vectors $\boldsymbol{a} = 2\boldsymbol{i} - 5\boldsymbol{j} + \boldsymbol{k}$ and $\boldsymbol{b} = p\boldsymbol{i} - 2\boldsymbol{j} + 4\boldsymbol{k}$ are perpendicular. Find the value of p.

6 $\boldsymbol{u} = \begin{pmatrix} 8 \\ 0 \\ 4 \end{pmatrix}$ and $\boldsymbol{v} = \begin{pmatrix} 4 \\ 0 \\ 1 \end{pmatrix}$. Calculate the angle between the vectors $\boldsymbol{u} + \boldsymbol{v}$ and $\boldsymbol{u} - \boldsymbol{v}$.

7 O is the origin, P(−2, −1, 1) and Q(−1, 1, 2).

a Calculate the exact values of:

(i) $|\boldsymbol{p}|$ **(ii)** $|\boldsymbol{q}|$ **(iii)** $\angle$POQ.

b What kind of triangle is POQ?

8 $\triangle$ABC has vertices A(2, 1, 5), B(3, −2, 4) and C(−3, 4, 1).

a Find, in component form: **(i)** $\overrightarrow{AB}$ **(ii)** $\overrightarrow{AC}$.

b Calculate: **(i)** $\overrightarrow{AB}.\overrightarrow{AC}$ **(ii)** lengths AB and AC

(iii) $\angle$BAC **(iv)** $\angle$CBA **(v)** $\angle$ACB.

9 Show that the angle between the vectors $\boldsymbol{i} - \boldsymbol{j} + 2\boldsymbol{k}$ and $\boldsymbol{i} + \boldsymbol{k}$ is exactly $\frac{\pi}{6}$.

10 Use a suitable scalar product to check that the triangle with vertices A(2, −3, 4), B(5, −8, 13) and C(4, 0, 5) is right-angled. (Sketch each angle to help you to choose the correct sense of each vector, $\overrightarrow{AB}$ or $\overrightarrow{BA}$, etc.)

11 A 'space' quadrilateral has vertices A, B, C, D as shown. M_1, M_2, M_3, M_4 are the midpoints of the sides.

a Write down the coordinates of M_1, M_2, M_3 and M_4.

b Prove that $M_1M_2M_3M_4$ is a parallelogram.

c Calculate the acute angles in $M_1M_2M_3M_4$.

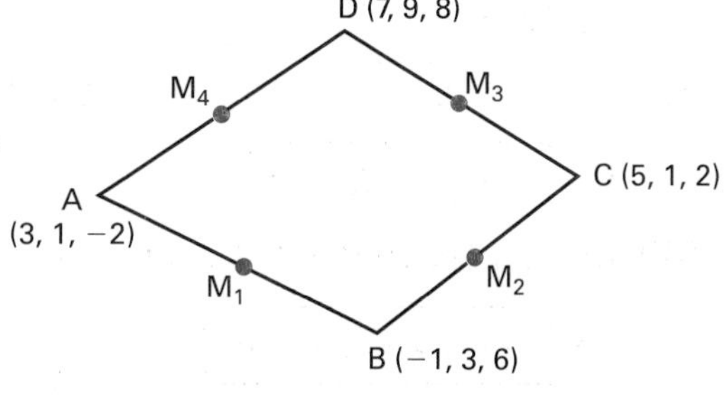

12 OABCDEFG is a cube with edges 8 cm long. M is the midpoint of DE, N is the midpoint of EA and P divides EF in the ratio 3:1.

a Find the coordinates of M, N and P.

b In △MNP, calculate, correct to 1 decimal place:

(i) the length of the shortest side

(ii) the size of the smallest angle (using scalar product).

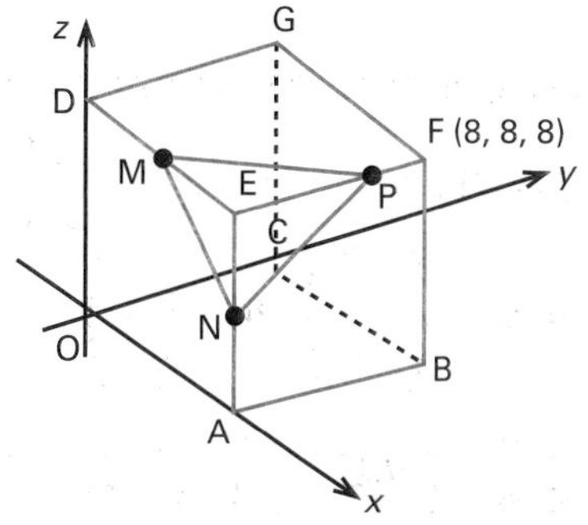

13 Quadrilateral PQRS has vertices P(−2, 0, −5), Q(1, 6, −8), R(7, 9, 4) and S(7, 3, 16).

a Find point T on PR such that $\frac{PT}{TR} = \frac{5}{4}$.

b Show that Q, T, S are collinear.

c Calculate the acute angle between the diagonals of PQRS.

14 P is (−1, 1, 6) and Q(5, 4, 6). R divides PQ in the ratio 2:1.

a Find the coordinates of R.

b S is (4, 1, 4). Show that ∠PRS = 90°, using:

(i) scalar product (ii) the converse of Pythagoras' Theorem.

15 A potash alum crystal is shaped like an octahedron. In a suitable coordinate system its vertices are A(2, −4, 4), B(7, −2, 6), C(8, 2, 2), D(3, 0, 0), E(−3, 10, 12) and F(13, −12, −6).

a Find the coordinates of the midpoints of AC and EF.

b Show that these space diagonals, AC and EF, bisect each other at right angles.

c Show that ABCD is a rhombus.

d Find the exact value of cos BAD.

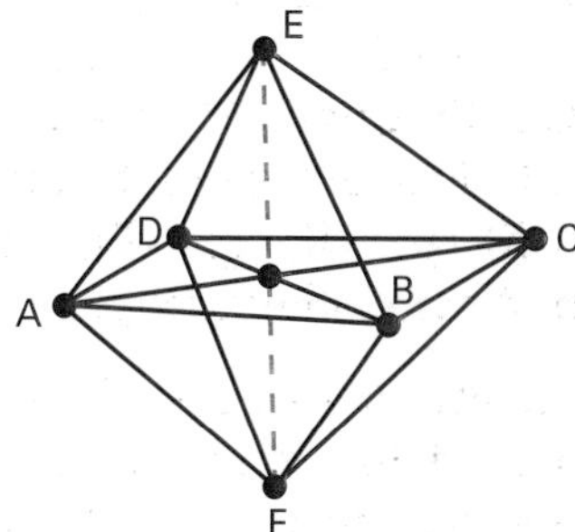

Some results using scalar product

1 Using $\boldsymbol{a}.\boldsymbol{b} = |\boldsymbol{a}||\boldsymbol{b}|\cos\theta$:

(i) $\boldsymbol{a}.\boldsymbol{a} = |\boldsymbol{a}||\boldsymbol{a}|\cos 0° = |\boldsymbol{a}||\boldsymbol{a}| \times 1 = a^2$, where $a = |\boldsymbol{a}|$

So $\boxed{\boldsymbol{a}.\boldsymbol{a} = a^2}$

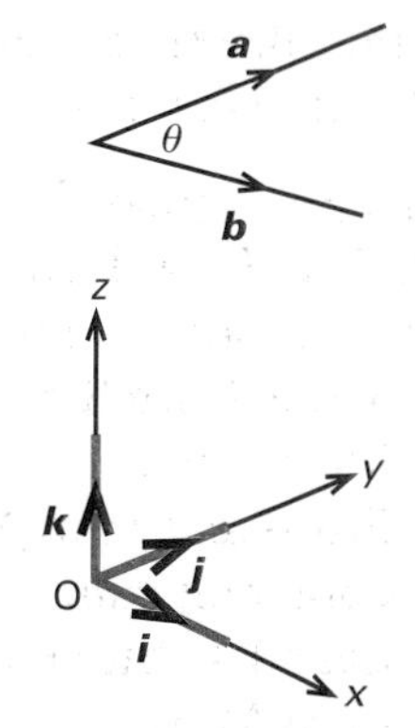

(ii) $\boldsymbol{i}^2 = \boldsymbol{i}.\boldsymbol{i} = |\boldsymbol{i}||\boldsymbol{i}|\cos 0° = 1 \times 1 \times 1 = 1$

So $\boxed{\boldsymbol{i}^2 = \boldsymbol{j}^2 = \boldsymbol{k}^2 = 1}$

(iii) $\boldsymbol{i}.\boldsymbol{j} = |\boldsymbol{i}||\boldsymbol{j}|\cos 90° = 1 \times 1 \times 0 = 0$

So $\boxed{\boldsymbol{i}.\boldsymbol{j} = \boldsymbol{i}.\boldsymbol{k} = \boldsymbol{j}.\boldsymbol{k} = 0}$

2 If $\boldsymbol{a} = \begin{pmatrix} x_1 \\ y_1 \\ z_1 \end{pmatrix}$, $\boldsymbol{b} = \begin{pmatrix} x_2 \\ y_2 \\ z_2 \end{pmatrix}$ and $\boldsymbol{c} = \begin{pmatrix} x_3 \\ y_3 \\ z_3 \end{pmatrix}$,

then $\boldsymbol{a}.(\boldsymbol{b} + \boldsymbol{c}) = x_1(x_2 + x_3) + y_1(y_2 + y_3) + z_1(z_2 + z_3)$, and
$\boldsymbol{a}.\boldsymbol{b} + \boldsymbol{a}.\boldsymbol{c} = (x_1x_2 + y_1y_2 + z_1z_2) + (x_1x_3 + y_1y_3 + z_1z_3)$.

It follows that $\boxed{\boldsymbol{a}.(\boldsymbol{b} + \boldsymbol{c}) = \boldsymbol{a}.\boldsymbol{b} + \boldsymbol{a}.\boldsymbol{c}}$

Example Parallel vectors **b** and **c** are inclined at 60° to vector **a**.
$|\boldsymbol{a}| = 3$, $|\boldsymbol{b}| = 2$, $|\boldsymbol{c}| = 4$. Evaluate $\boldsymbol{a}.(\boldsymbol{a} + \boldsymbol{b} + \boldsymbol{c})$.

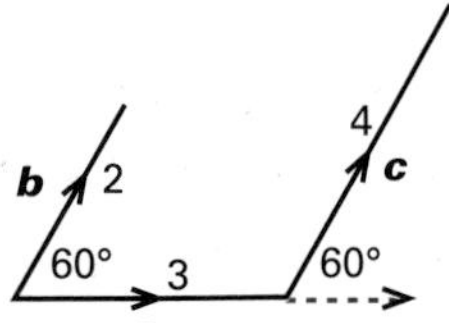

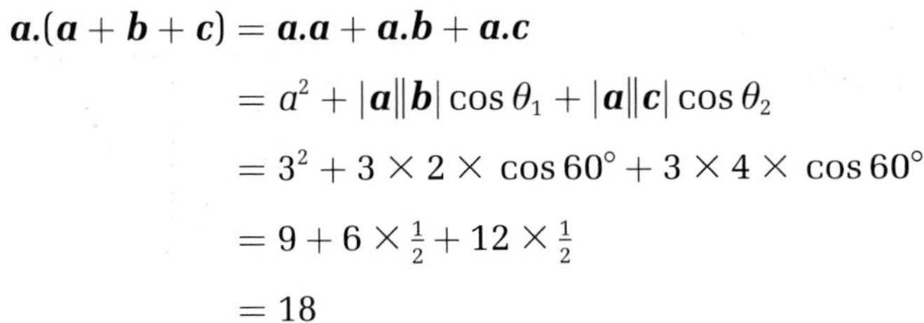

$$\begin{aligned} \boldsymbol{a}.(\boldsymbol{a} + \boldsymbol{b} + \boldsymbol{c}) &= \boldsymbol{a}.\boldsymbol{a} + \boldsymbol{a}.\boldsymbol{b} + \boldsymbol{a}.\boldsymbol{c} \\ &= a^2 + |\boldsymbol{a}||\boldsymbol{b}| \cos\theta_1 + |\boldsymbol{a}||\boldsymbol{c}| \cos\theta_2 \\ &= 3^2 + 3 \times 2 \times \cos 60° + 3 \times 4 \times \cos 60° \\ &= 9 + 6 \times \tfrac{1}{2} + 12 \times \tfrac{1}{2} \\ &= 18 \end{aligned}$$

EXERCISE 10

1 Evaluate:
a $\boldsymbol{i}^2 + \boldsymbol{j}^2 + \boldsymbol{k}^2$ b $\boldsymbol{i}.\boldsymbol{j} + \boldsymbol{i}.\boldsymbol{k} + \boldsymbol{j}.\boldsymbol{k}$ c $\boldsymbol{i}.(\boldsymbol{i} + \boldsymbol{j})$ d $\boldsymbol{j}.(\boldsymbol{i} + \boldsymbol{k})$ e $\boldsymbol{i}.(\boldsymbol{i} + \boldsymbol{j} + \boldsymbol{k})$.

2 Evaluate $\boldsymbol{a}.(\boldsymbol{a} + \boldsymbol{b})$, given:
a $|\boldsymbol{a}| = 2$, $|\boldsymbol{b}| = 3$ and $\theta = 90°$
b $|\boldsymbol{a}| = 1$, $|\boldsymbol{b}| = 1$ and $\theta = 60°$
c $|\boldsymbol{a}| = |\boldsymbol{b}| = \frac{1}{2}$ and $\theta = 120°$.

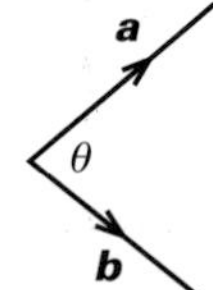

3 Vectors **a** and **b** make an angle of $\dfrac{\pi}{6}$ radians. $|\boldsymbol{a}| = 3$ and $|\boldsymbol{b}| = 4$.
Show that $\boldsymbol{a}.(\boldsymbol{a} + \boldsymbol{b}) = 9 + 6\sqrt{3}$.

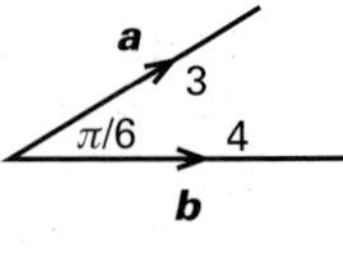

4 $\boldsymbol{a} = \begin{pmatrix} -1 \\ 0 \\ 2 \end{pmatrix}$, $\boldsymbol{b} = \begin{pmatrix} 1 \\ 1 \\ -1 \end{pmatrix}$ and $\boldsymbol{c} = \begin{pmatrix} 2 \\ -2 \\ -1 \end{pmatrix}$. Evaluate $\boldsymbol{a}.(\boldsymbol{b} + \boldsymbol{c})$.

5 This equilateral triangle has sides 3 units in length.
a Write down the size of the angle between **p** and **q**.
b Calculate **p.q**.
c Calculate the size of the angle between **q** and **r**.
d Evaluate: (i) $\boldsymbol{q}.(\boldsymbol{q} + \boldsymbol{r})$ (ii) $\boldsymbol{p}.(\boldsymbol{q} + \boldsymbol{r})$.

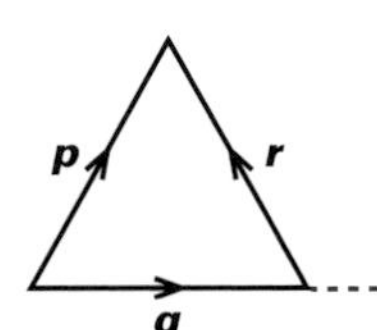

6 The two equal sides of this isosceles triangle are each 1 unit in length. Evaluate:

a $\boldsymbol{a}.\boldsymbol{c} + \boldsymbol{b}.\boldsymbol{c}$ **b** $\boldsymbol{c}.(\boldsymbol{a} - \boldsymbol{b})$.

7 In these diagrams, $|\boldsymbol{a}| = |\boldsymbol{b}| = \sqrt{2}$.

(i)

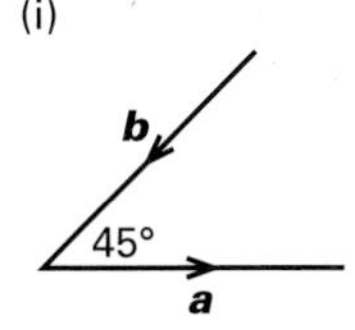

(ii)

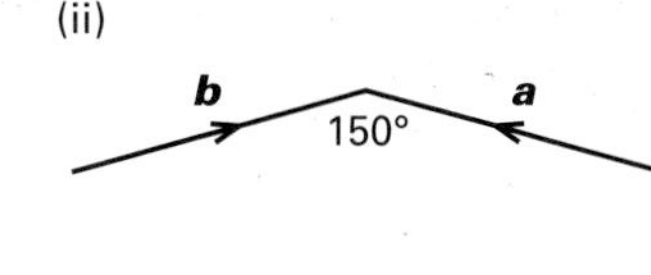

a Make sketches to show the angles between the vectors $\boldsymbol{a}$ and $\boldsymbol{b}$.

b Show that for **(i)** $\boldsymbol{a}.(\boldsymbol{a} + \boldsymbol{b}) = 2 - \sqrt{2}$, and for **(ii)** $\boldsymbol{a}.(\boldsymbol{a} + \boldsymbol{b}) = 2 - \sqrt{3}$.

8 $\triangle$PQR is equilateral, with sides 2 units long. M is the midpoint of PQ. Evaluate $\boldsymbol{a}.(\boldsymbol{b} + \boldsymbol{c})$.

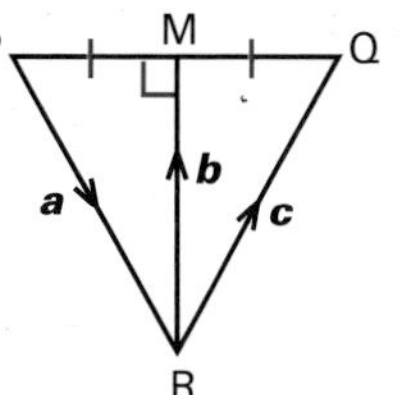

Challenges

1 a Simplify $\boldsymbol{a}.(\boldsymbol{b} - \boldsymbol{c}) + \boldsymbol{b}.(\boldsymbol{c} - \boldsymbol{a}) + \boldsymbol{c}.(\boldsymbol{a} - \boldsymbol{b})$.

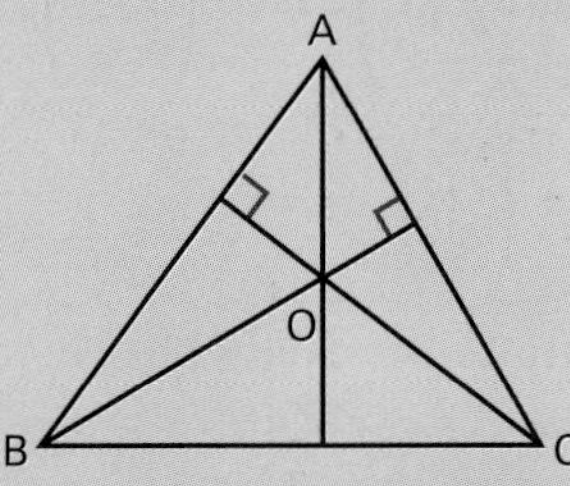

b In $\triangle$ABC, BO and OC are perpendicular to AC and AB respectively. If $\boldsymbol{a}$, $\boldsymbol{b}$, $\boldsymbol{c}$ denote the position vectors of A, B, C with respect to O as origin, show that $\boldsymbol{b}.(\boldsymbol{c} - \boldsymbol{a}) = 0$ and $\boldsymbol{c}.(\boldsymbol{a} - \boldsymbol{b}) = 0$.

c Hence show by vector algebra that $\boldsymbol{a}.(\boldsymbol{b} - \boldsymbol{c}) = 0$. What can you conclude about AO and BC?

d State your conclusion in a form which is true for every triangle.

2 Use vectors to prove that the three perpendicular bisectors of the sides of a triangle are concurrent.

CHAPTER 1 REVIEW

1 a Write down the component form of $\overrightarrow{AB}$ for:

(i) A(−1, 2, −3) B(3, −2, 5)

(ii) A(2, 4, −1) B(3, −2, −2).

b Calculate the distance AB for each pair of points.

2 $\begin{pmatrix} 3a+1 \\ 9 \\ 1-b \end{pmatrix} = \begin{pmatrix} b-2 \\ 9 \\ -4a-5 \end{pmatrix}$.

Find a and b.

3 The centre of the cuboid is at O, and the edges are parallel to the axes.

a Write down:

(i) the coordinates of B and E

(ii) the components of OA and EB.

b Calculate the lengths of OA and EB.

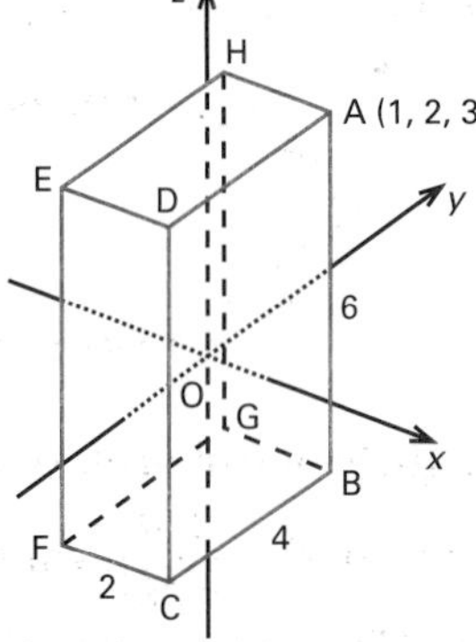

4 $\boldsymbol{u} = \begin{pmatrix} 1 \\ 0 \\ 2 \end{pmatrix}$ and A is the point (3, 1, −2).

Find the coordinates of the point B such that $\overrightarrow{AB}$ is parallel to $\boldsymbol{u}$ and in the same direction, and has three times the length of $\boldsymbol{u}$.

5 △ABC has vertices A(2, 1, 1), B(−2, 3, 3) and C(2, 5, −1). M, N and D are the mid-points of AB, AC and BC, respectively.

a Find the coordinates of M, N and D.

b Show that BDNM is a parallelogram but not a rhombus.

6 Prove that the points A(3, −1, 0), B(5, 2, 5) and C(9, 8, 15) are collinear, and find the value of $\frac{AB}{BC}$.

7 D is (2, 0, −3) and E is (12, 10, 7). Find point P on DE such that $\frac{DP}{PE} = \frac{3}{2}$.

8 $\frac{AP}{PB} = \frac{3}{-2}, \frac{BQ}{QC} = \frac{2}{3}$ and R is the midpoint of CA.

a Find the coordinates of P, Q and R.

b Show that P, Q, R are collinear, and find $\frac{PQ}{QR}$.

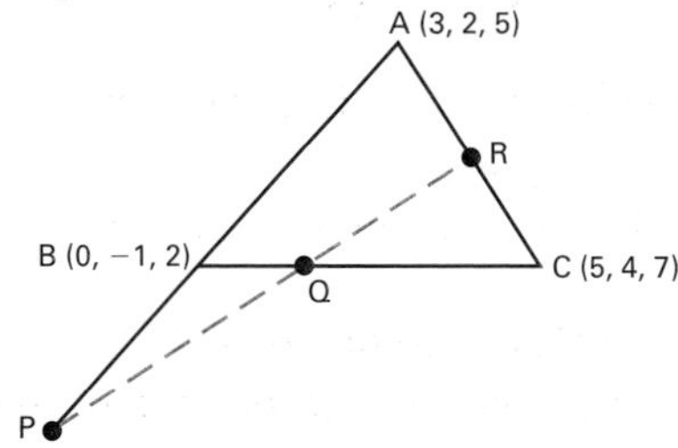

9 Find the two unit vectors of the form $a\boldsymbol{i} + \frac{1}{3}\boldsymbol{j} - \frac{1}{3}\boldsymbol{k}$.

10 Calculate $\boldsymbol{a}.\boldsymbol{b}$ for these pairs of vectors:

a $\boldsymbol{a} = \begin{pmatrix} 1 \\ 0 \\ -3 \end{pmatrix}, \boldsymbol{b} = \begin{pmatrix} 2 \\ -1 \\ 5 \end{pmatrix}$

b $\boldsymbol{a} = \begin{pmatrix} 2 \\ 3 \\ 1 \end{pmatrix}, \boldsymbol{b} = \begin{pmatrix} -1 \\ 2 \\ 4 \end{pmatrix}$

11 Calculate the angle between $\boldsymbol{u} = 2\boldsymbol{i} + \boldsymbol{j} - 2\boldsymbol{k}$ and $\boldsymbol{v} = \boldsymbol{i} + 2\boldsymbol{j} + \boldsymbol{k}$.

12 Show that $\boldsymbol{p} = 2\boldsymbol{i} + 3\boldsymbol{j} - \boldsymbol{k}$ and $\boldsymbol{q} = 3\boldsymbol{i} - \boldsymbol{j} + 3\boldsymbol{k}$ are perpendicular.

13 Calculate ∠BAC, where A is (3, 1, 4), B(2, 3, 1) and C(5, 4, 8).

14 A is (−1, 2, 5) and B(8, 11, −16). P divides AB in the ratio 1:2. C is (1, 6, −2).

a Find the coordinates of P.

b Prove that ∠APC = 90°.

c Q divides AB in the ratio 2:1. Prove that Q and A are equidistant from C.

CHAPTER 1 SUMMARY

1 A vector is a quantity which has magnitude and direction. It can be represented by a directed line segment.

2 The vector $v = \overrightarrow{AB}$ has components parallel to the x, y and z axes.

For example, $v = \begin{pmatrix} 1 \\ 2 \\ -3 \end{pmatrix} =$

$\boldsymbol{i} + 2\boldsymbol{j} - 3\boldsymbol{k}$ in terms of the three unit vectors $\boldsymbol{i}$, $\boldsymbol{j}$ and $\boldsymbol{k}$.

3 The magnitude of vector

$v = \begin{pmatrix} a \\ b \\ c \end{pmatrix}$ is $|v| = \sqrt{(a^2 + b^2 + c^2)}$.

4 Vectors can be added:

(i) geometrically, 'nose-to-tail'

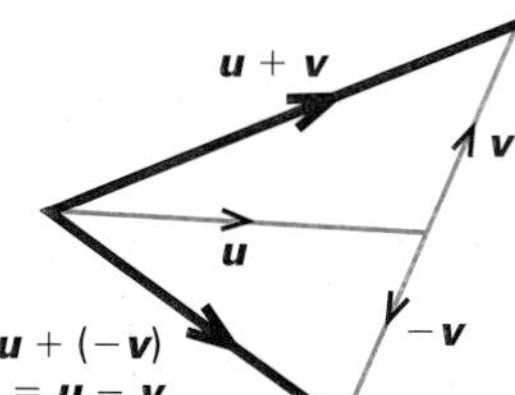

(ii) using components

$$\begin{pmatrix} a \\ b \\ c \end{pmatrix} + \begin{pmatrix} p \\ q \\ r \end{pmatrix} = \begin{pmatrix} a + p \\ b + q \\ c + r \end{pmatrix}$$

5 The position vector of A is $\boldsymbol{a} = \overrightarrow{OA}$, and $\overrightarrow{AB} = \overrightarrow{OB} - \overrightarrow{OA} = \boldsymbol{b} - \boldsymbol{a}$.

6 The distance formula

If A is $(x_1, y_1\ z_1)$ and B is (x_2, y_2, z_2),

then: $\overrightarrow{AB} = \boldsymbol{b} - \boldsymbol{a} = \begin{pmatrix} x_2 - x_1 \\ y_2 - y_1 \\ z_2 - z_1 \end{pmatrix}$,

and $|\overrightarrow{AB}| = \sqrt{((x_2 - x_1)^2 + (y_2 - y_1)^2 + (z_2 - z_1)^2)}$.

7 Collinear points and parallel lines

a If $\overrightarrow{AB} = k\,\overrightarrow{BC}$, then A, B and C are collinear (B is common).

b If $\overrightarrow{AB} = k\,\overrightarrow{CD}$, $k \neq 0$, then AB $\|$ CD.

8 If a point P divides a line AB in the ratio 1:2 then $\overrightarrow{AP} = \frac{1}{2}\overrightarrow{PB}$, and $\boldsymbol{p} - \boldsymbol{a} = \frac{1}{2}(\boldsymbol{b} - \boldsymbol{p})$ etc.

A ——P—————— B (AP : PB = 1 : 2)

Scheme A B / 1 2 (crossed) $\boldsymbol{p} = \frac{1}{3}(2\boldsymbol{a} + \boldsymbol{b})$

9 The position vector of the midpoint of AB is $\boldsymbol{m} = \frac{1}{2}(\boldsymbol{a} + \boldsymbol{b})$.

10 The scalar product of two vectors $\boldsymbol{a}$ and $\boldsymbol{b}$ is:

(i) $\boldsymbol{a}.\boldsymbol{b} = |\boldsymbol{a}||\boldsymbol{b}|\cos\theta$, or

(ii) $\boldsymbol{a}.\boldsymbol{b} = x_1x_2 + y_1y_2 + z_1z_2$.

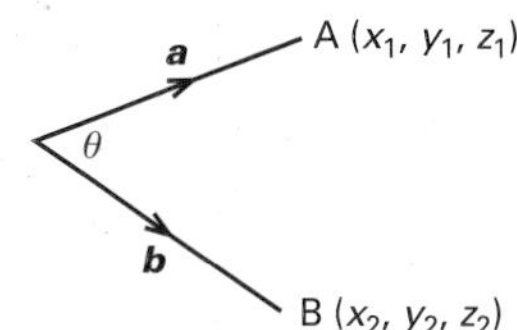

11 The angle between vectors $\boldsymbol{a}$ and $\boldsymbol{b}$ is given by: $\cos\theta = \dfrac{\boldsymbol{a}.\boldsymbol{b}}{|\boldsymbol{a}||\boldsymbol{b}|}$, where $\boldsymbol{a}$ and $\boldsymbol{b}$ point *out* from the vertex of the angle.

12 For three vectors $\boldsymbol{a}$, $\boldsymbol{b}$ and $\boldsymbol{c}$, $\boldsymbol{a}.(\boldsymbol{b} + \boldsymbol{c}) = \boldsymbol{a}.\boldsymbol{b} + \boldsymbol{a}.\boldsymbol{c}$.

Note All these results can be adapted for 2 dimensions by omitting the z-coordinates of the vectors, and using vectors in the 2-dimensional x, y-plane as on pages 192–5.

2 Further Differentiation and Integration

The derivatives of sin x and cos x

A practical problem

A weight is bobbing up and down at the end of a spring. Its displacement y cm from OX at time t seconds is $y(t) = \sin t$.
What is its velocity at time t?
When is it stationary?

The velocity is $\frac{dy}{dt} = \frac{d}{dt}(\sin t)$, so we have to find the derivative of the sine function in order to answer these questions.

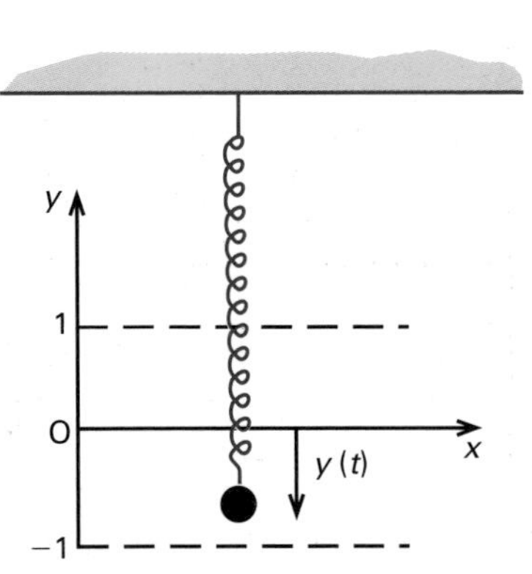

CLASS DISCUSSION/EXERCISE 1

1 Using the graph of the derived function

In the chapter Introduction to Differentiation, we saw that, given the graph $y = f(x)$ of a function f, we can sketch the graph of the derived function f' by using the fact that the gradient of the tangent at the point $(x, f(x))$ on the graph $y = f(x)$ is $f'(x)$. The same method can be used to find the derivatives of sin x and cos x.

Note In calculus, sin x and cos x always mean the sine and cosine of an angle of x radians.

In the first diagram on page 219, tangents are drawn to the sine curve, and their gradients have been measured at $x = 0, \frac{\pi}{4}, \frac{\pi}{2}, \ldots$ and recorded in this table.

x	0	$\pi/4$	$\pi/2$	$3\pi/4$	π	$5\pi/4$	$3\pi/2$	$7\pi/4$	2π
Gradient of tangent $= f'(x)$	1	0.7	0	−0.7	−1	−0.7	0	0.7	1

These points have been plotted in the second graph, and the part of the graph of the derived function f' from $x = 0$ to $x = 2\pi$ has been drawn.

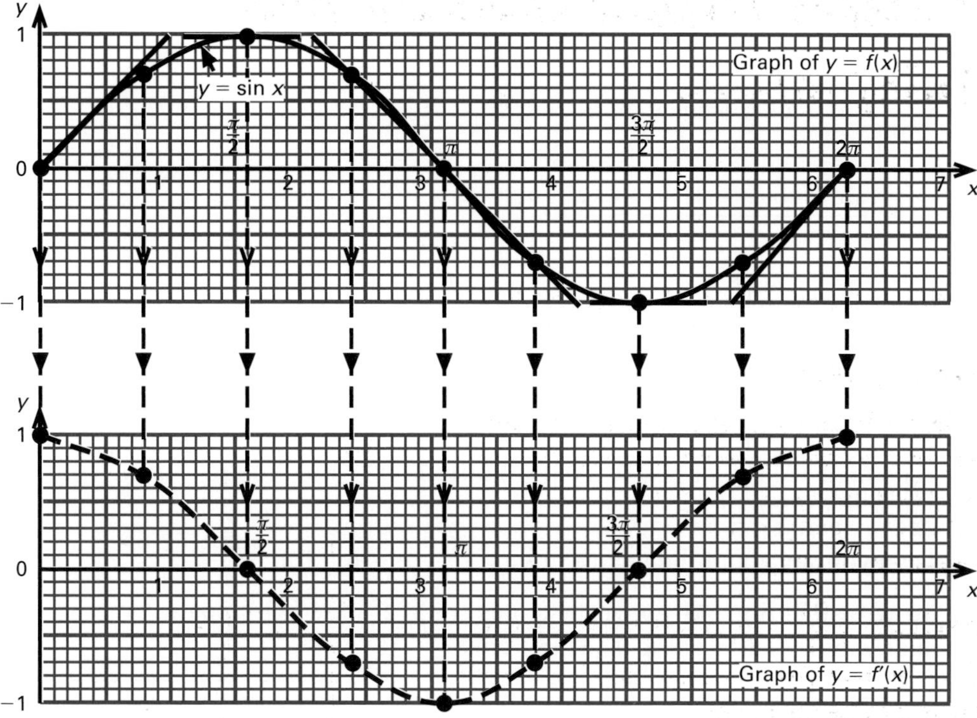

Do you recognise this as the graph of $y = \cos x$, for $0 \leqslant x \leqslant 2\pi$? This suggests that:

If $f(x) = \sin x$, $f'(x) = \cos x$. In differential notation, $\frac{d}{dx}(\sin x) = \cos x$.

a Using the same scales, draw the graph of $f(x) = \cos x$ on squared paper, for $0 \leqslant x \leqslant 2\pi$.

b Measure the gradients of the tangents at $x = 0, \frac{\pi}{2}, \pi, \frac{3\pi}{2}$ and 2π, and complete a table.

c Use the points to draw the graph of the derived function f'. You should obtain the graph $y = -\sin x$. This suggests that:

If $f(x) = \cos x$, $f'(x) = -\sin x$. In differential notation, $\frac{d}{dx}(\cos x) = -\sin x$.

a Draw the graphs $y = \sin x$ and $y = (\sin(x + 0.01) - \sin x)/0.01$, using radians.

b Insert the graph $y = \cos x$ on the same screen. What can you deduce?

c Now draw the graphs $y = \cos x$ and $y = (\cos(x + 0.01) - \cos x)/0.01$.

d The second graph is approximately of the form $y = a \sin x$. What is the value of a? What can you deduce?

2 Using the definition of a derivative

Take $f(x) = \sin x$.

$$f'(x) = \lim_{h \to 0} \frac{f(x+h) - f(x)}{h} = \lim_{h \to 0} \frac{\sin(x+h) - \sin x}{h}$$

$$= \lim_{h \to 0} \frac{\sin x \cos h + \cos x \sin h - \sin x}{h}$$

$$= \lim_{h \to 0} \frac{\sin x(\cos h - 1) + \cos x \sin h}{h}$$

$$= \sin x \lim_{h \to 0} \left(\frac{\cos h - 1}{h}\right) + \cos x \lim_{h \to 0} \left(\frac{\sin h}{h}\right) \quad \ldots \quad \text{(A)}$$

What happens to $\frac{\cos h - 1}{h}$ and $\frac{\sin h}{h}$ as $h \to 0$?

a Calculate their values for $h = 0.1, 0.01, 0.001, 0.0001$ and $0.000\,01$, *using your calculator in radian mode.*

b What can you say about the values of $\lim_{h \to 0} \frac{\cos h - 1}{h}$ and $\lim_{h \to 0} \frac{\sin h}{h}$?

c Do you agree that line (A), above, becomes $\cos x$? If so, $f'(x) = \cos x$.

In a similar way, if $f(x) = \cos x$, $f'(x) = -\sin x$.

Using differential notation, $\frac{d}{dx}(\sin x) = \cos x$ and $\frac{d}{dx}(\cos x) = -\sin x$

Example 1 Differentiate $5 \sin x - 3 \cos x$.

$\frac{d}{dx}(5 \sin x - 3 \cos x) = 5\frac{d}{dx}(\sin x) - 3\frac{d}{dx}(\cos x) = 5 \cos x + 3 \sin x.$

Example 2 Find the equation of the tangent to the curve $y = 3 + 2 \sin x$ at $x = 0$.

$\frac{dy}{dx} = 2 \cos x \Rightarrow$ gradient of tangent at $x = 0$ is $2 \cos 0 = 2 \times 1 = 2$.

If $x = 0$, $y = 3 + 2 \times 0 = 3$, so the point is $(0, 3)$.

The equation of the tangent at $(0, 3)$ with gradient 2 is $y - 3 = 2(x - 0)$, i.e.

$y = 2x + 3$

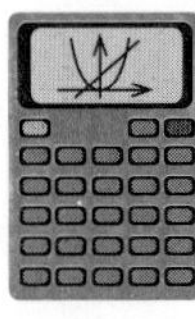

a Given $f(x) = \sin x - \cos x$, write down $f'(x)$, and draw the graphs $y = f(x)$ and $y = f'(x)$.

b Check these corresponding aspects:

$y = f(x)$ .... increasing ... stationary ... decreasing

$y = f'(x)$ ... positive ...... zero .... negative.

EXERCISE 2A

Differentiate in questions **1–4**.

1 **a** $\sin x$ **b** $3\sin x$ **c** $2\sin x$ **d** $1-\sin x$

2 **a** $\cos x$ **b** $2\cos x$ **c** $\frac{1}{2}\cos x$ **d** $1-\cos x$

3 **a** $5\cos x$ **b** $6\sin x$ **c** $\sin x-\cos x$

4 **a** $3\cos x-\sin x$ **b** $4\sin x+7\cos x$

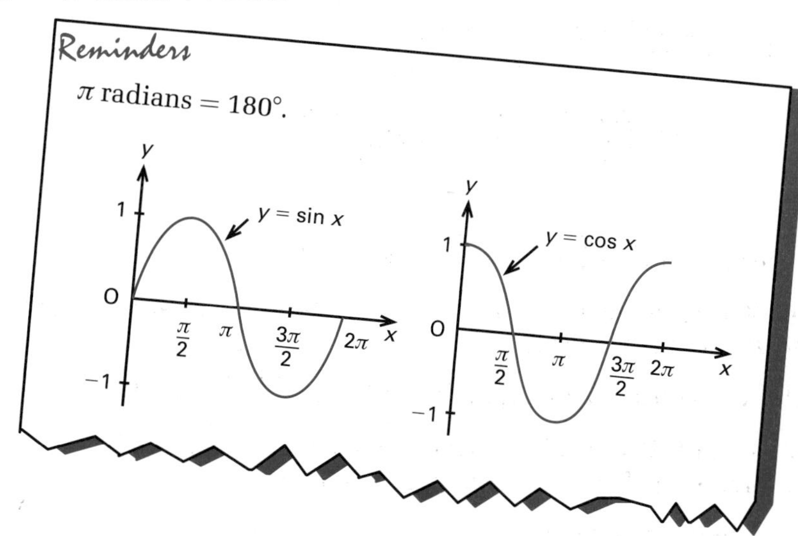

5 Use the sine and cosine graphs to write down the value of:

a $\sin\frac{\pi}{2}$ **b** $\sin\pi$ **c** $\cos 0$ **d** $\cos\pi$

e $\cos\frac{\pi}{2}$ **f** $\sin 2\pi$ **g** $\cos\frac{3\pi}{2}$ **h** $\cos 2\pi$.

6 Use the triangles to write down the value of:

a $\sin\frac{\pi}{4}$ **b** $\cos\frac{\pi}{4}$

c $\sin\frac{\pi}{6}$ **d** $\cos\frac{\pi}{3}$.

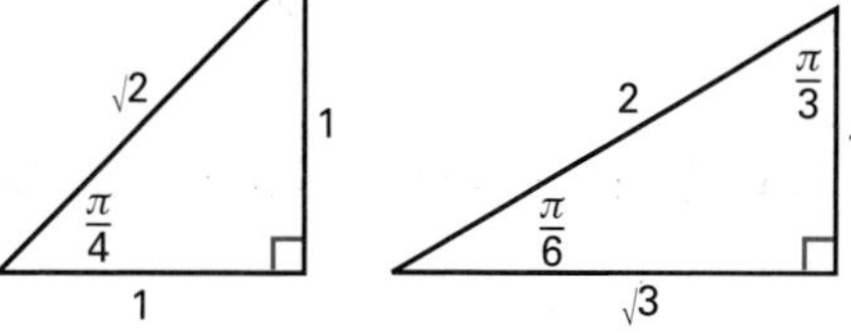

7 Find the gradient of the tangent to the curve $y=\sin x+\cos x$ at:

a $x=0$ **b** $x=\frac{\pi}{2}$ **c** $x=\frac{\pi}{4}$.

8 Find the gradient, then the equation, of the tangent to the curve:

a $y=2\sin x$ at $x=\frac{\pi}{2}$ **b** $y=1+\cos x$ at $x=\pi$.

9 Use differentiation to show that the function $f(x)=5\sin x$ has a maximum turning value of 5 at $x=\frac{\pi}{2}$ and a minimum turning value of -5 at $x=\frac{3\pi}{2}$.

10 As in question **9**, show that $f(x)=5\cos x$ has a maximum turning value of 5 at $x=0$ and a minimum turning value of -5 at $x=\pi$.

11 Show that one of the following functions is always increasing, and the other is always decreasing.
a $f(x) = 2x + \cos x$ **b** $f(x) = \sin x - 2x$

12 Find the equation of the tangent to the curve:
a $y = 3x - \cos x$ at $x = 0$ **b** $y = 3x^2 + \sin x + 2$ at $x = 0$.

Example Find the derivative of $f(x) = \dfrac{1 - x\cos x}{2x}$.

$$f(x) = \frac{1 - x\cos x}{2x} = \frac{1}{2x} - \frac{x\cos x}{2x} = \tfrac{1}{2}x^{-1} - \tfrac{1}{2}\cos x \Rightarrow f'(x) = -\tfrac{1}{2}x^{-2} + \tfrac{1}{2}\sin x$$

EXERCISE 2B

Calculate $f'(x)$ in questions **1–4**.

1 a $f(x) = 5x^2 - 2\sin x$ **b** $f(x) = \dfrac{1}{x} - 3\cos x$

2 a $f(x) = \sqrt{x} + \cos x$ **b** $f(x) = \dfrac{1}{\sqrt{x}} - \sin x$

3 a $f(x) = 9\cos x + 8\sin x$ **b** $f(x) = \tfrac{1}{2}\sin x - \tfrac{1}{3}\cos x$

4 a $f(x) = \dfrac{2 + x\sin x}{x}$ **b** $f(x) = \dfrac{3 + x^2\cos x}{x^2}$

5 Calculate:
a the gradient of the tangent to the curve $y = x + \sin x$ at: **(i)** $x = 0$ **(ii)** $x = \dfrac{\pi}{2}$
b the acute angle, in degrees, between these tangents, correct to 1 decimal place.

6 Calculate the gradient, then the equation, of the tangent to the curve
$y = \dfrac{x^2}{2\pi} + 2\sin x$ at: **a** $x = 0$ **b** $x = \pi$.

Reminders

Relating the angles to π or 2π (whichever is nearer), and using the all–sin–tan–cos diagram:

(i) $\sin\dfrac{2\pi}{3} = \sin\left(\pi - \dfrac{2\pi}{3}\right) = +\sin\dfrac{\pi}{3} = \dfrac{\sqrt{3}}{2}$

(ii) $\cos\dfrac{5\pi}{4} = \cos\left(\pi + \dfrac{\pi}{4}\right) = -\cos\dfrac{\pi}{4} = -\dfrac{1}{\sqrt{2}}$

(iii) $\sin\dfrac{11\pi}{6} = \sin\left(2\pi - \dfrac{\pi}{6}\right) = -\sin\dfrac{\pi}{6} = -\tfrac{1}{2}$

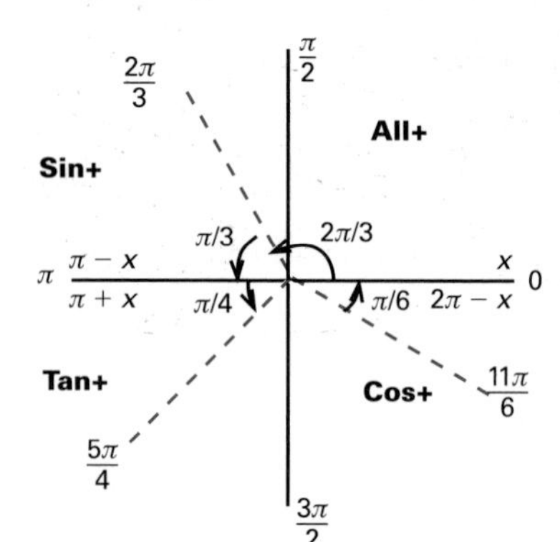

7 Simplify:

a $\sin\frac{3\pi}{4}$ **b** $\cos\frac{3\pi}{4}$ **c** $\sin\frac{5\pi}{6}$ **d** $\cos\frac{5\pi}{6}$

e $\sin\frac{4\pi}{3}$ **f** $\cos\frac{4\pi}{3}$ **g** $\sin\frac{5\pi}{3}$ **h** $\cos\frac{5\pi}{3}$.

8 Find the gradient of the tangent to the curve:

a $y = 2\cos x$ at $x = \frac{2\pi}{3}$ **b** $y = x - \cos x$ at $x = \frac{5\pi}{3}$.

9 Calculate the rate of change of $f(x) = 2\cos x + 4\sin x$ at $x =$

a $\frac{\pi}{2}$ **b** π **c** $\frac{5\pi}{3}$ **d** $\frac{5\pi}{4}$.

10 The height of the ocean above or below mean sea-level is given by $y(t) = 2\sin t$, measured in metres at t hours.

a What is the difference in metres between high tide and low tide?

b Find the rate of rise or fall at time t.

c At what level is this rate at maximum (numerical) value?

11 The displacement of the weight on the spring on page 218 is $y(t) = \sin t$ after t seconds, and its velocity is $\frac{dy}{dt}$.

a Calculate, correct to 2 decimal places, the velocity after 1 second. (Remember angles are in radians, so use RAD mode on your calculator.)

b After what time is the velocity first zero?

Display the graphs and tangents in questions **5** and **8** of Exercise 2B and find the approximate points of contact.

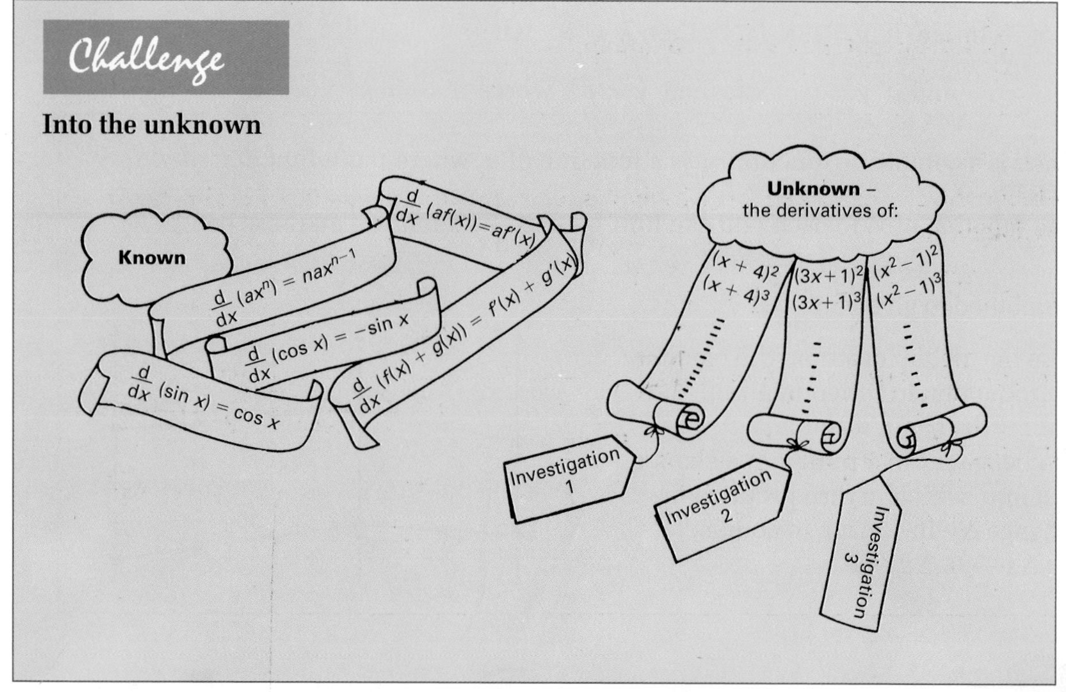

In each list on page 223: (i) multiply out the brackets
(ii) differentiate, using known rules
(iii) factorise, if possible.

Can you discover patterns and predict derivatives?

y	$\frac{dy}{dx}$
$(x + 4)^2$	$2(x + 4)$
$(3x + 1)^3$	$9(3x + 1)^2$
$(ax + b)^n$	?
$(x^2 - 1)^2$	$4x(x^2 - 1)$
$(ax^2 + b)^n$	?

As a further challenge, test any rule you have found on the derivative of $(x^2 + 3x + 4)^2$.

The chain rule for differentiation – algebraic functions

In the challenge above you may have found that:

if $y = (3x + 1)^2$, $\frac{dy}{dx} = 6(3x + 1) = 2 \times 3(3x + 1)$,

if $y = (3x + 1)^3$, $\frac{dy}{dx} = 9(3x + 1)^2 = 3 \times 3(3x + 1)^2$, and deduced that

if $y = (ax + b)^n$, $\frac{dy}{dx} = na(ax + b)^{n-1}$.

The *chain rule* described below will enable you to differentiate many types of *composite function*, including the ones above.

For example, if $y = (3x + 1)^2$, then $y = u^2$, where $u = 3x + 1$,

and if $y = (\sin x)^3$, then $y = u^3$, where $u = \sin x$.

Each is a composite function; y is a function of u, where u is a function of x, so y is a function of x. In each you can find $\frac{dy}{du}$ and $\frac{du}{dx}$, but how can these be combined to give you $\frac{dy}{dx}$?

Use the 'delta' idea from the chapter Introduction to Differentiation, and follow the chain reaction.
A change Δx in x produces a change Δu in u, which in turn produces a change Δy in y. And, of course, as $\Delta x \to 0$, $\Delta u \to 0$.

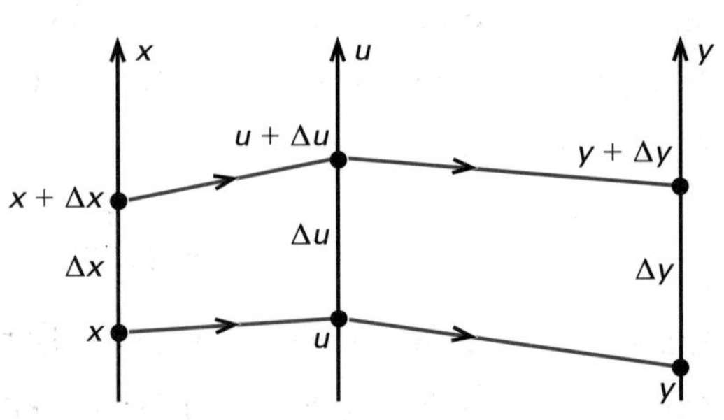

$$\frac{\Delta y}{\Delta x} = \frac{\Delta y}{\Delta u} \times \frac{\Delta u}{\Delta x}, \text{ so}$$

$$\lim_{\Delta x \to 0} \frac{\Delta y}{\Delta x} = \lim_{\Delta u \to 0} \frac{\Delta y}{\Delta u} \times \lim_{\Delta x \to 0} \frac{\Delta u}{\Delta x} (\Delta u \neq 0),$$

i.e. $\dfrac{\mathrm{d}y}{\mathrm{d}x} = \dfrac{\mathrm{d}y}{\mathrm{d}u}\dfrac{\mathrm{d}u}{\mathrm{d}x}$, the chain rule for differentiation.

The chain rule in function notation

If $y = f(g(x))$, a composite function, then $y = f(u)$, where $u = g(x)$.

$\dfrac{\mathrm{d}y}{\mathrm{d}x} = \dfrac{\mathrm{d}y}{\mathrm{d}u}\dfrac{\mathrm{d}u}{\mathrm{d}x}$ becomes $\dfrac{\mathrm{d}}{\mathrm{d}x} f(g(x)) = f'(u)\dfrac{\mathrm{d}}{\mathrm{d}x}(g(x)) = f'(g(x))\dfrac{\mathrm{d}}{\mathrm{d}x}(g(x))$,

that is $\dfrac{\mathrm{d}}{\mathrm{d}x} f(\text{- - -}) = f'(\text{- - -})\dfrac{\mathrm{d}}{\mathrm{d}x}(\text{- - -})$.

same function.

In particular, $\dfrac{\mathrm{d}}{\mathrm{d}x}(\text{- - -})^n = n(\text{- - -})^{n-1}\dfrac{\mathrm{d}}{\mathrm{d}x}(\text{- - -})$.

Examples

1 $\dfrac{\mathrm{d}}{\mathrm{d}x}(3x+1)^2 = 2(3x+1)\dfrac{\mathrm{d}}{\mathrm{d}x}(3x+1) = 6(3x+1)$

2 $\dfrac{\mathrm{d}}{\mathrm{d}u}(2-u^2)^{1/3} = \frac{1}{3}(2-u^2)^{-2/3}\dfrac{\mathrm{d}}{\mathrm{d}u}(2-u^2) = \dfrac{-2u}{3}(2-u^2)^{-2/3}$

3 $\dfrac{\mathrm{d}}{\mathrm{d}x}\left(\dfrac{1}{2x^3+1}\right) = \dfrac{\mathrm{d}}{\mathrm{d}x}(2x^3+1)^{-1} = (-1)(2x^3+1)^{-2} \times 6x^2 = \dfrac{-6x^2}{(2x^3+1)^2}$.

EXERCISE 3A

In questions **1–7**, differentiate with respect to the relevant variables.

1 a $(x+1)^2$ **b** $(x-1)^3$ **c** $(x+5)^4$

2 a $(3x+1)^2$ **b** $(2x-3)^3$ **c** $(1-5x)^2$

3 a $(1+u^2)^3$ **b** $(4-u^2)^2$ **c** $(2u^2-1)^3$

4 a $(3x-1)^{-2}$ **b** $(x^2+2)^{-1}$ **c** $(x^3-5)^{-3}$

5 a $\dfrac{1}{2x+3}$ **b** $\dfrac{2}{1-u}$ **c** $\dfrac{3}{4t+5}$

6 a $(2x+1)^{1/2}$ **b** $(3u-2)^{1/3}$ **c** $(x^2+3)^{1/2}$

7 a $(x^2+x)^3$ **b** $(x-x^3)^2$ **c** $(x^2+2x)^{-1}$

8 $f(x) = (2x + 1)^3$. Find the value of: **a** $f'(1)$ **b** $f'(-1)$.

9 $f(x) = (1 - x)^4$. Find the value of: **a** $f'(0)$ **b** $f'(1)$.

10 Find the equation of the tangent to the curve $y = (x^2 + 9)^{1/2}$ at the point where $x = 4$.

11 Find the equation of the tangent to the curve $y = \sqrt{(x^2 + 16)}$ at the point where $x = -3$.

12 Find the stationary point on the curve $y = 9x - (2x - 1)^{3/2}$, and determine its nature.

EXERCISE 3B

In questions **1–5**, differentiate with respect to the relevant variables, and express the answers with positive indices.

1 a $(1 - x)^5$ **b** $\dfrac{1}{1 + 2x}$ **c** $\dfrac{2}{(1 - 3x)^2}$

2 a $\sqrt[3]{(1 + 6x)}$ **b** $\dfrac{3}{\sqrt[3]{(9 - x)}}$ **c** $\left(1 + \dfrac{1}{u}\right)^4$

3 a $5(x^2 + x + 1)^2$ **b** $\dfrac{1}{y^2 - y - 1}$ **c** $\sqrt{(2z^2 - 4z + 6)}$

4 a $\sqrt{x} + \sqrt{(x + 1)}$ **b** $\dfrac{1}{2x} + \dfrac{1}{2x - 1}$

5 a $\left(x + 1 + \dfrac{1}{x}\right)^2$ **b** $\sqrt{((y - 2)(y + 1))}$

6 $f(x) = 2(3x - 4)^4$. Find the value of $f'(1)$.

7 $g(x) = (3 - 2x + x^2)^3$. Find the value of $g'(1)$.

8 Find the stationary value of the function $f(x) = 8x - (2x - 1)^{4/3}$, and determine its nature.

9 Find the equation of the tangent to the curve $y = 1 - \dfrac{1}{x + 1}$ at the point where $x = -\frac{1}{2}$.

10 In a model of a lung, air is drawn from a box, and the spherical balloon expands.

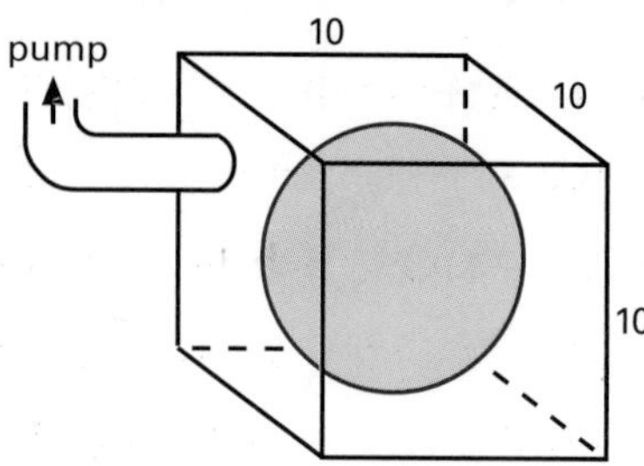

a Show that when the unoccupied space in the box is V cm^3, the radius r cm of the balloon is $r = \left[\dfrac{3}{4\pi}(1000 - V)\right]^{1/3}$.

(For a sphere, $V = \frac{4}{3}\pi r^3$.)

b Find an expression for $\dfrac{dr}{dV}$, and calculate its value, correct to 2 significant figures, when $V = 600$.

The chain rule for differentiation – trigonometric functions

The chain rule can be used in the same way here:

$\frac{d}{dx}\sin(\text{- - -}) = \cos(\text{- - -})\frac{d}{dx}(\text{- - -})$, and $\frac{d}{dx}\cos(\text{- - -}) = -\sin(\text{- - -})\frac{d}{dx}(\text{- - -})$

Examples

1 $\frac{d}{dx}\sin 3x = \cos 3x\frac{d}{dx}(3x) = 3\cos 3x$

2 $\frac{d}{dx}\sin^3 x = 3\sin^2 x\frac{d}{dx}(\sin x) = 3\sin^2 x\cos x$

3 $\frac{d}{dx}\cos(2x+3) = -\sin(2x+3) \times 2 = -2\sin(2x+3)$

a Display the graphs $y = \sin 2x$ and $y = (\sin 2(x + 0.01) - \sin 2x)/0.01$.

b As the second graph is approximately the graph of the derived function of $\sin 2x$, deduce the equation of the derived function.

EXERCISE 4A

Differentiate the following (p and q are constants in **3a**, **4a** and **8a**).

1 a $\sin 2x$ **b** $\sin 4x$ **c** $\sin\frac{1}{2}x$

2 a $\cos 3x$ **b** $\cos 5x$ **c** $\cos\frac{1}{2}x$

3 a $\sin(px+q)$ **b** $\sin(2x-3)$ **c** $\sin(5-x)$

4 a $\cos(px+q)$ **b** $\cos(3x-1)$ **c** $\cos(1-x)$

5 a $\sin(x^2-1)$ **b** $\cos(1-x^2)$ **c** $\sqrt{\sin x}$

6 a $\frac{1}{\sin t}$ **b** $\frac{2}{\cos t}$ **c** $\frac{3}{4\sin t}$

7 a $\sin^2 x$ **b** $\cos^2 x$ **c** $\sin^4 x$

8 a $\sin px + \cos qx$ **b** $\sin^2 u + \cos^2 u$

9 a $\sin^3 x$ **b** $\cos^4 x$ **c** $\sin 7x$

10 a $(1+\sin x)^2$ **b** $(4-3\cos x)^2$

11 a $\sqrt{(1+\sin x)}$ **b** $\sqrt{(1+\cos x)}$. Express your answers in root form.

12 a $2\cos^2 x - 1$ **b** $1 - 2\sin^2 x$ **c** $2\sin x\cos x$

13 a $\frac{1}{x} - \frac{1}{\sqrt{\sin x}}$ **b** $\frac{1}{2x} - \frac{1}{\sqrt{\cos x}}$. Express your answers with positive indices.

EXERCISE 4B

1 Given $f(x) = (1 + \sin x)^2$, calculate $f'(x)$ at:

a $x = 0$ **b** $x = \frac{\pi}{2}$ **c** $x = \pi$.

2 $f(x) = x + \sin x$.

a Show that the graph of f has a point of inflexion at $x = \pi$.

b Explain why f is a never decreasing function.

3 $f(x) = x - \cos x$, $0 \leqslant x \leqslant 2\pi$. Find the stationary point of the graph of f, and investigate its nature.

4 **a** Find:

(i) the gradients of the tangents to the curve $y = \sin x$ at $x = 0$ and $x = \pi$

(ii) the angle between these tangents.

b Show that:

(i) the equation of the tangent at $x = \pi$ is $x + y = \pi$

(ii) if this tangent cuts the x-axis at A and the y-axis at B, then $AB = \pi\sqrt{2}$ in length.

5 The gradients of the tangents at $x = \frac{\pi}{3}$ to the curves $y = \sin x$ and $y = \sin 2x$ are m_1 and m_2.

a Find the values of m_1 and m_2.

b Calculate the acute angle between the tangents, to the nearest degree.

6 **a** Show that the graphs $y = \sin x$ and $y = \cos x$ intersect at $x = \frac{\pi}{4}$.

b Find the gradients of the tangents to the curves at this point.

c Calculate the acute angle between the tangents, to the nearest degree.

7 **a** Show that the curve $y = \sin x + \cos x$ has stationary points where $\tan x = 1$.

b Find the SPs, and their nature, for $0 \leqslant x \leqslant 2\pi$.

c Sketch the curve for $0 \leqslant x \leqslant 2\pi$.

Further integration

So far, this chapter has extended *differentiation* to trigonometric and composite functions. We now extend *integration* to deal with trigonometric and composite functions also.

> *(i) A standard integral*
>
> $\frac{d}{dx}(ax+b)^{n+1} = (n+1)(ax+b)^n a$, so $\int (ax+b)^n \, dx = \frac{(ax+b)^{n+1}}{(n+1)a} + c$,
>
> where a, b and n are constants with $a \neq 0$ and $n \neq -1$.
>
> *Example* $\int (2x+3)^{1/2} \, dx = \frac{(2x+3)^{3/2}}{\frac{3}{2} \times 2} + c = \frac{1}{3}(2x+3)^{3/2} + c$

EXERCISE 5

1 Copy and complete:

a $\int (2x-7)^3 \, dx = \frac{(2x-7)^4}{4 \times \ldots} + c = \ldots$

b $\int (3-6x)^{-1/2} \, dx = \frac{(3-6x)^{1/2}}{\frac{1}{2} \times \ldots} + c = \ldots$

Integrate in questions **2–6**.

2 a $(x+1)^4$ **b** $(2x+1)^3$ **c** $(3x-2)^2$

3 a $(x-3)^4$ **b** $(3-x)^4$ **c** $(1-2x)^2$

4 a $(5x+4)^3$ **b** $(4x-3)^6$ **c** $(2-3x)^5$

5 a $(x+5)^{-2}$ **b** $(3x-2)^{-4}$ **c** $(5-2x)^{-3}$

6 a $(2x+1)^{1/2}$ **b** $(3x-7)^{4/3}$ **c** $(1-4x)^{-3/2}$

7 Find:

a $\int (u-3)^{-2} \, du$ **b** $\int \sqrt{(v+4)} \, dv$ **c** $\int \frac{dt}{(2t+3)^4}$ **d** $\int \frac{dx}{\sqrt{(4x-1)}}$

Evaluate the integrals in questions **8–10**.

8 a $\int_0^1 (2x+1)^3 \, dx$ **b** $\int_{-1}^1 (1-x)^3 \, dx$

9 a $\int_0^4 \sqrt{(4-x)} \, dx$ **b** $\int_1^2 \frac{dx}{(x+2)^2}$

10 a $\int_{-1}^3 \frac{dx}{\sqrt{(2x+3)}}$ **b** $\int_{-1}^4 (3x+4)^{3/2} \, dx$

11 Find the general solution of:

a $\dfrac{dy}{dx} = (3 - 4x)^5$ **b** $\dfrac{du}{dt} = \sqrt{(2t + 1)}$

c $\dfrac{dy}{dv} = \dfrac{1}{(1 - 2v)^3}$ **d** $\dfrac{dr}{dt} = \dfrac{2}{\sqrt[3]{(1 - t)}}$

12 Find the particular solution of each differential equation:

a $\dfrac{dy}{dx} = \dfrac{1}{(x - 1)^2}$, given that $y = 3$ when $x = 2$

b $\dfrac{dy}{dx} = \sqrt{(x + 1)}$, given that $y = 20$ when $x = 8$.

(ii) Integrals of trigonometric functions

1 $\dfrac{d}{dx}(\sin x) = \cos x$, so $\displaystyle\int \cos x \, dx = \sin x + c$

2 $\dfrac{d}{dx}(\cos x) = -\sin x$, so $\displaystyle\int \sin x \, dx = -\cos x + c$

As extensions of these, you can easily check by differentiation that where a and b are constants ($a \neq 0$):

3 $\displaystyle\int \cos(ax + b)\, dx = \frac{1}{a}\sin(ax + b) + c$

4 $\displaystyle\int \sin(ax + b)\, dx = -\frac{1}{a}\cos(ax + b) + c$

Examples

1 $\displaystyle\int (\sin x + 5)\, dx = -\cos x + 5x + c$

2 $\displaystyle\int 3\cos\left(6x + \frac{\pi}{10}\right) dx = 3 \times \tfrac{1}{6}\sin\left(6x + \frac{\pi}{10}\right) + c = \tfrac{1}{2}\sin\left(6x + \frac{\pi}{10}\right) + c$

EXERCISE 6

Integrate in questions **1–5**.

1 a $\sin x$ **b** $\cos x$ **c** $3\cos x$ **d** $4\sin x$

2 a $\cos 2x$ **b** $\sin 3x$ **c** $\cos 5x$

3 a $4\cos 4x$ **b** $6\sin 2x$ **c** $3\cos 3x$

4 a $-\sin 6x$ **b** $-\cos 2x$ **c** $a\cos ax$

5 a $\cos \tfrac{1}{2}x$ **b** $\sin \tfrac{1}{2}x$ **c** $a\sin ax$

In questions **6–11**, find:

6 a $\int \cos(x+2)\,dx$ **b** $\int \sin(2x-1)\,dx$

7 a $\int \cos(3x-1)\,dx$ **b** $\int \sin(2-x)\,dx$

8 a $\int \sin(3x+4)\,dx$ **b** $\int a\cos(ax+b)\,dx$

9 a $\int (\sin x - \cos x)\,dx$ **b** $\int (2\cos x + 3\sin x)\,dx$

10 a $\int (\sin 2x + \cos 3x)\,dx$ **b** $\int (\cos 5\theta + \sin 3\theta)\,d\theta$

11 a $\int (t^2 + 2\cos 2t)\,dt$ **b** $\int 4\sin(3-4u)\,du$

12 $\cos 2x = 2\cos x^2 - 1 = 1 - 2\sin^2 x$.

a Use this identity to express $\cos^2 x$ in terms of $\cos 2x$ and find $\int \cos^2 x\,dx$.

b Similarly find $\int \sin^2 x\,dx$.

c From **a** and **b** find $\int(\sin^2 x + \cos^2 x)\,dx$. Explain your answer.

13 Using $\sin 2x = 2\sin x\cos x$, find $\int \sin x\cos x\,dx$.

14 Find the general solution of:

a $\frac{dy}{dx} = 2\sin 2x$ **b** $\frac{dy}{dx} = \cos\left(1+\frac{x}{3}\right)$

c $\frac{dy}{dx} = 4\sin\left(2x+\frac{\pi}{3}\right)$ **d** $\frac{dy}{dx} = 6\cos\left(3x-\frac{\pi}{2}\right)$

15 For each of these differential equations find the particular solution satisfying the given conditions.

a $\frac{dy}{dx} = 3\sin 3x$, given that $y = 2$ when $x = \frac{\pi}{3}$

b $\frac{dy}{dt} = \sin\left(t-\frac{\pi}{4}\right) + \cos\left(t-\frac{\pi}{4}\right)$, given that $y = 1$ when $t = \frac{\pi}{4}$.

(iii) Definite trigonometric integrals

Examples Evaluate these integrals. Show the area represented by the integral in **1** in a sketch.

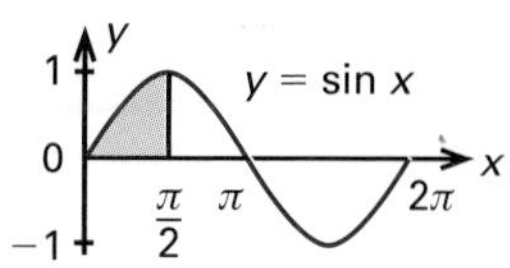

1 $\int_0^{\pi/2} \sin x\,dx = [-\cos x]_0^{\pi/2} = \left(-\cos\frac{\pi}{2}\right) - (-\cos 0) = 0 - (-1) = 1$

2 $\int_{\pi/6}^{\pi/4} (1+\sin 2x)\,dx = \left[x - \tfrac{1}{2}\cos 2x\right]_{\pi/6}^{\pi/4} = \left(\frac{\pi}{4} - \frac{1}{2}\cos\frac{\pi}{2}\right) - \left(\frac{\pi}{6} - \frac{1}{2}\cos\frac{\pi}{3}\right)$

$= \left(\frac{\pi}{4} - 0\right) - \left(\frac{\pi}{6} - \frac{1}{2}\times\frac{1}{2}\right) = \frac{\pi}{12} + \frac{1}{4}.$

EXERCISE 7

1 Check the values of these integrals.

a $\int_0^{\pi/2} \cos x \, dx = 1$ **b** $\int_0^{2\pi} \cos x \, dx = 0$

c $\int_0^{\pi} \sin x \, dx = 2$ **d** $\int_0^{2\pi} \sin x \, dx = 0$

e $\int_{3\pi/2}^{2\pi} \cos x \, dx = 1$ **f** $\int_{\pi/2}^{3\pi/2} \sin x \, dx = 0$

Evaluate the integrals in questions **2–4**.

2 a $\int_0^{\pi/4} \sin 2x \, dx$ **b** $\int_0^{\pi/3} \cos 3x \, dx$

3 a $\int_0^{\pi/4} \cos 2x \, dx$ **b** $\int_0^{\pi/8} \sin 4x \, dx$

4 a $\int_0^{\pi} (\sin t + \cos t) \, dt$ **b** $\int_0^{\pi/4} (\sin 4x + \cos 4x) \, dx$

5 Calculate the area of each shaded region.

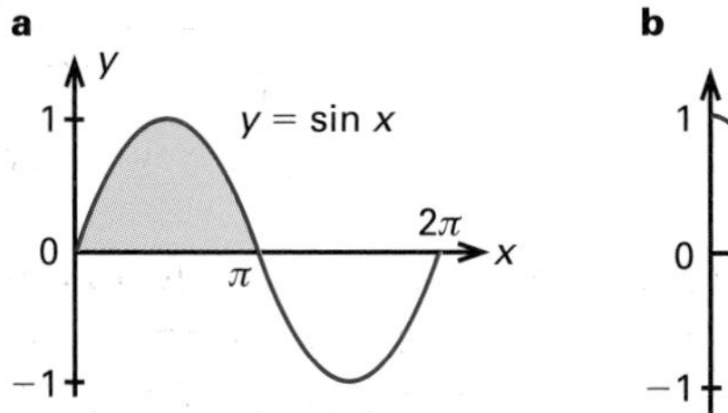

6 Calculate the total area of the shaded region in each diagram.

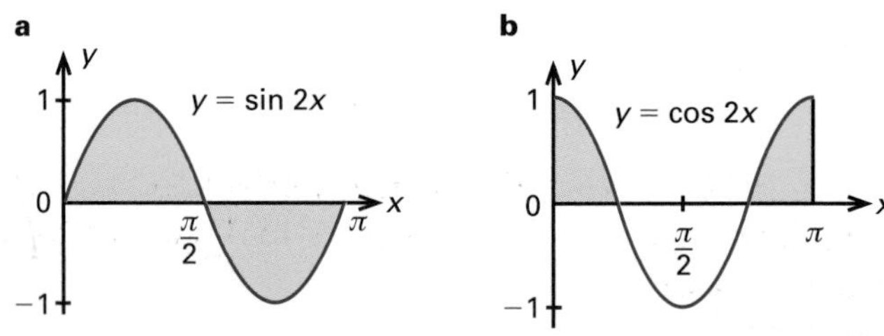

Evaluate the integrals in questions **7** and **8**.

7 a $\int_0^{2\pi} \cos \tfrac{1}{2}x \, dx$ **b** $\int_0^{2\pi} \sin \tfrac{1}{2}x \, dx$

8 a $\int_0^{\pi/4} \cos\left(2t + \frac{\pi}{2}\right) dt$ **b** $\int_{\pi/6}^{\pi/4} \sin\left(2t - \frac{\pi}{3}\right) dt$

9 Show that:

a the curve $y = \sin x$ and the line $y = \frac{2}{\pi}x$ intersect at $(0, 0)$ and $\left(\frac{\pi}{2}, 1\right)$

b the enclosed area is $1 - \frac{\pi}{4}$.

10 **a** Show that these curves intersect at $x = \frac{\pi}{4}$ and $x = \frac{5\pi}{4}$.

b Calculate the areas A and B.

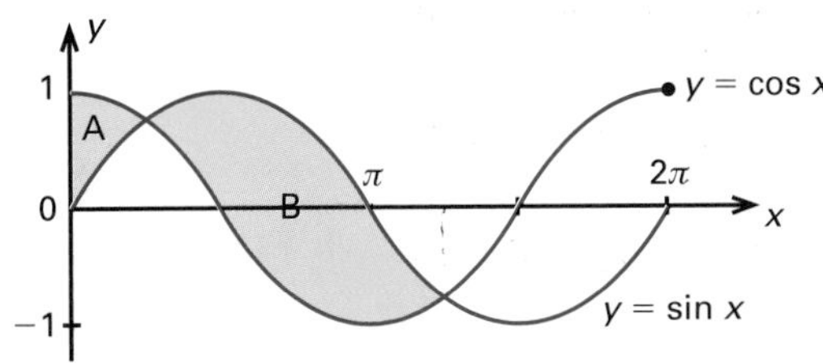

11 Calculate the area enclosed by the x-axis and:

a $y = \cos 3x$, for $0 \leqslant x \leqslant \frac{\pi}{2}$

b $y = \sin 3x$, for $0 \leqslant x \leqslant \frac{\pi}{2}$.

12 **a** Find the x-values at the three points of intersection of the curves $y = \sin x$ and $y = \sin 2x$ for $0 \leqslant x \leqslant \pi$.

b Calculate the areas A and B.

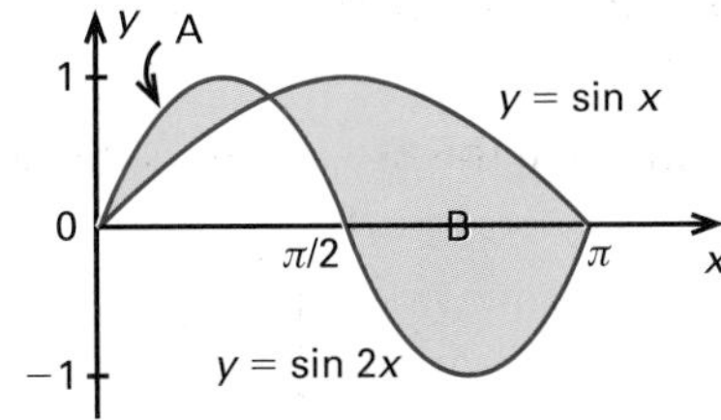

13 **a** Find the x-values of the three points of intersection P, Q, R, in order from left to right, of the curves $y = \sin x$ and $y = \cos 2x$ for $0 < x < 2\pi$.

b Calculate the area enclosed by the curves for values of x from:

(i) P to Q **(ii)** Q to R.

Challenges

1 **a** Writing $\sin 3A = \sin(2A + A)$, and expanding this, show that $\sin^3 A = \frac{1}{4}(3 \sin A - \sin 3A)$.

b Hence integrate $\sin^3 A$.

2 In a similar way, find a formula for $\cos^3 A$, and hence integrate $\cos^3 A$.

CHAPTER 2 REVIEW

1 Differentiate:
a $2\sin x$ **b** $3\cos x$ **c** $5\sin x - 4\cos x$
d $2\cos x + \frac{1}{2x}$ **e** $2\sqrt{x} - 4\sin x$.

2 Write down the value of:
a $\sin\frac{\pi}{6}$ **b** $\cos\frac{3\pi}{2}$
c $\sin\frac{4\pi}{3}$ **d** $\cos 2\pi$.

3 A curve has equation $y = 2\cos x$. Calculate:
a the gradient of the tangent at $x = \frac{\pi}{4}$
b the angle between the tangent and OX, correct to 0.1°
c the equation of the tangent.

4 a Use differentiation to show that the curve $y = 2 + 2\sin x$ has two stationary points for $0 \leqslant x \leqslant 2\pi$, and determine their nature.
b Sketch the curve.

5 Differentiate:
a $(x-5)^2$ **b** $(2x+1)^3$
c $(1-x)^{-2}$ **d** $(x^2+2)^{1/3}$
e $\sqrt{(x-x^3)}$ **f** $\frac{1}{x^4 - x^2 + 1}$.

6 a Show that the function $f(x) = x + 2\cos\frac{1}{2}x$ is never decreasing.
b Find the stationary value of f for $0 \leqslant x \leqslant 2\pi$.

7 a Use differentiation to find the SPs of $f(x) = \cos 2x$, for $0 \leqslant x \leqslant \pi$, and determine their nature.
b Sketch the graph of f, for $0 \leqslant x \leqslant \pi$.

8 Find the stationary value of the function f given by $f(x) = x - 2\sqrt{(x-1)}$, $x \geqslant 1$, and determine its nature.

9 Differentiate:
a $\sin(2x+3)$ **b** $\sin^4 x$
c $\sqrt{\cos x}$ **d** $\frac{1}{x} - \frac{1}{\sin x}$
e $(2-3x)^2 + \cos(2-3x)$.

10 A curve has equation $y = 1 + \cos^2 x$.
a Show that:
(i) $\frac{dy}{dx} = -\sin 2x$
(ii) the equation of the tangent at $x = \frac{\pi}{3}$ is $4y + 2\sqrt{3}x = 5 + \frac{2\pi}{\sqrt{3}}$.
b Find the stationary points, $0 \leqslant x \leqslant \pi$, and their nature.

11 Integrate:
a $x^2 + x + 1$ **b** $x^{1/2} + x^{-2}$
c $(x+3)^4$ **d** $\frac{1}{(x-1)^3}$
e $(3t+5)^3$ **f** $(1-4v)^2$
g $(6x-3)^{1/2}$ **h** $\frac{1}{\sqrt{(2x+1)}}$.

12 Find:
a $\int 4\sin x\,dx$
b $\int(\cos x - \sin x)\,dx$
c $\int \cos 2u\,du$
d $\int \sin 3x\,dx$
e $\int(\cos 5x - \sin 2x)\,dx$
f $\int \cos(3t+2)\,dt$.

13 Find $f(x)$, given:
a $f'(x) = 6x^2 - 2\sin 6x$
b $f'(x) = 2 + \cos 4x$.

14 Find the general solution of:
a $\frac{dy}{dx} = 3 - 2\sin 2x$
b $\frac{dy}{dx} = 2\cos 4x - 3\sin 3x$.

15 Evaluate:
a $\int_{-1}^{4} \frac{dt}{\sqrt{(3t+4)}}$ **b** $\int_{\pi/6}^{\pi/3} \sin 3u\,du$.

16 Calculate $\int_0^{\pi} \cos 2x\,dx$, and use a sketch to explain the result.

17 Calculate the area enclosed by the x-axis, the curve $y = 6\cos 3x$ and the line $x = -\frac{\pi}{18}$.

CHAPTER 2 SUMMARY

1 In calculus, angles are measured in radians

π radians $= 180°$

The sine and cosine curves:

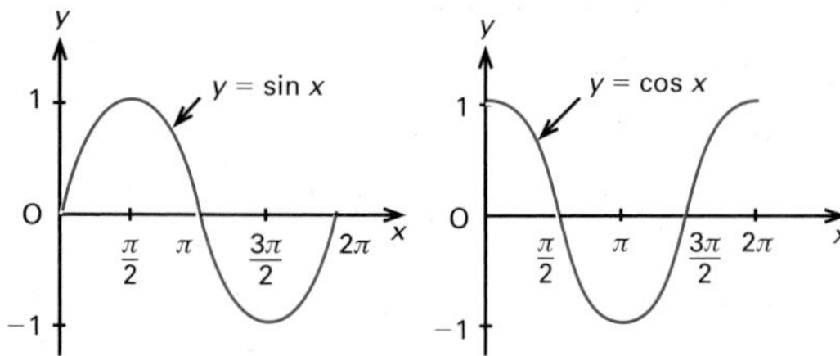

Special angles:

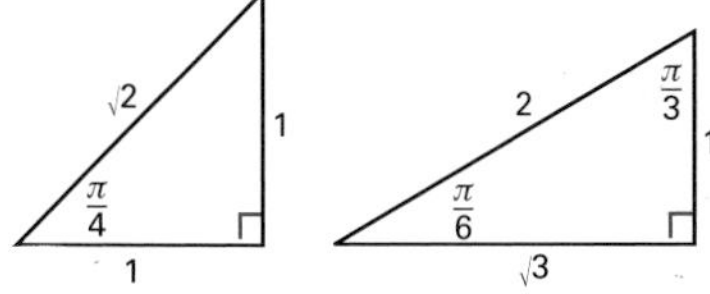

2 The derivatives of sin x and cos x

$$\frac{d}{dx}(\sin x) = \cos x;$$

$$\frac{d}{dx}(\cos x) = -\sin x$$

3 The chain rule for differentiating composite functions

If $y = f(g(x))$ and $u = g(x)$, then

$$\frac{dy}{dx} = \frac{dy}{du}\frac{du}{dx} \text{ or } \frac{d}{dx} f(\ldots) = f'(\ldots)\frac{d}{dx}(\ldots)$$

For example,

$$\frac{d}{dx}(\ldots)^n = n(\ldots)^{n-1} \times \frac{d}{dx}(\ldots),$$

$$\text{so } \frac{d}{dx}(ax+b)^n = na(ax+b)^{n-1}$$

$$\frac{d}{dx}\sin(\ldots) = \cos(\ldots) \times \frac{d}{dx}(\ldots)$$

$$\frac{d}{dx}\cos(\ldots) = -\sin(\ldots) \times \frac{d}{dx}(\ldots)$$

4 Some special integrals

$$\int (ax+b)^n\,dx = \frac{(ax+b)^{n+1}}{(n+1)a} + c,\ n \neq -1,\ a \neq 0.$$

$$\int \cos x\,dx = \sin x + c; \quad \int \sin x\,dx = -\cos x + c$$

$$\int \cos(ax+b)\,dx = \frac{1}{a}\sin(ax+b) + c,\ a \neq 0$$

$$\int \sin(ax+b)\,dx = -\frac{1}{a}\cos(ax+b) + c,\ a \neq 0$$

3 The Exponential and Logarithmic Functions

Growth and decay

Harry puts £100 into a bank account which pays interest at the rate of 12% per annum. His money increases by 12%, that is by a factor of 1.12 each year.
If £$A(n)$ is the amount in his account after n years, then:

$A(0) = 100 \qquad = 100 \times 1.12^0$
$A(1) = A(0) \times 1.12 = 100 \times 1.12 \qquad = 100 \times 1.12^1$
$A(2) = A(1) \times 1.12 = 100 \times 1.12 \times 1.12 \qquad = 100 \times 1.12^2$
$\dots \qquad \dots$
$A(n) = 100 \times 1.12^n$

This is a growth function.

EXERCISE 1 (Growth)

1 Use the function $A(n) = 100 \times 1.12^n$ to calculate the amount in Harry's account after:
a 1 year **b** 2 years **c** 5 years **d** 10 years.

2 Sally puts £100 in a bank account which gives interest of 7% per annum.
a Copy and complete this growth function for the amount in her account after n years: $A(n) = 100 \times \cdots$
b Show that she will have nearly doubled her money in ten years.

3 The Safe and Secure Building Society calculates the amount in Asha's account by using the function $A(n) = 600 \times 1.1^n$.
a How much did Asha deposit?
b What rate of interest were they paying?
c How much would she have after three years?

4 The 1990 census showed that Newtown's population was 70 000, and that it was growing at the rate of 2% per annum.
a Calculate the population one year later.
b Which of the following gives the population after n years?
(i) $P(n) = 1.02^n$
(ii) $P(n) = 70\,000 \times 1.02^n$
(iii) $P(n) = 70\,000 \times 0.02^n$
c What would the population be in the year 2000, correct to 2 significant figures?

5 Ulanda's population in 1990 was 100 million, and was growing at 6% per annum.
a Construct a growth function for the population in millions n years later.
b Estimate the population in the year 2000.

6 Some cells reproduce very rapidly. One population of 500 cells increases by 80% per hour.
a Construct a growth function for the number of cells after h hours.
b Estimate the number of cells after 6 hours.

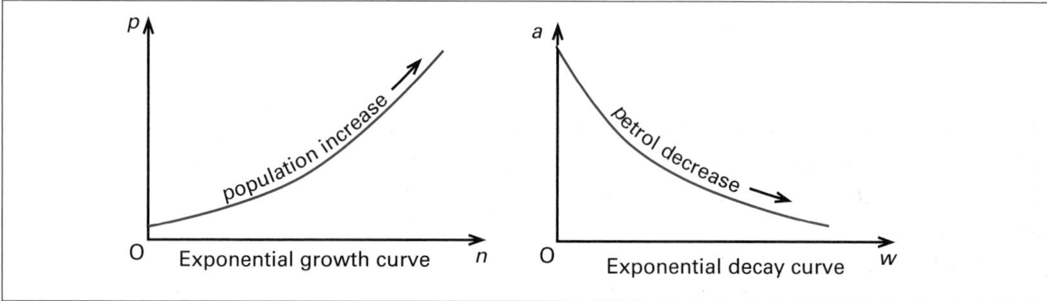

a Display the graph of the decay function $y = 5(0.8)^x$, $x \geqslant 0$.
b Explore other similar types of graph.

EXERCISE 2 (Decay)

1 Leaving the cap off the petrol can was a big mistake, as the petrol evaporated at the rate of 20% per week. Initially the can was full.
The amount of petrol in the can, in litres, after w weeks is given by $A(w) = 5(0.8)^w$, where A is a decay function.
Calculate the amount of petrol after:
a 1 week **b** 10 weeks, correct to 2 decimal places.

2 An open can is filled with 1000 ml of fluid which evaporates at the rate of 40% per week. The amount of fluid, in ml, after w weeks is $A(w) = 1000(0.6)^w$.
a How much is left after 1 week?
b Use 'trial and improvement' to find how many weeks it will take for the volume of fluid to be less than 1 ml.

3 8000 gallons of oil are lost in an oil spill in Blue Sky Bay. At the beginning of each week a filter plant removes 67% of the oil present.
a Construct a decay function for the amount of oil in the bay, in gallons, after x weeks: $A(x) = \cdots (0.33)^x$.
b Calculate the amount after: **(i)** 1 week **(ii)** 4 weeks.
c After how many complete weeks will there be less than 10 gallons left?

4 Radium has a half-life of 1600 years. This means that a given mass of radium will decay steadily and be halved in 1600 years.

a Check that, starting with 5 g of radium, the decay function for the mass after t years is $R(t) = 5(0.5)^{t/1600}$.

b Calculate its mass after:

(i) 400 years **(ii)** 16 000 years, to the nearest milligram.

5 A radioactive element has a half-life of only 20 years.

a Write down a decay function for 8 g after t years, $E(t) = \cdots (\cdots)^{t/20}$, and check it for $t = 20$.

b Calculate the mass after 10 years, to the nearest gram.

6 Plutonium 239 has a half-life of 24 400 years.

a Construct a decay function for 1 kg of plutonium.

b Estimate its mass after 100 000 years, to the nearest gram.

7 The half-life of C^{14}, the radioactive form of carbon, is 5720 years.

a If 1 g is originally present, construct the function that models the amount left after t years.

b Bones discovered in an archaeological dig contain 25% of their original C^{14} content. Check that the bones are about 11 440 years old.

A special exponential function – the number e

What do you think happens to the value of $\left(1 + \frac{1}{n}\right)^n$ as n becomes larger and larger?

$\frac{1}{n}$ appears to 'fight against' $(\ldots)^n$. There is a surprising outcome. Investigate it by copying and completing this table (1–10 to 2 decimal places, 100–1 000 000 to as many as your calculator gives).

n	1	2	3	4	5	10	100	1000	1 000 000
$\left(1 + \frac{1}{n}\right)^n$	2								

What can you now say about the value of $\left(1 + \frac{1}{n}\right)^n$ as $n \to \infty$?

In fact, $\lim\limits_{n\to\infty}\left(1 + \frac{1}{n}\right)^n$ does exist, and is denoted by the letter e. Use the $\boxed{e^x}$ key, with $x = 1$, to check that $e = 2.718\,281\,828$, correct to 10 significant figures. e is a never-ending decimal like π (3.141 592 ...), another well-known mathematical constant. $f(x) = e^x$ is called the exponential function, base e, often denoted by $\exp(x)$.

a Display the graph $y = 2^x$, $-2 \leqslant x \leqslant 2$ and $0 \leqslant y \leqslant 4$, and its approximate derivative $y = (2^{(x+0.01)} - 2^x)/0.01$. Compare and comment on the graphs.

b Repeat **a** for the graph $y = 3^x$ and its derived graph $y = (3^{(x+0.01)} - 3^x)/0.01$.

c Can you find a number a, $2 < a < 3$, where the derived graph of $y = a^x$ is $y = a^x$ itself? Investigate this by drawing $y = a^x$ and $y = (a^{(x+0.01)} - a^x)/0.01$ for $a = 2.5, 2.8; 2.6, 2.7$; etc.

In fact the function and its derivative are equal when $a = 2.718\,281\,828\ldots$, that is, the number e. If $f(x) = e^x$, $f'(x) = e^x$ also.

EXERCISE 3

1 a Write down the value of e (e^1) as accurately as the $\boxed{e^x}$ key on your calculator gives it.

b Round the value to 4 significant figures.

2 Calculate, correct to 3 significant figures:

a e^2 **b** e^{-1} **c** e^{20}.

3 a Copy and complete this table:

x	-2	-1	0	1	2	2.5	3	3.5	4
e^x	0.14								

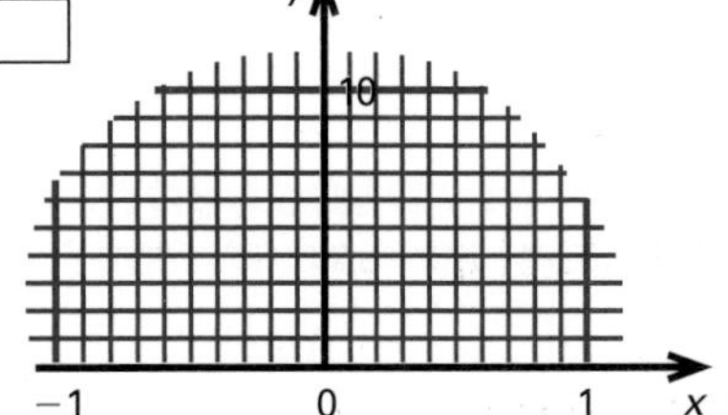

b On squared paper draw the graph $y = e^x$ for $-2 \leqslant x \leqslant 4$, for the scales shown.

c Use your graph to estimate values of:

(i) $e^{1.6}$ (ii) $e^{2.8}$ (iii) $e^{3.2}$ (iv) $e^{-0.5}$.

d Check your answers to **c** by calculator.

4 Lengths of chain are hung between posts in the park.

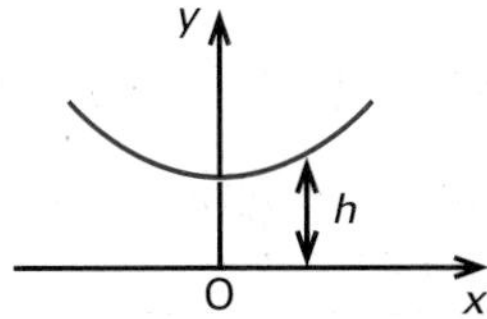

The height, h feet, of a point on the curve above the x-axis is given by $h(x) = 3(e^{x/3} + e^{-x/3})$. Calculate its height when:

a $x = 0$ **b** $x = 3$, correct to 2 decimal places.

5 The speed at which a rumour spreads in a school is exponential. Central High School has 1000 students. If two of them start a rumour, then t days later N students will have heard it, where $N(t) = 2e^{1.24t}$.

a Check that at the beginning, when $t = 0$, only two students are involved.

b Taking Monday as $t = 1$, how many students have heard the rumour by Friday?

6 Due to inflation, prices increase annually. The price, P, of items after t years is given by $P(t) = P_0 e^{0.05t}$, where P_0 is the original price.

a If a $\frac{1}{2}$ litre of milk costs 35p now, how much will it cost in one year's time?
b If a rail fare is £20 now, how much will it be in ten years?

7 A van hire company calculates the depreciation in the value of its vans using the formula $V(t) = V_0 e^{-0.16t}$.

a A new van costs £18 000. Calculate its value after five years.
b How much does the van's value fall during the fifth year?

8 Atmospheric pressure changes with altitude according to the formula $A(h) = 1.03e^{-0.0001h}$, where $A(h)$ is the pressure in kg/cm^2 h metres above sea-level.

a What is the pressure at sea-level?
b Mount Everest is 8848 m high. Calculate the atmospheric pressure at the top, correct to 3 significant figures.

9 A charge q_0 on a condenser of capacity C discharges through a resistance R. The charge $q(t)$ at time t seconds is given by $q(t) = q_0 e^{-t/RC}$.

a Show in a sketch how $q(t)$ varies with t.
b Find t in the form kRC, k a constant, when the charge is:
(i) $\frac{1}{2}q_0$ **(ii)** $\frac{1}{10}q_0$.

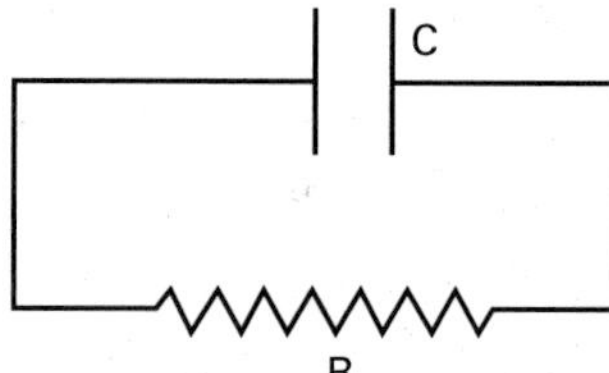

Linking the exponential function and the logarithmic function

In the chapter on Algebraic Functions and Graphs in Unit 1 we saw that the function $f(x) = a^x$ has an inverse function, called the logarithmic function to base a, denoted by $\log_a$, so that $y = a^x \Leftrightarrow x = \log_a y$. Using the form $y = a^x \Rightarrow \log_a y = x$:
(i) $1 = a^0 \Rightarrow \log_a 1 = 0$ (log 1 to any base = 0)
(ii) $a = a^1 \Rightarrow \log_a a = 1$ (the log of a number to that base = 1)

Examples **1** $25 = 5^2 \Rightarrow \log_5 25 = 2$, in logarithmic form
2 $\frac{1}{2} = 2^{-1} \Rightarrow \log_2 (\frac{1}{2}) = -1$
3 $\log_3 9 = 2 \Rightarrow 9 = 3^2$, in exponential form

EXERCISE 4

1 Write each of the following in logarithmic form. For example, $100 = 10^2 \Rightarrow \log_{10} 100 = 2$. Then use the log key on your calculator to check your answer.

a $10\,000 = 10^4$ **b** $1000 = 10^3$ **c** $10 = 10^1$
d $1 = 10^0$ **e** $0.1 = 10^{-1}$ **f** $0.01 = 10^{-2}$

Reminder
$y = a^x \Leftrightarrow \log_a y = x$
x is the index of the power a^x.

2 Write in logarithmic form.

a $81 = 3^4$ **b** $9 = 3^2$ **c** $32 = 2^5$ **d** $64 = 4^3$
e $36 = 6^2$ **f** $5 = 5^1$ **g** $1 = 6^0$ **h** $\frac{1}{2} = 2^{-1}$
i $\frac{1}{9} = 3^{-2}$ **j** $x^2 = 12$ **k** $y^4 = 20$ **l** $z^{1/2} = 10$

3 Write in exponential form, and check. For example, $\log_7 49 = 2$, so $49 = 7^2$.

a $\log_2 4 = 2$ **b** $\log_4 16 = 2$ **c** $\log_3 27 = 3$
d $\log_5 5 = 1$ **e** $\log_6 1 = 0$ **f** $\log_{10} 100 = 2$

4 Write in exponential form, and check where you can.

a $\log_9 3 = \frac{1}{2}$ **b** $\log_8 4 = \frac{2}{3}$ **c** $\log_{100} 10 = \frac{1}{2}$
d $\log_a a = 1$ **e** $\log_a 1 = 0$ **f** $\log_a c = b$

5 Express in exponential form, then solve each equation for x.

a $\log_x 9 = 2$ **b** $\log_x 125 = 3$ **c** $\log_x 64 = 2$
d $\log_x 7 = 1$ **e** $\log_x \frac{1}{4} = 2$ **f** $\log_2 x = 3$
g $\log_4 x = 0.5$ **h** $\log_2 x = 6$ **i** $\log_7 x = -1$
j $\log_{10} x = -2$ **k** $\log_2 4 = x$ **l** $\log_3 81 = x$
m $\log_4 1 = x$ **n** $\log_5 5 = x$ **o** $\log_{10} 10^6 = x$

6 Find the values of these logarithms.

a $\log_3 27$ **b** $\log_4 64$ **c** $\log_4 2$ **d** $\log_3 (\frac{1}{9})$

7 Use the [log] key on your calculator to find the value, correct to 2 decimal places of:

a $\log_{10} 6$ **b** $\log_{10} 29$ **c** $\log_{10} 0.3$ **d** $\log_{10} 0.07$.

8 If $\log_{10} x = 0.2$, then $x = 10^{0.2} = 1.58$, correct to 2 decimal places. In the same way, calculate x, given:

a $\log_{10} x = 0.5$ **b** $\log_{10} x = 1.2$ **c** $\log_{10} x = 0.01$.

9 **a** Use this table of values, and the scales shown, to draw the graph $y = \log_{10} x$ for $0.1 \leqslant x \leqslant 6$.

x	0.1	0.2	0.5	1	2	3	4	5	6
$\log_{10} x$		−0.70							0.78

b (i) Is $f(x) = \log_{10} x$ an increasing or a decreasing function?

(ii) Copy and complete: If $x_1 > x_2$, then $\log_{10} x_1 \ldots \log_{10} x_2$.

c Use your calculator to explore the values of $\log_{10} x$ as:

(i) $x \to 0$ (ii) $x \to \infty$.

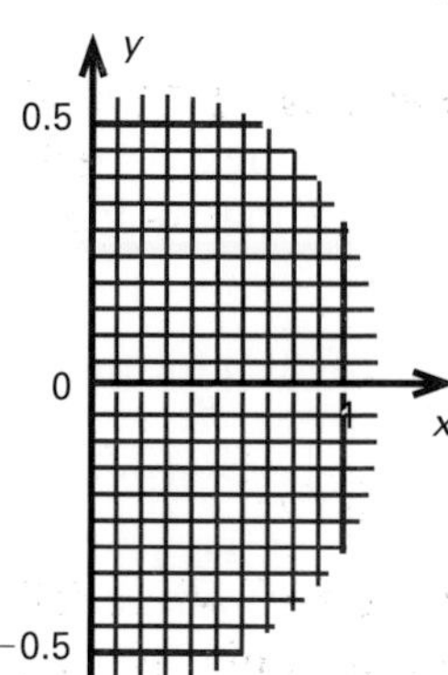

10 **a** Use your graph to estimate, correct to 1 decimal place, the value of x when:

(i) $\log_{10} x = 0.2$ (ii) $\log_{10} x = 0.5$ (iii) $\log_{10} x = 0.7$.

b Check your answers to part **a** by calculator.

Rules of logarithms

Do you remember these rules of indices?

1 $a^m \times a^n = a^{m+n}$ **2** $a^m \div a^n = a^{m-n}$ **3** $(a^m)^p = a^{mp}$

There are three corresponding rules for logarithms.

1 $\log_a xy = \log_a x + \log_a y$ **2** $\log_a \frac{x}{y} = \log_a x - \log_a y$ **3** $\log_a x^p = p \log_a x$

Proofs

Let $\log_a x = m$ and $\log_a y = n$, so that $x = a^m$ and $y = a^n$.

1 $xy = a^m \times a^n = a^{m+n}$

so $\log_a xy = m + n$

$= \log_a x + \log_a y$

2 $\frac{x}{y} = a^m \div a^n = a^{m-n}$

so $\log_a \frac{x}{y} = m - n$

$= \log_a x - \log_a y$

3 $x^p = (a^m)^p = a^{mp}$

so $\log_a x^p = mp$

$= p \log_a x$

Example 1

$\log_3 12 + \log_3 3 - \log_3 4$

$= \log_3 \left(\frac{12 \times 3}{4}\right)$

$= \log_3 9$

$= 2$

Example 2

$2 \log_a 4 - 4 \log_a 2$

$= 2 \log_a 2^2 - 4 \log_a 2$

$= 4 \log_a 2 - 4 \log_a 2$

$= 0$

Example 3

$\log_2 \left(\frac{1}{x}\right)$

$= \log_2 1 - \log_2 x$

$= 0 - \log_2 x$

$= -\log_2 x$

EXERCISE 5

1 Simplify the following (all have the same base). For example,
$\log 5 + \log 2 = \log (5 \times 2) = \log 10$, and $\log 12 - \log 3 = \log \left(\frac{12}{3}\right) = \log 4$.

a $\log 7 + \log 2$ **b** $\log 5 + \log 3$ **c** $\log 10 + \log 1$
d $\log 2 + \log 3 + \log 4$ **e** $\log 12 - \log 2$
f $\log 8 - \log 4$ **g** $\log 6 + \log 1 - \log 3$

2 Simplify the following. For example, $\log 50 - 2 \log 5 = \log 50 - \log 5^2 = \log \left(\frac{50}{25}\right) = \log 2$.

a $\log 2 + 2 \log 3$ **b** $\log 4 + 3 \log 2$ **c** $\log 8 - 2 \log 2$
d $\log 25 - \log 5$ **e** $\log 27 - 3 \log 3$ **f** $2 \log 3 + 3 \log 2$

3 Simplify, then evaluate:

a $\log_8 2 + \log_8 4$ **b** $\log_6 2 + \log_6 3$ **c** $\log_5 100 - \log_5 4$
d $\log_4 18 - \log_4 9$ **e** $2 \log_2 4 - 3 \log_2 2$ **f** $2 \log_6 2 + 2 \log_6 3$
g $2 \log_{10} 5 + 2 \log_{10} 2$ **h** $3 \log_3 3 + \frac{1}{2} \log_3 9$ **i** $5 \log_8 2 + \log_8 4 - \log_8 16$
j $\log_2 \left(\frac{1}{2}\right) - \log_2 \left(\frac{1}{4}\right)$

4 Solve for x:

a $\log_a x + \log_a 2 = \log_a 10$ **b** $\log_a x - \log_a 5 = \log_a 20$

c $\log_a x + 3\log_a 3 = \log_a 9$

5 In an earthquake, the amount of energy released (E) is given by a number (R) on the Richter scale. For two earthquakes, $\log_{10}\left(\frac{E_1}{E_2}\right) = 1.5(R_1 - R_2)$. Calculate E_1, given that $E_2 = 10^6$, $R_2 = 4.3$ and $R_1 = 6.3$.

6 The volume of sound (loudness) is measured in decibels. If I_0 is the intensity of sound you can just hear, and I is the intensity for x decibels, then $10\log_{10}\left(\frac{I}{I_0}\right) = x$. Calculate I when $I_0 = 25$ and $x = 20$.

Challenge

A new key to open a new door!

a Using the e^x and ln keys on your calculator, copy and complete these tables.

x	0	0.5	1	1.25	1.5	1.75
e^x						

x	1	2	3	4	5	6
$\ln x$						

b Draw the graphs $y = e^x$ and $y = \ln x$ on the same sheet of 2 mm squared paper, using a scale of 2 cm to 1 unit on each axis.

c Draw the line of symmetry. What is its equation?

d What does the symmetry tell you about the functions e^x and $\ln x$? Investigate the connection between them.

Solving exponential equations

Example 1 Solve $5^x = 4$, correct to 2 decimal places.

Take logarithms to base 10 of both sides.

$$\log_{10} 5^x = \log_{10} 4$$

$$x\log_{10} 5 = \log_{10} 4$$

$$x = \frac{\log_{10} 4}{\log_{10} 5} = 0.86$$

Example 2 A formula for calculating compound interest is $A = PR^n$. Calculate n when $A = 250$, $P = 100$ and $R = 1.08$.

$A = PR^n$, so $250 = 100 \times 1.08^n$.

$$1.08^n = 2.5$$

$$n\log_{10} 1.08 = \log_{10} 2.5$$

$$n = \frac{\log_{10} 2.5}{\log_{10} 1.08} = 11.91$$

EXERCISE 6

1 Solve these equations, correct to 2 decimal places.
a $4^x = 25$ **b** $1.5^x = 7.5$ **c** $2^x = 0.3$
d $1.2^x = \pi$ **e** $0.7^x = 0.19$ **f** $5^x = 10^6$

2 Express each equation in the form $a^x = \ldots$, and then solve it, correct to 2 decimal places.
a $10 \times 3^x = 40$ **b** $250 \times 1.2^x = 1000$
c $8 \times 0.6^x = 16$ **d** $123 = 19 \times 1.5^x$

3 Find the least positive integer n for which:
a $3^n > 1000$ **b** $5^n > 6^7$ **c** $10^n > 2^{10}$.

4 A house is worth £150 000, and its value increases by 6% per annum. After t years its value is given by $V(t) = 150\,000(1.06)^t$.
a Calculate its value after 5 years.
b After how many years will its value exceed £300 000 for the first time?

5 The number of pairs of breeding gulls in a nature reserve is given by $P(t) = 500(1.09)^t$, where t is the time in years since records began.
a How many pairs were there initially?
b At what annual rate is the population increasing?
c After how many years will the population exceed 2000 pairs for the first time?

6 The number of dodos was given by $D(t) = 500(0.65)^t$, t years after records began. After how many years was the population reduced to fewer than two birds, and so to extinction?

7 $x = 20^{19}$ and $y = 19^{20}$. Find whether $x > y$ or $y > x$ by means of:
a the $\boxed{y^x}$ key on your calculator
b taking logarithms of both sides of the equation.

When the growth or decay base is e, the calculation is simpler if logarithms to base e (instead of 10), given by the $\boxed{\ln}$ key on your calculator, are used.

Example Rumours spread among N students after t days according to the model $N(t) = 2e^{1.24t}$. After how many days had 250 students heard the rumour?

$$2e^{1.24t} = 250$$

$$e^{1.24t} = 125$$

$$1.24t\log_e e = \log_e 125 \quad \text{(and, of course, } \log_e e = 1\text{)}$$

$$t = \frac{\log_e 125}{1.24} = 3.89. \qquad \text{Answer 3.89 days (nearly 4 days).}$$

EXERCISE 7

1 Solve these equations, correct to 2 decimal places.
a $e^t = 10$ **b** $e^{3t} = 120$ **c** $3.9e^{1.2t} = 74.9$

2 A population of mice increases according to the formula $M(t) = 6e^{0.18t}$, t the time in months.
a How many mice were there at the beginning?
b How many months will it be until there are 90 mice?

3 Scientists were trying to find the reason for stegosaurs becoming extinct. They set up the model $S(t) = 1000e^{-0.107t}$, t in years.
a How many creatures were there at the beginning?
b How many complete years are there before only one stegosaur is left?

4 Marsha is a television producer. She has to convince her authority that her programme will attract at least 500 000 viewers. She argued that viewing figures were growing according to the formula $V(t) = 100\,000e^{0.095t}$, t in weeks. How long should it take to reach her target viewing figures?

5 When taken from the oven, a bowl of pasta cools according to the model $T(t) = 100e^{-0.36t}$, t in minutes, T in °C.
a What was its temperature on leaving the oven?
b The room temperature is 20 °C. How long, to the nearest minute, will the pasta take to cool down to room temperature?

6 The intensity I of a light source after passing through d metres of fog is given by $I = I_0e^{-0.14d}$, where I_0 is the initial intensity. In what distance (nearest necessary metre) will the intensity be reduced to one tenth of its original value?

Experiment and theory

In experimental work, data can often be modelled by equations of the form $y = ax^n$ and $y = ab^x$, with graphs like these:

(i)

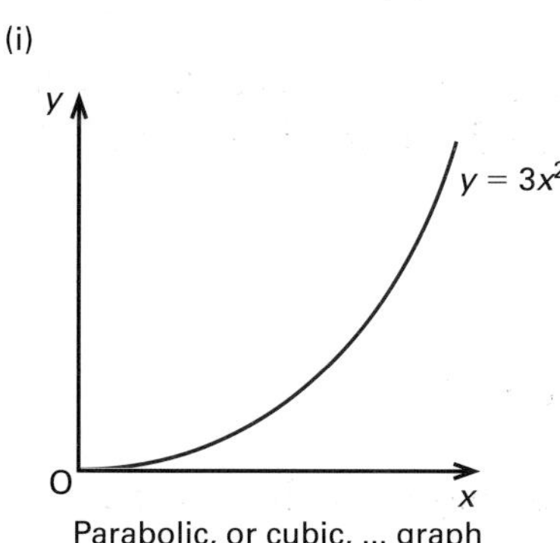

Parabolic, or cubic, ... graph

(ii)

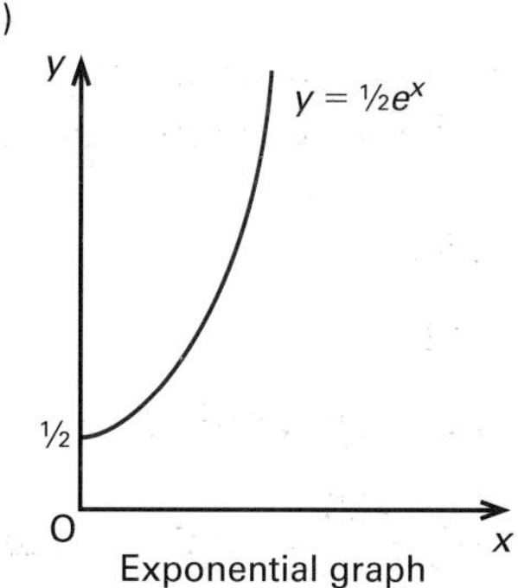

Exponential graph

Sometimes it is difficult to know which model to choose. One way to decide is to take logarithms.

(i) For $y = ax^n$,

$\log y = \log ax^n = \log a + \log x^n$

so $\log y = n \log x + \log a$,

like '$Y = mX + c$'.

(ii) For $y = ab^x$,

$\log y = \log ab^x = \log a + \log b^x$

so $\log y = x \log b + \log a$,

like '$Y = mx + c$'.

The graph of each is a straight line. By drawing the line, m and c can be found, and hence the equations obtained.

Example The table shows the result of an experiment. How are x and y related?

x	1.1	1.2	1.3	1.4	1.5	1.6
y	2.06	2.11	2.16	2.21	2.26	2.30

A quick sketch suggests an equation of the form $y = ax^n$.

Taking logarithms, $\log_{10} y = n \log_{10} x + \log_{10} a \ldots$ (1)

Comparing '$Y = mX + c$', (1) is the equation of a straight line.

Using a table of values of $\log_{10} x$ and $\log_{10} y$, we can draw the best-fitting straight line as shown, and find n and a.

$\log_{10} x$	0.04	0.08	0.11	0.15	0.18	0.20
$\log_{10} y$	0.31	0.32	0.33	0.34	0.35	0.36

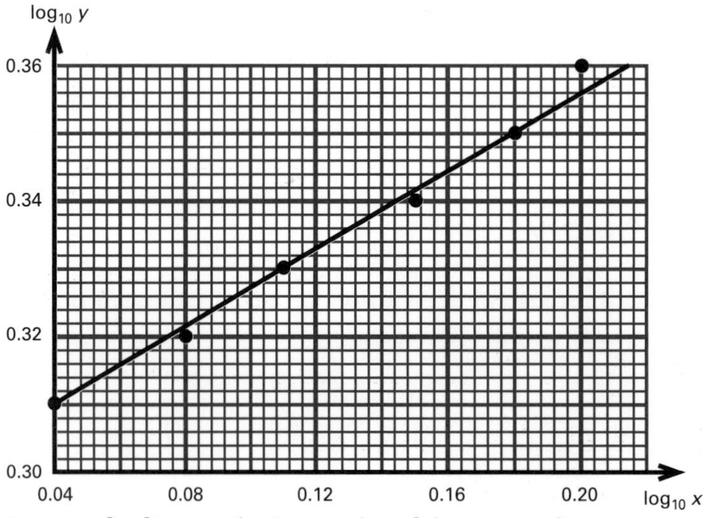

Take two points on the line ... (0.04, 0.31) and (0.18, 0.35).

From (1), $0.31 = 0.04n + \log_{10} a$

$0.35 = 0.18n + \log_{10} a$

Subtract: $0.04 = 0.14n$

$n = 0.29$, so $\log_{10} a = 0.30$ and $a = 10^{0.30} = 2.0$, to 1 decimal place.

So the relation between x and y, of the form $y = ax^n$, is approximately $y = 2x^{0.3}$.

EXERCISE 8

In questions **1** and **2**, assume that $y = ax^n$. Express this equation in logarithmic form, and use the graph to find a and n, correct to 1 decimal place. Hence write down the relation between x and y.

1

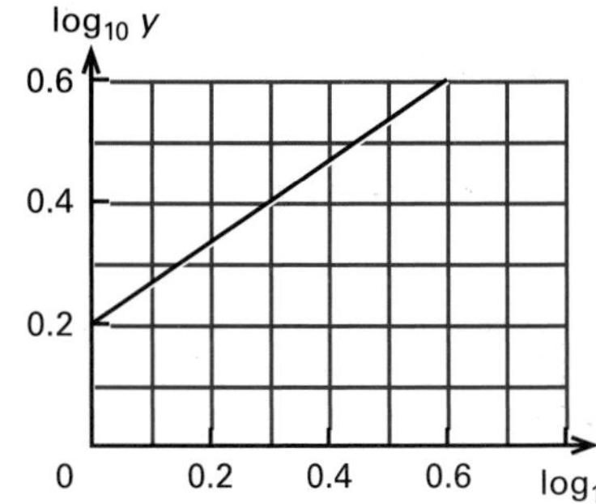

2

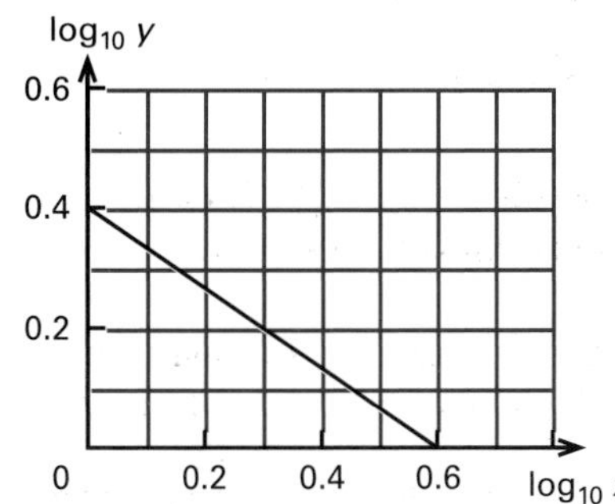

3 When $\log_{10} y$ is plotted against $\log_{10} x$, a best-fitting straight line has gradient 2 and passes through the point (0.6, 0.4). Fit this data to the model $y = ax^n$.

4 Repeat question **3** for a line which has gradient -1 and passes through (0.9, 0.2).

In questions **5** and **6**, assume that $y = ab^x$. Express this equation in logarithmic form, and use the graph to find a correct to 1 decimal place and b correct to 2 decimal places. Hence write down the relation between x and y.

5

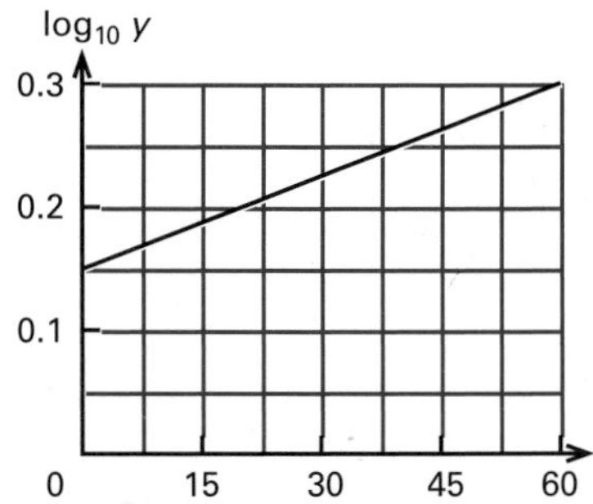

6

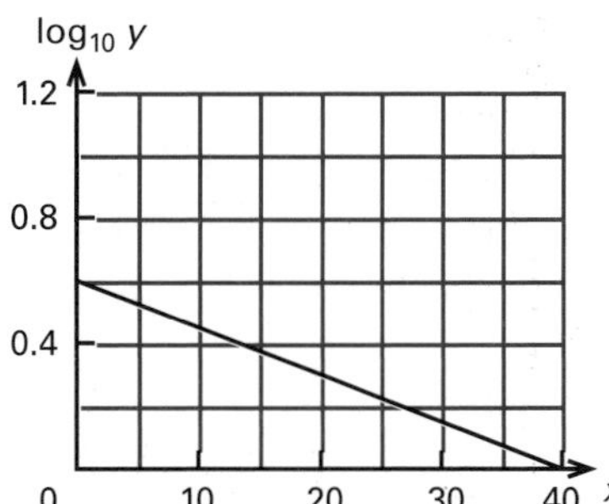

7 Find the relation $y = ax^n$ for this data:

x	10	20	30	40	50	60
y	9.49	13.42	16.43	18.98	21.21	23.24

8 Find the relation $y = ab^x$ for this data:

x	2.15	2.13	2.00	1.98	1.95	1.93
y	83.33	79.93	64.89	62.24	59.70	57.26

CHAPTER 3 REVIEW

1 a Copy and complete this table of values:

x	-2	-1	0	1	2
4^x	0.1	0.3			
4^{-x}					

b Using the scales in the diagram on page 239, draw the graphs $y = 4^x$ and $y = 4^{-x}$ for $-2 \leqslant x \leqslant 2$.

c Write down:

(i) the coordinates of the point where the graphs cross

(ii) the equation of their axis of symmetry.

2 A new type of grass spreads very fast, according to the formula $A(w) = 50(1.18)^w$, w in weeks, areas in m^2.

a What was the initial area?

b Calculate, to the nearest m^2, the area covered after:

(i) 5 weeks **(ii)** 10 weeks.

3 A bus costing £140 000 depreciates at 25% per year.

a Write down a function $V(t)$ that models its value after t years.

b When will its value fall below £4000?

4 Sketch the graphs:

a $y = e^x$ **b** $y = -e^x$

c $y = e^x + 1$.

5 The equation of a curve is $y = ae^x$. If it passes through the point $(0, \frac{1}{2})$, find the value of a.

6 Change to logarithmic form:

a $y = 5^3$ **b** $u = e^{-2}$

c $a = b^{1/2}$ **d** $v = 10^t$.

7 Change to exponential form:

a $2 = \log_e x$

b $3u = \log_{10} v$

c $2x = \log_a y$.

8 Simplify:

a $\log_2 16$ **b** $\log_3 27$

c $\log_9 3$ **d** $\log_{16} 2$.

9 Sketch the graphs:

a $y = \log_{10} x$

b $y = 1 + \log_{10} x$

c $y = \log_{10}(x + 1)$.

10 This is the graph $y = \log(x - a)$. What is the value of a?

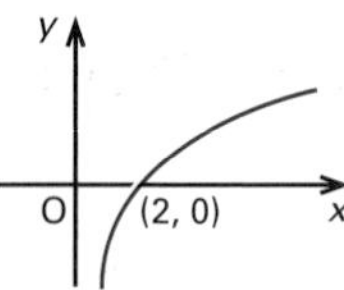

11 Simplify:

a $\log_3 4 + \log_3 6 - \log_3 8$

b $\log_5 50 - \log_5 2$

c $2\log_3 12 - 4\log_3 2$

d $\log_a a^3 - \log_a a^2$.

12 Solve these equations for y in terms of x:

a $\log_a 3 + \log_a y = x$

b $\log_e y - 2\log_e x = 1$.

13 The sketch shows part of the graph $y = a\log_{10}(x + b)$. Find the values of a and b.

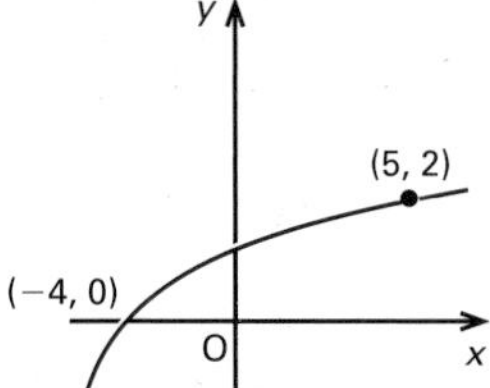

14 Find the least positive integer n for which $9^n > 10^{30}$.

15 The atmospheric pressure (P), x thousands of feet above sea-level, is given by $P = P_0 e^{-0.034x}$, where P_0 is the pressure at sea-level. Find the heights, in thousands of feet, correct to 1 decimal place, at which $P =$

a $\frac{1}{2}P_0$ **b** $\frac{1}{10}P_0$.

16 The population P of a town after n years is given by $P = 250\,000\,(1.2)^{0.1n}$.

a Calculate the population after 20 years.

b After how many years will the population be doubled?

17 Find an equation of the form $y = ax^n$ for the data shown in this graph.

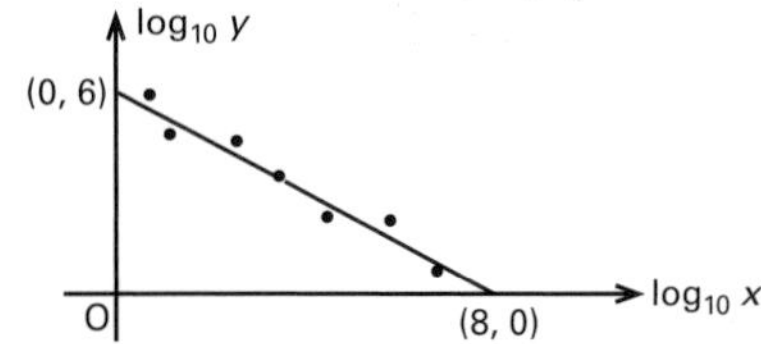

CHAPTER 3 SUMMARY

1 An exponential function is of the form $f(x) = a^x$, $a \neq 1$.

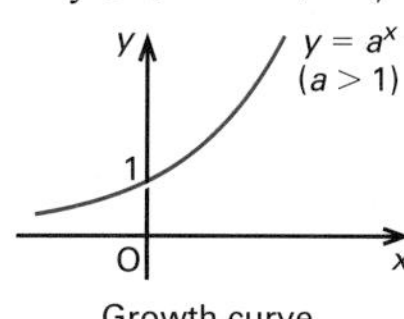

Growth curve

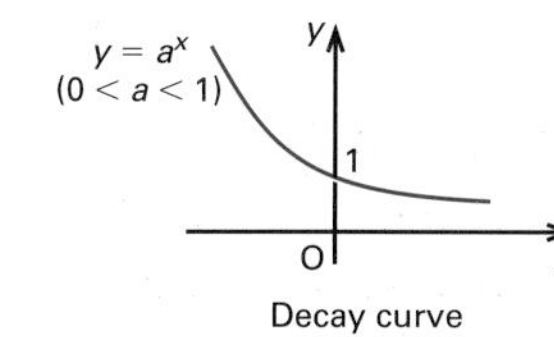

Decay curve

2 $f(x) = e^x$ is the exponential function with base e, where $e = 2.718$, correct to 3 decimal places.

3 The exponential function $f(x) = a^x$ and the logarithmic function $l(x) = \log_a x$ are inverse functions:

$$y = a^x \Leftrightarrow \log_a y = x$$

also, $\log_a 1 = 0$ and $\log_a a = 1$.

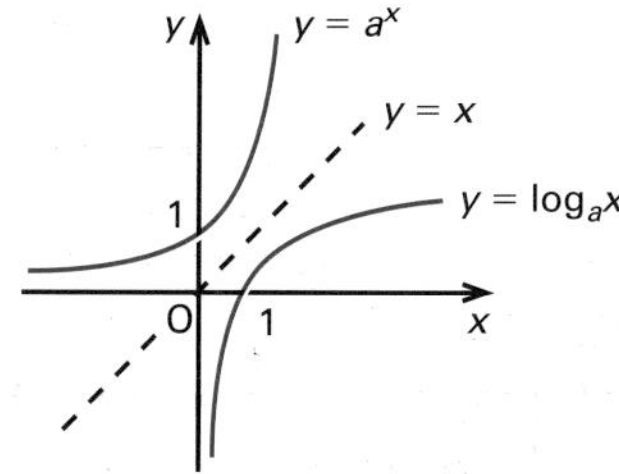

4 RULES OF LOGARITHMS

$$\log_a xy = \log_a x + \log_a y;$$

$$\log_a \frac{x}{y} = \log_a x - \log_a y;$$

$$\log_a x^p = p \log_a x$$

5 EXPONENTIAL EQUATIONS

a $5^x = 4$. Take logs to base 10, $\boxed{\log}$.

b $N(t) = 2e^{1.2t}$. Take logs to base e, $\boxed{\ln}$.

6 (i) The graph of $\log_{10} y$ against $\log_{10} x$ is a straight line $\Leftrightarrow y = ax^n$.

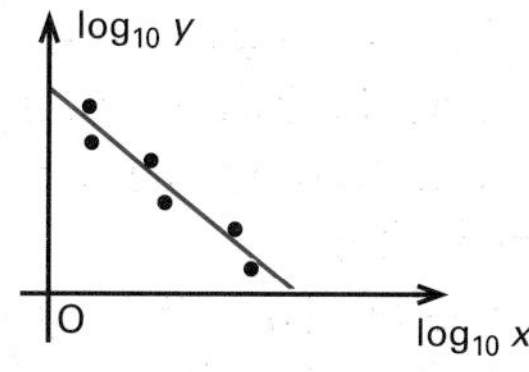

(ii) The graph of $\log_a y$ against x is a straight line $\Leftrightarrow y = ab^x$.

4 The Wave Function $a \cos x + b \sin x$

CLASS DISCUSSION: COMBINING WAVES

In speech, music, electronic circuits, vibrations, etc., wave forms can be very complicated since they may represent the sum of a large number of wave forms of different periods. A simple musical sound will normally consist of a basic note and its harmonics. Phenomena like these have complicated graphs. In this chapter a method is developed for combining waves of the form $a \cos x$ and $b \sin x$ where a and b are constants.

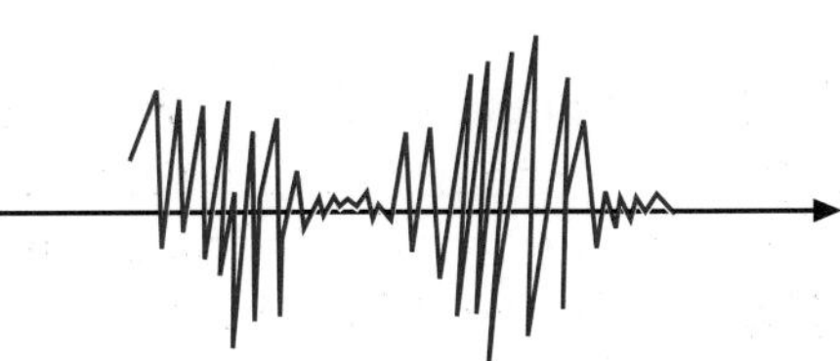

Example Investigate the graph $y = \cos x + \sin x$ for $0 \leqslant x \leqslant 2\pi$.

x	0	$\pi/4$	$\pi/2$	$3\pi/4$	π	$5\pi/4$	$3\pi/2$	$7\pi/4$	2π
$\cos x$	1	$1/\sqrt{2}$	0	$-1/\sqrt{2}$	-1	$-1/\sqrt{2}$	0	$1/\sqrt{2}$	1
$\sin x$	0	$1/\sqrt{2}$	1	$1/\sqrt{2}$	0	$-1/\sqrt{2}$	-1	$-1/\sqrt{2}$	0
y	1	$2/\sqrt{2}$*	1	0	-1	$-2/\sqrt{2}$*	-1	0	1

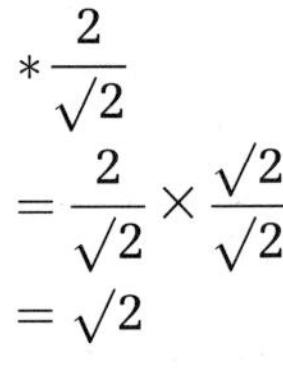

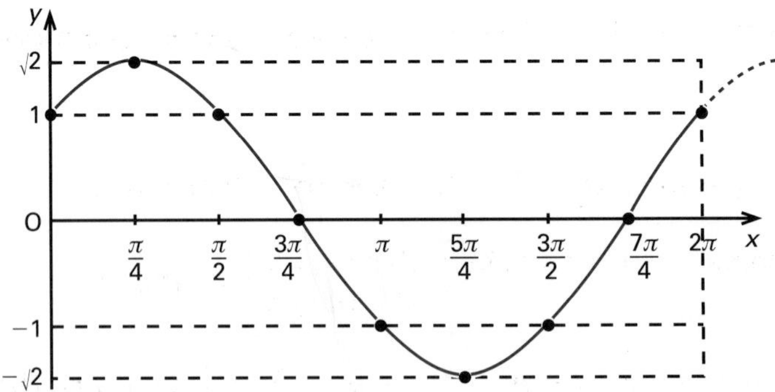

The graph is like $y = \cos x$, but its amplitude is $\sqrt{2}$, and it is displaced $\dfrac{\pi}{4}$ to the right. This suggests that its equation is $y = \sqrt{2} \cos\left(x - \dfrac{\pi}{4}\right)$.

Check $$\sqrt{2}\cos\left(x-\frac{\pi}{4}\right) = \sqrt{2}\left(\cos x\cos\frac{\pi}{4} + \sin x\sin\frac{\pi}{4}\right)$$
$$= \cos x + \sin x.$$
$$\text{So } \cos x + \sin x = \sqrt{2}\cos\left(x-\frac{\pi}{4}\right),$$

The two waves, $y = \cos x$ and $y = \sin x$, have been combined into one wave, $y = \sqrt{2}\cos\left(x-\frac{\pi}{4}\right)$.

Use the entries in the table on page 250 to draw the graph $y = \cos x - \sin x$ for $0 \leqslant x \leqslant 2\pi$.

a Show that the graph $y = \cos x + \sin x$ is like the graph $y = \cos x$ moved to the right and with a larger amplitude.

b Zoom in on the maximum turning point, and obtain an approximation α for the shift to the right (from the x-coordinate) and R for the amplitude (from the y-coordinate).

c Use the approximations to display $y = R\cos(x - \alpha)$, and compare with $y = \sqrt{2}\cos\left(x-\frac{\pi}{4}\right)$.

Expressing a *cos*x + b *sin*x *in the form* R *cos*(x ± α), *or* R *sin*(x ± α)

Reminders

$\cos(A + B) = \cos A\cos B - \sin A\sin B$ $\quad$ $\sin(A + B) = \sin A\cos B + \cos A\sin B$

$\cos(A - B) = \cos A\cos B + \sin A\sin B$ $\quad$ $\sin(A - B) = \sin A\cos B - \cos A\sin B$.

General method

Let $a\underline{\cos x} + b\underline{\sin x} = R\cos(x - \alpha) = R\underline{\cos x}\cos\alpha + R\underline{\sin x}\sin\alpha$.

Equating coefficients of $\cos x$ and $\sin x$, $\left.\begin{aligned} R\cos\alpha &= a \\ R\sin\alpha &= b \end{aligned}\right\} \cdots (1).$

Squaring and adding, $R^2(\cos^2\alpha + \sin^2\alpha) = a^2 + b^2$, from which $R = \sqrt{(a^2 + b^2)}$, taking $R > 0$.

Also, $\tan\alpha = \dfrac{R\sin\alpha}{R\cos\alpha} = \dfrac{b}{a}$ (from (1)), and the quadrant of α is found from the signs of $\cos\alpha$ and $\sin\alpha$.

So $a\cos x + b\sin x = R\cos(x - \alpha)$, where $R = \sqrt{(a^2 + b^2)}$ and $\tan\alpha = \dfrac{b}{a}$.

The graph of the function is:

$y = a\cos x + b\sin x = R\cos(x - \alpha)$.

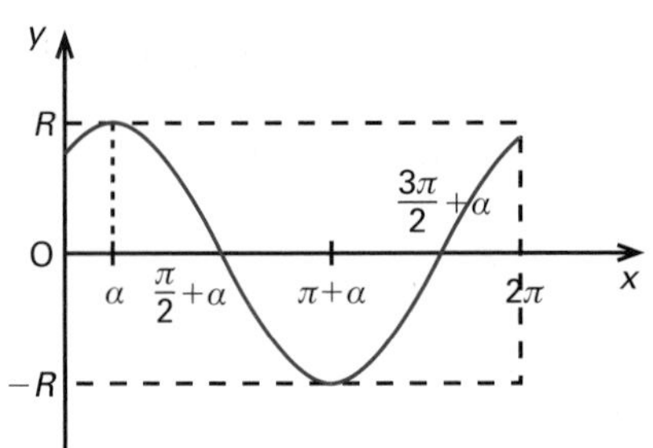

R is the *amplitude* of the function, the maximum height of a wave. α is the *phase angle*, the amount by which $y = R\cos x$ is moved to get $y = R\cos(x - \alpha)$. You saw examples of this in the chapter on Compound Angle Formulae.

Example Express $\cos x - \sin x$ in the form $R\cos(x - \alpha)$, and sketch the graph of the function. Let $\cos x - \sin x = R\cos(x - \alpha)$
$= R\cos x\cos\alpha + R\sin x\sin\alpha$.

Sin+	All+ ✓
$\pi - \alpha$	α
$\pi + \alpha$	$2\pi - \alpha$
Tan+ ✓	Cos+ ✓✓

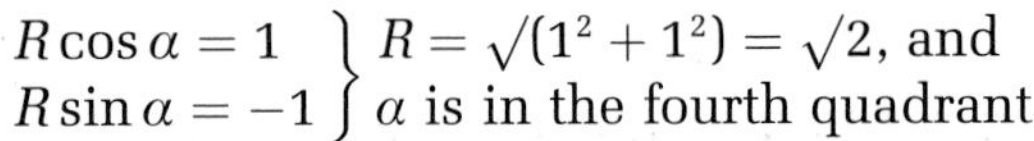

$\left.\begin{array}{l} R\cos\alpha = 1 \\ R\sin\alpha = -1 \end{array}\right\}$ $R = \sqrt{(1^2 + 1^2)} = \sqrt{2}$, and α is in the fourth quadrant.

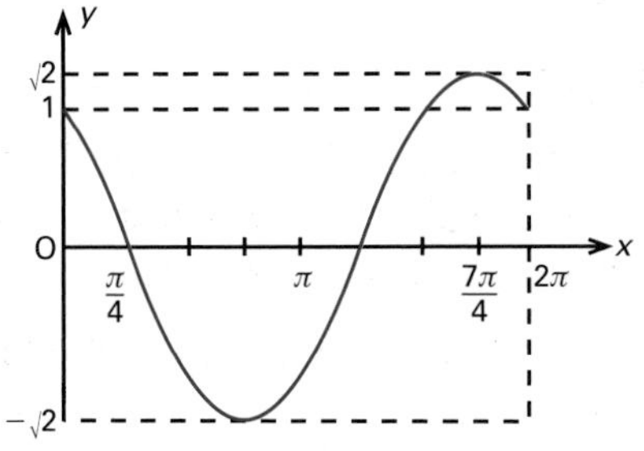

$$\tan\alpha = \frac{R\sin\alpha}{R\cos\alpha} = -1, \text{ so } \alpha = 2\pi - \frac{\pi}{4} = \frac{7\pi}{4}.$$

So $\cos x - \sin x = \sqrt{2}\cos\left(x - \frac{7\pi}{4}\right)$.

The amplitude is $\sqrt{2}$, and the phase angle is $\frac{7\pi}{4}$.

Draw the graphs of some of the functions in Exercise 1A, and zoom in to find R, $\alpha°$ (DEG mode) or R, α (RAD mode) as appropriate.

In these exercises, give angles in degrees to the nearest degree, and angles in radians correct to 2 decimal places, where these are not exact.

EXERCISE 1A

1 In each of the following:
 (i) square and add, to find R $(R > 0)$
 (ii) divide to find $\tan\alpha$, then $\alpha (0 \leqslant \alpha \leqslant 2\pi)$.
 a $R\cos\alpha = 1$, $R\sin\alpha = 1$ **b** $R\cos\alpha = 1$, $R\sin\alpha = -1$
 c $R\cos\alpha = \sqrt{3}$, $R\sin\alpha = 1$

2 Copy and complete:

$$\sqrt{3}\cos x - \sin x = R\cos(x - \alpha),\ 0 \leqslant x \leqslant 2\pi$$
$$= R\cos x \cos\alpha + R\sin x \sin\alpha$$

$$\left.\begin{array}{l} R\cos\alpha = \ldots \\ R\sin\alpha = \ldots \end{array}\right\} R^2 = \ldots,\ R = \ldots$$

S	A
T	C

$$\tan\alpha = \frac{-1}{\ldots} = \ldots$$

$$\alpha = 2\pi - \ldots = \ldots$$

So $\sqrt{3}\cos x - \sin x = 2\cos\left(x - \dfrac{11\pi}{6}\right)$.

3 Show that $2\cos x - 2\sin x = 2\sqrt{2}\cos\left(x - \dfrac{7\pi}{4}\right), 0 \leqslant x \leqslant 2\pi$, using $R\cos(x - \alpha)$.

4 Express each of the following in the form $R\cos(x - \alpha)$, $0 \leqslant x \leqslant 2\pi$.
a $\cos x + \sin x$ **b** $\cos x - \sqrt{3}\sin x$
c $\sqrt{3}\cos x + \sin x$ **d** $2\cos x + 2\sin x$

5 Show that $4\cos x^\circ - 3\sin x^\circ \doteqdot 5\sin(x - 233)^\circ$, $0 \leqslant x \leqslant 360$, using $R\sin(x - \alpha)^\circ$.

6 Express each of the following in the form $R\sin(x - \alpha)^\circ$, $0 \leqslant x \leqslant 360$.
a $3\cos x^\circ - 4\sin x^\circ$ **b** $8\cos x^\circ + 6\sin x^\circ$
c $-\cos x^\circ + 2\sin x^\circ$ **d** $-\sin x^\circ - 3\cos x^\circ$

7 Express $3\cos x^\circ + 4\sin x^\circ$ in each of these forms, for $0 \leqslant x \leqslant 360$:
a $R\cos(x - \alpha)^\circ$ **b** $R\cos(x + \alpha)^\circ$
c $R\sin(x - \alpha)^\circ$ **d** $R\sin(x + \alpha)^\circ$.

EXERCISE 1B

1 Electric currents $I_1 = \cos 300t^\circ$ and $I_2 = \sqrt{3}\sin 300t^\circ$ are fed into an ammeter. Express the resultant $I_1 + I_2$ in the form $R\cos(300\,t - \alpha)^\circ$.

2 Express each of these in the form $R\cos(kx - \alpha)$:
a $\cos 2x + \sin 2x$ (let $\cos 2x + \sin 2x = R\cos(2x - \alpha)$)
b $\sin 3x - \cos 3x$.

3 Express each of these in the given form, for $0 \leqslant \theta \leqslant 2\pi$, using radian mode on your calculator:
a $3\cos 2\theta - 4\sin 2\theta$; $R\cos(2\theta - \alpha)$
b $2\sin 2\theta + \cos 2\theta$; $R\sin(2\theta - \alpha)$.

4 The displacement of a wave after t seconds is given by $10\cos 20t^\circ + 30\sin 20t^\circ$.
a Express this in the form $R\sin(20t + \alpha)^\circ$.
b Sketch the graph of the wave against t for $0 \leqslant t \leqslant 18$, showing where the curve cuts the t-axis, and any stationary points.

Maxima and minima of $a\cos x + b\sin x$

Example Find the maximum value of f, and the minimum value of g, along with the corresponding values of x, for $0 \leqslant x \leqslant 360$, given:
a $f(x) = 5\sin(x + 60)°$ **b** $g(x) = 2\cos(3x - 30)°$.

a Maximum value is 5, when $\sin(x + 60)° = 1$.

Then $x + 60 = 90, 450, \ldots$

$x = 30, (390), \ldots$

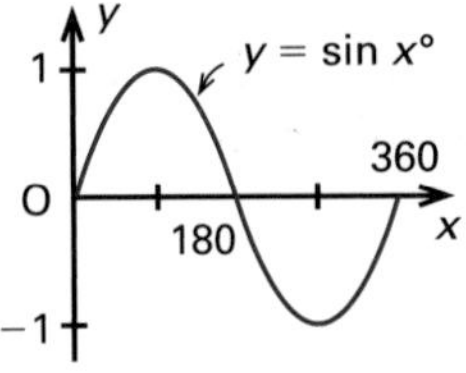

b Minimum value is -2, when $\cos(3x - 30)° = -1$.

Then $3x - 30 = 180, 540, 900, \ldots$

$3x = 210, 570, 930, \ldots$

$x = 70, 190, 310$

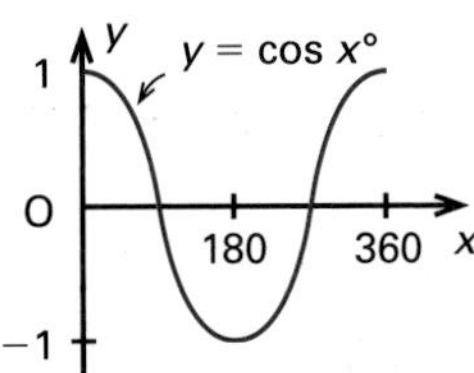

EXERCISE 2

1 Write down the maximum and minimum values of:
a $\sin x°$ **b** $\cos x°$ **c** $4\sin x°$
d $3\cos x°$ **e** $5\sin(x + 75)°$ **f** $2\cos(x - 45)°$.

In questions **2–6**, find the maximum and minimum values of the functions, and the corresponding values of x or θ.

2 For $0 \leqslant x \leqslant 360$:
a $2\sin x°$ **b** $3\cos x°$.

3 For $0 \leqslant x \leqslant 360$:
a $5\sin(x - 30)°$ **b** $10\cos(x + 60)°$.

4 For $0 \leqslant x \leqslant 2\pi$:
a $6\sin\left(x - \frac{\pi}{2}\right)$ **b** $7\cos\left(x + \frac{\pi}{4}\right)$.

5 For $0 \leqslant x \leqslant 360$:
a $2\sin(2x - 90)°$ **b** $3\cos(2x + 60)°$.

6 For $0 \leqslant \theta \leqslant \pi$:
a $4\sin\left(3\theta - \frac{\pi}{3}\right)$ **b** $5\cos\left(3\theta + \frac{\pi}{4}\right)$.

Example Find the maximum and minimum values of $f(x) = -3\sin x° - 4\cos x° + 10$, for $0 \leqslant x \leqslant 360$, and the corresponding values of x, using $R\sin(x+\alpha)°$.

Let $-3\sin x° - 4\cos x° = R\sin(x+\alpha)° = R\sin x°\cos\alpha° + R\cos x°\sin\alpha°$

$$\left.\begin{array}{l} R\cos\alpha° = -3 \\ R\sin\alpha° = -4 \end{array}\right\} \begin{array}{l} R = \sqrt{((-3)^2 + (-4)^2)} = 5, \text{ and} \\ \alpha \text{ is in the third quadrant.} \end{array}$$

✓ Sin+	All+
$(180 - x)°$	$x°$
$(180 + x)°$	$(360 - x)°$
✓✓ Tan+	Cos+ ✓

$\tan\alpha° = \dfrac{R\sin\alpha°}{R\cos\alpha°} = \dfrac{-4}{-3}$, so $\alpha = 180 + 53 = 233$ (to nearest degree)

$f(x) = 5\sin(x+233)° + 10.$

Its maximum value $= 5 + 10 = 15$, when $\sin(x+233)° = 1$.

$x + 233 = 90, 450, \ldots$

$x = (90 - 233), 450 - 233, \ldots$

$x = 217$

Its minimum value $= -5 + 10 = 5$, when $\sin(x+233)° = -1$.

$x + 233 = 270$

$x = 37$

Draw the graphs of some of the functions in Exercises 3A and 3B, and find approximate maximum and minimum values and corresponding values of x, using the calculator in appropriate mode.

EXERCISE 3A

1 Express each function in the form $R\cos(x-\alpha)°$, and find its maximum and minimum values, and the corresponding values of x for $0 \leqslant x \leqslant 360$.
a $12\cos x° + 5\sin x°$ **b** $7\cos x° - 24\sin x°$

2 Using $R\sin(x-\alpha)$ find the maximum and minimum values of f and g, and the corresponding values of x for $0 \leqslant x \leqslant 2\pi$.
a $f(x) = 1 + \sqrt{2}\cos x - \sqrt{2}\sin x$
b $g(x) = 2 + \sqrt{3}\sin x - \cos x$

3 The equations of these graphs are $y_1 = a\cos bx°$ and $y_2 = c\sin dx°$.

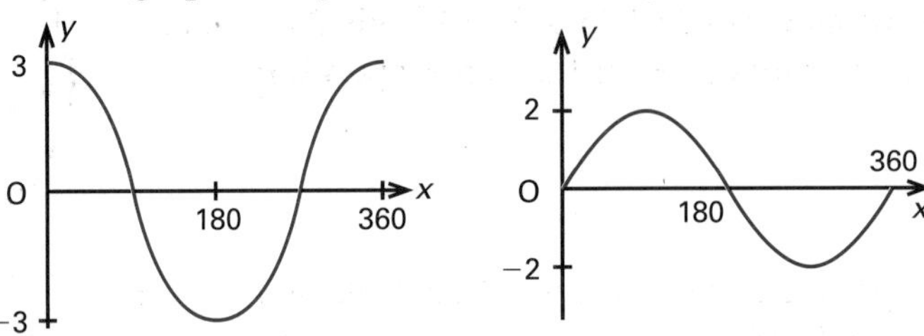

a Write down the values of a, b, c and d.
b A new wave is formed from $y_1 + y_2$. Write down its equation, and express it in the form $k\sin(x - \alpha)°$, $0 \leqslant x \leqslant 360$.
c Find its maximum and minimum values and the corresponding values of x.

4 Repeat question **3** for these graphs:

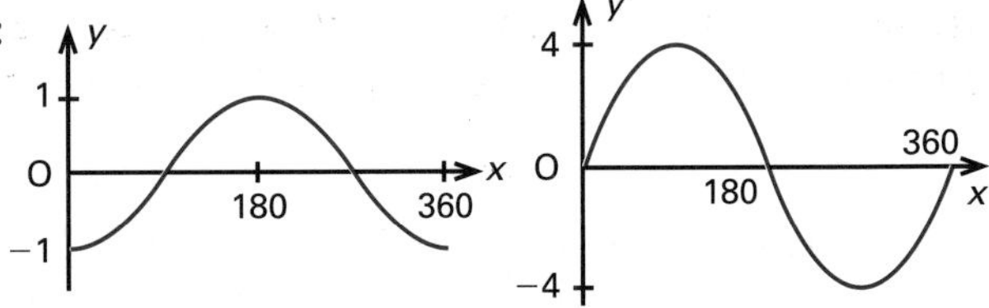

5 Repeat question **2**, using $R\cos(2x - \alpha)$, for:
a $f(x) = 4\cos 2x + 3\sin 2x + 5$
b $g(x) = \cos 2x - 2\sin 2x + \sqrt{5}$.

6 **a** Show that $9\cos x + 12\sin x = 15\cos(x - 0.93)$.
b Find the maximum value of $\dfrac{1}{20 + 9\cos x + 12\sin x}$ and the corresponding value of x, for $0 \leqslant x \leqslant 2\pi$.

EXERCISE 3B

1 A bracing spar of length 2 m is placed horizontally between two perpendicular walls. For maximum strength it has to be placed so that it covers the maximum distance on the walls, i.e. so that OA + OB is a maximum.

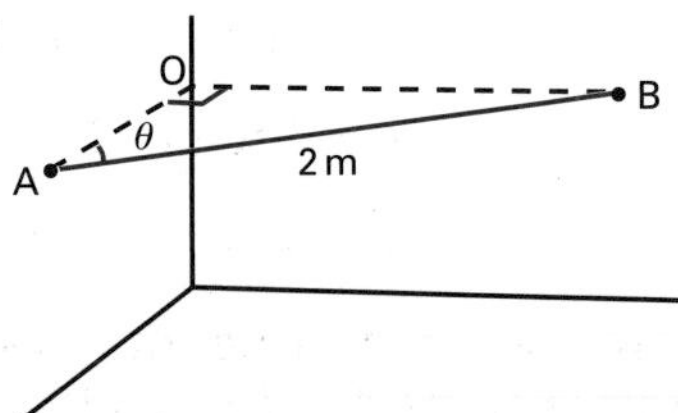

a Prove that $OA + OB = 2(\cos\theta + \sin\theta)$, where $0 < \theta < \dfrac{\pi}{2}$.
b Find the maximum value of OA + OB, and the corresponding value of θ.

2 **a** In the diagram, show that:
(i) $\angle DEF = x°$ (ii) $BE = 2.5\cos x° + 6\sin x°$.
b Find the maximum value of BE, and the corresponding value of x.

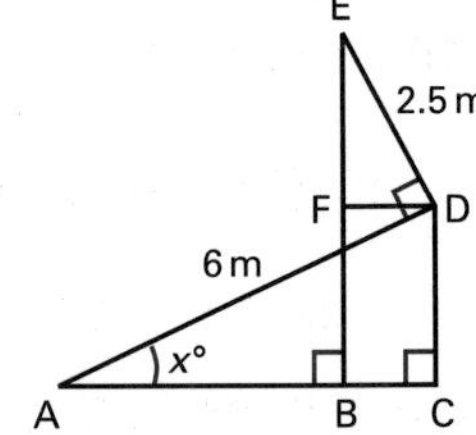

3 The height of the sea in metres above mean sea-level t hours after midnight is given by $H = 10\sqrt{5}(2\sin 30t° + \cos 30t°)$. Express H in the form $R\cos(30t - \alpha)°$, and find the times of high and low water during the first 12 hours.

4 O is the centre of the circle.

a Prove that the perimeter of $\triangle$COD is $P = 1 + \sin 2\theta + \cos 2\theta$.

b Find the maximum value of P, and the corresponding value of θ.

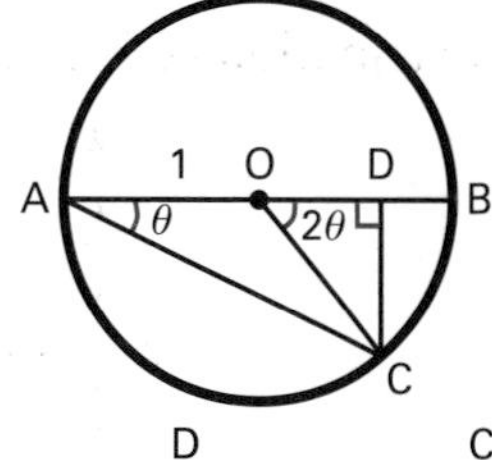

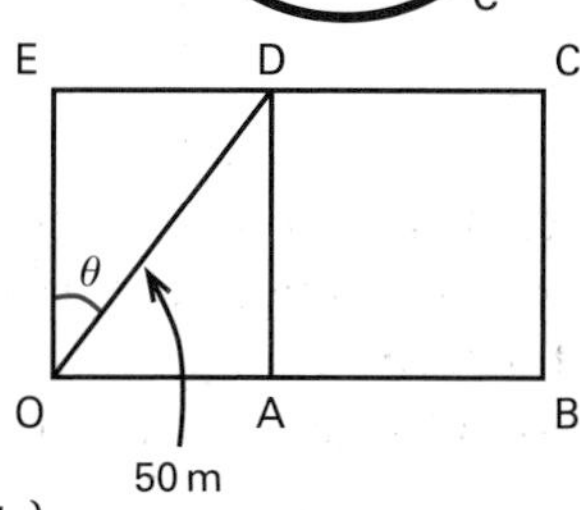

5 A rectangular car park is being planned. It consists of a square part ABCD and a rectangular part OADE, where OD = 50 m. The problem is to choose the value of θ that makes the area S m^2 of the car park a maximum.

a Show that $S = 2500(\sin\theta\cos\theta + \cos^2\theta)$.

b Express S in the form $R\cos(2\theta - \alpha) + c$.
(Remember, $\sin 2\theta = 2\sin\theta\cos\theta$ and $\cos 2\theta = 2\cos^2\theta - 1$.)

c Find the maximum value of S, and the corresponding value of θ.

Trigonometric equations

Example Solve the equation $\sin 2x° + 3\cos 2x° + 1 = 0$, for $0 \leqslant x \leqslant 180$.
Let $\sin 2x° + 3\cos 2x° = R\cos(2x - \alpha)° = (R\cos\alpha°)\cos 2x° + (R\sin\alpha°)\sin 2x°$.

$$\left.\begin{array}{l} R\cos\alpha° = 3 \\ R\sin\alpha° = 1 \end{array}\right\} \begin{array}{l} R = \sqrt{(3^2 + 1^2)} = \sqrt{10}, \text{ and} \\ \alpha \text{ is in the first quadrant} \end{array}$$

✓ Sin+	✓✓ All+
Tan+	Cos+ ✓

$\tan\alpha° = \frac{1}{3}$, so $\alpha = 18$, to the nearest degree.

The equation is $\sqrt{10}\cos(2x - 18)° = -1$

$$\cos(2x - 18)° = -\frac{1}{\sqrt{10}}$$

✓ Sin+ (180 − x)°	All+ x°
(180 + x)° Tan+ ✓	Cos+

$$2x - 18 = 180 - 72 \text{ or } 180 + 72^*$$

$$2x = 126 \text{ or } 270$$

$$x = 63 \text{ or } 135 \quad \text{(to nearest degree).}$$

*If the range of values of x was $0 \leqslant x \leqslant 360$, additional values $180 - 72 + 360$ and $180 + 72 + 360$ would be needed here.

In radian measure:
$\alpha = 0.32$ radian

$$\sqrt{10}\cos(2x - 0.32) = -1$$

$$\cos(2x - 0.32) = \frac{-1}{\sqrt{10}}$$

$$2x - 0.32 = \pi - 1.25 \text{ or } \pi + 1.25$$

$$2x = 2.21 \text{ or } 4.71$$

$x = 1.11$ or 2.36, correct to 2 decimal places.

a Draw the graph $y = \sin 2x° + 3\cos 2x° + 1$, for $0 \leqslant x \leqslant 180$. Zoom in to find the roots of $\sin 2x° + 3\cos 2x° + 1 = 0$, to the nearest degree or to 1 decimal place.

b Check the answers to some questions in Exercise 4.

EXERCISE 4

1 Express the left-hand side of each equation in the form $k\cos(x - \alpha)°$, where $0 \leqslant x \leqslant 360$, then solve the equation.

a $\cos x° + \sin x° = 1$ **b** $3\cos x° + 4\sin x° = 5$
c $9\sin x° - 12\cos x° = 10$ **d** $2\cos x° + 3\sin x° = -1$

2 Use the form $k\sin(x - \alpha)°$ to help you to solve the equations below, for $0 \leqslant x \leqslant 360$.

a $\sqrt{3}\cos x° - \sin x° = 0$ **b** $6\sin x° - 8\cos x° = 10$

3 Use $k\cos(x + \alpha)$ to solve the following equations for $0 \leqslant x \leqslant 2\pi$.

a $\cos x - \sin x = 1$ **b** $\sqrt{3}\sin x + \cos x = 1$

4 **a** Express $3\sin x° - 4\cos x°$ in the form $k\sin(x - \alpha)°$.
b Hence find the values of x, for $0 \leqslant x \leqslant 360$, for which:
(i) $3\sin x° - 4\cos x° = 2$
(ii) $3\sin x° - 4\cos x° \geqslant 2$.

5 Solve, for $0 \leqslant x \leqslant 180$:
a $2\sin(2x - 20)° = 1$
b $6\cos(3x + 60)° - 3 = 0$.

6 Use any of $k\cos(2x \pm \alpha)°$ or $k\sin(2x \pm \alpha)°$ to solve, for $0 \leqslant x \leqslant 180$:
a $\cos 2x° - \sin 2x° = 1$ **b** $3\cos 2x° + 4\sin 2x° + 1 = 0$.

7 **a** Express $4\cos x° - 3\sin x°$ in the form $R\sin(x + \alpha)°$ for $0 \leqslant x \leqslant 360$.
b Find the maximum and minimum values of the function, and the corresponding values of x.
c Sketch the function for $0 \leqslant x \leqslant 360$.
d Solve, for $0 \leqslant x \leqslant 360$:
(i) $4\cos x° - 3\sin x° = 0$ **(ii)** $4\cos x° - 3\sin x° < 0$.

8 Repeat question **7** for the function $8\sin\theta + 5\cos\theta$ for $0 \leqslant \theta \leqslant 2\pi$.

Challenge

The sun is setting behind the lone rectangular standing-stone, casting a shadow with parallel sides.

a Show that the width of the shadow $D = 5\sin\theta° + 2\cos\theta°$.

b Find θ (to the nearest degree) when $D = 4$.

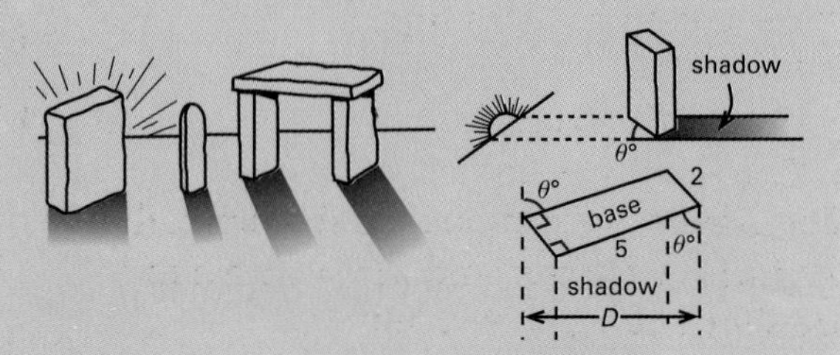

CHAPTER 4 REVIEW

1 Find $R\,(>0)$ and $\alpha°$ (to the nearest degree) for each of these pairs of equations:

a $R\cos\alpha° = -1$, $R\sin\alpha° = 1$

b $R\cos\alpha° = 1$, $R\sin\alpha° = \sqrt{3}$

c $R\cos\alpha° = 3$, $R\sin\alpha° = 4$

d $R\cos\alpha° = -5$, $R\sin\alpha° = 12$.

2 Show that:

a $\cos x° - \sin x° = \sqrt{2}\cos(x - 315)°$

b $\sqrt{3}\cos x° + \sin x° = 2\cos(x - 30)°$.

3 Show that, in radian measure:

a $\cos x + \sin x = \sqrt{2}\cos\left(x - \frac{\pi}{4}\right)$

b $-\cos x + \sqrt{3}\sin x = 2\cos\left(x - \frac{2\pi}{3}\right)$.

4 Show that $\cos x - \sin x =$

a $\sqrt{2}\cos\left(x - \frac{7\pi}{4}\right)$, using $R\cos(x - \alpha)$

b $\sqrt{2}\cos\left(x + \frac{\pi}{4}\right)$, using $R\cos(x + \alpha)$.

5 Express each of the following in the given form.

a For $0 \leqslant x \leqslant 2\pi$:

(i) $3\sin x - 3\cos x$, $R\cos(x - \alpha)$

(ii) $3\cos x + \sqrt{3}\sin x$, $R\sin(x + \alpha)$.

b For $0 \leqslant x \leqslant 360$:

(i) $-3\cos x° + 4\sin x°$, $R\cos(x + \alpha)°$

(ii) $5\sin x° + 2\cos x°$, $R\sin(x - \alpha)°$.

6 In an electric circuit the current is given by the formula
$I = 6\cos 250t° + 3\sin 250t°$.

a Express this in the form $R\sin(250t + \alpha)°$.

b State the amplitude and phase angle of the current.

7 Find the maximum and minimum values of these functions, and the corresponding values of x, for $0 \leqslant x \leqslant 360$:

a $1 + \sin x° - 2\cos x°$

b $2\sqrt{2} - \sin x° - \cos x°$.

8 The graphs of functions f and g defined by $f(x) = a\sin mx°$ and $g(x) = b\cos nx°$ are shown, for $0 \leqslant x \leqslant 360$.

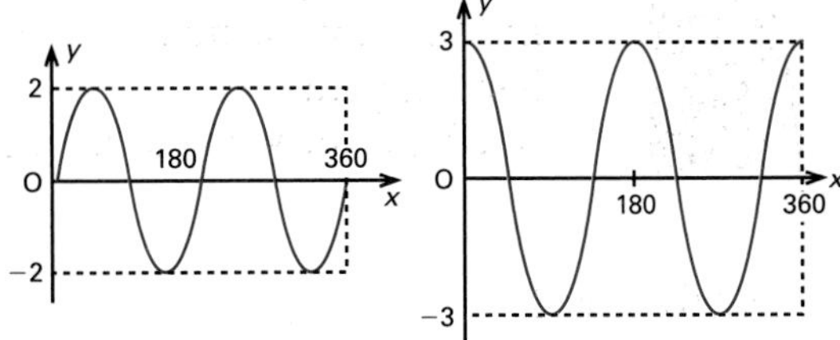

a Write down the values of a, m, b and n.

b A function h is defined by $h(x) = f(x) + g(x)$. Express $h(x)$ in the form $k\sin(px + q)°$, and state the values of k, p and q.

9 Solve these equations, **a** and **b** to the nearest degree and **c** correct to 2 decimal places.

a $3\cos x° - \sin x° = 2$, for $0 \leqslant x \leqslant 360$

b $\sin 2x° + 2\cos 2x° = 1$, for $0 \leqslant x \leqslant 180$

c $3\cos\theta + \sin\theta = 2$, for $0 \leqslant \theta \leqslant 2\pi$

10 There are 50 cm lengths of carpet at the top and bottom of the stairs. The staircase contains 4 risers and 3 treads on the steps.

a Show that the total length of carpet is $L = 120\cos\theta° + 160\sin\theta° + 100$ cm.

b Find the maximum value of L, and the value of θ when L is a maximum.

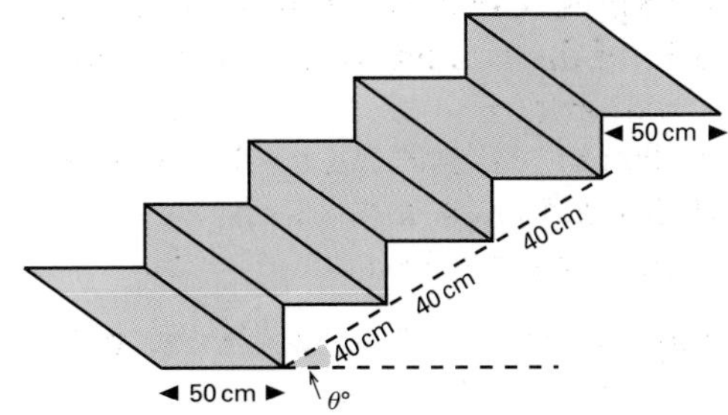

11 A right-angled triangular plot of ground has 40 metres of fencing round it.

a Prove that $h = \dfrac{40}{\cos\theta° + \sin\theta° + 1}$.

b Find the minimum value of h, and the corresponding value of θ.

CHAPTER 4 SUMMARY

1 Some reminders

a

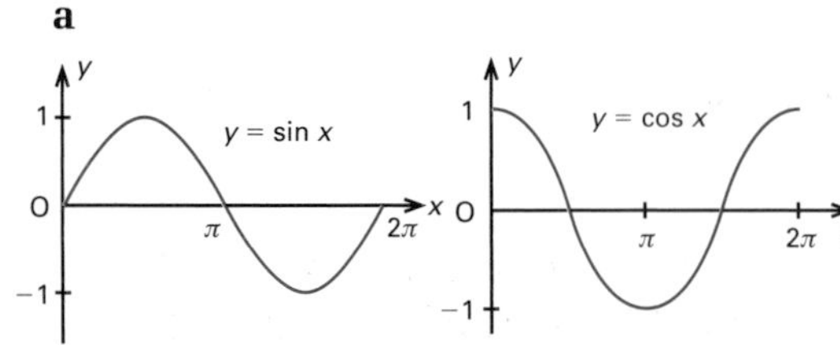

b Signs of trigonometric functions:

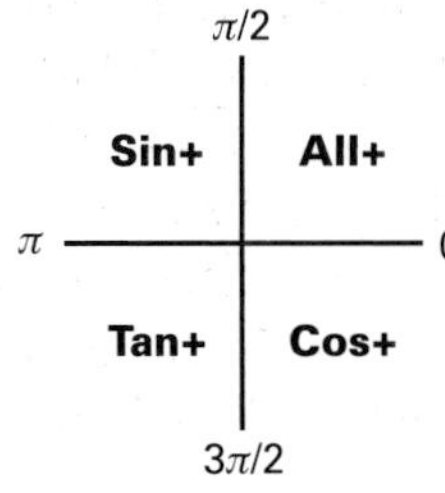

c $\cos(A+B) = \cos A\cos B - \sin A\sin B$
$\cos(A-B) = \cos A\cos B + \sin A\sin B$
$\sin(A+B) = \sin A\cos B + \cos A\sin B$
$\sin(A-B) = \sin A\cos B - \cos A\sin B$

d $\sin(-A) = -\sin A$
$\cos(-A) = \cos A$

e $\tan A = \dfrac{\sin A}{\cos A}$

f π radians $= 180°$
2π radians $= 360°$

2 The graph $y = 3\cos\left(x - \dfrac{\pi}{4}\right)$ has amplitude 3, period 2π and phase angle $\dfrac{\pi}{4}$. The graph $y = 3\cos x$ is displaced to the right by the phase angle $\dfrac{\pi}{4}$.

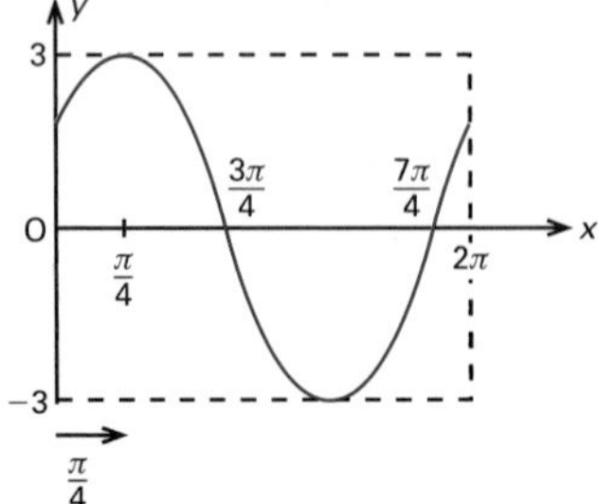

3 The functions $a\cos x$ and $b\sin x$ can be combined as a single function such as $R\cos(x - \alpha)$, where $R = \sqrt{(a^2 + b^2)}$, $\tan\alpha = \dfrac{b}{a}$ and the quadrant for α is determined by the signs of $\cos\alpha$ and $\sin\alpha$.
Similarly, the curves $y = a\cos x$ and $y = b\sin x$ can be combined into a single curve $y = R\cos(x - \alpha)$.

4 Maximum and minimum values of $a\cos x + b\sin x$, expressed in the form $R\cos(x \pm \alpha)$ or $R\sin(x \pm \alpha)$ are:

a maximum value R, when $\cos(x \pm \alpha) = 1$ or $\sin(x \pm \alpha) = 1$

b minimum value $-R$, when $\cos(x \pm \alpha) = -1$ or $\sin(x \pm \alpha) = -1$.

5 Solutions of the equation $a\cos x + b\sin x = c$ can be obtained by using the form $R\cos(x \pm \alpha) = c$ or $R\sin(x \pm \alpha) = c$.

5 Revision Exercises

CHAPTER REVISION EXERCISES

CHAPTER 1 REVISION

1 $\boldsymbol{u} = \begin{pmatrix} 1 \\ 2 \end{pmatrix}$ and $v = \begin{pmatrix} 3 \\ -2 \end{pmatrix}$. Draw these vectors on squared paper, along with the vectors $\boldsymbol{u} + v$ and $\boldsymbol{u} - v$.

2 $\boldsymbol{p} = \begin{pmatrix} -1 \\ -1 \\ -1 \end{pmatrix}$, $\boldsymbol{q} = \begin{pmatrix} 3 \\ 2 \\ -1 \end{pmatrix}$ and $\boldsymbol{r} = \begin{pmatrix} -2 \\ 7 \\ 3 \end{pmatrix}$.

Find as column vectors:

a $\boldsymbol{p} + \boldsymbol{q} + \boldsymbol{r}$ **b** $3\boldsymbol{p} - 2\boldsymbol{q} + \boldsymbol{r}$.

3 P is (3, 1, −1), Q(−6, −2, 2), A(1, 7, −2) and B(−2, 6, −1). Show that:

a PQ passes through the origin

b PQ is parallel to AB.

4 Prove that A, B and C in each set of points below are collinear, and find $\frac{\text{AB}}{\text{BC}}$ for each.

a A(−3, 2, 4), B(−1, 6, 1), C(3, 14, −5)

b A(−1, 0, 2), B(3, 2, 1), C(15, 8, −2)

c A(5, −2, 1), B(3, 2, 1), C(0, 8, 1)

5 Show that the triangle with vertices P(1, 1, 2), Q(1, 2, 3) and R(0, 2, 3) is right-angled.

6 Find the coordinates of P, given:

a A(−3, −7, 2), B(0, −4, 5) and AP:PB = 1:2

b A(−1, 0, 5), B(5, −3, 2) and AP:PB = 2:1

c A(0, 1, 2), B(−5, −4, −3) and AP:PB = 2:3.

7 △ABC has vertices A(2, −2, 3), B(−1, 1, −6) and C(0, −2, −7).

a Find the coordinates of:

(i) P, dividing AB in the ratio 1:2

(ii) Q, the midpoint of AC

(iii) R, where $\overrightarrow{CR} = \overrightarrow{BC}$.

b Prove that P, Q and R are collinear, and find the value of PQ:QR.

8 $\boldsymbol{s} = \boldsymbol{i} - \boldsymbol{j} + 2\boldsymbol{k}$, $\boldsymbol{t} = 2\boldsymbol{i} + 2\boldsymbol{j}$ and $\boldsymbol{u} = 3\boldsymbol{j} - 4\boldsymbol{k}$. Calculate the exact values of:

a $|\boldsymbol{s}|$ **b** $|\boldsymbol{t}|$ **c** $|\boldsymbol{u}|$

d $|\boldsymbol{s} + \boldsymbol{t}|$ **e** $|\boldsymbol{s} - \boldsymbol{t}|$

9 A is (−2, 2, 4) and B is (−4, −2, 2). Show that △OAB is equilateral, where O is the origin.

10 $\boldsymbol{a} = 2\boldsymbol{i} - 3\boldsymbol{j} + \boldsymbol{k}$ and $\boldsymbol{b} = \boldsymbol{i} - \boldsymbol{j} - 4\boldsymbol{k}$. Calculate the angle between $\boldsymbol{a} + \boldsymbol{b}$ and $\boldsymbol{a} - \boldsymbol{b}$.

11 $\begin{pmatrix} a \\ b \\ c \end{pmatrix}$ is perpendicular to both $\begin{pmatrix} 0 \\ 1 \\ -1 \end{pmatrix}$ and $\begin{pmatrix} 2 \\ 1 \\ -1 \end{pmatrix}$. Show that $a = 0$ and $b = c \, (\neq 0)$.

12 See next page.

12 The origin is at the midpoint of the side AF of this cuboid, whose edges are parallel to the axes. C is the point (4, 2, 4).

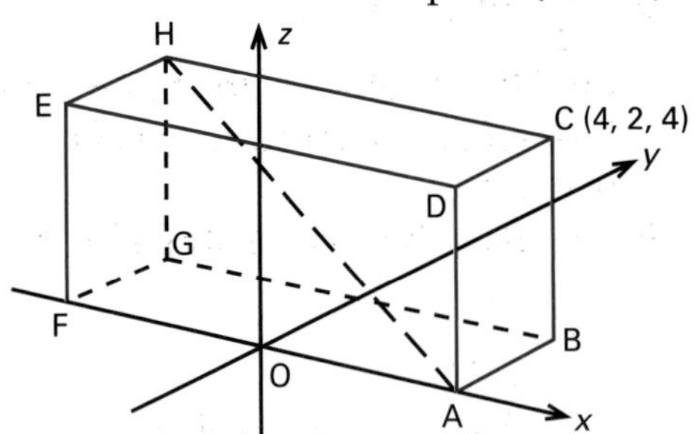

Find:

a the coordinates of A and H

b the length of AH

c $\angle$HOC.

13 ΔRST has vertices R(2, 3, -3), S(0, 1, -4) and T(-2, 2, -2). Prove that it is right-angled and isosceles by using:

a the distance formula

b scalar product.

14 A(3, 5, 8), B(4, 3, 4) and C(6, h, k) are collinear.

a Find h and k.

b Calculate AB:BC.

15 The sides of the equilateral triangle are 2 units long. Calculate:

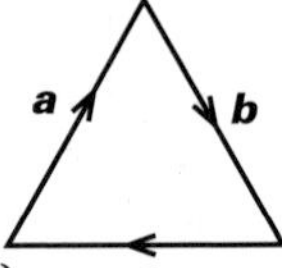

a $\boldsymbol{a}.\boldsymbol{b}$ **b** $\boldsymbol{a}.\boldsymbol{c}$

c $\boldsymbol{a}.(\boldsymbol{b}+\boldsymbol{c})$ **d** $\boldsymbol{a}.(\boldsymbol{a}+\boldsymbol{b}+\boldsymbol{c})$

CHAPTER 2 REVISION

1 Write down the value of:

a $\sin 2\pi$ **b** $\cos \dfrac{\pi}{3}$

c $\cos \dfrac{2\pi}{3}$ **d** $\sin \dfrac{\pi}{2}$

e $\cos \dfrac{\pi}{2} + \sin \dfrac{3\pi}{2}$

f $\sin^2 \dfrac{\pi}{4} + \cos^2 \dfrac{3\pi}{4}$.

Differentiate in questions **2–7**.

2 **a** $8 \sin x$

b $\frac{1}{2} \cos x$

c $3 \cos x + 4 \sin x$

d $1 - 2 \cos x$

e $3 - 2 \sin x + \cos x$

3 **a** $(3x+4)^5$ **b** $(1-2x)^3$

c $(2x+1)^{1/2}$ **d** $\sqrt[3]{(6x+9)}$

e $(4x+5)^{-3}$ **f** $(1-x)^{-1}$

4 **a** $\dfrac{1}{2x+1}$ **b** $\dfrac{1}{3(1-3x)^2}$

c $\dfrac{1}{\sqrt[3]{(1-9x)}}$

5 **a** $(x^2+7)^5$ **b** $\dfrac{1}{1+2x^2}$

c $\dfrac{2}{\sqrt{(x^2+x+1)}}$

6 **a** $\sin \frac{1}{2}x$

b $\cos(4x+2)$

c $\sin(6-2x)$

d $2 \sin 2x + 3 \cos 3x$

e $5 \cos(\pi x - 1)$

7 **a** $\cos^4 x$ **b** $(1+\cos x)^4$

c $(1+\sin x)^{-2}$ **d** $\dfrac{1}{2 \sin x}$

e $\dfrac{2}{\sqrt{(1+\cos x)}}$ **f** $\dfrac{1}{\sin x} + \dfrac{1}{\cos x}$

8 Calculate the rate of change of the function $f(x) = \dfrac{1}{1+\sin x}$, $0 \leqslant x \leqslant \pi$,

at: **a** $x = 0$ **b** $x = \dfrac{\pi}{2}$.

9 **a** Find the stationary values of the function $f(x) = x + \dfrac{1}{x}$, and determine their nature.

b Show that the function is increasing for $x > 1$ and $x < -1$.

10 Find the equation of the tangent to the curve $y = \sqrt{x} + \dfrac{1}{\sqrt{x}}$ at the point where $x = 4$.

11 Show that the function $f(x) = 2x + \sqrt{(20 - x^2)}$ has a stationary value at $x = 4$, and investigate its nature.

12 Integrate:
a $(x+1)^3$ **b** $(2x+3)^4$
c $(1-2x)^{-2}$ **d** $\sqrt{(2x+1)}$
e $(2x-1)^{-1/2}$ **f** $(1-x)^4$.

13 Evaluate:
a $\displaystyle\int_0^1 \frac{du}{(2-u)^2}$ **b** $\displaystyle\int_{-2}^1 \sqrt{(u+3)}\,du$.

14 Find:
a $\int 5\cos x\,dx$
b $\int 6\sin x\,dx$
c $\int 6\sin 3x\,dx$
d $\int \cos(4x+3)\,dx$
e $\int \sin(1-2x)\,dx$.

15 Evaluate:
a $\displaystyle\int_0^{\pi/3} \sqrt{3}\cos x\,dx$
b $\displaystyle\int_0^{\pi/4} \sqrt{2}\sin x\,dx$
c $\displaystyle\int_0^{\pi/2} (\sin x + \cos x)\,dx$
d $\displaystyle\int_{\pi/2}^{\pi} (3\sin x - 4\cos x)\,dx$.

16 Find a, for $0 \leqslant t \leqslant 2\pi$, given:
a $\displaystyle\int_0^a \cos t\,dt = 1$ **b** $\displaystyle\int_0^a \sin t\,dt = 2$.

17 Find the area enclosed by the x-axis, the curve $y = 1 - \cos x$ and the lines $x = \frac{\pi}{2}$ and $x = \pi$.

18 **a** Find the x-values of the three points of intersection of these curves, for $0 \leqslant x \leqslant 2\pi$.
b Calculate the area enclosed by the curves.

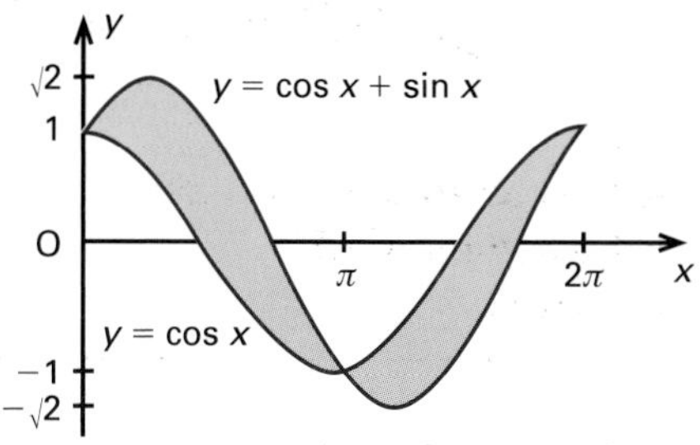

19 **a** If $f(x) = \sin^2 x$, show that $f'(x) = \sin 2x$.
b Investigate the stationary points of $y = f(x)$ for $0 \leqslant x \leqslant \pi$.
c Sketch, for $0 \leqslant x \leqslant \pi$, the graph of: **(i)** f **(ii)** the derived function f'.

CHAPTER 3 REVISION

1 Under water the temperature falls 2% every metre, said Joseph. His formula was $T = S \times (0.98)^d$, where T is the water temperature, S the surface temperature and d the depth in metres.
a If $S = 18$, calculate, correct to 1 decimal place, the temperature at a depth of: **(i)** 5 m **(ii)** 20 m.
b At what depth does the temperature fall below 10°?

2 A population of penguins increases at 6% per annum. There are P penguins to start with.
a Write down an expression for their population Q after n years.
b If $P = 5000$, calculate Q after ten years.

3 The value of a plane belonging to an airline depreciates according to the formula $V = 1.8e^{-0.223t}$, where V is the value in £million after t years.
a What is the plane's initial value?
b Calculate its value after one year, correct to 3 significant figures.
c What is the annual rate of depreciation?

4 On the same diagram, sketch:
a $y = e^x$ **b** $y = e^x + 2$
c $y = 2e^x$.

5 Write in logarithmic form:
a $16 = 4^2$ **b** $125 = 5^3$
c $3 = 27^{1/3}$ **d** $\frac{1}{x} = x^{-1}$.

6 Write in exponential form:
a $\log_2 32 = 5$ **b** $\log_5 5 = 1$
c $\log_7 x = y$.

7 Write in exponential form, then solve for x:

a $\log_x 196 = 2$ **b** $\log_3 x = 4$
c $\log_x 8 = 3$ **d** $\log_x 2 = 0.5$
e $\log_2 64 = x$ **f** $\log_x (\frac{1}{5}) = -1$.

8 Simplify:

a $\log_6 12 + \log_6 3$
b $\log_{10} 25 + \log_{10} 8 - \log_{10} 2$
c $4 \log_3 3 - \log_3 9$
d $3 \log_2 4 - 2 \log_2 2$.

9 The sketch shows part of the graph $y = \log_4 x$.

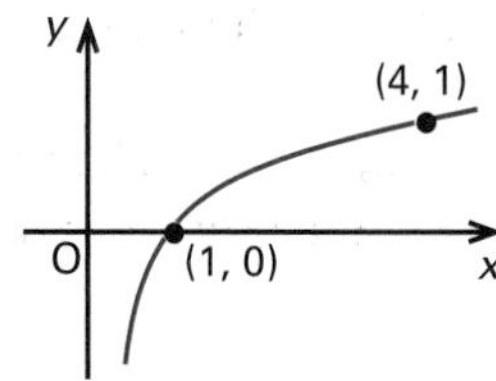

Make sketches of:

a $y = \log_4 \left(\frac{1}{x}\right)$
b $y = \log_4 4x$
c $y = 4^x$

10 Solve, correct to 1 decimal place:

a $4^x = 7$ **b** $6^x = 3$
c $2^{5x} = 80$ **d** $x = 2.5^{0.5}$
e $5 \times 6^x = 12$.

11 Calculate, correct to 2 decimal places:

a $\log_{10} e$ **b** $\log_e 10$ **c** e^{π}.

12 The mass of a radioactive element decreases at a rate given by $m_t = m_0 e^{-0.01t}$, where t is in years. Calculate:

a the mass of 500 g, to the nearest gram, after 100 years
b the half-life of the element, to the nearest year.

13 The price £C of a motorbike increases annually according to the formula $C = 8000e^{0.06t}$, where t is in years. Phil's savings £S increase according to the formula $S = 5000e^{0.1t}$.
Make an equation, and solve it to find in which year Phil can afford to buy the bike.

14 By graphing $\log_{10} y$ against $\log_{10} x$ or $\log_{10} y$ against x, find the values of a and b, given:

a $y = ax^b$

x	1	2	3	4	5
y	3	8.49	15.59	24	33.54

b $y = ab^x$

x	1	2	3	4	5
y	5.6	22.4	89.6	358.4	1434

CHAPTER 4 REVISION

1 Assuming that $R > 0$ and $0 \leqslant \alpha \leqslant 360$, find the exact value of R and the value of α to the nearest degree, given:

a $R\cos\alpha° = 1$, $R\sin\alpha° = 1$
b $R\cos\alpha° = -1$, $R\sin\alpha° = 1$
c $R\cos\alpha° = \sqrt{3}$, $R\sin\alpha° = -1$
d $R\cos\alpha° = -4$, $R\sin\alpha° = -3$.

2 Show that:

a $3\cos\theta + 3\sin\theta = 3\sqrt{2}\sin\left(\theta + \frac{\pi}{4}\right)$
b $-\sin x° - \sqrt{3}\cos x° = 2\cos(x + 150)°$.

3 Express each of the following in the form shown, giving α correct to the nearest degree $(0 \leqslant \alpha \leqslant 360)$:

a $7\cos x° + 5\sin x°$, $R\cos(x - \alpha)°$
b $-3\cos x° + 2\sin x°$, $R\sin(x - \alpha)°$.

4 Express each of these in the form shown $(0 \leqslant \theta \leqslant 2\pi)$:

a $6\cos\theta - 6\sin\theta$, $R\sin(\theta - \alpha)$
b $\sqrt{3}\cos\theta - \sin\theta$, $R\cos(\theta + \alpha)$.

5 **a** Find the intersections of the graph $y = 2\sin(x + 30)°$ with the axes, for $0 \leqslant x \leqslant 360$, also its maximum and minimum values and the corresponding values of x.
b State the amplitude and period, and sketch the graph.

6 a These two wave functions are added together.

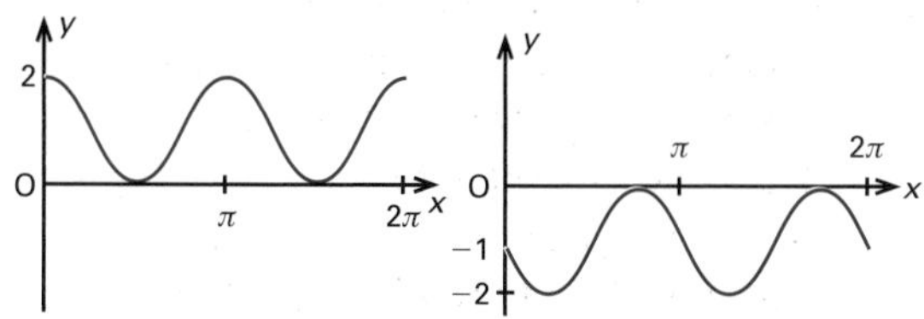

Find the equation of the combined wave in the form $y = a\cos mx + b\sin nx$.

b Express the combined equation in the form $R\cos(2x - \alpha)$, and find the maximum and minimum heights of the wave and the corresponding values of x, for $0 \leqslant x \leqslant 2\pi$.

7 Find the maximum and minimum values, and the corresponding values of x (to the nearest degree where necessary), for $0 \leqslant x \leqslant 360$, of:

a $8\cos x° + 6\sin x° - 4$

b $\dfrac{1}{8 + \sqrt{8}\sin x° + \sqrt{8}\cos x°}$.

8 Calculate the maximum and minimum values of $5\cos\theta - 12\sin\theta$, for $0 \leqslant \theta \leqslant 2\pi$, and the corresponding values of θ.

9 Solve, for $0 \leqslant x \leqslant 360$:

a $3\cos x° - 2\sin x° = -1$

b $15\cos x° + 8\sin x° = 17$.

10 The displacement, x cm, of a point on a sliding mechanism from a fixed point O is given by $x = 3\sin 2t - 4\cos 2t$, $t \geqslant 0$. By expressing x in the form $P\sin(2t - \alpha)$, where angles are in radians, find:

a the maximum displacement

b the first time when the point is at its maximum positive displacement

c the first time when its displacement is 2 cm.

11 Forces of 5 units and 12 units act at right angles at O on a body as shown.

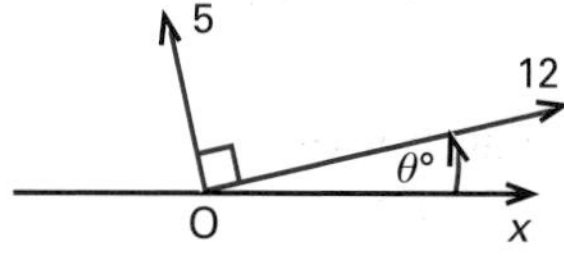

a Show that the combined effect of the force at O in the direction OX is $F(\theta) = 12\cos\theta° - 5\sin\theta°$, $0 \leqslant \theta \leqslant 360$.

b Investigate values of θ for maximum and minimum values of F.

GENERAL REVISION EXERCISES

REVIEW A

1 P is the point (2, 3, −1), Q is (0, 2, 1) and R(−4, 6, −3).

a Express $\overrightarrow{PQ}$ and $\overrightarrow{PR}$ in component form.

b Calculate:

(i) ∠QPR, correct to 0.1°

(ii) the area of △PQR.

2 Differentiate:

a $(3-2x)^4$ **b** $\sqrt{(2x-1)}$

c $\frac{1}{(3t+4)^5}$.

3 Simplify:

a $2\log_4 5 + 3\log_4 2 - 2\log_4 10$

b $\log_a \frac{a^2 \times a^3}{a}$.

4 Solve these simultaneous equations for k and α: $k\sin\alpha° = 2$ and $k\cos\alpha° = 3$, where $k > 0$ and $0 \leqslant \alpha \leqslant 360$, finding α correct to 0.1.

5 Simplify:

a $\int (3x+1)^4\,dx$ **b** $\int \frac{dx}{\sqrt{(2-x)}}$

c $\int_0^{\pi/4} \cos 2x\,dx$.

6 In the cuboid, OA = AB = 2 cm and BC = 4 cm. M, N and P are the mid-points of edges OA, BC and CD.

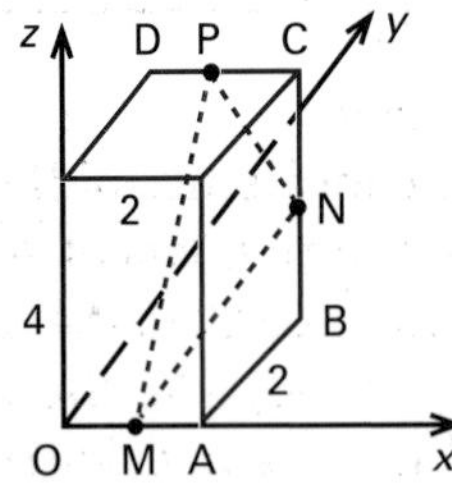

a Using the axes shown, write down the coordinates of A, B, C, M, N and P.

b Show that $\cos \text{PMN} = \frac{2\sqrt{5}}{5}$.

7 a Show that the function f given by $f(x) = x + \sin x$ is never decreasing.

b Find the gradient of the tangent to the curve $y = x + \sin x$ at:

(i) $x = \frac{\pi}{2}$ **(ii)** $x = \frac{3\pi}{2}$.

8 a Express $E(x) = 3\sin x° - 4\cos x°$ in the form $R\cos(x-\alpha)°$, $R > 0$ and $0 \leqslant \alpha \leqslant 360$.

b Find the maximum and minimum values of E, and the corresponding values of x, for $0 \leqslant x \leqslant 360$.

9 In an experiment, the number n of plant cells after t hours was given by $n = 25e^{1.2t}$

a Calculate the number of cells:

(i) initially **(ii)** after 2 hours.

b After how many whole minutes was the number of cells doubled?

10 $\boldsymbol{u} = \begin{pmatrix} -2 \\ -5 \\ -1 \end{pmatrix}$, $\boldsymbol{v} = \begin{pmatrix} 2 \\ -2 \\ 6 \end{pmatrix}$ and $\boldsymbol{w} = \begin{pmatrix} 6 \\ -6 \\ 18 \end{pmatrix}$. Show that:

a $\boldsymbol{u}$ is perpendicular to $\boldsymbol{v}$

b $\boldsymbol{v}$ is parallel to $\boldsymbol{w}$.

11 Solve:

a $\log_2(x^2 - 7x) = 3$

b $\log_6 2x + \log_6 3x - \frac{1}{2}\log_6 x^2 = 2$.

12 Calculate the area between the curve $y = \sin 2x$ and the x-axis for $0 \leqslant x \leqslant \frac{\pi}{2}$.

13 a Express $\sqrt{3}\cos x + \sin x$ in the form $R\sin(x+\alpha)$.

b Hence solve the equation $\sqrt{3}\cos x + \sin x = \sqrt{3}$, for $0 \leqslant x \leqslant 2\pi$.

14 Quadrilateral PQRS has vertices P(2, −3, 1), Q(6, 1, −3), R(−2, 2, 2) and S(−6, −2, 6).

a Find the coordinates of M, the mid-point of PQ, and N, which divides RM in the ratio 2:1.

b Prove that Q, N and S are collinear, and find the ratio in which N divides QS.

15 This is a sketch of $y = a\log_3(x - b)$.

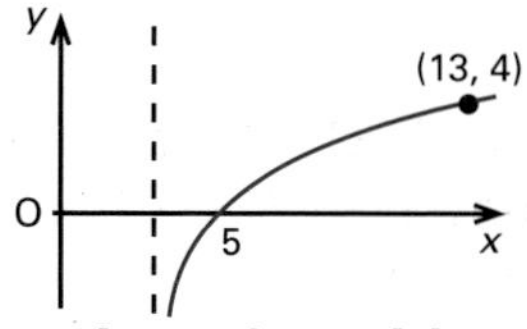

a Find the values of a and b.

b If the point $(k, 2)$ lies on the graph, find k.

16 a On the same diagram sketch $y = 1 + \sin x$ and $y = 1 - \sin x$ for $0 \leqslant x \leqslant \pi$.

b Calculate the area enclosed by the two curves.

17 $|\boldsymbol{a}| = 1$. Calculate the value of $\boldsymbol{a}.(\boldsymbol{a} + \boldsymbol{b} + \boldsymbol{c})$.

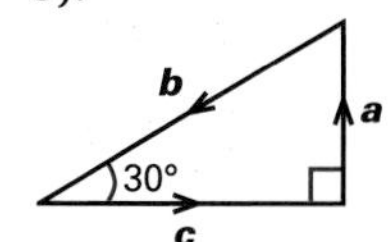

18 An experiment on the insulation of wires of thickness t mm at voltages V kilovolts gave these results:

t	2	3	5	10	14	18
V	153	200	282	450	562	666

a Show that a table of values of $\log_{10} t$ and $\log_{10} V$ gives approximately a straight line graph.

b Assuming that $V = kt^m$, calculate the values of k and m, correct to 2 significant figures.

c Predict the voltage for a 25 mm insulation.

REVIEW B

1 The gradient of the tangent to a curve at P(x, y) is given by $\frac{dy}{dx} = \sqrt{(2x + 1)}$.

If the point (4, 12) lies on the curve, find its equation.

2 Q is the point $(5, -2, 1)$ and S is $(-3, 22, -15)$.

a Find the coordinates of R which divides QS in the ratio 3:5.

b P is $(-3, 6, -3)$. Express $\overrightarrow{PQ}$, $\overrightarrow{PR}$ and $\overrightarrow{PS}$ in component form, and show that $\angle QPR = \angle RPS$.

3 Differentiate:

a $(2x + 1)^3 - \dfrac{1}{(2x + 1)^3}$

b $\sin(2x + 1) - \cos(2x + 1)$.

4 Vector $\boldsymbol{p}$ has components $\frac{2}{3}, \frac{2}{3}$ and $-\frac{1}{3}$ and $\boldsymbol{q}$ has components $\frac{2}{3}, -\frac{1}{3}$ and $\frac{2}{3}$. Show that:

a $\boldsymbol{p}$ and $\boldsymbol{q}$ have unit length

b $\boldsymbol{p}$ and $\boldsymbol{q}$ are perpendicular.

5 Find:

a $\displaystyle\int (x^4 + \frac{1}{x^4} - \sin x)\,dx$

b $\displaystyle\int_0^{\pi} \cos\tfrac{1}{2}x\,dx$.

6 $1 \times 2 \times 1$ unit bricks are stacked as shown.

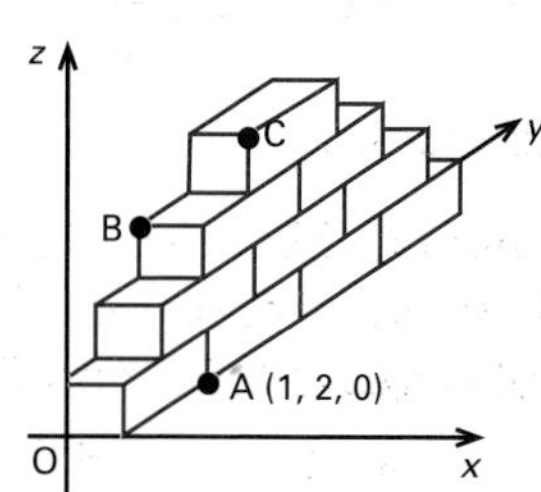

a Write down:

(i) the coordinates of B and C

(ii) the components of $\overrightarrow{AB}$ and $\overrightarrow{AC}$.

b Calculate $\angle BAC$, to the nearest degree.

c If D is $(-8, -6, -5)$, show that D, B, C are collinear, and calculate DB:BC.

7 a On the same diagram, sketch the graphs $y = e^x$ and $y = 4 - x$.

b Solve the equation $e^x = 4 - x$, correct to 1 decimal place.

8 a Express $E = \sqrt{3}\sin x° + \cos x°$ in the form $R\cos(x - \alpha)°$, $R > 0$ and $0 \leqslant \alpha \leqslant 360$.

b Write down the maximum and minimum values of E, and the corresponding values of x.

c Solve for x when $E = 1$, and $0 \leqslant x \leqslant 360$.

9 a A is $(-1, 4, -1)$, B$(2, 1, -4)$ and C$(4, 3, -6)$. Calculate $\angle$ABC, correct to $0.1°$.

b P divides CB externally in the ratio 3:1. Show that:

(i) P is the point $(1, 0, -3)$

(ii) AP is perpendicular to CB.

10 The mass in grams of a radioactive element decreases at a rate given by $m_t = m_0 e^{-0.03t}$, where t is the time in years. The initial mass is 500 g.

a Find:

(i) the mass after 100 years, to the nearest gram

(ii) the half-life of the element, to the nearest year.

b Sketch a decay curve to show the above information.

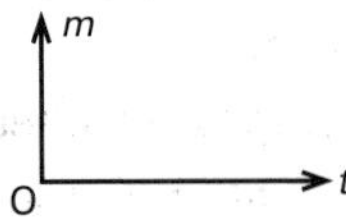

11 a Prove that the equation $\log_2(x^2 + a) - 2\log_2(x - 1) = 1$ is equivalent to the quadratic equation $x^2 - 4x + (2 - a) = 0$.

b Deduce that the given equation has real roots only if $a \geqslant -2$.

12 AB (1 unit long), AC (2 units long) and AD (3 units long) are at 60° to each other. $\overrightarrow{AB} = \mathbf{u}$, $\overrightarrow{AC} = \mathbf{v}$, and $\overrightarrow{AD} = \mathbf{w}$.
Evaluate:

a $\mathbf{u}.\mathbf{v}$, $\mathbf{u}.\mathbf{w}$ and $\mathbf{v}.\mathbf{w}$

b $\mathbf{u}.\mathbf{u} + \mathbf{v}.\mathbf{v} + \mathbf{w}.\mathbf{w}$

c $(\mathbf{u} + \mathbf{v} + \mathbf{w}).(\mathbf{u} + \mathbf{v} + \mathbf{w})$

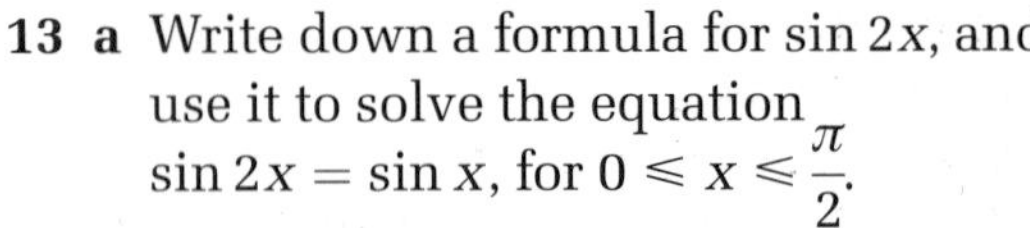

13 a Write down a formula for $\sin 2x$, and use it to solve the equation $\sin 2x = \sin x$, for $0 \leqslant x \leqslant \frac{\pi}{2}$.

b Find the shaded area enclosed by the curves $y = \sin 2x$ and $y = \sin x$.

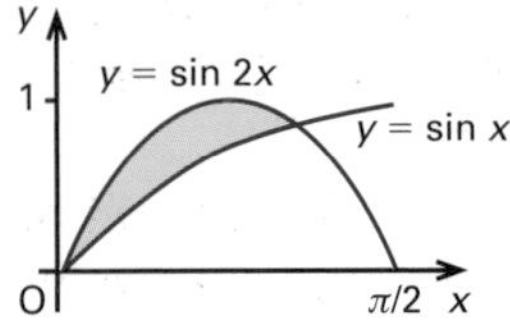

14 a Express $\sin\theta - \cos\theta$ in the form $R\sin(\theta - \alpha)$, $R > 0$ and $0 \leqslant \alpha \leqslant 2\pi$.

b Hence sketch the graph $y = \sin\theta - \cos\theta$ for $0 \leqslant \theta \leqslant 2\pi$.

c Solve the equation $\sin\theta - \cos\theta = -1$, $0 \leqslant \theta \leqslant 2\pi$.

15 $\frac{d^2y}{dx^2}$ denotes the derivative of $\frac{dy}{dx}$, i.e. $\frac{d}{dx}\left(\frac{dy}{dx}\right)$. The general solution of the equation $\frac{d^2y}{dx^2} + n^2y = 0$ is $y = A\cos nx + B\sin nx$, where n, A and B are constants.

a Write down the general solution if $\frac{d^2y}{dx^2} + 9y = 0$.

b Find the particular solution if $y = 1$ and $\frac{dy}{dx} = 3$ when $x = \frac{2\pi}{3}$.

REVIEW C

1 A is $(2, -3, 4)$, B$(-4, 6, -2)$ and C$(-8, 12, -6)$.

a Show that A, B and C are collinear.

b Find the ratio in which B divides AC.

c Find the point D which divides AC externally in the same ratio.

2 Differentiate:

a $\dfrac{1}{\sqrt[3]{(3x + 4)}}$

b $\sin(2x - 3) + \cos(3 - 2x)$.

3 Show that if $a\cos\theta + b\sin\theta = R\cos(\theta - \alpha)$, then $R\sin(\theta - \alpha) = a\sin\theta - b\cos\theta$.

4 Integrate:

a $x^2 - 2\cos 2x$

b $2\sin 3x\cos 3x$.

5 $\triangle$ABC has vertices A(1, 2, 0), B(3, −1, 4) and C(−2, 2, 2).

a Find the coordinates of:

(i) D, the midpoint of BC

(ii) S, which divides AD in the ratio 2:1.

b Show that S has position vector $\frac{1}{3}(\boldsymbol{a} + \boldsymbol{b} + \boldsymbol{c})$, where $\boldsymbol{a}$, $\boldsymbol{b}$, $\boldsymbol{c}$ are the position vectors of A, B, C.

6 Given $f(x) = \sin x$ and $g(x) = \sin 2x$, sketch the graphs, for $0 \leqslant x \leqslant 2\pi$:

a (i) $y = f(x)$ (ii) $y = f'(x)$

b (i) $y = g(x)$ (ii) $y = g'(x)$.

7 The number of bacteria in a colony after n days is given by $P(n) = 5000\,(10^{-n/6})$.

a What was the initial number of bacteria?

b What percentage has disappeared in 6 days?

c How many are left after $1\frac{1}{2}$ days?

d After how many whole days are there fewer than 100 left?

8 The velocity of a piston in a cylinder is given by $\dfrac{dx}{dt} = 6\cos 2t$. If the piston starts ($t = 0$) at A(2, 0), find its displacement $x(t)$ and its acceleration at time t.

9 The current $i(t)$ in this circuit at time t is given by $i(t) = \dfrac{E}{R} + \left(i_0 - \dfrac{E}{R}\right)e^{-(R/L)t}$.

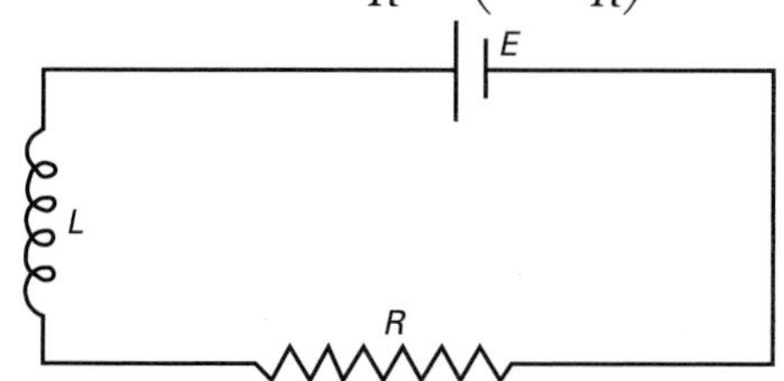

a Check that $i(0) = i_0$, the initial current.

b What happens to $i(t)$ as $t \to \infty$?

c Show in a sketch how $i(t)$ varies with t.

10 It can be shown that for the curve $y = xe^{-x^2}$, $\dfrac{dy}{dx} = (1 - 2x^2)e^{-x^2}$.

a Find the x-coordinates of its stationary points.

b State the values of x for which the curve is: **(i)** rising **(ii)** falling.

11 A is (2, 0, 3), B(1, 1, 0) and C(5, 2, −1).

a Show that $\angle$ABC is a right angle.

b Find the coordinates of D so that ABCD is a rectangle.

12 If two stars or planets have magnitudes m_1, m_2, and brightnesses b_1, b_2, then $\log_{10}\dfrac{b_1}{b_2} = 0.4(m_2 - m_1)$. Calculate, to the nearest whole number, $\dfrac{b_1}{b_2}$ for Venus (brightness b_1), with magnitude $m_1 = -4.4$, and Sirius (brightness b_2), with magnitude $m_2 = -1.4$.

13 A is (−3, 1, −5), B(5, 3, −1), C(−2, 0, −6) and D(4, 4, 0).

a Using midpoints, check that AB and CD bisect each other.

b Calculate, correct to 1 decimal place, the acute angle between AB and CD.

14 Find the maximum and minimum values of $2 + 2\cos x° - \frac{3}{2}\sin x°$, and the corresponding values of x, correct to 0.1°, for $0 \leqslant x \leqslant 360$.

15 Two of the shapes OMNQP, where MNQP is a square, make a new type of lawnmower blade.

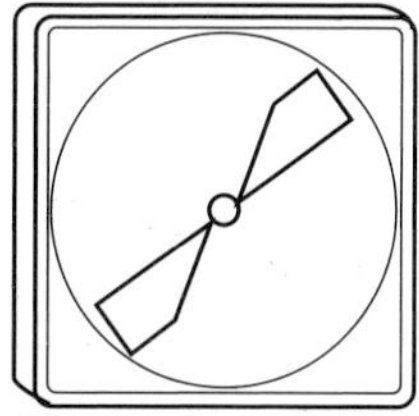

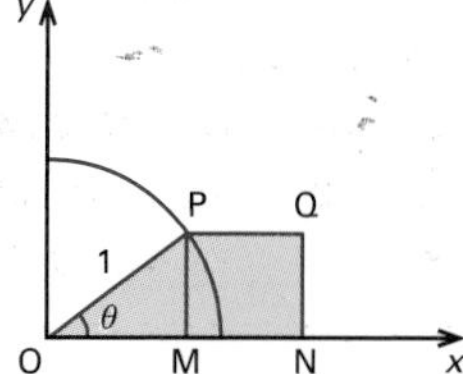

a Show that the area of OMNQP is $A = \sin^2\theta + \frac{1}{4}\sin 2\theta$.

b Express A in the form $R\cos(2\theta - \alpha) + c$, α correct to 1 decimal place.

c Find the maximum area, and the corresponding value of θ, correct to 1 decimal place.

REVIEW A

1 $\triangle ABC$ has vertices A(7, 6), B(−1, 2) and C(3, −2). M is the midpoint of AB and N is the midpoint of AC. Show that:
a MN is parallel to BC **b** $MN = \frac{1}{2}BC$.

2 $y(x)$ is such that $\frac{dy}{dx} = 5 - 6x^2$ and $y(-1) = 4$. Find $y(x)$.

3 Factorise $2x^3 - 3x^2 + x - 6$.

4 $\tan A = \frac{4}{3}$, and angle A is acute. Find the exact values of cos A and cos 2A.

5 For each of the graphs $y = f(x)$ below draw separate sketches to show the graphs of:
(i) $y = f(x) - 1$ (ii) $y = -f(x)$
(iii) $y = f'(x)$.

a **b**

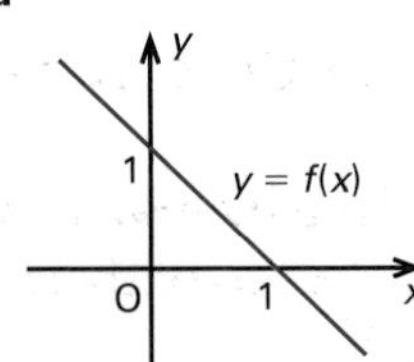

6 Find the equation of the tangent to the curve $y = x + \frac{2}{\sqrt{x}}$ at the point where $x = 4$.

7 Write down the largest domain and range of the function f defined by $f(x) = 3 + \sqrt{x}$.

8 In the triangle in question **1**, the altitude AD meets BC at D. Find the coordinates of D.

9 Differentiate $\sin(3x + 1) + (2 - 3x)^{1/3}$.

10 Each edge of this cube is 10 cm long. Calculate, correct to 0.1°, the angle between:
a BH and the base plane ABCD
b the planes HDB and HDAE.

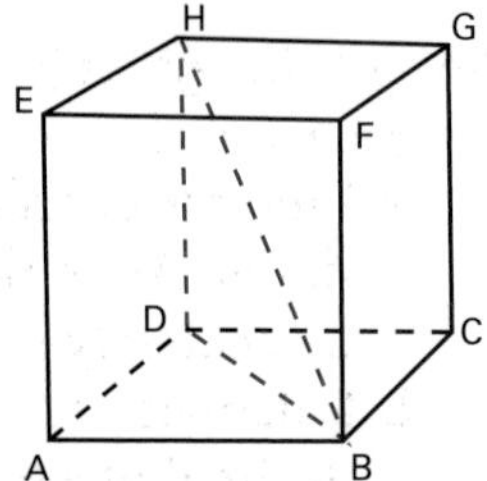

11 $f(x) = x^2 + a$ and $g(x) = 2x - 1$.
a Show that
$f(g(x)) - g(f(x)) = 2x^2 - 4x + (2 - a)$.
b Find a for which the equation
$f(g(x)) - g(f(x)) = 0$ has equal roots.

12 A is the point (−3, 2, −3) and B is (0, −2, 2). Find:
a the components of vector $\overrightarrow{AB}$
b the length of AB, in simplest surd form.

13 For which values of x is the function $f(x) = 2x^3 + 3x^2 - 12x + 1$:
a stationary
b increasing
c decreasing?

14 $u_{n+1} = 0.8u_n + 5$, and $u_1 = 50$, is a recurrence relation.
a List u_2, u_3 and u_4.
b Explain why the sequence has a limit, and calculate its value.

15 **a** Evaluate:
(i) $\int_0^{\pi/4} \cos 2x \, dx$
(ii) $\int_0^{\pi/4} \sin 2x \, dx$.
b Show sketches of the areas which these integrals can represent.

16 Solve the equation $6\cos^2 x° - \cos x° - 2 = 0$ for $0 \leqslant x \leqslant 360$, correct to 0.1° where necessary.

17 A population of 5 million increased at an annual rate of 5%.
a Calculate the population, to the nearest million, ten years later.
b After how many complete years did the population first exceed 10 million?

18 Find k if the roots of $2kx^2 - 6kx + (k + 7) = 0$ are:
a equal
b real and distinct.

19 a Find the equation of the tangent to the circle $x^2 + y^2 - 4x + 6y - 37 = 0$ at A(3, 4).

b Find also the equation of the parallel tangent.

20 a Express $2\cos x^\circ + \sqrt{5}\sin x^\circ$ in the form $R\cos(x - \alpha)^\circ$, with $R > 0$ and α correct to 0.1°.

b Solve the equation $2\cos x^\circ + \sqrt{5}\sin x^\circ = 1.5$, correct to 0.1°, for $0 \leqslant x \leqslant 360$.

21 a Simplify:

(i) $\log_6 9 + \log_6 8 - \log_6 2$

(ii) $2\log_a 2 + \log_a(\frac{1}{4})$.

b Find the least positive integer n for which $1.25^n > 7000$.

REVIEW B

1 Solve the equation $x^3 - 9x + 10 = 0$, giving the roots correct to 2 decimal places where necessary.

2 The equations of the sides of △ABC are: AB $3x - 2y + 1 = 0$, BC $x + 8y + 9 = 0$ and CA $2x + 3y - 8 = 0$.

a Prove that the triangle is right-angled.

b Find the coordinates of the right-angle vertex.

3 a Sketch the graph $y = x^4 + 4x^3$.

b For what values of a has the equation $x^4 + 4x^3 = a$ no real roots?

4 A sequence is defined by $u_{n+1} = mu_n + c$. If $u_0 = 0$, $u_1 = 2$ and $u_2 = 4$, find the values of:

a m and c **b** u_3.

5 Differentiate $\dfrac{1}{2x+1} - 3\cos^3 x$.

6 Two gearwheels are shown on a plan by a circle with centre A and equation $x^2 + y^2 - 16x + 28 = 0$, touching a circle with centre B $(0, k)$ and radius 4 units. Find:

a the centre A and radius of the first circle

b possible values of k and equations of the circle centre B.

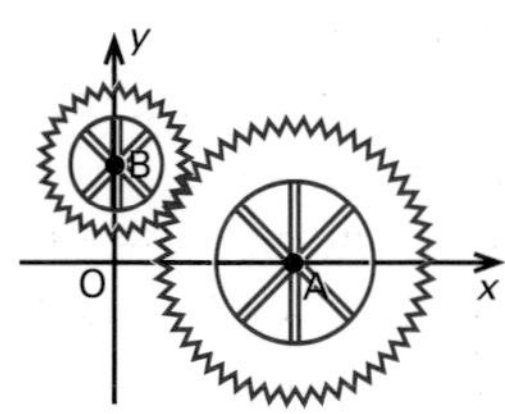

7 Solve the equation $3\sin\theta - 2\cos 2\theta + 1 = 0$, for $0 \leqslant \theta \leqslant 2\pi$, correct to 2 decimal places.

8 A is $(1, a, 2)$, B$(3, 4, 5)$, C$(2, -2, 3)$ and D$(b, 2, -1)$. If AB is perpendicular to CD, find the relation between a and b.

9 Integrate $\sqrt{(3 - x)} - \sin(3x + 2)$.

10 Express each of the following in the form $a(x + p)^2 + q$, then give its maximum or minimum value and the corresponding value of x.

a $x^2 + 2x + 5$

b $2x^2 - 8x + 1$

c $4 - 6x - x^2$

11 △PQR has vertices P(6, 3), Q(−4, 1) and R(4, −7).

a Find the equations of the medians PS and QT, and the coordinates of their point of intersection, K.

b Show that K lies on the third median RU.

12 For what values of t is $\boldsymbol{a} = t\boldsymbol{i} + \frac{1}{2}\boldsymbol{j} - \frac{1}{2}\boldsymbol{k}$ a unit vector?

13 Write down the equations of these curves:

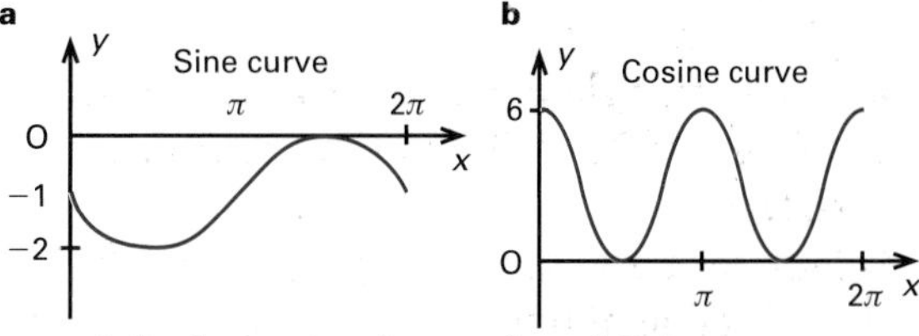

14 A is the point (5, 2, 1) and B is (9, 10, 13).

a Find the coordinates of P and Q which divide AB in the ratios 1:3 and 3:1 respectively.

b Calculate the length of PQ, correct to 1 decimal place.

C·O·U·R·S·E · R·E·V·I·S·I·O·N

15 $\cos A = \dfrac{1}{2\sqrt{2}}$, and $0° < A < 90°$.
Find the exact values of $\sin 2A$ and $\cos 2A$.

16 Find the values of a for which the line $y = x + a$ is a tangent to the circle $x^2 + y^2 = 2$.

17 **a** $f(x) = x^4 + x^3 - 3x^2 - x + 2$. Solve $f(x) = 0$.
b Find the values of x at stationary points of the curve $y = f(x)$, correct to 1 decimal place where necessary.
c Sketch the graph $y = f(x)$.

18 Evaluate $\displaystyle\int_{-1}^{2} (4 - 2x)\,dx$, and illustrate this as the area of a region of the x, y-plane.

19 $\triangle ABC$ has vertices A(1, 3, 5), B(−4, −2, 0) and C(−1, −3, −3).
a Show that $\angle ABC$ is obtuse.
b Find the coordinates of P, Q and R on the sides such that AP:PB = 2:3, BQ:QC = −3:2 and R is the midpoint of AC.
c Show that P, Q and R are collinear.

20 **a** Express $\sqrt{3}\cos x - \sin x$ in the form $R\sin(x - \alpha)$, with $R > 0$.
b Solve $\sqrt{3}\cos x - \sin x + 1 = 0$, for $0 \leqslant x \leqslant 2\pi$.

21 $f(x) = \sin^2 x$, $0 \leqslant x \leqslant 2\pi$.
a Write down the maximum and minimum values of f, and the corresponding values of x.
b Sketch the graph $y = f(x)$.
c Find the area enclosed by the graph and the x-axis for $0 \leqslant x \leqslant 2\pi$.

REVIEW C

1 P is the point $(2p, p^2)$ and Q is $(2q, q^2)$. Find, in simplest form, expressions for:
a the midpoint of PQ
b the gradient of PQ.

2 The shaded region represents the under-surface of the nose-cone of a new Formula 1 racing car. If 1 unit = 10 cm, calculate the area of the surface.

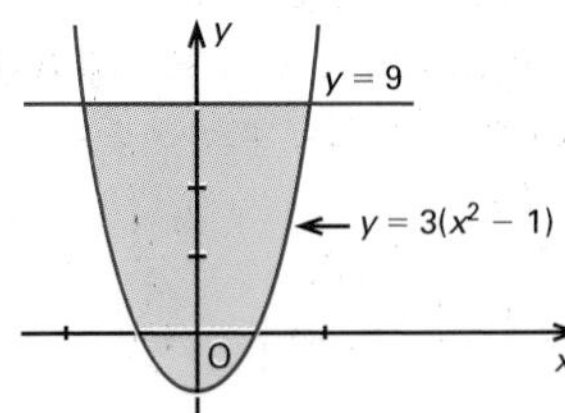

3 $\triangle ABC$ has vertices A(9, 0), B(−3, 6) and C(3, 8).
a Find the equations of the perpendicular bisectors of AB and BC, and their point of intersection S.
b Show that a circle, centre S, passes through A, B and C.

4 Solve the equations:
a $2\sin(2x - 50)° = 1$, $0 \leqslant x \leqslant 360$
b $3\cos\left(2x + \dfrac{\pi}{6}\right) = 1$, $0 \leqslant x \leqslant \pi$,
correct to 1 decimal place.

5 The parabola through B, O and C is symmetrical about the y-axis.

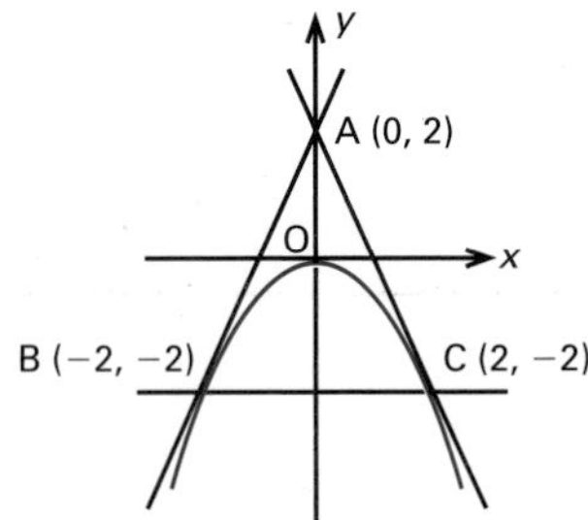

a Find the equations of AB, AC, BC and the parabola.
b The three lines and the parabola are reflected in the x-axis. Find the equations of their images.
c The images in **b** are translated 2 units in the $\overrightarrow{OY}$ direction. Write down the equations of the new positions of the lines and the parabola.

6 **a** Find the equation of the locus of P(x, y) for which AP = PB, where A is the point (−2, −3) and B is (4, 1).

b Verify that this is the equation of the perpendicular bisector of AB.

7 $f(x) = 3x - 2$, $g(x) = \dfrac{1}{x+1}$ and $h(x) = \dfrac{2x+3}{4x-3}$. Find, in simplest form:

a $f(g(x))$ **b** $g(f(x))$

c $g(h(x))$ **d** $h(g(x))$.

8 Garden planners base their designs on a coordinate grid. For one garden they plan a straight path from P(−2, 3) to Q(6, −5), across a circular plot having PQ as diameter.

a Find the equation of the circle, and of the diameter RS perpendicular to PQ.

b Find the coordinates of R and S.

c What shape is PRQS? Justify your answer.

9 **a** Given $y = e^{-0.12x}$, calculate x, correct to 1 decimal place, when $y = 0.15$.

b The graph illustrates the law $y = kx^n$. Find k and n, correct to 1 decimal place.

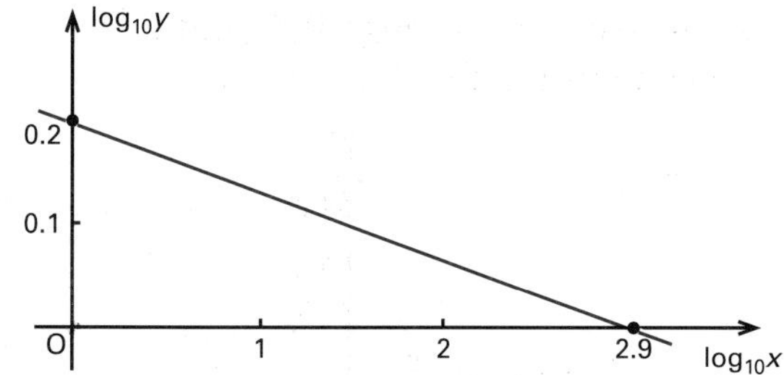

10 **a** Show that $\cos(A - B) - \cos(A + B) = 2 \sin A \sin B$.

b Evaluate $\displaystyle\int_0^{\pi/4} \sin x \sin 3x \, dx$.

11 **a** Express $E = 3 \sin 20t° - 4 \cos 20t°$ in the form $R \cos(20t - \alpha)°$, with $R > 0$ and α correct to the nearest degree.

b Solve the equation $E = 1$, for $0 \leqslant t \leqslant 40$, to the nearest degree.

12 Interpret $\displaystyle\int_0^1 \sqrt{(1 - x^2)} \, dx$ as the area of a region of the x, y-plane, and hence evaluate the integral.

13 A tetrahedron has vertices A(4, 2, 5), B(2, 0, −1), C(0, −2, 3) and D(6, −4, −1). M_1, M_2, M_3 and M_4 are midpoints of AB, BC, CD and DA.

a Prove that M_1M_3 and M_2M_4 bisect each other.

b Find the acute angle between M_1M_3 and M_2M_4, correct to 0.1°.

14 A function f is defined by $f(\theta) = 8 \sin^3 \theta + 3 \cos 2\theta$, for $0 \leqslant \theta \leqslant 2\pi$.

a Find $f'(\theta)$, and solve the equation $f'(\theta) = 0$.

b Make a table of values of f for the roots of $f'(\theta) = 0$.

c Deduce the maximum and minimum values of f for $0 \leqslant \theta \leqslant 2\pi$.

15 The lengths of the sides of a triangle are: AB $4x$ cm, BC $2x$ cm and CA $3x$ cm. Show that:

a $\sin C = 2 \sin A$

b $2 \cos A + 7 \cos C = 0$.

·A·N·S·W·E·R·S·

UNIT 1

1 The straight line

Page 2 Exercise 1

1 a 2 **b** 14 **c** −1 **d** 7
e −3 **f** −6 **g** 1 **h** −1

2 $\sqrt{(2+1)^2+(-7)^2} = \sqrt{9+49} = \sqrt{58} = 7.6$

3 a 5 **b** 13 **c** 25 **d** 10

4 P on edge, Q inside, R outside

5 $AB = \sqrt{50} = BC$

6 a OA 5 km, AB 10 km, BC 10 km, CO 8.5 km
b 33.5 km

7 a $(5, 3\frac{1}{2})$ **b** $(3\frac{1}{2}, 6)$
c $(4\frac{1}{2}, 14)$ **d** $(0, 1)$

8 $(1, 4)$; $AM = \sqrt{26} = MB$

9 $(2, -2)$; $AM = \sqrt{10} = MB$

10 a S(1, 4), T(3, 3) **b** $\frac{1}{2}$

11 $PQ^2 = 100 = QR^2 + PR^2$

12 a $AV = \sqrt{10} = AK$, $TV = \sqrt{58} = TK$
b $(-2, 3)$

13 $BC^2 > AC^2 > AB^2$

Page 4 Exercise 2A

1 a 1 **b** 2 **c** 1 **d** 2 **e** 0 **f** −1

2 MN $\frac{1}{2}$, PQ − 3, RS 0, TU −1, VW not defined, ZA $\frac{1}{3}$
b (i) slopes up from left to right
(ii) slopes down from left to right

3 0.8, 1.6, −1

4 $m_{AB} = m_{DC} = \frac{1}{4}$, $m_{AD} = m_{BC} = -2$

5 $m_{EF} = m_{HG} = -\frac{1}{3}$

6 $m_{PK} = 1$, $m_{PM} = -\frac{1}{3}$

7 a $m_{AB} = m_{BC} = 1$, and B is common
b $m_{DO} = m_{OE} = \frac{1}{2}$, and O is common

8 a (i) 1 **(ii)** 45° **b (i)** 2 **(ii)** 63°
c (i) −4 **(ii)** 104° **d (i)** $-\frac{1}{3}$ **(ii)** 162°

9 a $m_{FG} = m_{KH} = -\frac{1}{2}$, $m_{KF} = m_{HG} = 2$
b $FH^2 = 50 = FG^2 + GH^2$, or $FH^2 = KG^2 = 50$

Page 5 Exercise 2B

1 a (i) $\frac{1}{3}$ **(ii)** 2 **(iii)** 1 **(iv)** $\frac{1}{3}$ **(v)** $-\frac{5}{3}$ **(vi)** 0
b AB, FG **c** MN **d** AB, OC, DE, FG

2 a 3, 72° **b** −3, 108°
c −1, 135° **d** $\frac{3}{4}$, 37°

3 $m_{DG} = m_{EF} = -\frac{3}{2}$

4 a $m_{PQ} = m_{QR} = \frac{1}{3}$, and Q is common
b $m_{SQ} = m_{QT} = -1$, and Q is common
c $m_{PS} = m_{TR} = 1$, so PS‖TR; by alternate angles the △s are equiangular, so similar

5 a 1 **b** −3.7 **c** −0.5

6 a −0.3 **b** −0.1 **c** −0.5

Page 7 Exercise 3

1 b, c

2 a AB, IJ; EF, KL
b AB, GH; GH, IJ; CD, EF; CD, KL

3 a (i) 4 **(ii)** $-\frac{1}{4}$ **b (i)** −1 **(ii)** 1
c (i) $\frac{1}{3}$ **(ii)** −3 **d (i)** $\frac{3}{4}$ **(ii)** $-\frac{4}{3}$
e (i) $-2\frac{1}{2}$ **(ii)** $\frac{2}{5}$

4 a $y = -\frac{1}{3}x$ **b** $y = \frac{1}{5}x$ **c** $y = -10x$
d $y = -\frac{3}{2}x$ **e** $y = 2x$ **f** $y = -x$

5 a (iii), (iv) **b** (i), (ii)

6 $m_{AB} = 1$, $m_{CD} = -1$, so $m_{AB} \times m_{CD} = -1$

7 a 2, $k/6$ **b** −3

8 a $m_{CD} \times m_{DB} = \frac{1}{2} \times (-2) = -1$, so ∠CDB = 90°;
$m_{AC} \times m_{AB} = -2 \times \frac{1}{2} = -1$, so ∠CAB = 90°
b $AB^2 + AC^2 = 40 = BC^2 = DB^2 + DC^2$

9 $m_{PQ} = m_{RS} = -\frac{1}{3}$, and $m_{QR} = m_{SP} = 3$, so opposite sides are parallel; $m_{PQ} \times m_{PS} = -1$, so all angles are 90°

10 $AB^2 = 26 = BC^2$, so AB = BC; 1

11 ∠SKT = 90°, so angle in semi-circle, or OK = OS = OT, equal radii

Page 8 Exercise 4

1 a (i) $y = 4x + 2$ **(ii)** $y = 4x - 1$ **(iii)** $y = 4x$
b (i) $y = -x + 2$ **(ii)** $y = -x - 5$ **(iii)** $y = -x$

2 a 1, 6, $y = x + 6$ **b** $-\frac{1}{2}$, −3, $y = -\frac{1}{2}x - 3$

3 a 1, $y = x + 4$ **b** 2, $y = 2x + 2$
c $-\frac{2}{3}$, $y = -\frac{2}{3}x + 3$ **d** −4, $y = -4x - 2$

4 a $y = x - 6$ **b** $y = -x - 6$

5 a $y = x + 2$, on **b** $y = -2x - 1$, not on
c $y = \frac{1}{3}x - 4$, not on **d** $y = -\frac{2}{3}x + 2$, on

6 a (i) $y = x$ **(ii)** $y = -x$
b (i) $y = 2x$ **(ii)** $y = -\frac{1}{2}x$
c (i) $y = -3x$ **(ii)** $y = \frac{1}{3}x$

7 a $\frac{1}{4}$ **b (i)** $y = \frac{1}{4}x + 5$ **(ii)** $y = -4x + 5$

8 a $y = \frac{1}{2}x + 5$, yes **b** $y = 4x - 1$, no

9 a 63° **b** 108°

10 a $y = 2x + 4$; 2, 4 **b** $y = -3x + 6$; −3, 6
c $y = \frac{2}{3}x + 2$; $\frac{2}{3}$, 2 **d** $y = -x + 5$; −1, 5

11 a **b**

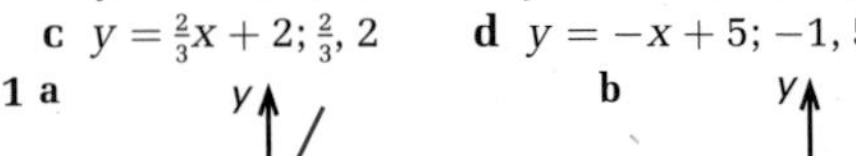

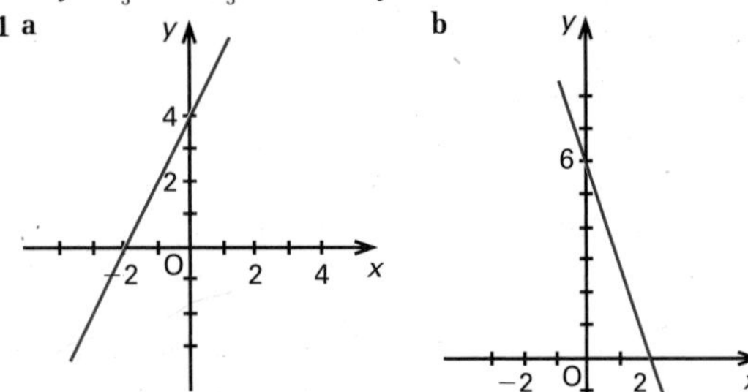

c

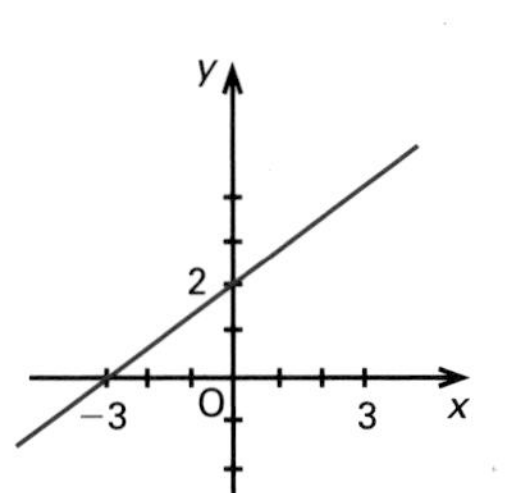

d

12 a (i) $y = -3x - 6$
(ii) $y = -3x + 6$
(iii) $y = 3x - 6$
b (i) $y = 3x$ (ii) $y = 3x + 8$

Page 10 Exercise 5

1 a $2x - y - 1 = 0$ b $2x - y + 1 = 0$
c $2x - 3y + 6 = 0$ d $4x + 5y - 5 = 0$
e $x + 6y + 4 = 0$ f $6x - 4y - 3 = 0$

2 a

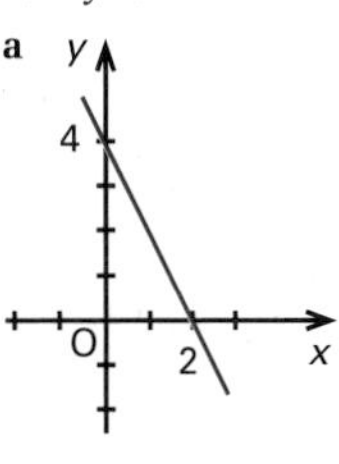

b

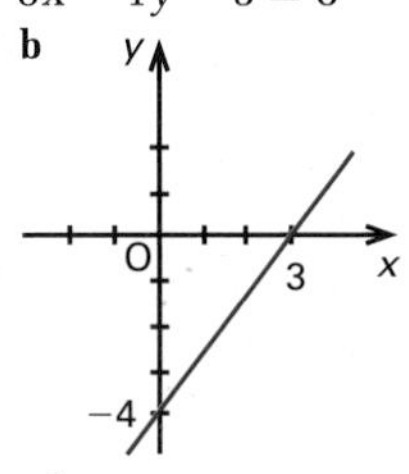

c

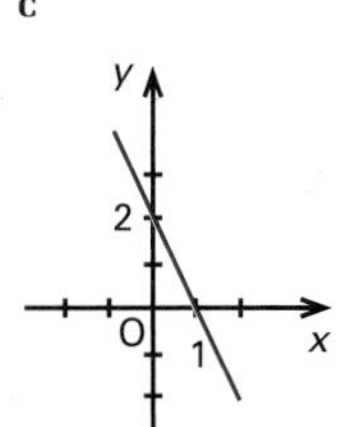

d

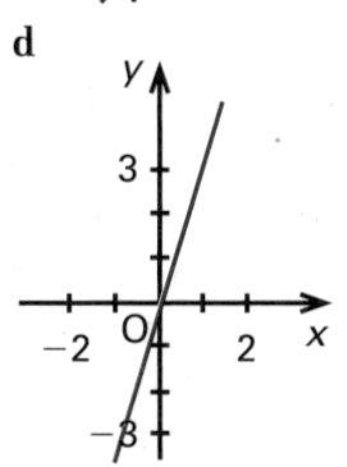

3 a $y = 2$ b $x = 1$

4 $x = 2, x = 4, y = 1, y = 4$

5 a $\frac{4}{5}, -2$ b 39°, 117° c 78°

6 a, c, e

7 a 2 b $b = -2a + 3$

8 a $h = 6, k = 0$ b gradient = 3

10 a $3x - 2y = 5$
b of first degree in x and y; product of gradients = −1

11 a $3x + y = 5$ b as for **10b**

Page 11 Exercise 6

1 a $y - 3x = 1$ b $y - 2x = 3$
c $y + 5x = -10$ d $y + x = 2$
e $3y - 2x = 16$ f $4y + x = 13$

2 a $y - 2x = -2$ b $y - 3x = 3$
c $3y - x = 9$ d $5y + 2x = 1$

3 a $\frac{2}{3}, 3y - 2x = 7$ b $-\frac{1}{4}, 4y + x = 18$
c $-\frac{3}{2}, 2y + 3x = 13$ d $-\frac{1}{3}, 3y + x = -5$

4 a $y - x = 1$ b $y - 3x = -13$
c $y + x = -5$ d $2y - 3x = -9$

5 a $2y + x = 4$ b $4y + x = 21$
c $y + 2x = 10$ d $2y - 3x = -15$

6 a $y - 2x = 4$ b $y + 3x = 14$
c $2y + x = -2$

7 a $(1, -1)$ b 3 c $y - 3x = -4$

8 $5y + 2x = 13, 4y - 5x = -5, y + 7x = 18$

9 a (i) $-\frac{2}{3}$ (ii) $\frac{3}{2}$ b $2y - 3x = -11$

10 $4y + x = 11, 3y - 2x = 5, y + 3x = 6$

11 a $m_{ST} = m_{VU} = \frac{1}{2}$, $m_{VS} = m_{UT} = \frac{7}{3}$; so opposite sides are parallel
b ST $2y - x = 7$, VU $2y - x = -4$, VS $3y - 7x = 27$, UT $3y - 7x = -17$

12 a (i) $m_{AC} = -\frac{2}{3}$ (ii) $m_{BD} = \frac{3}{2}$
b $2y - 3x = -11$ c (i) $(5, 2)$ (ii) $(1, -4)$

13 a AS $y + 3x = 22$, BL $y + 3x = 52$
b $3y - x = 26$ c $y = 7$ d $3y + x = 16$

Page 14 Exercise 7A

1 a $(1, 2)$ b $(0, 5)$ c $(-1, 1)$

2 $(6, 0), (0, -4)$

3 $(1, 7), (1, 0), (0, 5)$

4 a $2y + x = 6$ b $(0, 3), (6, 0)$

5 a $y + x = 2$ b $(1, 1)$

6 a VT, $3y - 4x = 5$; SU, $y = 3$ b $(1, 3)$

7 a (i) $y - 4x = 4$ (ii) $2y - x = 8$ b $(0, 4)$

8 a $m_{AB} = \frac{1}{3}$, $m_{BC} = -\frac{1}{2}$
b $y + 3x = 34$, $y - 2x = -16$ c $(10, 4)$

Page 15 Exercise 7B

1 a (i) $y = x$, $3y + x = -10$ (ii) $(-\frac{5}{2}, -\frac{5}{2})$
b the altitudes are concurrent (pass through the same point)

2 a (i) $2y + x = 10$ (ii) $y - 2x = 0$
b at D(2, 4)
c 027°, 4.47 km

3 a (i) PQ, $y + 2x = 8$; QR, $y = 1$ (ii) D$(\frac{7}{2}, 1)$
b S lies on $3y - 4x = -11$

4 a (i) $3y - 2x = 6$ (ii) $2y + 3x = 30$
b (i) $y = 3$ (ii) $(8, 3)$ (iii) 361 m

5 a (i) A(−5, 3), B(5, 7), C(1, −5)
(ii) $4y + x = 7$, $7y - 8x = 9$, $y + 10x = 5$
b S$(\frac{1}{3}, \frac{5}{3})$ lies on CR

6 a $m_{OA} = -\frac{4}{3}$, $m_{OB} = -\frac{3}{4}$
b $4y - 3x = 25$, $3y - 4x = -25$
c $(25, 25)$ d 35 cm
e P(−15, −5), Q$(\frac{5}{2}, -5)$ f 17.5 cm

7 B(8, 8), D(8, 4), F$(8, 6\frac{2}{3})$, H(8, 0)

Page 17 Review

1 a 10 b $\frac{4}{3}$ c 53°

2 a G(1, 4), H(3, 2)

3 a parallel b perpendicular
c parallel d perpendicular
e parallel f perpendicular

4 a (4, 0), (0, −6) **b** $y = \frac{3}{2}x - 6$; $\frac{3}{2}$
5 KL 3, 0, $y = 4$; LM 6.7, −2, $y + 2x = 6$; MN 6.7, $-\frac{1}{2}$, $2y + x = 0$; NK 3, undefined, $x = -2$
6 a (i) 26.6° **(ii)** 123.7° **b** 82.9°
7 K, Z, V
8 10, $-\frac{3}{4}$, $4y + 3x = -6$
9 yes
10 a (i) $4y - 3x = 16$ **(ii)** $3y + 4x = 37$
b product of gradients $= \frac{3}{4} \times (-\frac{4}{3}) = -1$; (4, 7)
11 a (i) $-\frac{2}{3}$ **(ii)** $\frac{3}{2}$ **b** $2y - 3x = -6$
12 a (5, −1) **b** $4y + x = 1$
13 a (i) $3y - x = 6$, $y + 3x = 22$ **(ii)** (6, 4)
14 P(−3, 2), Q(5, 4), R(−1, −2)
15 (5, 3)
16 $y = 1.39x$, $y = -0.72x$

2.1 Composite and inverse functions

Page 20 Exercise 1

1 Rows: 1, 1, 1, 1; −1, undefined, 0, −1; −5, $-\frac{1}{2}$, 4, $\frac{1}{7}$
2 a {5, 6, 7} **b** {−3, −1, 1}
c {4, 1, 0} **d** $\{1, \frac{1}{2}, \frac{1}{3}\}$
e {0, 25, 100}
3 a, b and **d** represent functions
4 a $4x^2$ **b** $(x+1)^2$ **c** x^2 **d** $1/x^2$
5 a $2x + 3$ **b** $4x + 1$ **c** $x + 1$ **d** $2x - 1$
7 b $3x^2 + 12x + 11$
c $6x + 6$
8 a $x < 0$ **b** $x < 1$ **c** $x < -2$
d 0 **e** 5 **f** 0, −1
9 a $\frac{x-1}{x}$ **b** $\frac{1}{1+x}$ **c** $1 - x$ **d** $\frac{1}{x}$
10 a $\frac{x+1}{-x}$ **b** $\frac{1}{x-1}$ **c** $\frac{1}{x}$ **d** $-\frac{1}{x}$
11 3 **12** $1\frac{1}{3}$

Page 21 Exercise 2

1 a $-1 \leqslant x \leqslant 2$, $-1 \leqslant y \leqslant 5$
b $1 \leqslant x \leqslant 3$, $1 \leqslant y \leqslant 4$
c $-3 \leqslant x \leqslant 2$, $-2 \leqslant y \leqslant 2$
d $-2 \leqslant x \leqslant 3$, $-2.5 \leqslant y \leqslant 15$
2

a

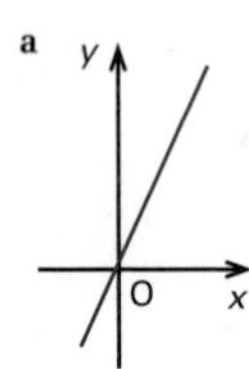

Range R

b

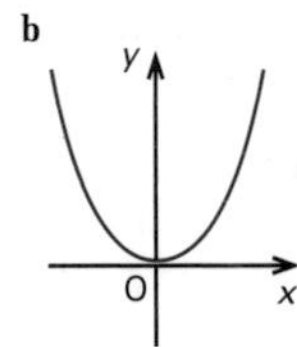

Range $y \geqslant 0$

c

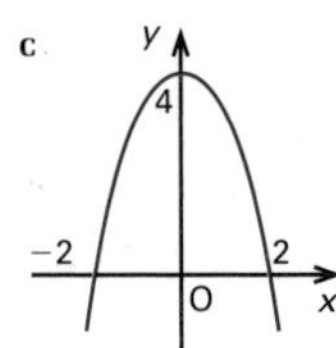

Range $y \leqslant 4$

3 a is right-hand curve, range $y \geqslant 1$
b is whole parabola, range $y \geqslant 1$

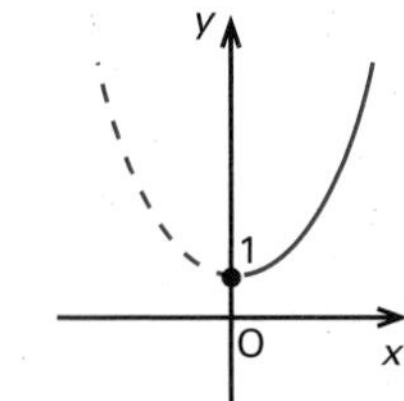

4

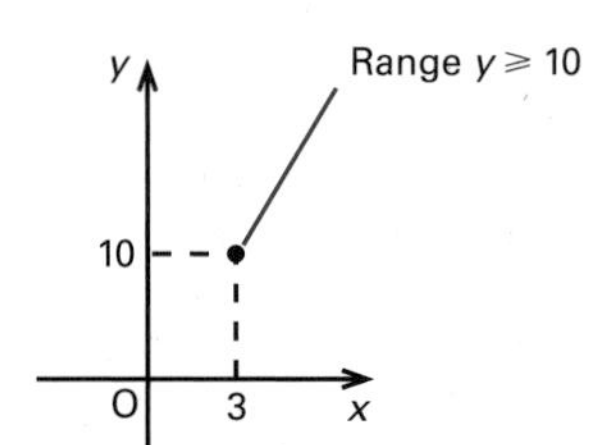

5

a

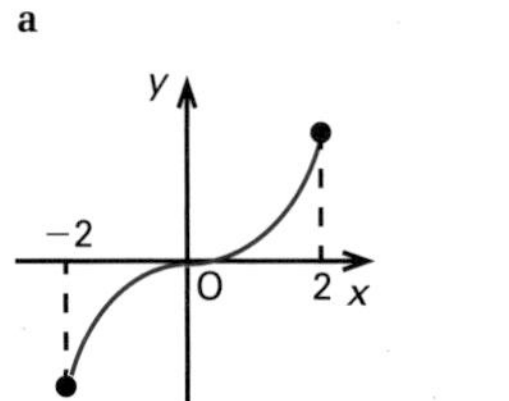

Range $-8 \leqslant y \leqslant 8$

b

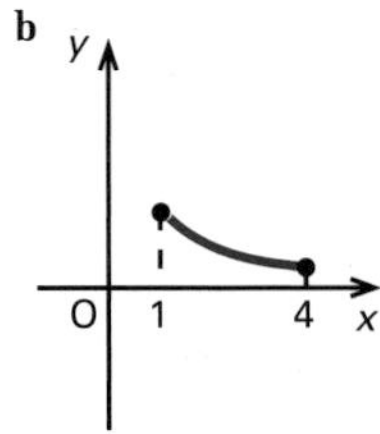

Range $\frac{1}{4} \leqslant y \leqslant 1$

6 a

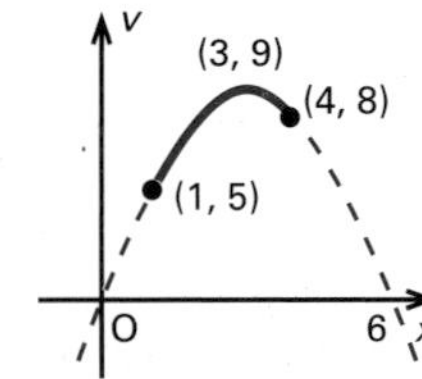

b Domain $1 \leqslant x \leqslant 4$, range $5 \leqslant v \leqslant 9$
c max 9 cm³ when length is 3 cm, min 5 cm³ when length is 1 cm

7 a

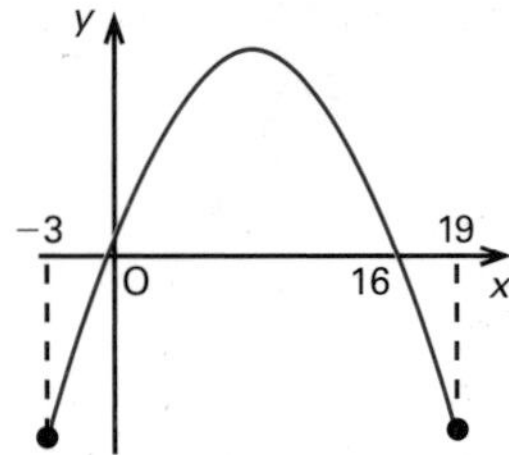

b $-28\frac{1}{2} \leqslant y \leqslant 32$ **(i)** 32 m **(ii)** $60\frac{1}{2}$ m
8 a (i) $C \doteqdot 2a$ **(ii)** $C \doteqdot 200/9a$. In **(i)** pipe too large and costly; in **(ii)** too small to deliver enough water
b $C \geqslant 13\frac{1}{3}$ **c** £$13\frac{1}{3}$ million

Page 23 Exercise 3

1 5, 4, 3, 2; 25, 16, 9, 4

2 **a** 5, 10 **b** 6, 12 **c** 7, 14 **d** $2(x+5)$

3 **a** 3 **b** 18 **c** 1 **d** -2
e 1 **f** -2 **g** 0 **h** -18
i $3x-2$ **j** $3(x-2)$ **k** $x-4$ **l** $9x$

4 **a** (i) $x+5$ (ii) $x+5$
b (i) $6x+11$ (ii) $6x+7$
c (i) x^6 (ii) x^6
d (i) $(x-2)^2$ (ii) x^2-2
e (i) $3x^3$ (ii) $27x^3$
f (i) $2x^2+11$
(ii) $(2x+5)^2+3 = 4x^2+20x+28$
g (i) $2\sin x$ (ii) $\sin 2x$
h (i) $1-\cos^2 x$ (ii) $\cos(1-x^2)$

5 **a** $15x+3a+1, 15x+5+a$ **b** 2

6 **a** $4x^2+4$ **b** $2(x^2+4)$ **c** $4x$
d $(x^2+4)^2+4$, or x^4+8x^2+20

7 **a** (i) $(x+2)^2$ (ii) x^2+2
b (i) $3x-16$ (ii) $3x-6$
c (i) $x^2-15x+56$ (ii) x^2-x-7
d (i) $4x^4-1$ (ii) $(4x^2-1)^2$
e (i) $9x^2-6x+2$ (ii) $3x^2+2$
f (i) $\frac{1}{3x}$ (ii) $\frac{3}{x+1}-1=\frac{2-x}{x+1}$
g (i) $\frac{2x}{3}$ (ii) $\frac{3x}{2}$
h (i) $-\frac{1}{x}$ (ii) $\frac{x-2}{x-1}$

8 **a** x **b** $\frac{1-x}{x}$ **c** $\frac{1}{x-1}$ **d** $\frac{x}{1-2x}$

Page 24 Challenges

1 In general, $g(f(x)) \neq f(g(x))$

2 In all cases, where the compositions are meaningful, $h\circ(g\circ f) = (h\circ g)\circ f$.
First example: $(g\circ f)(x) = 2x+1$, $(h\circ g)(x) = x^2+2x+1$, with $[h\circ(g\circ f)](x) = [(h\circ g)\circ f](x) = 4x^2+4x+1$
Second example: $(g\circ f)(x) = 6x+11$, $(h\circ g)(x) = 3x+6$, with $[h\circ(g\circ f)](x) = [(h\circ g)\circ f](x) = 6x+15$

Page 25 Exercise 4

1 **a** no **b** no **c** yes **d** yes

3 no

4 **b** Rows: 10, $10^2, \ldots, 10^6$; 1, 2, …, 6

5 For each graph there are different values of x for which $f(x)$ is the same

6 **a** $f(-1) = f(1) = -3$, for example; so there is no inverse function
b $y \geqslant -4$
c Take $x \geqslant 0$, for example, giving the right-hand half of the parabola. Take $x \geqslant 1$, etc., or $x \leqslant 0$, etc.

7

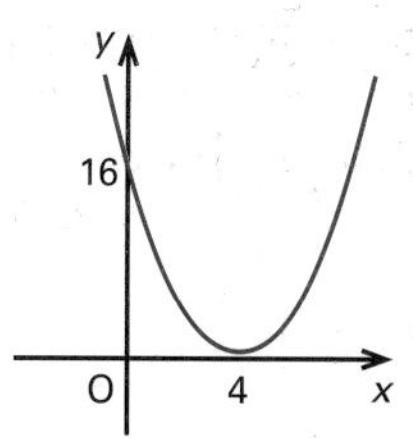

a $f(3) = f(5) = 1$, etc. **b** $y \geqslant 0$
c $x \geqslant 4$ or $x \geqslant 5$ etc., or $x \leqslant 4$ etc.

8 **a** $f^{-1}(x) = \frac{1}{4}x$ **b** $f^{-1}(x) = x-2$
c $f^{-1}(x) = x+5$ **d** $f^{-1}(x) = 5x$
e $f^{-1}(x) = x^{1/2}$ **f** $f^{-1}(x) = x^{1/3}$

9 **a** (i)

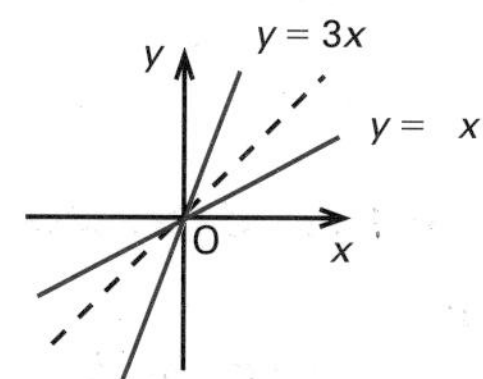

(ii) $f^{-1}(x) = \frac{1}{3}x$

b (i)

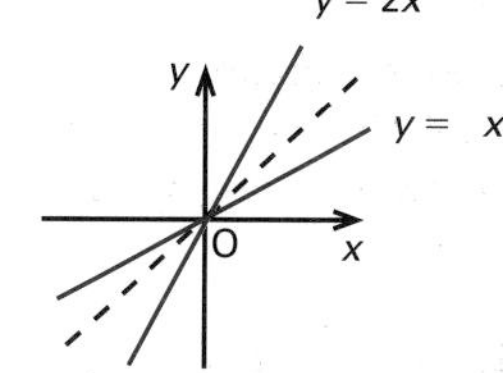

(ii) $f^{-1}(x) = 2x$

c (i)

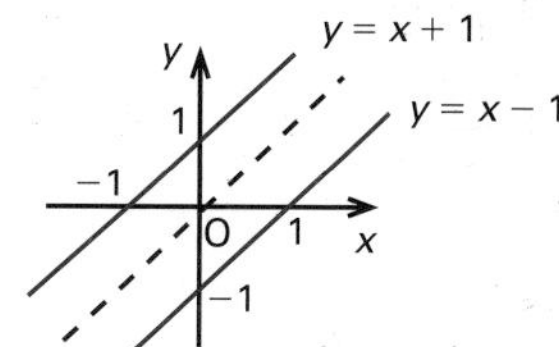

(ii) $f^{-1}(x) = x-1$

d (i)

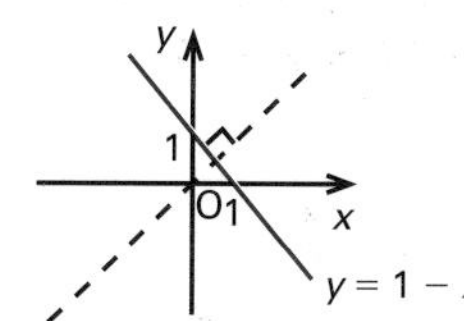

(ii) $f^{-1}(x) = 1-x$

10 a Row: 1, 2, 4, 8

b–d

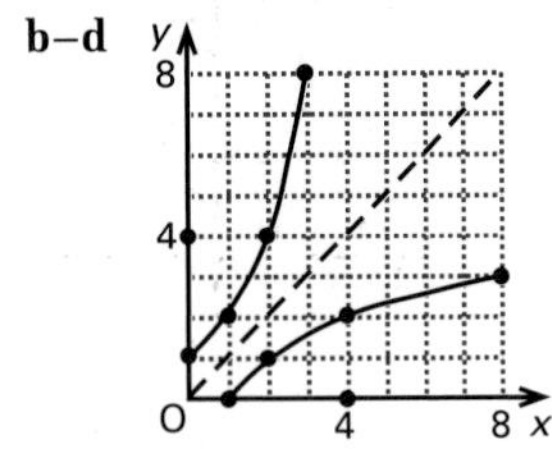

c Rows: 1, 2, 4, 8;
0, 1, 2, 3

Page 28 Review

1 a $\{4, 7, 10, 13\}$ **b** $\{0, 1, 2, 3\}$
c $\{2, 11\}$ **d** $-1 \leqslant y \leqslant 1$

2 a $x \geqslant -1$ **b (i)** $\sqrt{x}$ **(ii)** $2\sqrt{x}$

3 a (i) $-2 \leqslant x \leqslant 4$ **(ii)** $-1 \leqslant y \leqslant 2$
b (i) $-2 \leqslant x \leqslant 1$ **(ii)** $-1 \leqslant y \leqslant 7$

4 a $x \leqslant 2$ **b** $x \geqslant 2$ or $x \leqslant -2$
c R, except -1 **d** R, except 0 and 2

5 a

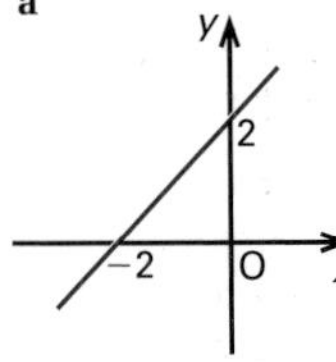

Range R

b

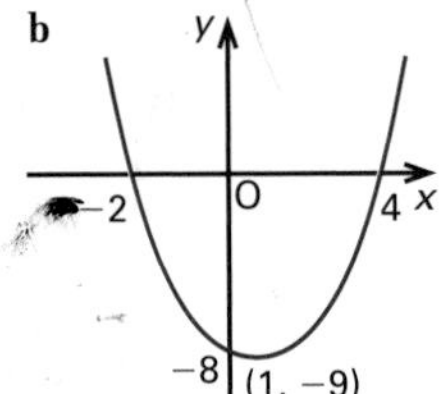

Range $y \geqslant -9$

6 a (i) $(3x+5)^2$ **(ii)** $3x^2+5$
(iii) $9x+20$ **(iv)** x^4

b (i) $\dfrac{1}{2x-1}$ **(ii)** $\dfrac{2}{x}-1$ **(iii)** $4x-3$ **(iv)** x

c (i) $2x-1$ **(ii)** $2x$ **(iii)** x **(iv)** $4x-1$

d (i) $\dfrac{x}{1-x}$ **(ii)** $x-1$ **(iii)** x **(iv)** $\dfrac{x-1}{2-x}$

7 a $\dfrac{4x^2-4x+2}{4x^2-4x}$ **b** 0, 1

8 b 1

9 a (i)

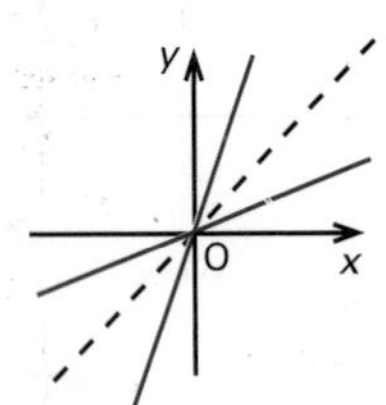

(ii) $f^{-1}(x) = \frac{1}{3}x$

b (i)

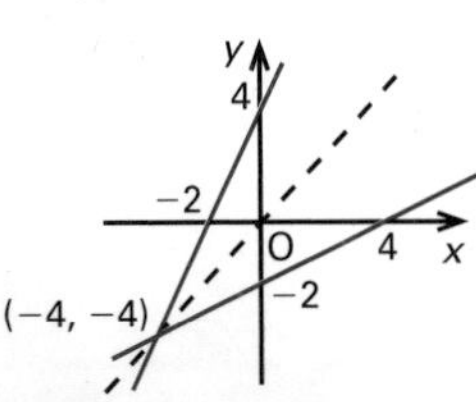

(ii) $g^{-1}(x) = \frac{1}{2}x - 2$

c (i)

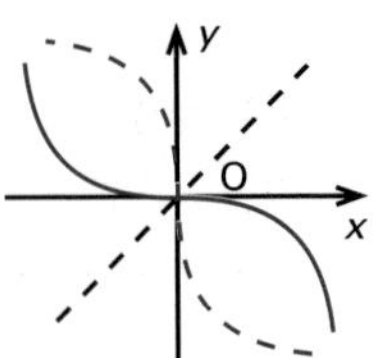

(ii) $h^{-1}(x) = -x^{1/3}$

10 a $0 \leqslant s \leqslant 70$ **b** $0 \leqslant n \leqslant 68$

c $s = \dfrac{20n}{88-n}$; 24 mph

2.2 Algebraic functions and graphs

Page 30 Exercise 1A

1 $(x+4)^2-16$ **2** $(x+1)^2-1$
3 $(x-3)^2-9$ **4** $(x-1)^2-1$
5 $(x+1)^2+4$ **6** $(x+3)^2-10$
7 $(t-5)^2-5$ **8** $(p-1)^2-6$
9 $(u+2)^2-5$ **10** $(v-1)^2+4$
11 $8-(x+1)^2$ **12** $14-(x-3)^2$
13 $5-(t+2)^2$ **14** $30-(t-5)^2$
15 $18-(x+4)^2$ **16** $2-(x-1)^2$

Page 30 Exercise 1B

1 $2(x+2)^2-7$ **2** $3(x-1)^2-5$
3 $2(t+1)^2+2$ **4** $5(p-2)^2-13$
5 $2(c+1)^2+1$ **6** $4(d-2)^2-13$
7 $(x+\frac{1}{2})^2+\frac{3}{4}$ **8** $(x-\frac{1}{2})^2+\frac{3}{4}$
9 $2(x+\frac{1}{4})^2+\frac{7}{8}$ **10** $2(x-\frac{3}{4})^2+\frac{7}{8}$
11 $4\frac{1}{4}-(y-\frac{3}{2})^2$ **12** $4\frac{1}{4}-(y+\frac{1}{2})^2$

Page 31 Challenge

a 100 m², 10 m, 10 m
b 200 m², 20 m, 10 m
c 400 m², 20 m, 20 m

Page 31 Exercise 2

1 a -12, $x=-4$ **b** 2, $x=2$
c -1, $x=-1$ **d** -25, $x=5$

2 a 11, $x=-2$ **b** 24, $x=4$

3 $(x+1)^2+6$, $\frac{1}{6}$

4 b (i) 2 **(ii)** 3

5 a $h = 80-(t-5)^2$ **b** 80 m, 5 s

6 a 50 mph **b** £5

Page 33 Exercise 3

1 b 1, at $x=2$

c

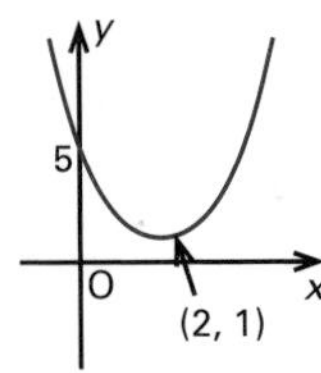

2 b 4, at $x = 1$

c

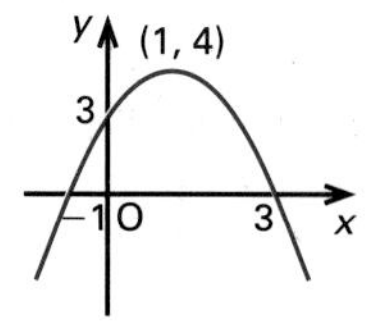

3 a (i) $(x + 2)^2 + 6$

(ii) min 6, at $x = -2$

(iii)

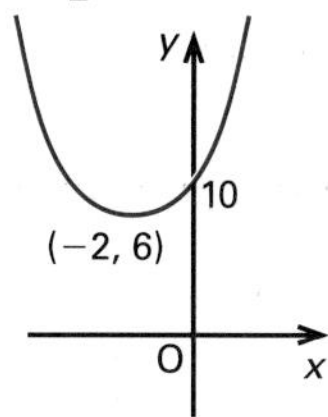

b (i) $(x - 1)^2$

(ii) min 0, at $x = 1$

(iii)

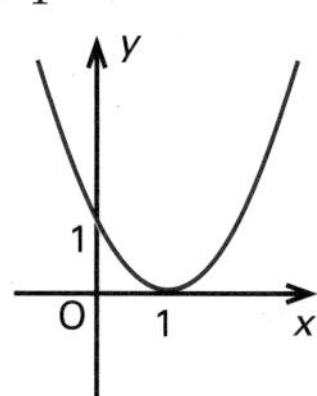

c (i) $9 - (x + 1)^2$

(ii) max 9, at $x = -1$

(iii)

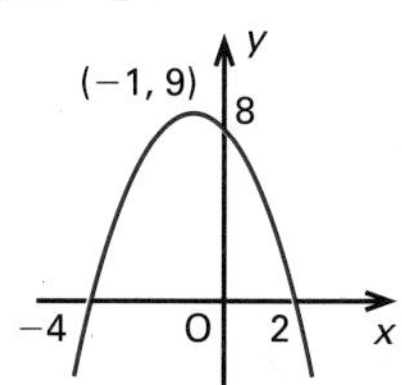

d (i) $16 - (x - 2)^2$

(ii) max 16, at $x = 2$

(iii)

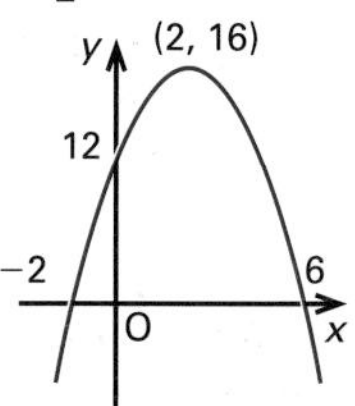

4 a

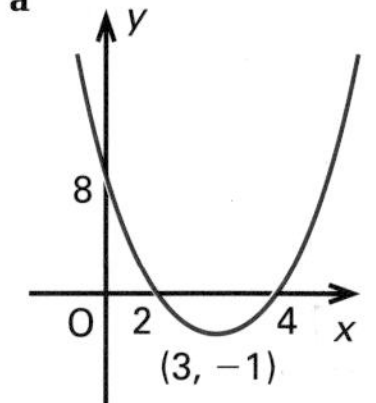

b

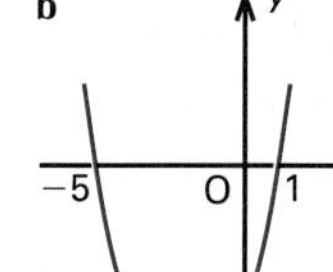

c

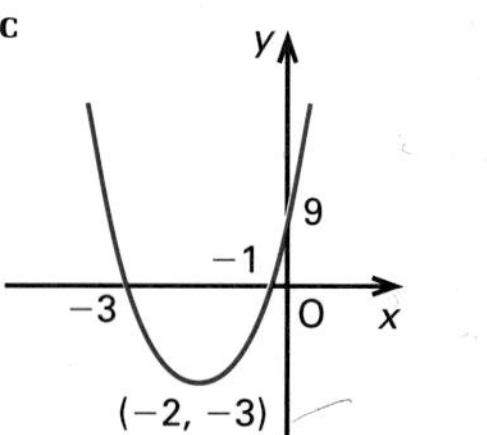

d

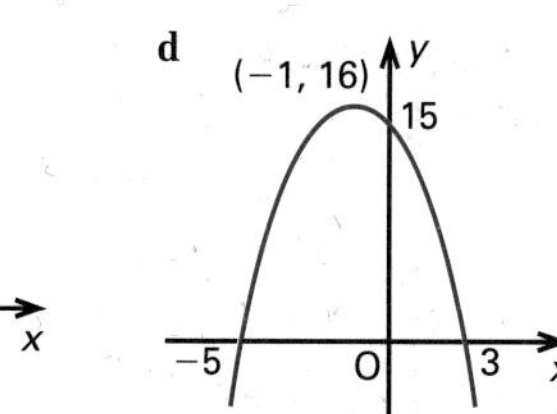

Page 34 Exercise 4

1	**a** (ii)	**b** (i)	**c** (iii)	**d** (iv)
3	**a** (i)	**b** (vii)	**c** (viii)	**d** (iii)
	e (ii)	**f** (iv)	**g** (vi)	**h** (v)

4 **a** **b**

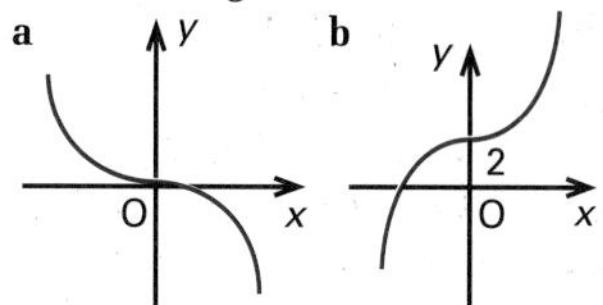

c **d**

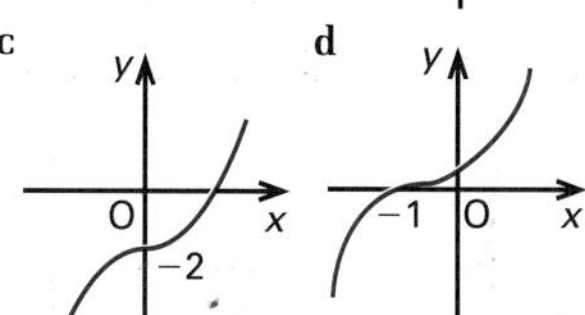

e **f**

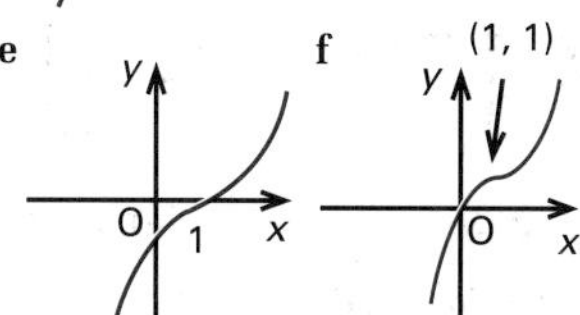

5 **a** **b**

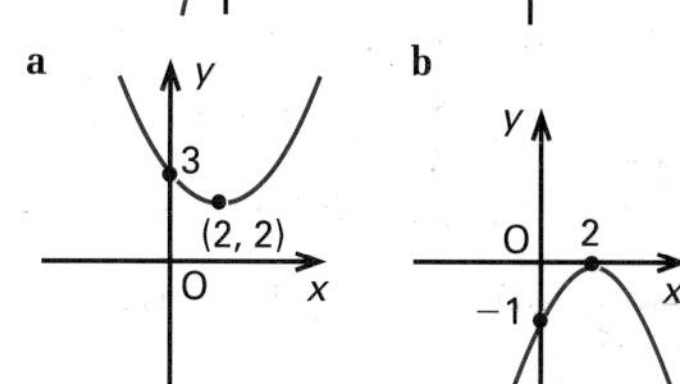

c **d**

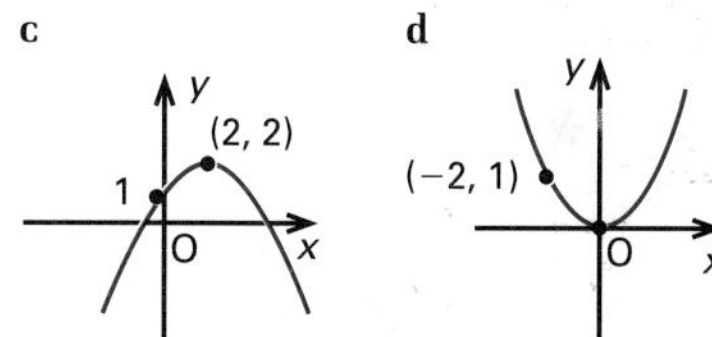

6 **a** **b**

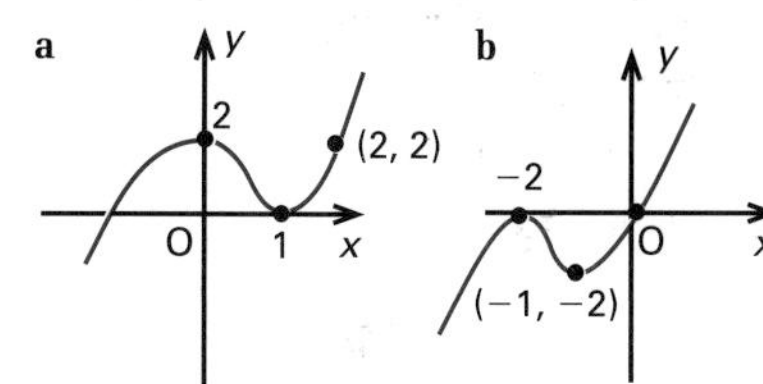

c d

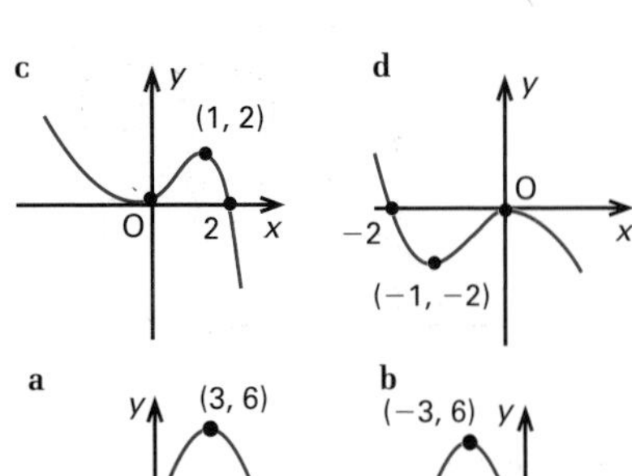

7 a

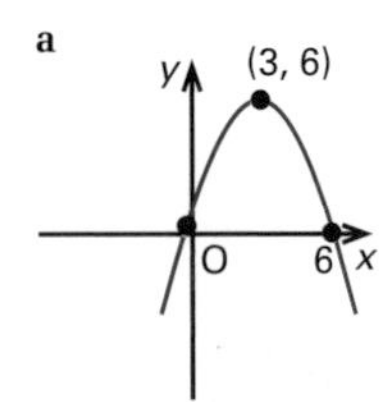

b

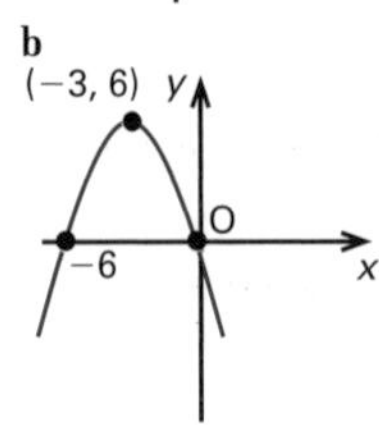

c

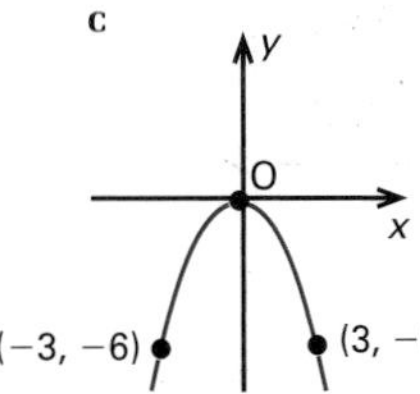

d

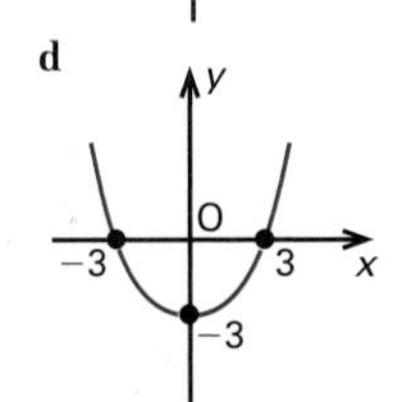

8 a

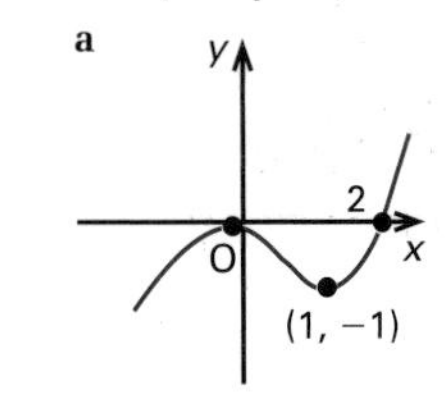

b

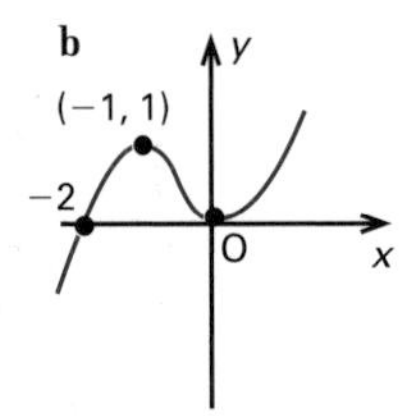

c d

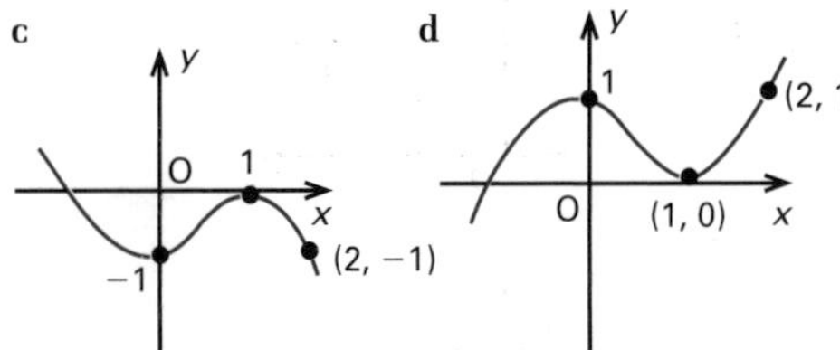

9 a b

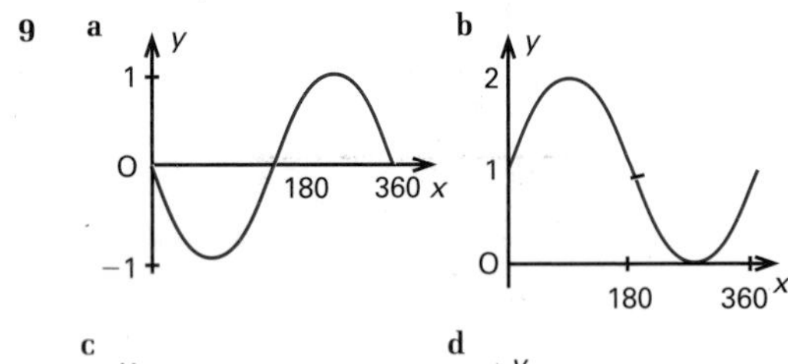

c d

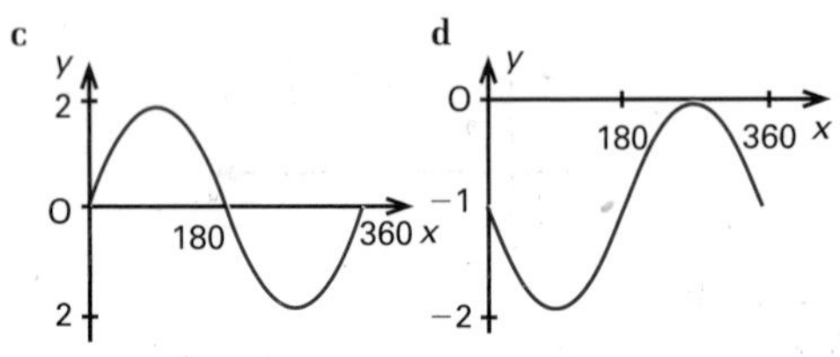

10 a

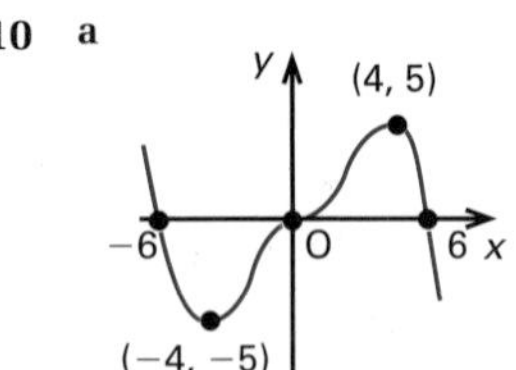

b

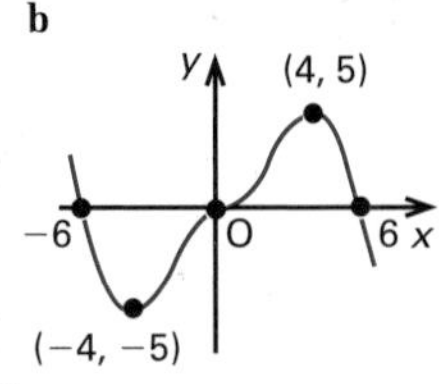

c

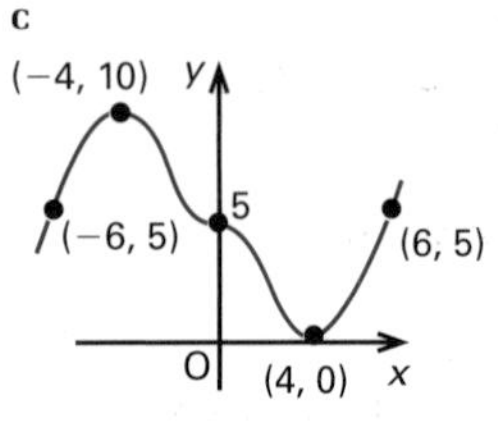

d

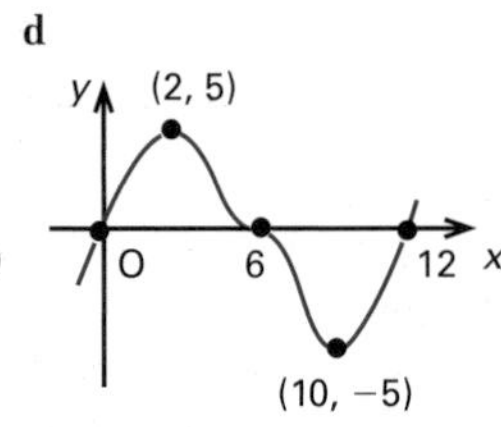

11 a

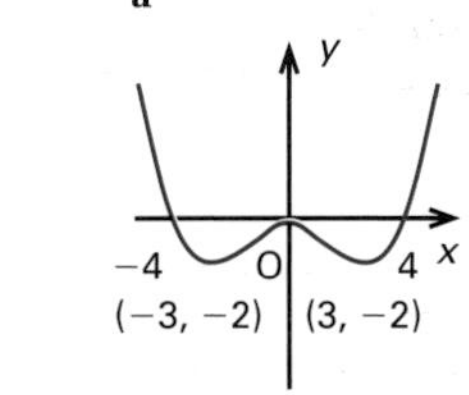

b (i) (ii)

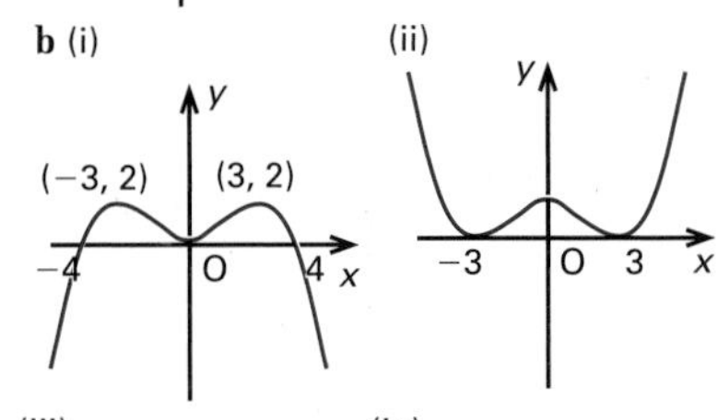

(iii) (iv)

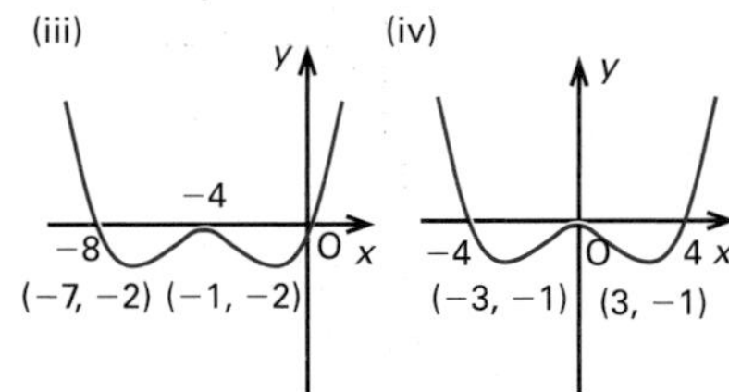

Page 37 Exercise 5

1 **a** 25 **b** 5 **c** 1 **d** 0.2

2 **a** 9 **b** 1 **c** 81 **d** 3

3 **a** 2.89 **b** 6.41 **c** 1.53

4 **a** 25 **b** 27 **c** 53.97

5 **a** 3, 9, 27

c they pass through (0, 1), rise steadily from left to right, have x-axis as asymptote, and $y \to \infty$ as $x \to \infty$

6 a 4, 2, 1, 0.5

b

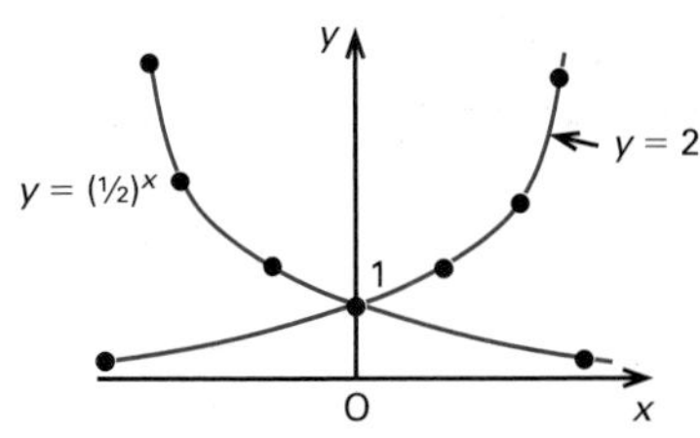

c the y-axis

7 a (i) 8 (ii) 64 (iii) 1024 (iv) 1

b unfolded

c you cannot have half a fold

8 a 1, 3, 9, 27, 81, 243, 729 **b** $N(x) = 3^x$

c (i) 59 000 (ii) 3 490 000 000

9 a 5, 2.5, 1.25, 0.625, 0.3125

b $20 \times (\frac{1}{2})^x = 20 \times 2^{-x}$

c 0.0098 ... $\doteqdot$ 0.01 (1 cm)

d No. Due to loss of energy by air resistance, sound and heat losses, etc.

10 a (i) £1000 (ii) £444.44 **b** seventh

Page 39 Exercise 6

1

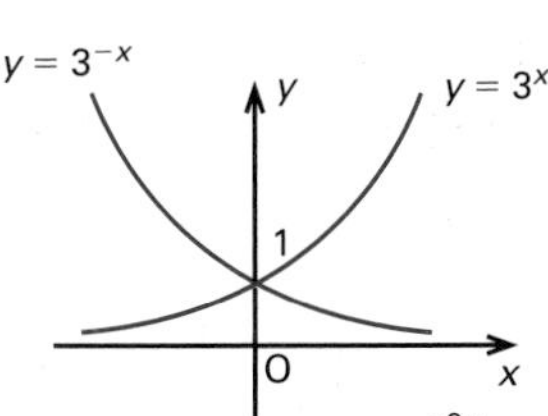

2 a $2^0 = 1$ **b**

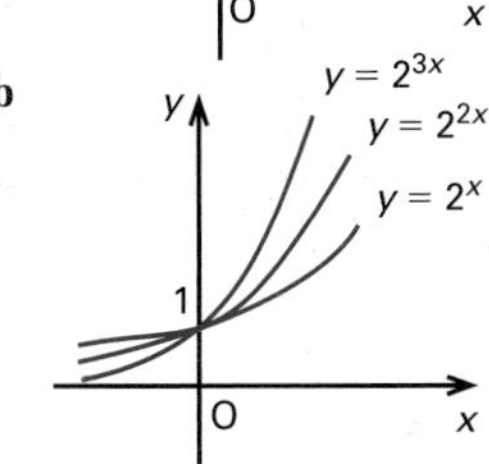

3

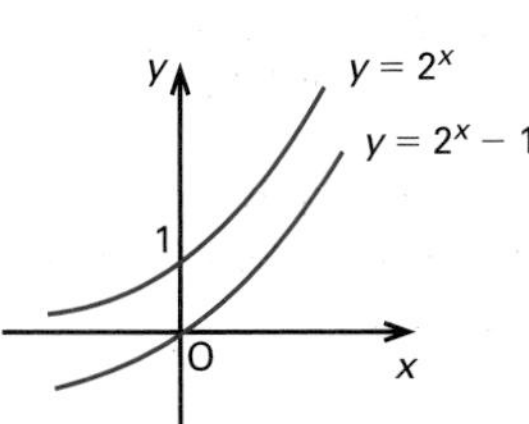

4 $x = 0$

5

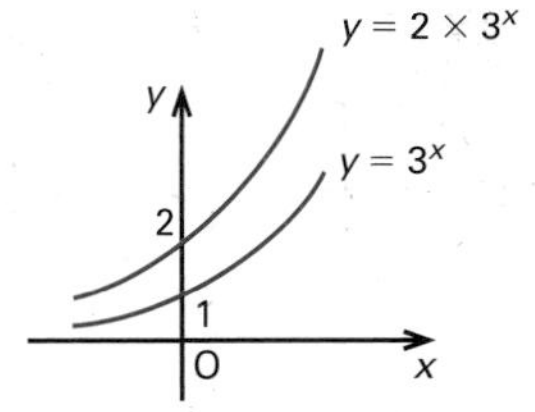

6 4

7 a $a = 3$ **b** $b = 2$

8 4.2

Page 42 Exercise 7

1

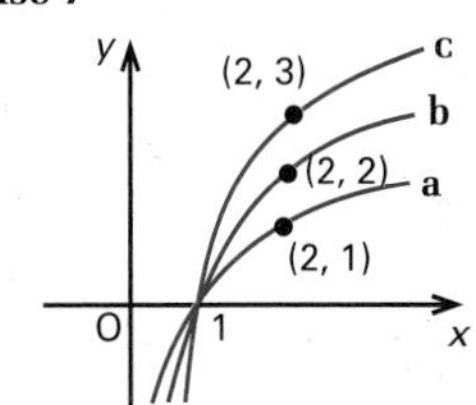

2

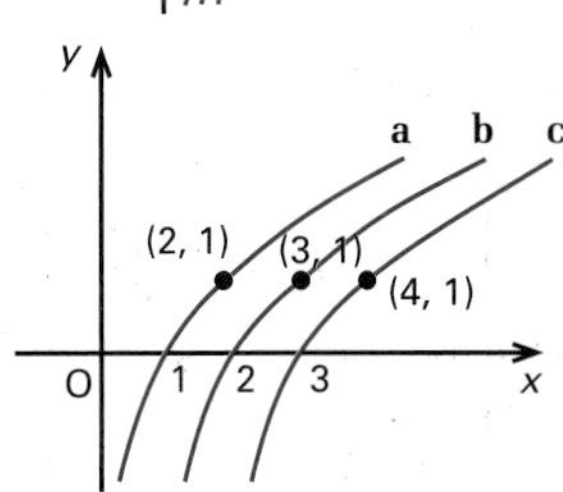

3 a

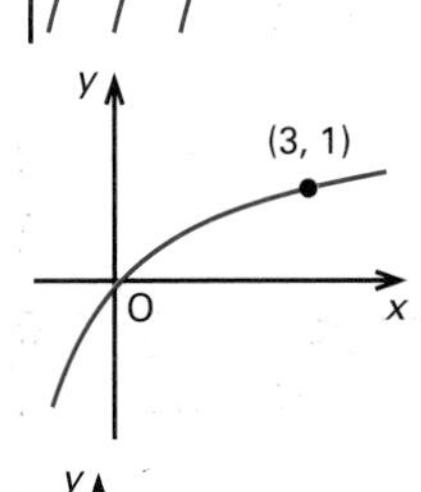

b

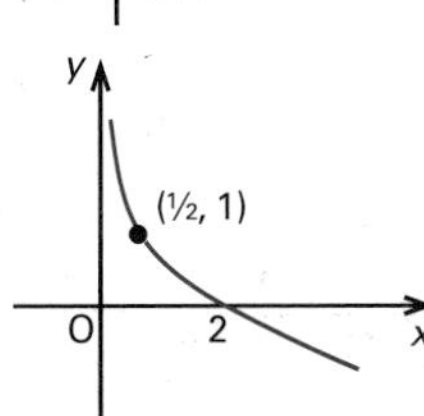

4 a

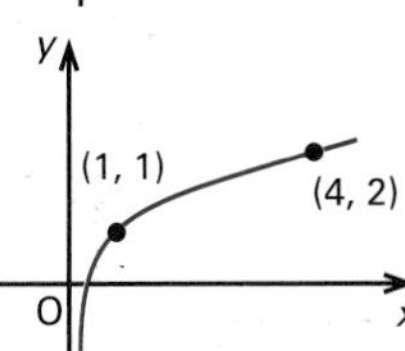

b $(\frac{1}{4}, 0)$

5 a

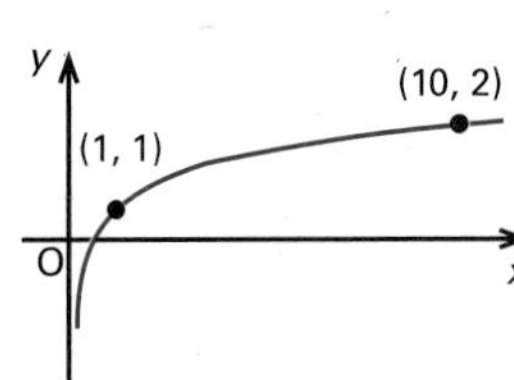

b $(\frac{1}{10}, 0)$

6 **a** to **b** translation of 1 unit in the direction $\overrightarrow{OX}$, **a** to **c** reflection in the x-axis, **a** to **d** translation of 1 unit in the direction $\overrightarrow{YO}$

7 3

8 2

9 **a**

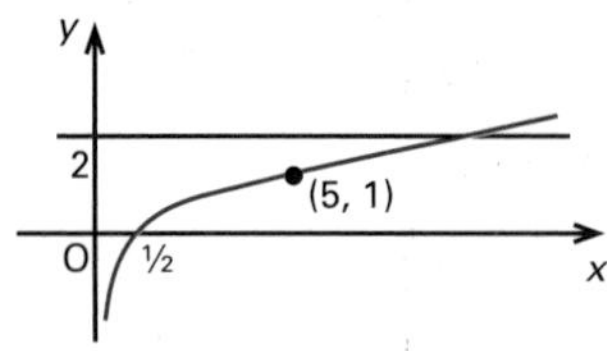

b (50, 2)

10 $a = 3, b = 4$

11 $a = 1, b = 2$

12 **a**

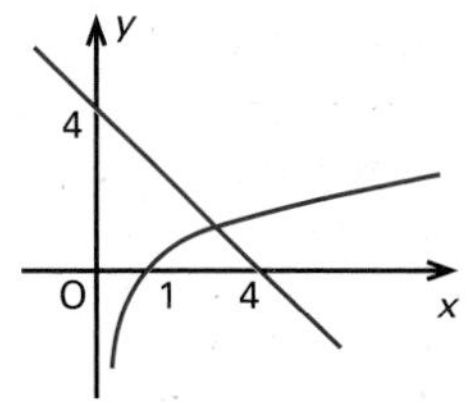

b $4 - x = \log_{10} x$ **d** 3.46

Page 43 Review

1 **a** $(x+5)^2 - 10$ **b** $2(x-2)^2 - 11$

2 **a** $10 + (x-10)^2$, min 10, $x = 10$ **b** 1

3 **a** $(2, -16)$

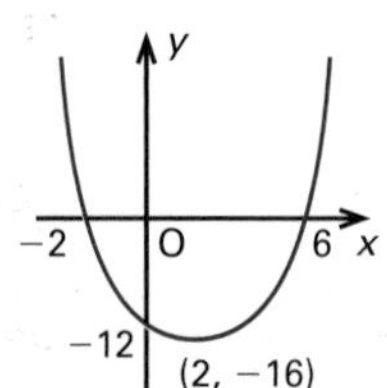

4 **a** $y = -f(x)$ **b** $y = f(x) - 9$ **c** $y = f(x+3) - 9$

5 **a** (v) **b** (ii) **c** (iii) **d** (iv) **e** (i) **f** (vi)

6

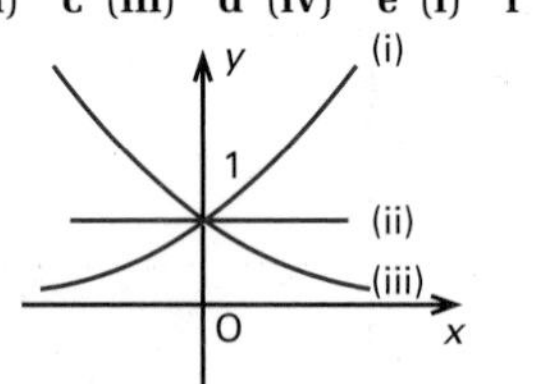

7 $y = 5^{-x}$

8

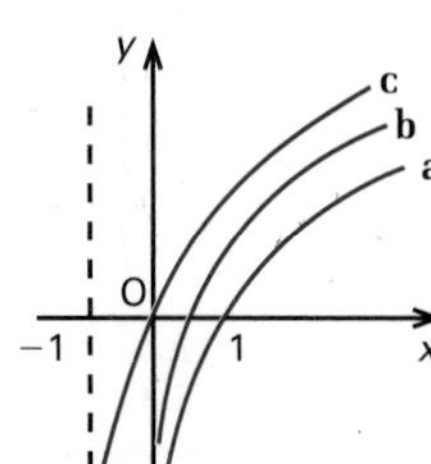

9

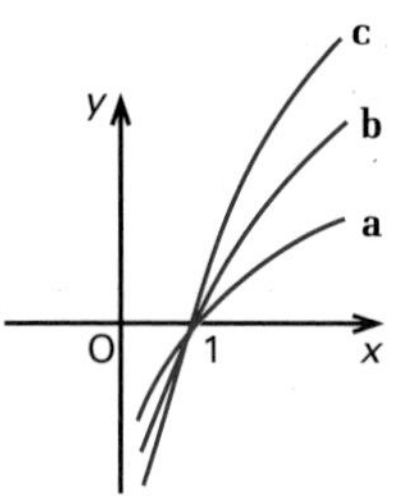

10 4

11 4

2.3 Trigonometric functions and graphs

Page 45 Exercise 1

1 **a** 90° **b** 30° **c** 60° **d** 360° **e** 120° **f** 270°

2 **a** $\pi/3$ **b** $\pi/2$ **c** $2\pi/3$ **d** $\pi/4$ **e** $3\pi/4$

3 **a** 1 **b** 0 **c** −1 **d** 0

4 **a** −1 **b** 1 **c** 0 **d** 0

5 **a** Sides 1, 1, $\sqrt{2}$ (hypotenuse); 1, $\sqrt{3}$, 2 (hypotenuse)

b Rows: $\frac{1}{2}$, $1/\sqrt{2}$, $\sqrt{3}/2$; $\sqrt{3}/2$, $1/\sqrt{2}$, $\frac{1}{2}$; $1/\sqrt{3}$, 1, $\sqrt{3}$

6 **a** 0.5, 0.71, 1.73 **b** same as **a**

7 **a** 0.38 **b** 0.95 **c** 0.73 **d** 0.5

8 **a** $\frac{1}{2} + \sqrt{3}/2$ **b** $\sqrt{3}/2 + \frac{1}{2}$ **c** 2 **d** 0 **e** 0 **f** 5 **g** 1 **h** $3\frac{1}{3}$

Page 48 Exercise 2

1 **a** $\frac{3}{5}, \frac{4}{5}, \frac{3}{4}$ **b** $\frac{3}{5}, -\frac{4}{5}, -\frac{3}{4}$ **c** $-\frac{3}{5}, -\frac{4}{5}, \frac{3}{4}$ **d** $-\frac{3}{5}, \frac{4}{5}, -\frac{3}{4}$

3 **a** positive **b** negative **c** positive **d** positive **e** positive **f** negative

4 **a** $\pi/2$ **b** $5\pi/6$ **c** $\pi/2$ **d** $\pi/4$ **e** $5\pi/3$ **f** $7\pi/6$

5 **a** $\sin\pi/3 = \sqrt{3}/2$ **b** $-\cos\pi/4 = -1/\sqrt{2}$ **c** $\tan\pi/3 = \sqrt{3}$ **d** $-\cos\pi/6 = -\sqrt{3}/2$ **e** $-\sin\pi/3 = -\sqrt{3}/2$ **f** $-\tan\pi/4 = -1$

6 Rows: 0, 1, 0, −1, 0; 1, 0, −1, 0, 1; 0, –, 0, –, 0

7 **b**

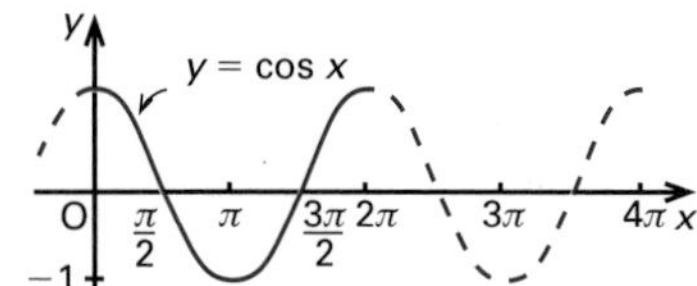

8 **a** 1, −1 **b** 1, −1 **c** 2, 0 **d** 3, 1 **e** 4, 2 **f** 4, 0 **g** 4, 0 **h** 1, −3

9 **a** $\tan(\pi + \theta) = \dfrac{-y}{-x} = \dfrac{y}{x} = \tan\theta$

b π radians

c as given graph, with one more branch to the left

Page 50 Exercise 3

1 a (i) 1, −1; 1; 2π

(ii)

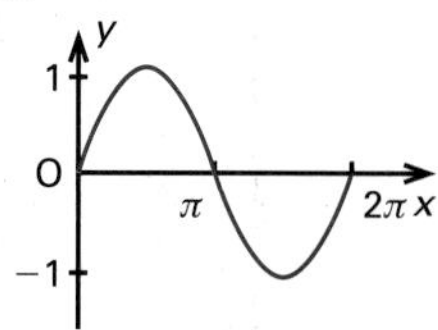

b (i) 3, −3; 1, 2π

(ii)

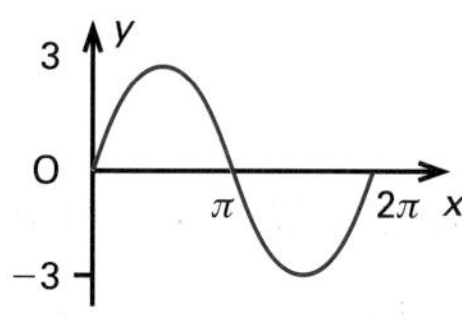

c (i) 1, −1; 3, $2\pi/3$

(ii)

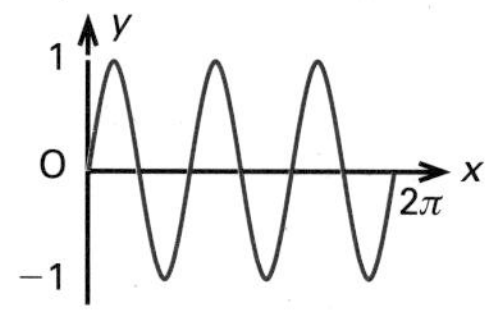

2 a (i) 1, −1; 1; 2π

(ii)

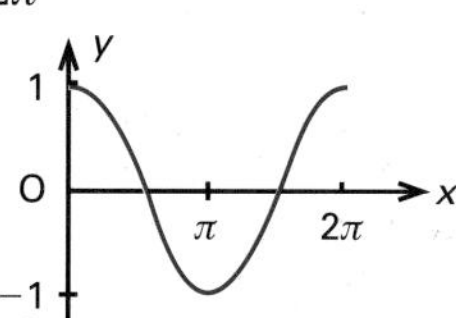

b (i) 1, −1; 1; 2π

(ii)

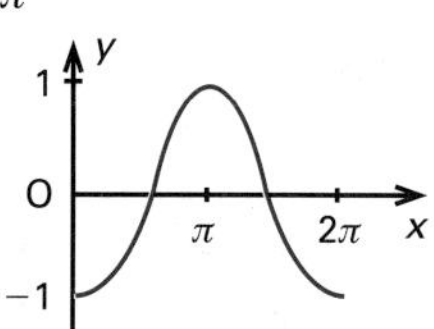

c (i) 0, −2; 1, 2π

(ii)

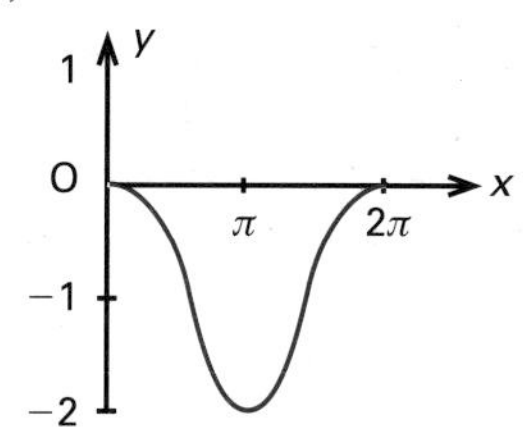

3 a (i) 3, −3; 2; π

(ii)

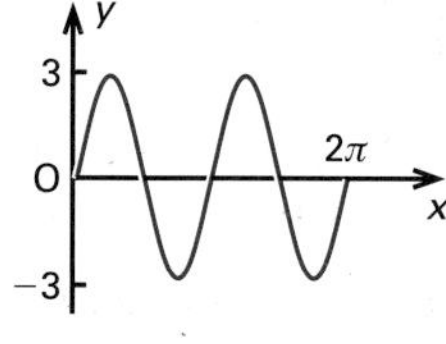

b (i) 2, −2; 3; $2\pi/3$

(ii)

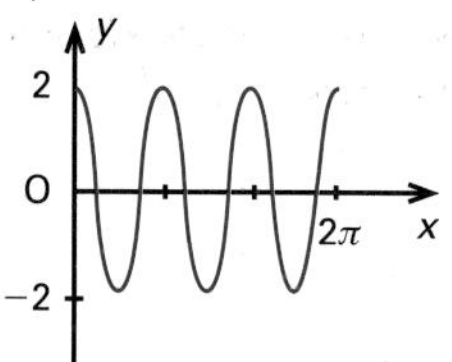

c (i) 1, −1; $\frac{1}{2}$; 4π

(ii)

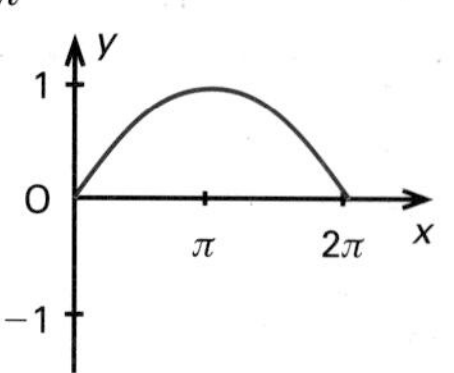

4 a $y = \sin 3x$; $2\pi/3$ radians

b $y = 3\cos x$; 2π radians

c $y = \frac{1}{2}\sin 2x$; π radians

d $y = 2\cos\frac{1}{2}x$; 4π radians

5 a 1, −1 **b** 2, 0 **c** 2, 0

d 1, −1 **e** 4, 2 **f** 4, 2

6 a

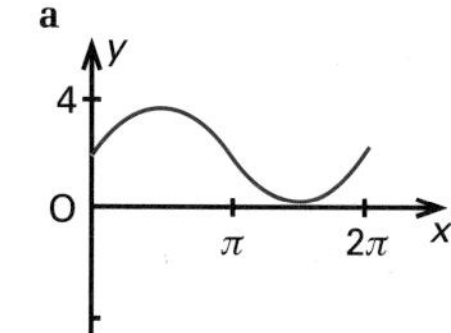

b

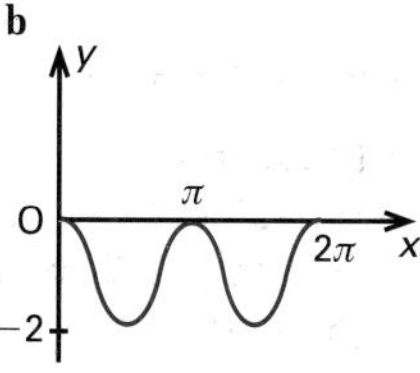

c

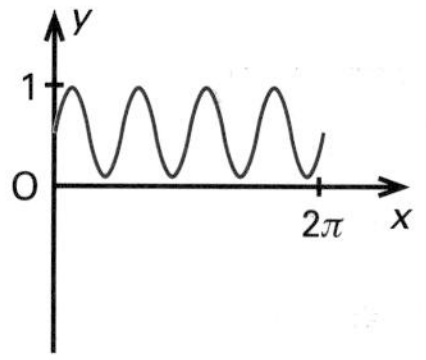

d

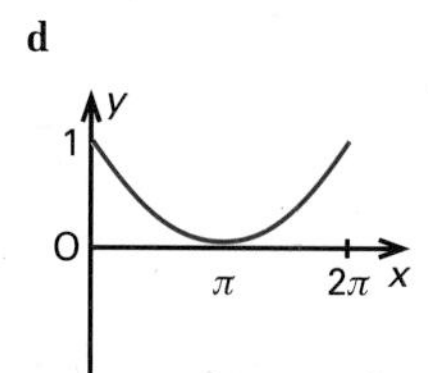

7 a $3\pi/4$ **b** $\pi/3$ **c** 0

8 a $(\pi/3, 2)$ **b** $(\pi/2, 5)$

9 a 6 m **b**

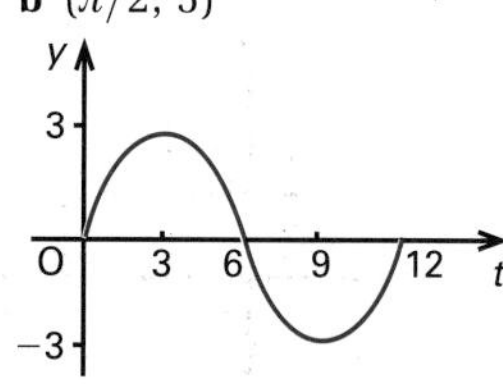

10 a $\frac{2}{3}$ m **b** $2\pi/3$ s **c**

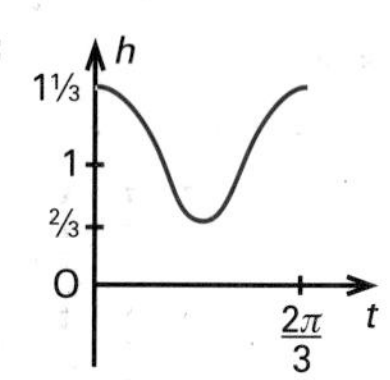

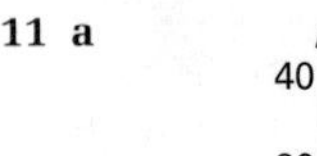

11 a

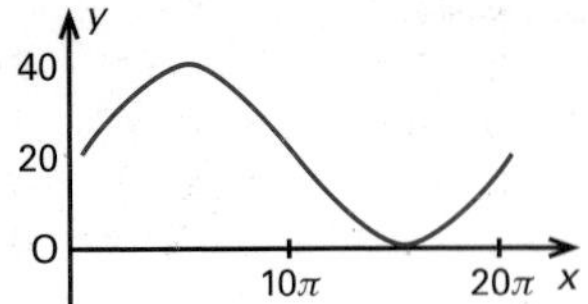

b 40 m, 63 m

Page 53 Exercise 4

1 a (i) 90 **(ii)** 180 **(iii)** 0, 180, 360
b (i) $\pi/2$ **(ii)** π **(iii)** $0, \pi, 2\pi$

2 a $\pi/4, 3\pi/4$ **b** $5\pi/4, 7\pi/4$
c $2\pi/3, 4\pi/3$ **d** $\pi/6, 11\pi/6$

3 a $\pi/4, 5\pi/4$ **b** $3\pi/4, 7\pi/4$
c $\pi/3, 4\pi/3$ **d** $5\pi/6, 11\pi/6$

4 a 210, 330 **b** 60, 300
c 240, 300 **d** 45, 315

5 a 45, 225 **b** 0, 180, 360

6 a 20, 40, 140, 160, 260, 280
b 30, 90, 150, 210, 270, 330

7 a (i) 44, 136 **(ii)** 22, 68, 202, 248
(iii) 15, 45, 135, 165, 255, 285

b

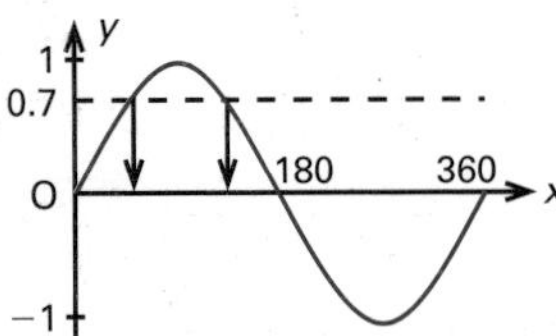

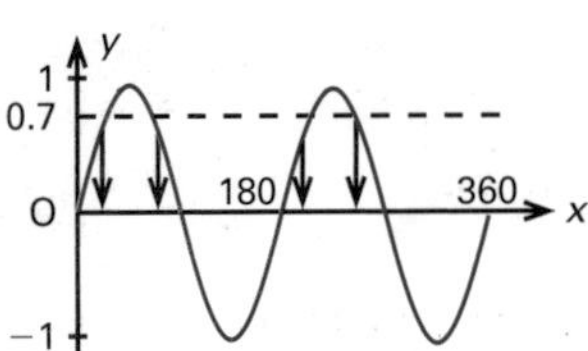

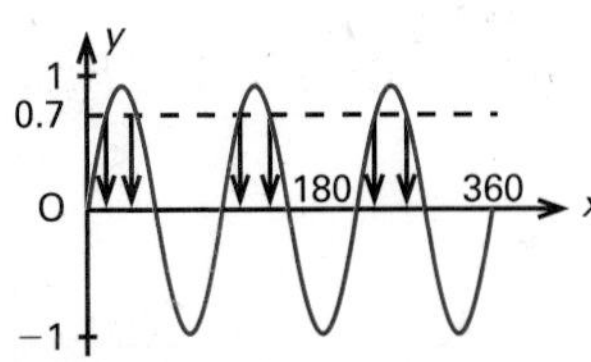

Page 54 Exercise 5

1 a 60, 120, 240, 300 **b** 30, 150, 210, 330
c 60, 120, 240, 300

2 a 90 **b** 0, 360 **c** 60, 180, 300 **d** 210, 330

3 a 0.58, 2.56, 3.72, 5.70
b 0.89, 2.25(6), 4.03, 5.39
c 1.18, 1.96, 4.32, 5.10
d 1.82, 4.96, 1.25, 4.39
e 3.48, 5.94, 3.67, 5.76
f 1.37, 4.91, 2.30, 3.98

4 a 90, 180, 270 **b** 0, 90, 180, 360
c 19, 161, 210, 330 **d** 53, 180, 307

5 b 60, 300

6 a $\pi/6, 5\pi/6$ **b** $\pi/3, 2\pi/3$

7 after 1 hour

8 after $\pi/9$ seconds

9 5.2 m, 26.2 m

Page 55 Exercise 6

1 a 63, 137 **b** 46, 274

2 a 60, 240 **b** 120, 300

3 a 45, 105, 225, 285 **b** 1, 139, 181, 319

4 a 2.1 **b** 2.4

5 a 0.6, 1.8 **b** 0.6, 2.0

6 a 0.2, 1.4 **b** 0.8, 2.9

Page 56 Review

1 a $\pi/3$ **b** $2\pi/3$ **c** $5\pi/6$
d $3\pi/2$ **e** $7\pi/4$

2 a 90° **b** 30° **c** 270° **d** 45° **e** 57.3°

3 a 0 **b** 1 **c** $1/\sqrt{2}$ **d** $1/\sqrt{2}$
e $-\frac{1}{2}$ **f** $\sqrt{3}$ **g** $\frac{1}{2}$ **h** 0

4 a + **b** − **c** − **d** − **e** − **f** +

5 a −0.64 **b** −1.43 **c** −0.84
d 0.59 **e** 0.31 **f** −3.08

6 a (i) 1, −1; 3; $2\pi/3$
(ii)

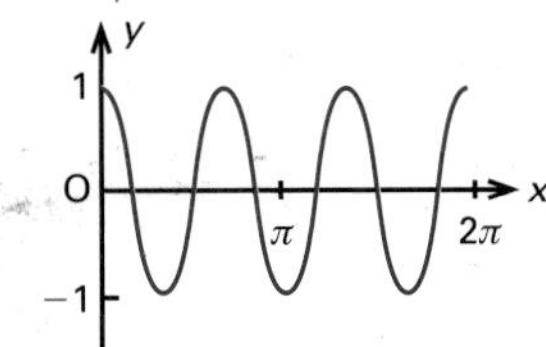

b (i) 3, −3; 2; π
(ii)

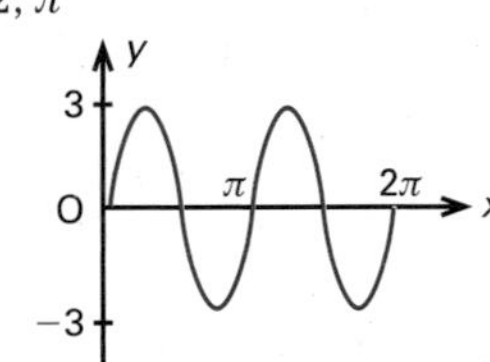

c (i) 4, 0; 1; 2π
(ii)

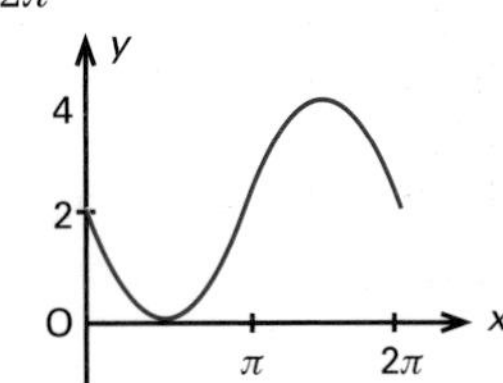

d (i) 4, 2; $\frac{1}{2}$; 4π
(ii)

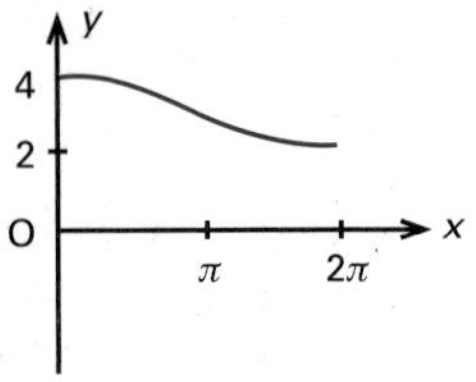

7 a (i) $y = 3\cos 2x$; π **(ii)** $\pi/6, 5\pi/6$
b (i) $y = 2\sin x + 3$; 2π **(ii)** 3.99, 5.43

8 $a = 1, b = -2, c = 2$

9 a 14.5, 165.5 **b** 30, 150, 210, 330
c 101.3, 281.3

10 a $3\pi/2$
b $\pi - \pi/6 = 5\pi/6, \pi + \pi/6 = 7\pi/6$
c $\pi/2, 3\pi/2, 1.23, 5.05$
d $0.73, 2.41, 3.39, 6.03$
11 a $4, 96$ **b** $175, 355$
12 a 0.8 **b** $1.0, 1.8$
13 a $\frac{1}{2}$ m **b** $\pi/18$ second
14 a $2, 0$ **b** $1, 0$ **c** $1, -3$

3.1 Introduction to differentiation

Page 58 Class Discussion/Exercise 1

1 a 10 m/s **b** 0 m/s **c** 10 m/s
2 a $\frac{4-1}{2-1} = 3$
b (i) m_{PQ}: 2.8, 2.6, 2.4, 2.3, 2.2, 2.1
(ii) they get closer to 2
(iii) 2
3 a m_{PQ}: 2.09, 2.08, …, 2.01, 2.009, 2.008, …
b yes
4 $\frac{(1+h)^2 - 1}{(1+h) - 1} = \frac{1 + 2h + h^2 - 1}{1 + h - 1} = \frac{h(2+h)}{h} = 2 + h$
5 a 4 **b** 10 **c** −2

Page 62 Exercise 2

1 a $3x^2$ **b** $2x$ **c** $5x^4$ **d** $4x^3$ **e** 1
2 a $10x$ **b** $6x^2$ **c** $12x^3$ **d** 8 **e** 0
3 a $2x + 4$ **b** $3x^2 - 2$ **c** $5x^4 + 1$
4 a $4t^3 + 6t$ **b** $3p^2 - 2$ **c** $7u^6$
5 a $3x^2 + 2x + 1$ **b** $6x - 6x^5$
6 a $x - 1$ **b** $x^2 + 5$
7 a $3y^2 - 4y + 3$ **b** $1 - 2v + 3v^2$
8 a $2x + 2$ **b** $2x + 10$ **c** $2x - 6$ **d** $8x + 4$
9 a $2x + 5$ **b** $2x$
10 a $-2x + 5$ **b** $4x^3 + 8x$
11 a $-25u^4 + 100u^9$ **b** $6v^2 - 6v + 5$
12 a 3 **b** 11 **c** −5
13 a 1 **b** 2 **c** 6
14 a $3a^2$ **b** $4a$ **c** $2a - 2$
15 a 32 **b** 3
16 a 8 **b** 10 **c** −36 **d** 12 **e** 0, 3, 27

Page 62 Exercise 3

1 a $\frac{1}{x^5}$ **b** $\frac{1}{y}$ **c** $\frac{1}{u^2}$ **d** v^3 **e** $2w$
2 a x^{-1} **b** x^{-3} **c** x^{-4} **d** $\frac{1}{2}x^{-1}$ **e** $\frac{1}{3}x^{-2}$
3 a $y^{1/2}$ **b** $y^{1/3}$ **c** $y^{4/3}$ **d** $y^{-1/2}$ **e** $\frac{1}{2}y^{-1/3}$
4 a x^2 **b** y^{-1} **c** z^{-2}
d 1 **e** u^4 **f** v^{-1}
g $6p^{-5}$ **h** $10a^2$ **i** $2y^{1/2}$
5 a x^2 **b** y^4 **c** 1 **d** t **e** $u^{2/3}$
f $v^{1/2}$ **g** x **h** $\frac{1}{2}y^{-2}$ **i** $\frac{1}{2}t^{1/2}$ **j** $\frac{2}{3}u^2$
6 a $\frac{1}{4}$ **b** 3 **c** −2 **d** 10 **e** 64 **f** 1
7 a $x^{3/2} + x^{1/2}$ **b** $y - 1$ **c** $1 + 2x^{1/2} + x$
d $x - 2 + \frac{1}{x}$ **e** $t^{2/3} - 1$

Page 64 Exercise 4A

1 a $-2x^{-3}$ **b** $-5x^{-6}$ **c** $-4x^{-5}$ **d** $-x^{-2}$
2 a $-3x^{-4}$ **b** $-8x^{-9}$ **c** $-6x^{-7}$ **d** $-10x^{-11}$
3 a $\frac{3}{2}x^{1/2}$ **b** $\frac{5}{2}x^{3/2}$ **c** $\frac{1}{2}x^{-1/2}$ **d** $\frac{2}{3}x^{-1/3}$
4 a $-\frac{1}{2}x^{-3/2}$ **b** $-\frac{1}{4}x^{-5/4}$ **c** $-\frac{2}{3}x^{-5/3}$ **d** $-\frac{1}{3}x^{-4/3}$
5 a $x^{-2}, -2x^{-3}$ **b** $x^{-1}, -x^{-2}$
c $x^{-3}, -3x^{-4}$ **d** $x^{-5}, -5x^{-6}$
6 a $x^{2/3}, \frac{2}{3}x^{-1/3}$ **b** $x^{1/2}, \frac{1}{2}x^{-1/2}$
c $x^{-1/2}, -\frac{1}{2}x^{-3/2}$ **d** $x^{5/4}, \frac{5}{4}x^{1/4}$
7 a $-\frac{1}{x^2}$ **b** −1 **c** $-\frac{1}{4}$ **d** −4
8 a $\frac{5}{3}x^{2/3}$ **b** 0 **c** $\frac{5}{3}$ **d** 15
9 a −2 **b** $-\frac{1}{4}$ **c** 2
10 a $\frac{1}{2}$ **b** $\frac{1}{4}$ **c** $\frac{1}{6}$
11 a $3x^{-1}, -3x^{-2}$ **b** $\frac{1}{2}x^{-1}, -\frac{1}{2}x^{-2}$
c $2x^{-1/2}, -x^{-3/2}$ **d** $6x^{-1/3}, -2x^{-4/3}$
e $\frac{2}{3}x^{-2}, -\frac{4}{3}x^{-3}$
12 a −4 **b** $-\frac{1}{4}$ **c** −3 **d** $\frac{3}{4}$
13 a −1 **b** $-\frac{1}{16}$

Page 65 Exercise 4B

1 a $2 - \frac{1}{x^2}$ **b** $12x^2 - \frac{2}{x^3}$ **c** $5 + \frac{1}{2x^2}$
2 a $\frac{1}{3} - \frac{3}{x^2}$ **b** $\frac{1}{2x^{1/2}} + \frac{1}{2x^{3/2}}$ **c** $3 + \frac{1}{x^2}$
3 a $4x + \frac{2}{x^3}$ **b** $\frac{1}{3x^{2/3}} - \frac{1}{3x^{4/3}}$ **c** $2x - \frac{2}{x^3}$
4 a $\frac{4}{x^2}$ **b** $1 + \frac{1}{x^2}$ **c** $\frac{1}{2} + \frac{1}{2x^2}$
5 a $\frac{3}{x^2}$ **b** $-\frac{4}{x^2} - \frac{8}{x^3}$ **c** $-\frac{2}{x^3}$
6 a $\frac{1}{2x^{1/2}}$ **b** $2x - 1$ **c** $\frac{1}{3x^{2/3}}$ **d** $\frac{1}{x^{1/2}} + 1$
7 $4\frac{3}{4}$
8 $f'(x) = -\frac{1}{3}x^{-4/3} + \frac{1}{3}x^{-2/3}$ etc.

Page 67 Exercise 5A

1 a (i) −2 (ii) 0 (iii) 2 **b**

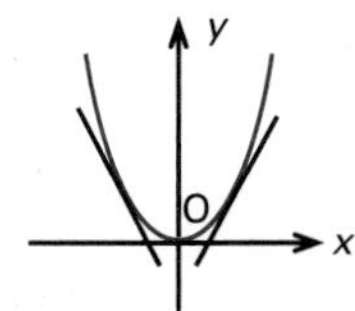

2 a (i) 3 (ii) 0 (iii) 3 **b**

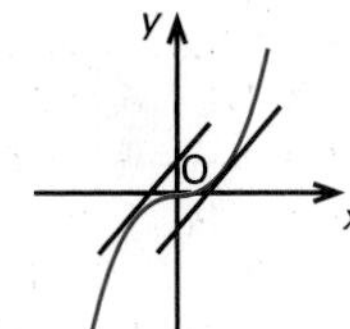

3 a 12, $y = 12x - 12$ **b** 4, $y = 4x - 1$
c 4, $y = 4x - 3$ **d** $\frac{1}{4}$, $4y = x + 4$
e $\frac{3}{2}$, $2y = 3x - 1$ **f** 2, $y = 2x + 3$
g 12, $y = 12x + 28$ **h** 0, $y = 0$
4 a $(3, -2)$ **b** $y = 2x - 8$

5 a (3, 9), (−3, −9)
b $y = 9x - 18$, $y = 9x + 18$
6 a (−2, 1) **b** $y = -8x - 15$
7 a (i) 63° (ii) 117° (iii) 0°
b

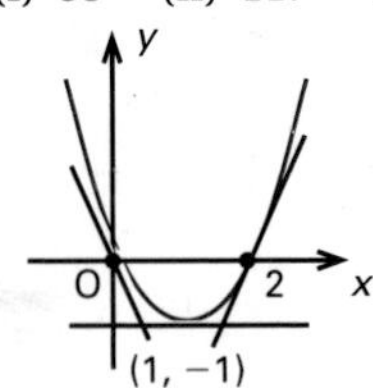

8 a $4x$ **b** $6t^{1/2}$ **c** $1 + u^{-2}$

Page 67 Exercise 5B

1 at A, $y = 2x + 2$; at B, $y = x + 1$
2 a at A, $y = 5x - 10$; at B, $y = x - 2$
b (2, 0)
3 a 3, −3 **b** 72°, 108° **c** 36°
4 a $\frac{dy}{dx} = 3(x - 2)^2 \geqslant 0$ **b** (2, 9)
5 b (−3, −18)
6 $8y = -8x + 5$
7 a $\frac{1}{3x^{2/3}}$ **b** $2x + \frac{2}{x^3}$ **c** $\frac{1}{t^{1/2}} + \frac{1}{t^{3/2}}$ **d** $\frac{2}{u^2} - \frac{2}{u^3}$

Page 68 Challenge

a $-1/a^2$ **c** the area is always 2

Page 69 Exercise 6

1 **a**

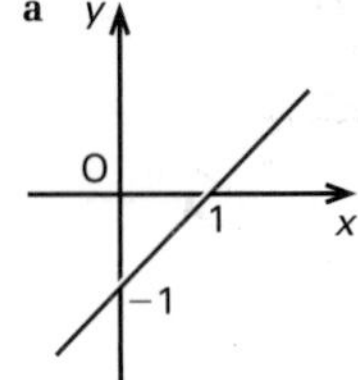

b

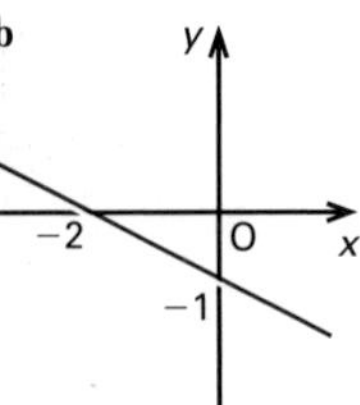

2 **a**

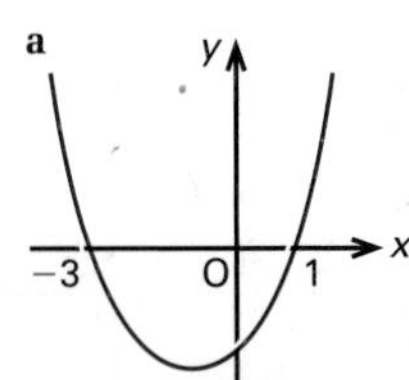

b

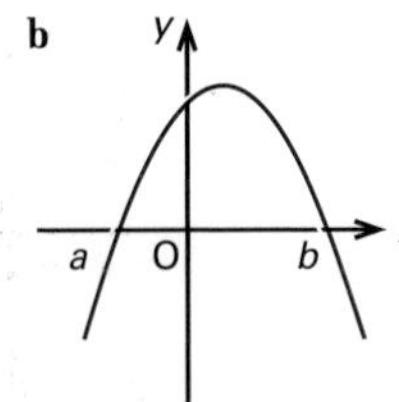

3 **a**

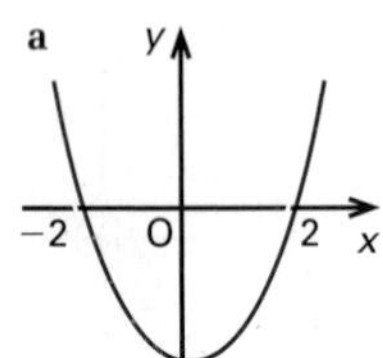

b

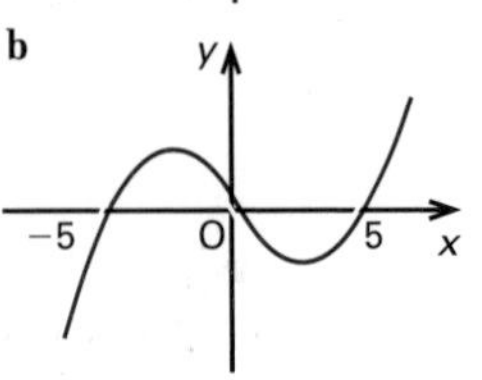

4 **a**

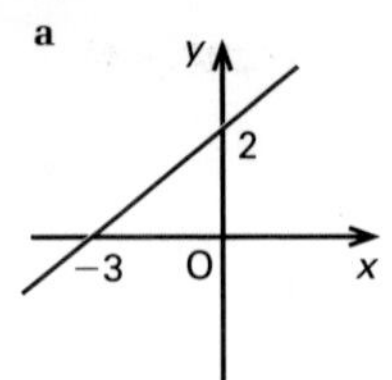

b

5 a 2 **b**

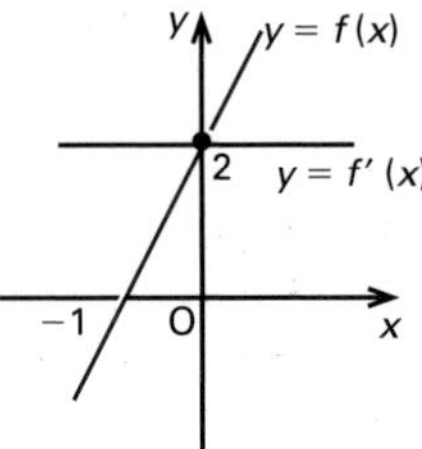

6

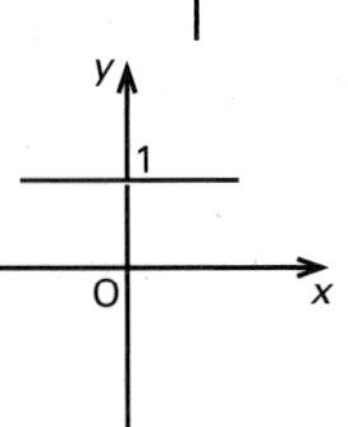

7 **a**

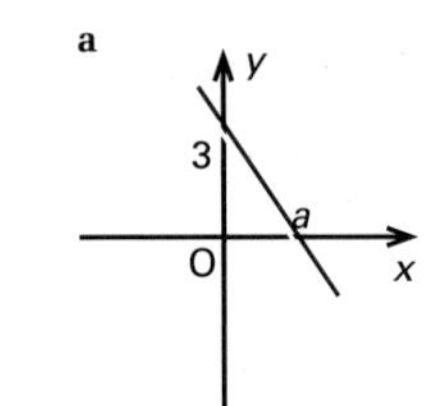

b

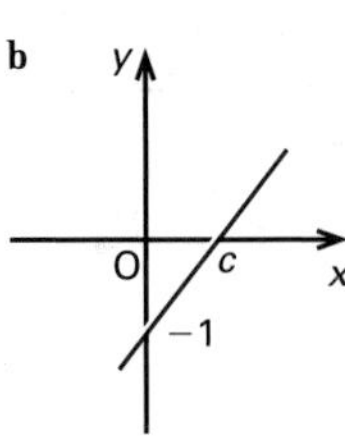

8 **a**

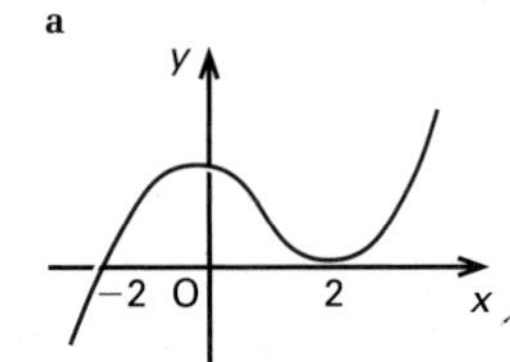

b

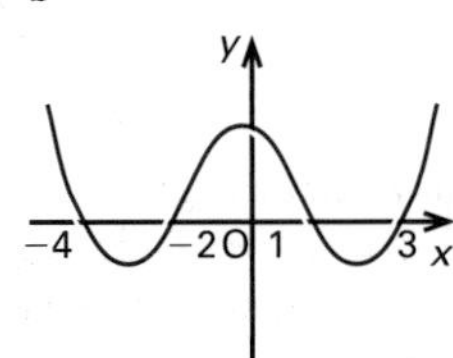

9 **a** (example)

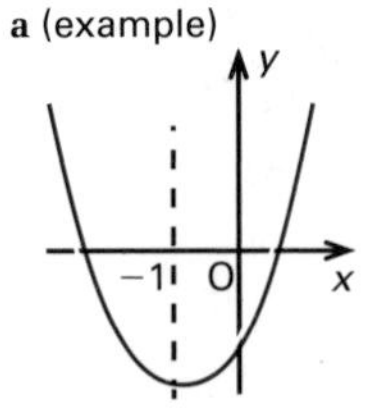

Quadratic, with SP on $x = -1$

b (example)

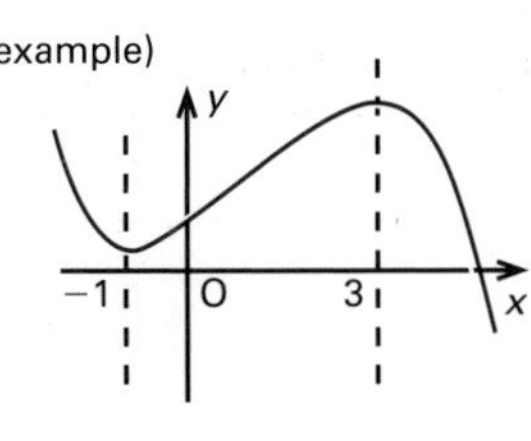

Cubic, with SPs on $x = -1$, $x = 3$

3.2 Using differentiation

Page 72 Exercise 1

1 (0, 0), min TP
2 (2, −4), min TP
3 (1, 2), min TP
4 (2, 9), max TP
5 (0, 0), PI
6 (0, 4), max TP
7 (0, 1), max TP
8 (2, 0), min TP

9 a (1, 0), (−2, 0) **b** max (−2, 0), min (0, −4)

c

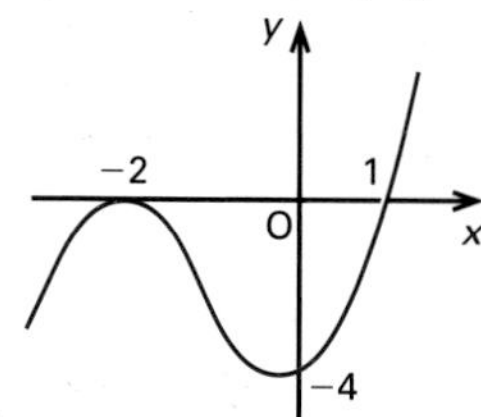

d $x \geqslant 1$ and $x = -2$

Page 73 Exercise 2

1 a (0, 1), min TP **b** dec $x < 0$, inc $x > 0$

2 a (0, 3), max TP **b** inc $x < 0$, dec $x > 0$

3 a (0, 0), PI **b** inc $x < 0$ and $x > 0$

4 a (−1, −2), min TP; (1, 2), max TP

b inc $-1 < x < 1$, dec $x < -1$ and $x > 1$

5 a (0, 0), PI; (1, −1), min TP

b dec $x < 0$ and $0 < x < 1$, inc $x > 1$

6 a (−1, 4), (1, 4), min TPs; (0, 5), max TP

b inc $-1 < x < 0$ and $x > 1$, dec $x < -1$ and $0 < x < 1$

7 a no SPs **b** always increasing

8 a (−1, 4), max TP; (0, 2), PI; (1, 0), min TP

b inc $x < -1$ and $x > 1$, dec $-1 < x < 0$ and $0 < x < 1$

9 a $\frac{dy}{dx} = -\frac{4}{x^2} < 0$ **b** $y = -x + 4$

d

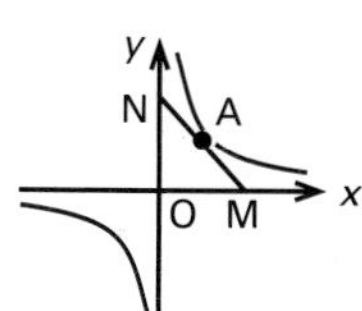

Page 73 Challenge

a C_1 increases, C_2 decreases

b $(2, 4 + a)$; minimum cost £$(4 + a)$ when diameter is 2 m

Page 75 Exercise 3

1

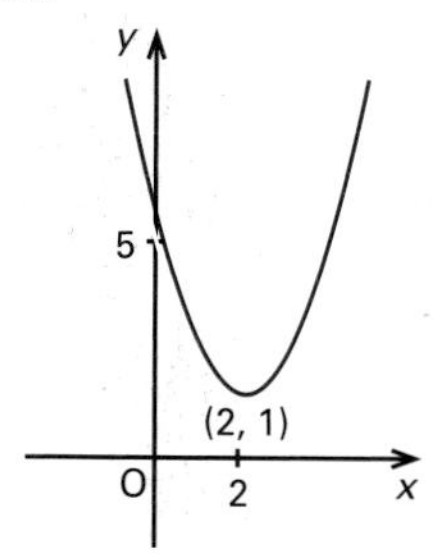

2

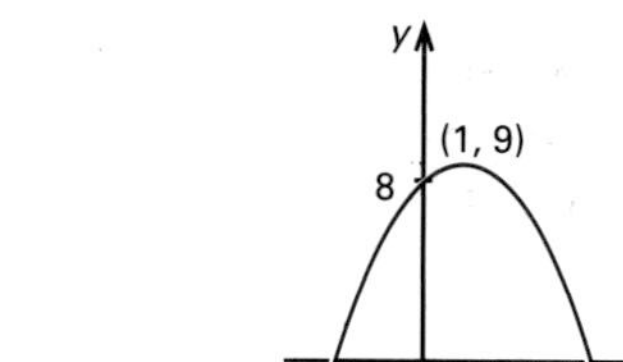

3

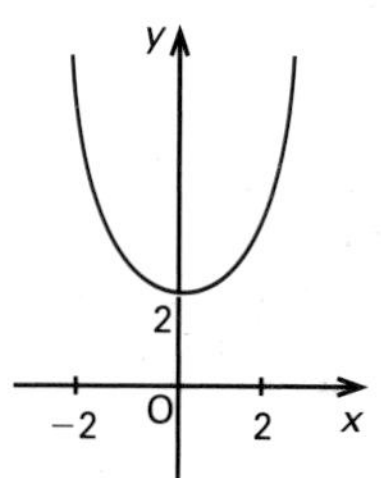

4

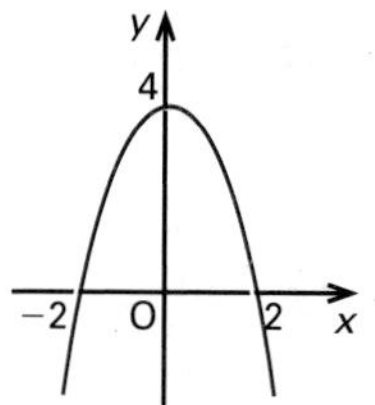

5

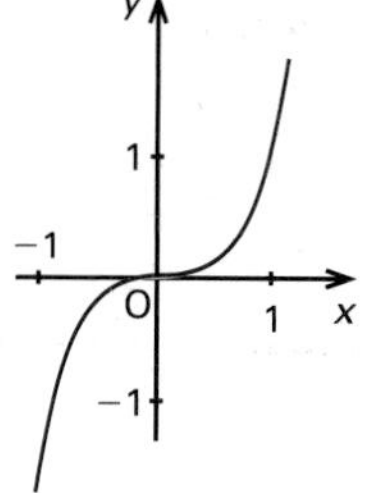

6

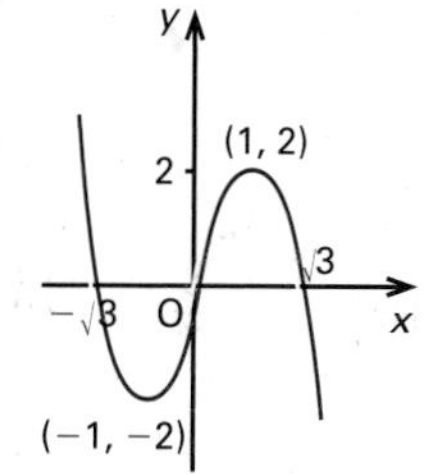

7

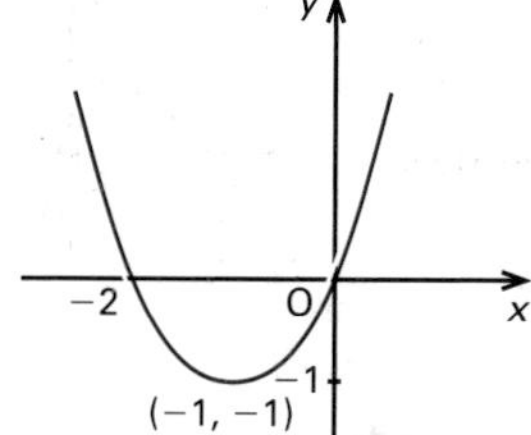

8

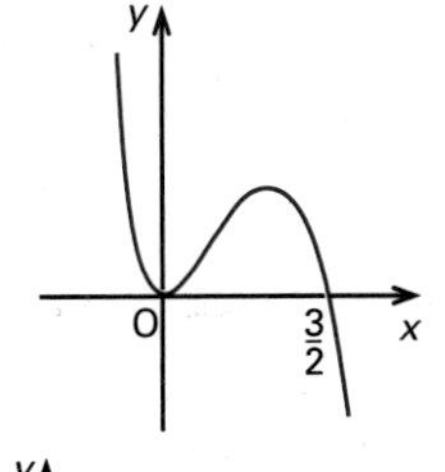

9

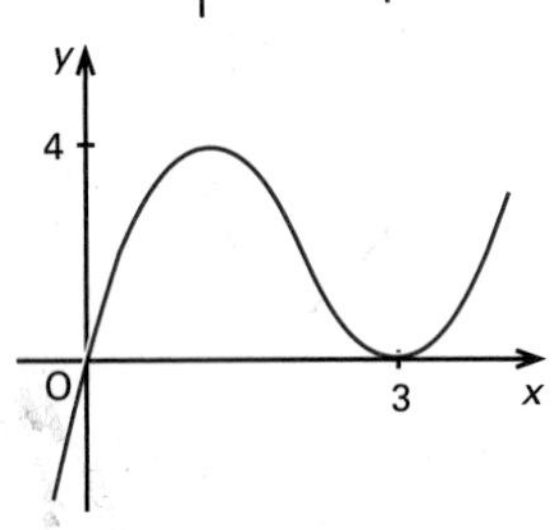

10

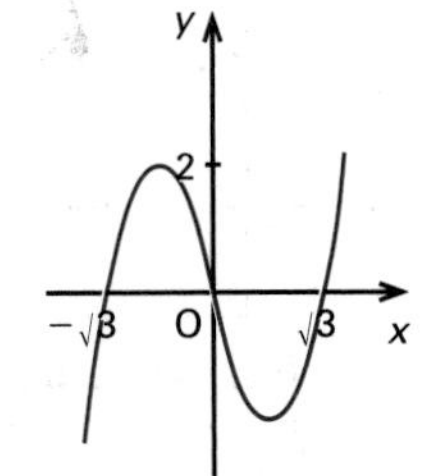

11

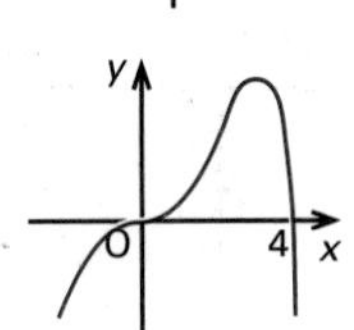

12

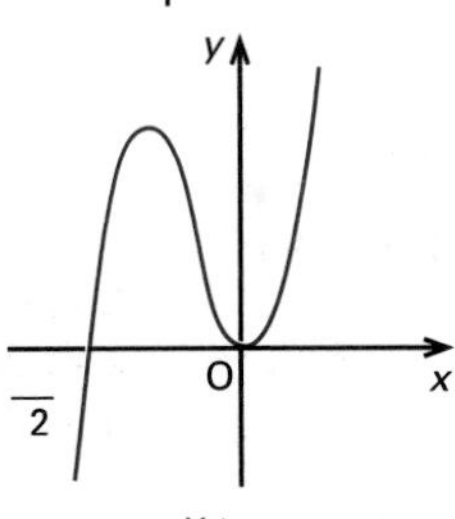

13

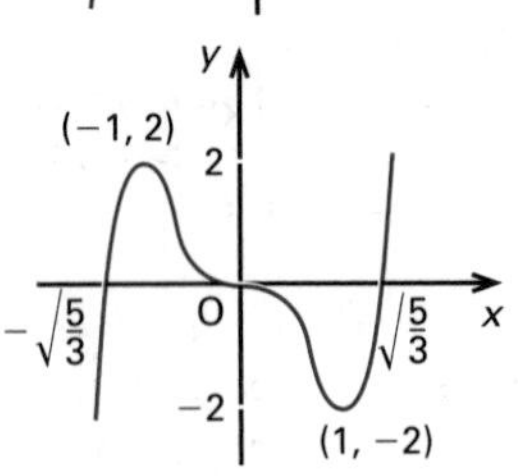

14

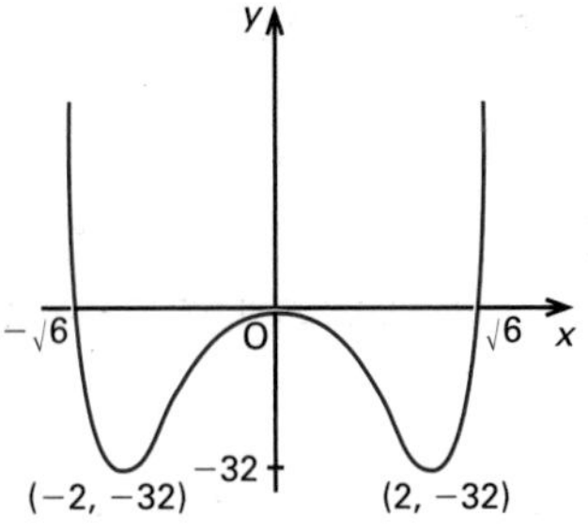

15

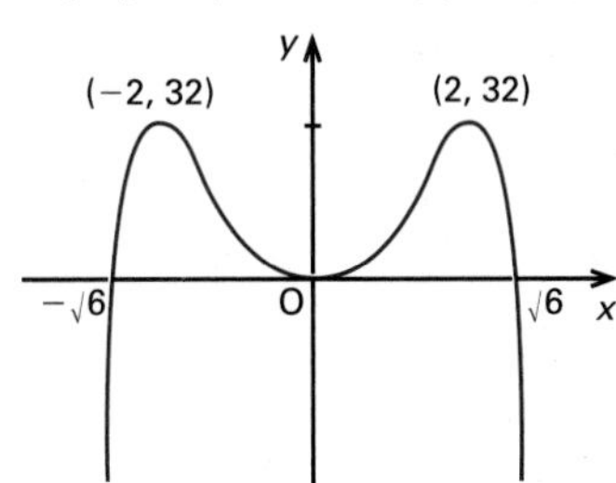

Page 76 Exercise 4

1 a $f(-2)$ **b** $f(0)$, $f(2)$ **c** $f(-1)$, $f(1)$

2 a **(i)** 3, −3 **(ii)** max 5 **(iii)** 5, −3

b **(i)** −2, 18 **(ii)** max 2, min −2 **(iii)** 18, −2

c **(i)** 17, 189 **(ii)** min −64, PI(0, 0) **(iii)** 189, −64

d **(i)** −49, 0 **(ii)** max 32, min 0 **(iii)** 32, −49

e **(i)** −11, −27 **(ii)** max 16, PI(0, 0) **(iii)** 16, −27

f **(i)** 56, −56 **(ii)** max 2, min −2, PI(0, 0) **(iii)** 56, −56

Page 76 Exercise 5A

1 b $x = y = 6$

2 b $x = -25$, $y = 25$

3 $x = y = 6$

4 b 225 cm^2, 15 cm, 15 cm

5 b 10 cm, 10 cm

6 b 11 cm by 22 cm

7 a $A = 2xy + x^2$ **c** $x = y = 4$

Page 77 Exercise 5B

1 b 2 **2 b** 3 cm by 3 cm by 1.5 cm

3 b 5 **4 b** 46 cm^2

5 b 16 m^2 **6 b** $r = 4$, $h = 8$

Page 79 Exercise 6

1 a $\frac{dy}{dx} = kx^2$ **b** $\frac{dy}{dx} = \frac{k}{\sqrt{x}}$

2 $\frac{dN}{dt} = kN$, $k > 0$

3 $\frac{dQ}{dt} = -kQ$, $k > 0$

4 a $A = x^2$ **b** $\frac{dA}{dx} = 2x$

5 a $V = x^3$ **b** $\frac{dV}{dx} = -3x^2$

6 a $\frac{dV}{dr} = 4\pi r^2$ **b** $\frac{dV}{dr} = -4\pi r^2$

7 a $F = \frac{k}{x^2}, k > 0$ **b** $\frac{dF}{dx} = -\frac{2k}{x^3}$
8 24 g/s
9 $1\frac{1}{4}$ wpm
10 660 bacteria/second
11 a $\frac{1}{4}$ metre/hour
b it decreases; no, the ground is waterlogged
12 24π mm²/mm

Page 81 Exercise 7

1 a $v = -14 + 4t, a = 4$ **b** $-2, 4$
c to left on x-axis
2 a $v = 7 - 2t, a = -2$ **b** $1, -2$
c to right on x-axis
3 a 6, 0 **b (i)** 1 **(ii)** 1
4 a $-12, 0$ **b (i)** 2 **(ii)** 0
5 a $a = 6, -6$ **b** $v = 12$
6 $t = 2, a = 24$
7 a $v = 80 - 8t$ **b** 400 m
8 a $v = 120 - 6t$ **b** 1200 m
9 a $d\theta/dt = 4 + 3t - t^2$ **b** 16
10 a to right of O on x-axis, moving to right, accelerating
b to left of O on x-axis, moving to left, decelerating

Page 82 Review

1 a $6x^5$ **b** $20x$ **c** $3x^2 - 6x + 4$
2 a $-x^{-2}$ **b** $-20x^{-5}$ **c** $-2x^{-3}$ **d** $-\frac{1}{2}x^{-2}$
3 a $\frac{1}{2}y^{-1/2}$ **b** $-\frac{1}{3}y^{-4/3}$ **c** $\frac{2}{3}y^{-1/3}$ **d** $-y^{-5/4}$
4 a $1 - t^{-2}$ **b** $1 - 2t^{-2}$ **c** $-2t^{-3} - \frac{1}{2}t^{-3/2}$
5 a $1 - 2u$ **b** $2u + 1$ **c** $8u + 20$
6 a (i) -8 **(ii)** -4 **(iii)** -12 **b** $2, -5$
7 a $\frac{dy}{dx} = 4x^3$ **b** $\frac{dy}{dx} = -3x^{-4}$ **c** $\frac{dy}{dx} = x^{-1/2}$
8 a $y = -2x - 4$ **b** $y = -2$
9 a $y = -2x + 2, y = 2x - 2$ **b** $(1, 0)$
10 a $y = x + 4$ **b** midpoint of AB is $(0, 4)$
11 a $\frac{1}{16}$ **b** -4
12 a $a = -2, b = 7$
13 a 4 s **b** 130 m
c (i) $0 < t < 4$ **(ii)** $4 < t < 8$
14 a (0, 9), max TP
b $(-1, 4)$, max TP; $(1, -4)$, min TP
c (0, 0), PI
15 a (i) $x < 0$ **(ii)** $x > 0$
b (i) $x < -1$ and $x > 1$ **(ii)** $-1 < x < 1$
c (i) $x < 0$ and $x > 0$ **(ii)** never

16 a

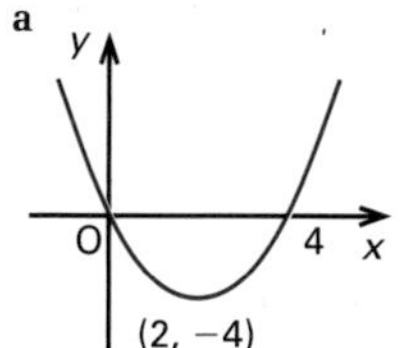

b

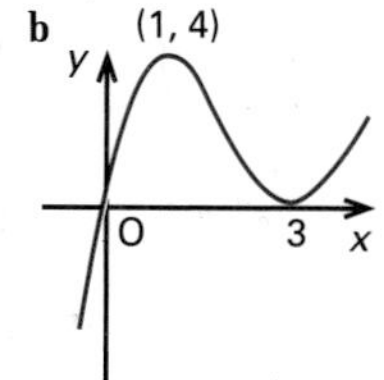

c

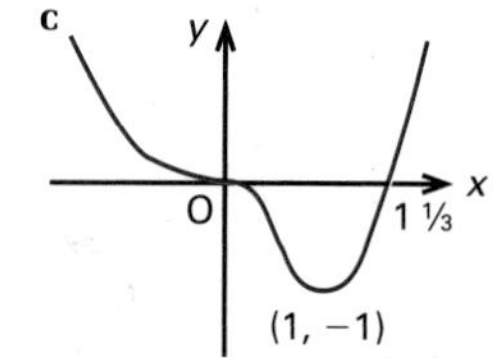

17 1, 9
18 a 74 mm **b** 16 mm/s, 14 mm/s² **c** $9\frac{3}{4}$ mm/s
19

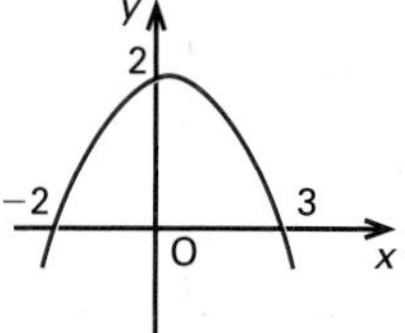

20 a $(-1, 0), (2, 0)$ **b** max $(-1, 0)$, min $(1, -4)$
c

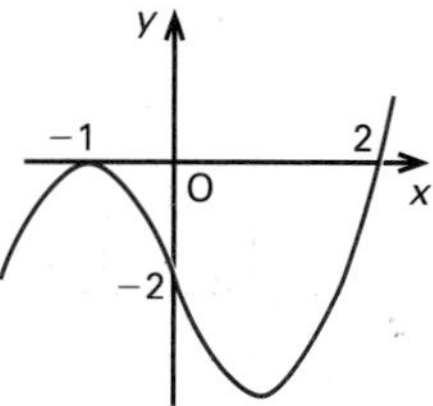

d $x \leq 2$

4 Sequences

Page 84 Class Discussion

a add 2 **b** subtract 1
d square the previous term **e** multiply by -3
g add 10 **h** add 4

Page 85 Exercise 1

1 a 2, 4, 6, 8, 10 **b** 4, 7, 10, 13, 16
c 3, 5, 9, 17, 33 **d** 2, 5, 10, 17, 26
e $\frac{1}{3}, \frac{1}{9}, \frac{1}{27}, \frac{1}{81}, \frac{1}{243}$ **f** $0, -1, -2, -3, -4$
2 a 16, 8, 4 **b** 5
3 a $u_n = 5n$ **b** $u_n = 5n - 1$
c $u_n = 2n + 1$ **d** $u_n = 2n - 3$
e $u_n = 2^n$ **f** $u_n = 3^n$
g $u_n = 7n - 7$ **h** $u_n = 10n - 20$
i $u_n = -2n + 12$ **j** $u_n = -3n + 23$
k $u_n = -n + 11$
4 a 3, 6, 12, 24 **b** 5, 7, 9, 11
c 10, 8, 6, 4 **d** 256, 128, 64, 32
e 1, 4, 13, 40

5 a $u_{n+1} = u_n + 5,\ u_1 = 5$
b $u_{n+1} = u_n + 5,\ u_1 = 4$
c $u_{n+1} = u_n + 2,\ u_1 = 3$
d $u_{n+1} = u_n + 2,\ u_1 = -1$
e $u_{n+1} = 2u_n,\ u_1 = 2$
f $u_{n+1} = 3u_n,\ u_1 = 3$
g $u_{n+1} = u_n + 7,\ u_1 = 0$
h $u_{n+1} = u_n + 10,\ u_1 = -10$
i $u_{n+1} = u_n - 2,\ u_1 = 10$
j $u_{n+1} = u_n - 3,\ u_1 = 20$
k $u_{n+1} = u_n - 1,\ u_1 = 10$
6 70, 90, 130, 210
7 a $u_{n+1} = u_n + 2,\ u_0 = 3$
b 5, 7, 9, 11, 13 **c** $u_n = 2n + 3$
8 a 1, 1, 2, 3, 5, 8, 13, 21, 34, 55
b 1, 2, 1.5, 1.666 ..., 1.6, 1.625, 1.615 ..., 1.619 ..., 1.617 ... The values increase and decrease alternately, tending to a limit between 1.617 and 1.619

Page 86 Exercise 2

1 a $u_n = 2n + 2$ **b** $u_n = 6n - 5$
c $u_n = 100 - 10n$ **d** $u_n = 16 - 7n$
2 a (i) 7, 10, 13, 16 **(ii)** $u_n = 3n + 4$
b (i) 1, 2, 3, 4 **(ii)** $u_n = n$
c (i) 8, 6, 4, 2 **(ii)** $u_n = 10 - 2n$
d (i) 99, 98, 97, 96 **(ii)** $u_n = 100 - n$
e (i) 26, 35, 44, 53 **(ii)** $u_n = 9n + 17$
f (i) −3, 4, 11, 18 **(ii)** $u_n = 7n - 10$
3 a $p_{n+1} = p_n + 25,\ p_0 = 200$
b 225, 250, 275, 300
c $p_n = 25n + 200$ **d** £800
4 a $r_{n+1} = r_n + 200,\ r_0 = 12\,340$
b 12 540, 12 740, 12 940, 13 140
c $r_n = 200n + 12\,340$
d after 9 weeks
5 a $L_{n+1} = L_n + 1500,\ L_0 = 10\,000$
b 9500, 11 500, 13 500, 15 500; $W_n = 2000n + 7500$
c 11 500, 13 000, 14 500, 16 000; $L_n = 1500n + 10\,000$
d 5

Page 88 Exercise 3

1 a $V_{n+1} = 0.9V_2,\ V_n = 10\,000$
b 9000, 8100, 7290, 6561
c $V_n = 0.9^n \times 10\,000$ **d** £3500
2 a $u_{n+1} = 2u_n,\ u_0 = 100$
b 200, 400, 800, 1600 **c** $u_n = 2^n \times 100$
3 a £800 **b** $A_{n+1} = 1.1A_n,\ A_0 = 800$
c 880, 968, 1064.80, 1171.28
d $A_n = 1.1^n \times 800$ **e** £8667.76
4 a $H_{n+1} = 1.05H_n,\ H_0 = 100$
b 105, 110, 116 **c** $H_n = 1.05^n \times 100$
5 a $A_{n+1} = 1.07A_n,\ A_0 = 1000$
b 1070, 1144.90, 1225.04
c $A_n = 1.07^n \times 1000$ **d** in the 11th year

6 a $u_{n+1} = 0.94u_n,\ u_0 = 40$; 31.2
b $u_n = 0.94^n \times 40$; 9.1
7 a $T_n = 0.4^n \times 200,\ P_n = 0.1^n \times 200,\ N_n = 0.6^n \times 200$
b 4, 2 and 6 weeks
8 a $P_n = 1.045^n \times 210,\ M_n = 1.08^n \times 190$ **b** 3
9 a $A_{n+1} = 0.9A_n$ **b** $A_n = 0.9^n A_0$ **c** 7

Page 89 Exercise 4

1 a 6 **b** 8 **c** 5 **d** 11
2 a **c** and **d** are finite, **a** and **b** are infinite
b 1, 2, 4, 5, 10, 20; 1, 2, 4, 11, 22, 44
3 a $0, \frac{1}{2}, \frac{2}{3}, \frac{3}{4}, \frac{4}{5}$
b 0.9, 0.99, 0.999, 0.9999, 0.999 99, 0.999 999
c 1
d $\frac{1}{n} \to 0$ as $n \to \infty$, so $1 - \frac{1}{n} \to 1$ as $n \to \infty$
4 a 0.49 g **b** 0.12 g **c** less than 0.65 g
5 a 0 **b** 2 **c** 3 **d** 1 **e** 2 **f** 1
6 a $S_n - rS_n = a - ar^n,\ S_n(1 - r) = a(1 - r^n)$
b $S_n = \dfrac{a}{1 - r}$
c (i) 200 **(ii)** $13\frac{1}{2}$ **(iii)** $5\frac{1}{3}$ **(iv)** 100

Page 91 Exercise 5

1 a (i) 6, 8, 9 **(ii)** yes, $-1 < 0.5 < 1$ **(iii)** 10
b (i) 16, 25, 38.5 **(ii)** no, $1.5 > 1$
c (i) 38, 14.8, 24.08 **(ii)** yes, $-1 < -0.4 < 1$
(iii) 21.43
d (i) 5.1, 9.61, 14.571 **(ii)** no, $1.1 > 1$
e (i) 48, 46.2, 44.58 **(ii)** yes, $-1 < 0.9 < 1$
(iii) 30
f (i) 30, −14, 21.2 **(ii)** yes, $-1 < -0.8 < 1$
(iii) $5\frac{5}{9}$
g (i) −1, −4.6, −6.76 **(ii)** yes, $-1 < 0.6 < 1$
(iii) −10
h (i) 38, −154, 614 **(ii)** no, $-4 < -1$
2 a $M_{n+1} = 0.3M_n + 300,\ M_0 = 1000$
b 433 **c** $-1 < 0.3 < 1$
d 429, to nearest whole number
3 a $B_{n+1} = 0.9B_n + 30,\ B_0 = 200$
b 241
c about 300 $(-1 < 0.9 < 1)$
4 a $d_{n+1} = 0.3d_n + 1.2,\ d_0 = 1$
b 1.71 m
c no; limit of depth is $1\frac{5}{7}$ m $\doteqdot$ 1.71 m $(-1 < 0.3 < 1)$, and d_n increases towards this limit
5 a if p_n is the pressure after n days, $p_{n+1} = 0.89p_n + 3,\ p_0 = 26$. The limit is $27\frac{3}{11} \doteqdot 27.3$ $(-1 < 0.89 < 1)$; this is safe since it is less than 28. However, the pressure did fall to 23.14 in day 1, perhaps unsafe.

6 Let G_n be the number of gallons after n days. Option **a**: $G_{n+1} = 0.25G_n + 1600$, $G_0 = 1750$; limit $2133\frac{1}{3} (-1 < 0.25 < 1) > 2000$, not possible. Option **b**: $G_{n+1} = 0.25G_n + 1300$, $G_0 = 1750$; limit $1733\frac{1}{3}$, acceptable. Option **c**: $G_{n+1} = 0.25G_n + 1000$, $G_0 = 1750$; limit $1333\frac{1}{3} < 1340$, not permissible. Option **b** should be selected.

Page 92 Exercise 6

1 **a** $u_{n+1} = 4u_n - 10$, 430
b $u_{n+1} = 3u_n + 2$, 161
c $u_{n+1} = \frac{1}{2}u_n + 32$, 60.5
d $u_{n+1} = \frac{1}{3}u_n + 8$, 13
e $u_{n+1} = 10u_n - 90$, 10 010
f $u_{n+1} = \frac{2}{3}u_n + 1$, $8\frac{1}{3}$

2 **a** **c** $(-1 < \frac{1}{2} < 1)$, **d** $(-1 < \frac{1}{3} < 1)$ and **f** $(-1 < \frac{2}{3} < 1)$
b 64, 12, 3 respectively

3 **a** $a = 3, b = 2$ **b** 11, 14, 17

4 **a** $a = 5, b = -2$ **b** 3, 8, 13, 18, 23, 28

5 **a** $r = 3$ or -3, $a = \frac{2}{3}$
b 2, 6, 18, 54; −2, 6, −18, 54

6 **a** $m = 2, c = 1$ **b** 63

7 **a** $b = 3$; 201

8 **b** **(i)** 1, 2, 7, 32, 157, 782
(ii) 1, 2, 7, 32, 93, 206

Page 93 Review

1 **a** **(i)** 8, 13, 18, 23 **(ii)** $u_n = 5n + 3$
b **(i)** 5, 1, −3, −7 **(ii)** $u_n = 9 - 4n$
c **(i)** 2, 4, 8, 16 **(ii)** $u_n = 2^n$
d **(i)** 6, 3, $\frac{3}{2}$, $\frac{3}{4}$ **(ii)** $u_n = (\frac{1}{2})^{n-1} \times 6$

2 **a** $u_{n+1} = u_n + 2$, $u_0 = 10$
b 12, 14, 16, 18 **c** $u_n = 2n + 10$

3 **a** $A_{n+1} = 1.12A_n$, $A_0 = 2000$
b 2240, 2508.80, 2809.86, 3147.04
c $A_n = 1.12^n \times 2000$ **d** £6211.70

4 **a** $B_{n+1} = 1.02B_n$, $B_0 = 600$
b $B_n = 1.02^n \times 600$ **c** £760.95

5 **a** Limit for $A_{n+1} = 0.65A_n + 100$ is 285.71, so the answer is no

6 **a** $u_{n+1} = 0.95u_n + 40$ **b** 636
c yes, as the limit is 800

7 **a** **(i)** 5, 6.5, 7.55 **(ii)** $-1 < 0.7 < 1$ **(iii)** 10
b **(i)** 100, −73, 68.86 **(ii)** $-1 < -0.82 < 1$
(iii) 4.95

8 **a** 6 **b** 7

9 **a** $a = -2, b = 3$ **b** −31

10 **a** $-1 < \frac{1}{2} < 1$, so limit is 1, i.e. $t_n \to 1$ as $n \to \infty$.

5 Revision exercises

Page 95 Chapter 1 Revision

1 **a** $(1, \frac{1}{2})$ **b** 13 **c** $\frac{5}{12}$ **d** $\frac{5}{12}, -\frac{12}{5}$

2 **a** 3, $\frac{1}{4}$ **b** **(i)** 71.6°, 14.0° **(ii)** 57.6°

3 **a** **(i)** $m_{DE} = -\frac{1}{5} = m_{EF}$, and E is a common point
b $y - 5x = 22$

4 **a** $AB^2 = 17 = BC^2$, $AD^2 = 85 = DC^2$
b $(4\frac{1}{2}, \frac{1}{2})$

5 **a** **(i)** $y - x = -2$ **(ii)** $y + 2x = 18$
b $(\frac{20}{3}, \frac{14}{3})$

6 **a** **(i)** $4y - 3x = -10$ **(ii)** $3y + 4x = 5$
b −9 **c** (−4, 7)

7 **a** $3y + 4x = -7$ **b** 10 km

8 **a** $y + 3x = 60$ **b** (18, 6)
c $3y - x = 120$

9 **a** $y + 2x = 10$, $7y - x = 10$ **b** (4, 2)

10 **a** 354 m **b** it lands in the stream

Page 96 Chapter 2.1 Revision

1 Rows: −1, $\frac{1}{2}$, 0, 1; 8, −1, −, 25; 2, 1, −, 1

2 **a** $-2 \leqslant y \leqslant 6$ **b** $y \geqslant 0$
c $1 \leqslant y \leqslant 4$ **d** $y > 11$

3 **a** $-2x - 1$ **b** $1 - x$
c $2x - 1$ **d** $1 + 2x$

4 **a** $-\dfrac{1}{x}$ **b** $\dfrac{1}{x}$ **c** $\dfrac{x}{x-1}$ **d** $\dfrac{1+x}{x}$

5 **a** **(i)** 5 **(ii)** −2 not in domain
(iii) 14 **(iv)** 7
b 3, $-\frac{1}{2}$

6 **a** **(i)** $-2 \leqslant x \leqslant 2$ **(ii)** $-1 \leqslant y \leqslant 3$
(iii) yes (In **a** and **c**, elements in domain and range are in one-to-one correspondence)
b **(i)** $-2 \leqslant x \leqslant 1$ **(ii)** $-1 \leqslant y \leqslant 2$ **(iii)** no
c **(i)** $0 \leqslant x \leqslant 3$ **(ii)** $0 \leqslant y \leqslant 9$ **(iii)** yes
d **(i)** $-2 \leqslant x \leqslant 3$ **(ii)** $-4 \leqslant y \leqslant 6$ **(iii)** no

7 **a** **(i)** $2(x + 2)$ **(ii)** $2x + 2$ **(iii)** $x + 4$ **(iv)** $4x$
b **(i)** $x^2 - 1$ **(ii)** $(x - 1)^2$ **(iii)** x^4 **(iv)** $x - 2$
c **(i)** $1 - \dfrac{1}{x}$ **(ii)** $\dfrac{1}{1-x}$ **(iii)** x **(iv)** x
d **(i)** $\dfrac{1}{x-2}$ **(ii)** $\dfrac{2-x}{x-1}$ **(iii)** $x - 2$ **(iv)** $\dfrac{x-1}{2-x}$

8 $a = 2, b = -3$; −5

9 **a** **b**

y = 2x + 3
y = ½x − 3⁄2
(−3, −3)
f⁻¹(x) = ½x − 3⁄2
(4, 4)
y = ½x + 2
y = 2x − 4
f⁻¹(x) = 2x − 4

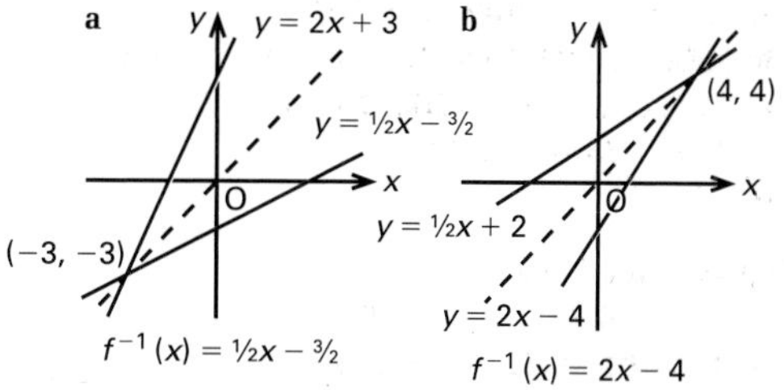

10 **a** $1 - 2x^2$, $(1 - 2x)^2$ **b** **(i)** ±2 **(ii)** 0, $\frac{2}{3}$

11 **a** 1 **b** $x^4 - 4x^3 + 10x^2 - 12x + 12$

12 $L(x) = \sqrt{(2500 + (x - 2)^2)}$
b $(x - 2)/50$, $2 \leqslant x \leqslant 7$
c $50 \leqslant L(x) \leqslant 50.25$

Page 97 Chapter 2.2 Revision

1 **a** $(x + 1)^2 + 4$ **b** $(x - 3)^2 - 9$
c $7 - (x + 2)^2$

2 **a** min −10, $x = 4$ **b** max 30, $x = 5$

3 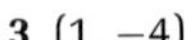 (1, −4)

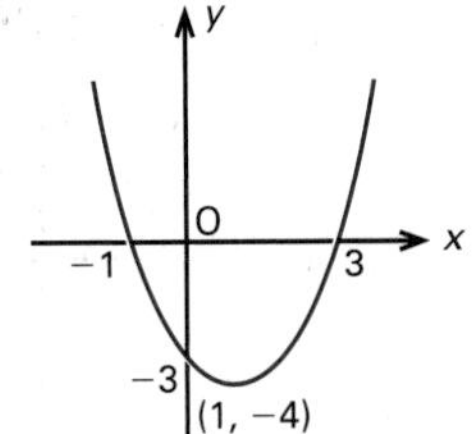

4 a b

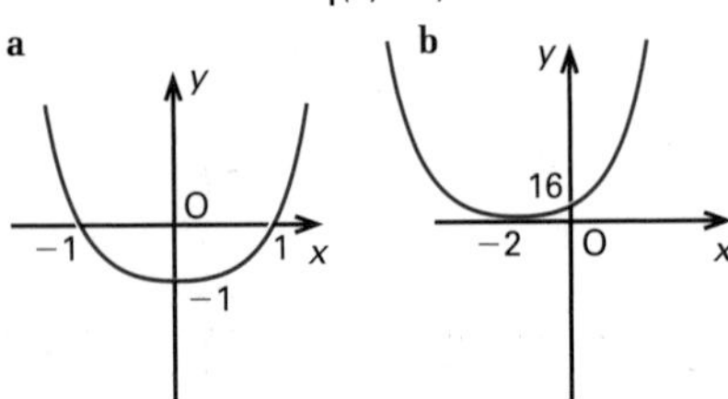

c

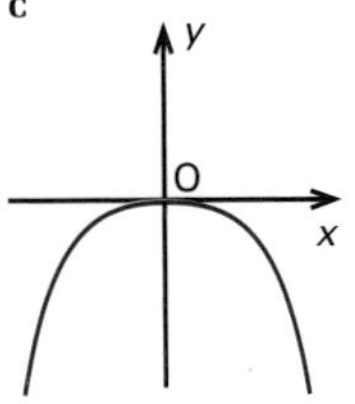

d

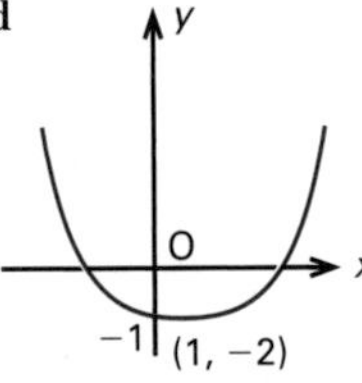

5 a

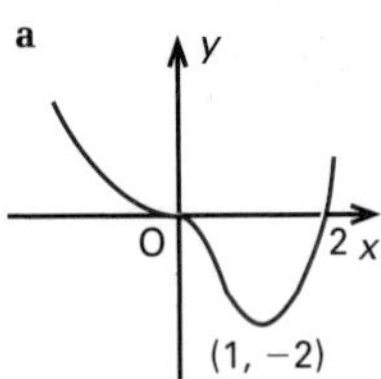

b

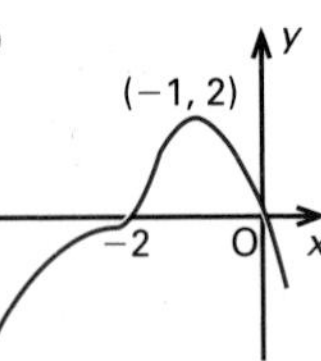

c

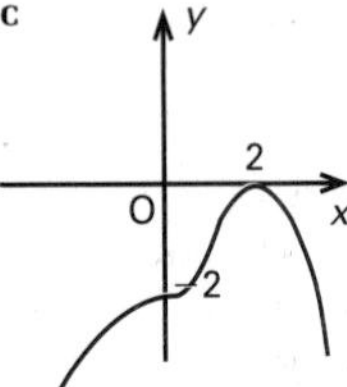

d

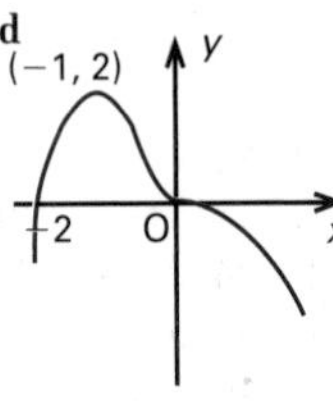

6 **a** $y = x(6 - x)$ **b** $y = 3x^3$
c $xy = 4$ **d** $y = x(x - 2)(x + 2)$

7

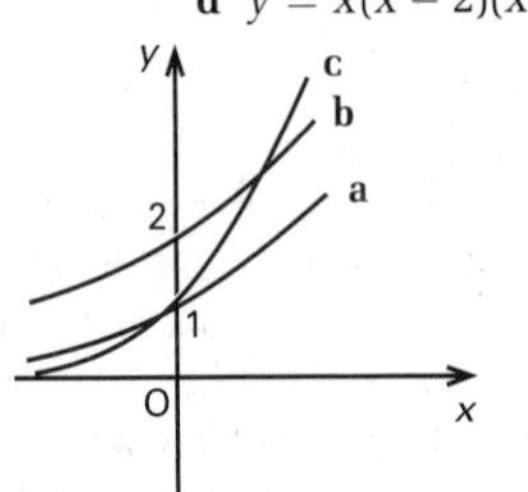

8 1
9 3
10 **a** (i) **b** (iv) **c** (iii) **d** (ii)
11 3
12 $a = 3\frac{1}{3}$, $b = 4$

Page 98 Chapter 2.3 Revision

1 Rows (missing values): 90, 135, 330; π, $\pi/3$, $5\pi/3$

2 **a** $-1/\sqrt{2}$ **b** 1 **c** $\sqrt{3}/2$
d $-\sqrt{3}/2$ **e** $\sqrt{3}$ **f** $\sqrt{3}$
g $\sqrt{3}/2$ **h** $-\sqrt{3}/2$

3 **b** $\frac{2}{3}$

4 −3

5 **a** −0.174 **b** 0.342 **c** −1.43
d 0.588 **e** −0.383 **f** −0.727

6 **a** $\frac{3}{4}$ **b** 1 **c** 4 **d** 1

7 a

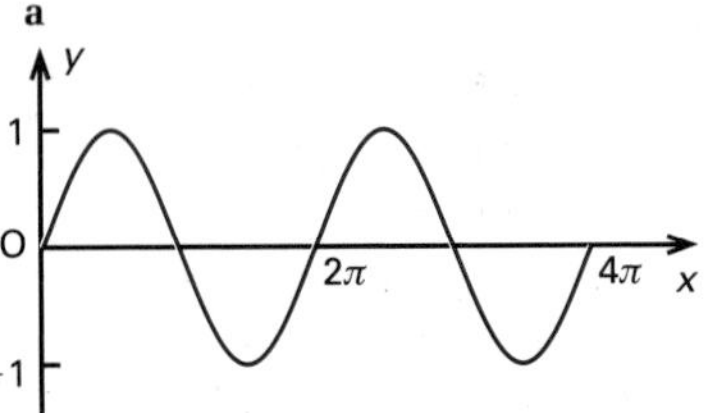

b

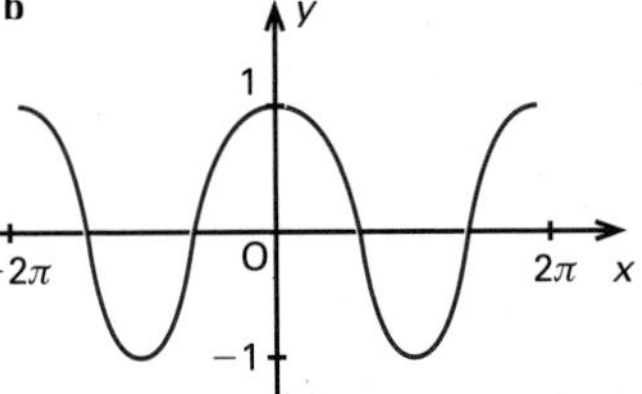

c

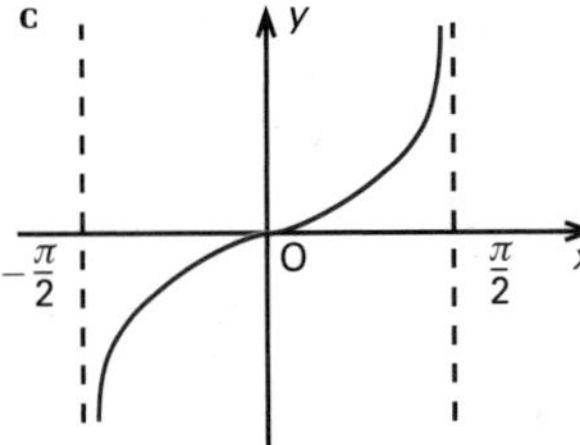

8 **a** $y = 3\sin 2x$ **b** $y = 3 - \cos x$

9 **a** (i) 1, −1; 2; π
(ii)

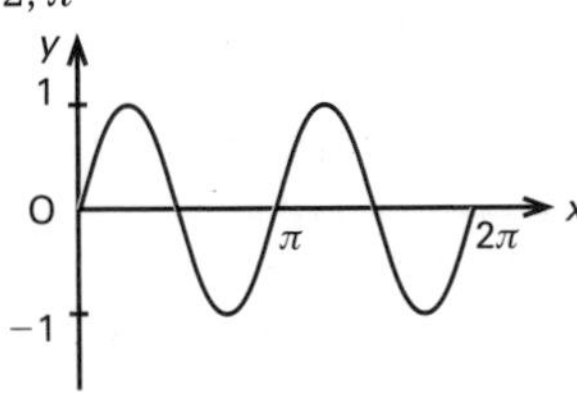

b (i) 2, −2; $\frac{1}{2}$; 4π
(ii)

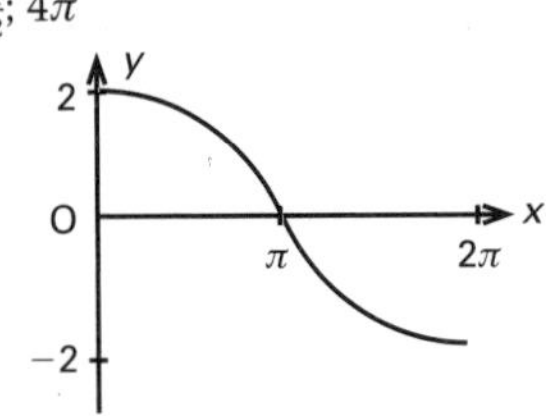

c (i) 4, 2; 4; $\pi/2$

(ii)

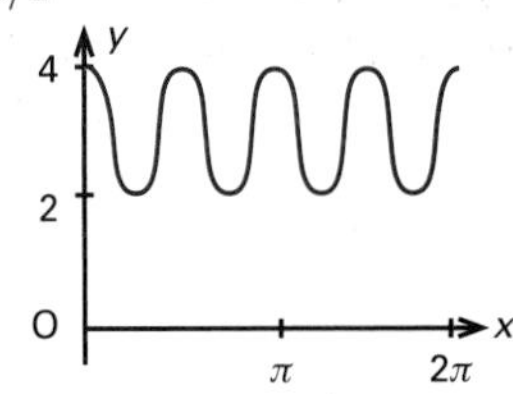

d (i) 0, -2; 1; 2π

(ii)

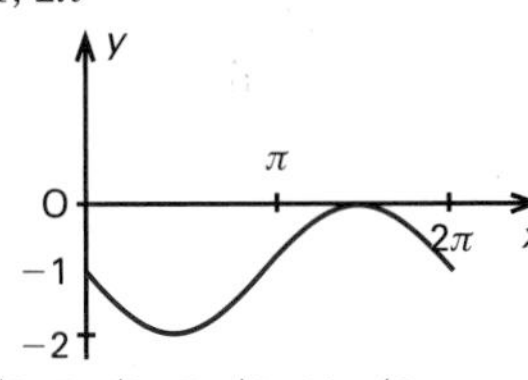

10 a π **b** $\pi/6, 5\pi/6, 7\pi/6, 11\pi/6$
11 a 60, 180, 300 **b** 90, 210, 330
12 a 1.57, 3.48, 5.94 **b** 0.84, 1.91, 4.37, 5.44
13 a 189, 331 **b** 175, 355
14 a 0.8 **b** 0.7, 1.7
15 Graph is $y = 6\cos 4x + 1$; $\pi/12, 5\pi/12$
16 $(\pi/4, 1/\sqrt{2})$, i.e. $(0.79, 0.71)$; $(5\pi/4, -1/\sqrt{2})$, i.e. $(3.93, -0.71)$
17 a $(2\pi/3, 3), (5\pi/3, -3)$
b $(5\pi/3, 2), (2\pi/3, -2)$

Page 100 Chapter 3 Revision

1 a $8x - 5$ **b** $x + 3x^3$ **c** $x^{-3/4}$
2 a $-2x + 4$ **b** $18x + 6$ **c** $3x^2 - 4x + 1$
3 a $-6x^{-4}$ **b** $-\frac{1}{4}x^{-2}$
c $-2x^{-3/2}$ **d** $1 + x^{-1/2}$
4 a $\frac{dy}{dx} = 3x^2 - 3x^{-4}$ **b** $\frac{dy}{dx} = 2 - 4x^{-2}$
c $\frac{dy}{dx} = 1$ **d** $\frac{dy}{dx} = x^{-1/2} - \frac{1}{4}x^{-3/2}$
5 a 8 **b** -8 **c** 10
6 a $\frac{1}{4}$ **b** $4y = x + 8$
7 a $(-2, -8)$ **b** $y = -2x - 12$
8 $9y = 8x + 6, 9y = 8x - 6$
9 31 m/s
10 b zero at $x = 3$, otherwise positive
11 a $y = 3x - 2$ **b** $(0, -2)$
12 $y = 9x - 16, y = 9x + 16$
13 a $y = 2x, y = -2x + 4$ **b** $(1, 2)$ **c** 53°
14 a $(4, -4)$, min TP
b $(-2, 0)$, min TP; $(0, 16)$, max TP; $(2, 0)$, min TP
15 a $x > 4$ **b** $-2 < x < 0$ and $x > 2$

16 a

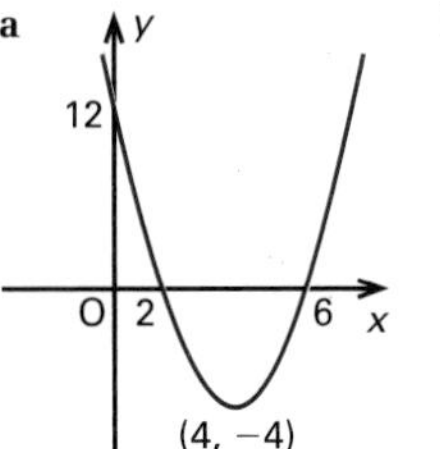

b

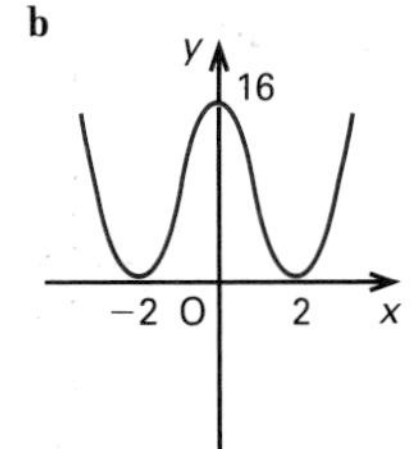

c d

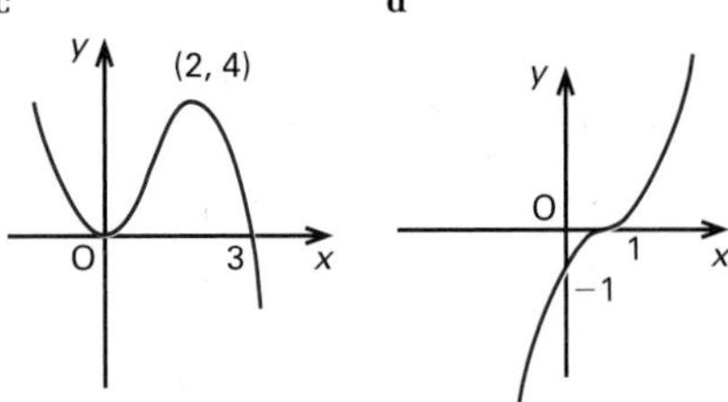

17 b 12 m
18 a

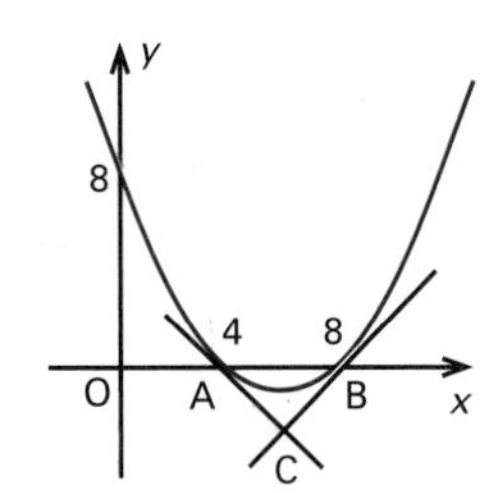

b 90°
19 a $-1, 7$ **c** -6 m/s

Page 101 Chapter 4 Revision

1 a 0, 3, 6 **b** 5, 7, 11
c 12, 10, 8 **d** 40, 16, 6.4
e 11, 25, 53 **f** 40, 34, 33.4
g 30, 18, 10.8
2 a (i) 7, 9, 11, 13 **(ii)** $u_n = 2n + 5$
b (i) 27, 24, 21, 18 **(ii)** $u_n = 30 - 3n$
c (i) 11, 21, 31, 41 **(ii)** $u_n = 10n + 1$
d (i) 15, 10, 5, 0 **(ii)** $u_n = 20 - 5n$
3 a $D_0 = 4$
b 2.8, 1.96, 1.372
c $D_{n+1} = 0.7D_n, D_0 = 4$
d $D_n = 0.7^n \times 4$
e between 5 and 6 pm
4 Let P_n = population of slugs per acre after n days. For Slugone, $P_n = 0.86^n \times 280$, so $P_7 \doteqdot 97$ (< 100); for Slugoff, $P_n = 0.85^n \times 280$, so $P_7 \doteqdot 89$ (< 100); for Slugrid, $P_n = 0.87^n \times 280$, so $P_7 \doteqdot 105$ (> 100). He should choose Slugoff or Slugone.
5 a (i) 4.6, 5.14, 5.626 **(ii)** yes, $-1 < 0.9 < 1$; 10
b (i) 54, 58.4, 63.24 **(ii)** no, $1.1 > 1$
c (i) 5, 3.5, 4.25 **(ii)** yes, $-1 < -\frac{1}{2} < 1$; 4
d (i) 4, 1, $-1\frac{1}{4}$ **(ii)** yes $-1 < \frac{3}{4} < 1$; -8

6 a $B_0 = 4500$
b 3425, 2726, 2272
c $B_{n+1} = 0.65B_n + 500$, $B_0 = 4500$
d $-1 < 0.65 < 1$, so limit exists, and is 1429; the business will collapse.

7 A, limit 10 125; B, limit 9833; C, limit 10 000. A and C are acceptable.

8 $a = \frac{1}{4}$, $b = \frac{3}{4}$, $u_4 = 1\frac{1}{2}$

Page 102 Review A

1 a $y = 4x - 4$ b $2y = 3x + 2$

2 $(x - 1)^2 + 2$; 2

3 a $\frac{3}{4}$, -3 b ± 1

4 a b

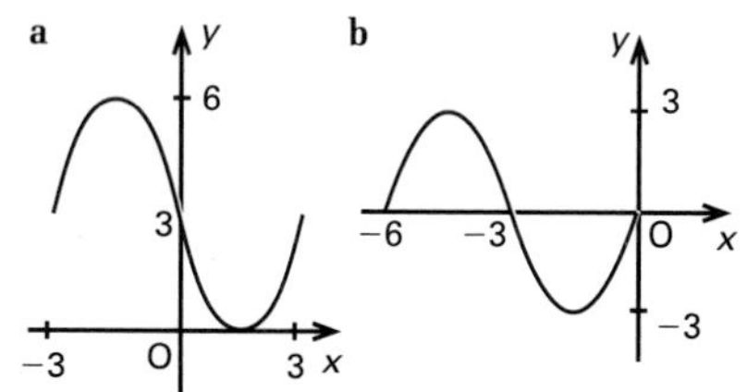

5 a $m = \frac{3}{4}$, $c = 0$ b 0

6 94 million

8 $(1, \frac{1}{2})$

9 a $(x + 3)^2 - 12$ b $(-3, -12)$
c

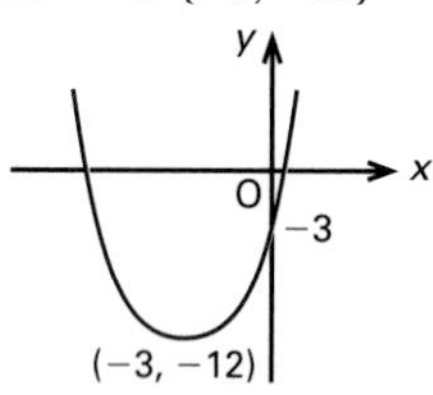

10 a $y = -2x - 2$ b $y = 4x$

11 a $y = 2\cos 4x°$ b 15, 75

12 86°

13 a

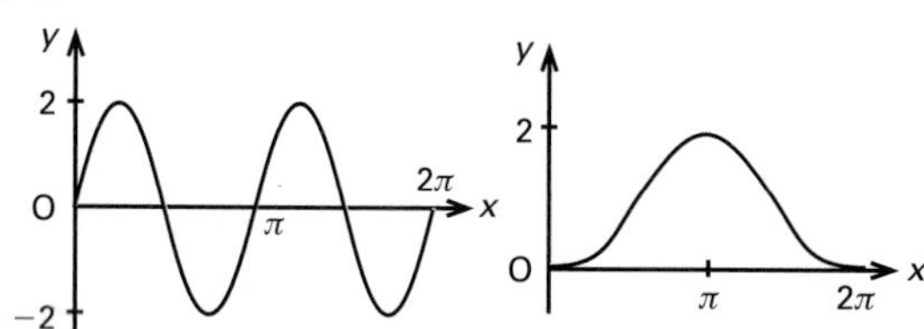

b (i) 2, at $x = \pi/4$ and $5\pi/4$; -2, at $x = 3\pi/4$ and $7\pi/4$
(ii) 2, at $x = \pi$; 0 at $x = 0$ and 2π

14 A(0, 2), B(−2, 4), C(4, 6)

15 a (i) at (−1, 0) and (5, 0)
(ii) max (−1, 0), min (3, −32)
b

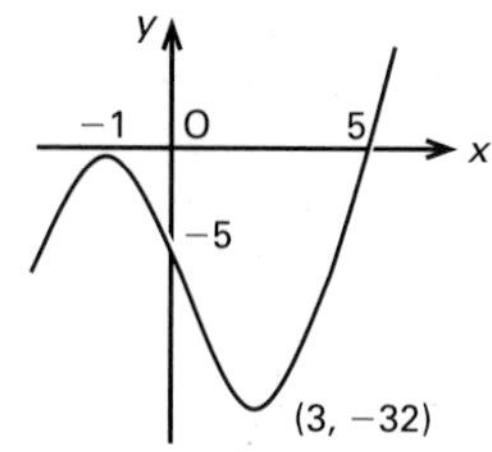

16 a 0, $\pi/6$, $5\pi/6$, π, 2π
b 60, 109.5, 250.5, 300

17 a (i) 0 m, 25 m/s (ii) 30 m, 5 m/s
b $31\frac{1}{4}$ m

Page 103 Review B

1 a $OP^2 = 2x^2 - 2x + 1$ c $1/\sqrt{2}$

2 $300 - (t - 10)^2$; 300 m after 10 s

3 a 53° b 30 ft

4 a $y + 6x = 3$, $y - 6x = -21$

5 a A(1, 2), B(−1, −1), C(7, −2)

6 (ii) $y = f(x - 4) - 2$ (ii) $y = -f(x) - 2$

7 a $4x - x^{-3}$ b $-x^{-3/2} - x^{-2}$

8

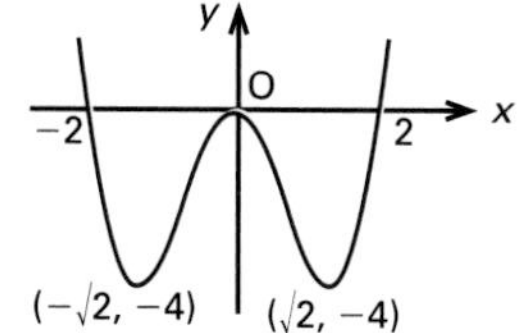

9 a 50, $u_{n+1} = 0.9u_n + 10$
b 63.55 c no; $u_n \to 100$ as $n \to \infty$

11 a $9 - 2(x + 2)^2$ b (i) max 9 (ii) min $\frac{4}{9}$

12

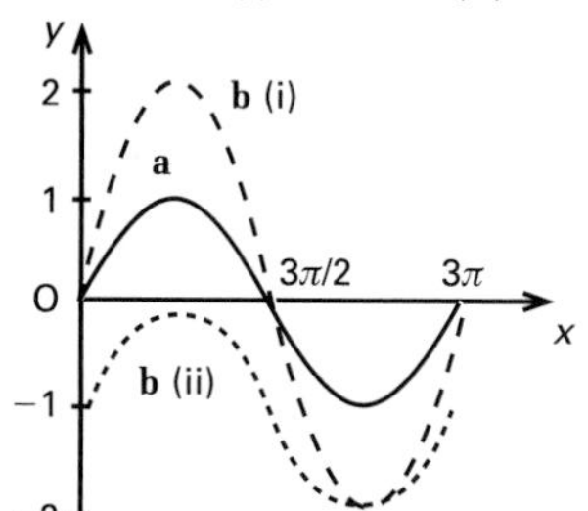

13 71.6°

14 a 16 cm/s, 14 cm/s² b 33 cm/s

15 $y = x^2 - x$

16 a 20, 110, 200, 290 b 1.0, 3.0

Page 104 Review C

1 b 0, −2

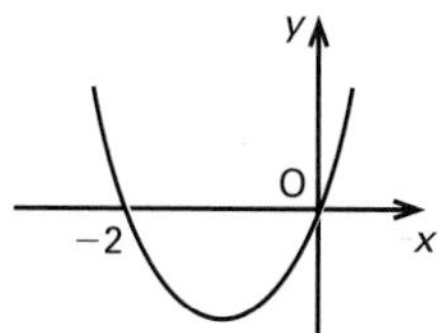

c $-2 \leqslant x \leqslant 0$

2 a 0.9, 1.23, 1.131 **b** $1\frac{2}{13}$
3 14
4 a $3y + 2x = 6$ **c** $(1, 1\frac{1}{3})$
5 a $2(x + a)^2 + (1 - 2a^2)$ **b** ± 2
6 a 30, 150, 210, 330 **b** 1.51, 4.65
7 a max $(-2, 16)$, min $(2, -16)$
b

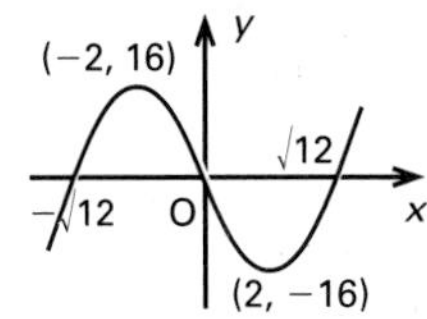

8 a $5y + 4x = 4$

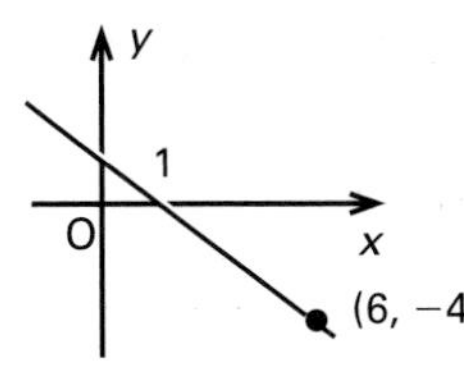

b $\frac{4}{5}$

9 a $a = 2, b = \pi/6$ **b** $(5\pi/3, -2)$
c $\pi/3, \pi$ (show the line $y = 1$)
10 a $P_{n+1} = 0.92P_n + 3$ **b** 3
c no; the limit is $37\frac{1}{2}$ units
11 a $3y - 2x = 13, 2y + 3x = 0$
b (i) Q(1, 5), R(4, −6) **(ii)** $\sqrt{130}$
12 $1, \frac{1}{9}$
13 c $w = h = 0.84$
14 a a, ar, ar^2, ar^3 **b** $a = \pm 2, r = \pm 3$
c 2, 6, 18, 54; −2, 6, −18, 54

UNIT 2

1.1 Polynomials

Page 106 Exercise 1

1 a 29 **b** 13 **c** −3 **d** 39 **e** 21
f −5 **g** 618 **h** −1 **i** 178
4 a 4.304 **b** 75.875 **c** −0.535 686

Page 108 Exercise 2

1 $x+3$, 1
2 $2x-5$, 7
3 x^2+1, −2
4 x^2+x+5, 6
5 $2t^2-2t+8$, 1
6 $3u^2+2u+10$, 0
7 $2x+2$, −1
8 $4x$, 3
9 x^2+x+1, 0
10 x^2-2x+4, 0
11 $t^5+t^4+t^3+t^2+t+1$, 2
12 a x, −3 **b** $x-2$, 9
c $2t^2+2t-2$, 1 **d** $\frac{3}{2}x^2-\frac{3}{4}x-\frac{5}{8}$, $\frac{45}{8}$

Page 109 Exercise 3

2 c f, g
3 $(x-1)^2(x+1)$
4 $(x+1)^2(x-2)$
5 $(x-1)(x-2)(x+3)$
6 $(x-2)(x^2+4)$
7 $(x+2)(x-3)(3x+1)$
8 $(x-3)(x+3)^2$
9 $(x+1)^3$
10 $(x+2)(2x+1)(3x-1)$
11 $(x-1)(x+1)(x-2)(x+2)$
12 $(x-1)(x+1)(x^2+1)$
14 $a=-4$; $(x+1)(x-2)(x+2)$
15 $k=10$; $(x-3)(x-1)(2x-1)$
16 $a=16$; $(x-4)(x+4)(x-5)$
17 $b=7$; $(x+3)(x-1)(x+5)$
18 $a=0$, $b=-1$
19 $x-1$, $x-2$
20 $2x-3$, $2x+1$
21 $p=-16$; $(2x-1)(x-4)^2$

Page 110 Exercise 4

1 1, −1
2 2, $\sqrt{2}$, $-\sqrt{2}$
3 2, −2
4 3, 4, −4
5 −3
6 3, −3, $1\frac{1}{2}$
7 $k=-2$; 1, 2
8 $(x+1)(x^2+2)=0$ has only one real root, −1
9 $k=30$; 3, 5
10 a $k=8$; $(x-1)(x+2)(x+7)$ **b** 1, −2, −7
11 a 2, 3, 4 **b** (2, 0), (3, 0), (4, 0)
12 (1, 0), (−2, 0)
13 a $x^3+x^2-36=0$
b only real root 3; 3 m
14 $y^3-6y^2+11y-6=0$; years 1, 2, 3
15 3 seconds (the real root of $t^3-6t-9=0$)
16 a 1 million years
b (i) 2 million years after end of first ice age
(ii) a further 3 million years
17 20 days

Page 112 Exercise 5

1 1.3 **2** 1.2 **3** 0.5
4 a 4.9 cm **b** 4.7 cm **c** 6.1 cm

Page 113 Review

1 a 6 **b** 0 **c** 20
2 a −2 **b** −10 **c** 826
3 a 252 **b** 64
4 a $3x^2+5x+12$, 19 **b** $2x^3-x^2+3x-8$, 31
c x^3+x^2-x+1, −3
5 a $(x+1)^2(x-3)$ **b** $(x-2)(x+3)(x-5)$
c $(x-2)(x+2)(2x^2+3)$ **d** $(x-3)(x^2+x+1)$
6 −10
8 −2, −3
9 −7, 2
10 a −5, 2, 3 **b** 0, −1, 2
11 a −3 **b** −3, −2, 1
12 (−6, 0), (−2, 0), (1, 0)
13 (1, 2), (−2, −10)
14 b 2.7
15 b −0.54
16 b 0.35 second
17 −1.9

1.2 Quadratic theory

Page 116 Exercise 1

1 a 6, −7, 1 **b** 1, 2, −3 **c** 2, 0, 0
d −1, 3, 4 **e** −3, 0, 7 **f** −10, 4, 0
2 a $(t+2)(t-1)$ **b** $(p-2)(p-4)$
c $(n-1)^2$ **d** $(x-1)(2x+3)$
e $(x-7)^2$ **f** $(y-2)(2y-3)$
g $(m+1)(m-1)$ **h** $(2n+3)(2n-3)$
i $(4+5r)(4-5r)$
3 a −3, 1 **b** −3, −2 **c** −15, −1
d −2, 4 **e** $\frac{1}{3}$ **f** −3, 3
g 0, $\frac{1}{2}$ **h** −2, 0 **i** $-\frac{1}{2}$, 3
j $1\frac{1}{2}$ **k** −3, 4 **l** −5, 3
m −1, 2 **n** −1, $-\frac{2}{3}$
4 a $x^2-3x+2=0$ **b** $x^2+7x+12=0$
c $x^2-2x-3=0$ **d** $x^2+5x=0$

Page 117 Exercise 2

1 a −2, −1 **b** −2, 3
2 a −3.24, 1.24 **b** −4.56, −0.44
c −2.35, 0.85 **d** 0.42, 1.58
3 a −1, $-\frac{2}{3}$ **b** −3.30, 0.30
c 0, 1 **d** 2, 3
e 1 **f** 0.76, 5.24
4 20
5 1.30
6 $(\sqrt{5}-1)/2$

Page 117 Challenges

1 $x = \pm 1.55$

2 sum of roots $= -\dfrac{b}{a}$, product of roots $= \dfrac{c}{a}$

Page 118 Exercise 3

1 a real and distinct **b** not real
c not real **d** equal
e real and distinct **f** equal
g real and distinct **h** real and distinct

2 a real and distinct
b equal
c not real

3 a not real
b real and distinct
c equal

4 a $p = 1$ **b** $p < 1$ **c** $p > 1$

5 -7 or 5

6 a (i) $a = 2$ **(ii)** -1
b (i) $b = \pm 6$ **(ii)** -1 for $b = 6$, 1 for $b = -6$
c (i) $c = 9$ **(ii)** -3

7 discriminant $= 1 + 4k^2 > 0$

8 a 3 or -3 **b** real and distinct

9 a 5 or 1 **b (i)** III **(ii)** II **(iii)** I

10 $\frac{1}{3}, -\frac{1}{9}$

11 $m > 3\frac{1}{3}$ or $m < -3\frac{1}{3}$

12 4

13 a ± 2 **b** 0, 3

Page 120 Exercise 4

1 $(2, 4)$

2 $y = 6x - 9$, $(3, 9)$

3 $(-2, 4)$

4 a $(0, 1)$ **b** $(2, 8)$ **c** $(1, 3)$ **d** $(-1, 4)$

5 $(\frac{1}{2}, 2)$

6 a $y = 4 - 2x$ **b** $(1, 2)$; $(\frac{1}{2}, 4)$ and $(-2, -1)$

7 $(-1, -2)$

8 yes, at $(1, 1)$

9 b ± 2; $y = 2x$, $y = -2x$

10 b -4 **c** $(2, -2)$

11 b -7 **c** $(1, -2)$

12 1

13 a ± 4 **b** $(2, -2), (-2, 2)$

14 a ± 2 **b** $(1, 1), (-1, -1)$

Page 121 Challenge

e.g.

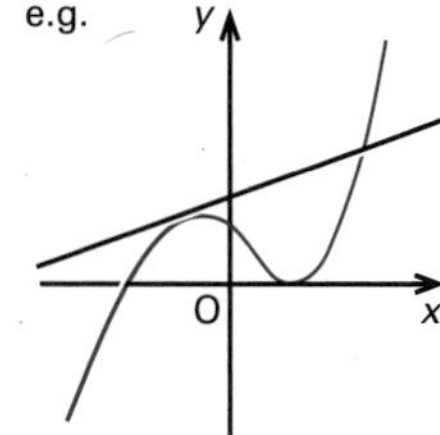

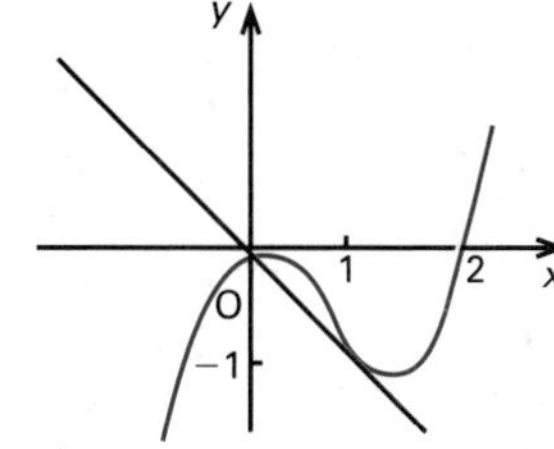

Page 122 Exercise 5

1 a $-1, 3$ **b** $x < -1$ or $x > 3$

2 a $-4, -1$ **b** $x \leqslant -4$ or $x \geqslant -1$

3 a $-3, 3$ **b** $x < -3$ or $x > 3$ **c** $-3 \leqslant x \leqslant 3$

4 $-1 < x < 1$

5 $x < 1$ or $x > 4$

6 $-2 \leqslant x \leqslant 3$

7 $x \leqslant 0$ or $x \geqslant 4$

8 $-5 < x < 5$

9 $x \leqslant -2$ or $x \geqslant \frac{1}{2}$

10 $-1 < x < 2$

11 $x \leqslant 0$ or $x \geqslant 1$

12 $x < 1$ or $x > 1$

13 $x \leqslant -5$ or $x \geqslant 1$

14 a $x(x + 1) < 6$ **b** $-3 < x < 2$

15 a (i) $-2 \leqslant x \leqslant 2$ **(ii)** $x < -2$ or $x > 2$
b (i) $x \leqslant -1$ or $x \geqslant 2\frac{1}{2}$ **(ii)** $-1 < x < 2\frac{1}{2}$

16 between 15 m and 20 m in breadth

Page 123 Review

1 a $(x + 3)(x - 1)$ **b** $(p + 3)(p - 4)$
c $(t + 1)(3t - 5)$

2 a $-3, 2$ **b** 3, 4 **c** $-\frac{2}{3}, \frac{1}{2}$

3 a $x^2 - 6x + 8 = 0$ **b** $x^2 + 5x + 6 = 0$
c $x^2 - 4x - 5 = 0$ **d** $6x^2 - 5x + 1 = 0$

4 8 m, 18 m

5 a $-1.24, 3.24$ **b** 0.68, 7.32
c $-0.82, 1.82$ **d** 0.23, 1.43

6 a (i) 1 **(ii)** real and distinct
b (i) -8 **(ii)** not real
c (i) 0 **(ii)** equal
d (i) 21 **(ii)** real and distinct
e (i) 1 **(ii)** real and distinct
f (i) 21 **(ii)** real and distinct

7 a -8 or 9 **b** $-8 < k < 9$

8 $k \leqslant 7$

9 $a < -\frac{1}{4}$

10 a $(1, -3), (3, 1)$ **b** $(-2, -3)$
c $(2, 4), (-1, -8)$; the line is a tangent

11 $t = 1\frac{3}{4}$; $(1\frac{1}{2}, 6\frac{1}{4})$

12 a $-1 \leqslant x \leqslant -\frac{1}{4}$ **b** all real values of x
c $-2 \leqslant x \leqslant 3$ **d** $x < 5$ or $x > 5$

13 a 9 **b (i)** ± 6 **(ii)** $a > 6$ or $a < -6$

14 £900 for $x = 100$

2 Integration

Page 126 Exercise 1

1 a $y = x^2 + c$ **b** $y = 2x^2 + c$
c $y = 3x^2 + x + c$

2 a $y = 3x + 3x^2 + 2$ **b** $y = 6x^2 + x - 10$
c $y = 5x - 4x^2 - 3$

3 a $y = 3x^2 + 2$ **b** $y = 4x^2 - 12$
c $y = x^2 - x - 1$ **d** $y = 2x^2 - 3x + 1$
e $y = x - x^3 + 8$ **f** $y = x^4 - 2$

4 a $y = 5x + 5x^2$ **b** 550 m

Page 127 Exercise 2A

1 a $\frac{1}{3}x^3 + c$ **b** $\frac{1}{4}x^4 + c$
c $\frac{1}{5}x^5 + c$ **d** $\frac{1}{6}x^6 + c$

2 **a** $\frac{1}{2}x^2 + c$ **b** $2x^2 + c$
c $2x^3 + c$ **d** $3x^4 + c$

3 **a** $5x + c$ **b** $8x + c$
c $x^2 + c$ **d** $x^3 + c$

4 **a** $\frac{1}{3}x^3 + \frac{1}{2}x^2 + c$ **b** $x^2 + x + c$

5 **a** $3x - 2x^2 + c$ **b** $x^3 - 4x + c$

6 **a** $x^4 + 2x^2 + c$ **b** $x - x^5 + c$

7 **a** $2x^3 - 2x^2 + 2x + c$ **b** $x^3 + 4x^2 - 5x + c$

8 **a** $\frac{1}{3}x^3 + 3x^2 + 9x + c$ **b** $\frac{1}{3}x^3 - 16x + c$

9 **a** $y = x^3 - 4x + c$
b $y = 2x^4 + x^2 + c$
c $y = x^6 - 2x^3 + c$
d $y = x - \frac{1}{2}x^2 + \frac{1}{3}x^3 - \frac{1}{4}x^4 + c$

10 **a** $y = x^3 - 3x^2 + x + 1$
b $y = x^4 - 2x^3 + 5x + 5$
c $y = \frac{1}{3}x^3 - \frac{1}{2}x^2 - 6x - 1$

11 **a** $x = 2t^2 + 2t$
b $x = t^3 - t^2 + 4$
c $x = t - 4t^2 + 2t^3 + 1$
d $x = \frac{1}{3}t^3 - t^2 + t + 9$

Page 128 Exercise 2B

1 **a** $-\dfrac{1}{2x^2} + c$ **b** $-\dfrac{1}{x} + c$
c $-\dfrac{1}{3x^3} + c$ **d** $-\dfrac{1}{4x^4} + c$

2 **a** $\frac{3}{4}x^{4/3} + c$ **b** $\frac{4}{7}x^{7/4} + c$
c $2x^{1/2} + c$ **d** $-\dfrac{2}{x^{1/2}} + c$

3 **a** $-\dfrac{6}{x} + c$ **b** $4x^{3/2} + c$
c $-\dfrac{1}{4x^2} + c$ **d** $x^{1/2} + c$

4 **a** $\frac{4}{5}t^{5/4} + c$ **b** $-\dfrac{1}{t^3} + c$ **c** $-\dfrac{2}{t} + c$

5 **a** $\frac{2}{3}u^{3/2} - 3u + c$ **b** $\frac{1}{2}u^2 + u + c$

6 **a** $\frac{1}{3}x^3 - \dfrac{1}{x} + c$ **b** $\frac{2}{3}x^{3/2} - 2x^{1/2} + c$

7 **a** $t - \dfrac{1}{t^2} + c$ **b** $2t^3 - 2t + c$

8 **a** $x^2 - x + 14$ **b** $3x^3 + 5$
c $2x + \dfrac{1}{x} + 5$ **d** $\frac{1}{2}x^2 + 2x^{1/2} - 2$
e $\frac{1}{3}x^{3/2} - 2x^{5/2} + 3$

9 **a** $y = x^4 - \dfrac{1}{x^2}$ **b** $y = u - \dfrac{1}{u} + 2\frac{1}{2}$

10 **a** $\frac{1}{5}p^5 - p + c$ **b** $\frac{4}{3}t^3 + 2t^2 + t + c$
c $\frac{1}{3}u^3 - 2u - \dfrac{1}{u} + c$ **d** $\frac{1}{3}v^3 + v + c$
e $\frac{2}{5}t^{5/2} + 4t^{1/2} + c$ **f** $\frac{1}{3}u^3 + 2u - \dfrac{1}{u} + c$

Page 129 Exercise 3

1 **a** $P = 5t + 6t^{4/3} + c$
b $P = 5t + 6t^{4/3} + 5000$
c 5136

2 **a** $P = 70x - 0.2x^2 - 1200$ **b** £120

3 **a** $V = 1400t + 30t^2$ **b** 17 000

4 **a** $N = 7x + 3x^2 + 42$ **b** 152

5 $y = 4x^2 - \frac{1}{3}x^3$, $42\frac{2}{3}$ cm

6 **a** $\dfrac{dw}{dt} = \frac{3}{4}(2 + t)$, $w = \frac{3}{2}t + \frac{3}{8}t^2 + 10$ **b** 82 g

7 **a** $\dfrac{ds}{dt} = 30 + 6t$, $s = 30t + 3t^2$ **b** 117 m

8 **a** $v = 400t - t^2$ **b** $\dfrac{dy}{dt} = 400t - t^2$
c $y = 200t^2 - \frac{1}{3}t^3$, 1666 700 m

Page 131 Exercise 4

1

a

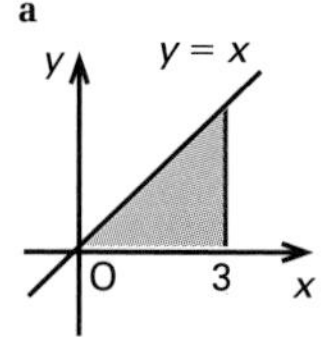

b

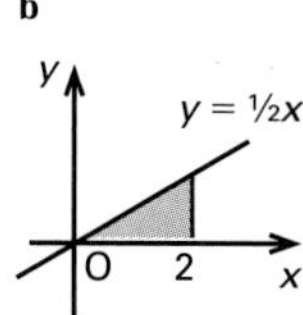

c

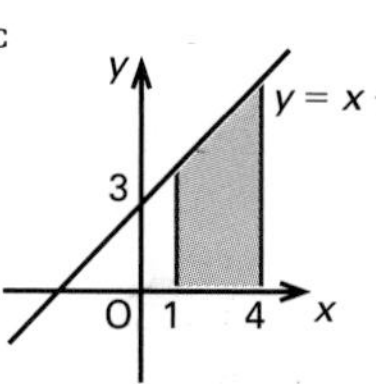

2

a

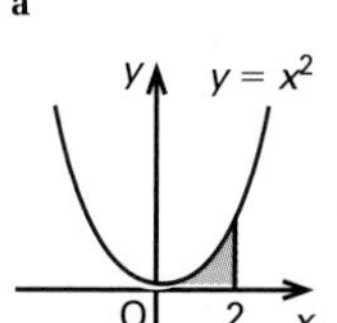

b

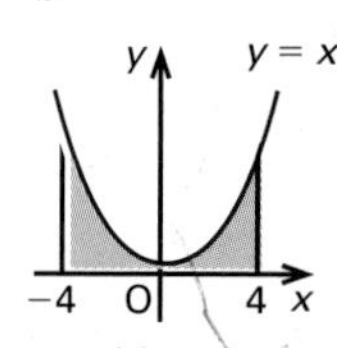

c

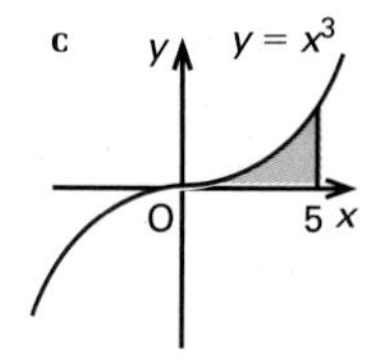

3

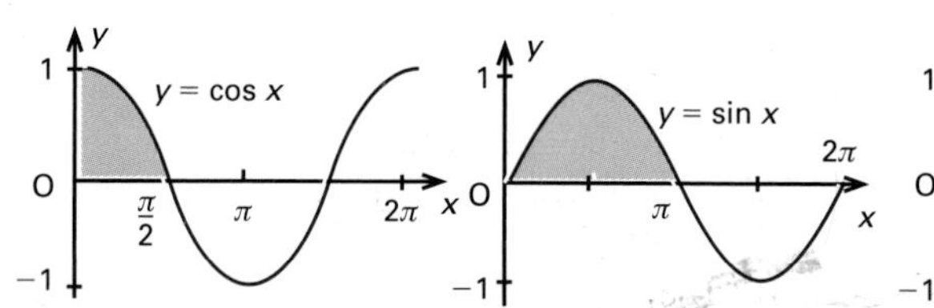

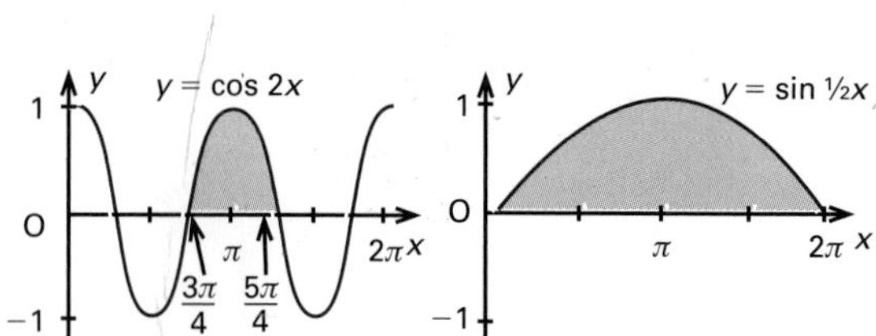

4 **a** $\displaystyle\int_0^6 (6 - x)\,dx$ **b** $\displaystyle\int_{-3}^3 (9 - x^2)\,dx$

5 **a** $\displaystyle\int_1^3 (\tfrac{1}{2}x + 1)\,dx$ **b** $\displaystyle\int_2^6 \frac{1}{x}\,dx$

6 **a** $\displaystyle\int_0^4 (4 - x)\,dx$ **b** $\displaystyle\int_0^3 (x^2 - 3x)\,dx$

7 a $\int_{3\pi/2}^{2\pi} \cos x \, dx$ **b** $\int_{\pi}^{2\pi} \sin x \, dx$

8 a $\int_{\pi/2}^{\pi} \sin 2x \, dx$ **b** $\int_{0}^{2} (4 - x^2)^{1/2} \, dx$

Page 133 Exercise 5

1 a 8 **b** 26 **c** 15
2 a $1\frac{1}{2}$ **b** 1 **c** 3
3 a 6 **b** 8 **c** $\frac{1}{3}$
4 a 5 **b** 4
5 a 12 **b** 8
6 a $2\frac{1}{3}$ **b** $2\frac{2}{3}$
7 a $\frac{2}{3}$ **b** $8\frac{2}{3}$
8 a 0 **b** 0
9 a $5\frac{1}{3}$ **b** $\frac{1}{2}$ **c** 2
10 a 8 **b** $3\frac{3}{4}$
11 a $1\frac{1}{2}$ **b** 5
12 a $\frac{1}{6}$ **b** 0
13 a each side $= -2$
14 a 2 **b** 4

Page 135 Exercise 6

1 a 25 **b** 12
2 a $2\frac{2}{3}$ **b** 7
3 a $20\frac{1}{4}$ **b** $5\frac{1}{3}$
4 a 36 **b** $1\frac{1}{3}$
5 a $97\frac{1}{5}$ **b** 18
6 $\frac{1}{3}$
7 $1\frac{1}{3}$
8 a 4, 9, 13 **b** 1, 16, 17

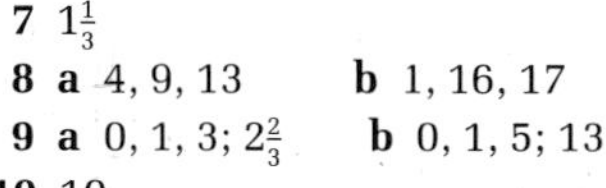

9 a 0, 1, 3; $2\frac{2}{3}$ **b** 0, 1, 5; 13
10 10
11 $4\frac{1}{4}$

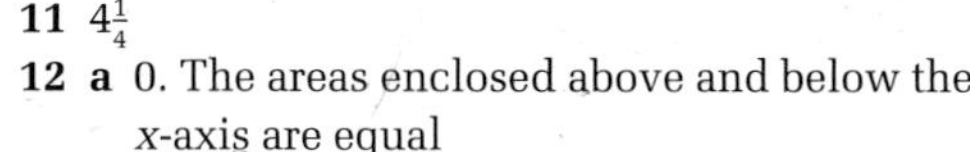

12 a 0. The areas enclosed above and below the x-axis are equal
b 8
13 a 32 **b** 2.5
14 a (i) $(-\sqrt{3}, 0)$, $(0, 0)$, $(\sqrt{3}, 0)$
(ii) max TP$(1, 2)$, min TP$(-1, -2)$
c (i) $4\frac{1}{2}$ **(ii)** $2\frac{1}{2}$

Page 137 Exercise 7

1 $\frac{1}{6}$

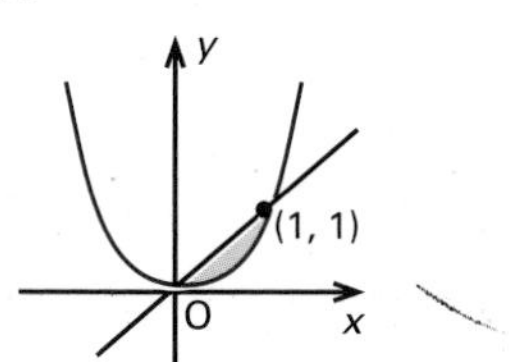

2 4

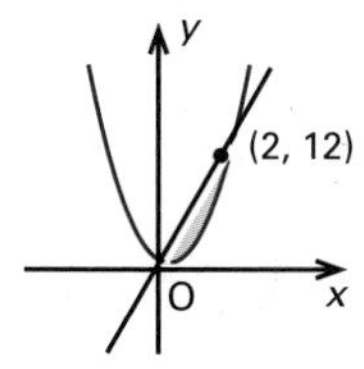

3 36

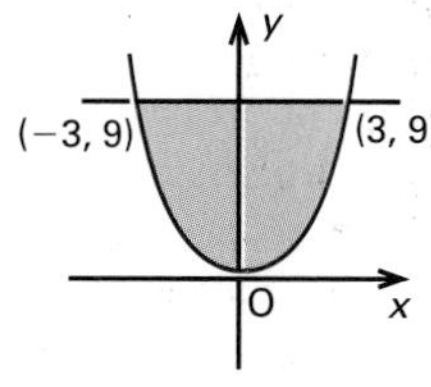

4 $2\frac{2}{3}$

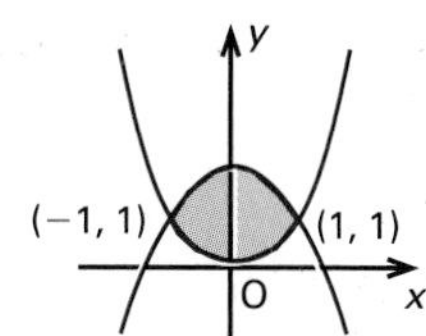

5 $\frac{1}{2}$

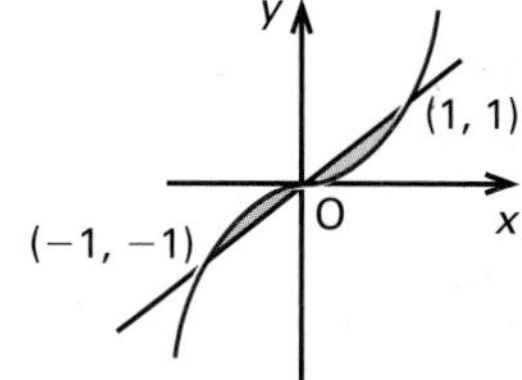

6 $\frac{1}{3}$

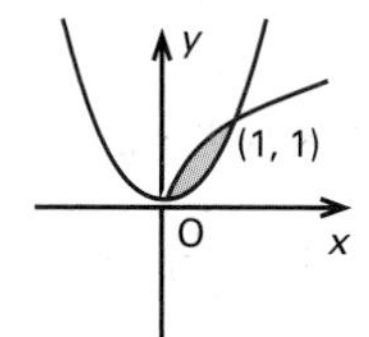

7 36

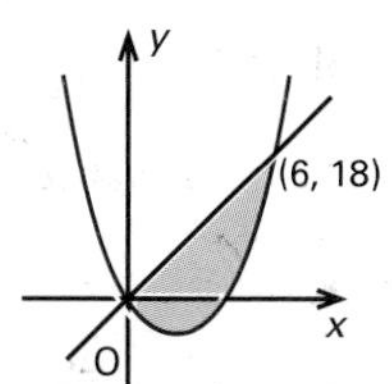

8 $1\frac{1}{3}$

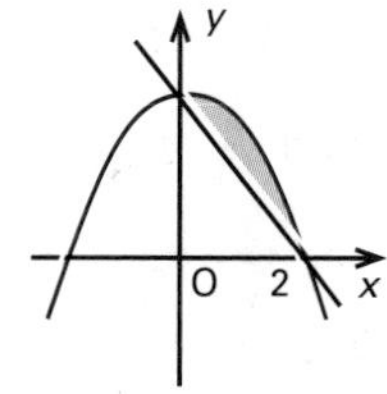

9 $10\frac{2}{3}$

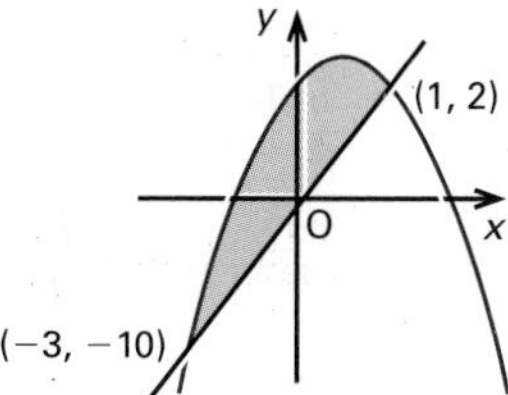

10 $21\frac{1}{3}$

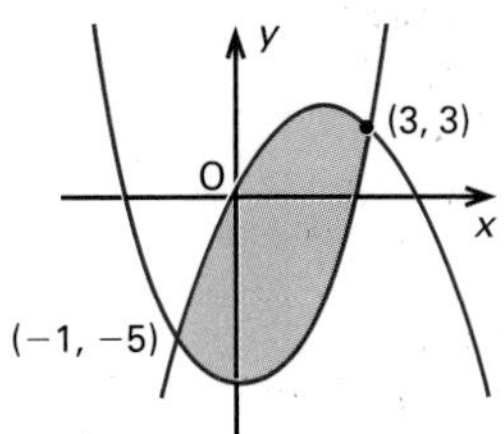

11 8

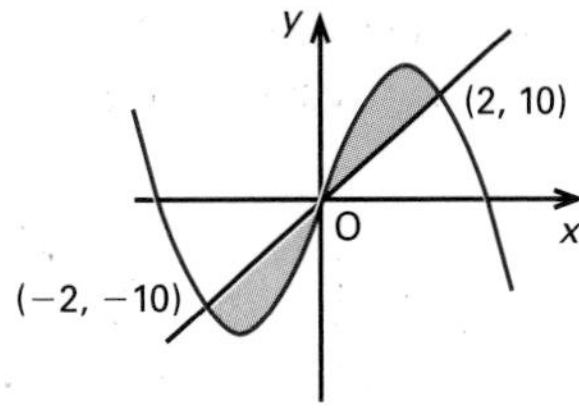

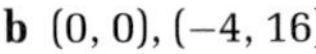

12 a $85\frac{1}{3}$ **b** $(0, 0), (-4, 16)$

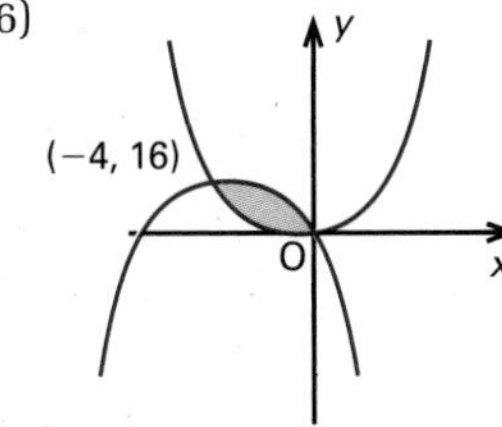

13 a $y = -x + 4$ **b** $\frac{5}{6}$

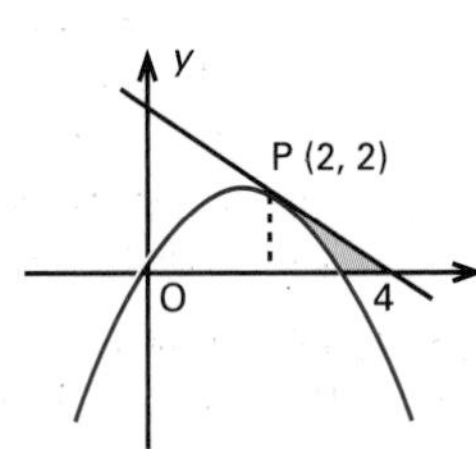

14 a $(-1\frac{1}{2}, 0)$ **b** $10\frac{5}{12}$

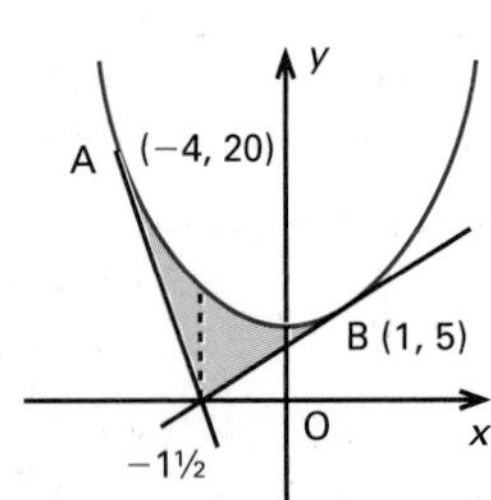

Page 138 Exercise 8

1 3600 m^2
2 9 cm^2
3 a $6\frac{2}{3}$ m^2 **b** yes
4 a A(−6, 0), B(6, 0) **b** 12 000 cm^2
5 40 cm^2
6 A 19 200 cm^2, B 17 100 cm^2
7 animal farm $46\frac{2}{3}$, picnic area $10\frac{1}{2}$, gardens $10\frac{1}{3}$

Page 140 Review

1 a $\frac{1}{3}x^3 + \frac{1}{2}x^2 + x + c$ **b** $2x^4 - 2x^2 - 2x + c$
c $\frac{2}{3}x^{3/2} + 2x^{1/2} + c$ **d** $-x^{-1} - \frac{1}{2}x^{-2} + c$
2 a $3x - x^3 + c$ **b** $\frac{1}{2}x^6 + x^2 + c$
3 a $2x^3 - 4x^2 + c$ **b** $-2x^{-1} - \frac{1}{3}x^3 + c$
4 a $x - \frac{1}{2}x^2 + c$ **b** $\frac{1}{3}x^3 - x + c$
5 a $y = 3x - x^2 + 2x^3 + 1$ **b** $y = \frac{3}{4}x^{4/3} + 2\frac{1}{4}$
6 a 15 **b** 20 **c** 1
7 a 5 **b** 2 **c** $\frac{1}{3}$ **d** 6
8 a $x^3 - x^{-2} + c$
b $2x^{3/2} + \frac{1}{2}x^{2/3} + c$
c $\frac{1}{3}x^3 + 2x - x^{-1} + c$
d $\frac{1}{4}x^4 + 2x^3 + \frac{11}{2}x^2 + 6x + c$
9 a $\int_0^2 x(2 - x)\,dx$ **b** $\int_2^5 \frac{dx}{x^2}$
c $\int_0^1 x^2(x - 1)\,dx$ **d** $\int_{-3}^{-1} (3 - 2x)\,dx$
10 a $1\frac{1}{3}$ **b** $\frac{3}{10}$ **c** $\frac{1}{12}$ **d** 14
11 $21\frac{1}{3}$ **12** 18 **13** $\frac{1}{2}$
14 6 **15** $20\frac{5}{6}$ **16** $\frac{2}{3}$
17 26.4 m^2

3.1 Calculations in 2 and 3 dimensions

Page 142 Exercise 1

1 a 28.7° **b** 14.2
2 a 10 m **b** 7 m
3 a 5.0 cm
4 a 131.1°
5 a 38.9° **b** 3051 m^2
6 a 40 m **b** 37 m
7 a 93 km **b** 076°
8–11 a Use the reminders, including the Sine Rule
11 b (i) $\sqrt{3}$: 1 **(ii)** $\sqrt{2}$: 1 **(iii)** 1:1
12 Use the Sine Rule, or area formulae, or Cosine Rule

Page 145 Exercise 2

1 a 10 cm **b** 26.6° **c** 39.8°
2 a ∠s TQP, VQR, PTQ
b ∠s VQR or WPS, TQP or WRS, PWS or QVR
3 a 45° **b** 35.3°
4 a (i) 5 m **(ii)** 2 m **(iii)** 22°
b (i) 12.8 m **(ii)** 17°
5 a ABCD is symmetrical about plane AMD
b 1.7 m, 0.6 m **c** 70.5°
6 a 9.4 m **b** 6.3 m **c** 41.9°
d 32.4°; no, it is more than 30°
7 Make a sketch showing angles $\alpha°, \beta°, \gamma°$; then start from the right-hand side of the equation
8 a (i) $x^2 + y^2$ **(ii)** $x^2 + y^2 + z^2$
b $\cos^2 \alpha° = x^2/(x^2 + y^2 + z^2)$ in △OAP, etc.

Page 147 Exercise 3

2

3 a (3, 2, 0) **b** A(4, 0, 1), B(2, 1, 2), C(0, 2, 3)

4 a O(0, 0, 0), R(2, 0, 0), Q(2, 1, 0), V(0, 1, 0), T(0, 0, 3), S(2, 0, 3), U(0, 1, 3)

b (i) 2.2 **(ii)** 3.6 **(iii)** 3.2

5 a B(3, 2, 0), C(3, 4, 0), D(−1, 4, 0), E(−1, 2, 3), F(3, 2, 3), G(3, 4, 3), H(−1, 4, 3)

b (i) $\sqrt{13}$, $\sqrt{20}$ $(2\sqrt{5})$, $\sqrt{25}(5)$ **(ii)** $\sqrt{29}$

6 a Q(12, 0, 0), R(12, 10, 0), S(0, 10, 0), T(6, 5, 0)

b (i) 15.6 **(ii)** 27.1° (27.2°)

7 a O(0, 0, 0), A(2, 0, 0), B(0, 0, 3), C(0, −2, 0)

b $AB = BC = \sqrt{13}$, $AC = \sqrt{8} = 2\sqrt{2}$; $\angle ABC = 46°$, $\angle ACB = \angle CAB = 67°$

8 a (i) 5 **(ii)** 13 **b** 67°

9 65°

Page 150 Review

1 4.9 km **2** 72.9° **3** 16.6 cm^2

4 c Use the Sine Rule

5 a 29° **b** 71 m **c** 64 m

6 a 10, 15.6 **b (i)** 39.8° **(ii)** 50.2°

7 a A(8, 0, 0), B(8, 6, 0), C(0, 6, 0), E(0, 0, 6), F(8, 0, 6), G(8, 6, 6), H(0, 6, 6)

b 9.4

8 a (9, 12, 8), E → X, N → Y, up → Z

b 15 km on a bearing 037°

3.2 Compound angle formulae

Page 153 Exercise 1

1 a $-\sin x°$ **b** $\cos y°$

c $\cos a°$ **d** $\sin a°$

e $\sin b°$ **f** $-\cos b°$

2 a $\sin\theta$ **b** $-\cos\theta$

c $-\sin\theta$ **d** $\sin\theta$

e $\cos\theta$ **f** $\cos\theta$

4 a $\sin x°$ **b** $\cos x°$

5 a $\tan A$ **b** $\tan B$

c $\tan 2C$ **d** 1

e 1 **f** $\cos^2 A$

g $\sin^2 B$ **h** $\sin^2 2C$

Page 154 Exercise 2

1 a $\cos X \cos Y - \sin X \sin Y$

b $\cos C \cos D + \sin C \sin D$

c $\cos M \cos N - \sin M \sin N$

d $\cos P \cos Q + \sin P \sin Q$

3 a $\cos C \cos D - \sin C \sin D$ **c** $\frac{56}{65}$

4 c $\frac{117}{125}$

5 a

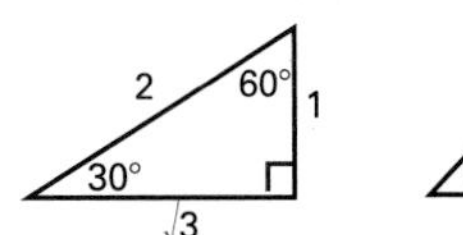

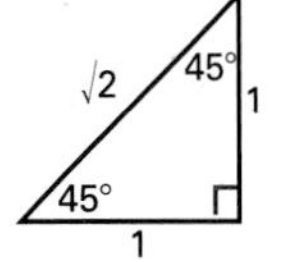

b

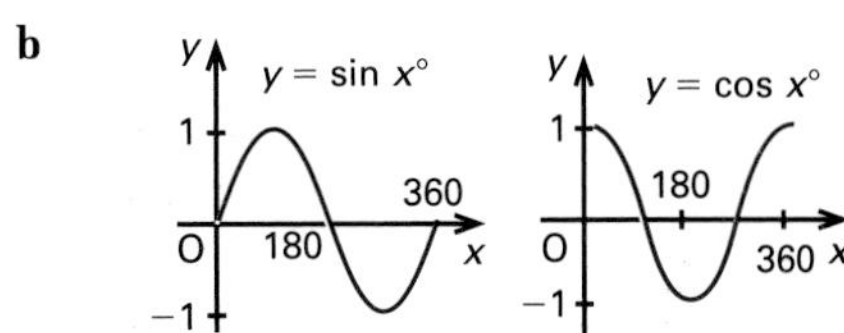

8 a $-\cos x°$ **b** $\cos y°$

c $\cos\theta$ **d** $\sin\theta$

11 a false **b** true

12 a $\cos(P + Q)$ **b** $\cos A$ **c** 0 **d** $\frac{1}{2}$

14 a AB = 130 cm, BC = 50 cm

b $\angle ABC = 180° - (x + y)°$ **c** $-\frac{33}{65}$

Page 156 Exercise 3

1 a $\sin P \cos Q + \cos P \sin Q$

b $\sin X \cos Y - \cos X \sin Y$

3 b $\frac{12}{13}, \frac{3}{5}$ **d** $\frac{16}{65}$

5 a $\sin x°$ **b** $\cos y°$

c $-\sin\theta$ **d** $-\sin\theta$

Page 157 Challenge

a $\tan(B - A) = \dfrac{\tan B - \tan A}{1 + \tan B \tan A}$ **c** 45°

Page 158 Exercise 4A

1 a $2\sin X \cos X$ **b** $2\sin\theta\cos\theta$

c $2\sin 2\theta \cos 2\theta$

2 a $\cos 2Y = \cos^2 Y - \sin^2 Y = 2\cos^2 Y - 1 = 1 - 2\sin^2 Y$

b $\cos 2\theta = \cos^2\theta - \sin^2\theta = 2\cos^2\theta - 1 = 1 - 2\sin^2\theta$

c $\cos 4\theta = \cos^2 2\theta - \sin^2 2\theta = 2\cos^2 2\theta - 1 = 1 - 2\sin^2 2\theta$

3 b $\frac{24}{25}$

4 a $2/\sqrt{5}$ **b** $\frac{4}{5}$ **c** $\frac{3}{5}$

5 a $1/\sqrt{10}$ **b** $\frac{3}{5}$ **c** $\frac{4}{5}$ **d** $\frac{24}{25}$

6 a $\sqrt{15}/8$ **b** $\frac{7}{8}$

8 a $\frac{1}{2}$ **b** $\frac{1}{2}$ **c** 1 **d** $\sqrt{3}/2$

9 a $\sin A = 2\sin\frac{1}{2}A\cos\frac{1}{2}A$

b $\cos A = \cos^2\frac{1}{2}A - \sin^2\frac{1}{2}A = 2\cos^2\frac{1}{2}A - 1$
$= 1 - 2\sin^2\frac{1}{2}A$

10 a (i) start with $\cos 2A = 1 - 2\sin^2 A$

Page 159 Challenge

a $\cos^4 x = \frac{3}{8} + \frac{1}{2}\cos 2x + \frac{1}{8}\cos 4x$

b $\sin^4 x = \frac{3}{8} - \frac{1}{2}\cos 2x + \frac{1}{8}\cos 4x$

Page 159 Exercise 4B

2 59.5°

8 a $\dfrac{\sin(i-\theta)°}{\sin R°} = \dfrac{\sin i°}{\sin r°}$

Page 161 Exercise 5

1 30, 90, 150, 270
2 0, 180, 360
3 60, 180, 300
4 90, 210, 330
5 90, 120, 240, 270
6 30, 150
7 60, 300
8 210, 330
9 (30, 1.5), (150, 1.5)
10 $\pi/2, 7\pi/6, 11\pi/6$
11 $\pi/6, 5\pi/6, 3\pi/2$
12 $0, \pi/3, \pi, 5\pi/3, 2\pi$
13 $\pi/2, 7\pi/6, 3\pi/2, 11\pi/6$
14 $\pi/3, \pi, 5\pi/3$
15 π
16 a (i) $y = \cos 2x + 3$
(ii) $y = 2\cos x + 2$
b $(0, 4), (\pi/2, 2), (3\pi/2, 2), (2\pi, 4)$
17 0, 104.5, 255.5, 360
18 30, 150, 199.5, 340.5
19 0.9, 2.1 $(2\pi/3)$, 4.2 $(4\pi/3)$, 5.4
20 0.8, 1.8, 4.5, 5.4

Page 163 Exercise 6

1 a $1, 2\pi$

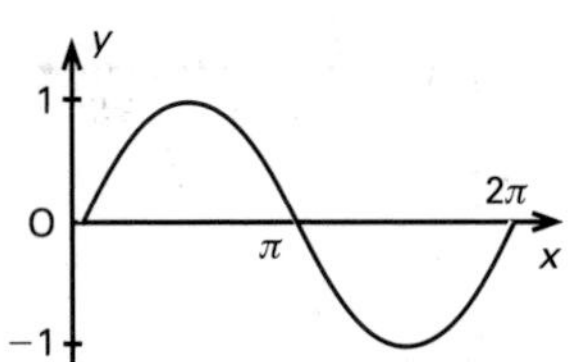

b $2, 2\pi$

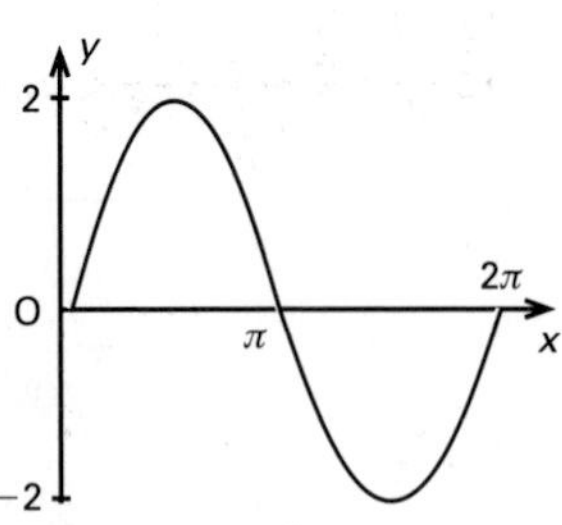

c $1, \pi$

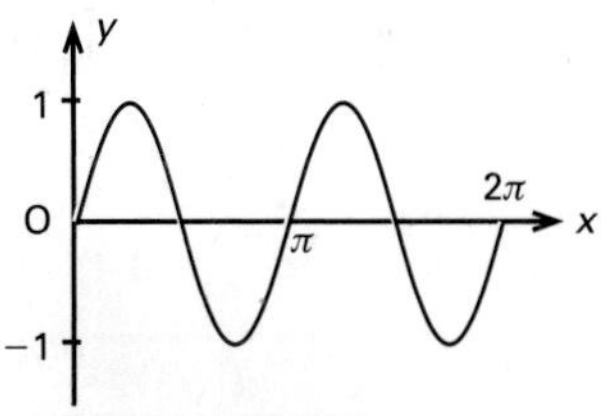

2 a $1, 2\pi$

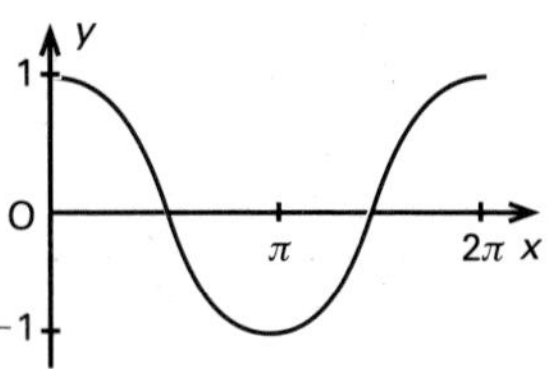

b $4, 2\pi$

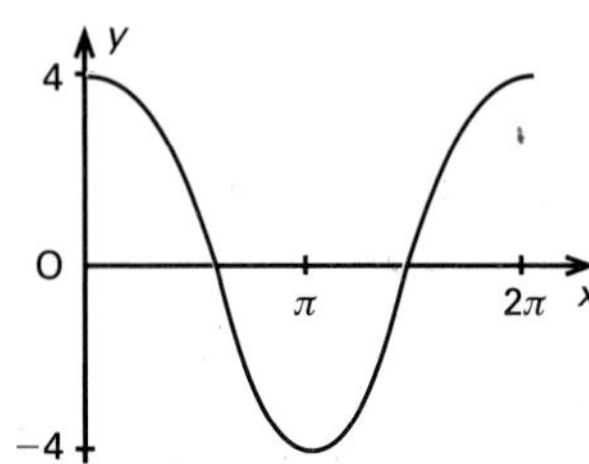

c $1, 2\pi/3$

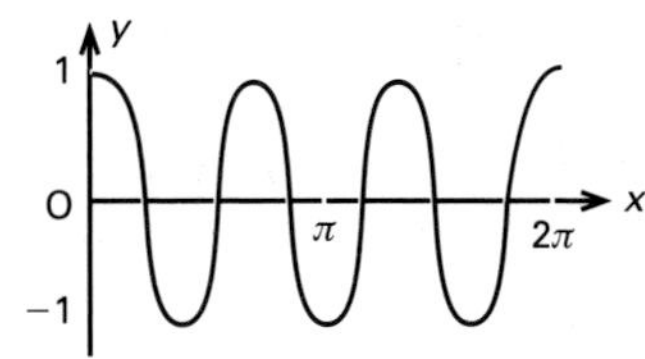

3 a (i) 1 **(ii)** $\pi/2$ **(iii)** $y = \cos 4x$
b (i) 5 **(ii)** π **(iii)** $y = 5\sin 2x$

4 a (i)

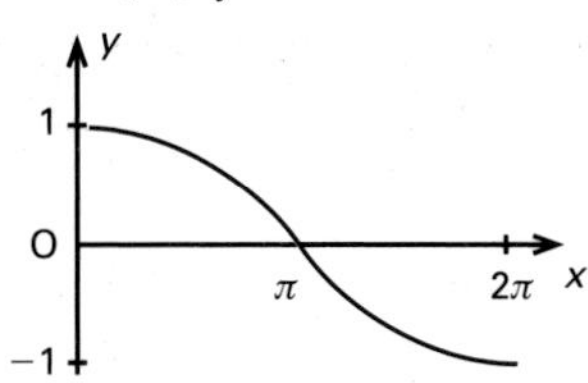

(ii) Max 1 at $x = 0$
Min −1 at $x = 2\pi$

b (i)

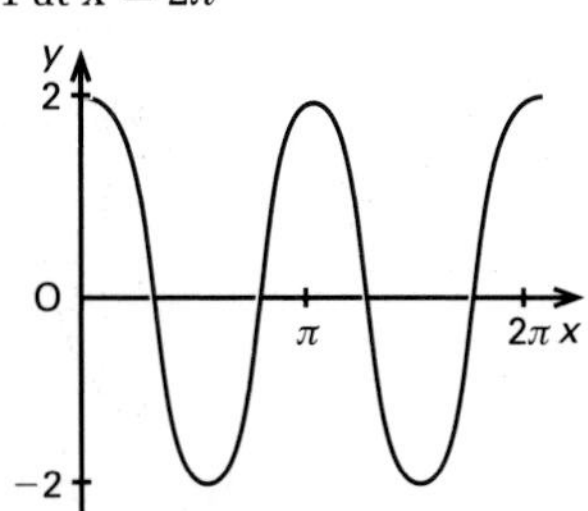

(ii) Max 2 at $x = 0, \pi, 2\pi$
Min −2 at $x = \pi/2, 3\pi/2$

5 a (i)

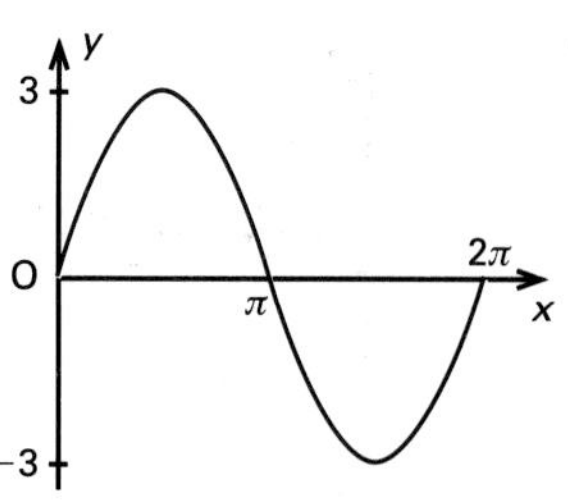

(ii) Max 3 at $x = \pi/2$
Min -3 at $x = 3\pi/2$

b (i)

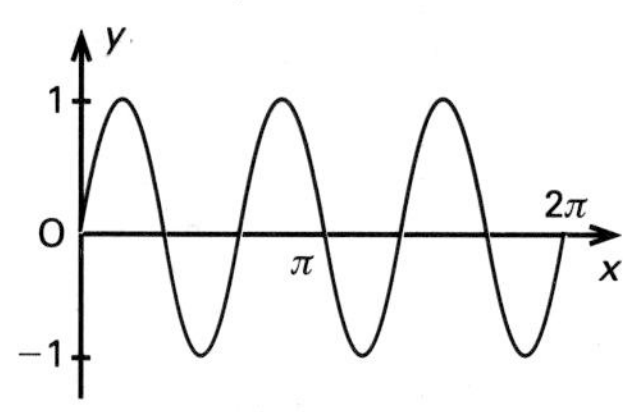

(ii) Max 1 at $x = \pi/6,\ 5\pi/6,\ 3\pi/2$
Min -1 at $x = \pi/2,\ 7\pi/6,\ 11\pi/6$

Page 165 Exercise 7

1

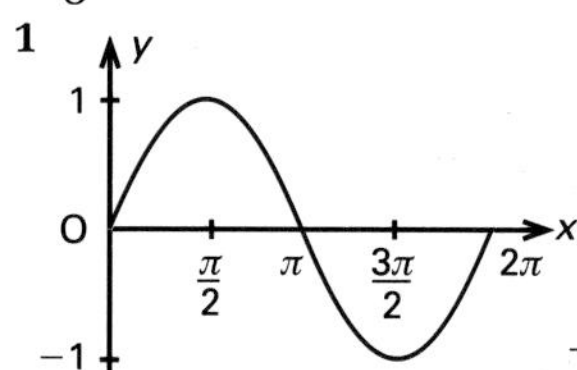

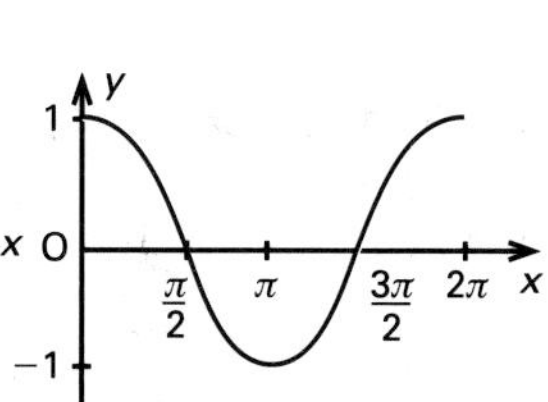

2 If $x = 0,\ y = 0$.
If $y = 0,\ x = 0,\ \pi,\ 2\pi$.
Max 1 at $x = \pi/2$.
Min -1 at $x = 3\pi/2$.

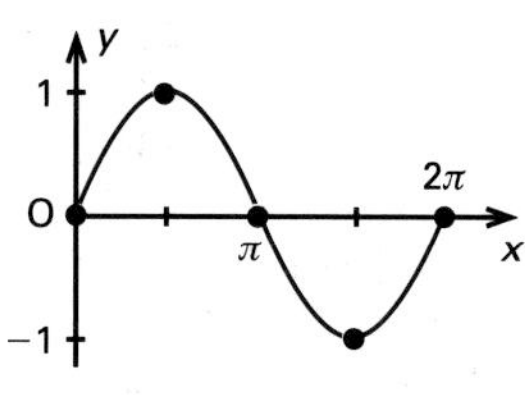

3 If $x = 0,\ y = -1$.
If $y = 0,\ x = \pi/2,\ 3\pi/2$.
Max 1 at $x = \pi$.
Min -1 at $x = 0,\ 2\pi$.

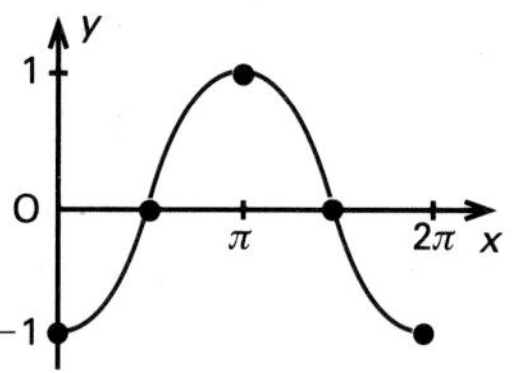

4 If $x = 0,\ y = 0$.
If $y = 0,\ x = 0,\ 180,\ 360$.
Max 1 at $x = 270$.
Min -1 at $x = 90$.

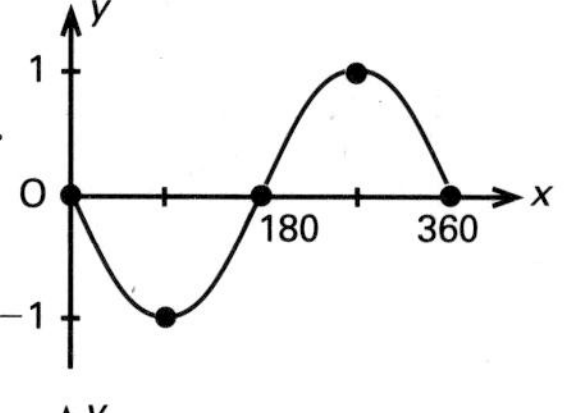

5 If $x = 0,\ y = 1$.
If $y = 0,\ x = 90,\ 270$.
Max 1 at $x = 0,\ 360$.
Min -1 at $x = 180$.

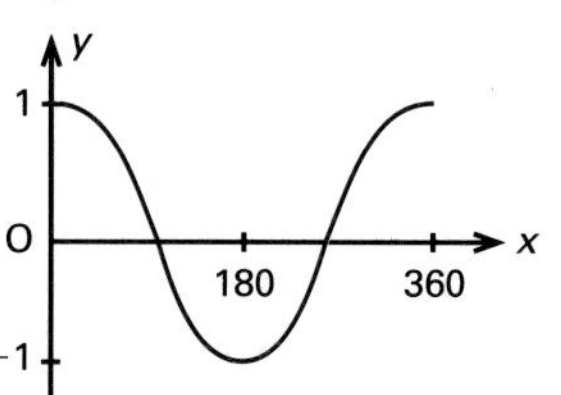

6 a $\pi/6$ radians to right

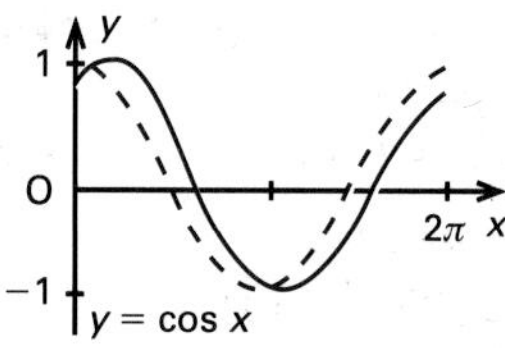

b $\pi/6$ radians to left

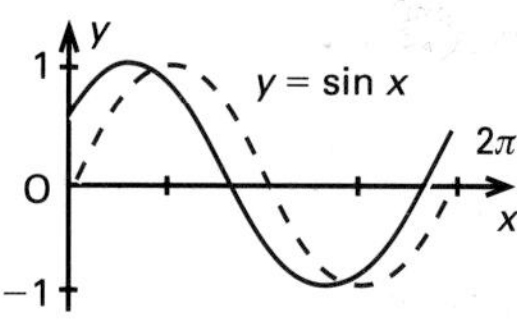

c 45° to left

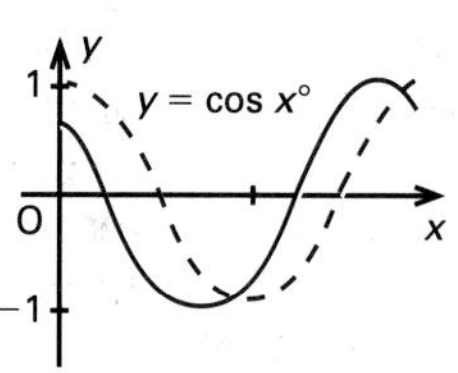

d 45° to right

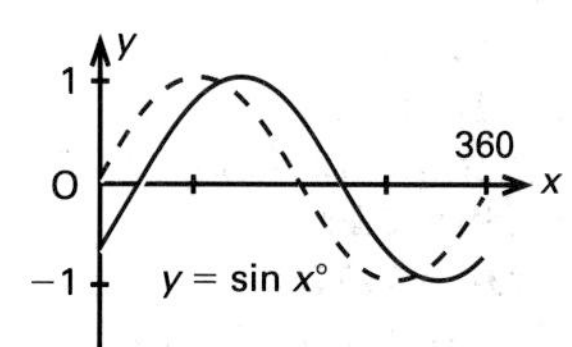

7 b

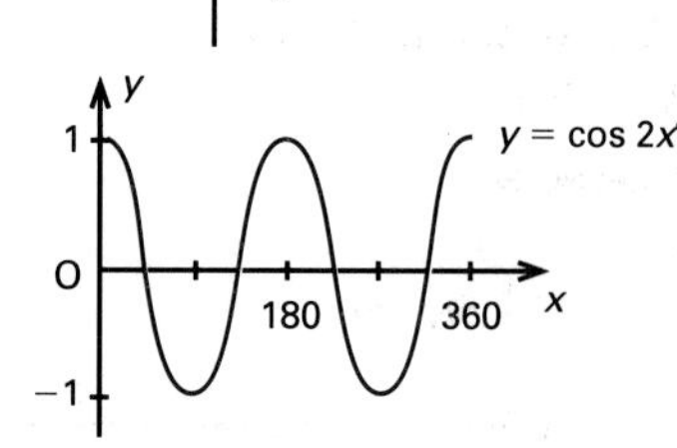

8

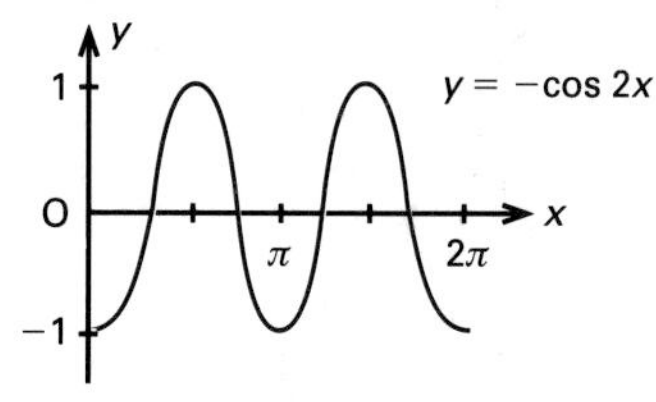

9 a

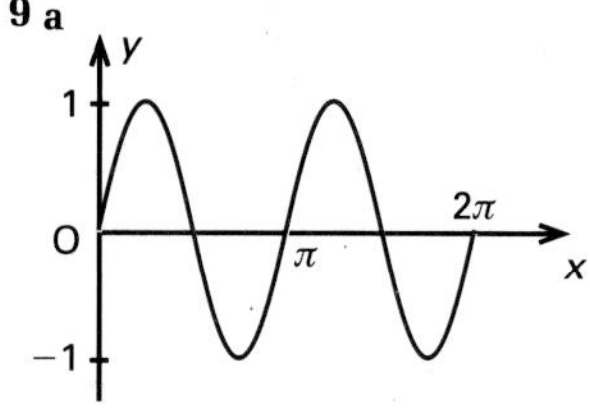

b

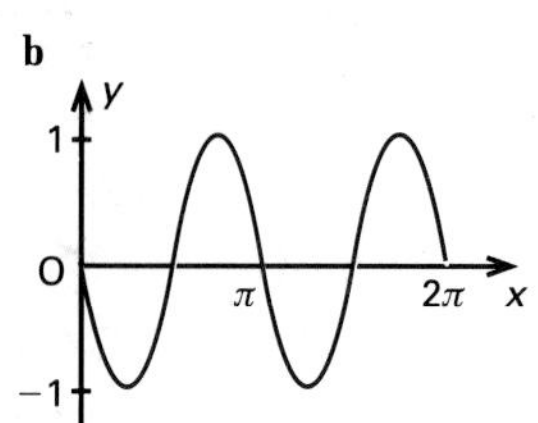

Page 166 Review

1 **a** $-\sin A$ **b** $\sin x°$
c $\cos B$ **d** $-\cos y°$
e $\cos a°$ **f** $\sin a°$

4 $\frac{16}{65}$

5 $\frac{56}{65}, \frac{33}{65}, \frac{56}{33}$

6 **a** (i) $2\cos X \sin Y$ (ii) $2\sin X \sin Y$

8 $\frac{3}{5}, \frac{24}{25}, -\frac{7}{25}$

9 **a** $\frac{3}{5}$ **b** $\frac{4}{5}$ **c** $\frac{3}{4}$

11 **a** $\sin^2 x = \frac{1}{2}(1 - \cos 2x)$
b $\cos^2 x = \frac{1}{2}(1 + \cos 2x)$

12 **a** $\sin \pi/3$ **b** $-\cos \pi/4$
c $-\sin \pi/4$ **d** $\cos \pi/3$

13 **a** 90, 270 **b** 0, 180, 210, 330, 360
c 120, 240

14 **a** 4.7 ($3\pi/2$) **b** 0.7, 3.1 (π), 5.6

15 (30, −0.5), (150, −0.5), (270, −2)

16 **a**

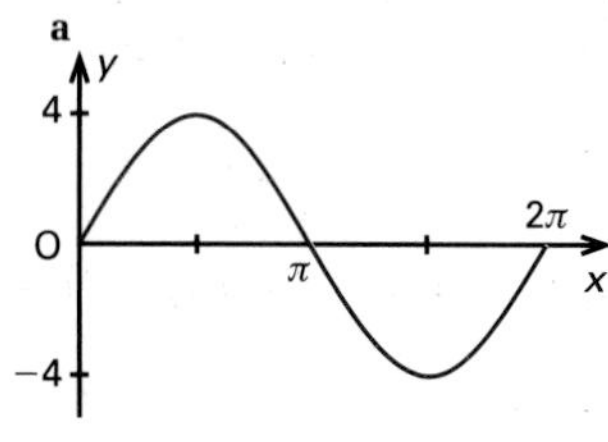

b

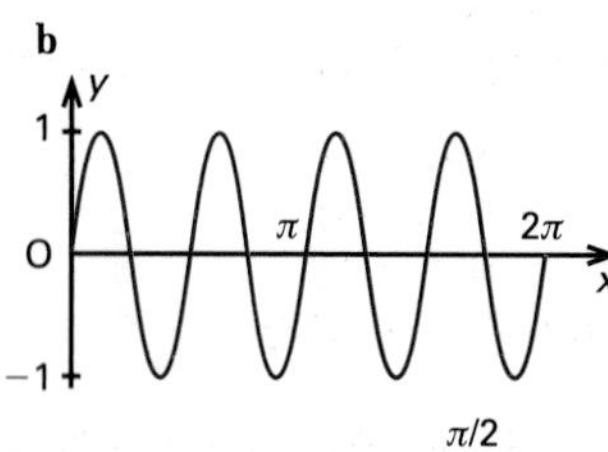

c

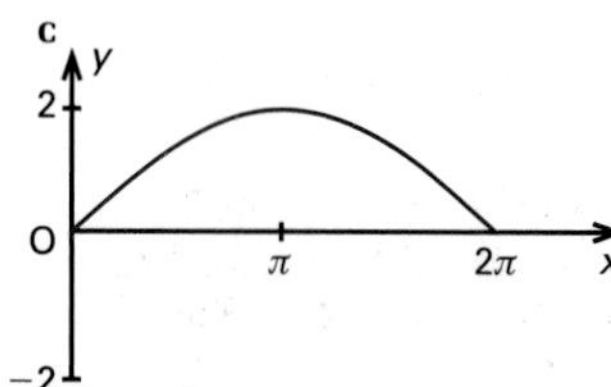

17 **a** If $y = 0$, $x = 2\pi/3, 5\pi/3$.
If $x = 0$, $y = \sqrt{3}$.
Max TP ($\pi/6$, 2).
Min TP ($7\pi/6$, −2).

b

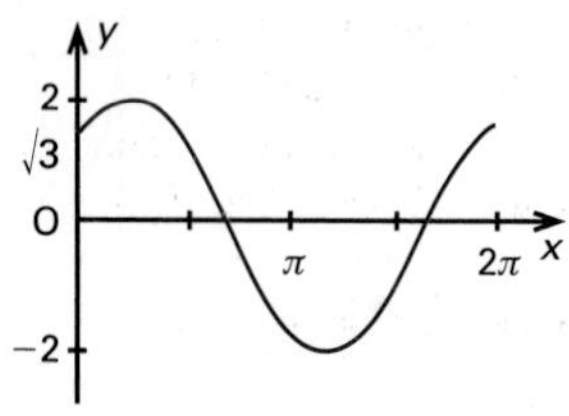

18 **a** If $y = 0$, $x = \pi/6, 7\pi/6$.
If $x = 0$, $y = -1$.
Max TP ($2\pi/3$, 2).
Min TP ($5\pi/3$, −2).

b

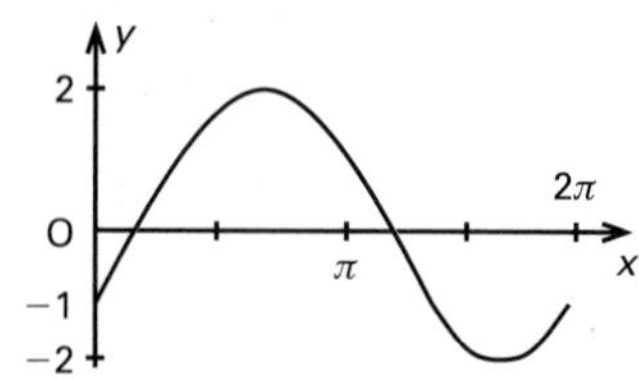

4 The circle

Page 168 Exercise 1

1 **a** (0, 0), 3 **b** (0, 0), 4 **c** (0, 0), 8
d (0, 0), 1 **e** (0, 0), 6 **f** (0, 0), 2

2 **a** $x^2 + y^2 = 25$ **b** $x^2 + y^2 = 49$
c $x^2 + y^2 = 144$ **d** $x^2 + y^2 = 400$
e $x^2 + y^2 = 3$

3 **a** $x^2 + y^2 = 25$ **b** $x^2 + y^2 = 41$
c $x^2 + y^2 = 18$ **d** $x^2 + y^2 = 49$

4 $x^2 + y^2 = 400$

5 **b** (i) $x^2 + y^2 = 25$ (ii) $x^2 + y^2 = 50$

6 **a** $12^2 + (-9)^2 = 144 + 81 = 225$
b (i) ±2 (ii) ±6

7 **a** all 5 units from O **b** $x^2 + y^2 = 25$
c $x^2 + y^2 = 6.25$

8 **a** $x^2 + y^2 = 4$ **b** $x^2 + y^2 = 100$
c $x^2 + y^2 = 196$

9 A on, B inside, C outside, D on, E on, F inside

10 **a** $x^2 + y^2 = 12.96$ **b** (i), (iii), (v)

11 $x^2 + y^2 = 289$

12 428 m²

Page 169 Challenge

1 **a** 5 **b** 0 **c** 2

2 **a** $\{(x, y): 49 < x^2 + y^2 \leqslant 100\}$
b $\{(x, y): 1 < x^2 + y^2 \leqslant 16\}$
c $\{(x, y): x^2 + y^2 \leqslant 16\}$
d $\{(x, y): x^2 + y^2 > 16\}$
e $\{(x, y): x^2 + y^2 \leqslant 100\}$

Page 170 Exercise 2A

1 **a** $(x - 2)^2 + (y - 7)^2 = 16$
b $(x - 3)^2 + (y + 1)^2 = 49$
c $(x + 1)^2 + y^2 = 100$
d $(x + 5)^2 + (y + 6)^2 = 1$

2 **a** (3, 1), 5 **b** (4, 4), 1 **c** (−5, 2), 2
d (−2, −1), 3 **e** (1, 0), 4 **f** (0, −3), 6

3 **a** $(x - 2)^2 + (y - 2)^2 = 13$
b $(x - 1)^2 + (y + 5)^2 = 40$
c $(x + 2)^2 + (y + 3)^2 = 80$
d $(x + 3)^2 + y^2 = 40$

4 (5, 5), $(x-5)^2+(y-5)^2=25$; (5, −5), $(x-5)^2+(y+5)^2=25$; (−5, −5), $(x+5)^2+(y+5)^2=25$; (−5, 5), $(x+5)^2+(y-5)^2=25$

5 $(x-1)^2+(y+1)^2=64$

6 a (1, 2), 5, $(x-1)^2+(y-2)^2=5$
b (−1, 1), 9 $(x+1)^2+(y-1)^2=9$

7 $(x-6)^2+(y-8)^2=29$

8 (3, 2), $\sqrt{13}$, $(x-3)^2+(y-2)^2=13$

Page 171 Exercise 2B

1 a DF‖y-axis, EF‖x-axis
b $(x-3)^2+(y-4)^2=8$

2 7

3 a (i) $(x+2)^2+(y+2)^2=4$
(ii) $(x-2)^2+(y-2)^2=4$
(iii) $(x-2)^2+(y+2)^2=4$
b (i) $x^2+(y-2)^2=4$
(ii) $(x+2)^2+(y-4)^2=4$

4 b The circles touch each other externally

5 a A(−7, −1), radius 10; B(3, −1), radius 10; C(−2, −1), radius 5
b $(x+7)^2+(y+1)^2=100$, $(x-3)^2+(y+1)^2=100$

6 a $y=1$ **b** $(x-15)^2+(y-7)^2=36$
c (i) $(x-3)^2+(y-3)^2=4$
(ii) $(x-13)^2+(y-7)^2=36$

Page 172 Exercise 3A

1 a yes; (2, 4), 2 **b** no
c yes; (4, 1), 2 **d** yes; (1, −1), $\sqrt{7}$
e no **f** yes; (−2, −3), 3
g no **h** yes; (−1, −1), 3

2 a (v) **b** (iv) **c** (iii) **d** (i) **e** (ii)

3 a (1, 4), 5
b A inside, B on, C outside, D inside

4 a 3 **b** −4 or 2

5 a (3, 2) **c** (7, −1)

6 a $2y=x+10$

7 a $y=-2x+4$, $y=3x-11$
b (3, −2)
c $(x-3)^2+(y+2)^2=25$

8 a $x^2+y^2-2x-2y-43=0$
b $x^2+y^2+8x-6y=0$

9 $(x-3)^2+(y-2)^2=25$

Page 173 Challenge

b $(x-2)^2+(y-3.5)^2=1$, $(x-3.5)^2+(y-2.75)^2=0.0625$ $(\frac{1}{16})$

Page 173 Exercise 3B

1 a (0, 0), 2; (4, −3), 1 **b** 2

2 a (0, 0), 3; (7, 0), 4
b distance between centres = sum of radii

3 distance between centres = difference between radii

4 b (−4, −1), $2\sqrt{5}$

5 a $x^2+y^2-16x+2y+45=0$
b coefficients of x^2 and y^2 are equal and 'g^2+f^2-c' $=20>0$; (8, −1), $2\sqrt{5}$

Page 174 Exercise 4

1 a $y=3x-10$ **b** $3y=2x+13$

2 a $y=x+4$ **b** A(−4, 0), B(0, 4) **c** $4\sqrt{2}$

3 a $y-2x=5$, $2y+x=5$ **b** (−1, 3)

4 a (−4, −1), 5 **b (i)** $\sqrt{178}$ **(ii)** $\sqrt{153}$

5 $5\sqrt{2}$

6 a $y=x-5$ **b** $y=3$
c $4y=7x-25$ **d** $y=4x+6$

7 a (−1, 7)

8 a $3y=4x$ at (0, 0), $3y+4x=18$ at (0, 6), $3y+4x=-32$ at (−8, 0)
b those at (0, 6) and (−8, 0) have gradient $-\frac{4}{3}$; $3y=4x+50$

Page 176 Exercise 5A

1 a yes, (−3, 1), (3, 1) **b** yes, (0, 2)
c no **d** yes, (−2, −2), (2, 2)
e yes, (−2, −1), (1, 2) **f** yes, (2, 1)

2 a (i) 6 **(ii)** 8 **b (i)** 24 **(ii)** 10
c (i) 1 **(ii)** 4
d (i) 0 **(ii)** 8. Circle touches x-axis

3 a (−1, 4) **b** (−3, 1), (1, 1)

4 a (1, 1), (5, 5) **b** $(x-3)^2+(y-3)^2=8$

5 $\sqrt{2}$

6 a (4, 3), (4, −3)
b $3y+4x=25$, $3y-4x=-25$
c $(6\frac{1}{4}, 0)$ **d** $3\frac{3}{4}$

7 a (−3, 1), (1, 3) **b** $(x+2)^2+(y-4)^2=10$

Page 177 Exercise 5B

1 a (3, 0) **b** (3, −1)
c (−2, 4) **d** (−1, 3)

2 b ±4 **c** (−2, −2), (2, 2)

3 5

4 b (i) 0, $1\frac{1}{3}$ **(ii)** $m<0$ or $m>1\frac{1}{3}$ **(iii)** $0<m<1\frac{1}{3}$

5 b (4, 2)

6 a $y+3x=-10$ **b** (−6, 8)

7 a $y=x+4$
b Q(1, 5), R(−5, −1) **c** $6\sqrt{2}$

8 b A(−2, 6), B(10, 10) **c** $4\sqrt{10}$

9 a $2y=x+8$ **b** A(2, 5), B(6, 7)
c 72° to 162°

Page 178 Challenge

a (−4, 3) **b** (3, 4) **c** (2, 0) **d** (1, 3)

Page 179 Review

1 a $x^2+y^2=49$ **b** (0, 0), 3

2 a (10, 0), (−10, 0); (0, 10), (0, −10)
b (5, 0), (−5, 0); (0, 5), (0, −5)

3 a (3, 1), 5 **b** A on, B inside, C outside

4 a (4, −3), 4 **b** $(x+5)^2+(y-7)^2=4$

5 $(x-2)^2+(y-2)^2=1$

6 $(x+3)^2+(y+5)^2=34$

7 a $(x-1)^2+(y-3)^2=9$
b (i) $(x-1)^2+(y+3)^2=9$
(ii) $(x+1)^2+(y-3)^2=9$
(iii) $(x+1)^2+(y+3)^2=9$
(iv) $(x-3)^2+(y-1)^2=9$
8 $2y=x+10$
9 $(8\frac{1}{3}, 0)$
10 a $(-4, 1)$, 5 **b** $2\sqrt{5}$
11 b sum of radii = distance between centres
12 (0, 1), (5, 6)
13 a $(x-4)^2+(y-2)^2=20$ **b** (0, 4), (2, 6)
14 $5y=-3x-5$
15 (1, −7)
16 $(x-4)^2+(y+2)^2=8$
17 a $2y=-5x+25$, $y=5$ **b** (3, 5)
c $(x-3)^2+(y-5)^2=58$

5 Revision exercises

Page 181 Chapter 1.1 Revision

1 a −1 **b** 5 **c** −15 **d** 0
2 a 239 **b** 35 **c** 0.264
3 33
4 $(x-3)(x^2+9x+24)+76$
5 a
6 a $(x-1)(x-2)(x+3)$
b $(x+1)(x+3)(2x-1)$
7 2; $(x+2)(x-1)(x+1)$
8 −8, 12; $(x-1)(x+3)(x-2)(x+2)$
9 $(2x-1)(x-1)(x+3)$
10 b $4x^2+6x+9$ has no factors
11 −1, 2
12 a 1, −2 **b** 1, −2, −3
13 b $-1, \frac{1}{3}, 1$
14 a (1, 2), (4, 2)
b the curves cross at (1, 2) and touch at (4, 2)
18 1.2

Page 182 Chapter 1.2 Revision

1 a $(x-2)(x+5)$ **b** $(2x-1)(x-2)$
c $(2x-3)^2$
2 a 1, 6 **b** $-1, -\frac{1}{3}$ **c** 10 **d** $-1, 2\frac{1}{2}$
3 8 cm, 12 cm
4 a $\frac{1}{3}$ **b** $-1\frac{1}{2}$, 2 **c** 0.19, 1.31
d no real roots
5 a 0, 200 **b** (100, −40)
6 a not real **b** real and distinct
c real and distinct **d** equal
7 $1\frac{1}{8}$
8 a 3 **b** none possible
9 b ±1
10 $-\frac{3}{4}$
11 a $y=mx-4$
b ±4; $y=4x-4$, $y=-4x-4$

12 a (i) $x<-5$ or $x>2$ **(ii)** $-5\leqslant x\leqslant 2$
b (i) $3<x<7$ **(ii)** $x\leqslant 3$ or $x\geqslant 7$
13 a $x^2+(3-y)x+(5+y)=0$
c length 11, breadth 3, area 33
14 a (i) 20 m **(ii)** 30 m
b at $x=0$, $y=4$; yes
c (i) $4\frac{1}{6}$ m **(ii)** 5 m

Pages 183 Chapter 2 Revision

1 a $x^4+\frac{2}{3}x^3+x+c$ **b** $\frac{1}{5}x^5-\frac{1}{2}x^2+3x+c$
c $2x-2x^2+2x^3+c$ **d** $\frac{1}{3}x^3-\frac{1}{2}x^2-2x+c$
2 a $2x^{1/2}+\frac{2}{3}x^{3/2}+\frac{2}{5}x^{5/2}+c$
b $\frac{1}{2}t^2-t+c$ **c** $-x^{-1}-x^{-2}+c$
d $x-4x^{-1}+c$ **e** $\frac{2}{3}t^{3/2}+2t^{1/2}+c$
3 a $3x^2+5x+2$ **b** $\frac{1}{16}x^4-2x^{-2}+3\frac{1}{2}$
4 a $2t^3+2t^{-2}+c$ **b** $\frac{2}{5}u^{5/2}+\frac{2}{7}u^{7/2}+c$
c $x^3-\frac{1}{3}x^{-1}+c$ **d** $\frac{1}{2}x^2+\frac{4}{3}x^{3/2}+x+c$
5 $y=x^2-x^{-1}-2$
6 a 28 **b** 9 **c** 18
8 a 36 **b** 28 **c** 14 **d** $-\frac{2}{3}$
9 a −3 or 2 **b** $\frac{1}{3}$ **c** 4
10 a 6

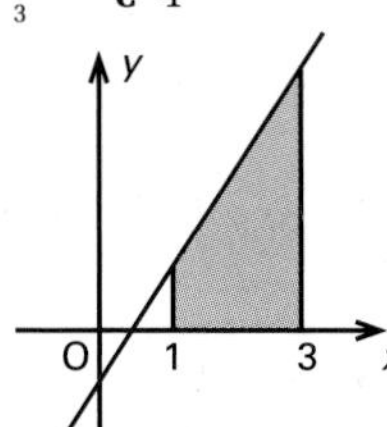

b $6\frac{2}{3}$

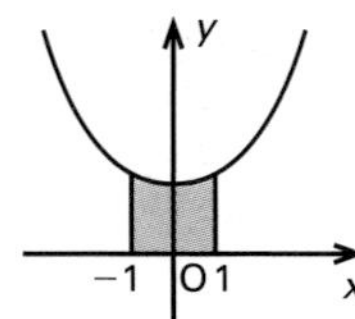

c 32

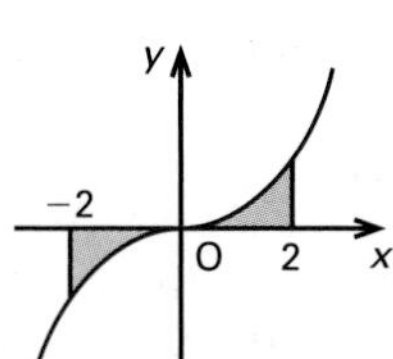

d $40\frac{1}{2}$

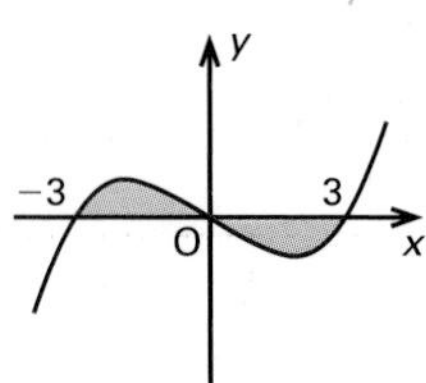

11 a 36 **b** $20\frac{5}{6}$
12 a 72 **b** 7:1
13 $10\frac{2}{3}$
14 32

15 $4\frac{1}{2}$
16 $21\frac{1}{3}$
17 $24\frac{2}{3}$
18 1

Page 184 Chapter 3.1 Revision

1 a $r^2 = R^2 - d^2$
b $\sin\theta° = r/R$, $\cos\theta° = d/R$, $\tan\theta° = r/d$
c $(90 - \theta)°$
3 a 67° **b** 13.8 cm
5 a P(5, 0, 0), Q(5, 4, 0), R(0, 4, 0), S(0, 0, 3), T(5, 0, 3), V(0, 4, 3), W(2.5, 2, 1.5)
b (i) 25.1° **(ii)** 36.9°
6 a B(40, 0, 0), C(40, 26, 0), D(0, 26, 0), M(12, 13, 0), E(12, 13, 10)
b 39.8°
7 a B(8, 0, 0), C(8, 8, 0), D(0, 8, 0), E(4, 4, 0), F(8, 4, 0)
b (i) 4 **(ii)** 68.2°
8 a 1.6 m **b** 40° **c** 1.3 m **d** 33° or 34°

Page 185 Chapter 3.2 Revision

1 a cos U cos V + sin U sin V
b sin H cos K − cos H sin K
c $2\sin t°\cos t°$
d $\cos^2 t° - \sin^2 t°$, $2\cos^2 t° - 1$, $1 - 2\sin^2 t°$
e $2\sin 2t°\cos 2t°$
2 a sin 20° **b** cos 40°
c tan 20° **d** −cos 80°
e −sin 80° **f** −tan 10°
3 a 1 **b** $1/\sqrt{2}$ **c** 1 **d** $-1/\sqrt{2}$
4 b (i) $\frac{24}{25}$ **(ii)** $\frac{7}{25}$ **(iii)** $\frac{336}{625}$
5 a $8/\sqrt{65}$ **b** $1/\sqrt{65}$ **c** $\frac{12}{13}$ **d** $\frac{5}{13}$
7 a $\cos^2 A = \frac{1}{2}(1 + \cos 2A)$
b $\sin^2 A = \frac{1}{2}(1 - \cos 2A)$
8 b 38.3°
9 a 90, 228.6, 270, 311.4
b 30, 90, 150 **c** 0, 180, 360
10 a $\pi/6$, $5\pi/6$ **b** 0, $\pi/6$, $5\pi/6$, π, 2π
c $\pi/2$, $3\pi/2$
11 (30, $\sqrt{3}/2$), (90, 0), (150, $-\sqrt{3}/2$), (270, 0)
12 $-\sqrt{3}\sin\theta$
14 a (i) $y = \sin x° + 1$ **(ii)** $y = 3\cos 2x°$
b A(30, 1.5), B(150, 1.5), C(221.8, 0.3), D(318.2, 0.3)
15

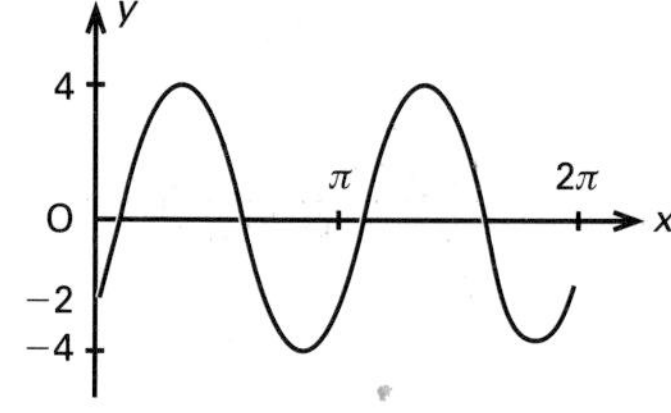

Page 186 Chapter 4 Revision

1 a $x^2 + y^2 = 36$ **b** $x^2 + y^2 = 16$
c $x^2 + y^2 = 29$
2 a $(x + 1)^2 + (y - 2)^2 = 49$
b $(x + 1)^2 + (y - 2)^2 = 5$
c $(x + 1)^2 + (y - 2)^2 = 4$
d $(x + 1)^2 + (y - 2)^2 = 1$
3 (1, 5), 2, $(x - 1)^2 + (y - 5)^2 = 4$
4 a (i) 1:2:3 **(ii)** 1:4:9
b $(x - 1)^2 + y^2 = 1$, $(x - 2)^2 + y^2 = 4$, $(x - 3)^2 + y^2 = 9$
c (i) $x = 0$ **(ii)** $y = 0$
5 a (5, 1), 6 **b** (−2, 3), 3
6 a $r^2 = 20$ for each circle
7 −15 or 2
9 $CM^2 + DM^2 = 25 + 144 = 169 = 13^2 = CD^2$. Hence right angle (converse of Pythagoras' Theorem)
10 a $\sqrt{10}$ **b** 12
11 b $y = -3x - 1$
12 a (−3, 4), (3, 4)
b $4y = 3x + 25$, $4y = -3x + 25$; $(0, 6\frac{1}{4})$
13 ±5
14 a (−6, 8) **b** $3\sqrt{10}$
15 a $(x - 3)^2 + (y - 2)^2 = 20$ **b** (1, 6), (5, −2)
16 a $(x - 10)^2 + y^2 = 100$, or $x^2 + y^2 - 20x = 0$
b $x^2 + (y - 2)^2 = 4$, or $x^2 + y^2 - 4y = 0$

Page 188 Review A

1 a $x^3 - x^2 + x + c$ **b** $\frac{2}{3}x^{3/2} - 2x^{1/2} + c$
2 −0.41, 2.41
3 a $x^2 + y^2 = 20$
b (i) $2y = x - 10$ **(ii)** (0, −5), (10, 0)
4 a $\frac{56}{65}$ **b** $\frac{24}{25}$
5 a $-\frac{1}{6}$ **b** $9\frac{1}{3}$
6 a $-4x^2 - 4x$, $3 - 2x^2$ **b** 2, −3
7 b (1, 2)

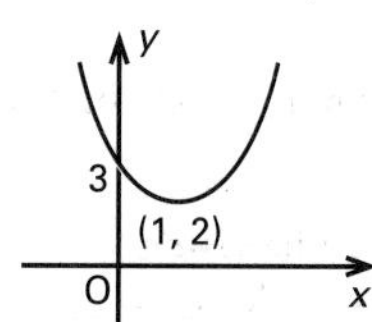

8 a $(x - 2)^2 + (y - 3)^2 = 18$ **b** (−1, 6)
9 a (i) $2\sin x°\cos x°$ **(ii)** $2\cos^2 x° - 1$
b (i) 0, 120, 180, 240, 360 **(ii)** 180

10 a

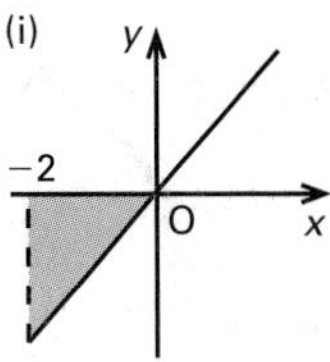

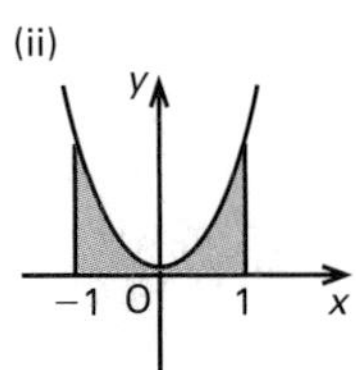

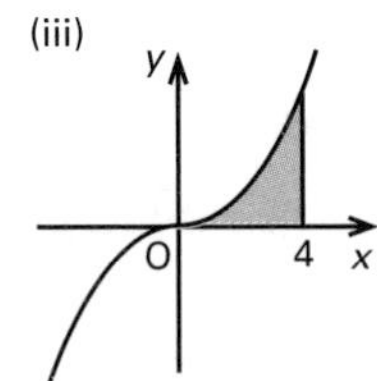

b (i) 2 (ii) $\frac{2}{3}$ (iii) 64

11 a A(12, 0, 0), B(12, 5, 0), F(12, 5, 4)
b (i) 17.1° (ii) 18.4°

12 a $-1 \leqslant x \leqslant 3$ **b** $x < -3$ or $x > 3$

13 a (2, 3), (−3, −2) **b** $\pm\sqrt{26}$

14 a

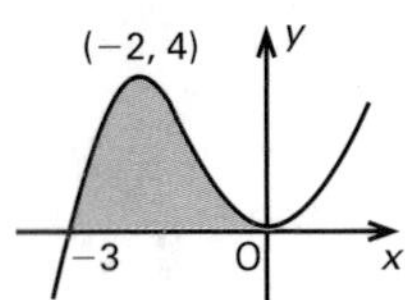

b $6\frac{3}{4}$

15 a A(−2, 0), B($\frac{1}{2}$, 0), C(4, 0)
b AB $12\frac{1}{2}$ km, BC $17\frac{1}{2}$ km

16 $(x-1)^2 + (y-3)^2 = 10$

17 a −2 **b** $p > -2$

Page 189 Review B

1 −6, 2

2 a $7\frac{1}{3}$ **b** 26

3 b (−2, 4), (2, 4)

4 a −2, 1 **b** (−1, 4), (1, 0)
c

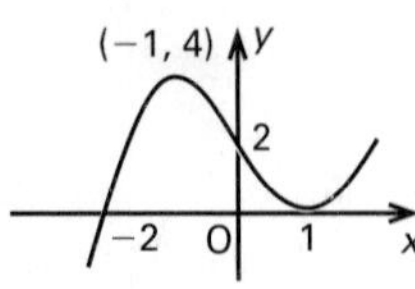

d (i) $x > 1$ or $x < -1$ (ii) $-1 < x < 1$

5 b $-\frac{3}{4}$

6 a $y = 2x + 5$
b (i) −5 (ii) $y = 2x$, $x^2 + (y+5)^2 = 5$

7 a $(x-1)(x-1)(x-4)$
b max (1, 0), min (3, −4)

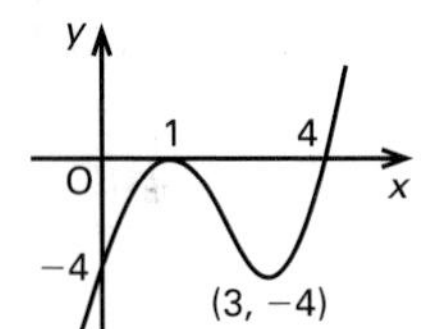

c $6\frac{3}{4}$

8 a 35, 80, 125, 170 **b** 0.72, 3.14, 5.56

9 14 m, 196 m

11 a

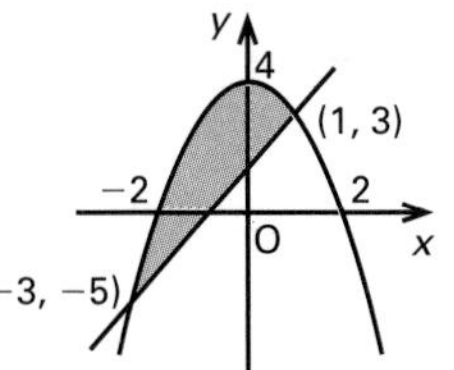

b $10\frac{2}{3}$

12 b $\frac{1}{2}r(t\sin\alpha + s\cos\alpha)$

13 a $f^{-1}(x) = 2x$

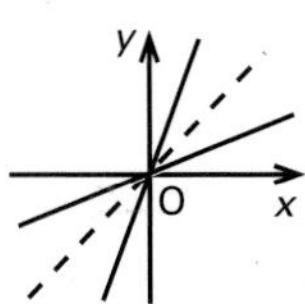

b $f^{-1}(x) = x + 1$

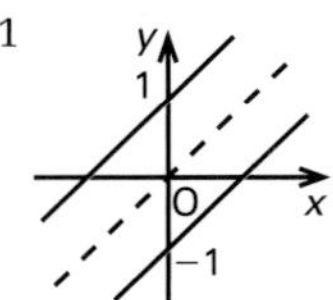

c $f^{-1}(x) = x^{1/4}$

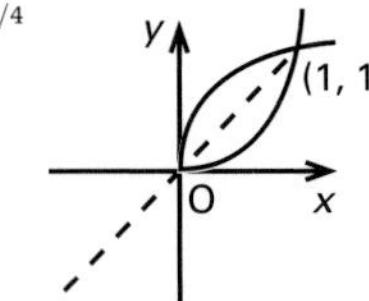

14 $(4, -5\frac{1}{3})$

15 a $\frac{x-2}{x-1}, -\frac{1}{x}$ **b** −0.6, 1.6

16 a $8x^2 + 8y^2 - 58x - 20y + 85 = 0$
b the coefficients of x and y are equal, and '$g^2 + f^2 - c$' > 0

Page 190 Review C

1 $\frac{1}{2}x^2 + 4x^{1/2} + 1$

2 a (1, 2) **b** $y = x - 7$

3 a $y = -4x + 9$ **b** $2\frac{2}{3}$

4 a (i) $\frac{1}{4}$ (ii) $k > \frac{1}{4}$ **b** 3

5 a $x^4 + 4x^3 + 5x^2 + 2x$, $x^4 + 2x^3 + 3x^2 + 2x$
b −1, 0

6 a $2y = -3x + 9$ **b** $(x-4)^2 + (y-5)^2 = 13$

7 b max 9, min 1

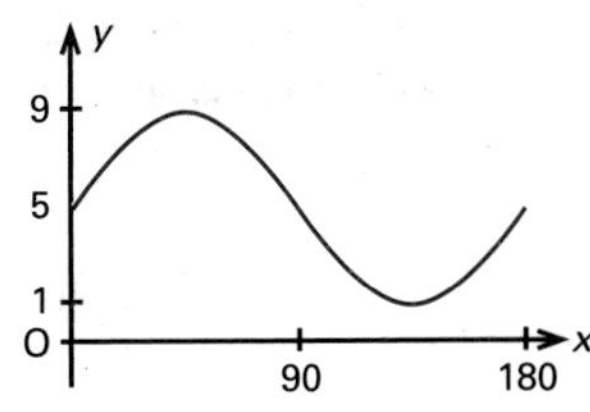

c 105, 165

8 9

9 a 14.5, 90, 165.5, 270 **b** 0.9, 5.4

10 a $g(a)h(b) + h(a)g(b)$

11 a (i) 39 m **(ii)** 30 m

12 $(x-5)^2 + (y+2)^2 = 17$

13 a (i) $\sin 2x$ **(ii)** $\frac{1}{2}(1 - \cos 2x)$

b $2\sin 2x - \sin 4x$

14 a $-2, -1, 1$

15 b $2\frac{11}{24}$

A·N·S·W·E·R·S

UNIT 3

1 Vectors

Page 193 Exercise 1

1 a $\overrightarrow{GF}$ **b** $\overrightarrow{HG}$ **c** $\overrightarrow{EH}$ **d** $\overrightarrow{HF}$

2 a $\overrightarrow{AB}, \overrightarrow{DC}, \overrightarrow{HG}$ **b** $\overrightarrow{AD}, \overrightarrow{EH}$ **c** $\overrightarrow{CA}, \overrightarrow{GE}$

3 $\boldsymbol{a} = \begin{pmatrix} 2 \\ 3 \end{pmatrix}$, $\boldsymbol{b} = \begin{pmatrix} 2 \\ -4 \end{pmatrix}$, $\boldsymbol{c} = \begin{pmatrix} 2 \\ 2 \end{pmatrix}$, $\boldsymbol{d} = \begin{pmatrix} -3 \\ 4 \end{pmatrix}$, $\boldsymbol{e} = \begin{pmatrix} 3 \\ -4 \end{pmatrix}$, $\boldsymbol{f} = \begin{pmatrix} -1 \\ -5 \end{pmatrix}$

4 a

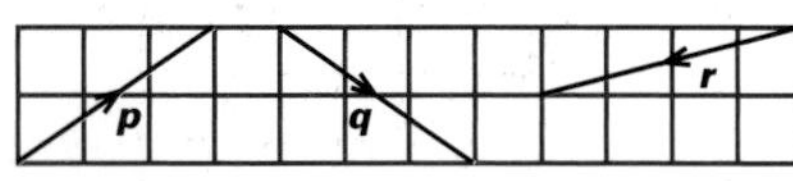

b both the same

5 $\overrightarrow{BA} = \begin{pmatrix} -2 \\ -1 \end{pmatrix}$, $\overrightarrow{DC} = \begin{pmatrix} 3 \\ -4 \end{pmatrix}$, $\overrightarrow{FE} = \begin{pmatrix} 1 \\ 6 \end{pmatrix}$

6 a (3, 2) **b** (4, 6) **c** (−1, 5) **d** (8, 0)

7 $\overrightarrow{KA} = \begin{pmatrix} 1 \\ 2 \end{pmatrix}$, $\overrightarrow{KB} = \begin{pmatrix} 2 \\ 1 \end{pmatrix}$, $\overrightarrow{KC} = \begin{pmatrix} 2 \\ -1 \end{pmatrix}$, $\overrightarrow{KD} = \begin{pmatrix} 1 \\ -2 \end{pmatrix}$, $\overrightarrow{KE} = \begin{pmatrix} -1 \\ -2 \end{pmatrix}$, $\overrightarrow{KF} = \begin{pmatrix} -2 \\ -1 \end{pmatrix}$, $\overrightarrow{KG} = \begin{pmatrix} -2 \\ 1 \end{pmatrix}$, $\overrightarrow{KH} = \begin{pmatrix} -1 \\ 2 \end{pmatrix}$

8 a (i) $\begin{pmatrix} 3 \\ 3 \end{pmatrix}$ **(ii)** $\begin{pmatrix} 3 \\ -3 \end{pmatrix}$ **(iii)** $\begin{pmatrix} -3 \\ 3 \end{pmatrix}$ **(iv)** $\begin{pmatrix} 0 \\ -6 \end{pmatrix}$ **(v)** $\begin{pmatrix} 0 \\ 6 \end{pmatrix}$

b (i) $\begin{pmatrix} -6 \\ 3 \end{pmatrix}$ **(ii)** $\begin{pmatrix} 6 \\ -3 \end{pmatrix}$

9 a since $\overrightarrow{AB} = \overrightarrow{DC}$, AB and CD are equal and parallel

b they are collinear and B is the midpoint of AE

Page 195 Exercise 2

1 a $|\boldsymbol{u}| = 5$ **b** $|\boldsymbol{v}| = 10$ **c** $|\boldsymbol{w}| = 13$

2 a (i) $\begin{pmatrix} 5 \\ 2 \end{pmatrix}$ **(ii)** 5.4

b (i) $\begin{pmatrix} -3 \\ 4 \end{pmatrix}$ **(ii)** 5

c (i) $\begin{pmatrix} 3 \\ 0 \end{pmatrix}$ **(ii)** 3

d (i) $\begin{pmatrix} 0 \\ -4 \end{pmatrix}$ **(ii)** 4

e (i) $\begin{pmatrix} -4 \\ -1 \end{pmatrix}$ **(ii)** 4.1

3 a 7 km **b** 8 km **c** 6 km

4 a 25 m/s **b** 15 m/s **c** 14 m/s

5 a (i) v **(ii)** v **b (i)** v **(ii)** v

6 ±4.6

Page 197 Exercise 3

1 a $\begin{pmatrix} 2 \\ 1 \\ 3 \end{pmatrix}$ **b** 3.7

2 a $\begin{pmatrix} 2 \\ 0 \\ 5 \end{pmatrix}$ **b** $\begin{pmatrix} 1 \\ 3 \\ -6 \end{pmatrix}$ **c** $\begin{pmatrix} 0 \\ 0 \\ 2 \end{pmatrix}$ **d** $\begin{pmatrix} -3 \\ -1 \\ -2 \end{pmatrix}$ **e** $\begin{pmatrix} -5 \\ 2 \\ -2 \end{pmatrix}$ **f** $\begin{pmatrix} 7 \\ -3 \\ -3 \end{pmatrix}$

3 a 5.4 **b** 6.8 **c** 2 **d** 3.7

4 a $\begin{pmatrix} x_B - x_A \\ y_B - y_A \\ z_B - z_A \end{pmatrix}$ **b** $\begin{pmatrix} x_A - x_B \\ y_A - y_B \\ z_A - z_B \end{pmatrix}$

5 a each $= \begin{pmatrix} 6 \\ 4 \\ 2 \end{pmatrix}$ **b** a parallelogram

6 a (i) each $= \begin{pmatrix} 5 \\ 1 \\ -6 \end{pmatrix}$ **(ii)** each = 7.9

b a rhombus

7 a (3, 4, 3) **b** $\begin{pmatrix} 4 \\ 2 \\ 3 \end{pmatrix}$ **c** 5.4

8 $AS^2 = BS^2 = CS^2 = 72$

9 PQ = PR = 14

10 $LM^2 = LN^2$; $LM^2 + LN^2 = 10 = MN^2$

11 (10, 7, 2)

12 (1, 6, 2)

13 a $x = 3, y = 5, z = 3$

b $x = 3, y = 2, z = 1$

14 a $\begin{pmatrix} 2 \\ 3 \\ -1 \end{pmatrix}$ **b** 3.7

c (5, 2, 1) **d** (3, 3, 4)

e $\begin{pmatrix} 2 \\ -1 \\ -3 \end{pmatrix}$ **f** 3.7

15 a C(2, 0, 3), D(2, 2, 3) **b** $\begin{pmatrix} -1 \\ -1 \\ -3 \end{pmatrix}$, 3.3

c 10.3 units **d** $\begin{pmatrix} 1 \\ 1 \\ -6 \end{pmatrix}$, 6.2

Page 200 Exercise 4

1 a (i) $\begin{pmatrix} 0 \\ 2 \\ 2 \end{pmatrix}$ **(ii)** 2.8

b (i) $\begin{pmatrix} 3 \\ 0 \\ 10 \end{pmatrix}$ **(ii)** 10.4

2

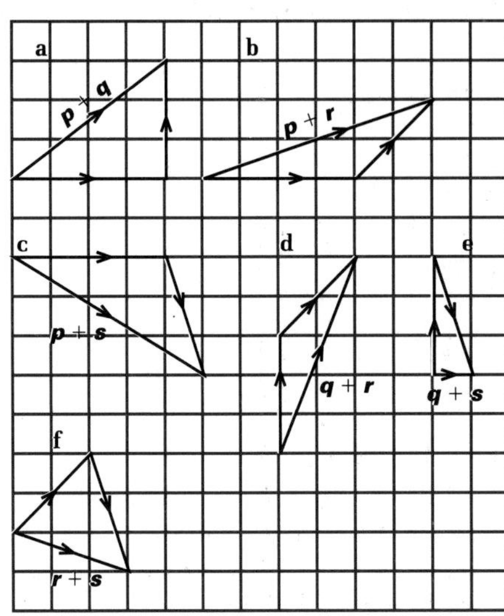

3 a $\begin{pmatrix} -3 \\ -2 \\ -1 \end{pmatrix}$ **b** $\begin{pmatrix} 1 \\ 0 \\ -4 \end{pmatrix}$

c $\begin{pmatrix} 2 \\ 3 \\ 4 \end{pmatrix}$ **d** $\begin{pmatrix} -a \\ -b \\ -c \end{pmatrix}$

4 same length, opposite direction

5 a $\begin{pmatrix} 6 \\ 5 \\ 1 \end{pmatrix}$ **b** $\begin{pmatrix} -3 \\ -2 \\ 1 \end{pmatrix}$

c $\begin{pmatrix} 3 \\ 3 \\ 2 \end{pmatrix}$

6

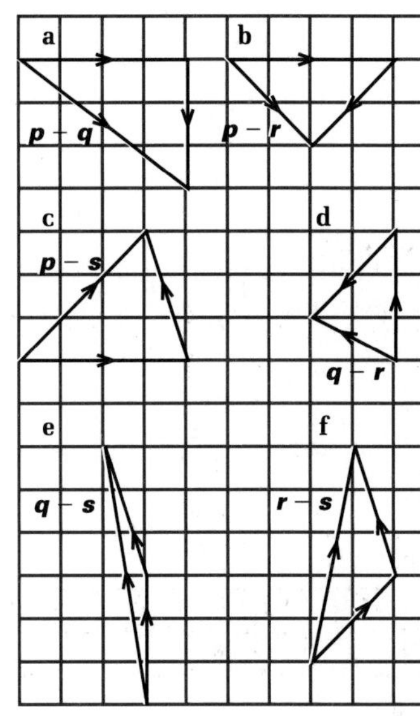

7 a (i) $\begin{pmatrix} 2 \\ -2 \\ 6 \end{pmatrix}$ **(ii)** $\begin{pmatrix} 6 \\ 12 \\ -6 \end{pmatrix}$ **(iii)** $\begin{pmatrix} 8 \\ 10 \\ 0 \end{pmatrix}$

b (i) $\begin{pmatrix} 0 \\ 2 \\ 4 \end{pmatrix}$ **(ii)** $\begin{pmatrix} 18 \\ -6 \\ 0 \end{pmatrix}$ **(iii)** $\begin{pmatrix} 18 \\ -4 \\ 4 \end{pmatrix}$

8 a $\begin{pmatrix} -4 \\ -1 \\ 8 \end{pmatrix}$ **b** 9

9

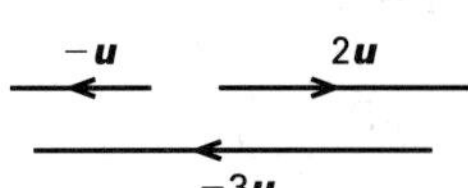

10 a $m = 4$, $n = -1$, $p = -\frac{1}{4}$

b (i) same direction, $|\boldsymbol{b}| = 4|\boldsymbol{a}|$

(ii) opposite directions, $|\boldsymbol{c}| = |\boldsymbol{a}|$

(iii) opposite directions, $|\boldsymbol{c}| = \frac{1}{4}|\boldsymbol{b}|$

11 a (i) $\boldsymbol{u} = 3\boldsymbol{v}$ **(ii)** $\boldsymbol{u} = -2\boldsymbol{v}$

b (i) same direction, $|\boldsymbol{u}| = 3|\boldsymbol{v}|$

(ii) opposite directions, $|\boldsymbol{u}| = 2|\boldsymbol{v}|$

12 a trapezium ($\overrightarrow{DC} = \frac{3}{2}\overrightarrow{AB}$)

13 a $\begin{pmatrix} 8 \\ 0 \\ -15 \end{pmatrix}$ **b** 17

Page 203 Exercise 5

1 a (i) $\begin{pmatrix} 1 \\ 3 \\ 3 \end{pmatrix}$ **(ii)** $\begin{pmatrix} 3 \\ 9 \\ 9 \end{pmatrix}$

b parallel, in the same direction, and $\overrightarrow{CD} = 3\overrightarrow{AB}$

2 a $\overrightarrow{RS} = 2\overrightarrow{PQ}$
b $\overrightarrow{RS}$ is parallel to $\overrightarrow{PQ}$, with the same direction, and RS = 2PQ

3 a $\overrightarrow{AB} = \begin{pmatrix} 1 \\ 2 \\ -3 \end{pmatrix}$, $\overrightarrow{BC} = \begin{pmatrix} 2 \\ 4 \\ -6 \end{pmatrix}$
b $\overrightarrow{BC} = 2\overrightarrow{AB}$, so
(i) $\overrightarrow{AB}$ and $\overrightarrow{BC}$ are parallel, in the same direction and with B in common
(ii) AB:BC = 1:2

4 a $\overrightarrow{OA} = \overrightarrow{AB}$, etc.
b (i) 1 (ii) 1:2

5 b (i) parallel, but in opposite directions
(ii) 1:3

6 It is S_3

7 $\overrightarrow{MN} = 2\overrightarrow{LM}$ etc.; 1:2

8 a (5, 5, 2) **b** (−5, −2, 0)

9 a (i) (−1, −1, 5) (ii) (2, 0, 8)
c PQ∥AC and PQ = $\frac{1}{2}$AC

10 a $\overrightarrow{OP} = \overrightarrow{RQ}$, or $\overrightarrow{PQ} = \overrightarrow{OR}$
b $\overrightarrow{AB} = \overrightarrow{DC}$, or $\overrightarrow{AD} = \overrightarrow{BC}$

11 a (i) $\frac{1}{3}$ (ii) $-\frac{1}{3}$

12 a (i) $\begin{pmatrix} 0.6 \\ 0.8 \\ 0.05 \end{pmatrix}$ (ii) $\begin{pmatrix} 1.2 \\ 1.6 \\ 0.10 \end{pmatrix}$
b $\overrightarrow{AB} = \frac{1}{2}\overrightarrow{BC}$, so AB∥BC and B is common
c (i) 1.0 (ii) 2.0

Page 205 Exercise 6

1 (0, 4, 4)
2 (−1, 2, 1)
3 a (4, 3, 8) **b** (2, 1, 2) **c** (6, 1, 2)
4 a S(−1, 2, −2), T(3, 2, 2) **b** $\overrightarrow{ST} = \frac{4}{5}\overrightarrow{QR}$
7 (9, −14, 11)
8 a P(2, 1, 3), Q(2, 0, 1), R(2, −3, −5)
b $\overrightarrow{QR} = 3\overrightarrow{PQ}$, and Q is common; 1:3
9 a S(1, 1, 3), T(1, −2, 0)
10 $\frac{AP}{PB} = \frac{m}{n}$, so $\overrightarrow{AP} = \frac{m}{n}\overrightarrow{PB}$, $n(\boldsymbol{p} - \boldsymbol{a}) = m(\boldsymbol{b} - \boldsymbol{p})$, etc.

Page 206 Exercise 7

1 a (i) $\begin{pmatrix} 1 \\ 2 \\ 8 \end{pmatrix}$ (ii) $\boldsymbol{i} + 2\boldsymbol{j} + 8\boldsymbol{k}$
b (i) $\begin{pmatrix} -1 \\ -5 \\ 2 \end{pmatrix}$ (ii) $-\boldsymbol{i} - 5\boldsymbol{j} + 2\boldsymbol{k}$
c (i) $\begin{pmatrix} 6 \\ 0 \\ -7 \end{pmatrix}$ (ii) $6\boldsymbol{i} - 7\boldsymbol{k}$

2 a $\begin{pmatrix} 1 \\ 0 \\ 0 \end{pmatrix}$ **b** $\begin{pmatrix} 0 \\ 2 \\ 0 \end{pmatrix}$ **c** $\begin{pmatrix} 0 \\ 0 \\ -1 \end{pmatrix}$ **d** $\begin{pmatrix} 1 \\ 1 \\ 0 \end{pmatrix}$
e $\begin{pmatrix} 1 \\ 1 \\ 1 \end{pmatrix}$ **f** $\begin{pmatrix} 1 \\ -1 \\ 0 \end{pmatrix}$ **g** $\begin{pmatrix} 2 \\ 0 \\ -2 \end{pmatrix}$

3 a $\boldsymbol{a} = \boldsymbol{i} + \boldsymbol{j} + 2\boldsymbol{k}$, $\boldsymbol{b} = \boldsymbol{i} + 4\boldsymbol{j} + 3\boldsymbol{k}$, $\boldsymbol{c} = -\boldsymbol{j} - 2\boldsymbol{k}$
b $\begin{pmatrix} 2 \\ 4 \\ 3 \end{pmatrix}$, $2\boldsymbol{i} + 4\boldsymbol{j} + 3\boldsymbol{k}$

4 a $\begin{pmatrix} 6 \\ 1 \\ 0 \end{pmatrix}$, $\begin{pmatrix} -2 \\ -3 \\ 2 \end{pmatrix}$ **b** $\sqrt{37}$, $\sqrt{17}$

5 a 13 **b** 3 **c** 15.2 **d** 11.2
6 a 7 **b** 9
7 $a = \pm 1/\sqrt{2}$
8 $a^2 + b^2 = \frac{3}{4}$
9 $v = -2\boldsymbol{u}$
10 a $6\boldsymbol{i} + 3\boldsymbol{j} + 2\boldsymbol{k}$ **b** 7
11 $\boldsymbol{i} + 4\boldsymbol{j} - 2\boldsymbol{k}$

Page 209 Exercise 8

1 a 6 **b** 0 **c** $10\sqrt{2}$ **d** −1
2 a $\sqrt{3}$ **b** $5\sqrt{2}$ **c** $-5\sqrt{2}$ **d** 0
3 a 8 **b** 1 **c** 5 **d** a
4 3 **5** 2
6 a

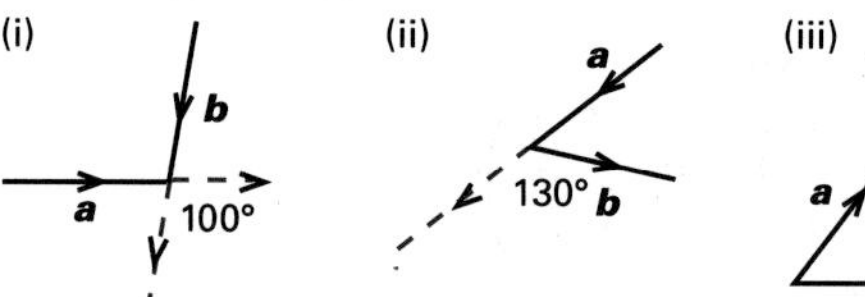

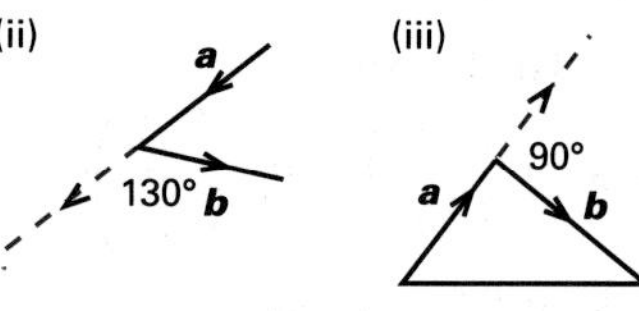

b (i) −4.3 (ii) −16.1 (iii) 0
7 a 14 **b** −2 **c** 2 **d** 5
8 −7
9 −5
10 a (7, −1, 3) **b** 54
11 a $M(2\frac{1}{2}, \frac{1}{2}, 1)$, $N(1\frac{1}{2}, -\frac{1}{2}, 3)$
b $\boldsymbol{a}.\boldsymbol{b} = 2$, $\boldsymbol{c}.\boldsymbol{d} = 8$

Page 212 Exercise 9

1 a 45° **b** 30° **c** 45° **d** 90°
2 a 90° **b** 120° **c** 180°
3 78.6°
4 $\boldsymbol{p}.\boldsymbol{q} = 0$
5 −7
6 14.3°
7 a (i) $\sqrt{6}$ (ii) $\sqrt{6}$ (iii) 60°
b equilateral
8 a (i) $\begin{pmatrix} 1 \\ -3 \\ -1 \end{pmatrix}$ (ii) $\begin{pmatrix} -5 \\ 3 \\ -4 \end{pmatrix}$
b (i) −10
(ii) AB = 3.3, AC = 7.1
(iii) 115.3° (iv) 45.3° (v) 19.5°
10 ∠A = 90°
11 a $M_1(1, 2, 2)$, $M_2(2, 2, 4)$, $M_3(6, 5, 5)$, $M_4(5, 5, 3)$
b $\overrightarrow{M_1M_2} = \overrightarrow{M_4M_3}$, or $\overrightarrow{M_1M_4} = \overrightarrow{M_2M_3}$
c 58.2°

12 **a** M(4, 0, 8), N(8, 0, 4), P(8, 6, 8)
b (i) MN = 5.7 cm (ii) 46.2°
13 **a** (3, 5, 0) **b** $\overrightarrow{QT} = \frac{1}{2}\overrightarrow{TS}$ etc. **c** 51.3°
14 **a** (3, 3, 6)
15 **a** both are (5, −1, 3)
b $\overrightarrow{AC}.\overrightarrow{EF} = 0$, so AC and EF are perpendicular and, by part **a**, they bisect each other
c $\overrightarrow{AB} = \overrightarrow{DC}$ and AB = AD **d** $\frac{5}{33}$

Page 214 Exercise 10

1 **a** 3 **b** 0 **c** 1 **d** 0 **e** 1
2 **a** 4 **b** $1\frac{1}{2}$ **c** $\frac{1}{8}$
4 −7
5 **a** 60° **b** $4\frac{1}{2}$ **c** 120° **d** (i) $4\frac{1}{2}$ (ii) 9
6 **a** 2 **b** 0
8 −5

Page 215 Challenges

1 **a** 0 **c** they are perpendicular
d the altitudes of a triangle are concurrent
2 Take BC as the x-axis and the perpendicular bisector of BC as the y-axis, and work in 2 dimensions.

Page 216 Review

1 **a** (i) $\begin{pmatrix} 4 \\ -4 \\ 8 \end{pmatrix}$ (ii) $\begin{pmatrix} 1 \\ -6 \\ -1 \end{pmatrix}$
b (i) 9.8 (ii) 6.2
2 $a = -3, b = -6$
3 **a** (i) B(1, 2, −3) E(−1, −2, 3)
(ii) $\overrightarrow{OA} = \begin{pmatrix} 1 \\ 2 \\ 3 \end{pmatrix}$, $\overrightarrow{EB} = \begin{pmatrix} 2 \\ 4 \\ -6 \end{pmatrix}$
b OA = 3.7, EB = 7.5
4 (6, 1, 4)
5 **a** M(0, 2, 2), N(2, 3, 0), D(0, 4, 1)
b $\overrightarrow{MN} = \overrightarrow{BD}$, MN ≠ ND
6 $\overrightarrow{BC} = 2\overrightarrow{AB}$, so parallel, and B is common; AB:BC = 1:2
7 (8, 6, 3)
8 **a** P(−6, −7, −4), Q(2, 1, 4), R(4, 3, 6)
b $\overrightarrow{PQ} = 4\overrightarrow{QR}$ etc.; PQ:QR = 4:1
9 $\pm\frac{1}{3}\sqrt{7}\boldsymbol{i} + \frac{1}{3}\boldsymbol{j} - \frac{1}{3}\boldsymbol{k}$
10 **a** −13 **b** 8
11 74.2°
12 $\boldsymbol{p}.\boldsymbol{q} = 0$
13 113.4°
14 **a** (2, 5, −2) **b** $\overrightarrow{PA}.\overrightarrow{PC} = 0$ **c** CQ = CA

2 Further differentiation and integration

Page 218 Class Discussion/Exercise 1

1 **b** Row: 0, −1, 0, 1, 0
2 **a** −0.049 958 ..., −0.000 49 ..., 0; 0.998 33 ..., 0.999 99 ..., 1
b the values are 0 and 1

Page 221 Exercise 2A

1 **a** $\cos x$ **b** $3\cos x$ **c** $2\cos x$ **d** $-\cos x$
2 **a** $-\sin x$ **b** $-2\sin x$ **c** $-\frac{1}{2}\sin x$ **d** $\sin x$
3 **a** $-5\sin x$ **b** $6\cos x$ **c** $\cos x + \sin x$
4 **a** $-3\sin x - \cos x$ **b** $4\cos x - 7\sin x$
5 **a** 1 **b** 0 **c** 1 **d** −1
e 0 **f** 0 **g** 0 **h** 1
6 **a** $1/\sqrt{2}$ **b** $1/\sqrt{2}$ **c** $\frac{1}{2}$ **d** $\frac{1}{2}$
7 **a** 1 **b** −1 **c** 0
8 **a** 0, $y = 2$ **b** 0, $y = 0$
9 Use $f'(x) = 5\cos x$ and a table of signs
11 **a** $f'(x) > 0$; increasing
b $f'(x) < 0$; decreasing
12 **a** $y = 3x - 1$ **b** $y = x + 2$

Page 222 Exercise 2B

1 **a** $10x - 2\cos x$ **b** $-x^{-2} + 3\sin x$
2 **a** $\frac{1}{2}x^{-1/2} - \sin x$ **b** $-\frac{1}{2}x^{-3/2} - \cos x$
3 **a** $-9\sin x + 8\cos x$ **b** $\frac{1}{2}\cos x + \frac{1}{3}\sin x$
4 **a** $-2x^{-2} + \cos x$ **b** $-6x^{-3} - \sin x$
5 **a** (i) 2 (ii) 1 **b** 18.4°
6 **a** 2, $y = 2x$ **b** −1, $y = -x + 3\pi/2$
7 **a** $1/\sqrt{2}$ **b** $-1\sqrt{2}$ **c** $\frac{1}{2}$ **d** $-\sqrt{3}/2$
e $-\sqrt{3}/2$ **f** $-\frac{1}{2}$ **g** $-\sqrt{3}/2$ **h** $\frac{1}{2}$
8 **a** $-\sqrt{3}$ **b** $1 - \sqrt{3}/2$
9 **a** −2 **b** −4 **c** $\sqrt{3} + 2$ **d** $-\sqrt{2}$
10 **a** 4 m **b** $2\cos t$ **c** at mean sea-level
11 **a** 0.54 cm/s **b** 1.57 s

Page 223 Challenge

$f(x)$	$f'(x)$
$(x+4)^2 = x^2+8x+16$	$2x+8 = 2(x+4)$
$(x+4)^3 = x^3+12x^2+48x+64$	$3x^2+24x+48 = 3(x+4)^2$
....	....
$(3x+1)^2 = 9x^2+6x+1$	$18x+6 = 6(3x+1)$
$(3x+1)^3 = 27x^3+27x^2+9x+1$	$81x^2+54x+9 = 9(3x+1)^2$
....	....
$(x^2-1)^2 = x^4-2x^2+1$	$4x^3-4x = 4x(x^2-1)$
$(x^2-1)^3 = x^6-3x^4+3x^2-1$	$6x^5-12x^3+6x = 6x(x^2-1)^2$

If $f(x) = (ax+b)^n$ then $f'(x) = na(ax+b)^{n-1}$
If $g(x) = (ax^2+b)^n$ then $g'(x) = 2nax(ax^2+b)^{n-1}$
$h(x) = (x^2+3x+4)^2$, $h'(x) = 2(2x+3)(x^2+3x+4)$

Page 225 Exercise 3A

1 a $2(x+1)$ **b** $3(x-1)^2$ **c** $4(x+5)^3$
2 a $6(3x+1)$ **b** $6(2x-3)^2$ **c** $-10(1-5x)$
3 a $6u(1+u^2)^2$ **b** $-4u(4-u^2)$
c $12u(2u^2-1)^2$
4 a $-6(3x-1)^{-3}$ **b** $-2x(x^2+2)^{-2}$
c $-9x^2(x^3-5)^{-4}$
5 a $-2(2x+3)^{-2}$ **b** $2(1-u)^{-2}$
c $-12(4t+5)^{-2}$
6 a $(2x+1)^{-1/2}$ **b** $(3u-2)^{-2/3}$
c $x(x^2+3)^{-1/2}$
7 a $3(x^2+x)^2(2x+1)$ **b** $2(x-x^3)(1-3x^2)$
c $-2(x^2+2x)^{-2}(x+1)$
8 a 54 **b** 6
9 a −4 **b** 0
10 $5y = 4x+9$
11 $5y = -3x+16$
12 max TP (5, 18)

Page 226 Exercise 3B

1 a $-5(1-x)^4$
b $\dfrac{-2}{(1+2x)^2}$ **c** $\dfrac{12}{(1-3x)^3}$
2 a $\dfrac{2}{(1+6x)^{2/3}}$ **b** $\dfrac{1}{(9-x)^{4/3}}$
c $-\dfrac{4}{u^2}\left(1+\dfrac{1}{u}\right)^3$
3 a $10(x^2+x+1)(2x+1)$
b $\dfrac{1-2y}{(y^2-y-1)^2}$ **c** $\dfrac{2(z-1)}{(2z^2-4z+6)^{1/2}}$
4 a $\dfrac{1}{2x^{1/2}}+\dfrac{1}{2(x+1)^{1/2}}$ **b** $-\dfrac{1}{2x^2}-\dfrac{2}{(2x-1)^2}$
5 a $2\left(x+1+\dfrac{1}{x}\right)\left(1-\dfrac{1}{x^2}\right)$ **b** $\dfrac{2y-1}{2(y^2-y-2)^{1/2}}$
6 −24
7 0
8 max TP (14, 31)
9 $y = 4x+1$
10 b $\dfrac{dr}{dV} = -\dfrac{1}{4\pi}\left[\dfrac{3}{4\pi}(1000-V)\right]^{-2/3}$; −0.0038

Page 227 Exercise 4A

1 a $2\cos 2x$ **b** $4\cos 4x$ **c** $\frac{1}{2}\cos\frac{1}{2}x$
2 a $-3\sin 3x$ **b** $-5\sin 5x$ **c** $-\frac{1}{2}\sin\frac{1}{2}x$
3 a $p\cos(px+q)$ **b** $2\cos(2x-3)$
c $-\cos(5-x)$
4 a $-p\sin(px+q)$ **b** $-3\sin(3x-1)$
c $\sin(1-x)$
5 a $2x\cos(x^2-1)$ **b** $2x\sin(1-x^2)$
c $\frac{1}{2}(\sin x)^{-\frac{1}{2}}\cos x$
6 a $-(\sin t)^{-2}\cos t$ **b** $2(\cos t)^{-2}\sin t$
c $-\frac{3}{4}(\sin t)^{-2}\cos t$
7 a $2\sin x\cos x$ **b** $-2\cos x\sin x$
c $4\sin^3 x\cos x$
8 a $p\cos px - q\sin qx$ **b** 0
9 a $3\sin^2 x\cos x$ **b** $-4\cos^3 x\sin x$
c $7\cos 7x$
10 a $2(1+\sin x)\cos x$
b $6(4-3\cos x)\sin x$
11 a $\dfrac{\cos x}{2\sqrt{(1+\sin x)}}$ **b** $\dfrac{-\sin x}{2\sqrt{(1+\cos x)}}$
12 a $-4\cos x\sin x$ **b** $-4\sin x\cos x$
c $2\cos 2x$
13 a $-\dfrac{1}{x^2}+\dfrac{\cos x}{2(\sin x)^{3/2}}$ **b** $-\dfrac{1}{2x^2}-\dfrac{\sin x}{2(\cos x)^{3/2}}$

Page 228 Exercise 4B

1 a 2 **b** 0 **c** −2
2 b $f'(x) = 1+\cos x \geqslant 0$
3 PI at $(3\pi/2, 3\pi/2)$
4 a (i) 1, −1 **(ii)** $\pi/2$
5 a $\frac{1}{2}$, −1 **b** 72°
6 b $1/\sqrt{2}$, $-1/\sqrt{2}$ **c** 71°

7 b max TP $(\pi/4, \sqrt{2})$, min TP $(5\pi/4, -\sqrt{2})$

c

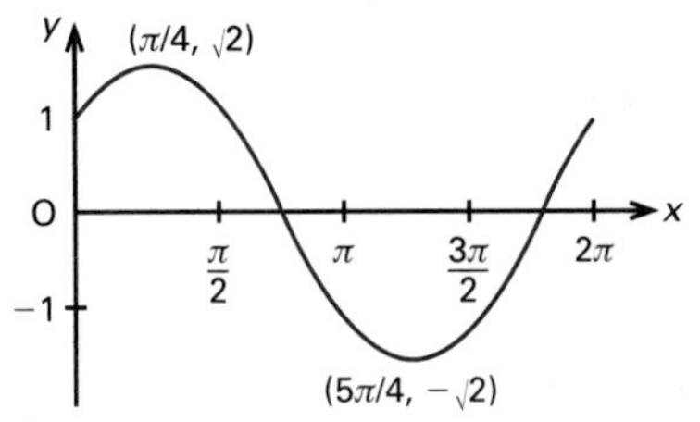

Page 229 Exercise 5

1 a $\dfrac{(2x-7)^4}{4 \times 2} + c = \frac{1}{8}(2x-7)^4 + c$

b $\dfrac{(3-6x)^{1/2}}{\frac{1}{2} \times -6} + c = -\frac{1}{3}(3-6x)^{1/2} + c$

2 a $\frac{1}{5}(x+1)^5 + c$ **b** $\frac{1}{8}(2x+1)^4 + c$

c $\frac{1}{9}(3x-2)^3 + c$

3 a $\frac{1}{5}(x-3)^5 + c$ **b** $-\frac{1}{5}(3-x)^5 + c$

c $-\frac{1}{6}(1-2x)^3 + c$

4 a $\frac{1}{20}(5x+4)^4 + c$ **b** $\frac{1}{28}(4x-3)^7 + c$

c $-\frac{1}{18}(2-3x)^6 + c$

5 a $-(x+5)^{-1} + c$ **b** $-\frac{1}{9}(3x-2)^{-3} + c$

c $\frac{1}{4}(5-2x)^{-2} + c$

6 a $\frac{1}{3}(2x+1)^{3/2} + c$ **b** $\frac{1}{7}(3x-7)^{7/3} + c$

c $\frac{1}{2}(1-4x)^{-1/2} + c$

7 a $-(u-3)^{-1} + c$ **b** $\frac{2}{3}(v+4)^{3/2} + c$

c $-\frac{1}{6}(2t+3)^{-3} + c$ **d** $\frac{1}{2}(4x-1)^{1/2} + c$

8 a 10 **b** 4

9 a $5\frac{1}{3}$ **b** $\frac{1}{12}$

10 a 2 **b** $136\frac{2}{5}$

11 a $y = -\frac{1}{24}(3-4x)^6 + c$

b $u = \frac{1}{3}(2t+1)^{3/2} + c$

c $y = \frac{1}{4}(1-2v)^{-2} + c$

d $r = -3(1-t)^{2/3} + c$

12 a $y = 4 - (x-1)^{-1}$ **b** $y = \frac{2}{3}(x+1)^{3/2} + 2$

Page 230 Exercise 6

1 a $-\cos x + c$ **b** $\sin x + c$

c $3\sin x + c$ **d** $-4\cos x + c$

2 a $\frac{1}{2}\sin 2x + c$ **b** $-\frac{1}{3}\cos 3x + c$

c $\frac{1}{5}\sin 5x + c$

3 a $\sin 4x + c$ **b** $-3\cos 2x + c$

c $\sin 3x + c$

4 a $\frac{1}{6}\cos 6x + c$ **b** $-\frac{1}{2}\sin 2x + c$

c $\sin ax + c$

5 a $2\sin\frac{1}{2}x + c$ **b** $-2\cos\frac{1}{2}x + c$

c $-\cos ax + c$

6 a $\sin(x+2) + c$ **b** $-\frac{1}{2}\cos(2x-1) + c$

7 a $\frac{1}{3}\sin(3x-1) + c$ **b** $\cos(2-x) + c$

8 a $-\frac{1}{3}\cos(3x+4) + c$ **b** $\sin(ax+b) + c$

9 a $-\cos x - \sin x + c$ **b** $2\sin x - 3\cos x + c$

10 a $-\frac{1}{2}\cos 2x + \frac{1}{3}\sin 3x + c$

b $\frac{1}{5}\sin 5\theta - \frac{1}{3}\cos 3\theta + c$

11 a $\frac{1}{3}t^3 + \sin 2t + c$ **b** $\cos(3-4u) + c$

12 a $\cos^2 x = \frac{1}{2}(1+\cos 2x)$; $\frac{1}{2}x + \frac{1}{4}\sin 2x + c$

b $\sin^2 x = \frac{1}{2}(1-\cos 2x)$; $\frac{1}{2}x - \frac{1}{4}\sin 2x + c$

c $x + c$; $\int(\sin^2 x + \cos^2 x)\,dx = \int 1\,dx = x + c$

13 $-\frac{1}{4}\cos 2x + c$

14 a $y = -\cos 2x + c$

b $y = 3\sin(1 + x/3) + c$

c $y = -2\cos(2x + \pi/3) + c$

d $y = 2\sin(3x - \pi/2) + c$

15 a $y = -\cos 3x + 1$

b $y = -\cos(t - \pi/4) + \sin(t - \pi/4) + 2$

Page 232 Exercise 7

2 a $\frac{1}{2}$ **b** 0

3 a $\frac{1}{2}$ **b** $\frac{1}{4}$

4 a 2 **b** $\frac{1}{2}$

5 a 2 **b** 1

6 a 2 **b** 1

7 a 0 **b** 4

8 a $-\frac{1}{2}$ **b** $\frac{1}{2} - \frac{1}{4}\sqrt{3}$

10 b A $\sqrt{2} - 1$, B $2\sqrt{2}$

11 a 1 **b** 1

12 a $0, \pi/3, \pi$ **b** A $\frac{1}{4}$, B $2\frac{1}{4}$

13 a $\pi/6, 5\pi/6, 3\pi/2$

b (i) $3\sqrt{3}/2$ (ii) $3\sqrt{3}/4$

Page 233 Challenges

1 a $\sin(2A + A) = \sin 2A\cos A + \cos 2A\sin A$
$= 2\sin A\cos^2 A + (1 - 2\sin^2 A)\sin A$
$= 2\sin A(1 - \sin^2 A) + (1 - 2\sin^2 A)\sin A$, etc.

b $-\frac{3}{4}\cos A + \frac{1}{12}\cos 3A + c$

2 a $\cos^3 A = \frac{1}{4}(3\cos A + \cos 3A)$

b $\frac{3}{4}\sin A + \frac{1}{12}\sin 3A + c$

Page 234 Review

1 a $2\cos x$ **b** $-3\sin x$

c $5\cos x + 4\sin x$ **d** $-2\sin x - \frac{1}{2}x^{-2}$

e $x^{-1/2} - 4\cos x$

2 a $\frac{1}{2}$ **b** 0 **c** $-\sqrt{3}/2$ **d** 1

3 a $-\sqrt{2}$ **b** 125.3°

c $y + \sqrt{2}x = \sqrt{2} + \pi\sqrt{2}/4$

4 a max TP $(\pi/2, 4)$, min TP $(3\pi/2, 0)$

b

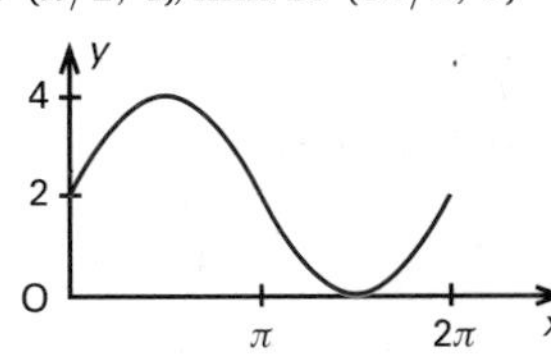

5 a $2(x-5)$ **b** $6(2x+1)^2$

c $2(1-x)^{-3}$ **d** $\frac{2}{3}x(x^2+2)^{-2/3}$

e $\frac{1}{2}(x-x^3)^{-1/2}(1-3x^2)$

f $-(x^4 - x^2 + 1)^{-2}(4x^3 - 2x)$

6 a $f'(x) = 1 - \sin\frac{1}{2}x \geqslant 0$

b π, at $x = \pi$

7 a (0, 1) and (π, 1) are max TPs; ($\pi/2$, -1) is a min TP

b

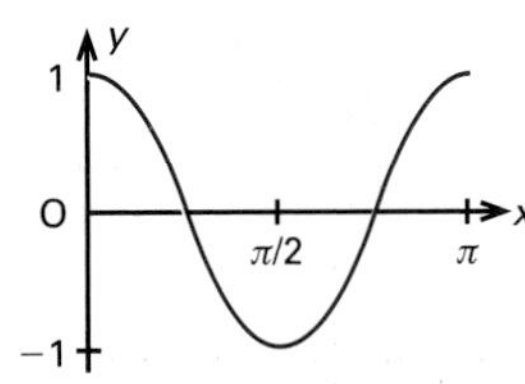

8 0, when $x = 2$; a min TV

9 a $2\cos(2x + 3)$ **b** $4\sin^3 x \cos x$
c $-\frac{1}{2}(\cos x)^{-1/2} \sin x$ **d** $-x^{-2} + (\sin x)^{-2} \cos x$
e $-6(2 - 3x) + 3\sin(2 - 3x)$

10 b max TPs (0, 2) and (π, 2); min TP ($\pi/2$, 1)

11 a $\frac{1}{3}x^3 + \frac{1}{2}x^2 + x + c$ **b** $\frac{2}{3}x^{3/2} - x^{-1} + c$
c $\frac{1}{5}(x + 3)^5 + c$ **d** $-\frac{1}{2}(x - 1)^{-2} + c$
e $\frac{1}{12}(3t + 5)^4 + c$ **f** $-\frac{1}{12}(1 - 4v)^3 + c$
g $\frac{1}{9}(6x - 3)^{3/2} + c$ **h** $(2x + 1)^{1/2} + c$

12 a $-4\cos x + c$ **b** $\sin x + \cos x + c$
c $\frac{1}{2}\sin 2u + c$ **d** $-\frac{1}{3}\cos 3x + c$
e $\frac{1}{5}\sin 5x + \frac{1}{2}\cos 2x + c$ **f** $\frac{1}{3}\sin(3t + 2) + c$

13 a $2x^3 + \frac{1}{3}\cos 6x + c$ **b** $2x + \frac{1}{4}\sin 4x + c$

14 a $y = 3x + \cos 2x + c$
b $y = \frac{1}{2}\sin 4x + \cos 3x + c$

15 a 2 **b** $\frac{1}{3}$

16 0, the areas above and below the x-axis are equal

17 3

3 The exponential and logarithmic functions

Page 236 Exercise 1

1 a £112 **b** £125.44 **c** £176.23 **d** £310.58
2 a $A(n) = 100 \times 1.07^n$ **b** $A(10) = 196.72$
3 a £600 **b** 10% **c** £798.60
4 a 71 400 **b** (ii) **c** 85 000
5 a $P(n) = 100 \times 1.06^n$ **b** 179 million
6 a $N(h) = 500 \times 1.8^h$ **b** 17 000

Page 237 Exercise 2

1 a 4 litres **b** 0.54 litre
2 a 600 ml **b** 14 weeks
3 a $A(x) = 8000\,(0.33)^x$
b (i) 2640 gallons **(ii)** 95 gallons
c 7
4 b (i) 4.204 g **(ii)** 5 mg
5 a $E(t) = 8\,(0.5)^{t/20}$, $E(20) = 4$ **b** 6 g
6 a $D(t) = (0.5)^{t/24\,400}$ **b** 58 g
7 a $D(t) = (0.5)^{t/5720}$
b put $t = 11\,440$ into the formula

Page 239 Exercise 3

1 a 2.718 281 828 **b** 2.718
2 a 7.39 **b** 0.368 **c** 485 000 000
3 a 0.37, 1, 2.72, 7.39, 12.18, 20.09, 33.12, 54.60
d (i) 4.95 **(ii)** 16.44 **(iii)** 24.53 **(iv)** 0.61
4 a 6 feet **b** 9.26 feet
5 b 985
6 a 37p **b** £33
7 a £8088 **b** £1403
8 a 1.03 kg/cm² **b** 0.425 kg/cm²
9 a

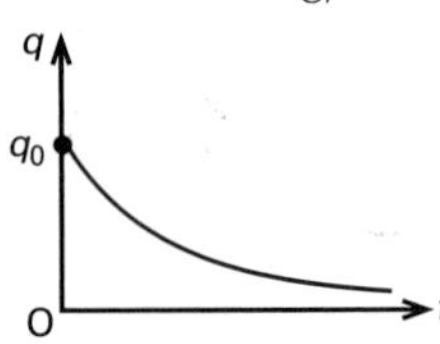

b (i) $0.7RC$ **(ii)** $2.3RC$

Page 240 Exercise 4

1 a $\log_{10} 10\,000 = 4$ **b** $\log_{10} 1000 = 3$
c $\log_{10} 10 = 1$ **d** $\log_{10} 1 = 0$
e $\log_{10} 0.1 = -1$ **f** $\log_{10} 0.01 = -2$
2 a $\log_3 81 = 4$ **b** $\log_3 9 = 2$
c $\log_2 32 = 5$ **d** $\log_4 64 = 3$
e $\log_6 36 = 2$ **f** $\log_5 5 = 1$
g $\log_6 1 = 0$ **h** $\log_2 (\frac{1}{2}) = -1$
i $\log_3 (\frac{1}{9}) = -2$ **j** $\log_x 12 = 2$
k $\log_y 20 = 4$ **l** $\log_z 10 = \frac{1}{2}$
3 a $4 = 2^2$ **b** $16 = 4^2$
c $27 = 3^3$ **d** $5 = 5^1$
e $1 = 6^0$ **f** $100 = 10^2$
4 a $3 = 9^{1/2}$ **b** $4 = 8^{2/3}$
c $10 = 100^{1/2}$ **d** $a = a^1$
e $1 = a^0$ **f** $c = a^b$
5 a $9 = x^2$, 3 **b** $125 = x^3$, 5
c $64 = x^2$, 8 **d** $7 = x^1$, 7
e $\frac{1}{4} = x^2$, $\frac{1}{2}$ **f** $x = 2^3$, 8
g $x = 4^{0.5}$, 2 **h** $x = 2^6$, 64
i $x = 7^{-1}$, $\frac{1}{7}$ **j** $x = 10^{-2}$, 0.01
k $4 = 2^x$, 2 **l** $81 = 3^x$, 4
m $1 = 4^x$, 0 **n** $5 = 5^x$, 1
o $10^6 = 10^x$, 6
6 a 3 **b** 3 **c** $\frac{1}{2}$ **d** −2
7 a 0.78 **b** 1.46 **c** −0.52 **d** −1.15
8 a 3.16 **b** 15.85 **c** 1.02
9 a Row: −1, −0.70, −0.30, 0, 0.30, 0.48, 0.60, 0.70, 0.78
b (i) increasing **(ii)** $\log_{10} x_1 > \log_{10} x_2$
c (i) $\log_{10} x \to -\infty$ **(ii)** $\log_{10} x \to +\infty$
10 a (i) 1.6 **(ii)** 3.2 **(iii)** 5.0

Page 242 Exercise 5

1 a log 14 **b** log 15 **c** log 10
d log 24 **e** log 6 **f** log 2 **g** log 2
2 a log 18 **b** log 32 **c** log 2
d log 5 **e** 0 **f** log 72
3 a 1 **b** 1 **c** 2 **d** $\frac{1}{2}$ **e** 1
f 2 **g** 2 **h** 4 **i** 1 **j** 1

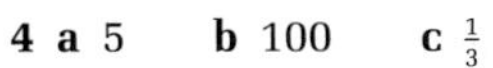

4 a 5 **b** 100 **c** $\frac{1}{3}$

5 10^9

6 2500

Page 243 Challenge

a 1, 1.65, 2.72, 3.49, 4.48, 5.75; 0, 0.69, 1.10, 1.39, 1.61, 1.79

b

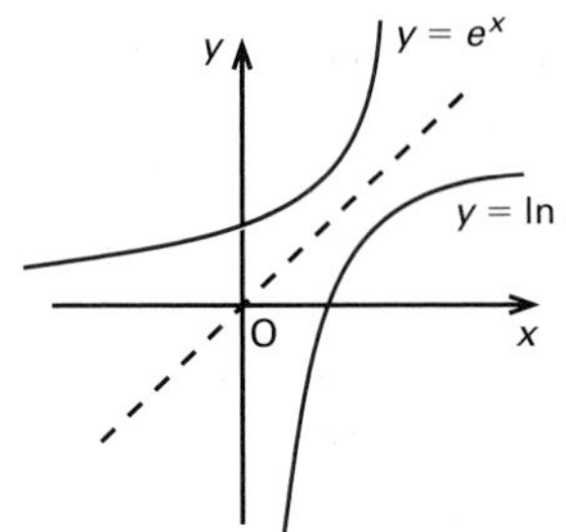

c $y = x$

d e^x and $\ln x$ are inverses of each other, so $\ln x$ is simply $\log_e x$.

Page 244 Exercise 6

1 a 2.32 **b** 4.97 **c** −1.74 **d** 6.28 **e** 4.66 **f** 8.58

2 a 1.26 **b** 7.60 **c** −1.36 **d** 4.61

3 a 7 **b** 8 **c** 4

4 a £200 734 **b** 12

5 a 500 **b** 9% **c** 17

6 13

7 $x < y$

Page 245 Exercise 7

1 a 2.30 **b** 1.60 **c** 2.46

2 a 6 **b** about 15

3 a 1000 **b** 65

4 17 weeks

5 a 100 °C **b** 5 minutes

6 17 m

Page 247 Exercise 8

1 $y = 1.6x^{0.7}$

2 $y = 2.5x^{-0.7}$

3 $y = 0.2x^2$

4 $y = 12.6x^{-1}$

5 $y = 1.4(1.01)^x$

6 $y = 4.0(0.97)^x$

7 $y = 3x^{0.5}$

8 $y = 2.2(5.3)^x$

Page 248 Review

1 a Rows: 1, 4, 16; 16, 4, 1, 0.3, 0.1

c (i) (0, 1) **(ii)** $x = 0$

2 a 50 m² **b (i)** 114 m² **(ii)** 262 m²

3 a $V(t) = 140\,000\,(0.75)^t$

b in the 13th year

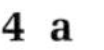

4 a

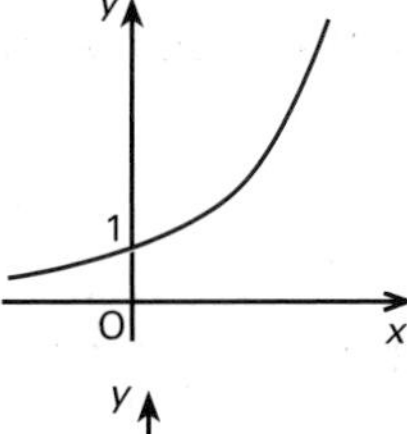

b

c

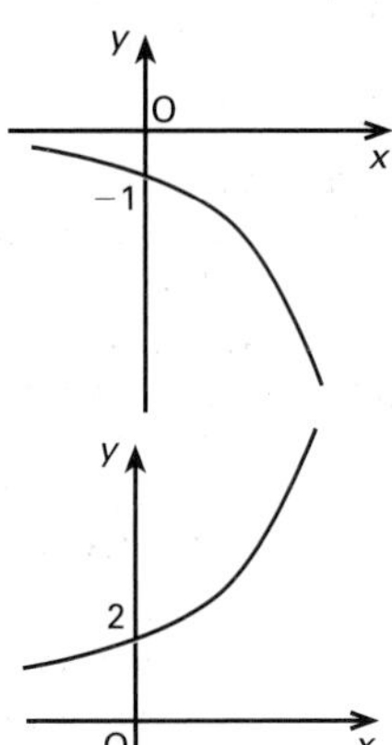

5 $\frac{1}{2}$

6 a $\log_5 y = 3$ **b** $\log_e u = -2$ **c** $\log_b a = \frac{1}{2}$ **d** $\log_{10} v = t$

7 a $x = e^2$ **b** $v = 10^{3u}$ **c** $y = a^{2x}$

8 a 4 **b** 3 **c** $\frac{1}{2}$ **d** $\frac{1}{4}$

9 a

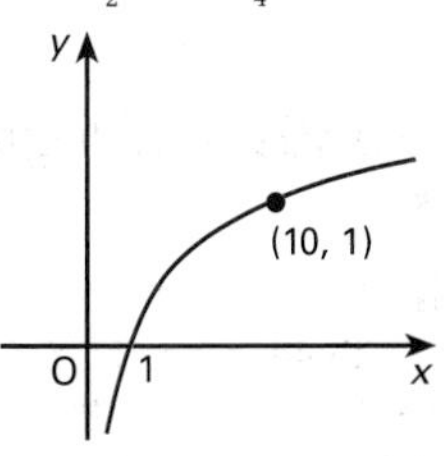

b

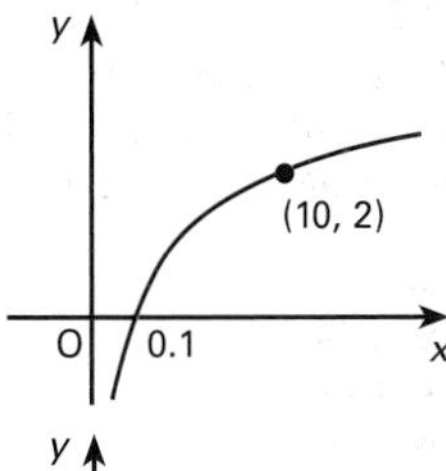

c

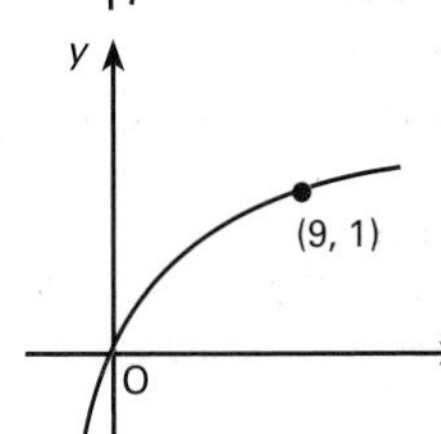

10 1

11 a 1 **b** 2 **c** 2 **d** 1

12 a $y = \frac{1}{3}a^x$ **b** $y = ex^2$

13 $a = 2,\ b = 5$

14 32

15 a 20.4 **b** 67.7
16 a 360 000 **b** about 38
17 $y = 10^6 x^{-3/4}$

4 The wave function *a* cos *x* + *b* sin *x*

Page 252 Exercise 1A

1 a (i) $\sqrt{2}$ (ii) $1, \pi/4$
b (i) $\sqrt{2}$ (ii) $-1, 7\pi/4$
c (i) 2 (ii) $1/\sqrt{3}, \pi/6$
2 $R\cos\alpha = \sqrt{3}$, $R\sin\alpha = -1$; $R^2 = 3 + 1 = 4$, $R = 2$; $\tan\alpha = -1/\sqrt{3}$, $\alpha = 2\pi - \dfrac{\pi}{6} = 11\pi/6$
3 $R = \sqrt{8} = 2\sqrt{2}$; $\tan\alpha = -1$, $\alpha = 2\pi - \pi/4 = 7\pi/4$
4 a $\sqrt{2}\cos(x - \pi/4)$ **b** $2\cos(x - 5\pi/3)$
c $2\cos(x - \pi/6)$ **d** $2\sqrt{2}\cos(x - \pi/4)$
5 $R\cos\alpha° = -3$, $R\sin\alpha° = -4$, $R = 5$, $\tan\alpha° = \frac{4}{3}$, $\alpha = 180 + 53 = 233$
6 a $5\sin(x - 217)°$ **b** $10\sin(x - 307)°$
c $\sqrt{5}\sin(x - 27)°$ **d** $\sqrt{10}\sin(x - 108)°$
7 a $5\cos(x - 53)°$ **b** $5\cos(x + 307)°$
c $5\sin(x - 323)°$ **d** $5\sin(x + 37)°$

Page 253 Exercise 1B

1 $2\cos(300t - 60)°$
2 a $\sqrt{2}\cos(2x - \pi/4)$ **b** $\sqrt{2}\cos(3x - 3\pi/4)$
3 a $5\cos(2\theta - 5.36)$ **b** $\sqrt{5}\sin(2\theta - 5.82)$
4 a $10\sqrt{10}\sin(20t + 18)°$
b

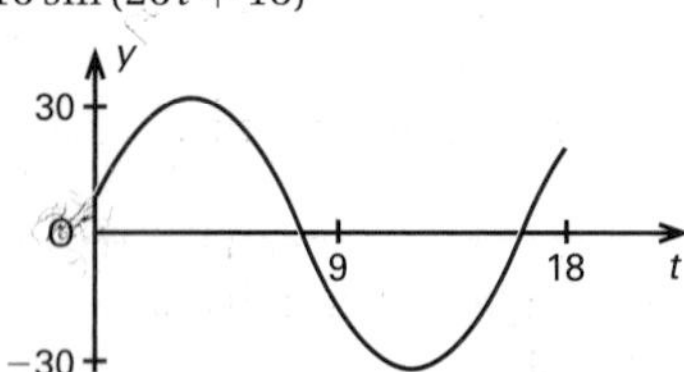

cuts t-axis at $t = 8.1, 17.1$; max 31.62 at $t = 3.6$, min -31.62 at $t = 12.6$

Page 254 Exercise 2

1 a 1, −1 **b** 1, −1 **c** 4, −4
d 3, −3 **e** 5, −5 **f** 2, −2
2 a max 2, $x = 90$; min −2, $x = 270$
b max 3, $x = 0, 360$; min −3, $x = 180$
3 a max 5, $x = 120$; min −5, $x = 300$
b max 10, $x = 300$; min −10, $x = 120$
4 a max 6, $x = \pi$; min −6, $x = 0, 2\pi$
b max 7, $x = 7\pi/4$; min −7, $x = 3\pi/4$
5 a max 2, $x = 90, 270$; min −2, $x = 0, 180, 360$
b max 3, $x = 150, 330$; min −3, $x = 60, 240$
6 a max 4, $\theta = 5\pi/18, 17\pi/18$; min −4, $\theta = 11\pi/18$
b max 5, $\theta = 7\pi/12$; min −5, $\theta = \pi/4, 11\pi/12$

Page 255 Exercise 3A

1 a $13\cos(x - 23)°$; max 13, $x = 23$; min −13, $x = 203$
b $25\cos(x - 286)°$; max 25, $x = 286$; min −25, $x = 106$
2 a $f(x) = 1 + 2\sin(x - 5\pi/4)$; max 3, $x = 7\pi/4$; min −1, $x = 3\pi/4$
b $g(x) = 2 + 2\sin(x - \pi/6)$; max 4, $x = 2\pi/3$; min 0, $x = 5\pi/3$
3 a $a = 3, b = 1, c = 2, d = 1$
b $y_1 + y_2 = 3\cos x° + 2\sin x° = \sqrt{13}\sin(x - 304)°$
c max $\sqrt{13}$, $x = 34$; min $-\sqrt{13}$, $x = 214$
4 a $a = -1, b = 1, c = 4, d = 1$
b $y_1 + y_2 = -\cos x° + 4\sin x° = \sqrt{17}\sin(x - 14)°$
c max $\sqrt{17}$, $x = 104$; min $-\sqrt{17}$, $x = 284$
5 a $f(x) = 5\cos(2x - 0.64) + 5$; max 10, $x = 0.32, 3.46$; min 0, $x = 1.89, 5.03$
b $g(x) = \sqrt{5}\cos(2x - 5.18) + \sqrt{5}$; max $2\sqrt{5}$, $x = 2.59, 5.73$; min 0, $x = 1.02, 4.16$
6 b 0.2, $x = 4.07$

Page 256 Exercise 3B

1 $2\sqrt{2}$ m at $\theta = \pi/4$
2 a (i) ∠DEF = ∠FDA (each is complement of ∠EDF) = ∠DAC (alternate)
(ii) BE = BF + FE = CD + FE = $6\sin x° + 2.5\cos x°$
b 6.5 m, 67°
3 $H = 50\cos(30t - 63)°$; high at $t = 2.1$ (0207), low at $t = 8.1$ (0807)
4 b $1 + \sqrt{2}$ at $\theta = \pi/8$
5 a $OE = 50\cos\theta$, $ED = 50\sin\theta$, so area OADE = $2500\sin\theta\cos\theta$. BC = OE = $50\cos\theta$, so area of square = $2500\cos^2\theta$, etc.
b $1250 + 1250\sqrt{2}\cos(2\theta - \pi/4)$
c $1250 + 1250\sqrt{2}$ at $\theta = \pi/8$

Page 258 Exercise 4

1 a 0, 90, 360 **b** 53
c 95, 191 **d** 162, 310
2 a 60, 240 **b** 143
3 a $0, 3\pi/2, 2\pi$ **b** $0, 2\pi/3, 2\pi$
4 a $5\sin(x - 53)°$
b (i) 77, 210 (ii) $77 \leqslant x \leqslant 210$
5 a 25, 85 **b** 0, 80, 120
6 a 0, 135, 180 **b** 77, 156
7 a $5\sin(x + 127)°$
b max 5, $x = 323$; min −5, $x = 143$
c

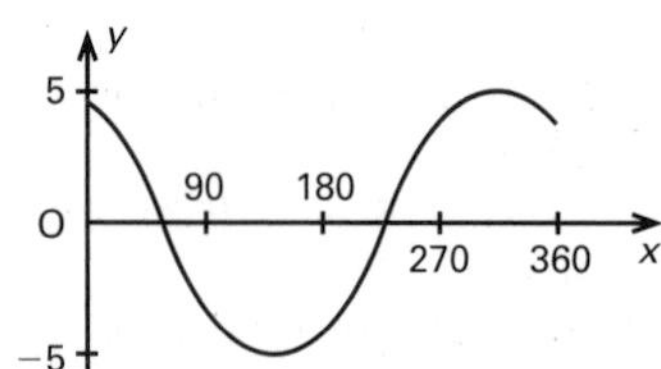

d (i) 53, 233 (ii) $53 < x < 233$

8 a $\sqrt{89}\sin(\theta + 0.56)$
b max $\sqrt{89}$, $\theta = 1.01$; min $-\sqrt{89}$, $\theta = 4.15$
c

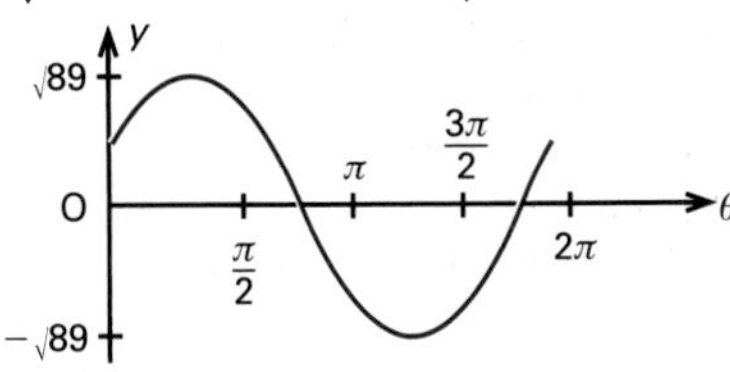

d (i) 2.58, 5.72 **(ii)** $2.58 < \theta < 5.72$

Page 258 Challenge
b 26

Page 259 Review
1 a $\sqrt{2}$, 135° **b** 2, 60°
c 5, 53° **d** 13, 113°
5 a (i) $3\sqrt{2}\cos(x - 3\pi/4)$
(ii) $2\sqrt{3}\sin(x + \pi/3)$
b (i) $5\cos(x + 233)°$
(ii) $\sqrt{29}\sin(x - 338)°$
6 a $3\sqrt{5}\sin(250t + 63)°$ **b** $3\sqrt{5}$, 63°
7 a max $1 + \sqrt{5}$ at $x = 153$; min $1 - \sqrt{5}$ at $x = 333$
b max $3\sqrt{2}$ at $x = 225$; min $\sqrt{2}$ at $x = 45$
8 a $a = 2$, $m = 2$, $b = 3$, $n = 2$
b $h(x) = \sqrt{13}\sin(2x + 56)°$; $k = \sqrt{13}$, $p = 2$, $q = 56$
9 a 32, 291 **b** 45, 162 **c** 1.21, 5.71
10 a each riser is $40\sin\theta°$ and each tread is $40\cos\theta°$
b 300 cm, 53
11 b $40/(1 + \sqrt{2})$ (= 16.6 m), 45

5 Revision exercises

Page 261 Chapter 1 Revision
1

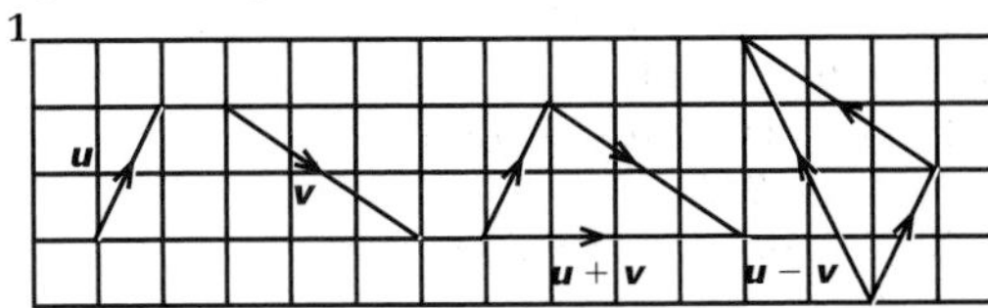

2 a $\begin{pmatrix} 0 \\ 8 \\ 1 \end{pmatrix}$ **b** $\begin{pmatrix} -11 \\ 0 \\ 2 \end{pmatrix}$
3 a $\overrightarrow{OQ} = -2\overrightarrow{OP}$, so parallel, and O is common
b $\overrightarrow{PQ} = 3\overrightarrow{AB}$ etc.
4 a $\overrightarrow{BC} = 2\overrightarrow{AB}$ etc.; 1: 2 **b** $\overrightarrow{BC} = 3\overrightarrow{AB}$; 1: 3
c $\overrightarrow{BC} = \frac{3}{2}\overrightarrow{AB}$; 2: 3
5 $\angle Q = 90°$ (using converse of Pythagoras' Theorem, or scalar product)
6 a (−2, −6, 3) **b** (3, −2, 3) **c** (−2, −1, 0)
7 a (i) (1, −1, 0)
(ii) (1, −2, −2)
(iii) (1, −5, −8)
b $\overrightarrow{QR} = 3\overrightarrow{PQ}$ etc.; 1: 3
8 a $\sqrt{6}$ **b** $2\sqrt{2}$ **c** 5 **d** $\sqrt{14}$ **e** $\sqrt{14}$
9 $OA^2 = OB^2 = AB^2 = 24$
10 97.2°
12 a A(4, 0, 0), H(−4, 2, 4)
b 9.2 **c** 83.6°
13 a $RS^2 + ST^2 = 18 = TR^2$, $RS^2 = ST^2$
b $\overrightarrow{ST}.\overrightarrow{SR} = 0$
14 a $h = -1$, $k = -4$ **b** 1:2
15 a −2 **b** −2 **c** −4 **d** 0

Page 262 Chapter 2 Revision
1 a 0 **b** $\frac{1}{2}$ **c** $-\frac{1}{2}$ **d** 1 **e** −1 **f** 1
2 a $8\cos x$ **b** $-\frac{1}{2}\sin x$
c $-3\sin x + 4\cos x$ **d** $2\sin x$
e $-2\cos x - \sin x$
3 a $15(3x + 4)^4$ **b** $-6(1 - 2x)^2$
c $(2x + 1)^{-1/2}$ **d** $2(6x + 9)^{-2/3}$
e $-12(4x + 5)^{-4}$ **f** $(1 - x)^{-2}$
4 a $-2(2x + 1)^{-2}$ **b** $2(1 - 3x)^{-3}$
c $3(1 - 9x)^{-4/3}$
5 a $10x(x^2 + 7)^4$ **b** $-4x(1 + 2x^2)^{-2}$
c $-(x^2 + x + 1)^{-3/2}(2x + 1)$
6 a $\frac{1}{2}\cos\frac{1}{2}x$ **b** $-4\sin(4x + 2)$
c $-2\cos(6 - 2x)$ **d** $4\cos 2x - 9\sin 3x$
e $-5\pi\sin(\pi x - 1)$
7 a $-4\cos^3 x\sin x$
b $-4(1 + \cos x)^3\sin x$
c $-2(1 + \sin x)^{-3}\cos x$
d $-\frac{1}{2}(\sin x)^{-2}\cos x$
e $(1 + \cos x)^{-3/2}\sin x$
f $-(\sin x)^{-2}\cos x + (\cos x)^{-2}\sin x$
8 a −1 **b** 0
9 a max TV −2 at $x = -1$; min TV 2 at $x = 1$
b $f'(x) = 1 - 1/x^2 > 0$ in each case
10 $16y = 3x + 28$
11 max value 10
12 a $\frac{1}{4}(x + 1)^4 + c$ **b** $\frac{1}{10}(2x + 3)^5 + c$
c $\frac{1}{2}(1 - 2x)^{-1} + c$ **d** $\frac{1}{3}(2x + 1)^{3/2} + c$
e $(2x - 1)^{1/2} + c$ **f** $-\frac{1}{5}(1 - x)^5 + c$
13 a $\frac{1}{2}$ **b** $4\frac{2}{3}$
14 a $5\sin x + c$ **b** $-6\cos x + c$
c $-2\cos 3x + c$ **d** $\frac{1}{4}\sin(4x + 3) + c$
e $\frac{1}{2}\cos(1 - 2x) + c$
15 a $1\frac{1}{2}$ **b** $\sqrt{2} - 1$ **c** 2 **d** 7
16 a $\pi/2$ **b** π
17 $1 + \pi/2$
18 a 0, π, 2π **b** 4

19 b (0, 0) and (π, 0) are min TPs, ($\pi/2$, 1) is a max TP

c

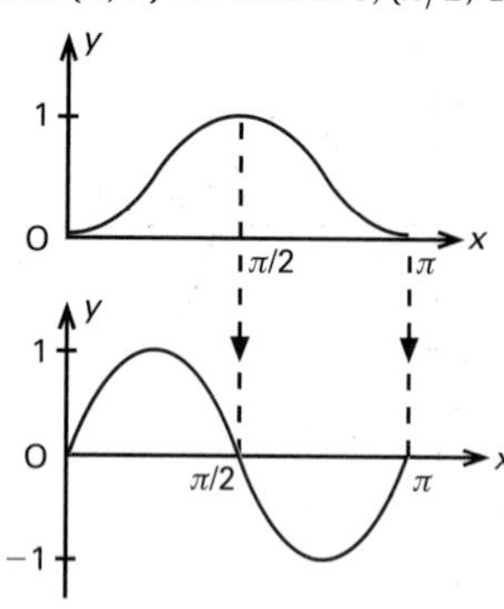

Page 263 Chapter 3 Revision

1 a (i) 16.3° (ii) 12.0°
b 30 m
2 a $Q = 1.06^n \times P$ **b** 8954
3 a £1.8 million **b** £1.44 million **c** 20%
4

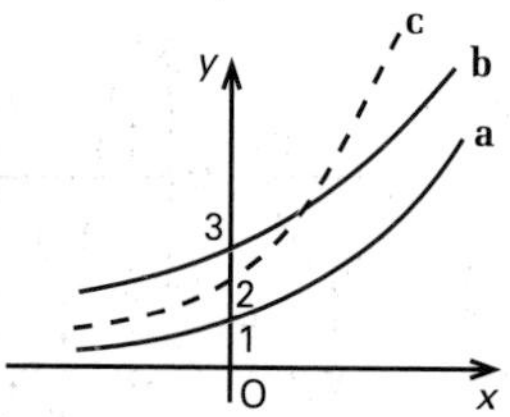

5 a $\log_4 16 = 2$ **b** $\log_5 125 = 3$
c $\log_{27} 3 = \frac{1}{3}$ **d** $\log_x \left(\frac{1}{x}\right) = -1$
6 a $32 = 2^5$ **b** $5 = 5^1$ **c** $x = 7^y$
7 a 14 **b** 81 **c** 2 **d** 4 **e** 6 **f** 5
8 a 2 **b** 2 **c** 2 **d** 4
9 a

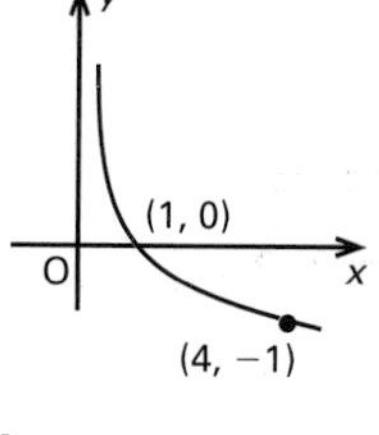

b

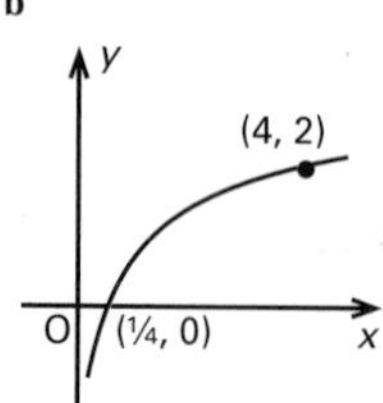

c

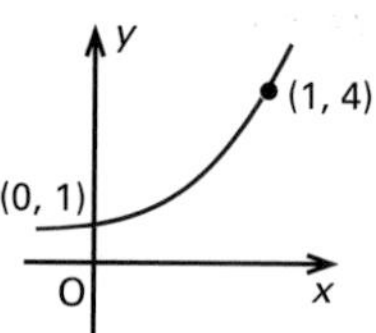

10 a 1.4 **b** 0.6 **c** 1.3 **d** 1.6 **e** 0.5
11 a 0.43 **b** 2.30 **c** 23.14
12 a 184 g **b** 69 years
13 12th
14 a $a = 3, b = 1.5$ **b** $a = 1.4, b = 4$

Page 264 Chapter 4 Revision

1 a $R = \sqrt{2}, \alpha = 45$ **b** $R = \sqrt{2}, \alpha = 135$
c $R = 2, \alpha = 330$ **d** $R = 5, \alpha = 217$
3 a $\sqrt{74}\cos(x - 36)°$ **b** $\sqrt{13}\sin(x - 56)°$
4 a $6\sqrt{2}\sin(\theta - 5\pi/4)$ **b** $2\cos(\theta + \pi/6)$
5 a If $x = 0$, $y = 1$. If $y = 0$, $x = 150, 330$. Max 2 at $x = 60$; min -2 at $x = 240$
b

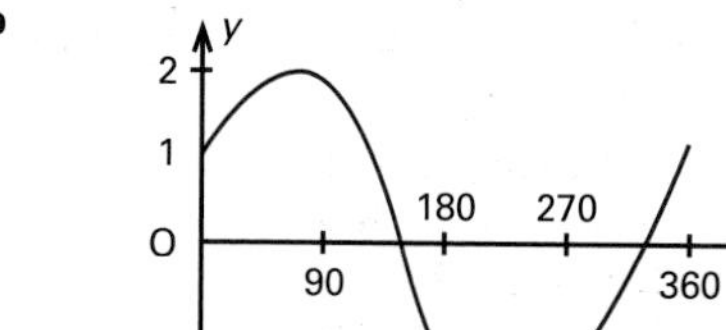

amplitude 2, period 360°
6 a $y = \cos 2x - \sin 2x$
b $\sqrt{2}\cos(2x - 7\pi/4)$; max $\sqrt{2}$ at $x = 7\pi/8, 15\pi/8$; min $-\sqrt{2}$ at $x = 3\pi/8, 11\pi/8$
7 a max 6 at $x = 37$; min -14 at $x = 217$
b max $\frac{1}{4}$ at $x = 225$; min $\frac{1}{12}$ at $x = 45$
8 max 13 at $\theta = 5.11$; min -13 at $\theta = 1.97$
9 a 72, 220 **b** 28
10 a 5 cm **b** 1.3 seconds **c** 0.7 second
11 b max 13 at $\theta = 337$; min-13 (in the direction XO) at $\theta = 157$

Page 266 Review A

1 a $\begin{pmatrix} -2 \\ -1 \\ 2 \end{pmatrix}, \begin{pmatrix} -6 \\ 3 \\ -2 \end{pmatrix}$
b (i) 76.2° (ii) 10.2
2 a $-8(3 - 2x)^3$ **b** $(2x - 1)^{-1/2}$ **c** $-15(3t + 4)^{-6}$
3 a $\frac{1}{2}$ **b** 4
4 $k = \sqrt{13}, \alpha = 33.7$
5 a $\frac{1}{15}(3x + 1)^5 + c$ **b** $-2(2 - x)^{1/2} + c$ **c** $\frac{1}{2}$
6 a A(2, 0, 0), B(2, 2, 0), C(2, 2, 4), M(1, 0, 0), N(2, 2, 2), P(1, 2, 4)
7 b (i) 1 (ii) 1
8 a $5\cos(x - 143)°$
b max 5 at $x = 143$, min -5 at $x = 323$
9 a (i) 25 (ii) 275 **b** 35
11 a $-1, 8$ **b** 6

12 1

13 a $2\sin(x+\pi/3)$ b $0, \pi/3, 2\pi$

14 a M(4, −1, −1,), N(2, 0, 0)

b $\overrightarrow{NS} = 2\overrightarrow{QN}$, 1:2

15 a $a = 2, b = 4$ b 7

16 a

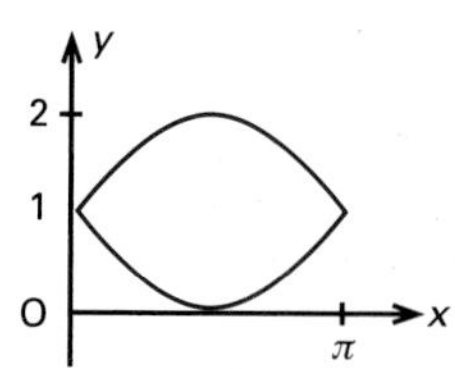

b 4

17 0

18 b $k = 96, m = 0.67$ c 830 kilovolts

Page 267 Review B

1 $y = \frac{1}{3}(2x+1)^{3/2} + 3$

2 a (2, 7, −5)

b $\overrightarrow{PQ} = \begin{pmatrix} 8 \\ -8 \\ 4 \end{pmatrix}, \overrightarrow{PR} = \begin{pmatrix} 5 \\ 1 \\ -2 \end{pmatrix}, \overrightarrow{PS} = \begin{pmatrix} 0 \\ 16 \\ -12 \end{pmatrix}$

3 a $6(2x+1)^2 + 6(2x+1)^{-4}$

b $2\cos(2x+1) + 2\sin(2x+1)$

5 a $\frac{1}{5}x^5 - \frac{1}{3}x^{-3} + \cos x + c$ b 2

6 a (i) B(0, 2, 3), C(1, 3, 4)

(ii) $\overrightarrow{AB} = \begin{pmatrix} -1 \\ 0 \\ 3 \end{pmatrix}, \overrightarrow{AC} = \begin{pmatrix} 0 \\ 1 \\ 4 \end{pmatrix}$

b 23° c 8:1

7 a

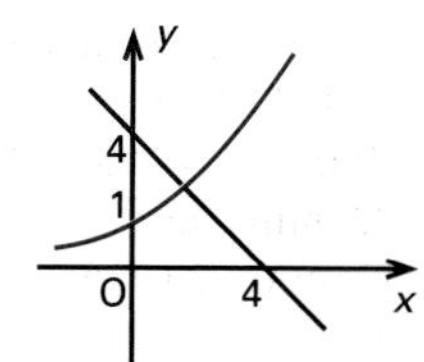

b 1.1

8 a $2\cos(x - 60)^\circ$

b max 2 at $x = 60$, min −2 at $x = 240$

c 120, 360

9 a 109.5°

10 a (i) 25 g (ii) 23 years

b

12 a 1, $1\frac{1}{2}$, 3 b 14 c 25

13 a $2\sin x\cos x$; 0, $\pi/3$ b $\frac{1}{4}$

14 a $\sqrt{2}\sin(\theta - \pi/4)$

b

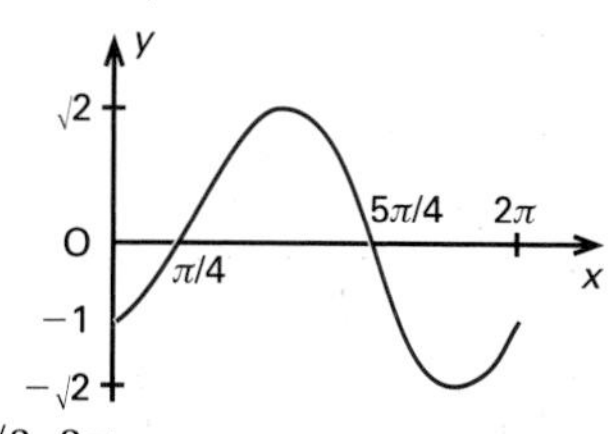

c $0, 3\pi/2, 2\pi$

15 a $y = A\cos 3x + B\sin 3x$

b $y = \cos 3x + \sin 3x$

Page 268 Review C

1 b 3:2 c (−28, 42, −26)

2 a $-(3x+4)^{-4/3}$

b $2\cos(2x-3) + 2\sin(3-2x)$

4 a $\frac{1}{3}x^3 - \sin 2x + c$ b $-\frac{1}{6}\cos 6x + c$

5 a (i) $(\frac{1}{2}, \frac{1}{2}, 3)$ (ii) $(\frac{2}{3}, 1, 2)$

6 a (i) b (i)

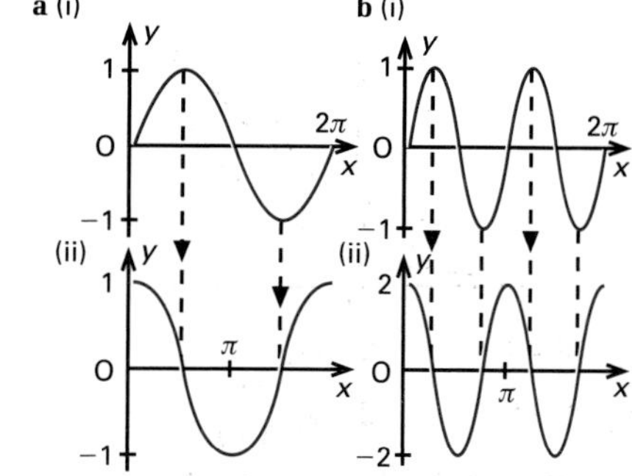

7 a 5000 b 90% c 2811 d 11

8 $3\sin 2t + 2, -12\sin 2t$

9 b $i(t) \to E/R$

c

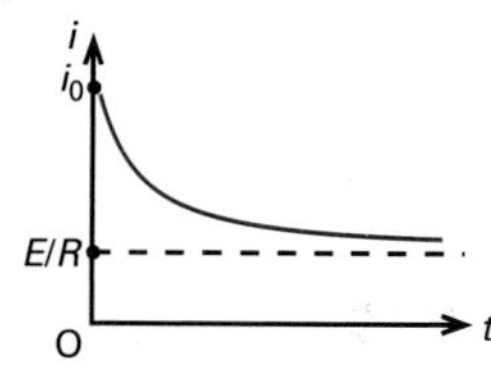

10 a $\pm 1/\sqrt{2}$

b (i) $-1/\sqrt{2} < x < 1/\sqrt{2}$

(ii) $x > 1/\sqrt{2}$ or $x < -1/\sqrt{2}$

11 b (6, 1, 2)

12 16

13 b 21.5°

14 $4\frac{1}{2}$ at $x = 323.1$, $-\frac{1}{2}$ at $x = 143.1$

15 b $\frac{1}{2} + (\sqrt{5}/4)\cos(2\theta - 2.7)$

c $\frac{1}{2} + \sqrt{5}/4$, 1.3

COURSE REVISION

Page 270 Review A

2 $y(x) = 5x - 2x^3 + 7$

3 $(x - 2)(2x^2 + x + 3)$

4 $\frac{3}{5}, -\frac{7}{25}$

5 a (i)

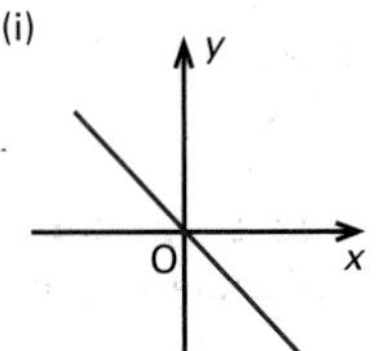

(ii)

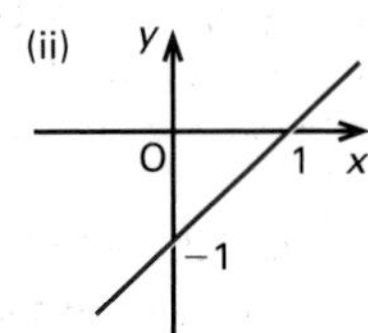

(iii)

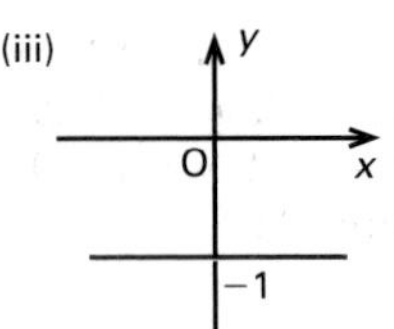

b (i)

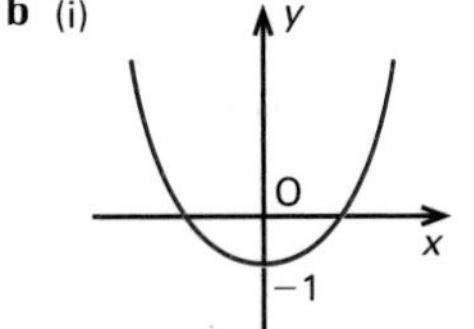

(ii)

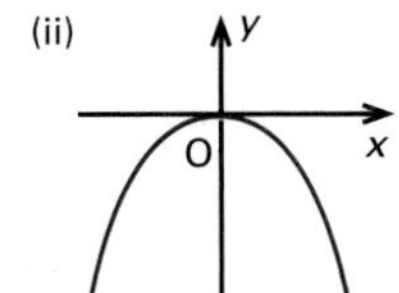

(iii) (assuming $f(x)$ is quadratic)

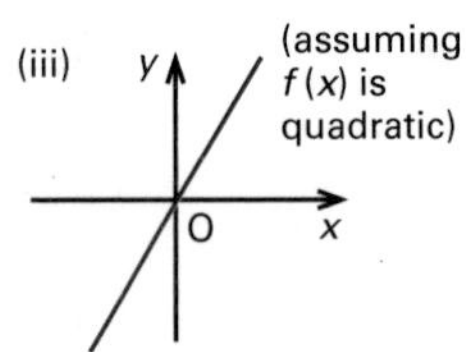

6 $7x - 8y + 12 = 0$

7 $x \geqslant 0,\ y \geqslant 3$

8 $(1, 0)$

9 $3\cos(3x + 1) - (2 - 3x)^{-2/3}$

10 a $35.3°$ **b** $45°$

11 b 0

12 a $\begin{pmatrix} 3 \\ -4 \\ 5 \end{pmatrix}$ **b** $5\sqrt{2}$

13 a $-2, 1$ **b** $x > 1, x < -2$ **c** $-2 < x < 1$

14 a 45, 41, 37.8 **b** $-1 < 0.8 < 1$; 25

15 a **(i)** $\frac{1}{2}$ **(ii)** $\frac{1}{2}$

b

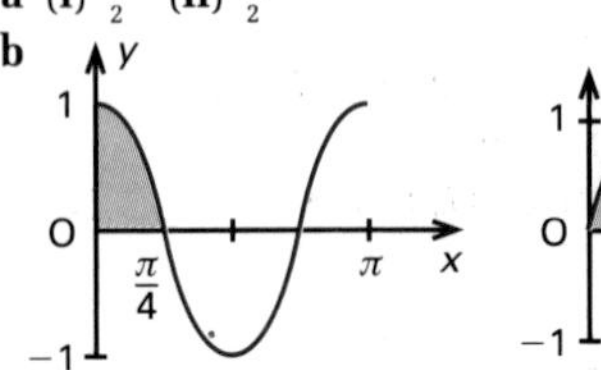

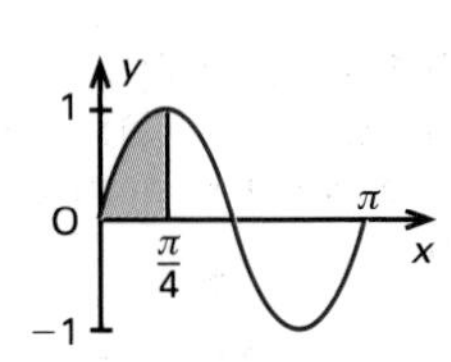

16 48.2, 120, 240, 311.8

17 a 8 million **b** 15

18 a 2 **b** $k < 0$ or $k > 2$

19 a $7y + x = 31$ **b** $7y + x = -69$

20 a $3\cos(x - 48.2)°$ **b** 108.2, 348.2

21 a **(i)** 2 **(ii)** 0 **b** 40

Page 271 Review B

1 2, 1.45, −3.45

2 b A(1, 2)

3 a

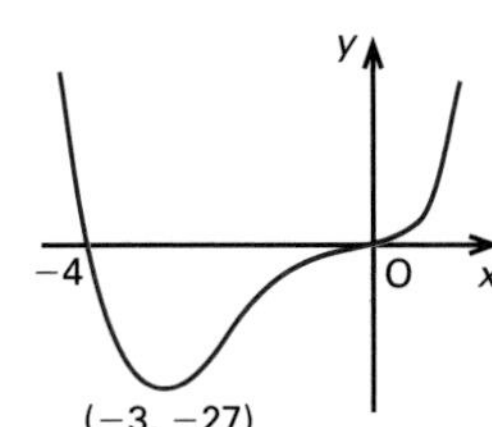

b $a < -27$

4 a 1, 2 **b** 6

5 $-2(2x + 1)^{-2} + 9\cos^2 x \sin x$

6 a (8, 0), 6 **b** ± 6, $x^2 + (y \pm 6)^2 = 16$

7 0.25, 2.89, 4.71

8 $b = 2a$

9 $-\frac{2}{3}(3 - x)^{3/2} + \frac{1}{3}\cos(3x + 2) + c$

10 a $(x + 1)^2 + 4$, min 4 at $x = -1$

b $2(x - 2)^2 - 7$, min −7 at $x = 2$

c $13 - (x + 3)^2$, max 13 at $x = -3$

11 a $y = x - 3$, $3y = -x - 1$; $(2, -1)$

12 $\pm\sqrt{2}/2$

13 a $y = -\sin x - 1$ **b** $y = 3 + 3\cos 2x$

14 a P(6, 4, 4), Q(8, 8, 10) **b** 7.5

15 $\frac{1}{4}\sqrt{7}, -\frac{3}{4}$

16 ± 2

17 a −2, −1, 1 **b** 1, −0.2, −1.6

c

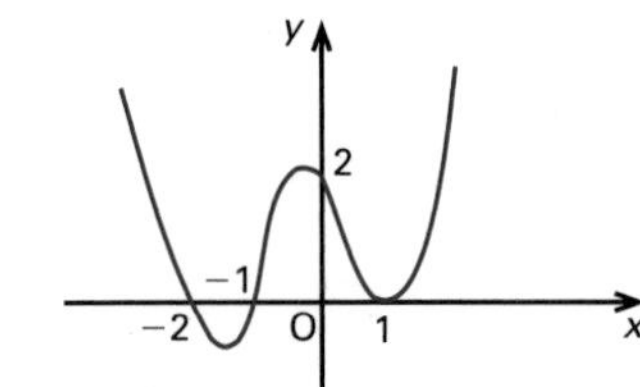

18 9

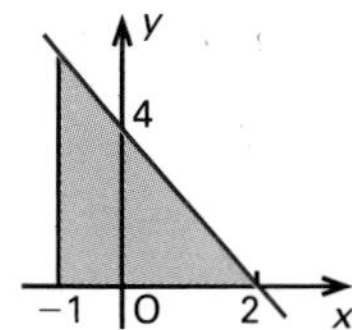

19 **b** P(−1, 1, 3), Q(5, −5, −9), R(0, 0, 1)

20 **a** $2\sin(x - 4\pi/3)$ **b** $\pi/2$, $7\pi/6$

21 **a** max 1 at $x = \pi/2, 3\pi/2$; min 0 at $x = 0, \pi, 2\pi$

b

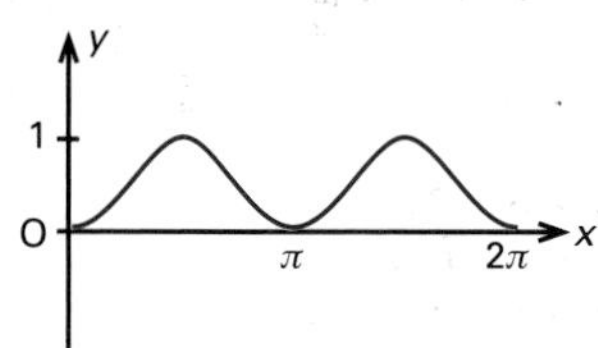

c π

Page 272 Review C

1 **a** $(p+q, \frac{1}{2}(p^2+q^2))$ **b** $\frac{1}{2}(p+q)$

2 3200 cm^2

3 **a** AB $y = 2x - 3$, BC $y = -3x + 7$, S(2, 1)

4 **a** 40, 100, 220, 280 **b** 0.4, 2.3

5 **a** $y = 2x + 2$, $y = -2x + 2$, $y = -2$, $y = -\frac{1}{2}x^2$

b $y = -2x - 2$, $y = 2x - 2$, $y = 2$, $y = \frac{1}{2}x^2$

c $y = -2x$, $y = 2x$, $y = 4$, $y = \frac{1}{2}x^2 + 2$

6 **a** $3x + 2y - 1 = 0$

7 **a** $\frac{1-2x}{x+1}$ **b** $\frac{1}{3x-1}$

c $\frac{4x-3}{6x}$ **d** $\frac{5+3x}{1-3x}$

8 **a** $(x-2)^2 + (y+1)^2 = 32$; $y = x - 3$

b (−2, −5), (6, 3) **c** a square

9 **a** 15.8 **b** $k = 1.6$, $n = -0.1$

10 **b** $\frac{1}{4}$

11 **a** $5\cos(20t - 143)°$ **b** 3, 11, 21, 29, 39

12 $y = \sqrt{(1 - x^2)}$ is upper half of circle $x^2 + y^2 = 1$; integral $= \pi/4$

13 **b** 86.6°

14 **a** $24\sin^2\theta\cos\theta - 6\sin 2\theta = 6\sin 2\theta(2\sin\theta - 1)$; 0, $\pi/6$, $\pi/2$, $5\pi/6$, π, $3\pi/2$, 2π

b second row: 3, 2.5, 5, 2.5, 3, −11, 3

c max 5, min −11